Fifth Edition

Computer Confluence
Concise Edition

Exploring Tomorrow's Technology

George Beekman
Oregon State University

Prentice Hall
Upper Saddle River, New Jersey 07458

Acquisitions Editor: Melissa Whitaker-Oliver
VP/Publisher: Natalie Anderson
Senior Development Editor: Lena Buonanno
Assistant Editor: Melissa Edwards
Media Project Manager: Cathleen Profitko
Marketing Assistant: Jason Smith
Associate Director, Manufacturing: Vincent Scelta
Production Manager: Gail Steier de Acevedo
Project Manager: Lynne Breitfeller
Manufacturing Buyer: Lynne Breitfeller
Full-Service Composition: Pre-Press Company
Design Manager: Pat Smythe
Interior and Cover Design: Jill Little
Printer: Von Hoffman Press

Photo, screen capture, and text credits appear on pages 311–313.

Library of Congress Cataloging-in-Publication Data

Beekman, George.
   Computer confluence exploring tomorrow's technology / George Beekman.—Concise, 5th ed.
     p. cm.
   ISBN 0-13-066187-2
    1. Computers. 2. Information technology. I. Title.

QA76.5 .B3652 2002
004—dc21
                                          2002016962

Pearson Education Limited (UK)
Pearson Education Australia Pty Ltd
Prentice Hall Canada Ltd
Pearson Educación de Mexico, S.A. de C.V.
Pearson Education Japan KK
Pearson Education China Ltd
Pearson Education Asia Pte Ltd

Copyright © 2003 by Prentice-Hall, Inc., Upper Saddle River, New Jersey 07458. All rights reserved. Printed in the United States of America. This publication is protected by Copyright and permission should be obtained from the publisher prior to any prohibited reproduction, storage in a retrieval system, or transmission in any form or by any means, electronic, mechanical, photocopying, recording, or likewise. For information regarding permission(s), write to: Rights and Permissions Department.

10 9 8 7 6 5 4 3 2
ISBN 0-13-066187-2

To
Rosie Beekman (1924–2002)
my first—and most important—teacher.

—G.E.B.

Brief Contents

Preface xii

Chapter 0   ReadMe   2
Chapter 1   Computer Currents: From Calculation to Connection   24
Chapter 2   Hardware Basics: Inside the Box   48
Chapter 3   Hardware Basics: Peripherals   68
Chapter 4   Software Basics: The Ghost in the Machine   98
Chapter 5   Computer Applications: Software Tools   126
Chapter 6   Networking and Telecommunication   162
Chapter 7   Inside the Internet and the Web   184
Chapter 8   From Internet to Information Infrastructure   208
Chapter 9   Computer Security and Risks   228
Chapter 10   Information Age Issues: Inventing the Future   256

The Concise Computer Consumer's Guide   281

Appendix: Correlation Guide to the ACM Code of Ethics and Professional Conduct   289

Glossary   295

Credits   311

Index   313

Contents

Preface xii

Chapter 0 ReadMe 2

Human Dreams and Dream Machines   3

PC Basics   4
- PC Hardware Basics   4
- **Using a Keyboard**   6
- **Using a Mouse**   7
- PC Software Basics   8
- **User's View: Using Microsoft Word with Microsoft Windows**   10
- **User's View: Using Microsoft Word with Mac OS**   12
- PC Network Basics   13

Internet Basics   13
- Email Basics   14
- **User's View: Communicating with Electronic Mail**   15
- World Wide Web Basics   16
- Web Search Basics   17
- Applying the Basics   18

Rules of Thumb: Navigating Computer Confluence   19

Computer Confluence QuickStart   20
- Launching the Computer Confluence CD-ROM   20
- Exploring the Computer Confluence Web Site   20

CrossCurrents: Brain Gain   21
Nick Montfort

Summary   22

Chapter Review   22
- Key Terms   22
- Interactive Quiz Questions   22
- Review Questions   23
- Discussion Questions   23
- Projects   23
- Sources and Resources   23

Chapter 1 Computer Currents: From Calculation to Connection 24

Charles Babbage, Lady Lovelace, and the Mother of All Computers   25

Living without Computers   26

Computers in Perspective: An Evolving Idea   26
- Before Computers   27
- The Information-Processing Machine   27
- The First Real Computers   27
- Evolution and Acceleration   28
- The Microcomputer Revolution   29

Computers Today: A Brief Taxonomy   30
- Mainframes and Supercomputers   30
- Workstations and PCs   31
- Portable Computers   32
- Embedded Computers and Special-Purpose Computers   33

Computer Connections: The Internet Revolution   34
- The Emergence of Networks   34
- The Internet Explosion   35

Living With Computers   37
- Explanations: Clarifying Technology   37
- Applications: Computers in Action   37
- Implications: Social and Ethical Issues   40

CrossCurrents: Tech's Double-Edged Sword   43
Steven Levy

Summary	44	Review Questions	45
Chapter Review	44	Discussion Questions	45
Key Terms	44	Projects	45
Interactive Quiz Questions	45	Sources and Resources	46

Chapter 2 Hardware Basics: Inside the Box 48

Thomas J. Watson, Sr., and the Emperor's New Machines	49	The Computer's Memory	60
		How it Works 2.4: Memory	62
What Computers Do	50	CrossCurrents: Bit Literacy	64
A Bit About Bits	51	*Mark Hurst*	
Bit Basics	51	Summary	65
How it Works 2.1: Binary Numbers	52	Chapter Review	65
Building with Bits	53	Key Terms	65
How it Works 2.2: Representing the World's Languages	55	Interactive Quiz Questions	65
Bits, Bytes, and Buzzwords	56	Review Questions	66
The Computer's Core: The CPU and Memory	56	Discussion Questions	66
		Projects	66
The CPU: The Real Computer	56	Sources and Resources	66
How it Works 2.3: The CPU	58		

Chapter 3 Hardware Basics: Peripherals 68

Steve Wozniak, Steve Jobs, and the Garage that Grew Apples	69	Output You Can Hear	81
		Controlling Other Machines	82
Input: From Person to Processor	70	Storage Devices: Input Meets Output	82
The Keyboard	70	Magnetic Tape	82
Pointing Devices	71	**Rules of Thumb: Ergonomics and Health**	83
Reading Tools	72	Magnetic Disks	84
Digitizing the Real World	74	Optical Disks	85
How it Works 3.1: Digitizing the Real World	76	**How it Works 3.4: Disk Storage**	86
		Solid-state Storage Devices	88
Output: From Pulses to People	77	Computer Systems: The Sum of Its Parts	89
Screen Output	77	Ports and Slots Revisited	89
Paper Output	78	Internal and External Drives	90
How it Works 3.2: Color Video	79	Expansion Made Easy: Emerging Interfaces	90
How it Works 3.3: Color Printing	81		

Rules of Thumb: Computer Consumer Concepts	91
Putting It All Together	92
Networks: Systems Without Boundaries	92
Software: The Missing Piece	92
CrossCurrents: Use It or Lose It	93
Arthur H. Bell, Ph.D.	
Summary	94
Chapter Review	94
Key Terms	94
Interactive Quiz Questions	95
Review Questions	95
Discussion Questions	95
Projects	95
Sources and Resources	96

Chapter 4 — Software Basics: The Ghost in the Machine 98

Linus Torvalds and the Software Nobody Owns	99
Processing with Programs	100
Food for Thought	100
A Fast, Stupid Machine	101
How it Works 4.1: Executing a Program	102
The Language of Computers	104
Software Applications: Tools for Users	105
Consumer Applications	105
Integrated Applications and Suites: Software Bundles	107
Vertical-Market and Custom Software	108
System Software: The Hardware-Software Connection	108
What the Operating System Does	108
How it Works 4.2: The Operating Systems	110
Utility Programs	110
Where the Operating System Lives	112
The User Interface: The Human-Machine Connection	112
Character-Based User Interfaces	113
Graphical User Interface Operating Systems	113
Why WIMP Won	114
Multiple User Operating Systems: UNIX and Linux	115
User's View: Connecting to a Multiuser Unix System	116
User's View: Using a Linux GUI	117
Hardware and Software Platforms	118
Tomorrow's User Interfaces	119
Rules of Thumb: Green Computing	121
CrossCurrents: 'Read the Manual!' What Manual?	122
Stephen Manes	
Summary	123
Chapter Review	123
Key Terms	123
Interactive Quiz Questions	124
Review Questions	124
Discussion Questions	124
Projects	124
Sources and Resources	124

Chapter 5 — Computer Applications: Software Tools 126

Bill Gates Rides the Digital Wave	127
Word Processing and Desktop Publishing	128
Word Processing	128
Desktop Publishing	129
User's View: Word Processing	130
Spreadsheets and other Simulation Software	132
Rules of Thumb: Beyond Desktop Tacky!	133
The Spreadsheet	133
User's View: Creating a Simple Worksheet	134
Statistical Software: Beyond Spreadsheets	136
Calculated Risks: Computer Modeling and Simulation	137
Graphics and Multimedia	138
Painting and Digital Image Processing	138
2-D and 3-D Drawing	138
Presentation Graphics: Brining Lectures to Life	139
Dynamic Media: Animation, Video, and Audio	139
User's View: Editing Photographic Images	140
User's View: Creating Presentation Graphics	142

Digital Video	142
How it Works 5.1: Data Compression	**144**
Interactive Multimedia	147
Databases: Electronic File Cabinets	148
Database Anatomy	149
Database Operations	149
User's View: Selecting, Sorting, and Reporting	**150**
Special-Purpose Databases	152
Database Management Systems	152
Databases and Privacy	153
Rules of Thumb: Dealing with Databases	**154**
Rules of Thumb: Your Private Rights	**155**
CrossCurrents: Counterfeit Freedom	156
Randall E. Stross	
Summary	157
Chapter Review	157
Key Terms	157
Interactive Quiz Questions	158
Review Questions	158
Discussion Questions	158
Projects	158
Sources and Resources	159

Chapter 6   Networking and Telecommunication   162

Arthur C. Clarke's Magical Prophecy	*163*
Linking Up: Network Basics	164
Basic Network Anatomy	164
Networks Near and Far	166
Communication Software	167
The Network Advantage	169
Email, Teleconferences, and Instant Messaging: Interpersonal Computing	170
The Postal Alternative	171
Bypassing the Telephone	171
Minimizing Meetings	171
Online Issues: Reliability, Security, Privacy, and Humanity	171
Converging Communication Technologies: From Messages to Money	173
Online Information Services	173
Rules of Thumb: Online Survival Tips	**174**
Video Teleconferencing	174
Fax Machines and Fax Modems	174
Voice Mail and Computer Telephony	175
The Global Positioning System	176
E-Money	176
Emerging Communication Technologies: Beyond Wires	176
Building Bandwidth	177
Fiber Optic Connections	177
Wireless Communication Takes Off	178
Digital Communication in Perspective	179
CrossCurrents: Time To Do Everything Except Think	180
David Brooks	
Summary	181
Chapter Review	181
Key Terms	181
Interactive Quiz Questions	182
Review Questions	182
Discussion Questions	182
Projects	182
Sources and Resources	182

Chapter 7   Inside the Internet and the Web   184

ARPANET Pioneers Build an Unreliable Network . . . on Purpose	*185*
Inside the Internet	186
Counting Connections	186
Internet Protocols	187
Internet Addresses	188
Internet Access Options	189
Inside Internet Applications: The Client-Server Connection	193
Inside the Web	194
Web Protocols: HTTP and HTML	194
Publishing on the Web	195
How it Works 7.1: The World Wide Web	**196**
From Hypertext to Multimedia	197

User's View: Building a Web Site	198	Chapter Review	205
Rules of Thumb: Weaving Winning Web Sites	201	Key Terms	205
		Interactive Quiz Questions	206
Dynamic Web Sites: Beyond HTML	202	Review Questions	206
Putting Protocols to Work	203	Discussion Questions	206
CrossCurrents: Machine Net	204	Projects	206
Cathy Benko		Sources and Resources	206
Summary	205		

Chapter 8   From Internet to Information Infrastructure   208

Tim Berners-Lee Weaves the Web for Everybody	209	Internet Issues: Ethical and Political Dilemmas	219
Internet Applications: Communication and Connection	210	Internet Everywhere: The Invisible Information Infrastructure	220
Search Engines	210	Cyberspace: The Electronic Frontier	221
Portals	211	CrossCurrents: The Day I Got Napsterized	223
Email on the Internet	211	*Steven Levy*	
Rules of Thumb: Working the Web	212	Summary	224
Mailing Lists	212	Chapter Review	224
Network News	212	Key Terms	224
Real-Time Communication	214	Interactive Quiz Questions	225
Rules of Thumb: Netiquette	215	Review Questions	225
Push Technology	216	Discussion Questions	225
Intranets, Extranets, and Electronic Commerce	217	Projects	225
Web Services	218	Sources and Resources	226
The Evolving Internet	218		
Internet2 and the Next Generation Internet	219		

Chapter 9   Computer Security and Risks   228

Kempelen's Amazing Chess-Playing Machine	229	Backups and Other Precautions	242
Online Outlaws: Computer Crime	230	Human Security Controls: Law, Management, and Ethics	242
The Computer Crime Dossier	230	**Security, Privacy, Freedom, and Ethics: The Delicate Balance**	242
Theft by Computer	231		
Software Piracy and Intellectual Property Laws	232	When Security Threatens Privacy	242
Software Sabotage: Viruses and Other Invaders	234	Justice on the Electronic Frontier	244
Hacking and Electronic Trespassing	236	**Rules of Thumb: Safe Computing**	245
Computer Security: Reducing Risks	238	**Rules of Thumb: Computer Ethics**	246
Physical Access Restrictions	238	**Security and Reliability**	246
Passwords	238	Bugs and Breakdowns	247
Firewalls, Encryption, and Audits	239	Computers at War	248
How it Works 9.1: Cryptography	240	Is Security Possible?	249

CrossCurrents: Now, Weapons of Mass Disruption? *George F. Will*	251	Review Questions	253
		Discussion Questions	253
		Projects	254
		Sources and Resources	254
Summary	252		
Chapter Review	252		
Key Terms	252		
Interactive Quiz Questions	253		

Chapter 10 Information Age Issues: Inventing the Future 256

Alan Kay Invents the Future	257	The Day After Tomorrow: Information Technology Meets Biology	270
Into the Information Age	258		
Where the Computers Work	258	Human Questions for a Computer Age	272
The Automated Factory	259	Will Computers Be Democratic?	272
How it Works 10.1: Information Flow in a Management Information System	**260**	Will the Global Village Be a Community?	272
		Will We Become Information Slaves?	273
The Automated Office	262	Standing On the Shoulders of Giants	273
The Electronic Cottage	262	CrossCurrents: Borg in the Mirror	274
Computers and Jobs	262	*Peter Cochrane*	
Tomorrow Never Knows	264	Summary	275
From Research to Reality: 21st Century Information Technology	265	Chapter Review	275
		Key Terms	275
Tomorrow's Hardware: Trends and Innovations	265	Interactive Quiz Questions	276
Tomorrow's Software: Evolving Applications and Interfaces	267	Review Questions	276
		Discussion Questions	276
Tomorrow's Service: Truly Intelligent Agents	268	Projects	276
Tomorrow's Way of Life: Transparent Technology	269	Sources and Resources	277

The Concise Computer Consumer's Guide 281

Appendix: Correlation Guide to the ACM Code of Ethics and Professional Conduct 289

Glossary 295

Credits 311

Index 313

About this Book

> **Confluence**
> 1: a **coming or flowing together**, meeting, or gathering at one point (a happy confluence of weather and scenery);
> 2a: the flowing together of **two or more streams**;
>   b: the **place of meeting** of two streams;
>   c: the **combined stream** formed by conjunction
> —*Merriam Webster's Collegiate Dictionary, Electronic Edition*

When powerful forces come together, change is inevitable. As we enter the 21st century, we're standing at the confluence of three powerful technological forces: computers, telecommunications, and electronic entertainment. The computer's digital technology is showing up in everything from telephones to televisions, and the lines that separate these machines are eroding. This **digital convergence** is rapidly—and radically—altering the world's economic landscape. Start-up companies and industries are emerging to ride the waves of change. Some thrive; others dive into oblivion. Meanwhile, older organizations reorganize, regroup, and redefine themselves to keep from being washed away.

Smaller computers, faster processors, smarter software, larger networks, new communication media—in the world of information technology, it seems like change is the only constant. In less than a human lifetime, this technological cascade has transformed virtually every facet of our society—and the transformation is just beginning. As old technologies merge and new technologies emerge, far-fetched predictions routinely come true. This headlong rush into the high-tech future poses a challenge for all of us: How can we extract the knowledge we need from the deluge of information? What must we understand about information technology to successfully navigate the waters of change that carry us into the future? *Computer Confluence: Exploring Tomorrow's Technology* is designed to aid travelers on their journey into that future.

What Is Computer Confluence?

Computer Confluence presents computers and information technology on three levels:

- Explanations: *Computer Confluence* clearly explains what a computer is and what it can (and can't) do; it clearly explains the basics of information technology, from multimedia PCs to the Internet and beyond.
- Applications: *Computer Confluence* illustrates how computers and networks can be used as practical tools to solve a wide variety of problems.
- Implications: *Computer Confluence* puts computers in a human context, illustrating how information technology affects our lives, our world, and our future.

The book consists of 11 chapters, numbered 0 through 10 in the grand tradition of computer science. Chapter 0, ReadMe, new to this edition, provides an introduction for students who have little or no experience with PCs and the Internet. The chapter also includes an orientation to the *Computer Confluence* book, CD-ROM, and Web site.

The book's focus flows from the concrete to the controversial and from the present to the future. Individual chapters have a similarly expanding focus. After a brief introduction, each chapter flows from basic concepts toward abstract, future-oriented questions and ideas.

About the Author

George Beekman is a Senior Instructor in the Department of Computer Science at Oregon State University. An innovative computer literacy course he created more than a decade ago served as the inspiration for *Computer Confluence*. He has since designed several classes in interactive multimedia and the social and ethical issues surrounding information technology. He coordinates multimedia components of OSU's New Media program, which focuses on the digital convergence of multimedia, telemedia, and print media.

George Beekman has taught workshops in computer literacy and multimedia for students, educators, and economically disadvantaged families from the Atlantic to Alaska. He has written more than 20 books on computers, information technology, and multimedia, as well as more than 100 articles and reviews for *Macworld* and other popular publications. In his spare time he runs, rides his bike, and plays music with his friends.

About this Edition

 Even if you're on the right track, **you'll get run over** if you just sit on it.
—Pat Koppman

The pace of change threatens to make even the most successful introductory computer classes irrelevant. *Computer Confluence Concise*, Fifth Edition, helps students and instructors deal with rapid changes by emphasizing big ideas, broad trends, and the human aspects of technology—critical concepts that tend to remain constant even while hardware and software change. Every edition of *Computer Confluence* is rewritten to reflect changes in the technological landscape. This edition places new emphasis on the latest Web technologies, electronic commerce, multimedia trends, and emerging software platforms such as Windows XP, Linux, and Mac OS-X, and Palm OS. Here's a list of highlights new to this edition:

Chapter 0, "ReadMe," is brand new. It addresses the most commonly reported problem of introductory computer concepts classes—the diverse backgrounds of students in those classes. Many instructors report that the majority of their new students have some

PC and Internet experience. These students don't need to be told about keyboarding, using a CD-ROM, or navigating a Web site. But if these topics aren't covered, the inexperienced students are at a distinct disadvantage. The ReadMe Chapter is designed for those beginners, so they can fill in the gaps in their knowledge before launching into the rest of the book, the CD-ROM, and the Web site. The chapter also includes an orientation to all three components of *Computer Confluence* that includes time-saving tips for everyone.

Chapter 1, "Computer Currents: From Calculation to Connection," has been streamlined and updated; some of the most basic material has been moved to Chapter 0.

Chapter 2, "Hardware Basics: Inside the Box," and Chapter 3, "Hardware Basics: Peripherals," have been updated with coverage of state-of-the-market hardware. There's a more practical emphasis on equipment that students will encounter in their day-to-day computing experience. An expanded section on disk technology helps students make sense of the ever-growing list of storage options, from rewritable CDs to DVD-R. This edition also includes updated coverage of USB and FireWire (IEEE 1394), modern I/O standards that are taking center stage in new machines. Chapter 3 now includes Computer Consumer Concepts, a Rules of Thumb box that illuminates the concepts *behind* PC buyer's guides.

Chapter 4, "Software Basics: The Ghost in the Machine," has been updated and streamlined. User's View boxes covering Windows XP and Mac OS X are now in Chapter 0. Chapter 4 includes examples and explanations of Linux, UNIX, and other operating systems to provide a broader perspective for students familiar with PCs. The chapter includes an updated Rules of Thumb box, Green Computing, containing tips for minimizing our technological impact on the environment.

Chapter 5, "Computer Applications: Software Tools," contains updated examples showing the latest versions of Microsoft Office, Adobe Photoshop, and other applications in action.

Chapter 6, "Networking and Telecommunication," has been reorganized and updated to reflect changes in this dynamic industry. A new section on wireless communication introduces several important wireless technologies.

Chapter 7, "Inside the Internet and the Web," and Chapter 8, "From Internet to Information Infrastructure," replace the previous edition's Chapter 7. The new Chapter 7 includes clear explanations of basic Internet technology, including protocols, addresses, and connections. There's expanded coverage of DSL, cable modems, and wireless Internet connections. There's also more on dynamic Web tools, multimedia Web technology, and database-driven Web sites. The chapter includes a new Rules of Thumb box, Weaving Winning Web Sites. Chapter 8 opens with a new profile of Web visionary Tim Berners-Lee. The chapter focuses on the ways people put the Internet to work, including expanded coverage of search engines, portals, email, newsgroups, teleconferencing, peer-to-peer computing, grid computing, and electronic commerce.

Chapter 9, "Computer Security and Risks," has been updated with the latest data on computer crime and security. The chapter now includes discussions of *fair use*, the potential for abuse of intellectual property laws, and several controversial cases involving the Digital Millennium Copyright Act. There's more of an ethical emphasis in the expanded and updated section called "Security, Privacy, Freedom, and Ethics: The Delicate Balance."

Chapter 10, "Information Age Issues: Inventing the Future," is updated and streamlined. Since the short-term future of technology is explored throughout the book, this chapter looks further down the road, with discussions of optical computing, sensory computing, ubiquitous computing, microtechnology, nanotechnology, biotechnology, and artificial life. As in previous editions, the chapter ends by giving this futuristic technology a human context; the final pages raise difficult questions and pose ethical challenges for all of us.

Crosscurrents articles that close each chapter are, with a few exceptions, new to this edition. They include some of the best short essays on our relationship to technology that have been published in the past year. Topics include the role of information technology in terrorism, the erosion of personal privacy, the abuse of intellectual property laws, software reliability, machine intelligence, and our future as borgs.

The CD-ROM has been updated with new multimedia material and interactive explorations.

The Web site (www.prenhall.com/beekman) is continually updated to reflect changes in the Web and the subject matter. New to the fifth edition is Prentice Hall Web support material, including a syllabus manager, student chat rooms, and self-assessment quizzes.

For the Student

If you're like most students, you aren't taking this course to read about computers—you want to use them. That's sensible. You can't really understand computers without some hands-on experience, and you'll be able to apply your computer skills to a wide variety of future projects. But it's a mistake to think that you're computer savvy just because you can use a PC to write term papers and surf the Internet. It's important to understand how people use and abuse computer technology, because that technology has a powerful and growing impact on your life. (If you can't imagine how your life would be different without computers, read the vignette called "Living without Computers" in Chapter 1.) Even if you have lots of computer experience, future trends are almost certain to make much of that experience obsolete—probably sooner than you think. In the next few years, computers are likely to take on entirely new forms and roles because of breakthroughs in artificial intelligence, voice recognition, virtual reality, interactive multimedia, networking, and cross-breeding with telephone and home entertainment technologies. If your knowledge of computers stops with a handful of PC and Internet applications, you may be standing still while the world changes around you.

When you're cascading through white water, you need to be able to use a paddle, but it's also important to know how to read a map, a compass, and the river. *Computer Confluence: Exploring Tomorrow's Technology* is designed to serve as a map, compass, and book of river lore to help you ride the information waves into the future.

Computer Confluence will help you understand the important trends that will change the way you work with computers and the way computers work for you. This book discusses the promise and the problems of computer technology without overwhelming you with technobabble.

Computer Confluence is intentionally nontechnical and down to earth. Occasional ministories bring concepts and speculations to life. Illustrations and photos make abstract concepts concrete. Quotes add thought-provoking and humorous seasoning.

Whether you're a hard-core hacker or a confirmed computerphobe, there's something for you in *Computer Confluence*. Dive in!

George Beekman

For the Instructor

Instructor Resources

Instructor's Resource CD-ROM
The **Instructor's Resource CD-ROM** that is available with *Computer Confluence* contains:

- Instructor's Manual in Word and PDF.
- Solutions to all questions and exercises from the book and web site
- PowerPoint lectures with PresMan software
- A Windows-based test manager and the associated test bank in Word format with over 1500 new questions

Tools for Online Learning

www.prenhall.com/beekman
This text is accompanied by a companion Web site at www.prenhall.com/beekman. This site brings you and your students a richer, more interactive Web experience. Features of this site include the ability for you to customize your homepage with real-time news headlines, current events, exercises, an interactive study guide, and downloadable supplements.

ONLINE Courseware for Blackboard, WebCT and Course Compass
Now you have the freedom to personalize your own online course materials!

Prentice Hall provides the content and support you need to create and manage your own online course in WebCT, Blackboard, or Prentice Hall's own Course Compass. Content includes lecture material, interactive exercises, e-commerce case videos, additional testing questions and projects.

CourseCompass www.coursecompass.com
CourseCompass is a dynamic, interactive online course-management tool powered exclusively for Pearson Education by Blackboard. This exciting product allows you to teach market-leading Pearson Education content in an easy-to-use, customizable format.

BlackBoard www.prenhall.com/blackboard
Prentice Hall's abundant online content, combined with Blackboard's popular tools and interface, result in robust Web-based courses that are easy to implement, manage, and use—taking your courses to new heights in student interaction and learning.

WebCT www.prenhall.com/webct
Course-management tools within WebCT include page tracking, progress tracking, class and student management, gradebook, communication, calendar, reporting tools, and more. GOLD LEVEL CUSTOMER SUPPORT, available exclusively to adopters of Prentice Hall courses, is provided free-of-charge upon adoption and provides you with priority assistance, training discounts, and dedicated technical support.

Train & Assess IT: www.prenhall.com/phit
Prentice Hall offers Performance Based Training and Assessment in one product, Train&Assess IT. The Training component offers computer-based training that a student can use to preview, learn, and review Microsoft Office applications and computer literacy skills. Web- or CD-ROM delivered, the training component offers interactive, multimedia, computer-based training to augment classroom learning. Built-in prescriptive testing suggests a study path based not only on student test results but also on the specific textbook chosen for the course.

The assessment component offers computer-based testing that shares the same user interface and is used to evaluate a student's knowledge about specific topics in Word, Excel, Access, PowerPoint, Windows, Outlook, and the Internet. It does this in a task-oriented environment to demonstrate proficiency as well as comprehension of the topics by the students.

EXPLORE IT: www.prenhall.com/phit
Prentice Hall offers computer based training just for computer literacy. Designed to cover some of the most difficult concepts, as well as some current topical areas—EXPLORE IT is a web and CD-ROM based product designed to compliment a course. Available for free with any Prentice Hall title, our new lab coverage includes: Troubleshooting, Programming Logic, Mouse and Keyboard Basics, Databases, Building a Web Page, Hardware, Software, Operating Systems, Building a Network and more!

Throughout **Computer Confluence**, special focus boxes compliment the text:

Human Connection

Human Connection boxes at the beginning of all chapters feature stories of personalities who made an impact on the world of computing, and in some cases, people whose lives were transformed by computers and information technology.

How It Works

How It Works boxes are designed to provide additional technical material for courses and students who need it. How does the CPU execute a program? Why does a color image look different on the screen than on a printout? How does compression make files smaller? How can messages be encrypted? Students will find answers to these

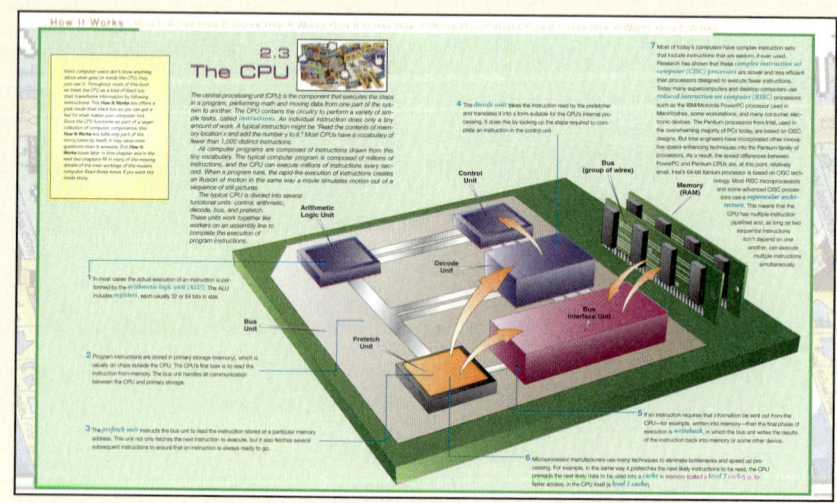

kinds of questions in the How It Works boxes. For classes where this kind of technical detail isn't necessary, students can safely skip these boxes without missing any critical information. How It Works boxes are numbered to make it easy for instructors to create customized reading assignments by specifying which are required and which are optional.

User's View

User's View boxes show the reader, through screens and text, what it's like to work with computer applications without getting bogged down in the details of button pushing. Featured applications are the latest versions of applications used by professionals, including Microsoft Office, Quark XPress, and Adobe Photoshop. These applications are available in similar versions on both Windows and Macintosh platforms.

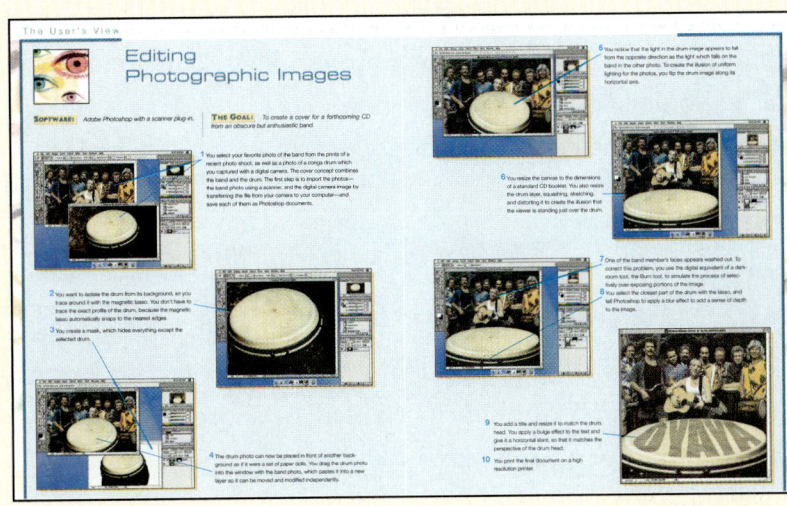

Crosscurrents

Crosscurrents boxes at the end of each chapter provide thought-provoking, timely, and sometimes controversial essays and articles by respected writers, analysts, and industry insiders. How is this technology changing our lives? What have we given up in return for a high-tech future? Who stands to gain the most, and who stands to lose the most, as we move into an information-based economy? How will future generations experience you digital works of art and literature? Is personal privacy history? Does our high-tech infrastructure make us more or less vulnerable to terrorists? Are digital implants in our medical future? These and other questions are raised—and wrestled with—in Crosscurrents

Rules of Thumb

Rules of Thumb boxes provide practical, nontechnical tips for avoiding the pitfalls and problems created by computer technology. How can you use graphics effectively and tastefully in a computer document? How can you minimize the health hazards of extended computer use? How can you protect your data from viruses and other software risks? What's the best way to communicate effectively with electronic mail? These are the types of questions that are answered in Rules of Thumb boxes.

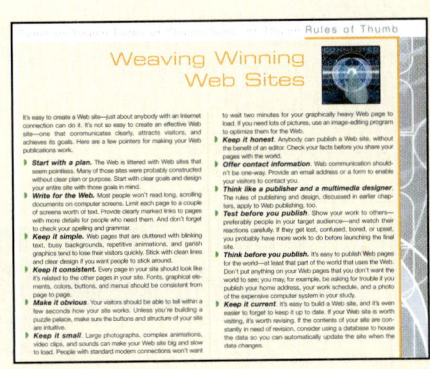

xix

ACM Guidelines

Appendix. The ACM Code of Ethics is the most widely known code of conduct specifically for computer professionals. This appendix reprints the code, along with detailed annotations that link specific tenants to related ethics material throughout the text.

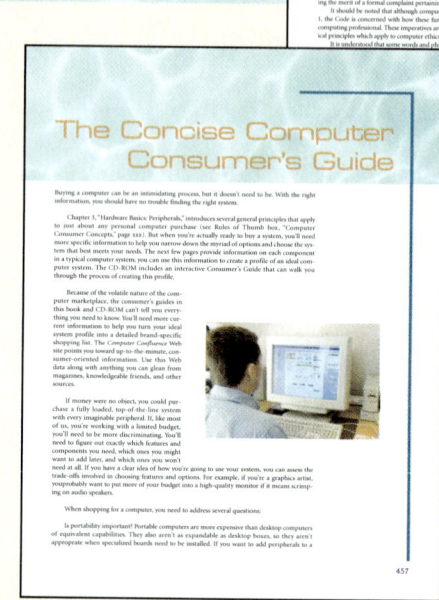

Concise Computer Consumer Guide

Concise Computer Consumer's Guide. For those students who are ready to buy a computer system, this guide provides up-to-date guidance on how to narrow down the myriad of options and make good decisions.

Companion Website at
www.prenhall.com/beekman

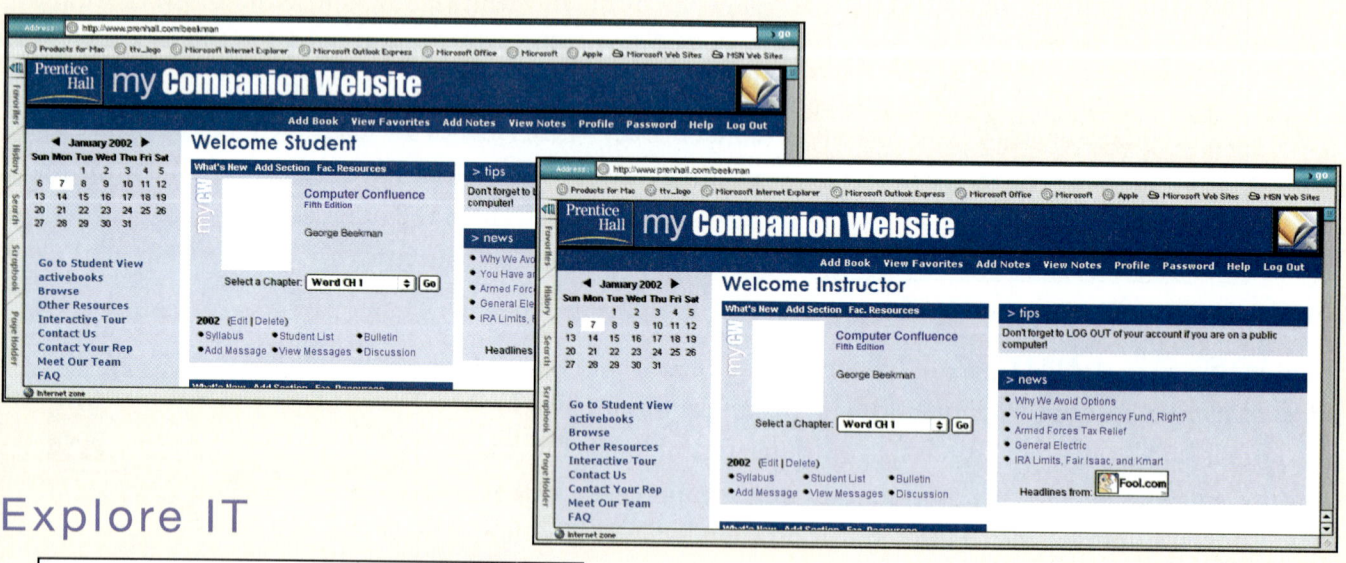

Explore IT

Acknowledgments

I'm deeply grateful to all of the people who've come together to make *Computer Confluence* a success. Their names may not be on the cover, but their high-quality work shows in every detail of this project.

I'm fortunate to be working with many of the same Prentice Hall people who helped with the fourth edition. Melissa Whitaker-Oliver, the Managing Editor for the Fourth Edition, took on the role of Acquisitions Editor for this new edition. In spite of the shortened publication schedule and the trauma that followed the terrorist tragedy of September 11, 2001, Melissa kept the project on track.

I'm especially indebted to Developmental Editor Lena Buonanno, who worked closely with me on the development of this fifth edition. Lena's skill, professionalism, patience, and attention to detail helped me to stay the course during the most trying of times. The book is much better thanks to her.

Many others brought their considerable talents to *Computer Confluence*. Patricia Smythe, design director, and Jill Little, designer, are the people most responsible for the design of the book. Lynne Breitfeller and Gail Steier de Acevedo worked on all aspects of production, helping ensure that the project could make all those nearly impossible deadlines. Editorial Assistant Mary Ann Broadnax played a central role at every step of this complex project. Abby Reip's patient and persistent research uncovered most of the excellent photos in these pages. The staff at Pre-Press produced the final book from all of the raw materials supplied by the others listed here. The details of the CD-ROM and the Web site were coordinated by Cathleen Profitko, media product manager. Content for the Web site is provided by Paul Berk.

I owe special thanks to members of my family who temporarily set aside many of their own personal and professional goals to help me with this project. My daughter, Johanna Beekman, helped organize the massive amounts of paper resources I've accumulated since the last edition.

It's not so easy to list the contributions of my wife Susan Grace. She was there to help in all kinds of ways, from research and organization to communication and collaboration. Just as importantly, she selflessly maintained the infrastructure of our home, our family, and our business, making it possible for me to meet the difficult deadlines of this project.

But the biggest contributions came from my son Ben Beekman, who served as my assistant throughout the project. As a college student, Ben is an ideal partner—he knows our readership from the inside. But Ben also knows the business of writing and the business of multimedia, and he's applied his expertise to every phase of this massive project—writing, research, information organization, screen shots, fact checking, graphic design, Web-page construction and editing, CD-ROM work, and more. I simply couldn't have completed this edition of *Computer Confluence* without his help.

All of this effort would be wasted if *Computer Confluence* didn't reach its intended audience. Thankfully, Sharon Turkovich, senior marketing manager, and her team have a strong track record for getting the good word out to the right people.

There are others who contributed to *Computer Confluence* in all kinds of ways, including critiquing chapters, answering technical questions, tracking down obscure references, guiding me through difficult decisions, and being there when I needed support. There's no room here to detail their contributions, but I want to thank the people who gave time, energy, talent, and support during the years that this book was under development, including Scobel Wiggins, Jim Folts, Jan Dymond, Mike Quinn, Michelle Artery, Nicole Mahan, Mark Dinsmore, Dave Trenkel, Paul Thurrott, Gary Brent, Robert Rose, Marion Rose, Maureen Allaire, Michelle Baxter, Natalie Anderson, Sherry Clark, Mike Johnson, Walter Rudd, Cherie Pancake, Bruce D'Ambrosio, Bernie Feyerham, Rajeev Pandey, Dave Stuve, Clay Cowgill, Keith Vertanen, Megan Slothover, Claudette Hastie-Baehrs, Shjoobedebop, Sujita, Isaiah Jones, Inner Strength, Oyaya, Breitenbush, Oregon Public Broadcasting, KLCC, and all of the editors and others who helped with previous editions of *Computer Confluence*. Thanks also to all the hardware and software companies whose cooperation made my work easier. And most of all, thanks to my family, whose patience, support, love, and sacrifice inspired me every day through all these years.

Computer Confluence Academic Advisors

A special thanks to the *Computer Confluence* Academic Advisors, a group of dedicated professors from all areas of the United States and Canada who were committed to providing valuable feedback and suggestions for all parts of this text. *Computer Confluence*, Third Edition, benefited tremendously from your honest and insightful analyses. Their comments are also reflected in the new Fifth Edition.

> Warren Boe, University of Iowa; David Bozak, SUNY Oswego; Nancy Cosgrove, University of Central Florida; Allen Dooley, Pasadena City College; Dwight Graham, Prairie State College; Margaret Guertin, Boston University; Lynne Hanrahan, Salem State College; Edward Kaplan, Bentley College; Linda Kieffer, Eastern Washington University; Larry Lagerstrom, University of California, Berkeley; Doug MacDormand, Red Deer College; Virginia Phillips, Youngstown State University; Paul Ryburn, University of Memphis; Susan Switzer, Central Michigan University; Dale Underwood, Lexington Community College.

Academic Reviewers

Thanks to all of the dedicated educators who reviewed the manuscript at various stages of development; *Computer Confluence* and its accompanying CD-ROM are significantly more valuable educational tools as a result of your ideas, suggestions, and constructive criticism.

> William Allen, University of Central Florida; Dennis Anderson, Pace University; Revis L. Bell, St. Philip's College; William Boroski, Trident Technical College; Frederick Bounds, DeKalb College; Gary Brent, Scottsdale Community College; Judy Cameron, Spokane Community College; Mark Ciampa, Volunteer State Community College; Daniel Combellick, Scottsdale Community College; Elaine Cousins, University of Michigan at Ann Arbor; H. E. Dunsmore, Purdue University; Joseph Fahs, Elmira College; Pat Fenton, West Valley College; David Fickbohm, Golden Gate University; Blaine Garfolo, San Francisco State University; Wade Graves, Grayson County College; Ananda Gunawardena, University of Houston-Downtown; Dale Gust, Central Michigan University; Michael Hansen, Midlands Technical College; Sally Ann Hanson, Mercer County Community College; Shelly Hawkins, Duquesne University; Rachel E. Hinton, Broome Community College and Binghamton University; Edward Hom, Nassau Community College; Monte J. Johnson, St. Cloud State University; Trevor Jones, Duquesne University; Fred Klappenberger, Anne Arundel City College; Robert Kuhn, Muskingum Area Technical College; Larry Lagerstrom, University of California, Berkeley; Edward L. Lamie, California State University at Stanislaus; Deborah Ludford, Glendale Community College; Valerie A. Martin, Immaculata College; Brenda Mathews, University College of the Cariboo; Pat Mattsen, St. Cloud University; Maribeth L. McAnally, Texas A&M University-Commerce; Vicki McCullough, Palomar College; J. Michael McGrew, Ball State University; Doris McPherson, Schoolcraft College; Linda Wise Miller, University of Idaho; William Moates, Indiana State University; Angela Peace, NorthWest Arkansas Community

College; Sally Peterson, University of Wisconsin at Madison; Gerhard Plenert, Brigham Young University; Loreto Porte, Hostos City College; John Rezac, Johnson County Community College; Mike Quinn, Oregon State University; Jennifer Sedelmeyer, Broome City College; Margaret Sklar, Northern Michigan University; Raoul Smith, Northeastern University; Jayne Stasser, Miami University; Randy Stolze, Marist College; Tim Sylvester, Maricopa City College; John Telford, Salem State College; Dwight Watt, Athens Area Technical Institute; Patricia Wermers, North Shore City College; Alan Whitehurst, Brigham Young University; Tom Wiggen, University of North Dakota; Melissa Wiggins, Mississippi College; Floyd Jay Winters, Manatee City College; Rich Yankosky, Frederick City College.

ReadMe

When you purchase computer software, the software commonly comes with a file or document called "ReadMe" or "ReadMe First." The ReadMe file typically tells you things you should know before you use the software: a broad overview or orientation, tips for getting started and making the most of the product, and background information for bringing beginners up to speed before using the product. This short ReadMe chapter is like a ReadMe file. In the introduction you'll find instructions that will help you determine how to make the most efficient use of this chapter—and of the complete Computer Confluence package—based on your background, interests, and needs.

After you read this chapter you should be able to:

▼

Describe the basic parts of a PC and how they work together

Explain the relationship between hardware and software

Describe how the Internet extends the functionality of a PC

Use a Windows PC or Macintosh to explore the *Computer Confluence* CD-ROM

Use a Windows PC or Macintosh to explore the *Computer Confluence* Web site

▲

▼ In this chapter:

A basic introduction to computers and the Internet

Instructions for launching the *Computer Confluence* CD-ROM and opening the *Computer Confluence* Web site

. . . and more.

▼ On the CD-ROM:

An interactive tour of the CD's most useful tools

A self-test of PC and Internet basics

. . . and more.

▼ On the Web:

www.prenhall.com/beekman

A tour of the most important features of the Web site

A self-test of PC and Internet basics

. . . and more.

Human Dreams and Dream Machines

The obvious choices aren't the only choices.
Steve Roberts

In 1983 Steve Roberts realized he wasn't happy chained to his desk and his debts. He decided to build a new lifestyle that combined his passions—writing, adventure, computers, bicycling, learning, and networking. Six months later he hit the road on Winnebiko, a recumbent bike equipped with a laptop and solar panel. He connected each day to the CompuServe network through pay phones, transmitting magazine articles and book chapters.

Steve Roberts with BEHEMOTH

Years later Roberts was exploring America on BEHEMOTH (Big Electronic Human-Energized Machine . . . Only Too Heavy), a million-dollar bike with seven networked computers and wireless communication capability. Roberts pedaled 17,000 miles before pursuing a new dream: "life with no hills." His latest project is Microship, a high-tech craft that will allow him to extend his technomadic lifestyle to the ocean. "There's a *lot* of world to explore out there. Having had a taste of it, how could I spend my life in one place?"

Vaughn Rogers "wasn't into computers." Computers, he thought, were useful for typing papers, but they weren't exciting. *Art* was exciting to Rogers, who had been drawing all his life.

In 1995 he went with a friend to the Computer Clubhouse, a nonprofit educational center at the Science Museum in Cambridge, Massachusetts. He saw other teens using computers to create art, edit video, and mix music. Before long, Vaughn was doing his art at the Computer Clubhouse after school.

Vaughn Rogers in his own art work

Today 21-year-old Rogers studies visual communication and animation at Catherine Gibbs College. His goal is to work in computer animation and video, using his drawing talent enhanced with computer technology. He now works as an assistant manager at the Computer Clubhouse, helping others learn to use computers to pursue their passions.

When Patricia Walsh lost her sight at 14, she almost lost sight of her dreams. She had already completed the advanced mathematics and science classes at her high school, and she wanted to go further. She learned to read and write Braille, but Braille couldn't help with the equations and formulas she needed to study. Her PC could talk using text-to-speech software, but it had nothing to say about scientific graphs and charts.

Fortunately, Walsh met John Gardner, a blind physics professor at Oregon State University. Gardner was developing tools to make math and science accessible to visually impaired people. His Tiger Tactile Graphics and Braille Embosser printed equations, formulas, and graphs as raised patterns that could be read by touch. Using this technology, Walsh could read class notes emailed by her professors. Once again she could "see" the figures that were critical to her studies.

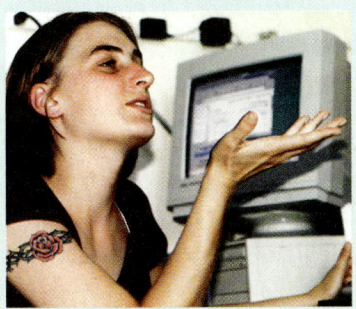
Patricia Walsh

Walsh started helping Gardner develop accessibility tools. She became a spokesperson for adaptive technology, telling others about tools that can open doors for people with disabilities. Walsh is now a junior at Winona University in Minnesota, where she uses the tools that she helped develop to pursue her dream. "Computers have allowed me to get in the mainstream. Now I can do what I used to love before I became blind. I've even become a CS major."

Steve Roberts, Vaughn Rogers, and Patricia Walsh would be living very different lives today if they hadn't connected with computers. Their stories are interesting and inspiring, but they aren't unique. Every day computer technology changes people's lives all around the world.

Sometimes it seems like everybody uses computers. In fact, the great majority of people on our planet have never touched a computer!

Most of the people who *do* use computers have fairly limited experience and ability—typically the basics of word processing, electronic mail, and finding information on the World Wide Web. The percentage of people who can go beyond the basics and harness the power of a modern PC is relatively small.

If you're a member of this tiny community of **power users,** the next few pages aren't for you. But before you move on to Chapter 1, take a look at the *Computer Confluence* Quick Start and Navigating *Computer Confluence* starting on page xxx. You'll find tips for getting the most out of this book and the companion CD and Web site. This chapter closes with a CrossCurrents article that will give you something to think about.

If you're a **casual computer user,** comfortable with the basic operation of a PC, a CD-ROM drive, and a Web browser, you may want to look through this chapter quickly and spend more time with the Quick Start, Navigating *Computer Confluence*, and CrossCurrents sections before moving on to Chapter 1, where the real story begins. (If you're not sure about your knowledge level, check out the questions at the end of the chapter. If you have trouble answering them, spend a little more time looking over this chapter before you move on.)

If you're a **beginner,** your experience is limited or out of date, you're uncomfortable with PC technology, or you just want to be thorough, this chapter is for you. Here you'll find the basic knowledge you'll need to bring you up to speed, so you're not struggling to catch up as you explore the rest of the book. You'll also learn what you need to know to take full advantage of the *Computer Confluence* CD-ROM and Web site. Along with this book, these resources can provide you with a rich multimedia introduction to the world of computers and information technology.

Whichever path you choose, don't wait until you're sitting in front of a computer to read *Computer Confluence*. Hands-on computer experience is important, but you won't need the computer to take advantage of this book. Wherever you are, just dive in.

Key terms in this chapter, and throughout the book, are highlighted in blue boldface. Secondary terms are highlighted in blue italics. In this chapter, the key terms are the ones that are critical for getting started with the Computer Confluence book, CD-ROM, and Web site; secondary terms are terms that are introduced briefly here and covered in more detail later.

PC Basics

> The beginning is the **most important part** of the work.
> —Plato

Computers come in all kinds of packages, from massive supercomputers to tiny computers embedded in cell phones, credit cards, and even microscopic machines and "smart" pills. But in this chapter, we'll focus on the typical desktop computer—the **personal computer**, or **PC**. We'll start with a look at the physical parts of a PC—the PC's **hardware**. This whirlwind tour will offer a quick, practical overview; you'll learn more in later chapters.

PC Hardware Basics

> **Hardware**: the parts of a computer that **can be kicked**.
> —Jeff Pesis

Modern desktop PCs don't all look alike, but under the skin, they're more alike than different. Every PC is built around a tiny *microprocessor* that controls the workings of the system. This **central processing unit**, or **CPU**, is usually housed in a box, called the *system unit* (or, more often, just "the computer" or "the PC") that serves as command central for the entire computer system. The CPU is the real computer—it controls the operation of all the other computer components. Some of these components are housed in the system unit with the *CPU*; others are *peripheral devices*—or simply *peripherals*—external devices connected via cables to the system unit.

The system unit includes built-in **memory** and a **hard disk** for storage and retrieval of information. The CPU uses memory for instant access to information while it's working. The built-in hard disk serves as a longer-term storage device for large quantities of information.

The PC's main hard disk is a permanent fixture in the system unit. Other types of disk drives work with *removable media*—disks that can be separated from their drives, just as an audio CD can be removed from a stereo system. A typical PC system unit includes a diskette drive and a CD-ROM drive (or some other kind of optical drive). A *diskette drive* (also known as a *floppy disk drive*) enables you to store small amounts of information on pocket-sized plastic-covered magnetic **diskettes**. A **CD-ROM drive** enables the computer to read and use information stored on 5-1/4-inch optical disks, including audio CDs and CD-ROMs (such as the one packaged with this book). Disk drives that are included in the system unit are called *internal drives*. (*External drives* can be attached to the system unit via cables. For example, a PC system might include an external hard disk for additional storage, a Zip drive for accessing removable Zip disks, and a CD-RW drive for reading and writing CDs.)

Other system unit components, including the video display card, the sound card, the network interface card, and the modem, communicate with external devices, with other computers, and with networks.

A standard desktop PC is made up of several components, including a system unit, a monitor, a keyboard, and a mouse. The system unit typically includes an internal hard drive, a CD-ROM drive, and a diskette drive.

But the PC's main purpose isn't to communicate with other machines—it's there to communicate with you. Four common *peripherals* aid this human-computer interaction:

- A **keyboard** enables you to type text and numerical data into the computer's memory.
- A **mouse** enables you to point to text, graphical objects, menu commands, and other items on the screen.
- A **monitor** displays text, numbers, and pictures from the computer's memory.
- A **printer** generates printed letters, papers, transparencies, labels, and other hard copies. (The printer might be directly connected to the computer, or it might be shared by several computers on a network.)

The next two pages illustrate the fundamentals of as basic PC keyboard and mouse. Chapter 3 explores peripherals in more detail.

Using a Keyboard

Typing letters, numbers, and special characters with a computer keyboard is similar to typing on a standard typewriter keyboard. But unlike a typewriter, the computer responds by displaying the typed characters on the monitor screen at the position of the line or rectangle called the cursor. Some keys on the computer keyboard—*cursor (arrow) keys*, the *Delete key*, the *Enter key*, *function keys (f-keys)*, and others—send special commands to the computer. These keys may have different names or meanings on different computer systems. This figure shows a typical keyboard on a Windows-compatible PC. Keyboards for Macintoshes and other types of systems have a few differences but operate on the same principles.

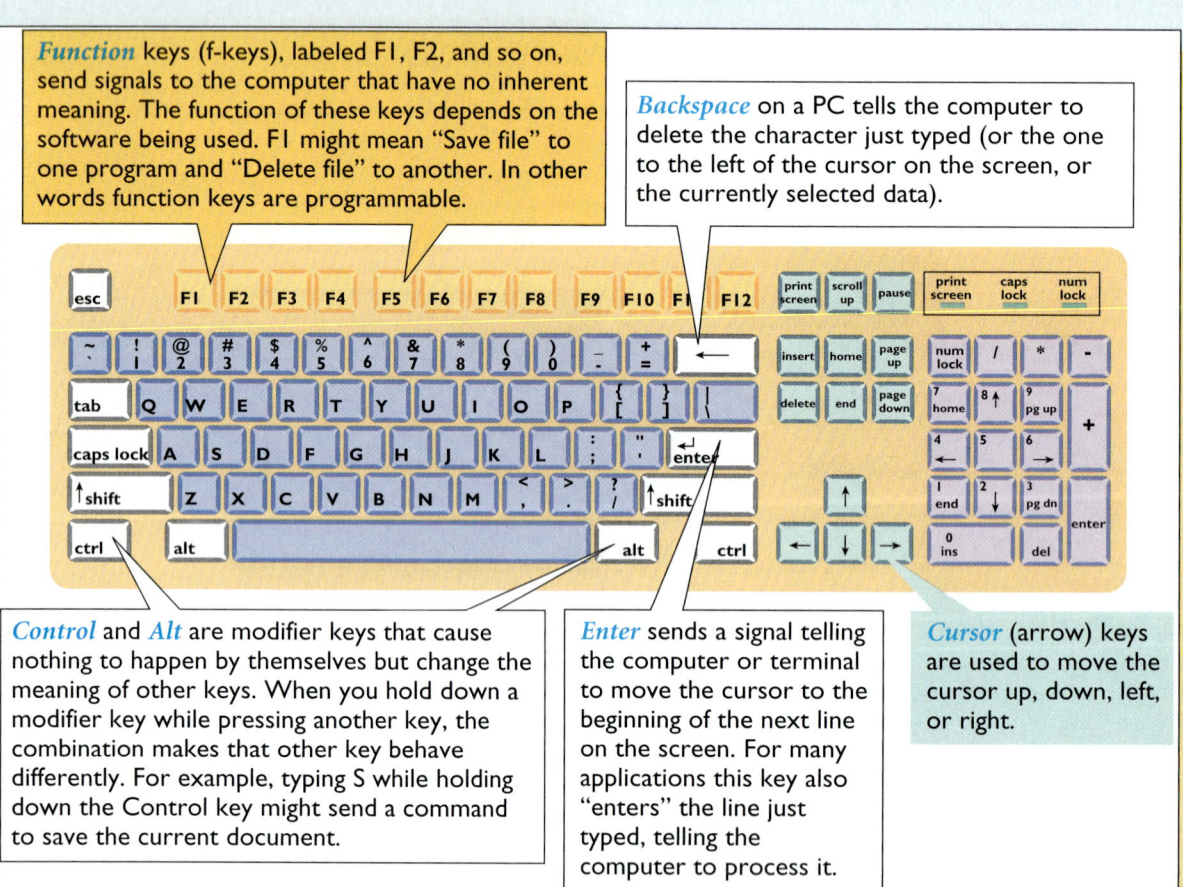

Function keys (f-keys), labeled F1, F2, and so on, send signals to the computer that have no inherent meaning. The function of these keys depends on the software being used. F1 might mean "Save file" to one program and "Delete file" to another. In other words function keys are programmable.

Backspace on a PC tells the computer to delete the character just typed (or the one to the left of the cursor on the screen, or the currently selected data).

Control and *Alt* are modifier keys that cause nothing to happen by themselves but change the meaning of other keys. When you hold down a modifier key while pressing another key, the combination makes that other key behave differently. For example, typing S while holding down the Control key might send a command to save the current document.

Enter sends a signal telling the computer or terminal to move the cursor to the beginning of the next line on the screen. For many applications this key also "enters" the line just typed, telling the computer to process it.

Cursor (arrow) keys are used to move the cursor up, down, left, or right.

Using a Mouse

The mouse enables you to perform many tasks quickly that might be tedious or confusing with a keyboard. As you slide the mouse across your desktop, a pointer echoes your movements on the screen. You can *click* the mouse—press the button while the mouse is stationary—or *drag* it—move it while holding the button down. On a two-button mouse, the left button is usually used for clicking and dragging. You can use these two techniques to perform a variety of operations.

Clicking the Mouse

If the pointer points to an onscreen *button*, clicking the mouse presses the button.

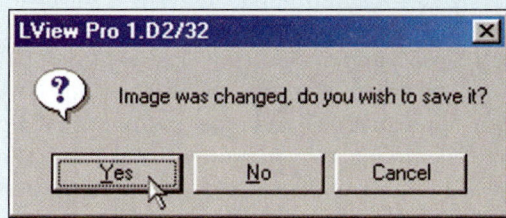

If the pointer points to a picture of a tool or object on the screen, clicking the mouse *selects* the tool or object; for example, clicking the pencil tool enables you to draw with the mouse.

If the pointer points to a part of a text document, it turns from an arrow into an *I-beam*; clicking repositions the flashing cursor.

Dragging the Mouse

If you hold the button down while you drag the mouse with a selected graphic tool (like a paintbrush), you can draw by remote control.

If you drag the mouse from one point in a text document to another, you select all the text between those two points so you can modify or move it. For example, you might select this movie title so you could italicize it.

You can drag the mouse to select a command from a *menu* of choices. For example, this command enables you to locate specific documents that are stored on your computer.

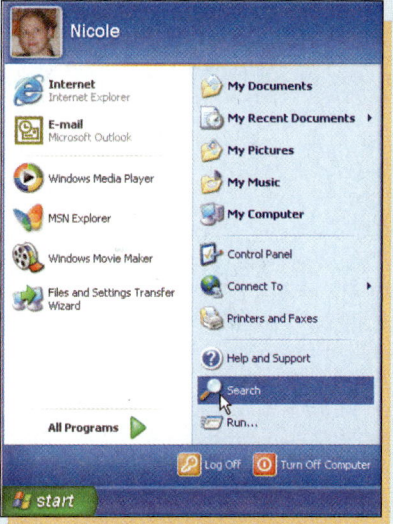

Other Mouse Operations

If you *double-click* the mouse—click twice in rapid succession—while pointing to an onscreen object, the computer will probably *open* the object so you can see inside it. For example, double-clicking this *icon* representing a letter causes the letter to open.

If you *right-click*—click the right mouse button—while pointing to an object, the computer will probably display a menu of choices of things you can do to the object. For example, if you right-click the letter icon, a menu appears at the pointer.

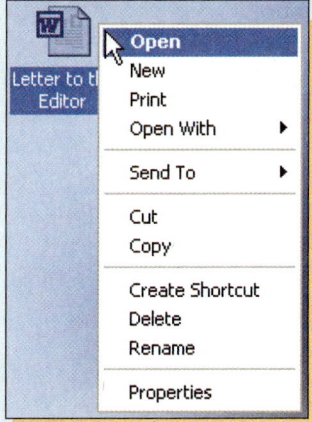

PC Software Basics

> Computers can figure out **all kinds of problems**, except the things in the world that **just don't add up**.
> —James Magary

All of this hardware is controlled, directly or indirectly, by the tiny CPU in the system unit. And the CPU is controlled by **software**—instructions that tell it what to do. **System software**, including the **operating system (OS)**, continuously takes care of the behind-the-scenes details and (usually) keeps things running smoothly. The operating system also determines what your screen display looks like as you work and how you tell the computer what you want it to do. Most PCs today use some version of the **Microsoft Windows** operating system; Macintosh computers use some version of Apple's **Mac OS**.

Application programs, also called simply **applications**, are the software tools that enable you to use a computer for specific purposes. Some applications are designed to accomplish well-defined short-term goals. For example, the *Computer Confluence* CD-ROM includes an application that supplements and expands on the material in this book using interactive quizzes, animated demos, video presentations, and other multimedia material. Other applications programs are more general and open-ended in their goals. For example, you can use a word processing program, such as Microsoft Word, to create memos, letters, term papers, novels, textbooks, or World Wide Web pages—just about any kind of text-based document. (In the PC world, a **document** is something created by an application, regardless of whether it has actually been printed. If you write a letter with the Microsoft Word application and save it as a disk file, the saved file is a Microsoft Word document.)

The User's View boxes on the following pages show examples of software at work. In these two simple examples, we'll use a word processing application to edit and print a term paper we created in an earlier session and stored as a document on the hard disk. In the first example, we'll use Microsoft Word on a PC with the Microsoft Windows XP operating system. In the second example we'll do the same thing using Microsoft Word on a Macintosh with Mac OS X. In both examples, we'll perform the following steps:

1. Locate the document on the hard disk.
2. **Open** the application—copy it from the computer's hard disk into memory so we can use it—and open the document.
3. Type some additional text at the end of the document.
4. Print the document.
5. Close the application.
6. Delete the document file from the hard disk.

Before we begin, a reminder and a disclaimer:

The reminder: The *User's View* examples are designed to give you a feel for the software, not to provide how-to instructions. You can learn how to use the software using lab manuals or other books on the subject, some of which are listed in *Sources and Resources* at the end of chapters in this book.

The disclaimer: These examples are intended to compare different types of interfaces—not to establish a favorite. The brand of software in a particular User's View box isn't as important as the general concepts built into that software. One of the best things about computers is that they offer lots of different ways to do things. These examples, and others throughout the book, are designed to expose you to possibilities. Even if you have no plans to use the operating systems or applications in the examples—*especially* if you have no plans to use them—you can learn something by looking at them as a curious observer.

Chapter 0 Read Me 9

Software makes it possible for PCs to be put to work in homes, schools, offices, factories, and farms.

The User's View

Using Microsoft Word with Microsoft Windows

SOFTWARE: *Microsoft Windows XP and Microsoft Word.*   **THE GOAL:** *To edit, print, and delete a term paper file.*

1 After the PC completes its startup process, you see a Login screen with a list of users. You click your user name from the list, so Windows will use your personal settings.

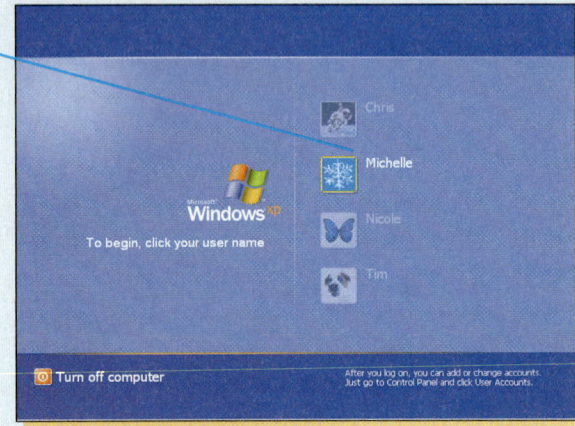

2 The Windows *desktop* appears—a screen that includes icons representing objects used in your work.

3 You click Start in the lower-left corner of the screen. The *Start menu* appears, enabling you to select from the applications and documents you use most frequently.

4 You select Microsoft Word, and click to open the program.

5 The Microsoft Word application opens, and you are presented with a blank document and a *task bar* containing buttons that represent frequently used commands and files.

6 You use the task bar to open your paper.

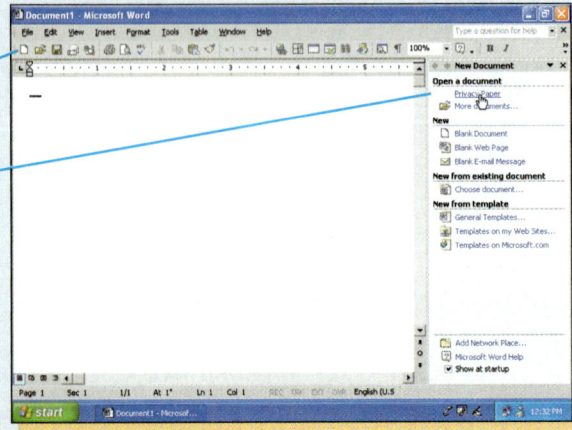

7 When you open the term paper document, Microsoft Word displays the term paper in a window.

8 You use the mouse to move the pointer to the end of the text; you click the mouse button. A flashing **cursor** (sometimes called an **insertion point**) indicates your location in the document.

9 You type additional text to be added at that point. As you type, the cursor moves to the right, leaving a trail of text in its wake. At the same time, those characters are stored in the computer's memory. If you mistype a character or string of characters, you can press Delete or Backspace to eliminate the typos.

10 As you type, the topmost lines **scroll** out of view to make room on the screen for the new ones. The text you've entered is still in memory, even though you can't see it on the screen. You can retrieve it anytime by scrolling backward through the text. In this respect a word processor document is like a modern version of ancient paper scrolls.

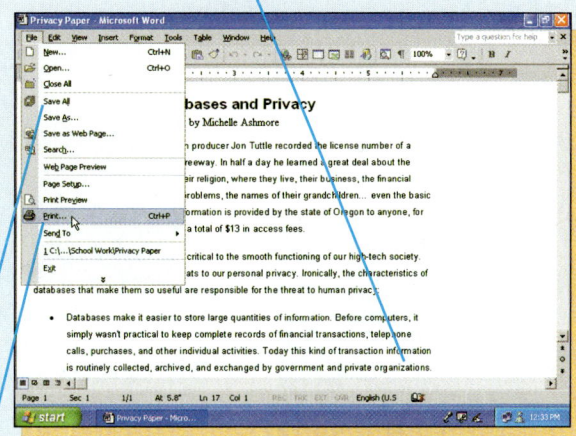

11 Every few minutes you select the Save command to save your document in a disk file containing your work so far. This provides insurance against accidental erasure of the text you've entered.

12 You choose the Print command to print the paper.

13 You select Print from the *dialog box* that appears.

14 You close the application by clicking the red Close button in the upper right corner of the window.

15 You return to the desktop. To locate your document in Windows Explorer, you open your Documents folder using the Start menu.

16 After you open the School Work folder which contains your paper, you can delete the printed file by dragging its icon over the Recycle Bin icon.

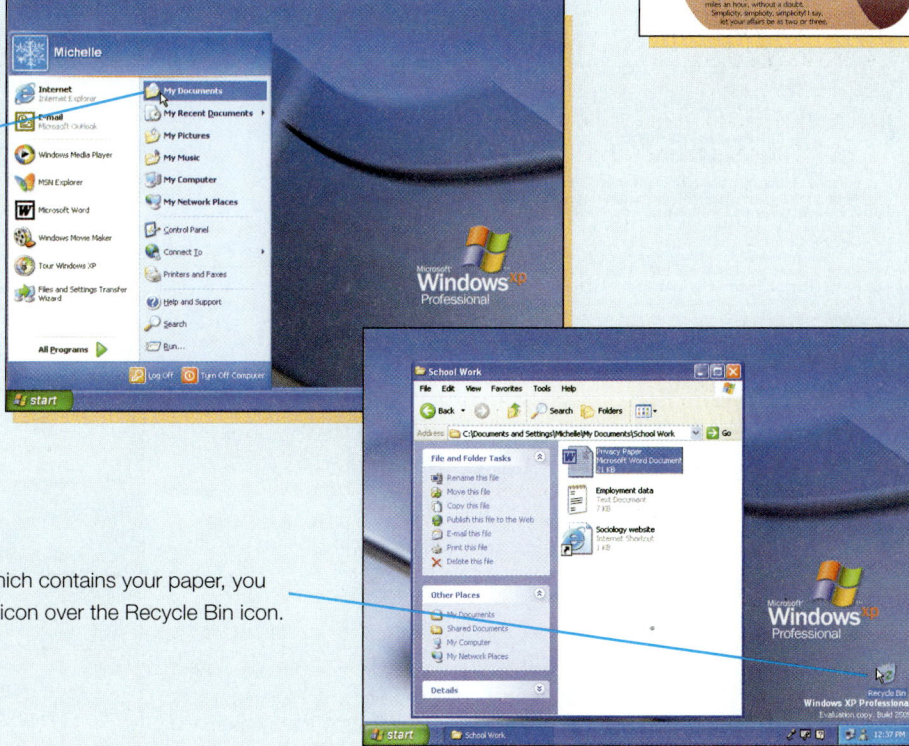

The User's View

Using Microsoft Word with Mac OS

SOFTWARE: *Mac OS X and Microsoft Word*

THE GOAL: *To edit, print, and delete a term paper file*

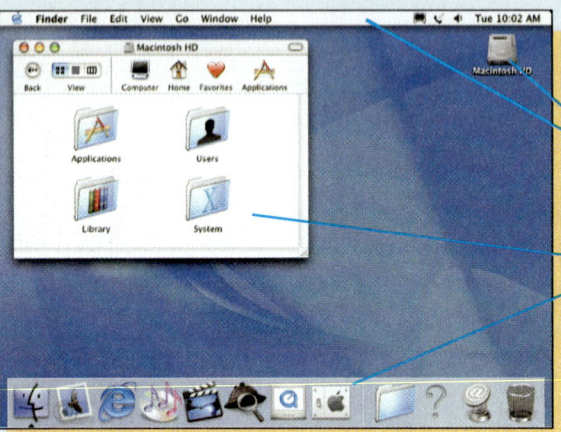

1. The Macintosh Login screen asks you to type in your name and **password** — a string of letters and numbers known only by you and the computer—to verify your identity. As you type your password, only asterisks appear on the screen, so there's no risk of anyone reading it over your shoulder.

2. Like the Windows desktop, the Macintosh desktop includes icons representing objects used in your work. The Macintosh menu bar spans the top of the screen.

3. An open window shows the contents of the hard disk called Macintosh HD. At the bottom of the screen is the *Dock*, which is a holding place for frequently used programs, documents, and folders. Folders, like their real-world counterparts, enable you to group related documents.

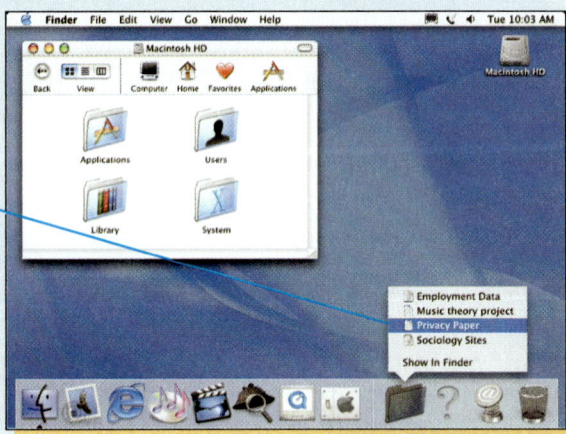

4. You click and hold the mouse button down on the School Work folder in the Dock. A pop-up menu enables you to select the term paper to open it.

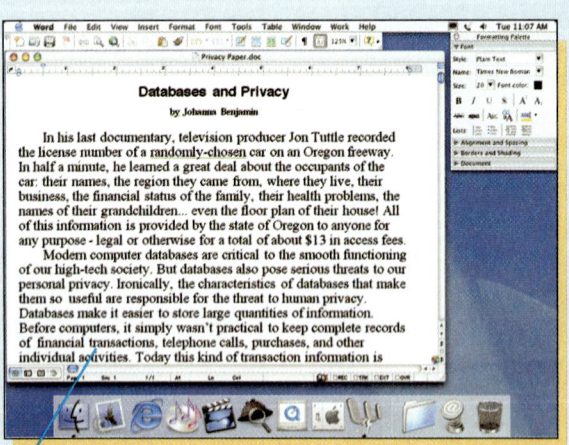

5. You edit and print the document; the process is similar for the Macintosh and Windows versions of Word.

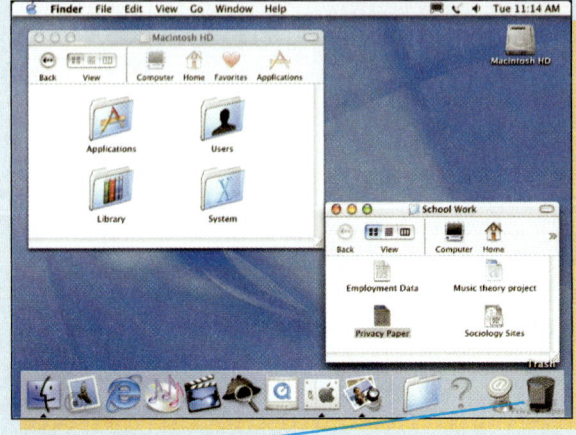

6. When you close the application (using the Quit command from the File menu), you return to the desktop. You can delete the printed file by dragging its icon over the Trash icon in the Dock. (Until you choose the Empty Trash command, you can change your mind and retrieve the file.)

PC Network Basics

> Networks aren't made of printed circuits, but of **people**.... **My terminal is a door** to countless, intricate pathways, leading to **untold numbers of neighbors**.
> —Cliff Stoll, in *The Cuckoo's Egg*

Today's PCs are powerful tools that can perform a variety of tasks that go far beyond the basic word processing examples illustrated here. In later chapters we'll explore many of these applications, from money management to multimedia. But a PC becomes even more powerful when it's connected to other computers through a network.

A computer may have a *direct connection* to a network—for example, cables might connect it to other computers, printers, and other devices in an office or student lab. These networked machines can easily and quickly share information with each other. When a computer isn't physically close to the other machines in the network, it can still communicate with those machines through a *remote access* connection. Using a *modem*, the remote computer can connect to the network through an ordinary phone line.

An entire computer network can be connected to other networks through cables, wireless radio transmissions, or other means. The *Internet* is an elaborate network of interconnected networks—a network that is dramatically changing the way people work, play, and communicate.

Networked computers in this lab allow students to share files, send messages, and connect to the Internet.

Internet Basics

> What interests me about it . . . is that it's a form of communication **unlike any other** and yet **the second you start doing it** you understand it.
> —Nora Ephron, Director of *You've Got Mail*

There was a time, not too many years ago, when word processing was the most popular computer activity among students. For most students, the computer was little more than a high-powered typewriter. Today a PC can be a window into the global system of interconnected networks known as the Internet, or just the *Net*.

The Internet is used by mom-and-pop businesses and multinational corporations that want to communicate with their customers, sell products, and track economic conditions; by kindergarteners and college students doing research and exploration; by consumers and commuters who need access to timely information, goods, and services; and by families and friends who just want to stay in touch. Most people connect to the Internet because it gives them the power to do things that they couldn't easily do otherwise.

Using the Internet you can

- Study material designed to supplement this book, including late-breaking news, interactive study aids, and multimedia simulations that can't be printed on paper.
- Send a message to 1 or 1,001 people, around town or around the world, and receive replies almost as quickly as the recipients can read the message and type a response.
- Explore vast libraries of research material, ranging from classic scholarly works to contemporary reference works.
- Find instant answers to time-sensitive questions such as "What's the weather like in Boston right now?" or "What software do I need to make my new computer work with my new printer?" or "Who won this morning's Olympic high-diving competition?" or "What did the United Nations secretary general say on National Public Radio's *All Things Considered* last night?" or "Where in the world is the Federal Express package I sent yesterday?"
- Get medical, legal, or technical advice from a wide variety of experts.
- Listen to live radio broadcasts from around the world.
- Participate in discussions or play games with people all over the globe who share your interests; with the right equipment, you can set aside your keyboard and communicate through live audio-video links.

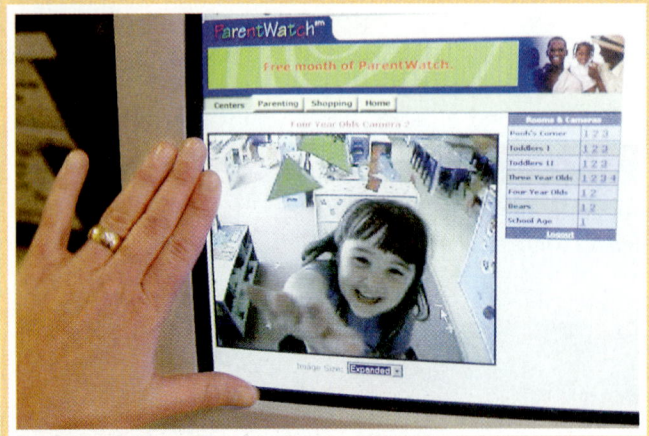

In Seattle, WA, (left) a mother checks on her four-year-old daughter from work using Internet-linked video cameras. In Philadelphia, PA, (right) the press corps at the Republican National Convention used the Internet to conduct and transmit live telecasts.

▸ Shop for obscure items such as out-of-print books and CDs that you can't find elsewhere.
▸ Download free software or music clips from servers all over the world onto your computer.
▸ Order a custom-built computer, car, or condominium.
▸ Track hourly changes in the stock markets and buy and sell stocks based on those changes.
▸ Take a course for college credit from a school thousands of miles away.
▸ Publish your own writings, drawings, photos, and multimedia works so Internet users all over the world can view them.
▸ Start your own business and have a worldwide clientele.

Every revolution has a dark side, and the Internet explosion is no exception. The Internet has plenty of worthless information, scams, and questionable activities. People who make the most of the Internet know how to separate the best of the Net from the rest of the Net. Every chapter of this book contains information that will help you to understand and use the Internet wisely. In this chapter we'll focus on the basics of the two most popular Internet applications: communicating with electronic mail and finding information on the World Wide Web.

Electronic mail (also called **email** or *e-mail*) is the application that lures many people to the Internet for the first time. Email programs make it possible for even casual computer users to easily send messages to family, friends, and colleagues. Because an email message can be written, addressed, sent, delivered, and answered in a matter of minutes—even if the correspondents are on opposite sides of the globe—email has replaced air mail for rapid, routine communication in many organizations. Closer to home, email makes it possible to replace time-consuming phone calls and meetings with more efficient online exchanges.

Email Basics

> Each person on the **"Internet"** has a unique email **"address"** created by **having a squirrel run** across a computer keyboard....
> —Dave Barry, humorist

Details vary, but the basic concepts of email are the same for almost all systems. When you sign up for an email account—through your school, your company, or a private **Internet service provider (ISP)**—you receive a **user name** (sometimes called a *login name* or *alias*) and a storage area for messages (sometimes called a *mailbox*). Any user can send a mail message to anyone else, regardless of whether the recipient is currently *logged in*—connected to the network. The message will be waiting in the recipient's *inbox* the next time he launches his email program and logs in. An email message can be addressed to one person or hundreds of people. Most email messages are plain text, without the kinds of formatting and graphic images found in printed documents. Messages can carry documents, pictures, multimedia files, and other computer files as *attachments*.

You can send messages to anyone on your local system or ISP by simply addressing the message to that person's user name. You can also send messages to anyone with access to Internet email, provided you know that person's Internet address. An Internet email address is

Chapter 0   Read Me

The User's View   The User's View   The   **The User's View**

Communicating with Electronic Mail

SOFTWARE: *America Online*

THE GOAL: *To catch up on your email. Using a PC, a modem, and America Online software, you're about to connect to America Online, an information service that serves as your electronic post office.*

1 When you double-click the America Online (AOL) icon, the application asks you to identify yourself with your user name and password.

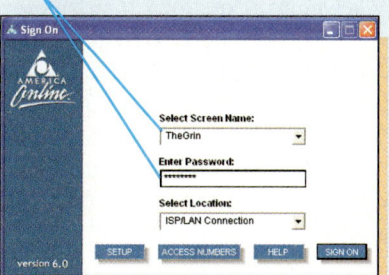

2 When you click the Sign On button, the software passes the necessary commands to the modem along with the network phone number and other information. You hear the dial tone, the touch-tone dialing signals, a high whistle, and a hiss as the modem dials and establishes the connection.

3 When a connection is made, AOL locates your screen name in its billing database and checks your password. If you typed the password correctly, you're greeted by an AOL headline screen and a digitized voice telling you that you have mail. You're now online—connected to the computer system and ready to communicate. You click the You've Got Mail icon to get your mail.

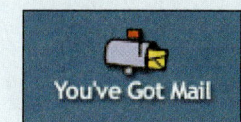

4 The New Mail window lists one new message; you click on the message title to read it.

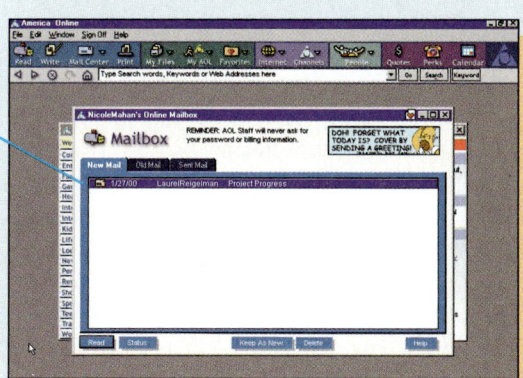

5 After reading the message, you click on the Reply icon.

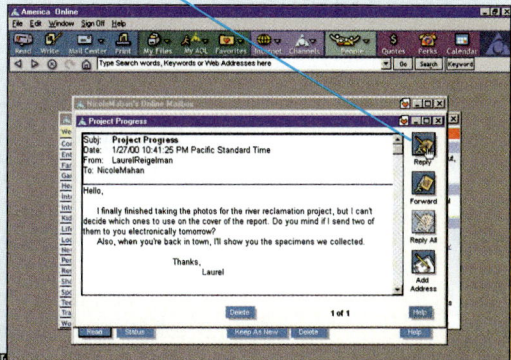

6 The software automatically fills in the address and subject.

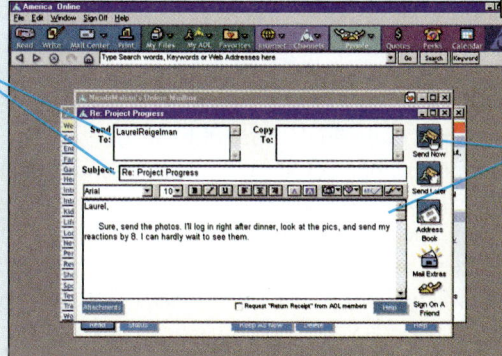

7 You type a message in the message box.

8 Then you click on Send to send the letter. Your message should be in Laurel Reigelman's mailbox waiting until Laurel Reigelman logs in. Your job is done so you can now explore other areas in America Online until you're ready to log off.

made up of two parts separated by an at sign (@): the person's user name and the *host name*—the name of the host computer, network, or ISP address where the user receives mail. Here's the basic form:

```
username@hostname
```

```
Here are a few examples of typical email addresses:
```

```
realgeorge999@aol.com
jandumont@engr.ucla.edu
enathab@pop3.ispchannel.com
```

Some organizations use standardized email addresses so it's easy to guess member addresses. For example, every employee at ABCXYZ Company might have an email address of the form *firstname_lastname@abcxyzco.com*. (The underscore character is sometimes used as a substitute for a space because spaces can't be embedded in email addresses).

It's important to address email messages with care—they can't be delivered if even a single character is mistyped. Fortunately, most email programs include address books, so users can look up email addresses by name and automatically address messages. Many World Wide Web sites, including Yahoo!, Excite, and search.com, offer free email search services and directories.

Many commercial Web sites offer free email accounts. Sometimes these free email services are subsidized by advertisers; sometimes they're provided to attract Web site visitors. Free email services are popular with users of public computers (for example, in libraries), people who don't receive email from their ISPs, people who want multiple email addresses not associated with their workplace, and travelers who want to check email on the road without lugging a laptop.

The example in the User's View box shows a simple email session using America Online—one of the most popular Internet Service Providers. AOL's software is unique, but the concepts illustrated in the example apply to all email programs.

World Wide Web Basics

Email may be the most popular Internet application, but the *World Wide Web (WWW)* opens up all kinds of other possible Internet activities. The *Web* is a huge portion of the Internet that includes a wealth of multimedia content accessible through simple point-and-click programs called *Web browsers*. Web browsers on PCs and other devices serve as windows into the Web's richly diverse information space.

The World Wide Web is made up of millions of interlinked documents called *Web pages*. A Web page is typically made up of text and images, like a page in a book. A collection of related pages stored on the same computer is called a *Web site*; a typical Web site is organized around a home page that serves as an entry page and a stepping off point for other pages in the site. Each Web page has a unique address, technically referred to as a *URL (uniform resource locator)*. For example, the URL for this book's home page is **http://www.prenhall.com/beekman**. You can visit the site by typing the exact URL into the address box of your Web browser.

At the heart of the Web is the concept of *hypertext*. A Web browser enables you to jump from one Web page to another by clicking *hyperlinks* (often called just *links*)—words, pictures, or menu items that act as buttons. For example, at the *Computer Confluence* Web site you can select chapter number to jump to pages related to that chapter. Within the chapter, you can click Multiple Choice to jump to a page containing practice quiz questions. Or you can click Chapter Connections to jump to a page full of hyperlinks that can take you to pages on other Web sites. These off-site pages contain articles, illustrations, audio clips, video segments, and other resources created by others. They reside on computers owned by of corporations, universities, libraries, institutions, and individuals around the world.

Text links are typically, but not always, underlined and displayed in a different color than standard text on the page. In the example shown here, the offsite chapter connection hyperlinks are underlined in blue; the Chapter Connection hyperlink is part of a white-on-black menu on the left side of the screen, and the original Chapter link is part of a pop-up menu.

You can explore an amazing variety of Web pages by clicking links. But this kind of random jumping isn't without frustrations. Some links lead to cobwebs—Web pages that haven't been kept up to date by their owners—and dead-ends—pages that have been removed or moved.

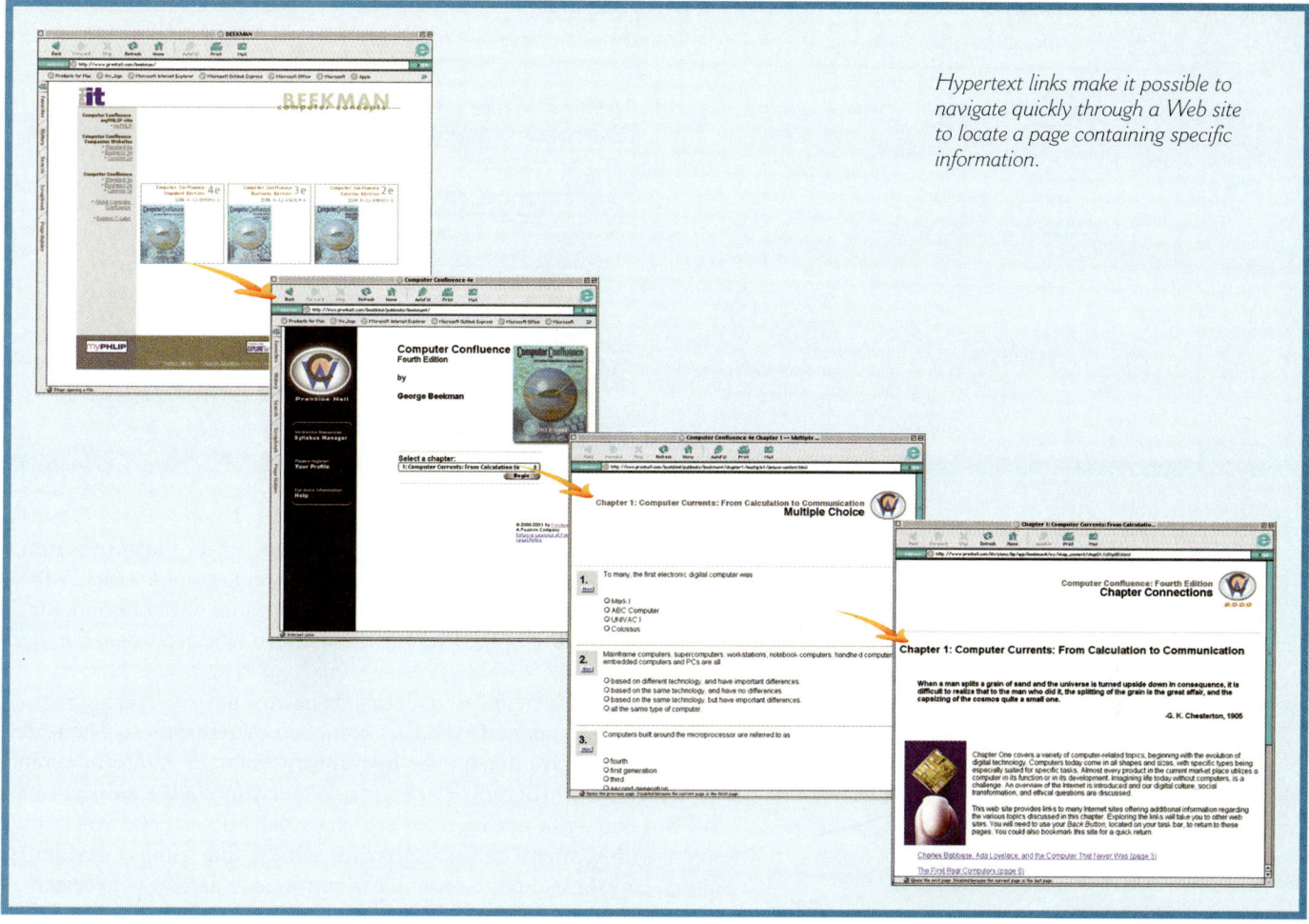

Hypertext links make it possible to navigate quickly through a Web site to locate a page containing specific information.

Even if a link is current, it may not be reputable or accurate; since anybody can create Web pages, they don't all have the editorial integrity of trusted print media.

It can also be frustrating to try to find your way back to pages you've seen on the Web. That's why browsers have *Back* and *Forward buttons*; you can retrace your steps and re-retrace your steps as often as you like. These buttons won't help, though, if you're trying to find an important page from an earlier session. Most browsers include tools for keeping personal lists of memorable sites, called *bookmarks* or *favorites*. When you run across a page worth revisiting, you can mark it with a Bookmark or Add to Favorites command. Then you can revisit that site anytime by selecting it from the list.

Web Search Basics

> The ability to **ask the right question** is more than half the battle of finding the answer.
> —Thomas J. Watson, founder of IBM

The World Wide Web is like a giant, loosely woven, constantly changing document created by thousands of unrelated authors and scattered about in computers all over the world. The biggest challenge for many Web users is extracting the useful information from the rest. If you're looking for a specific information resource, but you don't know where it is located on the Web, you might be able to find it using a *search engine*.

A search engine is built around a database that catalogs Web locations based on content. (Databases are covered later in the book; for now, you can just think of it as an indexed collection of information stored in a computer.) For some search engines, researchers organize and evaluate Web sites. Other search engines use software to search the Web and catalog information automatically. The usefulness of a search engine depends in part on the information in its database. But it also depends on how easy it is for people to find what they're looking for in the database.

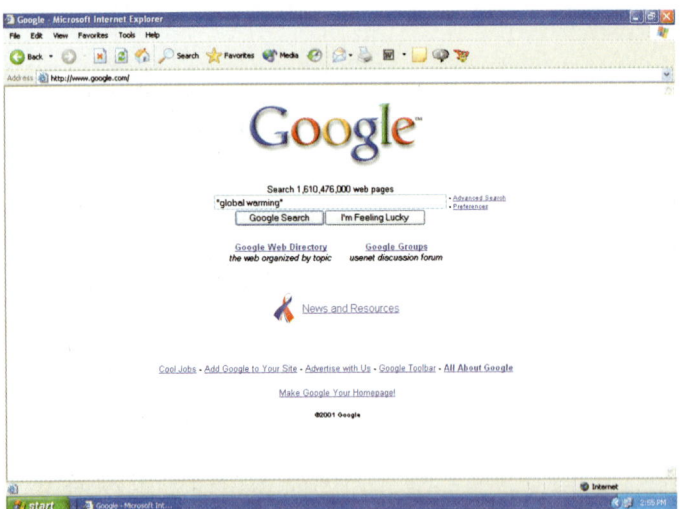

A search for the phrase "global warming" yields hundreds of hits on the Google search engine.

Yahoo's subject tree enables you to narrow your search by clicking categories within a subject.

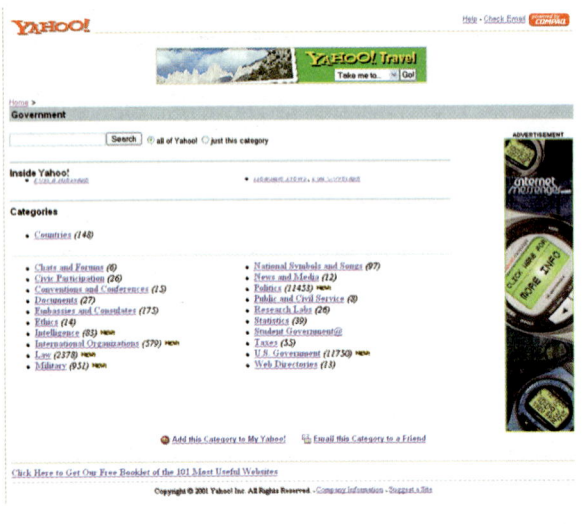

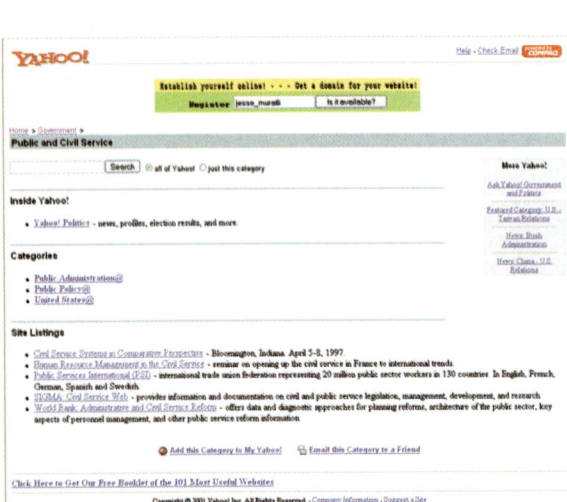

To find information with a typical search engine, you type a keyword or keywords into a search field, click a button, and wait a few seconds for your Web browser to display a list of *hits*—pages that contain requested keywords. A search engine can easily produce a list of hundreds or thousands of hits. Most search engines attempt to list pages in order from best to worst, but these automatic rankings aren't always reliable.

Another popular way to use a search engine is to repeatedly narrow the search using a *directory* or *subject tree*—a hierarchical catalog of Web sites compiled by researchers. The search engine at Yahoo! is probably the best-known example. A screen presents you with a menu of subject choices. When you click a subject—say, Government—you narrow your search to that subject, and you're presented with a menu of subcategories within that subject—Military, Politics, Law, Taxes, and so on. You can continue to narrow your search by proceeding through subject menus until you reach a list of selected Web sites related to the final subject. The sites are usually rank-ordered based on estimated value. The list of Web sites on a given index page is not exhaustive—there may be hundreds of pages related to the subject that aren't included in any directory. It's simply not possible to keep a complete index of all the pages on the ever-changing Web.

Popular search engines are located on Excite, Yahoo, and other Internet *portals*—Web sites designed as first-stop gateways for Internet explorers. The Windows and Macintosh operating systems include search engines. Internet Explorer, Netscape Communicator, and other Web browsers include Search buttons that connect to popular search engines. And many large Web sites include search engines that enable you to search for site-specific information.

Applying the Basics

> It is good to have **an end** to journey toward,
> but it is **the journey** that matters in the end.
>
> Ursula K. LeGuin, author of *The Dispossessed*

In a few pages, you've learned the bare-bones basic concepts behind the PC and the Internet. Now it's time to apply what you've learned in a practical, hands-on way. The next few pages guide you, step-by-step, through an opening session with the *Computer Confluence* CD-ROM and Web Site. They're followed by a few helpful rules of thumb for navigating through the remaining chapters of this book. Once you've completed this quick tour, you'll be ready to dive into the heart of *Computer Confluence*, starting with Chapter 1. So what are you waiting for?

Rules of Thumb

Navigating Computer Confluence

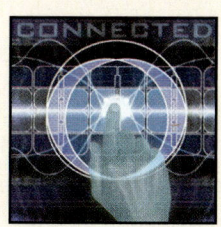

Here are a few pointers for exploring *Computer Confluence*. Take a minute to read these and you'll probably save hours later.

- **Know your boxes.** Text chapters include several types of boxes, each of which is designed to be read in a particular way.

- The **User's View** boxes show you what it's like to be in the driver's seat with some of today's most popular software. Even if you have experience with the software, take a little time to look over these boxes. Some key concepts are introduced here. These boxes can be especially helpful if they cover applications you aren't learning first-hand. A User's View box in the main text means "This is a good time to look over The User's View box." The *Computer Confluence* CD-ROM includes multimedia versions of many of these boxes.

- *Rules of Thumb* boxes (similar to this one) provide practical tips on everything from designing a publication to protecting your privacy. They bring concepts down to earth with useful suggestions that can save you time, money, and peace of mind.

- *How It Works boxes* are for those readers who want—or need—to know more about what's going on under the hood. These boxes use words and pictures to take you deeper into the inner workings without getting bogged down in technical detail. The *Computer Confluence* CD-ROM includes multimedia versions of many of these boxes as well as bonus How It Works features that aren't in the text. If your course objectives or personal curiosity doesn't motivate you to learn how it works, that's okay; you can skip every How It Works box and still understand the rest of *Computer Confluence*.

- *CrossCurrents boxes* showcase diverse, timely, and often controversial points of view on the technology and its impact on our lives. These short essays, which close each chapter, offer perspectives from some of the most important writers and thinkers on information technology.

- **Read it and read it again.** If possible, read each chapter twice: once for the big ideas and the second time for more detailed understanding. You may also find it helpful to survey each chapter's outline in the table of contents before reading the chapter for the first time.

- **Don't try to memorize every term the first time through.** Throughout the text, key terms are introduced in **boldface blue**, and secondary terms are *italicized in blue*. Use the Key Terms list at the end of each chapter to review and the glossary to recall any forgotten terms. The CD-ROM contains an interactive cross-referenced version of the glossary to find any term quickly.

- **Don't overanalyze examples.** *Computer Confluence* is designed to help you understand concepts, not memorize keystrokes. You can learn the nuts and bolts of working with computers in labs or at home. The examples in this text may not match the applications in your lab, but the concepts are similar.

- **Don't get stuck.** If a concept seems unclear on the first reading, make a note and move on. Sometimes ideas make more sense after you've seen the bigger picture. If you still don't understand the concept the second time through, check the CD-ROM and the Web site for further clarification. When in doubt, ask questions.

- **Remember that there's more than one way to learn.** Some of us learn best by reading, others learn best by exploring interactive examples, and still others learn best by discussing ideas with others, online or in person. *Computer Confluence* offers you the opportunity to learn in all of these ways. Use the learning tools that work best for you.

- **Get your hands dirty.** Try the applications while you're reading about them. Your reading and lab work will reinforce each other and help solidify your newfound knowledge.

- **Study together.** There's plenty to discuss here, and discussion is a great way to learn.

In a hurry? Turn the page. The next page will give you a quick start—just enough information so you can start using the CD-ROM, the Web site, and related computer applications right away.

Computer Confluence Quick Start

The first few chapters of this book provide you with a broad orientation to computers, CD-ROMs, the Internet, and related technology. In the meantime, this Quick Start provides the basics—without detailed explanations—so you can get started with the *Computer Confluence* CD-ROM and Web site right away.

Details vary from computer to computer, but the basics are generally the same. If you're working in a computer lab, you'll probably need a few additional lab instructions to supplement the steps in this Quick Start.

Launching the *Computer Confluence* CD-ROM

1. Turn on the computer. After a minute or so the screen will show icons that represent disks and other computer resources. It may also show open windows that reveal the contents of these resources. A row of menus appears at the top of each window (or, if you're using a Macintosh, at the top of the screen).

2. As you move the mouse around, the pointer on the screen moves in the same motion. (If you run out of space on the mouse pad or desk, you can lift the mouse and reposition it.) Point to an icon and click it by pressing the mouse button. (If there are two or more buttons, use the left button.) You'll click this way to select objects, press onscreen buttons, and navigate around the Web site and CD-ROM.

3. Insert the *Computer Confluence* CD-ROM in the CD-ROM drive. Press the drive's button to make the CD tray slide open. Place the CD, label side up, on the tray, being careful not to handle the other side. Close the CD tray by pressing the button again. (Some CD-ROM drives automatically close.) The *Computer Confluence* CD-ROM application may launch automatically, filling your screen with a Welcome screen. If it does, skip to Step 5.

4. The next step depends on your operating system software. If you're not sure, ask.

Windows

   a. Point to the icon called "My Computer" and double-click it (click twice in rapid succession with the left mouse button).
   b. Double-click the CD-ROM icon in the My Computer window.
   c. Double-click the CCWin.EXE icon.

Macintosh

   a. Point to the CCCD icon and double-click it (click twice in rapid succession).
   b. Double-click the CCMac icon in the CCCD window.

5. The application takes a few seconds to load into the computer's memory. When it does, a new window will open on your screen. On-screen instructions will guide you through the CD's contents.

Exploring the *Computer Confluence* Web Site

To explore the *Computer Confluence* Web site, you'll need a Web browser and an Internet connection. Your computer probably includes one or more of these browsers: Internet Explorer, Netscape Navigator, Netscape Communicator, or America Online's Web browser.

1. Locate the browser and double-click its icon. If you're using a modem to connect to the Internet, this will probably cause the modem to dial the appropriate number.

2. Point to the long rectangle at the top of the browser window. If the text in that window is black on a white background, double-click it to highlight it. Then type **www.prenhall.com/beekman** to replace the highlighted text. (Depending on your browser, you may be able to get the same results by simply typing **computerconfluence**.) Press Return or Enter.

3. If an error message appears, click the OK button, check your typing carefully, correct any errors, and press Return or Enter again. When you type it correctly, you'll be taken to the *Computer Confluence* opening screen.

4. If you're using your own computer, you can mark this page so you can return by selecting it from a menu rather than retyping its name. If you're using Internet Explorer, select Add to Favorites from the Favorites menu. If you're using Netscape Navigator or Communicator, select Add Bookmark from the Bookmark menu.

5. At the *Computer Confluence* site you can click on on-screen images and menus to select the edition of the book you're using, select a chapter, and then select activities within that chapter.

Brain Gain

Nick Montfort

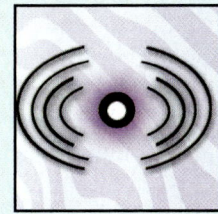

Every chapter of this book ends with an article that explores issues related to computer technology and its impact on our lives. Many of these articles present controversial points of view; all of them raise interesting, important questions. In this article, first published in the November, 2000 issue of Smart Business for the New Economy, *writer Nick Montfort discusses changes higher education will face as computers, the Internet, and related technologies evolve. Montfort presents visions of a future in which textbooks and classrooms might be replaced by virtual reality simulations and microscopic robots. Since you don't have a robot tutor, take some of your own time to read this thought-provoking article.*

At last, the intersection of education and technology is about to jump beyond the film-strip projector. Already, almost all U.S. public schools and just more than half of all public school classrooms have Internet access. In the next 10 years, concepts like virtual reality and distance learning will have a broad impact.

Students at high schools and universities already use the Internet as a reference tool. The more adventurous are now taking distance education courses using the Web. Jack Wilson, a professor at Rensselaer Polytechnic Institute in Troy, New York, says that traditional students, corporate trainees, and other learners will benefit in coming years from Internet classes and from meeting with far-away students in real time. While "18- to 21-year-old college students will probably still want to have the university experience," he says, live online classes will allow those students to learn and collaborate with others in different countries and take advantage of resources not available on campus. "Live online learning lets students in Hong Kong work with those in the United States on a routine basis," he says. As chairman of software developer LearnLinc (www.learnlinc.com, now part of a company called Mentergy), Wilson is putting his ideas into practice and helping others use live Internet learning.

Virtual environments have become the norm in networked entertainment, but they haven't found widespread use in education. Ray Kurzweil, author of *The Age of Spiritual Machines* (Viking, 1999), says that will change in the next 10 years. He says virtual environments will be ubiquitous by 2010, being used in many contexts, including secondary schools. Says Bruce Campbell of the University of Washington's Human Interface Technology Laboratory, "I think it might be another 15 years or so," noting that while the technology may be ready much sooner, it may not be accepted by educators.

Certain disciplines will benefit from virtual environments sooner than others will. Campbell says that fields such as chemistry, astronomy, physics, and meteorology "are the natural ones" for teaching through virtual environments. "They let you interact with things at a scale you can't easily interact with in the real world," he says.

John Sutherland of the University of Abertay in Dundee, Scotland, says other fields are appropriate for this technology as well. "Surgery is already a strong virtual learning environment," he says, "but primarily for very high-end operations that are rare, costly, and risky." Sutherland says virtual environments will probably not aid the teaching of abstract topics, such as computer programming.

Though virtual reality has yet to live up to the expectations that arose out of the cyberpunk fiction of the 1980s and '90s, an even more outlandish notion advanced by cyberpunks—downloading knowledge directly into the brain—is increasingly discussed with a straight face.

"In order to download knowledge, we will need the ability to directly access and augment the neural networks in which memory and knowledge are stored," Kurzweil says. To do this, he says we would use "massively distributed nanobot-based neural implants," tiny networked robots that will meld directly to our neurons to offer enhanced senses and improved cognitive capabilities. The implants could also provide a truly immersive virtual environment experience, or allow us to experience our usual senses. While Kurzweil asserts that the technology is about three decades away, he points out that 5mm-wide robots, called "smart dust," are already being developed at the University of California at Berkeley.

2004	2-D and 3-D simulations become standard tools in teaching some subjects.
2012	The average U.S. high schooler studies in at least one immersive virtual environment.
2020	Artificial intelligence teachers become better than the real thing.
2032	Nanobot neural implants enhance the brain directly.

DISCUSSION QUESTIONS

1. Which of the future visions presented here seem most realistic to you? Explain your answer.
2. Which of the future visions presented here seem most appealing to you? Explain your answer.

Summary

PCs come in a variety of shapes and sizes, but they're all made up of two things—the physical parts of the computer, called hardware, and the software instructions that tell the hardware what to do. The PC's system unit contains the CPU, which controls the other components, including memory, disk drives, and monitor screens. The keyboard and mouse enable a person to communicate with the computer, which sends information back to the person through displays on the monitor.

The computer's operating system software takes care of details of the computer's operation. Application software provides specific tools for computer users.

PCs can be networked to other computers using cables, radio waves, or other means. A computer can also connect to a network through standard phone lines using a modem.

The Internet is a global network of computer networks used for education, commerce, and communication. Electronic mail is the most popular Internet application. Email enables almost instant communication among Internet users.

A Web browser is a PC application that provides easy access to the World Wide Web — a wide-ranging array of multimedia information on the Internet. Web pages are interconnected by hyperlinks that make it easy to follow information trails. Search engines serve as indices for the Web, locating pages with subject matter that matches keywords.

The *Computer Confluence* CD-ROM and Companion Web site use PC multimedia and Internet technology to enhance and expand the information and ideas presented in this book.

Chapter Review

▼ Key Terms

(Terms introduced in this chapter will be revisited in later chapters.)

application program (p. 8)
button (p. 7)
CD-Rom drive (p. 5)
click (p. 7)
CPU (p. 4)
desktop (p. 10)
diskette (p. 5)
document (p. 8)
double-click (p. 7)
drag (the mouse) (p. 7)
electronic mail (email, e-mail) (p. 14)
hard disk (p. 5)
hardware (p. 4)
hyperlink (p. 16)
Internet (p. 13)
keyboard (p. 5)
memory (p. 5)
menu (p. 7)
monitor (p. 5)
mouse (p. 5)
open (p. 7)
operating system (OS) (p. 8)
password (p. 12)
personal computer (PC) (p. 4)
printer (p. 5)
save (p. 6)
search engine (p. 17)
software (p. 8)
user name (p. 14)
URL (uniform resource locator) (p. 16)
Web browser (p. 16)
Web page (p. 16)
Web site (p. 16)
World Wide Web (WWW) (p. 16)

▼ Interactive Quiz Questions

1. The *Computer Confluence* CD-ROM contains self-test quiz questions related to this chapter, including multiple choice, true or false, and matching questions.
2. The *Computer Confluence* Web site, www.prenhall.com/beekman, contains self-test exercises related to this chapter. Follow the instructions for taking a quiz. After you've completed your quiz, you can email the results to your instructor.

The Web site also contains open-ended discussion questions called Internet Explorations. Discuss one or more of the Internet Exploration questions at the section for this chapter.

▼ Review Questions

1. Briefly define or describe each of the key terms listed in the "Key Terms" section.
2. How are hardware and software related?
3. Which computer component is the most critical to the computer's functioning, and why?
4. Which two computer components are most often used by people for getting information into PCs?
5. What is the difference between operating system software and application software?
6. List some ways that a computer might be connected to a network.
7. Give examples of ways email can change the way you communicate with other people.
8. How can you use hyperlinks to explore the World Wide Web? Give an example.
9. How can you find a site on the Web if you don't know the URL?

▼ Discussion Questions

1. Spend some time exploring the *Computer Confluence* CD-ROM. What features of the software do you think will be most helpful to you? Why?
2. Spend some time exploring the *Computer Confluence* Web Site, www.prenhall.com/beekman. What features of the site do you think will be most helpful to you? Why?

▼ Project

1. Keep a log of your progress as you use the *Computer Confluence* book, CD-ROM, and Web site. Make notes on which features are most helpful and which are least helpful. When you finish the book and related material, you may want to send a summary of your log to the author c/o Prentice Hall. Your notes will help make future editions of *Computer Confluence* more useful for others.

Sources and Resources

At the end of every chapter of *Computer Confluence*, you'll find an annotated list of valuable resources for learning more about the subjects covered in the chapter. Some of these resources are magazines, journals, and other periodicals that with particularly good coverage of computers, the Internet, and the impact of technology on our lives. Some of the resources are books, both fiction and nonfiction, that provide insights into the world of information technology. Some are films and videos that vividly portray concepts and issues related to the technology. And, of course, some are Web sites that can take you far beyond the basic ideas covered in this book. If you want to learn more, start with these sources and resources.

1 | Computer Currents: From Calculation to Connection

After you read this chapter you should be able to:

▼

Characterize what a computer is and what it does

Describe several ways computers play a critical role in modern life

Discuss the circumstances and ideas that led to the development of the modern computer

Describe several trends in the evolution of modern computers

Comment on the fundamental difference between computers and other machines

Explain the relationship between hardware and software

Outline the four major types of computers in use today and describe their principal uses

Describe how the explosive growth of the Internet is changing the way people use computers and information technology

Discuss the social and ethical impact of information technology on our society

▲

▼ In this chapter:

The evolution of digital technology

The many faces and forms of computers

How the Internet changed everything

Our digital culture: social transformation and ethical questions

Self-study questions and projects

Minireviews of helpful resources for further study

…and more.

▼ On the CD-ROM:

Video lab highlighting a cutting edge internet company

An activity on a new security technology

Instant access to glossary and key word references

Interactive self-study quizzes

…and more.

▼ On the Web:

www.prenhall.com/beekman

Important documents tracing the history of computers, the Internet, and digital technology

Links to Web sites of the most important computer companies

A quick tour of some of the most popular and innovative sites on the Web

Self-study exercises

…and more.

Charles Babbage, Lady Lovelace, and the Mother of All Computers

The Analytical Engine has no **pretensions whatever** to originate anything. It can do **whatever** we know how **to order it** to perform.

—Augusta Ada King, Countess of Lovelace

The Analytical Engine Lady Lovelace referred to was the mother of all computers, conceived by Charles Babbage, a 19th-century mathematics professor at Cambridge University. Babbage was an eccentric genius known by the public for his war with street musicians. He calculated that they sapped him of 25 percent of his working power, and he strove to have them outlawed. But Babbage was more than a crank; his many inventions included the skeleton key, the speedometer, and… the computer.

Babbage's computer vision grew out of frustration with the tedious and error-prone process of creating mathematical tables. In 1823, he received a grant from the British government to develop a "difference engine"—a mechanical device for performing repeated additions. Two decades earlier, Joseph-Marie Charles Jacquard, a French textile maker, had developed a loom that could automatically reproduce woven patterns by reading information encoded in patterns of holes punched in stiff paper cards. After learning of Jacquard's programmable loom, Babbage abandoned the difference engine for a more ambitious enterprise: an **Analytical Engine** that could be programmed with punched cards to carry out any calculation to 20 digits of accuracy. Babbage's design included the four basic components found in every modern computer: components for performing the basic functions of input, output, processing, and storage.

Charles Babbage (1791–1871)

Analytical Engine

Augusta Ada King, Countess of Lovelace (sometimes erroneously called "Ada Lovelace"), the daughter of poet Lord Byron, visited Babbage and the Analytical Engine. Ada corresponded regularly with him. She is often called the first computer programmer, because she wrote a plan for using the Analytical Engine to calculate sequences of Bernoulli numbers. But programmer is probably the wrong term to describe her actual contribution. She was more of an interpreter and promoter of Babbage's visionary work.

Babbage was obsessed with completing the Analytical Engine. Eventually the government withdrew financial support; there simply wasn't enough public demand to justify the ever-increasing cost. The technology of the time was not sufficient to turn their ideas into reality. The world wasn't ready for computers, and it wouldn't be for another 100 years.

Augusta Ada King, Countess of Lovelace (1815–1852)

Computers are so much a part of modern life that we hardly notice them. But computers are everywhere, and we'd certainly notice them if they suddenly stopped working. Imagine…

Computer screens and television screens populate today's television control rooms.

Living without Computers

You wake up with the sun well above the horizon and realize your alarm clock hasn't gone off. You wonder if you've overslept. You have a big research project to finish today. The face of your digital wristwatch stares back at you blankly. The TV and radio are no help; you can't find a station on either one. You can't even get the time by telephone, because the telephone doesn't work either.

The morning newspaper is missing from your doorstep. You'll have to guess the weather forecast by looking out the window. No music to dress by this morning—your CD player refuses your requests. How about some breakfast? Your automatic coffeemaker refuses to be programmed; your microwave oven is on strike too.

You decide to go out for breakfast. Your car won't start. In fact, the only cars moving are at least 15 years old. The lines at the subway are unbelievable. People chatter nervously about the failure of the subway's computer-controlled scheduling device.

You duck into a coffee shop and find long lines of people waiting while cashiers handle transactions by hand. While you're waiting, you join the conversation that's going on around you. People seem more interested in talking to each other since all the usual tools of mass communication have failed.

You're down to a couple of dollars in cash, so you stop after breakfast at an automated teller machine. Why bother?

You return home to wait for the book you ordered online. You soon realize that you're in for a long wait; planes aren't flying because air traffic control facilities aren't working. You head for the local library to see if the book is in stock. Of course, it's going to be tough to find since the book catalog is computerized.

As you walk home, you speculate on the implications of a worldwide computer failure. How will people function in high-tech, high-rise office buildings that depend on computer systems to control everything from elevators to humidity? Will electric power plants be able to function without computer control? What will happen to patients in computerized medical facilities? What about satellites that are kept in orbit by computer-run control systems? Will the financial infrastructure collapse without computers to process and communicate transactions? Will the world be a safer place if all computer-controlled weapons are grounded?

Computers are used to coordinate thousands of Union Pacific trains in this high-tech Omaha control room.

This cart's built-in computer helps golfers navigate the course.

Our story could go on, but the message should be clear enough by now. Computers are everywhere, and our lives are affected in all kinds of ways by their operation—and nonoperation. It's truly amazing that computers have infiltrated our lives so thoroughly in such a short time.

Computers in Perspective: An Evolving Idea

> Consider the past and you shall **know the future**.
> —Chinese Proverb

While the computer has been with us for only about half a century, its roots go back to a time long before Charles Babbage conceived of the Analytical Engine in 1823. This extraordinary machine is built on centuries of insight and intellectual effort.

Before Computers

Computers grew out of a human need to quantify. Early humans were content to count with fingers or rocks. As cultures became more complex, so did their counting tools. The abacus (a type of counting tool and calculator used by the Babylonians, the Chinese, and others for thousands of years) and the Hindu-Arabic number system are examples of early calculating tools that had an immediate and profound effect on society. (Imagine trying to conduct business without a number system that allows for easy addition and subtraction.)

The Analytical Engine had little impact until a century after its invention, when it served as a blueprint for the first real programmable computer. Virtually every computer in use today follows the basic plan laid out by Babbage and Lady Lovelace.

The Information-Processing Machine

Like the Analytical Engine, the computer is a machine that changes information from one form to another. All computers take in information (**input**) and give out information (**output**) as shown here.

Because information can take many forms, the computer is an incredibly versatile tool, capable of everything from computing federal income taxes to guiding the missiles those taxes buy. For calculating taxes, the input to the computer might be numbers representing wages, other income, deductions, exemptions, and tax tables, and the output might be the number representing the taxes owed. If the computer is deploying a missile, the input might be radio and radar signals for locating the missile and the target, and the output might be electrical signals to control the flight path of the missile. Amazingly enough, the same computer could be used to accomplish both of these tasks.

How can a machine be so versatile? The computer's flexibility isn't hidden in **hardware**—the physical parts of the computer system. The secret of its functionality is in its **software**, or **programs**—the instructions that tell the hardware how to transform the input **data** (information in a form it can read) into the necessary output.

Whether a computer is performing a simple calculation or producing a complex animation, a program controls the process from beginning to end. In effect, changing programs can turn the computer into a different tool. Because it can be programmed to perform various tasks, the typical modern computer is a general-purpose tool.

The First Real Computers

Although Lady Lovelace predicted that the Analytical Engine might someday compose music, the scientists and mathematicians who designed and built the first working computers a century later had a more modest goal: to create machines capable of doing repetitive mathematical calculations. Here are some landmark examples:

> First we shape our tools, thereafter **they shape us**.
> —Marshall McLuhan

- In 1939 a young German engineer named Konrad Zuse completed the first programmable, general-purpose digital computer—a machine he built from electric relays to automate the process of doing engineering calculations. "I was too lazy to calculate and so I invented the computer," Zuse recalls. In 1941, Zuse and a friend asked the German government for funds to build a faster electronic computer to help crack enemy codes. The Nazi military establishment turned him down, confident that their aircraft could quickly win the war without the aid of sophisticated calculating devices.

- At about the same time, the British government was assembling a top-secret team of mathematicians and engineers to crack Nazi military codes. In 1943 the team, led by mathematician Alan Turing and others, completed Colossus, considered by many to be the first electronic digital computer. This special-purpose computer successfully broke codes, allowing British military intelligence to eavesdrop on even the most secret German messages throughout most of the war.
- In 1939, Iowa State University professor John Atanasoff, seeking a tool to help his graduate students solve long, complex differential equations, developed what could have been the first electronic digital computer, the Atanasoff-Berry Computer (ABC). His university neglected to patent Atanasoff's ground-breaking machine, and Atanasoff never managed to turn it into a fully operational product. The International Business Machines Corporation responded to his queries by telling him "IBM will never be interested in an electronic computing machine."
- Harvard professor Howard Aiken was more successful in financing the automatic general-purpose calculator he was developing. In 1944, with a million dollars from IBM, he completed the Mark I. This 51-foot-long, 8-foot-tall monster used noisy electromechanical relays to calculate five or six times faster than a person could, but it was far slower than a modern $5 pocket calculator.
- After consulting with Atanasoff and studying the ABC, John Mauchly teamed up with J. Presper Eckert to help the U.S. effort in World War II by constructing a machine to calculate trajectory tables for new guns. The machine was the ENIAC (Electronic Numerical Integrator and Computer), a 30-ton behemoth with 18,000 vacuum tubes that failed at an average of once every seven minutes. When it was running, it could calculate 500 times faster than the existing electromechanical calculators—about as fast as a modern pocket calculator. Nevertheless, it failed in its first mission: It wasn't completed until two months after the end of the war. Still, it convinced its creators that large-scale computers were commercially feasible. After the war, Mauchly and Eckert started a private company called Sperry and created UNIVAC I, the first general-purpose commercial computer. UNIVAC I went to work for the U.S. Census Bureau in 1951.

J. Presper Eckert (middle) and CBS news correspondent Walter Cronkite (right) confer while UNIVAC I tallies votes in the 1952 presidential election. After counting 5 percent of the votes, UNIVAC correctly predicted that Eisenhower would win the election, but CBS cautiously chose to withhold the prediction until all votes were counted. In the 2000 presidential election incorrect, premature computer projections (and faulty human decision-making) caused a public relations nightmare for the major TV networks.

Evolution and Acceleration

> Invention breeds **invention**.
> —Ralph Waldo Emerson

Computer hardware evolved rapidly from those early days, with new technologies replacing old every few years. Historians marked major hardware changes in the first decades of the computer age by defining four **generations of computers**. UNIVAC I and other computers in the early 1950s were, according to this common classification scheme, first-generation computers. This was the era of machines built around vacuum tubes—light-bulb-sized glass tubes that housed switching circuitry. First-generation machines were big, expensive, and finicky. Only a big institution like a major bank or the U.S. government could afford a computer, not to mention the climate-controlled computer center needed to house it and the staff of technicians needed to program it and keep it running. But with all their faults, first-generation computers quickly became indispensable tools for scientists, engineers, and other professionals.

The **transistor**, invented in 1948, could perform the same function as a vacuum tube by transferring electricity across a tiny resistor. Transistors were first used in a computer in 1956, an event generally viewed as the beginning of the computer's second generation. Computers that used transistors were radically smaller, more reliable, and less expensive than tube-based computers. Because of improvements in software at about the same time, these machines were also much easier and faster to program and use. As a result, computers became more widely used in business as well as in science and engineering.

But America's fledgling space program, determined to surpass the Soviet satellite successes of the 1950s, needed computers that were even smaller and more powerful than the second-generation machines, so researchers developed technology that enabled them to pack hundreds of transistors into a single integrated circuit on a tiny silicon chip. By the mid-1960s, transistor-based computers were replaced by smaller, more powerful third-generation machines built around the new integrated circuits.

Integrated circuits rapidly replaced early transistors for the same reasons that transistors superseded vacuum tubes:

- *Reliability*. Machines built with integrated circuits were less prone to failure than their predecessors, because the chips could be rigorously tested before installation.
- *Size*. Single chips could replace entire circuit boards containing hundreds or thousands of transistors, making it possible to build much smaller machines.
- *Speed*. Because electricity had shorter distances to travel, the smaller machines were markedly faster than their predecessors.
- *Efficiency*. Since chips were so small, they used less electrical power. As a result, they created less heat.
- *Cost*. Mass production techniques made it easy to manufacture inexpensive chips.

These three devices define the first three computer generations. The vacuum tube (left) housed a few switches in a space about the size of a light bulb. The transistor (middle) allowed engineers to pack the same circuitry in a semiconductor package that was smaller, cooler, and much more reliable. The first silicon chips packed several transistors' worth of circuitry into a speck much smaller than a single transistor.

Just about every breakthrough in computer technology since the dawn of the computer age has presented similar advantages over the technology it replaced.

The relentless progress of the computer industry is illustrated by Moore's Law. In 1965 Gordon Moore, the chairman of Intel, predicted half-seriously that the power of a silicon chip of the same price would double about every 18 months for at least two decades. So far Moore's prediction has been uncannily accurate!

The Microcomputer Revolution

> Computer cost-effectiveness has risen **100 millionfold** since the late 1950s— a 100,000-fold rise in **power** times a thousandfold drop in **cost**.
> —George Gilder

The inventions of the vacuum tube, the transistor, and the silicon chip had tremendous impact on our society, which is why they're used as computer-generational boundaries by many historians. But none of these had a more profound effect than the invention in 1971 of the first microprocessor—the critical components of a complete computer housed on a tiny silicon chip. The development of the microprocessor by Intel engineers marked the beginning of the fourth generation of computers and the end of an era when it made sense to count computer generations. The microprocessor's invention caused immediate and radical changes in the appearance, capability, and availability of computers.

The research and development costs for the first microprocessor were awesome. But once the assembly lines were in place, silicon computer chips could be mass produced cheaply. The raw materials were certainly cheap enough; silicon, the main ingredient in beach sand, is the second most common element (behind oxygen) in the Earth's crust.

U.S. companies soon flooded the marketplace with watches and pocket calculators built around inexpensive microprocessors. The economic effect was immediate: Mechanical calculators and slide rules became obsolete overnight; electronic hobbyists became wealthy entrepreneurs, and California's San Jose area gained the nickname Silicon Valley when dozens of microprocessor manufacturing companies sprouted and grew there.

The microcomputer revolution began in the late 1970s when companies like Apple, Tandy, and Commodore introduced low-cost, typewriter-sized computers as powerful as many of the room-sized computers that had come before. Personal computers, or PCs, as microcomputers

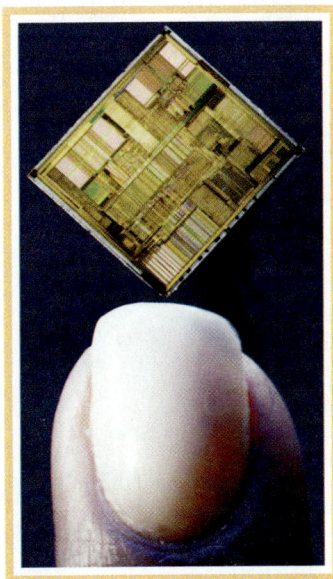

Today a single chip the size of your fingernail can contain the equivalent of millions of transistors.

The microcomputer revolution didn't just increase the number of computers in offices; it opened up entirely new possibilities for computer habitats. This police officer uses a computer to record case notes and track crime information. David Solove uses a portable computer, a digital camera, and a scanner to produce an online diary of circus life for his family and friends. The marine biologist uses a laptop computer to record research notes and analyze data in the field.

have come to be known, are now common in offices, factories, homes, schools, and just about everywhere else. Because chip manufacturers have been so successful at obeying Moore's Law, microcomputers have steadily increased in speed and power during the last two decades. At the same time, personal computers have taken over many tasks formerly performed by large computers, and every year people find new, innovative ways to harness these tiny workhorses.

The 1950s and 1960s represented an era of *institutional computing*. Corporations and government institutions used the large, expensive computers of the time to transform and streamline their operations, and the world changed as a result. Small computers had an even greater impact on society during the decades that followed—the *personal computer era*. Still, desktop computers haven't completely replaced big computers, which have also evolved. Today's world is populated with a variety of computers, each particularly well suited to specific tasks.

Computers Today: A Brief Taxonomy

> An IBM electronic calculator speeds through **thousands of intricate computations** so quickly that on many complex problems, it's just like having **150 extra engineers...**
> —IBM ad showing dozens of slide-rule-toting engineers in *National Geographic*, February, 1952

People today work with mainframe computers, supercomputers, workstations, notebook computers, handheld computers, embedded computers, and, of course, PCs. Even though they're based on the same technology, these machines have important differences.

Mainframes and Supercomputers

Computer-driven display systems are important fixtures in meeting rooms.

Before the microcomputer revolution, most information processing was done on **mainframe computers**—room-sized machines with price tags to match. Today large organizations, such as banks and airlines, still use mainframes for big computing jobs. Today's mainframes are smaller and cheaper than their ancestors; a typical mainframe today might be the size of a refrigerator and cost around a million U.S. dollars. These industrial-strength computers are largely invisible to the general public, because they're hidden away in climate-controlled rooms.

But the fact that you can't see them doesn't mean you don't use them. When you make an airline reservation or deposit money in your bank account, a mainframe computer is involved in the transaction. Your travel agent and your bank teller communicate with a mainframe using a computer **terminal**—a combination keyboard and screen that transfers information to and from the computer. The computer might be in another room or another country.

A mainframe computer can communicate with several users simultaneously through a technique called **timesharing**. For example, a timesharing system allows travel agents all over the country to make reservations using the same computer and the same information at the same time.

Timesharing also makes it possible for users with diverse computing needs to share expensive computing equipment. Many research scientists and engineers, for example, need more mathematical computing power than they can get from personal computers. Their computing needs might require a powerful mainframe computer. A timesharing machine can simultaneously serve the needs of scientists and engineers in different departments working on a variety of projects.

Terminals like the one in the photo on the right make it possible for ticket agents all over the world to send information to a single mainframe computer like the one shown on the left.

Many researchers can't get the computing power they need from a mainframe computer; traditional "big iron" simply isn't fast enough for their calculation-intensive work such as weather forecasting, telephone network design, simulated car crash testing, oil exploration, computer animation, and medical imaging. These power users need to have access to the fastest, most powerful computers made. Super fast, super powerful computers are called **supercomputers** or **high-performance computers**.

Until a few years ago people commonly referred to another class of multiuser machine called the *minicomputer*. According to traditional definitions minicomputers were smaller and less expensive than mainframes but larger and more powerful than personal computers. But most of today's mainframes are no bigger than yesterday's minicomputers, and most desktop computers are more powerful than those early minis. By most accounts, the minicomputer is history.

The Blue Mountain supercomputer at the U.S. Department of Energy's Los Alamos National Laboratory can perform 1.6 trillion operations per second. The machine is used to simulate nuclear tests and perform intensive calculations for other research projects.

Workstations and PCs

For many applications the minicomputer has been replaced by a **server**—a computer designed to provide software and other resources to other computers over a network. Just about any computer can be used as a server, but some computers are specifically designed with this purpose in mind. (Networks and servers are discussed later in this chapter and in later chapters.)

For other applications, such as large-scale scientific data analysis, the minicomputer has been replaced by the workstation—a high-end desktop computer with massive computing power at a fraction of the cost. **Workstations** are widely used by scientists, engineers, financial analysts, designers, and animators whose work involves intensive computations. Although many workstations are capable of supporting multiple users simultaneously, in practice they're typically used by only one person at a time.

Of course, like many computer terms, *workstation* means different things to different people. Some people refer to all desktop computers and terminals as workstations. Those who reserve the term for the most powerful desktop machines admit that the line separating workstations and high-end personal computers is fading. As workstations become less expensive and personal computers become more powerful, the line becomes as much a marketing distinction as a technical one.

This engineer uses a workstation to analyze the temperature distribution in electronic telecommunications equipment.

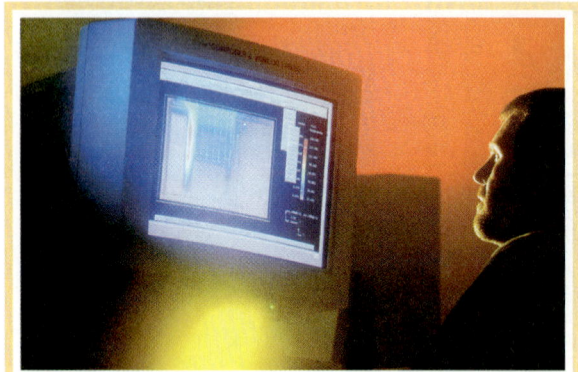

Most computer users don't need the power of a scientific workstation to do their day-to-day business. A modern **personal computer (PC)** has plenty of computing power for word processing, accounting, and other common applications. No surprise there—today's personal computers are far more powerful than the mainframes that dominated the world of computing a human generation ago. A personal computer, as the name implies, is almost always dedicated to serving a single user.

A word about terminology: The terms *personal computer* and *PC* occasionally generate confusion because in 1981 IBM named its desktop computer the IBM Personal Computer. That's why the terms *personal computer* and *PC* often are used to describe only IBM computers or machines compatible with IBM hardware. ("The office has a network of Macs and PCs.") But in another context, PC might describe any general-purpose single-user computer. ("Every student needs a PC to connect to the Internet.")

Portable Computers

Two decades ago the terms *personal computer* and *desktop computer* were interchangeable; virtually all PCs were desktop computers. Today, however, one of the fastest growing segments of the PC market involves machines that aren't tied to the desktop—**portable computers**.

Of course, portability is a relative term. The first "portable" computers were 20-pound suitcases with fold-out keyboards and small TV-like screens. Today those "luggable" computers have been replaced by flat-screen, battery-powered **laptop computers** that are so light you can rest one on your lap while you work or carry it in a briefcase when it's closed.

Today's laptop, commonly called a **notebook computer**, weighs between 3 and 8 pounds. Many laptops compare favorably with powerful desktop PCs. Extra-light, stripped down notebooks are sometimes called **subnotebooks**. To keep size and weight down, manufacturers often leave out some components that would be standard equipment on desktop machines. For example, some laptops don't have built-in CD-ROM or diskette drives. Some have expansion bays that allow these devices to be inserted one at a time. Most have ports that allow external drives to be attached with cables. A few models can be expanded with **docking stations**. A docking station enables a user to connect the laptop to an external monitor, keyboard, mouse, and disk drives. Many mobile workers use docking stations to turn their laptops into full-featured desktop PCs when they return to their offices. Even without docking stations, a laptop can be easily connected to peripherals and networks when it's deskbound.

Handheld computers, which are small enough to tuck into a jacket pocket, serve the needs of users who value mobility over a full-sized keyboard and screen. Docking **cradles** for handheld computers enable them to share information with desktop and laptop PCs.

Personal computers today come in a variety of forms. Apple's iMac includes the CPU, monitor, and storage devices in an all-in-one device; only the keyboard and mouse are separate. IBM's NetVista PC is a more traditional design, with monitor separate from the system unit containing the CPU and storage.

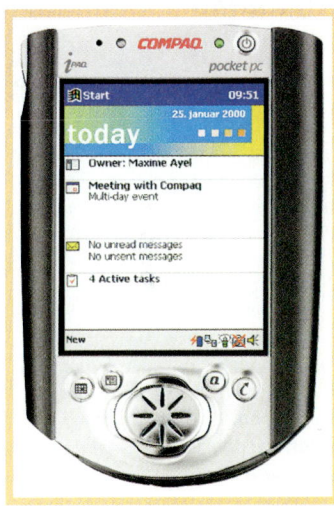

Handheld computers are sometimes called **personal digital assistants (PDAs)** or **palmtop computers**.

Size notwithstanding, most portable computers in all their variations are general-purpose computers built around microprocessors similar to those that drive desktop models. But portability comes at a price—portable computers generally cost more than comparable desktop machines. They're also more difficult to upgrade when newer hardware components become available.

Embedded Computers and Special-Purpose Computers

Not all computers are general-purpose machines. Many are **special-purpose (dedicated) computers** that perform specific tasks, ranging from controlling the temperature and humidity in a high-rise office building to monitoring your heart rate while you work out. **Embedded computers** enhance all kinds of consumer goods: wristwatches, toys, game machines, stereos, video cassette recorders, and ovens. In fact, more than 90 percent of the world's microprocessors are hidden inside common household and electronic devices! Because of embedded computers, a typical new car probably has more computing power than the salesperson's PC! Embedded computers are also used in industry, the military, and science for controlling a variety of hardware devices, including robots. Ninety percent of all microprocessors are embedded in some kind of consumer or electronic device other than a PC.

Most special-purpose computers are, at their core, similar to general-purpose personal computers. But unlike their desktop cousins, these special-purpose machines typically have their programs etched in silicon so they can't be altered. When a program is immortalized on a silicon chip, it becomes **firmware**—a hybrid of hardware and software.

The portable computers shown here represent just a small sample of sizes and types available today. Apple's Titanium Powerbook G4 (above left) is a full-featured multimedia computer in a slim, sleek package. The IBM ThinkPad (above right) can be converted from a laptop to a desktop PC using the docking station shown here. The Handspring Visor Prism is a handheld computer designed to accept input from a stylus; it's shown here in a cradle that provides a communication link to a PC. The RIM Blackberry is a handheld computer designed for email communication using a tiny keyboard. The Compaq iPac Pocket PC uses a version of the Windows operating system designed for handheld computers.

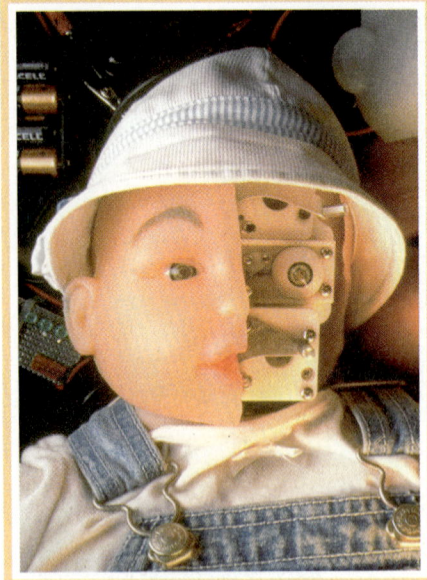

Computer Connections: The Internet Revolution

Embedded computers are so common in today's world that they're all but invisible. This experimental children's doll is a robot in disguise. The Independence™ 3000 IBOT Transporter™ is an intelligent wheelchair that allows disabled people to climb and descend stairs, "stand up" on two wheels, and even stroll on the beach. The dashboard computer in this car provides maps and navigation information for the driver.

> All persons are caught in an **inescapable network of mutuality**, tied in a single garment of destiny. Whatever affects **one** directly, affects **all** indirectly. . . .
> —Martin Luther King, Jr.

We've seen how breakthroughs in switching, storage, and processor technology have produced new types of computers. Each of these technological advances had an impact on our society as people found new ways to put computers to work. Most historians stopped counting computer generations after the microcomputer became commonplace; it was hard to imagine another breakthrough having as much impact as the tiny microprocessor. But while the world was still reeling from the impact of the microcomputer revolution, another information technology revolution was quietly building up steam: a network revolution. If current trends continue, we may look back on the 1990s as the beginning of the era of *interpersonal computing*.

The Emergence of Networks

The first computers were large, expensive, self-contained machines that could process only one job at a time. As demand for computing power grew, computer scientists searched for ways to make scarce computer resources more accessible. The invention of timesharing in the 1960s allowed multiple users to connect to a single mainframe computer through individual terminals. When personal computers started replacing terminals, many users found they had all the computing power they needed on their desktops. Still, there were advantages to linking some of these computers in local-area networks (LANs). When clusters of computers were networked, they could share scarce, expensive resources. For example, a single high-speed printer could meet the needs of an entire office if it was connected to a network. As a bonus, people could use computers to send and receive messages electronically through the networks.

The advantages of electronic communication and resource sharing were multiplied when smaller networks were joined to larger networks. Emerg-ing telecommunication technology eventually allowed wide-area networks (WANs) to span continents and oceans. A remote computer could connect to a network through standard telephone lines by using a **modem**—an electronic device that could translate computer data into signals compatible with the telephone system. Banks, government agencies, and other large, geographically distributed institutions gradually built information-processing systems to take advantage of long-distance networking technology. But for most computer users outside of these organizations, networking was not the norm. People saw computers as tools for doing calculations, storing data, and producing paper documents—not as communication tools.

There were exceptions: A group of visionary computer scientists and engineers, with financial backing from the U.S. government, built an experimental network called ARPANET in 1969. This groundbreaking network would become the Internet—the global collection of networks that radically transformed the way the world uses computers.

Computer Time Line

These *Time* covers symbolize changes in the way people saw and used computers as they evolved through the last half of this century. Notice that the beginning of each new "era" doesn't mean the end of the old ways of computing; today we live in a world of institutional, personal, and interpersonal computing.

1950 — 1975 — 1995

Institutional Computing Era
(Starting approximately 1950)

Characterized by a few large, expensive mainframe computers in climate-controlled rooms; controlled by experts and specialists; used mainly for data storage and calculation.

Personal Computing Era
(Starting approximately 1975)

Characterized by millions of small, inexpensive microcomputers on desktops in offices, schools, homes, factories, and almost everywhere else; controlled mostly by independent users; used mostly for document creation, data storage, and calculation.

Interpersonal Computing Era
(Starting approximately 1995)

Characterized by networks of interconnected computers in offices, homes, schools, vehicles, and almost everywhere else; controlled by users (clients) and network operators; used mostly for communication, document creation, data storage, and calculation.

The Internet Explosion

> It is **not proper** to think of networks as connecting computers. Rather they connect people using computers to **mediate**. The **great success of the Internet** is not technical, but **its human impact**.
> —Dave Clark, Internet pioneer, now a senior research scientist at MIT

In its early years, the Internet was the domain of researchers, academics, and government officials. It wasn't designed for casual visitors; users had to know cryptic commands and codes that only a programmer could love. In the 1990s, Internet software took giant leaps forward in usability.

In the early 1950s, the first computers were changing the military, and a few government agencies and big businesses. By 1980, the microcomputer revolution was transforming offices, schools, and some homes. In the early 21st century, the network revolution is likely to have an even bigger impact on our society.

Electronic mail (email) programs first attracted nontechnical people to the Internet. Email software made it easy to send messages across the office or around the world without learning complex codes.

But the biggest changes came in the early 1990s with the development of the **World Wide Web (WWW)**, a vast tract of the Internet accessible to just about anyone who could point to buttons on a computer screen. The **Web**, as it's often called, led the Internet's transformation from a text-only environment into a multimedia landscape incorporating pictures, animation, sounds, and video. Millions of people connect to the Web each day through **Web browsers**—programs that, in effect, serve as navigable windows into the Web. Hypertext links loosely tie together millions of Web pages created by diverse authors, making the Web into a massive, ever-changing global information storehouse.

Widespread email and Web use have led to astounding Internet growth in the last decade. In 1994, three million people were connected; seven years later more than 400 million people had connections. More than half of all American households are

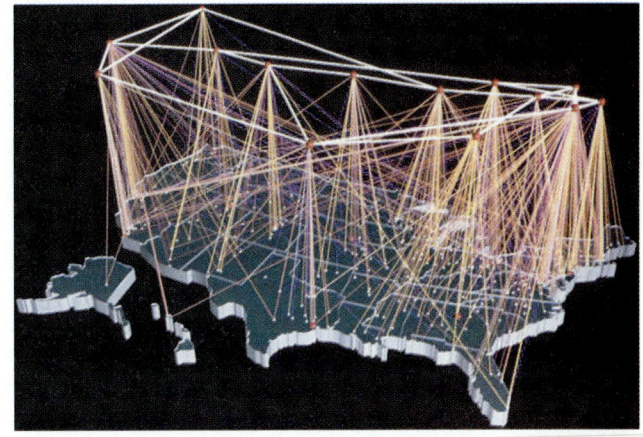

This computer-generated 3-D map represents major Internet connections in the United States.

connected to the Internet; before the first decade of the 21st century is over, 90 percent of U.S. households will likely be connected, making the Internet almost as universal as the television and the telephone. The United States leads the world in Internet activity, but the rest of the world is catching up. About one-fifth of all Europeans were online in 2001, and their numbers are rising quickly.

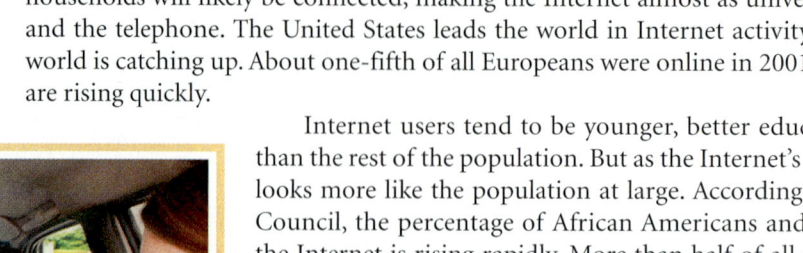

A passenger in a Sao Paulo, Brazil, cab accesses the Internet through a wireless connection.

Internet users tend to be younger, better educated, and wealthier than the rest of the population. But as the Internet's population grows, it looks more like the population at large. According to the U.S. Internet Council, the percentage of African Americans and Hispanics who use the Internet is rising rapidly. More than half of all active Internet users are now female. And while there are still some areas, even in the United States, with no Internet access, those are becoming harder to find. In just about any city on Earth, you can rent time on a PC to check your email or explore the Web.

The Internet is growing faster than television, radio, or any other communication technology that came before it. This growth is largely fueled by the rapid expansion of commerce on the Web. The U.S. Internet economy generates hundreds of billions of dollars in revenues and millions of jobs each year.

The Internet has become so pervasive that many organizations have rebuilt their entire information-processing systems around Internet technology. A growing number of companies are replacing their aging mainframe-and-PC-based systems with **intranets**—private intraorganizational networks based on Internet technology. Intranets mimic the Internet in the ways in which they enable people to transmit, share, and store information within an organization.

Many people believe we'll soon use computers mostly as gateways to intranets and the Internet. In fact, several companies, including IBM, Sun, and Hewlett Packard, are developing and marketing stripped-down computers designed to function mainly as network terminals. These companies don't all agree on exactly what these boxes should include, how much they should be able to do without the aid of a server, or even what they should be called. You might hear people referring to **network computers**, *NCs*, *thin clients*, *net PCs*, or *Windows terminals* when they talk about network-centric machines.

The Wyse Winterm thin client is designed to function only as part of a network, providing network access without the high maintenance costs of traditional PCs.

In spite of their different names and designs, all these machines share two common characteristics: They cost less than typical PCs, because they contain less hardware, and they are easier to maintain, because much of the software can be stored on a central server. Like a TV, a network computer is designed to receive information from elsewhere. But unlike a TV, an NC allows you to send and receive information; it's a two-way connection to the wired world.

Network computers make economic sense in many workplaces, but most of them are not designed for use in homes. But some manufacturers now sell **information appliances** (or *Internet appliances*) that enable home and office users to connect to the Internet without a full-blown PC. (Some people use the terms *Internet appliance* and *information appliance* to refer to network computers in offices and homes; the terminology is, at this point, as fluid as the technology.) For example, Internet telephones have screens and keyboards to enable easy access to email and the Web. **Set-top boxes**, including some game consoles, provide Internet access through television sets. Some handheld computers provide wireless access to the Internet. Even a few cellular phones can display Internet data on tiny screens. Who knows? Future homes and businesses may have dozens of devices—computers, telephones, televisions, stereos, security systems, and even kitchen appliances—continually connected to the Internet, monitoring all kinds of data that can have an impact on our lives and our livelihoods. Whatever happens, it's clear that the Internet is going to play an increasing role in our future.

Millions of homes may soon be connecting to the Internet using televisions through set-top boxes like this one.

Living with Computers

> Just as Michelangelo's contemporaries couldn't have foreseen **abstract expressionism**, we **can't foresee** how people will use the computing medium in the future.
>
> —Clement Mok, in *Designing Business*

In less than a human lifetime, computers have evolved from massive, expensive, error-prone calculators like the Mark I and ENIAC into (mostly) dependable, versatile machines that have worked their way into just about every nook and cranny of modern society. The pioneers who created and marketed the first computers did not foresee these spectacular advances in computer technology.

Thomas Watson, Sr., the founding father of IBM, declared in 1953 that the world would not need more than five computers! And the early pioneers certainly couldn't have predicted the extraordinary social changes that resulted from the computer's rapid evolution. In the time of UNIVAC, who could have imagined Sun workstations, Sony PlayStations, handheld Palms, smart bombs, or dot-coms?

Technological breakthroughs encourage further technological change, so we can expect the rate of change to continue to increase in coming decades. In other words, the technological and social transformations of the past five decades may be dwarfed by the changes that occur over the next half century! It's just a matter of time, and not very much time, before today's state-of-the-art PCs and Palms look as primitive as ENIAC looks to us today. Similarly, today's high-tech society just hints at a future world that we haven't begun to imagine.

What do you really need to know about computers today? The remaining chapters of this book, along with the accompanying CD-ROM and Web site, provide answers to that question by looking at the technology on three levels: explanations, applications, and implications.

Explanations: Clarifying Technology

You don't need to be a computer scientist to coexist with computers. But your encounters with technology will make more sense if you understand a few basic computer concepts. Computers are evolving at an incredible pace; many hardware and software details change every few years. And the Internet is evolving even faster; some suggest that one normal year is equal to several "Internet years." But most of the underlying concepts remain constant as computers and networks evolve. If you understand the basics, you'll find that it's a lot easier to keep up with the changes.

Applications: Computers in Action

Many people define *computer literacy* as the ability to use computers. But because computers are so versatile, you can learn no single set of skills to become computer literate in every situation. **Application programs**, also known simply as **applications**, are the software tools that enable you to use a computer for specific purposes. Many computer applications in science, government, business, and the arts are far too specialized and technical to be of use or of interest to people outside the field. On the other hand, some applications are so flexible that nearly anyone can use them.

Regardless of your background or aspirations, you can almost certainly benefit from knowing a little about the following applications:

- *Word processing and desktop publishing*. Word processing is a critical skill for anyone who communicates in writing—on paper or on the Web. Desktop-publishing software can transform written words into polished, visually exciting publications.
- *Spreadsheets and other number-crunching applications*. In business, the electronic spreadsheet is the personal computer application that pays the rent—or at least calculates it. If you work with numbers of any kind, spreadsheets and statistical software can help you turn those numbers into insights.
- *Databases*. Word processors may be the most popular standalone-PC applications, but databases reign supreme in the world of mainframes. Of course, databases are widely used on PCs, too. Even if you don't have database software on a PC, you can apply database-searching skills to find books in your library—or just about anything on the Internet.

11th century movable type, decimal number system, musical notation

12th century modern abacus

15th century Gutenberg's printing press

16th century algebraic symbols, lead pencil

17th century calculus, Pascal's calculator, probability, binary arithmetic, newspapers, mailboxes

18th century typewriter, three-color printing, industrial revolution

19th century automated loom, Analytical Engine, telegraph, vacuum tube, cathode ray tube, telephone, color photograph, Hollerith's data-processing machine, radio, sound recordings

Early 20th century assembly-line automated production, analog computer, television, motion pictures

1939 Atanasoff creates the first digital computer

1939 Zuse completes first programmable, general-purpose computer

1945 Von Neumann proposes storing programs as data

1946 Mauchly and Eckert design ENIAC

1954 IBM makes first mass-produced computer

1955 Sony introduces portable transistor radio

1956 Bell Labs build first transistorized computer

1962 DEC introduces minicomputer

1962 first timesharing operating system

1963 Doug Engelbart patents mouse

1969 first person on moon

1969 First microprocessor

1970 ROM developed

1975 Cray-1 supercomputer is introduced

1977 Xerox pioneers graphical user interface

1984 Apple introduces the Macintosh

1984 Volkswagen loses hundreds of millions to computer fraud

1988 First fiber-optic trans-Atlantic cable

1990 Microsoft introduces Windows 3.0 for IBM-compatible computers

1992 several pen-based computers and hand-held communications devices introduced

1993 computer companies, phone companies, and cable TV companies form alliances to create new interactive media

1996 PCs outsell TVs in the U.S. for the first time

1996 Palm handheld computer introduces as "Pilot" by US Robotics

1996 WebTV ships boxes that allow Internet access via TVs

1998 Sharp introduces wristwatch PC

1998 Apple's iMac starts trend toward stylish designer computers

1999 Yugoslav hackers attack one of NATO's computer servers

1999 Internet stock explosion pushes Dow past 10,000

2000 Hackers form a corporation to advise corporations on security

2000 Arizona holds first Internet primary election

2000 Love Bug email virus infiltrates millions of computers worldwide within hours of release

2001 Napster music-sharing Web site loses legal battle over copyrighted music

2001 Peer-to-peer computing takes off in spite of Napster's legal problem

The floodgates are open, and information technology ideas are flowing faster all the time.

1943 Turing's Colossus computer breaks Nazi codes

1944 Aiken completes the Mark I

1947 Shockley, Brittain, and Ardeen invent the transistor

1949 Orwell writes 1984, a novel about totalitarianism and computers

1951 computerized banking begins

1957 U.S..S.R. launches Sputnik; U.S. responds by forming ARPA

1959 Jack Kilby and Robert Noyce develop the integrated circuit

1960 laser invented

1964 first prosecuted computer crime

1967 software first sold separately

1969 first nationwide network (ARPANET)

1969 Bell Labs develops UNIX

1972 first home computer game; first email message sent

1974 first microcomputer

1974 first computer-controlled industrial robot

1977 Apple introduces the Apple II

1978 first spreadsheet program

1979 Pac Man appears

1981 IBM introduces its first personal computer

1986 desktop publishing takes off

1986 Connection Machine massively parallel computer introduced

1988 Internet worm cripples 6,000 computers for two days

1990 Hewlett-Packard and others introduce pocket computers

1991 many PC makers launch multimedia products

1991 World Wide Web introduced

1994 Apple introduces Power Macintosh using CPU developed by IBM

1994 White House announces its World Wide Web page

1994 Intel replaces thousands of Pentium processors because of bugs

1995 Microsoft introduces Windows 95 with $200 million marketing campaign

1997 Several companies introduce network computers for Internet access

1997 U.S. Supreme Court defends Internet free speech by striking down Communications Decency Act

1998 U.S. Justice Department sues Microsoft and Intel for separate antitrust violations

1999 free PCs offered to lure Internet subscribers for the first time

1999 Internet email outpaces the post office

1999 Y2K millennium bug captures public attention, costs businesses billions

2000 Denial of service attacks cripple many of the largest commercial Web sites

2000 Microsoft is found guilty of illegal monopolistic practices

2000 AOL buys Time Warner, creating the world's largest media company

2000 Internet economy takes a nose-dive when hundreds of dot-com businesses declare bankruptcy

2001 U.S. government settles Microsoft antitrust suit

2001 Terrorist attacks fuel explosion of interest in security

- *Computer graphics.* Computers make it possible to produce and manipulate all kinds of graphics, including charts, drawings, digital photographs—even realistic 3-D animation. As graphics tools become more accessible, visual communication skills become more important for all of us.
- *Multimedia.* Modern desktop computers make it easy to edit and manipulate audio and video, opening up creative possibilities for all kinds of potential artists. Multimedia software can combine audio and video with traditional text and graphics, adding new dimensions to computer communication. Interactive multimedia documents, including many Web sites, enable users to explore a variety of paths through media-rich information sources.
- *Telecommunication and networking.* A network connection is a door into a world of email, online discussion groups, Web-publishing ventures, and database sharing. If current trends continue, telecommunication—long-distance communication—may soon be the single most important function of computers.
- *Artificial intelligence.* Artificial intelligence is the branch of computer science that explores the use of computers in tasks that require intelligence, imagination, and insight—tasks that have traditionally been performed by people rather than machines. Until recently, artificial intelligence was mostly an academic discipline—a field of study reserved for researchers and philosophers. But that research is paying off today with commercial applications that exhibit intelligence, from basic speech recognition to sophisticated expert systems.
- *General problem solving.* People use computers to solve problems. Most people use software applications written by professional programmers. But some kinds of problems can't easily be solved with off-the-shelf applications; they require at least some custom programming. Programming languages aren't applications; they're tools that enable you to build and customize applications. Many computer users find their machines become more versatile and valuable when they learn a little about programming.

Implications: Social and Ethical Issues

> True **computer literacy** is not just **knowing how** to make use of computers and **computational ideas**. It is knowing **when it is appropriate** to do so.
> —Seymour Papert, in *Mindstorms*

Computers and networks are transforming the world rapidly and irreversibly. Jobs that existed for hundreds of years are eliminated by automation while new careers are built on emerging technology. Start-up businesses create multiple millionaires overnight, while older companies struggle to keep pace with "Internet time." Instant worldwide communication changes the way businesses work and challenges the role of governments. Computers routinely save lives in hospitals, keep space flights on course, and predict the weekend weather.

More than any other recent technology, the computer is responsible for profound changes in our society; we just need to imagine a world without computers to recognize their impact. Of course, computer scientists and computer engineers are not responsible for all the technological turbulence. Developments in fields as diverse as telecommunications, genetic engineering, medicine, and atomic physics contribute to the ever-increasing rate of social change. But researchers in all these fields depend on computers to produce their work.

The future is rushing toward you, and computer technology is a big part of it. It's exciting to consider the opportunities arising from advances in artificial intelligence, multimedia, robotics, and other cutting-edge technologies of the electronic revolution—opportunities in the workplace, the school, and the home. But it's just as important to pay attention to the potential risks. Here's a sampling of the kinds of issues we'll confront in this book:

- *The threat to personal privacy posed by large databases and computer networks.* When you use a credit card, buy an airline ticket, place a phone call, visit your doctor, send an email message, or explore the World Wide Web, you are leaving a trail of personal information in one or more computers. Who owns that information? Is it okay for the business or organization that collected the information to share it with others or make it public? Do you have the right to check its accuracy and change it if it's wrong? Do laws protecting individual privacy rights place undue burdens on businesses and governments?
- *The hazards of high-tech crime and the difficulty of keeping data secure.* Even if you trust the institutions and businesses that collect data about you, you can't be sure that data will remain secure in

their computer systems. Computer crime is at an all-time high, and law enforcement officials are having a difficult time keeping it under control. How can society protect itself from information thieves and high-tech vandals? How can lawmakers write laws about technology that they are just beginning to understand? What kinds of personal risk do you face as a result of computer crime?

- *The difficulty of defining and protecting intellectual property in an all-digital age.* Software programs, musical recordings, videos, and books can be difficult and expensive to create. But in our digital age, all of these can easily be copied. What rights do the creators of intellectual property have? Is a teenager who copies music files from the Web a computer criminal? What about a shopkeeper who sells pirated copies of Microsoft Office for $10? Or a student who posts a clip from *Star Wars* on his Web site? Or a musician who uses a two-second sample from a Beatles song in an electronic composition?

- *The risks of failure of computer systems.* Computer software is difficult to write, because it is incredibly complex. As a result, no computer system is completely fail-safe. Computer failures routinely cause communication problems, billing errors, lost data, and other inconveniences. But they also occasionally result in power blackouts, telephone system meltdowns, weapons failure, and other potentially deadly problems. Who is responsible for loss of income—or loss of life—caused by software errors? What rights do we have when buying and using software? How can we, as a society, protect ourselves from software disasters?

This robot security guard protects this museum from vandals and thieves. But does it threaten the jobs of other guards?

- *The threat of automation and the dehumanization of work.* Computers and the Internet fueled unprecedented economic growth in the last decade of the 20th century, producing plenty of new jobs for workers with the right skills. But the new information-based economy has cost many workers—especially older workers—their jobs and their dignity. And many workers today find that their jobs involve little more than tending to machines—and being monitored by bosses with high-tech surveillance devices. As machines replace people in the workplace, what rights do the displaced workers have? Does a worker's right to privacy outweigh an employer's right to read employee email or monitor worker actions? What is the government's role in the protection of worker rights in the high-tech workplace?

- *The abuse of information as a tool of political and economic power.* The computer age has produced an explosion of information, and most of that information is concentrated in corporate and government computers. The emergence of low-cost personal computers and the Internet makes it possible for more people to access information and the power that comes with that information. But the majority of the people on the planet have never made a phone call, let alone used a computer. Will the information revolution leave them behind? Do information-rich people and countries have a responsibility to share technology and information with the information-poor?

- *The dangers of dependence on complex technology.* One of the biggest news stories of 1999 was the impending threat of massive problems caused by the Y2K bug—the failure of some computer programs on January 1, 2000, because those systems represented the year with only two digits. People stockpiled food and fuel, hid cash and jewels, and prepared for the possibility that the power grid would fail, leaving much of the world's population helpless and hungry. Businesses and governments spent billions of dollars repairing and replacing computer systems, and the Y2K crisis never materialized. But the Y2K scare reminded us how much we have come to depend on this far-from-foolproof technology. Are we, as a society, addicted to computer technology? Should we question new technological innovations before we embrace them? Can we build a future in which technology never takes precedence over humanity?

Today's technology raises fascinating and difficult questions. But these questions pale in comparison to the ones we'll have to deal with as the technology evolves in the coming years:

- *The death of privacy.* Governments and private companies alike are installing extensive video surveillance networks to monitor security and track lawbreakers. Computer databases are accumulating more information about you all the time, and networks are making it easier to transmit, share, and merge that information. Will these converging technologies destroy the last of our personal privacy, as some experts have suggested? Is there anything we can do about it?

What impact will computer technology have on traditional cultures that have evolved for thousands of years without computers?

- *The blurring of reality.* Virtual reality (VR) is widely used by scientific researchers and computer gamers alike. But if VR doesn't live up to its name, it does suggest a future technology in which artificial environments look and feel real. Rapid developments in Internet technology are likely to lead us to shared virtual environments ranging from shopping malls to gaming centers. Already some people are suffering from computer and Internet addictions. Will these diseases become epidemics when VR feels like real life, only better? Will VR technology be abused by unscrupulous con artists? Should governments limit what's legal when just about anything is possible?
- *The evolution of intelligence.* Artificial intelligence research is responsible for many products, including software that can read books to the blind, understand spoken words, and play world-class chess. But tomorrow's machine intelligence will make today's smartest machines look stupid. What rights will human workers have when software can do their jobs better, faster, and smarter? What rights will smart machines have in a world run by humans? Will there come a time when humans aren't smart enough to maintain control of their creations?
- *The emergence of bio-digital technology.* Today thousands of people walk around with computer chips embedded in their bodies, helping them to overcome disabilities and lead normal lives. At the same time, researchers are attempting to develop computers that use biology, rather than electronics, as their underlying technology. As the line between organism and machine blurs, what happens to our vision of ourselves? What are the limits of our creative powers, and what are our responsibilities in using those powers?

For better and for worse, we will be coexisting with computers until death do us part. As with any relationship, a little understanding can go a long way. The remaining chapters of this book will help you gain the understanding you need to survive and prosper in a world of computers.

Tech's Double-Edged Sword

Steven Levy

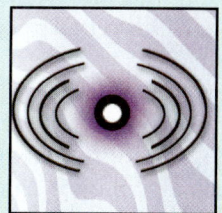

Is technology good, evil, both, or neither? Writer Steven Levy wrote this powerful essay in the wake of the terrorist attack on the World Trade Center and the Pentagon. The article, first published in the September 24, 2001, issue of Newsweek, *outlines the role technology played in that monumental tragedy. It raises some difficult questions about our relationship to technology in an uncertain future.*

From American Flight 77, en route to death and the Pentagon, lawyer Barbara Olson cell-phoned her husband, the U.S. solicitor general, and told him of the hijacking. On United Flight 93, both Jeremy Glick and Thomas Burnett Jr. called their wives and confided their (apparently successful) intentions to counterattack the hijackers. Others on the stolen planes, as well as dozens trapped in the World Trade Center towers, pulled out their cells to speak one more time to a wife or parent and say "I love you."

The recipients of those calls, while justifiably inconsolable, are undoubtedly grateful for the final opportunity to hear those voices. But before we celebrate another irreplaceable use of wireless communications, consider this: according to government officials, within hours of the explosions, mobile phones of suspected terrorists linked to Osama bin Laden were buzzing with congratulations for the murderous acts. *They use them, too.*

The contrast dramatizes a long-recognized truism: modern technologies that add efficiency, power and wonder to our lives inevitably deliver the same benefits to evildoers. The Internet is no exception. On Sept. 11 the Net seemed like a godsend. Email worked when phones didn't, allowing countless New Yorkers to assure worried friends and families around the world that they were still alive. Web sites were quickly home-brewed to carry lists of companies affected and family members missing. But there is also every likelihood that the terrorists had exploited the Internet as well, using easily available and virtually untraceable accounts on Yahoo or Hotmail, and meeting in ad hoc chat rooms.

Perhaps the terrorists cloaked their planning with cryptography, once an exotic technology, now a commonplace computer utility. Communications could also be shrouded with steganography (hiding messages between pixels of a graphic—a reputed bin Laden technique) or anonymizers (which make email untraceable). Such tools are lionized by freedom-loving "cypherpunks," who have shrugged off potential dark-side usage as a reasonable trade-off for the protection that crypto can provide just plain citizens; as with cars and telephones, the benefits way overwhelm the abuses.

So goes the attitude that has taken us to where we are today, in the best sense and now the worst sense. Technology drives civilization; it augments and amplifies human effort. Our own age is marked by computers and software, which have democratized formerly specialized pursuits. With the right software and the Web, anyone can be a publisher, a music distributor, a photo refinisher... the list is endless.

But the sophistication of our technology also leverages the efforts of those who would destroy. And the very structure of our society—a dense thicket of connections, where skyscrapers hold thousands of workers, "just in time" factories rely on next-day deliveries and air-traffic controllers manage hundreds of planes at once—allows a single act of terror to generate torrents of disruption and pain.

Thus a barely armed band of 19 can slam our nation with the force of many armies. The implements they used were strictly off the shelf. We don't know if they practiced their aeronautical skills by flying into virtual Twin Towers on Microsoft Flight Simulator (which was quickly taken off the shelves). But they did apparently train by renting time on computer-powered flight simulators that democratize the experience of flying a 767. Then, by way of the dime-store technology of small sharpened blades, they were able to take charge of sophisticated commercial airlines. Suddenly those benign carriers were powerful, targetable bombs.

It was a nightmarish fulfillment of science-fiction writer William Gibson's proclamation that the street finds its own uses for technology. The more powerful our tools are, the more dangerous they are when turned against us. For centuries we've accepted that. It's simply the downside of tech.

Sun Microsystems chief scientist Bill Joy has been pondering this downside while writing a book tentatively called "Why the Future Doesn't Need Us." Coincidentally, Joy was in lower Manhattan in the early part of last week. As bad as it was, Joy believes, the tragedy was nothing like what might be possible with biological weaponry. The coming age of biotech will undoubtedly make programmable bacteria and viruses more accessible—to doctors, business and bio-terrorists. "The things I'm worried about haven't happened yet," says Joy.

Virtually no one dares ask whether the balance of technology might tilt too far toward empowering the evil. Who would have a clue of how to address that situation? Human beings have a track record of pursuing what they see as progress and asking questions later. While refusing to think the Unthinkable, we create the circumstances that allow it to occur.

Should we be giving the Unthinkable more consideration as we drive technology ever further? The answer seems obvious. Yet it almost goes without saying that any safeguards we institute won't be perfect. What assurance do we have that future terrorists will not feast on the contents of Pandora's box? "Knowledge itself is dangerous," says Joy. "Scientific information we pursue in an unfettered way is a weapon. And we're not ready to deal with that." Maybe after last week, we are closer.

DISCUSSION QUESTIONS

1. Do you think it's possible to keep technology out of the hands of terrorists and other "evil" people? Explain your answer.
2. Do you think we should be "giving the Unthinkable more consideration" as we develop new technologies? Explain your answer.

Summary

While the basic idea behind a computer goes back to Charles Babbage's 19th-century plan for an Analytical Engine, the first real computers were developed during the 1940s. Computers have evolved at an incredible pace since those early years, becoming consistently smaller, faster, more efficient, more reliable, and less expensive. At the same time, people have devised all kinds of interesting and useful ways to put computers to work to solve problems.

Computers today, like their ancestors, are information-processing machines designed to transform information from one form to another. When a computer operates, the hardware accepts input data from some outside source, transforms the data by following instructions called software, and produces output that can be read by a human or by another machine.

Computers today come in all shapes and sizes, with specific types being well suited for particular jobs. Mainframe computers and supercomputers provide more power and speed than smaller desktop machines, but they are expensive to purchase and operate. Timesharing makes it possible for many users to work simultaneously at terminals connected to these large computers. At the other end of the spectrum, workstations, personal computers, and a variety of portable devices provide computing power for those of us who don't need a mainframe's capabilities. Microprocessors aren't just used in general-purpose computers; they're embedded in appliances, automobiles, and a rapidly growing list of other products.

Connecting to a network enhances the value and power of a computer—it can share resources with other computers and facilitate electronic communication with other computer users. Some networks are local to a particular building or business; others connect users at remote geographic locations. The Internet is a collection of networks that connects the computers of businesses, public institutions, and individuals around the globe. Email provides hundreds of millions of people with instant world-wide communication capabilities. With Web browsing software, those same Internet users have access to millions of Web pages on the World Wide Web. The Web is a distributed network of interlinked multimedia documents. Although it started out as a tool for researchers and scholars, the Web has quickly become a vital center for entertainment and commerce.

Computers and information technology have changed the world rapidly and irreversibly. We can easily list dozens of ways in which computers make our lives easier and more productive. Personal computer applications, such as word processing, spreadsheets, graphics, multimedia, and databases, continue to grow in popularity. Emerging technologies, such as artificial intelligence, offer promise for future applications. At the same time, computers threaten our privacy, our security, and perhaps our way of life. As we rush into the information age, our future depends on computers and on our ability to understand and use them in productive, positive ways.

Chapter Review

▼ Key Terms

analytical engine (p. 25)
application program (application) (p. 37)
data (p. 27)
embedded computer (p. 33)
firmware (p. 33)
handheld computer (p. 32)
hardware (p. 27)
high-performance computer (p. 31)
input (p. 27)
information appliance (p. 36)
integrated circuit (p. 29)
intranet (p. 36)

laptop computer (p. 32)
mainframe computer (p. 30)
microcomputer revolution (p. 29)
microprocessor (p. 29)
Moore's Law (p. 29)
network computer (NC) (p. 36)
notebook computer (p. 32)
output (p. 27)
personal computer (PC) (p. 29)
personal digital assistant (PDA) (p. 33)
program (p. 27)
server (p. 31)
set-top box (p. 36)

silicon chip (p. 29)
software (p. 27)
special-purpose (dedicated) computer (p. 33)
supercomputer (p. 31)
terminal (p. 30)
timesharing (p. 31)
transistor (p. 28)
Web browser (p. 35)
workstation (p. 31)
World Wide Web (WWW (p. 35))

▼ Interactive Quiz Questions

1. The *Computer Confluence* CD-ROM contains self-test quiz questions related to this chapter, including multiple choice, true or false, and matching questions.
2. The *Computer Confluence* Web site, www.prenhall.com/beekman, contains self-test exercises related to this chapter. Follow the instructions for taking a quiz. After you've completed your quiz, you can email the results to your instructor.

    The Web site also contains open-ended discussion questions called Internet Explorations. Discuss one or more of the Internet exploration questions at the section for this chapter.

▼ Review Questions

1. Provide a working definition of each of the key terms listed in the "Key Terms" section. Check your answers in the glossary.
2. List several ways you interact with computers in your daily life.
3. Why was the Analytical Engine never completed during Charles Babbage's lifetime?
4. Outline the evolution of the computer from World War II to the present.
5. How are hardware and software related?
6. What is the most important difference between a computer and a calculator?
7. What is the difference between a mainframe and a microcomputer? What are the advantages and disadvantages of each?
8. What kinds of computer applications require the speed and power of a supercomputer? Give some examples.
9. What types of computers typically employ timesharing?
10. List several common personal computer applications.
11. Why is it important for people to know about and understand computers?
12. Describe some of the benefits and drawbacks of the computer revolution.

▼ Discussion Questions

1. What do people mean when they talk about the computer revolution? What is revolutionary about it?
2. How do you feel about computers? Examine your positive and negative feelings.
3. What major events before the 20th century influenced the development of the computer?
4. Suppose Charles Babbage and Lady Lovelace had been able to construct a working Analytical Engine and develop a factory for mass producing it. How do you think the world would have reacted? How would the history of the 20th century have been different as a result?
5. How would the world be different today if a wrinkle in time transported a modern desktop computer system, complete with software and manuals, onto the desk of Herbert Hoover? Adolf Hitler? Albert Einstein?
6. The automobile and the television set are two examples of technological inventions that changed our society drastically in ways that were not anticipated by their inventors. Outline several positive and negative effects of each of these two inventions. Do you think, on balance, that we are better off as a result of these machines? Why or why not? Now repeat this exercise for the computer.
7. Should all students be required to take at least one computer course? Why or why not? If so, what should that course cover?
8. Computerphobia—fear or anxiety related to computers—is a common malady among people today. What do you think causes it? What, if anything, should be done about it?
9. In your opinion what computer applications offer the most promise for making the world a better place? Which computer applications pose the most significant threats to our future well-being?

▼ Projects

1. Start a collection of news articles, cartoons, or television segments that deal with computers. Does your collection say anything about popular attitudes toward computers?
2. Trace computer-related articles through several years in the same magazine. Do you see any changes or trends?
3. Develop a questionnaire to try to determine people's attitudes about computers. Once you have people's answers to your questions, summarize your results.
4. Take an inventory of all the computers you encounter in a single day. Be sure to include embedded computers such as those in cars, appliances, entertainment equipment, and other machines.

Sources and Resources

Books

Dictionary of Computer and Internet Words: An A to Z Guide to Hardware, Software, and Cyberspace, edited by American Heritage Dictionaries (New York: Houghton Mifflin, 2001). It sometimes seems like the computer industry makes three things: hardware, software, and jargon. Many computer terms are too new, too obscure, or too technical to appear in standard dictionaries. Fortunately, several good dictionaries specialize in computer terminology. This is one of the most comprehensive and up to date. It covers PC, Macintosh, and Internet terms.

The Difference Engine: Charles Babbage and the Quest to Build the First Computer, by Doron Swade and Charles Babbage (New York: Viking Press, 2001). This book tells the story of the design of Babbage's visionary computing machine. It also reveals the problems Babbage faced getting funding for the ill-fated project. Swade led a team that built a working model of a Difference Engine for the 1991 Babbage bicentenary.

ENIAC: The Triumphs and Tragedies of the World's First Computer, by Scott McCartney (Walker and Co., 1999). This engaging book tells the human story of two pioneers and their struggles to be recognized for their monumental achievements in those early days of computing.

Crystal Fire: The Birth of the Information Age, by Michael Riordan and Lillian Hoddeson (New York: Norton, 1997). One of the defining moments of the information age occurred in 1947 when William Shockley and his colleagues invented the transistor. Crystal Fire tells the story of that earthshaking invention, clearly describing the technical and human dimensions of the story.

A History of Modern Computing, by Paul E. Ceruzzi (Cambridge, MA: MIT Press, 2000). This book traces the first fifty years of computer history, from ENIAC to internetworked PCs. The social context of the technology is clear throughout the book.

Fire in the Valley: The Making of the Personal Computer, Second Edition, 1999, by Paul Freiberger and Michael Swaine (Berkeley, CA: Osborne/McGraw-Hill, 1999). This book chronicles the early years of the personal computer revolution. The text occasionally gets bogged down in details, but the photos and quotes from the early days are fascinating. The 1999 film *Pirates of Silicon Valley* is based loosely on this book.

Accidental Empires: How the Boys of Silicon Valley Make Their Millions, Battle Foreign Competition, and Still Can't Get a Date, Revised Edition, by Robert X. Cringely (New York: Harper Business, 1996). Robert X. Cringely is the pen name for *InfoWorld*'s computer-industry gossip columnist. In this opinionated, irreverent, and highly entertaining book Cringely discusses the past, present, and future of the volatile personal computer industry. When you read the humorous, colorful characterizations of the people who run this industry, you'll understand why Cringely didn't use his real name. *Triumph of the Nerds,* a 1996 PBS TV show and video based loosely on this book, lacks much of the humor and insight of the book, but includes some fascinating footage of the pioneers reminiscing about the early days.

Faster—The Acceleration of Just About Everything, by James Gleick (New York: Pantheon Books, 1999). The title says it all. In this age of ever-faster computers, electronic organizers, and Internet time, we're setting speed records at just about everything—but at what cost? Well worth reading if you have time.

The Difference Engine, by William Gibson and Bruce Sterling (New York: Spectra, 1992). How would the world of the 19th century be different if Charles and Ada had succeeded in constructing the Analytical Engine 150 years ago? This imaginative mystery novel takes place in a world where the computer revolution arrived a century early. Like other books by these two pioneers of the "cyberpunk" school of science fiction, *The Difference Engine* is dark, dense, detailed, and thought-provoking.

Dave Barry in Cyberspace, by Dave Barry (New York: Fawcett Columnbine, 1996). Dave Barry, the irreverent humor columnist, turns his wit loose on the information revolution in this hilarious little book. Here's a typical chapter title: "A Brief History of Computing from Cave Walls to Windows 95—Not That This Is Necessarily Progress." Whether you think computers are frustrating or funny, you'll probably find a few good laughs here.

Periodicals

Wired (www.wired.com). This high-style monthly started out as "the first consumer magazine for the digital generation to track technology's impact on all facets of the human condition." Today *Wired* devotes more pages to the business of technology and less to the impact of technology, but it's still a thought-provoking, influential magazine.

Computerworld (www.computerworld.com). This venerable newsweekly has provided up-to-the-week news on computers for decades.

InfoWorld (www.infoworld.com). *Computerworld's* younger sibling covers business computing, including applications for mainframes, servers, and other behind-the-scenes machines that aren't covered in PC publications.

E-Week. In 2000 this newsweekly changed its name from *PC Week* to *E-Week* to reflect its expanded coverage of the electronic digital business world.

PC World (www.pcworld.com). Because the world of personal computers changes so rapidly, computer users depend on magazines to keep them up to date on hardware and software developments. This periodical is one of the most popular sources for keeping up with developments in the PC world. The companion Web site offers up-to-the-minute information along with archives from past issues.

PC Magazine (www.pcmag.com). *PC Magazine* is another popular PC periodical, containing news, reviews, and feature articles for a variety of interests.

Macworld (www.macworld.com). This is the premiere periodical for Mac users, covering hardware, software, and Internet issues with clear, dependable articles and reviews.

MacAddict (www.macaddict.com). This magazine for Macintosh true-believers tends to be slightly more technical—and more partisan—than *Macworld*.

Mobile Computing & Communication (www.mobilecomputing.com). This is a good source of news and information on portable computing devices, from laptops to palmtops, as well as mobile phones and other traveling companions.

Pen Computing (www.pencomputing.com). This magazine covers pen-based computers, from tiny Palm devices to full-sized pen PCs.

Web Pages

Some of the best sources and resources on computers and information technology are on the Internet's World Wide Web. But the Web is changing quickly, and new sites are appearing every day. The *Computer Confluence* Web pages include up-to-date links to many of the best computer-related resources on the Web. To find them, open your Web browsing software, enter the address **www.prenhall.com/beekman**, follow the on-screen buttons to the table of contents, select a chapter, and click the links that interest you.

2 Hardware Basics: Inside the Box

After you read this chapter you should be able to:

▼

Explain in general terms how computers store and manipulate information

Describe the basic structure and organization of a computer

Discuss the functions and interactions of a computer system's principal internal components

Explain why a computer typically has different types of memory and storage devices

▲

▼ **In this chapter:**

Bits and bytes: the nature of digital information

Inside the box: the computer's "brain" and memory

How it works: visual explanations of the computer's inner workings

Self-study questions and projects

Mini-reviews of helpful resources for further study

…and more.

▼ **On the CD-ROM:**

Activities highlighting how memory works

Animated tutorials explaining how CPU and memory work

Instant access to glossary and key word references

Interactive self-study quizzes

…and more.

▼ **On the Web:**

www.prenhall.com/beekman

Documents describing and illustrating CPU and memory technology

Links to binary number counting games

Articles on the evolution of the CPU and memory technology

Self-study exercises

…and more.

Thomas J. Watson, Sr., and the Emperor's New Machines

There is no invention—**only discovery**.
—Thomas J. Watson, Sr.

Thomas J. Watson, Sr. (1874–1956)

As president or, as he has been called, the "emperor" of IBM, Thomas J. Watson, Sr., created a corporate culture that fostered both invention and discovery. In 1914 he joined the ailing Computing-Tabulating-Recording Company as a salesperson. The company specialized in counting devices that used punched cards to read and store information. Ten years later Watson took it over, renamed it International Business Machines, and turned it into the dominant force in the information industry.

Thomas Watson has been called autocratic. He demanded unquestioning allegiance from his employees and enforced a legendary dress code that forbade even a hint of color in a shirt. But in many ways Watson ran his company like a family, rewarding loyal employees with uncommon favors. During the Depression he refused to lay off workers, choosing instead to stockpile surplus machines. As if to prove that good deeds don't go unrewarded, the director of the newly formed Social Security Administration bought Watson's excess stock.

Watson's first involvement with computers was providing financial backing for Howard Aiken's Mark I, the pioneering electromechanical computer developed in the early 1940s at Harvard. But Watson stubbornly refused to develop a commercial computer, even as UNIVAC I achieved fame and commercial contracts for the fledgling Sperry company.

Shortly after Watson retired from the helm of IBM in 1949, his son, Thomas Watson, Jr., took over. When Watson Senior died of a heart attack in 1956 at the age of 82, he still held the title of chairman of IBM. The younger Watson led IBM into the computing field with a vengeance, eventually building a computing empire that dwarfed all competitors for decades to come.

The conservative giant was slow to adjust to the rapid-fire changes of the '80s and '90s, making it possible for smaller, more nimble companies such as Compaq, Dell, Sun, and Microsoft to seize emerging markets. Massive revenue losses forced IBM to reorganize, replace many of its leaders, and abandon the company's longstanding no-layoffs policy. (IBM also abandoned the legendary dress code, opting for a more casual image.) Today, in spite of stiff competition (or perhaps *because* of it), IBM is a major source of innovation in the industry, with major research projects in everything from massive supercomputers to microscopic storage devices. Thomas Watson is long gone, but invention and discovery are alive and well at IBM.

Computers schedule airline flights, predict the weather, play music, control space stations, and keep the world's economic wheels spinning. How can one kind of machine do so many things?

To understand what really makes computers tick, you would need to devote considerable time and effort to studying computer science and computer engineering. Most of us don't need to understand every detail of a computer's inner workings, any more than a parent needs to explain wave and particle physics when a child asks why the sky is blue. We can be satisfied with simpler answers, even if those answers are only approximations of the technical truth. We'll spend the next three chapters exploring answers to the question, "How do computers do what they do?"

The main text of each of these chapters provides simple, nontechnical answers and basic information. How It Works boxes use text and graphics to dig deeper into the inner workings of the computer. Depending on your course, learning style, and level of curiosity, you may read these boxes as they appear in the text, read them after you've completed the basic material in the chapter, or (if you don't need the technical details) bypass some or all of them. You'll find interactive multimedia versions of many of these How It Works boxes on the *Computer Confluence* CD-ROM. Use the Sources and Resources section at each chapter's end for further explorations.

PCs are assembled in factories like this one at Dell Computer, Inc. In the next two chapters, we'll examine the components that make up the modern computer.

What Computers Do

> Stripped of its interfaces, **a bare computer** boils down to little more than a pocket calculator that can **push its own buttons** and **remember** what it has done.
> —Arnold Penzias, in *Ideas and Information*

The simple truth is that computers perform only four basic functions:

▶ *Receive input.* Computers accept information from the outside world.
▶ *Process information.* Computers perform arithmetic or logical (decision-making) operations on information.
▶ *Produce output.* Computers communicate information to the outside world.
▶ *Store information.* Computers move and store information in memory.

Every computer system contains hardware components—physical parts—that specialize in each of these four functions:

▶ **Input devices** accept input from the outside world. The most common input devices, of course, are keyboards and pointing devices such as mice.
▶ **Output devices** send information to the outside world. Most computers use a TV-like video monitor as their main output device and a printer to produce paper printouts.
▶ A **processor**, or **central processing unit (CPU)**, is, in effect, the computer's "brain." The CPU processes information, performing arithmetic calculations and making basic decisions by comparing information values.
▶ **Memory** and **storage devices** both store information, but they serve different purposes. The computer's **memory** (sometimes called *primary storage*) is used to store programs and data that need to be instantly accessible to the CPU. Storage devices (sometimes called *secondary storage*), including disk and tape drives, serve as long-term repositories for data. You can think of a storage device, such as a disk drive, as a combination input and output device because the computer sends information to the storage device (output) and later retrieves that information from it (input).

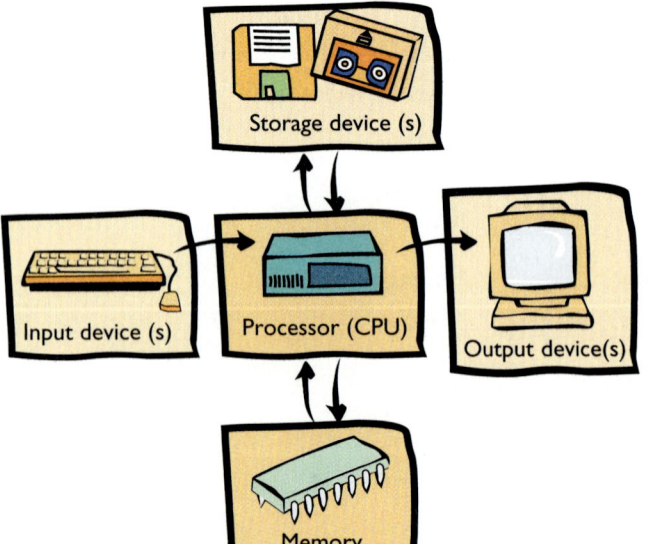

The basic components of every computer system include the central components (the CPU and memory), and peripherals (input, output, and storage devices).

These four types of components, when combined, make up the hardware part of a computer system. Of course, the system isn't complete without software—the instructions that tell the hardware what to do. But for now we concentrate on hardware. In this chapter, we focus on the central processing unit and the computer's memory; these components are at the center of all computing operations. In the next chapter, we look at the input, output, and storage devices—that is, the **peripherals** of the computer system. Because every computer hardware component is designed either to transport or to transform information, we start with a little bit of information about information.

A Bit About Bits

The term **information** is difficult to define because it has many meanings. According to one popular definition, information is communication that has value because it *informs*. This distinction can be helpful for dealing with data from televisions, magazines, computers, and other sources. But it's not always clear and it's not absolute. As Richard Saul Wurman points out, "Everyone needs a personal measure with which to define information. What constitutes information to one person may be data to another. If it doesn't make sense to you, it doesn't qualify."

> The great Information Age is really **an explosion of non-information**; it is an explosion of data. To deal with the increasing **onslaught of data**, it is **imperative** to distinguish between the two; information is **that which leads to understanding**.
> —Richard Saul Wurman, in *Information Anxiety 2*

At the opposite extreme, one communication theory defines information as anything that can be communicated, whether it has value or not. By this definition, information comes in many forms. The words, numbers, and pictures on these pages are symbols representing information. If you underline this sentence, you're adding new information to the page. Even the sounds and pictures that emanate from a television commercial are packed with information.

Some people attempt to strictly apply the first definition to computers, claiming that computers turn raw data, which has no value in its current form, into information, which is valuable. This approach emphasizes the computer's role as a business data-processing machine. But in our modern interconnected world, one computer's output is often another's input. If a computer receives a message from another computer, is the message worthless data or valuable information? And whose personal measure of value applies?

For our purposes, describing the mechanics of computers in these chapters, we lean toward the second, more subjective, approach and use the terms data and information more-or-less interchangeably. In later chapters we present plenty of evidence to suggest that not all computer output has value. In the end, it is up to you to decide what the real information is.

Bit Basics

Whatever you call it, in the world of computers information is **digital**: It's made up of discrete, countable units, so it can be subdivided. In many situations, people need to reduce information to simpler units to use it effectively. For example, a child trying to pronounce an unfamiliar word can sound out each letter individually before tackling the whole word.

A computer doesn't understand words, numbers, pictures, musical notes, or even letters of the alphabet. Like a young reader, a computer can't process information without dividing it into smaller units. In fact, computers can only digest information that has been broken into bits. A **bit** (binary digit) is the smallest unit of information. A bit can have one of two values. You can also think of these two values as yes and no, zero and one, on and off, black and white, or high and low.

If you think of the innards of a computer as a collection of microscopic on/off switches, it's easy to understand why computers process information bit by bit. Each switch stores a tiny amount of information: a signal to turn on a light, for example, or the answer to a yes/no question. (In modern integrated circuits, high and low electrical charges represent bits, but these circuits work the same as if they were really made up of tiny switches.)

Remember Paul Revere's famous midnight ride? His co-conspirators used a pair of lanterns to convey a choice between two messages, "One if by land, two if by sea"—a **binary**

How It Works

2.1 Binary Numbers

> This is the first of many **How It Works** boxes you'll find in this book. **How It Works** boxes provide more technical detail than you'll find in the main text. Nothing in the **How It Works** boxes is essential for understanding the matter in the rest of the book.

In a computer, all information—program instructions, pictures, text, sounds, or mathematical values—is represented by patterns of microscopic switches. In most cases these groups of switches represent numbers or numerical codes.

The easiest kind of switch to manufacture is an on/off toggle switch: It has just two settings, on and off, like an ordinary light switch. That's the kind of switch that's used in every modern computer.

Binary arithmetic follows the same rules as ordinary decimal arithmetic. But with only two digits available for each position, you have to borrow and carry (manipulate digits in other positions) more often. Even adding 1 and 1 results in a two-digit number. Multiplication, division, negative numbers, and fractions can also be represented in binary, but most people find them messy and complicated compared with decimal arithmetic.

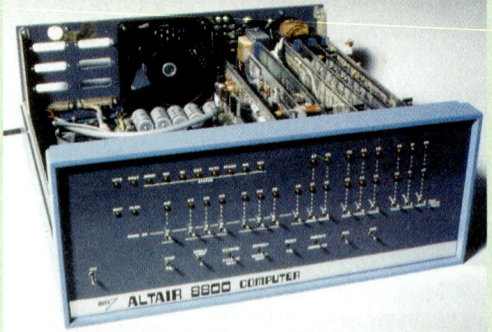

The MITS Altair, the first personal computer, came with no keyboard or monitor. It could only be programmed by using a bank of binary switches for input; binary patterns of lights provided the output.

1 In our decimal number system the position of a digit is important: In the number 7357, the 7 on the left stands for seven thousands, the other 7 for seven ones. The use of switches to represent numbers would be easy to understand if the switches each had 10 settings (0 through 9). The decimal number 67 might look like this:

choice. It's theoretically possible to send a message like this with just one lantern. But "One if by land, zero if by sea" wouldn't have worked very well unless there was some way to know exactly when the message was being sent. With two lanterns, the first lantern could say "Here is the message" when it was turned on. The second lantern communicated the critical bit's worth of information: land or sea. If the revolutionaries had wanted to send a more complex message, they could have used more lanterns. ("Three if by subway!")

In much the same way, a computer can process larger chunks of information by treating groups of bits as units. For example, a collection of 8 bits, called a **byte**, can represent 256 different messages ($256 = 2^8$). If you think of each bit as a light that can be either on or off, you can make different combinations of lights represent different messages. (Computer scientists usually speak in terms of 0 and 1 instead of on and off, but the concept is the same either way.) The computer has an advantage over Paul Revere in that it sees not just the number of lights turned on but also their order, so 01 (off–on) is different from 10 (on–off).

Chapter 2 Hardware Basics: Inside the Box

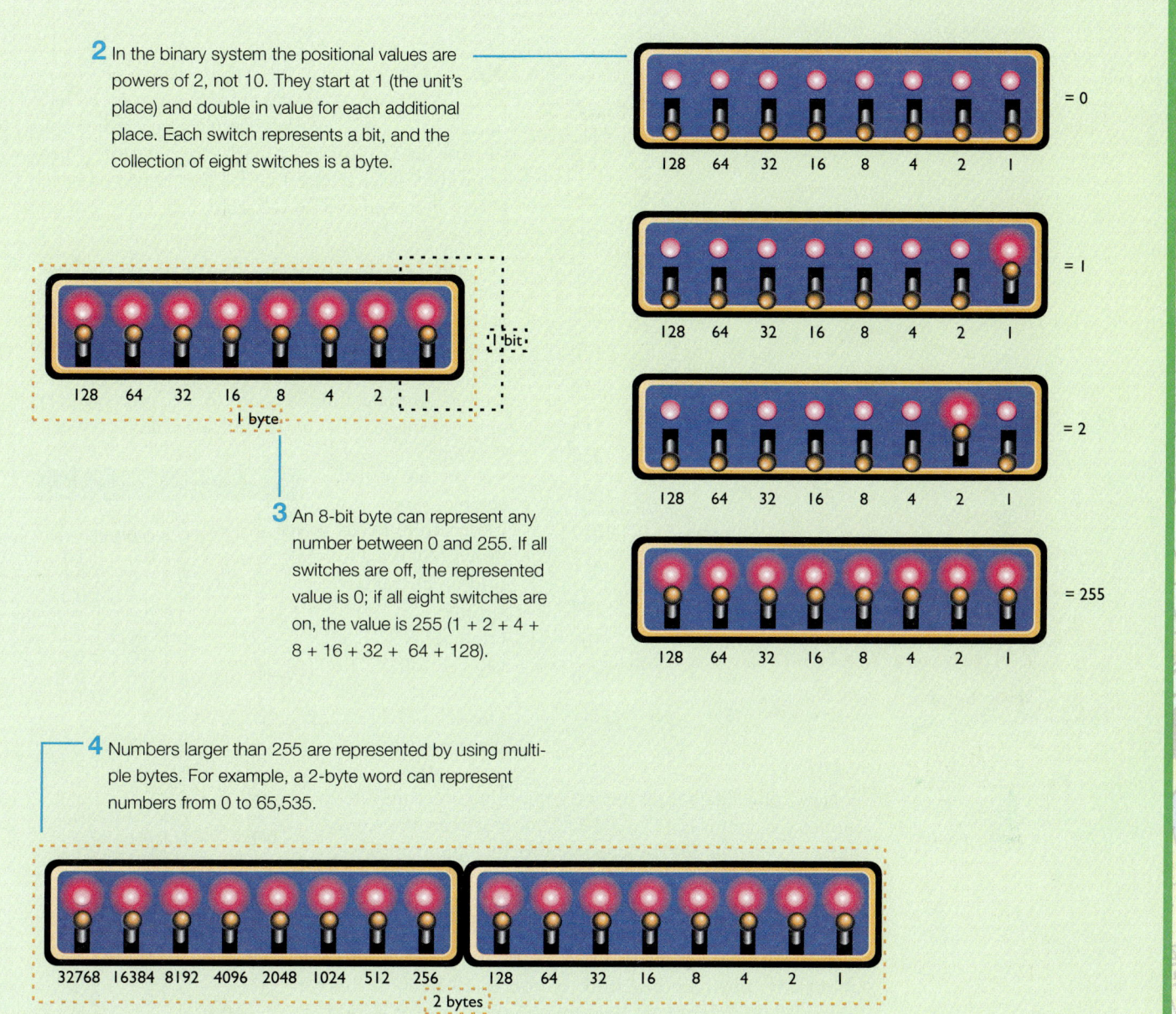

Building with Bits

> There's a **runaway market** for bits.
> —Russell Schweickart, astronaut

What does a bit combination like 01100110 mean to the computer? There's no single answer to that question; it depends on context and convention. A string of bits can be interpreted as a number, a letter of the alphabet, or almost anything else.

Bits as Numbers

Because computers are built from switching devices that reduce all information to 0s and 1s, they represent numbers using the *binary number system*—a system that denotes all numbers with combinations of two digits. Like the 10-digit decimal system you use every day, the binary system has clear, consistent rules for every arithmetic operation.

The people who worked with early computers had to use binary arithmetic. But today's computers include software that converts decimal numbers into binary numbers automatically, and vice versa. As a result, the computer's binary number processing is completely hidden from the user.

In the binary number system, every number is represented by a unique string of 0s and 1s.

Decimal representation	Binary representation
0	0
1	1
2	10
3	11
4	100
5	101
6	110
7	111
8	1000
9	1001
10	1010
11	1011
12	1100
13	1101
14	1110
15	1111

Bits as Codes

Today's computers work as much with text as with numbers. To make words, sentences, and paragraphs fit into the computer's binary-only circuitry, programmers have devised codes that represent each letter, digit, and special character as a unique string of bits.

The most widely used code, **ASCII** (an abbreviation of American Standard Code for Information Interchange, pronounced "as-kee"), represents each character as a unique 8-bit code. Out of a string of 8 bits, 256 unique ordered patterns can be made—enough to make unique codes for 26 letters (upper- and lowercase), 10 digits, and a variety of special characters.

As the world shrinks and our information needs grow, ASCII's 256 unique characters simply aren't enough. ASCII is too limited to accommodate Greek, Hebrew, Japanese, Chinese, and other languages. To facilitate multilingual computing, the computer industry is embracing **Unicode**, a coding scheme that supports 65,000 unique characters—more than enough for all major world languages.

Of course, today's computers work with more than characters. A group of bits can also represent colors, sounds, quantitative measurements from the environment, or just about any other kind of information that's likely to be processed by a computer. We explore other types of information in later chapters.

Bits as Instructions in Programs

So far we've dealt with the ways bits represent **data**—information from some outside source that's processed by the computer. But another kind of information is just as important to the computer: the programs that tell the computer what to do with the data you give it. The computer stores programs as collections of bits, just as it stores data.

Program instructions, like characters, are represented in binary notation through the use of codes. For example, the code 01101010 might tell the computer to add two numbers. Other groups of bits—instructions in the program—contain codes that tell the computer where to find those numbers and where to store the result. You learn more about how these computer instructions work in later chapters.

Character	ASCII binary code
A	01000001
B	01000010
C	01000011
D	01000100
E	01000101
F	01000110
G	01000111
H	01001000
I	01001001
J	01001010
K	01001011
L	01001100
M	01001101
N	01001110
O	01001111
P	01010000
Q	01010001
R	01010010
S	01010011
T	01010100
U	01010101
V	01010110
W	01010111
X	01011000
Y	01011001
Z	01011010
0	00110000
1	00110001
2	00110010
3	00110011
4	00110100
5	00110101
6	00110110
7	00110111
8	00111000
9	00111001

The capital letters and numeric digits are represented in the ASCII character set by 36 unique patterns of 8 bits. (The remaining 92 ASCII bit patterns represent lowercase letters, punctuation characters, and special characters.)

How It Works How It Works How It Works How It Works **How It Works**

2.2 Representing the World's Languages

The United States has long been at the center of the computer revolution; that's why the ASCII character set was originally designed to include only English-language characters. ASCII code numbers range from 0 to 127, but this isn't enough to handle all of the characters used in the languages of Western Europe, including accents and other diacritical marks.

The Latin I character set appends 128 additional codes onto the original ASCII 128 to accommodate additional characters.

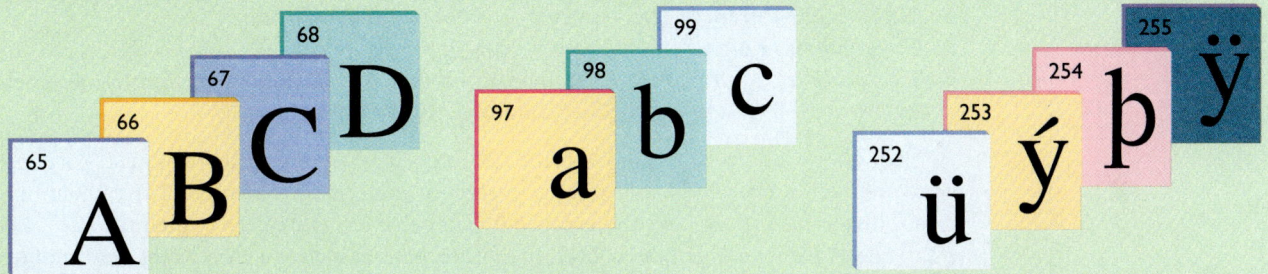

Both the ASCII and the Latin 1 character sets can use 8 bits—1 byte—to represent each character, but there's no room left for the characters used in languages such as Greek, Hebrew, Hindi, and Arabic, each of which has its own 50- to 150-character alphabet or syllabary. East Asian languages such as Chinese, Japanese, and Korean present bigger challenges for computer users. Chinese alone has nearly 50,000 distinct characters, of which about 13,000 are in current use.

A character set that uses two bytes, or 16 bits, per character allows for 256 x 256, or 65,536 distinct codes—more than enough for all modern languages. The emerging international standard double-byte character set called Unicode is designed to facilitate multilingual computing. In Unicode the first 256 codes (0 through 255) are identical to the codes of the Latin I character set. The remaining codes are distributed among the writing systems of the world's other languages.

Most major new software applications and operating systems are designed to be transported to different languages. Making a software application work in different languages involves much more than translating the words. For example, some languages write from right to left or top to bottom. Pronunciation, currency symbols, dialects, and other variations often make it necessary to produce customized software for different regions even when the same language is spoken.

Computer keyboards for East Asian languages don't have one key for each character. Using phonetic input, a user types a pronunciation for a character using a Western-style keyboard and then chooses the character needed from a menu of characters that appears on the screen. The software can make some menu choices automatically based on common language-usage patterns.

Bits, Bytes, and Buzzwords

> Even the most **sophisticated** computer is really only a large, well-organized **volume of bits**.
>
> —David Harel, in *Algorithmics: The Spirit of Computing*

Trying to learn about computers by examining their operation at the bit level is a little like trying to learn about how people look or act by studying individual human cells; there's plenty of information there, but it's not the most efficient way to find out what you need to know. Fortunately, people can use computers without thinking about bits. Some bit-related terminology does come up in day-to-day computer work, though. Most computer users need to have at least a basic understanding of the following terms for quantifying data:

- *Byte*: A grouping of 8 bits. If you work mostly with words, you can think of a byte as one character of ASCII-encoded text.
- *K (kilobyte or KB)*: About 1,000 bytes of information. For example, about 5K of storage is necessary to hold 5,000 characters of ASCII text. (Technically, 1K is 1,024 bytes because 1,024 is 2^{10}, which makes the arithmetic easier for binary-based computers. For those of us who don't think in binary, 1,000 is close enough.)
- *MB (megabyte or meg)*: Approximately 1,000K, or 1 million bytes.
- *GB (gigabyte or gig)*: Approximately 1,000MB.
- *TB (terabyte)*: Approximately 1 million megabytes. This astronomical unit of measurement applies to the largest storage devices commonly available today.

The abbreviations K, MB or meg, and GB or gig describe the capacity of memory and storage components. You would, for example, describe a computer as having 256MB of memory and a hard disk as having a 40GB storage capacity. The same terms are used to quantify sizes of computer files. A **file** is an organized collection of information, such as a term paper or a set of names and addresses, stored in a computer-readable form. For example, the text for this chapter is stored in a file that occupies about 70K of space on a disk.

To add to the confusion, people often measure data transfer speed or memory size in **megabits (Mb)** rather than megabytes (MB). A megabit, as you might expect, is approximately 1,000 bits—one-eighth the size of a megabyte. When you're talking in bits and bytes, a little detail like capitalization can make a significant difference.

The Computer's Core: The CPU and Memory

> The **microprocessor** that makes up your personal computer's *central processing unit*, or CPU, is the **ultimate computer brain**, **messenger**, **ringmaster**, and **boss**. All the other components—RAM, disk drives, the monitor—exist only to **bridge the gap** between you and the processor.
>
> —Ron White, in *How Computers Work*

It may seem strange to think of automated teller machines, video game consoles, and supercomputers as bit processors. But whatever it looks like to the user, a digital computer is at its core a collection of on/off switches designed to transform information from one form to another. The user provides the computer with patterns of bits—input—and the computer follows instructions to transform that input into a different pattern of bits—output—to return to the user.

The CPU: The Real Computer

The CPU, often called just the processor, performs the transformations of input into output. Every computer has at least one CPU to interpret and execute the instructions in each program, to do arithmetic and logical data manipulations, and to communicate with all the other parts of the computer system indirectly through memory.

A modern CPU is an extraordinarily complex collection of electronic circuits. When all of those circuits are built into a single silicon chip, as they are in most computers today, that chip is referred to as a *microprocessor*. In a desktop computer, the CPU is housed along with other chips and electronic components on a **circuit board**. The circuit board that contains a computer's CPU is called the *motherboard* or *system board*.

Many different kinds of CPUs are in use today; when you choose a computer, the type of CPU in the computer is an important part of the decision. Although there are many variations in design among these chips, only two factors are important to a casual computer user: compatibility and speed.

Compatibility

Not all software is **compatible** with every CPU; that is, software written for one processor may not work with another. Every processor has a built-in **instruction set**—a vocabulary of instructions the processor can execute. CPUs in the same family are generally designed so newer processors can process all of the instructions handled by earlier models. For example, Intel's Pentium 4 chip is **backward compatible** with the Pentium III, Pentium II, Pentium Pro, Pentium, 486, 386, and 286 chips that preceded it, so it can run most software written for those older CPUs. But software written for the PowerPC family of processors used in Macintosh computers won't run on the Intel processors found in most IBM-compatible computers; the Intel processors can't understand programs written for the PowerPC CPUs. Similarly, the Macintosh Power PC processor can't generally run Windows software. (In Chapter 4, "Software Basics: The Ghost in the Machine," you see how emulation software can partially overcome incompatibility problems by translating instructions written for one CPU into instructions that another can execute.)

The motherboard of a typical PC contains the CPU, memory, and several other important chips and components.

Speed

There's a tremendous variation in how fast different processors can handle information. Most computer applications, such as word processing, are more convenient to use on a faster machine. Many applications that use graphics or do computations, such as statistical programs, graphic design programs, and many computer games, require faster machines to produce satisfactory results.

A computer's speed is determined in part by the speed of its internal **clock**—the timing device that produces electrical pulses to synchronize the computer's operations. A computer's clock speed is measured in units called **megahertz (MHz)**, for millions of clock cycles per second. Ads for new computer systems often emphasize megahertz ratings as a measure of speed. But these numbers can be misleading; judging a computer's speed by its megahertz rating alone is like measuring a car's speed by the engine's RPM (revolutions per minute). A 700-MHz Celeron system isn't necessarily faster than a 600-MHz Pentium II or a 500-MHz PowerPC G4 chip; in fact, for some tasks, it's much slower.

Clock speed by itself doesn't adequately describe how fast a computer can process words, numbers, or pictures. Speed is also limited by the **architecture** of the processor—the design that determines how individual components of the CPU are put together on the chip. For example, newer chips can manipulate more bits simultaneously than older chips, which makes them more efficient, and therefore faster, at performing most operations. The number of bits a CPU can process at one time—typically 8, 16, 32, or 64—is sometimes

This inspector is adding a silicon wafer before it is sliced into many silicon chips.

The Intel Pentium 4 chip (left) contains intricate circuitry that looks like geometric colored patterns when magnified (right).

How It Works

2.3 The CPU

Most computer users don't know anything about what goes on inside the CPU; they just use it. Throughout most of this book we treat the CPU as a kind of black box that transforms information by following instructions. This **How It Works** box offers a peek inside that black box so you can get a feel for what makes your computer tick. Since the CPU functions as part of a larger collection of computer components, this **How It Works** box tells only part of the story; taken by itself, it may raise more questions than it answers. But **How It Works** boxes later in this chapter and in the next two chapters fill in many of the missing details of the inner workings of the modern computer. Read these boxes if you want the inside story.

The central processing unit (CPU) is the component that executes the steps in a program, performing math and moving data from one part of the system to another. The CPU contains the circuitry to perform a variety of simple tasks, called **instructions**. An individual instruction does only a tiny amount of work. A typical instruction might be "Read the contents of memory location x and add the number y to it." Most CPUs have a vocabulary of fewer than 1,000 distinct instructions.

All computer programs are composed of instructions drawn from this tiny vocabulary. The typical computer program is composed of millions of instructions, and the CPU can execute millions of instructions every second. When a program runs, the rapid-fire execution of instructions creates an illusion of motion in the same way a movie simulates motion out of a sequence of still pictures.

The typical CPU is divided into several functional units: control, arithmetic, decode, bus, and prefetch. These units work together like workers on an assembly line to complete the execution of program instructions.

Arithmetic Logic Unit

1 In most cases the actual execution of an instruction is performed by the **arithmetic logic unit (ALU)**. The ALU includes **registers**, each usually 32 or 64 bits in size.

Bus Unit

Prefetch Unit

2 Program instructions are stored in primary storage (memory), which is usually on chips outside the CPU. The CPU's first task is to read the instruction from memory. The bus unit handles all communication between the CPU and primary storage.

3 The **prefetch unit** instructs the bus unit to read the instruction stored at a particular memory address. This unit not only fetches the next instruction to execute, but it also fetches several subsequent instructions to ensure that an instruction is always ready to go.

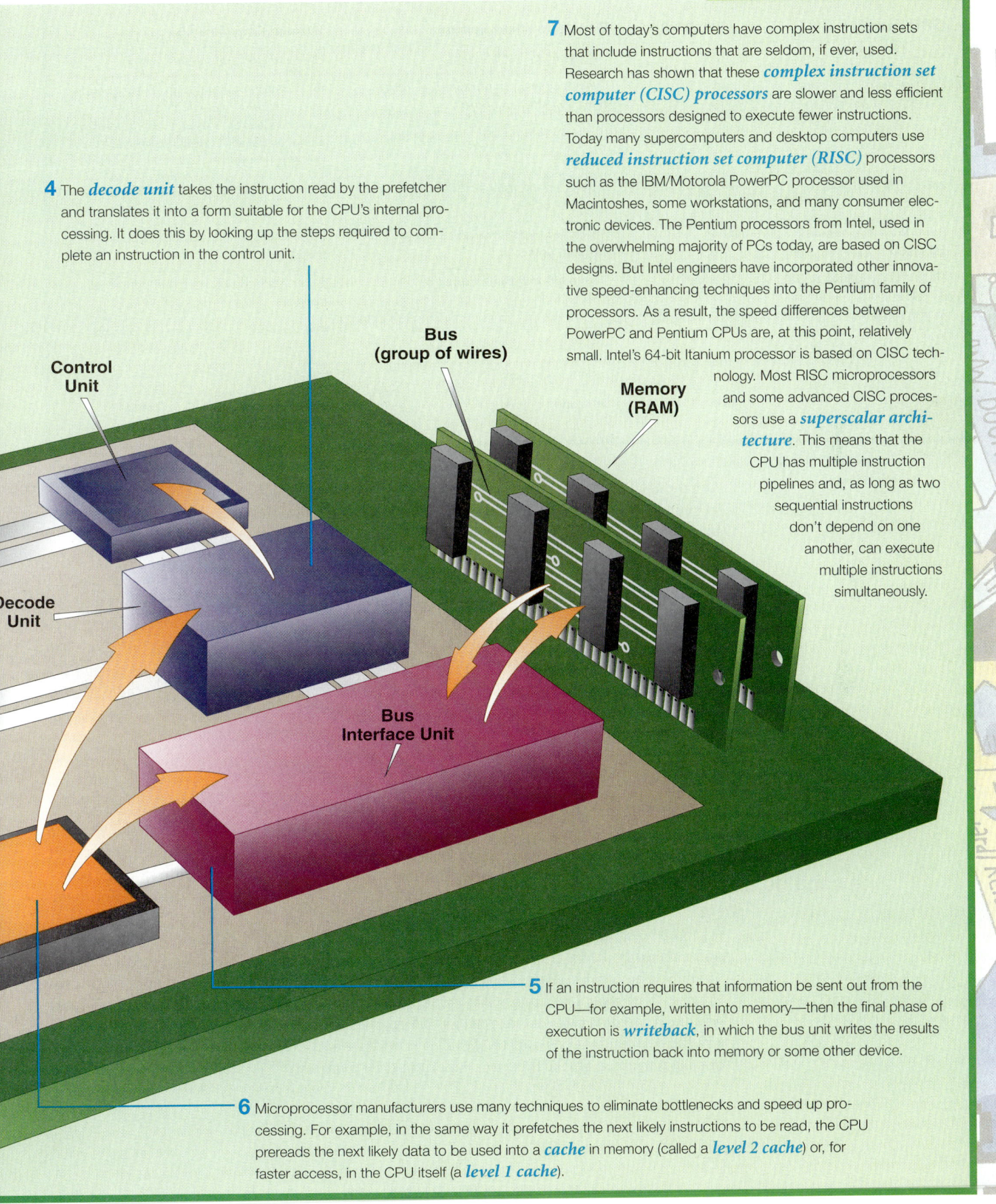

POPULAR CPU FAMILIES AND WHERE TO FIND THEM

CPU Family	Word Size	Developer/Manufacturer	Where They Are Used
Itanium Family	64 bit	Developed by Intel	High-end workstations and servers.
Pentium Family (including Celeron and Xeon)	32 bit	Developed and manufactured by Intel; clones by AMD and others.	IBM-compatible computers. (Pentium is used in mid- to high-end PCs and workstations; Celeron is used in less expensive computers; Xeon is used in high-end PCs and workstations.)
x86 Family (386, 486)	16 and 32 bit	Developed and manufactured by Intel; clones by others.	Older IBM-compatible computers.
PowerPC family, including G3 and G4	32 bit	Developed by IBM, manufactured by IBM and Motorola.	Macintoshes, network computers, special-purpose devices.
680x0 Family (68000, 68020, and others)	16 and 32 bit	Developed and manufactured by Motorola.	Older Macintoshes, computer-controlled devices.
MIPS	64 bit	Developed by Silicon Graphics, manufactured by many companies.	Workstations, servers, network computers, video game machines, other devices.
SPARC	64 bit	Developed by Sun.	Workstations.
ARM	32 bit	Developed by Intel.	Handheld computers, PDAs, special-purpose devices.

called the CPU's *word size*. More often, though, people use the number without a label, as in "The Itanium is Intel's first 64-bit processor." High-end workstations and servers today use 64-bit processors. Most PCs and Macintoshes use 32-bit processors. Some embedded and special-purpose computers still use 8- and 16 bit processors.

Because speed is so important, engineers and computer scientists are constantly developing techniques for speeding up a computer's ability to manipulate and move bits. One common techique for improving a computer's performance is to put more than one processor in the computer. Many personal computers, for example, have specialized subsidiary processors that take care of mathematical calculations or graphics displays. Most supercomputers have multiple processors that can divide jobs into pieces and work in parallel on the pieces. This kind of processing, known as **parallel processing** or **multiprocessing**, is becoming more commonplace throughout the computing world.

The Computer's Memory

"**What's one** and one and one and one and one and one and one and one and one and one?"

"**I don't know**," said Alice. "I lost count."

"**She can't do addition**," said the Red Queen.
—Lewis Carroll, in *Through the Looking Glass*

The CPU's main job is to follow the instructions encoded in programs. But like Alice in *Through the Looking Glass*, the CPU can handle only one instruction and a few pieces of data at a time. The computer needs a place to store the rest of the program and data until the processor is ready for them. That's what RAM is for.

RAM (*random access memory*) is the most common type of primary storage, or computer memory. RAM chips contain circuits that store program instructions and data temporarily. The computer divides each RAM chip into many equal-sized memory locations. Memory locations, like houses, have unique addresses so the computer can tell them apart when it is instructed to save or retrieve information. You can store a piece of information in any RAM location—you can pick one at random—and the computer can, if so instructed, quickly retrieve it. Hence the name random access memory.

The information stored in RAM is nothing more than a pattern of electrical current flowing through microscopic circuits in silicon chips. This means that when the power goes off the computer instantly forgets everything it was remembering in RAM. RAM is called **volatile memory** because information stored there is not held permanently.

This could be a serious problem if the computer didn't have another type of memory to store information that you don't want to lose. This **nonvolatile memory** is called **ROM (read-only memory)** because the computer can only read information from it; it can never write any new information on it. All modern computers include ROM that contains start-up instructions and other critical information. The information in ROM was etched in when the chip was manufactured, so it is available whenever the computer is operating, but it can't be changed except by replacing the ROM chip.

Other types of memory are available; most are seldom used outside of engineering laboratories. There are two notable exceptions:

- ▸ *CMOS* (complementary metal oxide semiconductor) is a special low-energy kind of RAM that can store small amounts of data for long periods of time on battery power. CMOS RAM stores the date, time, and calendar in a PC. (CMOS RAM is called *parameter RAM* in Macintoshes.)
- ▸ *Flash memory* chips, like RAM chips, can be written and erased rapidly and repeatedly. But unlike RAM, flash memory is nonvolatile; it can keep its contents without a flow of electricity. Cell phones, pagers, portable computers, handheld PDAs, and other digital devices use flash memory to store data that needs to be changed from time to time. Data flight recorders also use it. Flash memory is still too expensive to replace RAM and other common storage media, but it may in the future replace disk drives as well as memory chips.

It takes time for the processor to retrieve data from memory—but not very much time. The *access time* for most memory is measured in *nanoseconds*—billionths of a second. Compare this to hard disk access time, which is measured in *milliseconds*—thousandths of a second. Memory speed (access time) is another factor that affects the computer's overall speed.

Buses, Ports, and Peripherals

In a desktop computer, the CPU and memory chips are attached to circuit boards along with other key components. Information travels between components through groups of wires called **buses**. Buses typically have 8, 16, or 32 wires, or data paths; a bus with 16 wires is called a **16-bit bus** because it can transmit 16 bits of information at a time, twice as many as an 8-bit bus. Just as multilane freeways allow masses of automobiles to move faster than they could on single-lane roads, wider buses can transmit information faster than narrower buses. Newer, more powerful computers have wider buses so they can process information faster.

Buses connect to storage devices in **bays**—open areas in the system box for disk drives and other peripheral devices. Buses also connect to **expansion slots** (sometimes called just *slots*) inside the computer's housing. Users can customize their computers by inserting special-purpose circuit boards (called *cards*, or *expansion cards*) into these slots. Buses also connect to external **ports**—sockets on the outside of the computer chassis. The back of a computer typically has a variety of ports to meet a variety of needs. Some of these ports—the keyboard and mouse ports, for example—are connected directly to the system board. Others, such as the monitor port, are generally attached to an expansion card. In fact, many expansion cards do little more than provide convenient ports for attaching particular types of peripherals. Macintosh computers generally have

Slots and ports enable the CPU to communicate with the outside world via peripheral devices. Here a circuit board is being inserted into a slot. The panel holding the slot has been temporarily removed from the computer for easier viewing. The gray flat wire is a bus.

A portable computer typically has one or more slots to accommodate credit-card-sized PC cards like this one.

How It Works

2.4 Memory

Memory is the work area of the CPU. Think of memory as millions of tiny storage cells, each of which can contain a single byte of information. A typical personal computer has from 64 to 256 megabytes (million bytes) of memory. The information in memory includes program instructions, numbers for arithmetic, codes representing text characters, digital codes representing pictures, and other kinds of data.

Memory chips are usually grouped on small circuit boards called **SIMMs** (single in-line memory modules) and **DIMMs** (dual in-line memory modules) and are plugged into the motherboard.

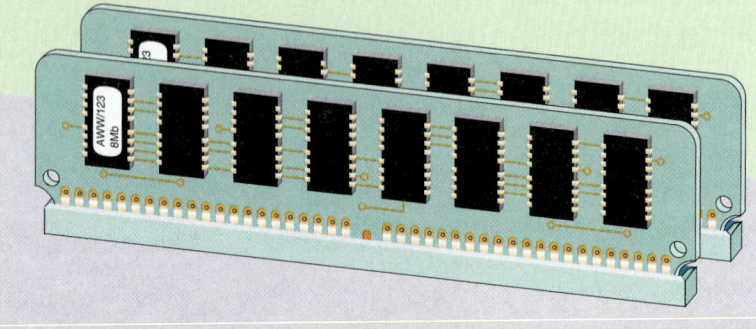

Two SIMMs plugged into a circuit board.

Like mailboxes in a row, bytes of memory have unique addresses that identify them and help the CPU keep track of where things are stored.

fewer expansion boards than their PC counterparts, because their system boards include more components as standard equipment.

In portable computers, where size is critical, most common ports go directly to the system board. Because portable computers don't have room for full-sized cards, many have slots for **PC cards**—credit-card-sized cards that contain memory, miniature peripherals, and additional ports. (When these cards were first released, they were known as *PCMCIA cards*. One writer suggested that this stood for "People Can't Memorize Computer Industry Acronyms." Thankfully, the name was shortened to PC cards.)

t Works How It Works How It Works How It Works How It Works How It Works

The CPU can only see into and access memory. Memory addresses make up the CPU's entire world, so any program that needs to be executed or data that needs to be modified must make its way into memory.

Most computer systems use ***memory-mapped I/O****, where information for input and output is stored in special areas of memory. For example, information to be displayed on the monitor screen is written into a special range of memory addresses that is continually scanned by the video subsystem.*

1 When you turn on the computer, the CPU automatically begins executing instructions stored in read-only memory (ROM). On most computer systems, ROM also contains parts of the operating system. The firmware programs in ROM are sometimes called the ***BIOS*** (basic input/output system).

2 The executing instructions help the system start up and tell it how to load the operating system—copy it from disk into memory.

3 Once executing instructions are loaded into memory, the CPU is able to execute them.

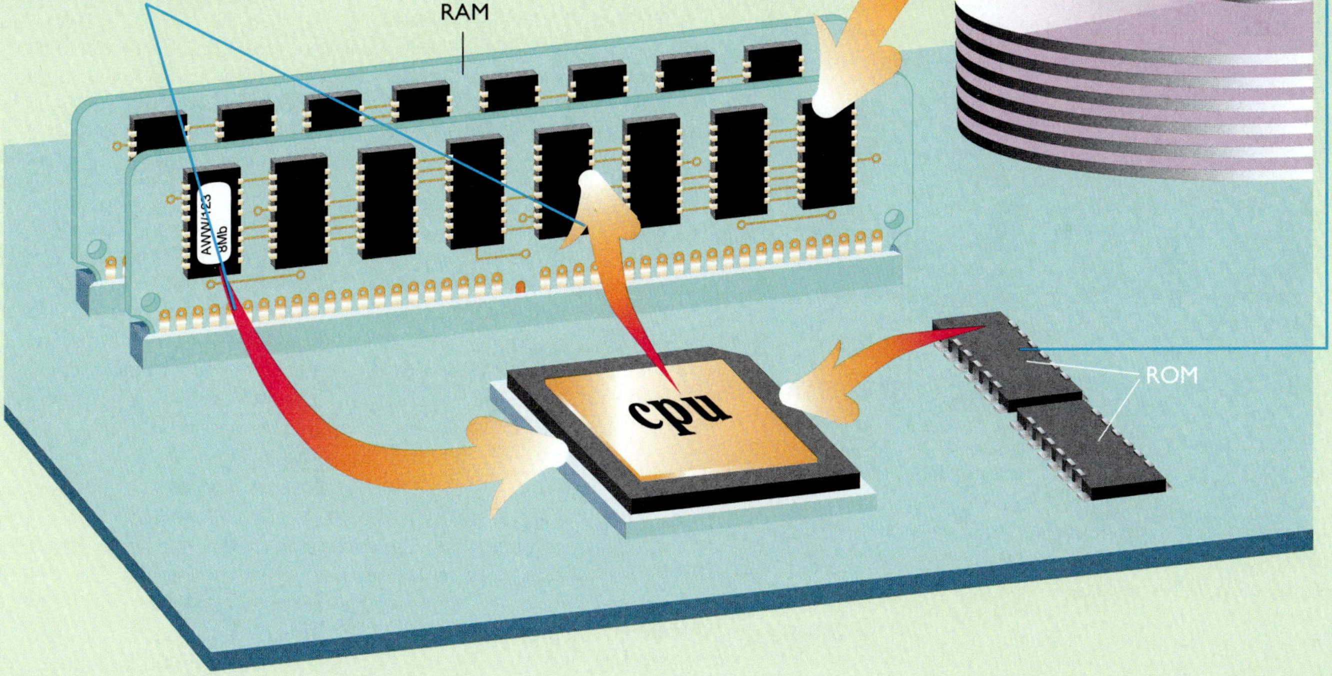

HARD DISK
RAM
AWW123
8Mb
cpu
ROM

Slots and ports make it easy to add external devices, or ***peripherals***, to the computer system so the CPU can communicate with the outside world and store information for later use. Without peripherals, CPU and memory together are like a brain without a body. Some peripherals such as keyboards and printers serve as communication links between people and computers. Other peripherals link the computer to other machines. Still others provide long-term storage media. In the next chapter, we explore a variety of input, output, and storage peripherals, and then revisit the slots and ports that connect those peripherals to the CPU and memory.

CrossCurrents

Bit Literacy

Mark Hurst

In Information Anxiety 2, Richard Saul Wurman explores a problem faced by many of us: too much information. In this edited article from that book, Consultant Mark Hurst of Creative Good discusses the problem and a solution: bit literacy.

Information anxiety is more important today than ever, thanks to the arrival of the bit. The tiniest one- or zero-pulse of digital data, the bit will affect our lives as much as the atom. Ten years ago, Americans may have felt some anxiety over the magazines and newspapers piling up at home, but today the anxiety is increasing as bits appear in all areas of our lives. Email, Web sites, e-newsletters, chat rooms, email, instant messages, and more email—all of these streams of bits can interrupt us, and keep us engaged, anywhere and anytime. Devices made to hold these bits are springing up, too: PDAs and cell phones bring us the bits when we're away from our PC.

For those who own a PC or a PDA, there is little escape from the bits. Even when we turn off the device, the bits pile up quietly, ready to flood us with anxiety when we return to the device. If anything, an escape from the bits can be dangerous. Take a week-long vacation without email, and upon return, a bloated inbox welcomes us back to work with seven times more bits.

And this is still *early* in the current explosion of digital information. One research study recently predicted that, within a few years, the number of emails we receive every day will increase to *forty* times its current volume. That's a lot of bits demanding our attention—just from email. It's likely that still other devices and other bitstreams will threaten the typical American with exponentially more information anxiety.

The problem of near-infinite bits, however, does have a solution. The solution is what I call "bit literacy." Bit literacy is an awareness of bits: what bits are, how they affect our lives, and how we can survive in a society permeated by bits. With that awareness, bit literate people are able to *control* the bits, and not be *controlled by* the bits, that are becoming central to our lives and jobs.

All of bit literacy can be distilled into a simple philosophy that allows people to regain their life, free from information anxiety, while still living in the bits. Here is the four-word philosophy:

Let the bits go.

That's right, let the bits go. Don't acquire them. Don't try to acquire them, and don't worry about acquiring them, since the bits will come to you. The bits touch our lives at so many points that it's impossible to escape them, and it's insane to try to acquire *all* of them. Instead, being bit literate means constantly working on *letting go* of as many of the bits as we can. Bit literacy allows us to clear a path of emptiness through the jungle of bits that surround and distract us; the emptiness allows us to see.

Here's a real-life example. Recently I visited a Web site where visitors can sign up to receive email newsletters, published by respected companies, on any number of topics. Internet news, sports commentary, entertainment gossip—all of these were available to me at the click of a button. I could get *all* of this information, delivered to my email inbox weekly . . . for free! And unlike subscriptions to paper magazines, these bits wouldn't clutter my apartment or need recycling. (I didn't sign up; I was there to unsubscribe from a newsletter.) So, one might reasonably ask, what's the problem with getting some potentially valuable or entertaining bits, if they don't clutter my living space, don't weigh me down, and don't cost a penny?

The problem is that the bits are different from paper-based information. Bits are more engaging, more immediate, more personal, and more abundant than other types of information. In the middle of lunch with a friend, we're interrupted by bits—perhaps a stock quote—and we instinctively reach for our PDAs to see what it is. Or we sit down to "read through some email" and blow through two hours like it was twenty minutes. Like the magazines and other anxiety-producing information, the bits call for our attention—but the bits call more loudly, more sweetly, more frequently, and in more areas of our lives.

These radically different qualities of bits mean that we must engage bits in a radically different way. Bit literacy is radical about letting the bits go. We can't let all the bits go—we must engage them first, and inevitably save the few most important bits—but our *default* behavior must be to let the bits go, rather than acquire and save them.

Here are some ways you can let the bits go: Keep your email inbox empty, by deleting your emails after saving the few that you *must* retain for later reference. Restrict the interruptions you allow on your cell phone and PDA, so that the interruptions that do come through are the important ones. And certainly don't open up any new bitstream—a newsletter, a ticker, or any other ongoing feed—unless it's vitally important. Instead, concentrate on letting go of the bits that find their way to you; the few remaining bits will be all the more valuable to you as a result.

I'd like to emphasize that last sentence: When a person becomes bit literate, what remains after all the letting go is *valuable*. I equate that with *meaningful*. Because—and here's the kicker—the bits by themselves aren't meaningful. Bits are just pointers to meaning, just containers of thoughts, just phantom images of the real item. The meaning is what lies behind the bits, what *drives* the bits. In their super-abundant quantities, swarming and overwhelming our consciousness, bits obscure the very meaning that created them. It's only after clearing out a path of emptiness that we can arrive at the meaning *behind* the bits.

DISCUSSION QUESTIONS:

1. Do you think information anxiety is a serious problem for many people? Explain your answer.
2. Do you think "bit literacy," as described by the author, makes sense? Explain your answer.

Summary

Whether it's working with words, numbers, pictures, or sounds, a computer is manipulating patterns of bits—binary digits of information that it can store in switching circuitry and that are represented by two symbols. Groups of bits can be treated as numbers for calculations using the binary number system. Bits can be grouped into coded messages that represent alphabetic characters, pictures, colors, sounds, or just about any other kind of information. Even the instructions computers follow—the software programs that tell the computer what to do—must be reduced to strings of bits before the computer accepts them. Byte, kilobyte, megabyte, and other common units for measuring bit quantities are used in descriptions of memory, storage, and file size.

The central processing unit (CPU) follows software instructions to perform the calculations and logical manipulations that transform input data into output. Not all CPUs are compatible with each other; each is capable of processing a particular set of instructions, so a program written for one family of processors can't be understood by a processor from another family. Engineers are constantly improving the clock speed and architecture of CPUs, making computers capable of processing information faster.

The CPU uses RAM (random access memory) as a temporary storage area—a scratch pad—for instructions and data. Another type of memory, ROM (read-only memory), contains unchangeable information that serves as reference material for the CPU as it executes program instructions.

The CPU and main memory are housed in silicon chips on one or more circuit boards inside the computer. Buses connect to slots and ports that enable the computer to communicate with peripherals.

Chapter Review

▼ Key Terms

architecture (p. 57)
ASCII (p. 54)
backward compatible (p. 57)
bay (p. 61)
binary (p. 51)
bit (p. 51)
bus (p. 59)
byte (p. 52)
central processing unit (CPU) (p. 50)
circuit board (p. 56)
compatible (p. 57)
digital (p. 51)

expansion slot (p. 61)
file (p. 56)
GB (gigabyte) (p. 56)
information (p. 51)
input device (p. 50)
K (kilobyte) (p. 56)
MB (megabyte) (p. 56)
memory (p. 50)
motherboard (p. 56)
multiprocessing (p. 60)
nonvolatile memory (p. 61)
output device (p. 50)

parallel processing (p. 60)
PC card (p. 62)
peripheral (p. 51)
port (p. 61)
processor (p. 50)
RAM (random access memory) (p. 60)
ROM (read-only memory) (p. 61)
storage device (p. 50)
TB (terabyte) (p. 56)
Unicode (p. 54)
volatile memory (p. 61)

▼ Interactive Quiz Questions

1. The *Computer Confluence* CD-ROM contains self-test quiz questions related to this chapter, including multiple choice, true or false, and matching questions.
2. The *Computer Confluence* Web site, **www.prenhall.com/beekman**, contains self-test exercises related to this chapter. Follow the instructions for taking a quiz. After you've completed your quiz, you can email the results to your instructor.

The Web site also contains open-ended discussion questions called Internet Explorations. Discuss one or more of the Internet Exploration questions at the section for this chapter.

Review Questions

1. Provide a working definition of each of the key words listed in the "Key Terms" section. Check your answers in the glossary.
2. Draw a block diagram showing the major components of a computer and their relationship. Briefly describe the function of each component.
3. Think of this as computer input: 123.4. The computer might read this as a number or as a set of ASCII codes. Explain how these concepts differ.
4. Why is information stored in some kind of binary format in computers?
5. Why can't you normally run Macintosh software on a PC with an Intel Pentium II CPU?
6. Clock speed is only one factor in determining a CPU's processing speed. What is another?
7. How does a RISC processor differ from a CISC processor?
8. Explain how parallel processing can increase a computer's speed; use an example or a comparison with the way people work if you like.
9. What is the difference between RAM and ROM? What is the purpose of each?
10. What is the difference between primary and secondary storage?

Discussion Questions

1. Why are computer manufacturers constantly releasing faster computers? How do computer users benefit from the increased speed?
2. How is human memory similar to computer memory? How is it different?

Projects

1. Collect computer advertisements from newspapers, magazines, and other sources. Compare how the ads handle discussions of speed. Evaluate the usefulness of the information in the ads from a consumer's point of view.
2. Interview a salesperson in a computer store. Find out what kinds of questions people ask when buying a computer. Develop profiles for the most common types of computer buyers. What kinds of computers do these customers buy, and why?

Sources and Resources

Books

Building IBM: Shaping an Industry and Its Technology, by Emerson W. Pugh (Cambridge, MA: MIT Press, 1995). This book traces IBM's history from Herman Hollerith's invention of the punch card machine more than a century ago. This thoroughly researched and clearly written book is a valuable resource for anyone interested in understanding IBM's history.

ThinkPad: A Different Shade of Blue, by Deboarh Dell and J. Gerry Purdy (Indianapolis: Sams, 2000). This is an insider's look at the making of IBM's wildly successful portable. Thomas Watson's philosophy inspired this product—a product that helped revive the company Watson founded.

Information Anxiety 2, by Richard Saul Wurman (Indianapolis: Que, 2001). This is a revised and updated version of Wurman's popular 1989 book. The style and organization are sometimes quirky, but the content is useful and thought-provoking. Wurman discusses the nature and value of information, and offers advice about how to cope with the explosion of non-information—"stuff that doesn't inform."

How Computers Work, Sixth Edition, by Ron White (Indianapolis: Que, 2001). The first edition of *How Computers Work* launched a series and inspired many imitators. Like its predecessor, this revised and expanded edition clearly illustrates with beautiful pictures and accessible prose how each component of a modern personal computer system works. If you're interested in looking under the hood, this is a great place to start. The book was produced on a Macintosh, but the explanations and illustrations are based on Wintel (Windows/Intel) computers. Still, most of the concepts apply to computers in general. A Windows-only CD-ROM includes a multimedia tour of a computer.

How the Mac Works: Millennium Edition, by John Rizzo and K. Daniel Clark (Indianapolis: Que, 2000). This book covers the basics of Macintosh anatomy in the same style as *How Computers Work*.

The Soul of a New Machine, by Tracy Kidder (Back Bay Books, 2000). This Pulitzer Prize winning book provides a journalist's inside look at the making of a new computer in the late

1970s, including lots of insights into what makes computers (and computer people) tick. It's still a good read more than two decades later.

The Essential Guide to Computing: The Story of Information Technology, by E. Garrison Walters (Upper Saddle River, NJ: Prentice Hall, 2001). This is a highly readable and surprisingly broad overview of computer technology, with coverage of hardware, software, and networks. The book provides historical and industry perspectives along with solid technical information that goes beyond the usual introductory books.

Personal Computers for Technology Students, by Charles Raymond (Upper Saddle River, NJ: Prentice Hall, 2001). This is a technical but readable text on the PC, from CPU to peripherals. It includes a useful glossary of acronyms, in case you need to know what SRAM or SVGA stands for.

Computer Sourcebook, by Alfred and Emily Glossbrenner (New York: Random House, 1997). This massive book is an eclectic collection of facts, figures, lists, and anecdotes related to PCs. Reading this book may give you the feeling that these two prolific authors are allowing you to rummage through their file cabinets. Want to learn how to get free computer magazine subscriptions? How to get help when something goes wrong with your PC? How to choose a backup system? You're almost certain to find plenty of useful information here, along with quite a bit that's of little value.

Peter Norton's Inside the PC, Eighth Edition, by Peter Norton and John Goodman (Indianapolis: Sams, 1999). Norton's name is almost a household word among PC enthusiasts, many of whom consider Norton Utilities to be indispensable software. This book offers clear, detailed explanations of the inner workings of the PC, from CPU to peripherals, from hardware to software. You don't need to be a technical wizard to understand and learn from this book.

World Wide Web Pages

Most computer hardware manufacturers have World Wide Web pages on the Internet. Use a Web browser such as Netscape Navigator or Microsoft Internet Explorer to visit some of these sites for information about the latest hardware from these companies. It's not hard to guess the Web addresses of computer companies; most follow the pattern suggested by these examples:

www.ibm.com

www.apple.com

www.dell.com

The *Computer Confluence* Web site, www.prenhall.com/beekman, will guide you to these and other hardware pages of interest.

3 Hardware Basics: Peripherals

After you read this chapter you should be able to:

▼

List several examples of input devices and explain how they can make it easier to get different types of information into the computer

List several examples of output devices and explain how they make computers more useful

Explain why a typical computer has different types of storage devices

Diagram how the components of a computer system fit together

▲

▼ In this chapter:

Why the letters on a keyboard are all mixed up

Pointing, painting, typing, and talking to your computer

Why onscreen pictures look different when you print them

Sound in, sound out

How a PC can hurt your health, and how to protect yourself

Self-study questions and projects

Mini-reviews of helpful resources for further study

… and more.

▼ On the CD-ROM:

Interactive activities on how input devices work

Instant access to glossary and key word references

Interactive self-study quizzes

…and more.

▼ On the Web:

www.prenhall.com/beekman

Documents describing and illustrating a variety of state-of-the-art peripherals

Links to the most important computer peripheral companies

Self-study exercises

… and more.

Steve Wozniak, Steve Jobs, and the Garage that Grew Apples

It's **not** like we were all smart enough to see a **revolution coming**.
Back then, I thought there might be a revolution in **opening** your garage door,
balancing your checkbook, **keeping** your recipes, that sort of thing.
There are **a million people** who study markets and analyze economic trends,
people who are **more brilliant than I am**, people who worked for
companies like Digital Equipment and IBM and Hewlett-Packard.
None of them foresaw what was going to happen, either.

—Steve Wozniak

What Steve Wozniak ("the Woz") and all those other people failed to foresee was the personal computer revolution—a revolution that he helped start. Wozniak, a brilliant engineer with an eye for detail, worked days as a calculator technician at Hewlett-Packard; he was refused an engineer's job because he lacked a college degree. At night he designed and constructed a scaled-down computer system that would fit the home hobbyist's budget. When he completed it in 1975, he offered it to HP; they turned it down.

Steve Wozniak and Steve Jobs.

Wozniak took his invention to the Homebrew Computer Club in Palo Alto, where it caught the imagination of another college dropout, Steven Jobs. A free-thinking visionary, Jobs persuaded Wozniak to quit his job in 1976 to form a company and market the machine, which they named the Apple I. Jobs raised $1,300 in seed capital by selling his Volkswagen, and Apple Computer, Inc., was born in Jobs's garage.

With the help and financial backing of businessman A.C. Markkula, the two Steves turned Apple into a thriving business. Wozniak created the Apple II, a more refined machine, and invented the first personal computer disk operating system so computers wouldn't be dependent on cassette tapes for storage. Jobs assumed the leadership role in the company. Because it put computing power within everyone's reach, the Apple II became popular in businesses, homes, and especially schools. Apple became the first company in American history to join the Fortune 500 in less than five years. Still in his mid-twenties, Jobs was running a corporate giant. But troubled times were ahead for Apple.

When IBM introduced its PC in 1982, it overshadowed Apple's presence in the business world, where people were accustomed to working with IBM mainframes. Other companies developed PC clones, treating the IBM PC as a standard—a standard that Apple refused to accept. Inspired by a visit to Xerox's Palo Alto Research Center (PARC), Jobs worked with a team of Apple engineers to develop the Macintosh, a futuristic computer he hoped would leapfrog IBM's advantage. When Jobs insisted on focusing most of Apple's resources on the Macintosh, Wozniak resigned to pursue other interests.

Businesses failed to embrace the Mac, and Apple stockholders grew uneasy with Jobs's controversial management style. In 1985, a year and a half after the Macintosh was introduced, Jobs was ousted. He went on to form NeXT, a company that produced workstations and software. He later bought Pixar, the computer animation company that captured the public's attention with *Toy Story*, the first computer-generated full-length motion picture.

After Apple's fortunes declined under a string of CEOs, the company bought NeXT in 1997 and invited an older and wiser Jobs to retake the helm. He agreed to share his time between Pixar and Apple. Under his leadership, Apple has regained its innovative edge, releasing a flurry of successful products that combine high technology with high style. Apple's rising market share is small in a business world dominated by IBM-compatible PCs running Microsoft Windows. Still, Apple retains an almost fanatically loyal customer base focused mainly in homes and creative markets, such as publishing, graphic design, multimedia, and education. While Jobs continues to lead Apple and Pixar, Woz is content to teach computing skills to kids in his community.

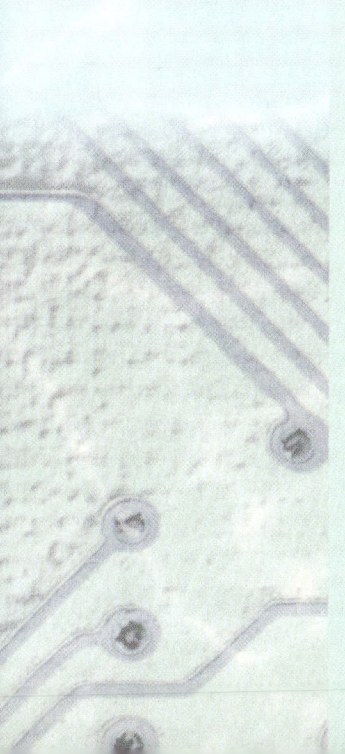

The Apple II's phenomenal success wasn't due to a powerful processor or massive memory; the machine had at its core a relatively primitive processor and only 16K of memory. The Apple II was more than a processor and memory; it included a keyboard, a monitor, and disk and tape drives for storage. While other companies sold computer kits to tinkerers, the two Steves delivered complete computer systems to hobbyists, schools, and businesses. They recognized that a computer wasn't complete without peripherals.

In this chapter we'll complete the tour of hardware we started in the last chapter. We've seen the CPU and memory at the heart of the system unit; now we'll explore the peripherals that radiate out from those central components. We'll start with input devices, then move on to output devices, and finish with a look at external storage devices. As usual, the main text provides the basic overview; if you want or need to know more about the inner workings, consult the *How It Works* boxes scattered throughout the chapter.

Input: From Person to Processor

> A computer terminal is **not** some **clunky old** television with a typewriter in front of it. It is an **interface** where the **mind** and **body** can **connect** with the **universe** and **move bits** of it about.
> —Douglas Adams, author of *The Hitchhiker's Guide to the Galaxy*

The nuts and bolts of information processing are usually hidden from the user, who sees only the input and output, or as the pros say, *I/O*. This wasn't always the case. Users of the first computers communicated one bit at a time by flipping switches on massive consoles or plugging wires into switchboards; they had to be intimately familiar with the inner workings of the machines before they could successfully communicate with them. In contrast, today's users have a choice of hundreds of input devices, which make it easy to enter data and commands into their machines. Of these input devices, the most familiar is the computer **keyboard**.

The Keyboard

A standard computer keyboard has straight rows of keys.

An ergonomic keyboard puts the keys at an angle to allow your wrists to assume a more natural position while you type.

In spite of nearly universal acceptance as an input device, the QWERTY keyboard (named for the first row of letter keys) seems strangely out of place in a modern computer system. The original arrangement of the keys, chosen to reduce the likelihood of jammed keys on early typewriters, stays with us a century later, forcing millions of people to learn an awkward system just so they can enter text into their computers. Alternatives to the QWERTY key arrangements have been shown to be easier to learn and use. For example, on the Dvorak keyboard the most frequently typed letters are located closest to the fingers' resting positions. But technological traditions die hard, and the QWERTY keyboard is still standard equipment on virtually all PCs.

Some modern computer keyboards stray from the traditional typewriter design in other ways. Typing on a standard keyboard, with keys lined up in straight rows, forces you to hold your arms and wrists at unnatural angles. Evidence suggests that long hours of typing this way may lead to medical problems, including **repetitive-stress injuries** such as tendonitus and carpal tunnel syndrome. **Ergonomic keyboards** place the keys at angles that are easier on your arms and hands without changing the ordering of the keys.

Whether it's straight or ergonomic, a typical keyboard sends signals to the computer through a coiled cable. A **wireless keyboard** can send infrared signals (similar to those of a TV remote control) so it isn't tethered to the rest of the system by a cable.

Other variations on keyboard design include folding keyboards for use with palm-sized computers, miniature keyboards built into pocket-sized devices, one-handed keyboards for people who need to (or prefer to) keep one hand free for other work, and keyboards printed on membranes that can be rolled or folded like paper. Innovative ideas are still emerging from that ancient typewriter technology.

This portable keyboard, designed for use with a Handspring Visor PDA, folds so it can easily fit in your pocket.

This half keyboard enables the user to type with one hand so the other hand is free for other tasks, including pointing.

Some pocket computers have QWERTY keyboards even though they're too small for touch typing.

This fabric keyboard can be folded, crumpled, or even washed like a piece of clothing.

Pointing Devices

Computer users today use their keyboards mostly to enter text and numeric data. For other traditional keyboard functions such as sending commands and positioning the cursor, they typically use a **mouse**. The mouse is designed to move a pointer around the screen and point to specific characters or objects. The most common type of mouse has a ball on its underside that allows it to roll around on the desktop. Another type of mouse uses reflected light to detect movement. The mouse has one or more buttons that can be used to send signals to the computer, conveying messages such as "Perform this command," "Activate the selected tool," and "Select all the text between these two points." Many modern PC mice include a scrolling wheel between the two standard buttons.

It's virtually impossible to find a new computer today that doesn't come with a mouse as standard equipment, but there is one exception: The mouse is impractical as a pointing device on portable computers because these machines are often used where there's no room for a mouse to roam across a desktop. Portable computer manufacturers provide a variety of alternatives to the mouse as a general-purpose pointing device:

The most common type of computer mouse has two buttons. The Microsoft Mouse has multiple buttons and a scroll wheel to streamline the process of scrolling through text or graphical windows; other mice have a similar design. The Apple Mouse has no buttons, but the entire surface of the mouse serves as a button.

- The **touchpad** (sometimes called *trackpad*) is a small flat panel that's sensitive to light pressure. The user moves the pointer by dragging a finger across the pad.
- The **pointing stick** (often called TrackPoint, IBM's brand name for the device) is a tiny handle that sits in the center of the keyboard, responding to finger pressure by moving the pointer in the direction in which it's pushed. It's like a miniature embedded joystick.
- The **trackball** is like an upside-down mouse. It remains stationary while the user moves the protruding ball to control the pointer on the screen. (Trackballs are also available as space-saving mouse alternatives for desktop machines.)

Other pointing devices offer advantages for specific types of computer work (and play). Here are some examples:

- The **joystick** is a gearshift-like device that's a favorite controller for arcade-style computer games.
- The **graphics tablet** is popular with artists and designers. Most touch tablets are pressure sensitive, so they can send different signals depending on how hard the user presses on the tablet with a stylus. The stylus performs the same point-and-click functions as a mouse.
- The **touch screen** responds when the user points to or touches different screen regions. Computers with touch screens are frequently used in public libraries, airports, and shopping malls where many users are unfamiliar with computers. Touch screens are also used in many handheld computers and PDAs; a *stylus* can be used for pointing or writing on these tiny screens.

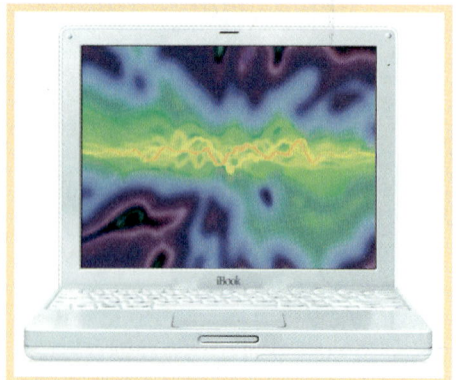

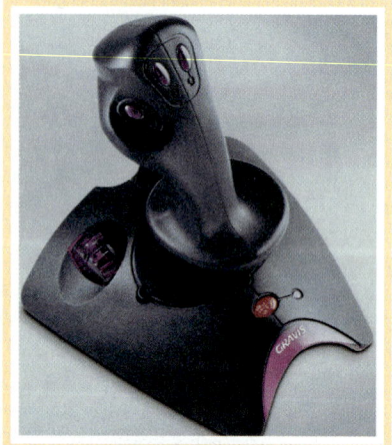

This Apple iBook (top left), like many portable computers, includes a built-in touchpad as a pointing device. The IBM ThinkPad (top center) has a tiny pointing stick (called a TrackPoint) embedded in its keyboard (above the B key) for positioning the cursor on the screen. Many video game machines and some portable and desktop PCs use trackballs (top right) for pointing devices. Joysticks (bottom left) are the chief weapons of the arcade army. Many computer artists find that drawing and painting are easier with a graphics tablet (bottom center) than with a mouse. Touch-screen monitors are ideal for kiosks, ATM machines, and self-serve checkout stands in stores and other public buildings (bottom right).

Reading Tools

In spite of their versatility, pointing devices are woefully inefficient for the input of large quantities of text into computers, which is why the mouse hasn't replaced the keyboard on the standard personal computer. Still, there are alternatives to typing for entering numbers and words into computers. Some types of devices allow computers to rapidly read marks, representing codes, specifically designed for computer input:

- **Optical-mark readers** use reflected light to determine the location of pencil marks on standardized test answer sheets and similar forms.
- **Magnetic-ink character readers** read those odd-shaped numbers printed with magnetic ink on checks.
- **Bar-code readers** use light to read **universal product codes (UPCs)**, inventory codes, and other codes created from patterns of variable-width bars. In many stores, bar-code readers are attached to **point-of-sale (POS) terminals**. These terminals send scanned information to a mainframe computer. The computer determines the item's price, calculates taxes and totals, and records the transaction for future use in inventory, accounting, and other areas.

Chapter 3 Hardware Basics: Peripherals

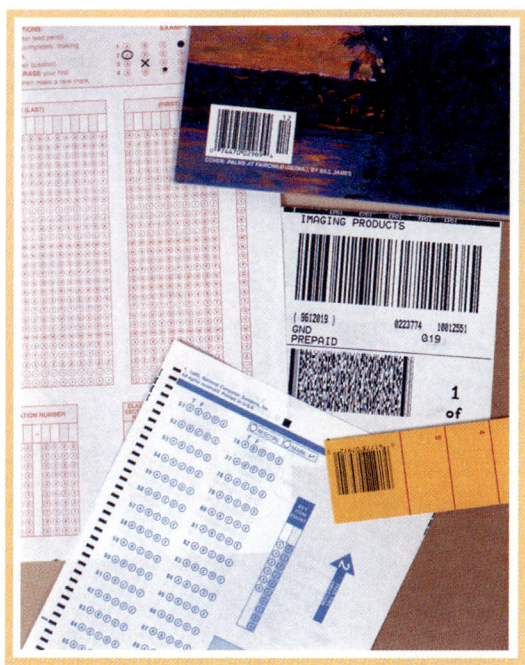

Computers use specialized input devices to read information stored as optical marks, bar codes, and specially designed characters.

This self-service POS terminal uses two input devices for gathering information about a purchase: a touch screen for entering commands and answering questions and a bar-code reader for scanning product information. Before the transaction is completed, another input device reads information encoded in the magnetic strip on the customer's credit card.

Because test forms, magnetic ink characters, and bar codes were designed to be read by computers, the devices that read them are extremely accurate. Reading text from books, magazines, and other printed documents is more challenging because of the great variety of printed text. **Optical character recognition (OCR)** is the technology of recognizing individual characters on a printed page, so they can be stored and edited as text.

Before a computer can recognize handwriting or printed text, it must first create a digital image of the page that it can store in memory. This is usually done with an input device known as a scanner. There are many types of scanners, as you'll see in the next section. A scanner doesn't actually read or recognize letters and numbers on a page—it just makes a digital "picture" of the page available to the computer. The computer can then use OCR software to interpret the black and white scanned patterns as letters and numbers.

Actually, a few special-purpose scanners take care of the OCR work themselves. **Pen scanners** look like highlighters, but they're actually wireless scanners that can perform character recognition on the fly. When you drag a pen scanner across a line of printed text, it creates a text file in its built-in memory, where it's stored until you transfer it into your computer's memory through a cable or infrared beam. A wireless pen scanner actually contains a small computer programmed to recognize printed text. This kind of optical character recognition isn't 100 percent accurate, but it's getting better all the time.

A pen scanner can capture text from a printed document and transfer it to a PC.

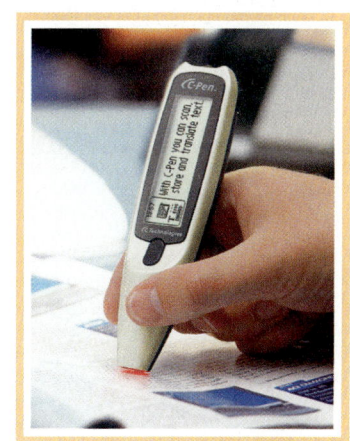

Handwriting recognition is far more difficult and error-prone than printed character recognition. But handwriting recognition has many practical applications today, especially in **pen-based computers**. A pen-based computer is a keyboardless machine that accepts input from a stylus applied directly to a flat-panel screen. The computer electronically simulates a pen and pad of paper. **Handwriting recognition software** translates the user's handwritten forms into ASCII characters. Most such systems require users to modify their handwriting so that it's consistent and unambiguous enough for the software to decipher reliably.

Personal digital assistants (PDAs) are pen computers that serve as pocket-sized organizers, notebooks, appointment books, and communication devices. These popular, verastile devices can also be programmed for specialized work ranging from sports scorekeeping to medical analysis.

The Palm OS software can recognize hand-drawn characters, but only if they're printed according to the rules of the Graffiti system (above). Pen input is used in handheld computers such as this Handspring Visor (center). The much larger Tablet PC (right) is a prototype of a full-featured Windows computer designed to accept pen input.

A smart whiteboard can send its contents to a PC, simplifying and streamlining the note-taking process for many meetings and classes.

Information workers who spend lots of time filling out forms use special-purpose pen-based systems. You've probably signed for a package or a credit card purchase using a pen-based computer system.

Handwriting recognition software can even be applied to notes scrawled on a whiteboard in a meeting room or classroom. A **smart whiteboard** can serve as an input device for a PC, so each board full of information is stored as a digital image on the computer's disk. If the writing is clear enough, handwriting recognition software can turn the whiteboard notes into a text file that can be emailed to meeting or class participants. (OCR and handwriting recognition are covered in more detail in later chapters.)

Digitizing the Real World

> The . . . **number-one peripheral device** is not a drive. It's not a printer, scanner, hub, or network. It's you, the user.
> —John K. Rizzo and K. Daniel Clark, in *How the Mac Works*

Before a computer can recognize handwriting or printed text, a scanner or other input device must **digitize** the information—convert it into a digital form. Because real-world information comes in so many forms, a variety of input devices have been designed for capturing and digitizing information. In this section we'll examine several of these devices, from common scanners to exotic sensors.

A **scanner** is an input device that can create a digital representation of a printed image. The most common models today are **flatbed scanners**, which look and work like photocopy machines, except that they create computer files instead of paper copies. Inexpensive flatbed scanners are designed for home and small business use. More expensive models used by graphics professionals are capable of producing higher-quality reproductions, and, with attachments, scan photographic negatives and slides. Some scanners, called **slide scanners**, can scan *only* slides and negatives. These special-

A slide scanner can produce high-quality digital reproductions from photographic negatives and slides.

Flatbed scanners capture and digitize images from external paper sources.

ized tools generally produce higher-quality results than flatbed scanners when scanning transparencies. *Drum scanners* are larger and more expensive than flatbeds; they're used in publishing applications where image quality is critical. At the other end of the spectrum, *sheet-fed scanners* are small, portable, and inexpensive. Regardless of its type or capabilities, however, a scanner converts photographs, drawings, charts, and other printed information into bit patterns that can be stored and manipulated in a computer's memory, usually using graphics software.

In the same way, a *digital camera* can capture snapshots of the real world as digital images. Unlike a scanner, a digital camera isn't limited to capturing flat printed images; it can record anything that a normal camera can. A digital camera looks like a normal camera. But instead of capturing images on film, a digital camera stores bit patterns on disks or other digital storage media.

A *video digitizer* is a collection of circuits that can capture input from a video camera, video cassette recorder, television, or other video source and convert it to a digital signal that can be stored in memory and displayed on computer screens. A *digital video camera* can send video signals directly into a computer without a video digitizer, because its video images are digitized when they're captured by the camera. Digital video input makes it possible for professionals and hobbyists to edit videos with a computer. Digital video is also used for multimedia applications such as Web page and CD-ROM development. And a growing number of businesses use video cameras and PCs for desktop *videoconferencing*. With videoconferencing software and hardware, people in diverse locations can see and hear each other while they conduct long-distance meetings; their video images are transmitted through networks. These video applications are discussed in more detail in later chapters.

Audio digitizers contain circuitry to digitize sounds from microphones and other audio devices. Digitized sounds can be stored in a computer's memory and modified with software. Of course, audio digitizers can capture spoken words as well as music and sound effects. But digitizing spoken input isn't the same thing as converting speech into text. Like scanned text input, digitized *voice input* is just data to the computer. *Speech recognition* software, a type of artificial

Consumer cameras like the one shown in the top-left photo sell for a few hundred dollars; professional models like this one in the top-center photo cost much more. A plug-in module turns the Handspring PDA into a digital camera in the top-right photo. Digital video cameras like the one in the bottom-left photo can deliver video data directly to a PC or Macintosh. A PC camera or Web cam like the one in the bottom-right photo can continuously feed still pictures or video directly to an attached PC.

How It Works

3.1 Digitizing the Real World

We live in an analog world, where we can perceive smooth, continuous changes in color and sound. Modern digital computers store all information as discrete binary numbers. To store analog information, such as an analog sound or image, in a computer we must digitize it—convert it from analog to digital form.

Digitizing involves using an input device, such as a desktop scanner or audio board, to take millions of tiny samples of the original. A sample of an image might be one pinpoint-sized area of the image; each sample from an audio source is like a brief recording of the sound at a particular instant.

The value of a sample can be represented numerically and therefore stored on a computer. A representation of the original image or sound can be reconstructed by assembling all the samples in sequence.

Scanners

A typical desktop scanner contains a camera similar to the kind found in many video camcorders. The scanner camera moves back and forth across an original image, recording for each sample the intensities of red, green, and blue light at that point. (Human eyes have receptors for red, green, and blue light; all colors are perceived as combinations of these three.) A single byte commonly represents the intensity of each color component; a 3-byte (24-bit) code represents the color for each sample. The scanner sends each digital code to the computer, where it can be stored and manipulated.

Audio Digitizers

Digital audio is commonplace today; the CD player is really a computer system designed to translate digital information on a compact disc into analog signals that can be amplified and sent to speakers. In digital audio recording using a PC, sound waves vibrate the diaphragm of a microphone connected to the computer, usually through a sound card. The position of the microphone diaphragm is sampled frequently—as much as 44,000 times each second—and its level is stored as a number. The faster the sampling frequency, the better the sound recording. Using more storage to represent finer gradations of the sound level also offers better sound. An 8-bit sample can represent 256 distinct levels; a 16-bit sample can represent 65,536 levels. Whether digitizing sounds or images, attempts to increase fidelity to the original usually increases storage requirements.

intelligence software, can convert voice data into words that can be edited and printed. Speech recognition software has been available for years, but until recently it wasn't reliable enough to be of much practical use. The latest products are still too limited to replace keyboards for most people. They generally must be trained to recognize individual voices; they typically require the speaker to carefully articulate each word, and they often work with only a limited vocabulary. Still, they're invaluable for people with disabilities and others who can't use their hands while they work. The promise and problems of automated speech recognition will be explored in later chapters.

Sensors designed to monitor temperature, humidity, pressure, and other physical quantities provide data used in robotics, environmental climate control, weather forecasting, medical monitoring, biofeedback, scientific research, and hundreds of other applications. Even our sense of smell can be simulated with sensors. Such sensors might soon be used to detect spoiled foods, land mines, chemical spills, or halitosis.

Computers can accept input from a variety of other sources, including manufacturing equipment, telephones, communication networks, and other computers. New input devices are being developed all the time as technologies evolve and human needs change. By stretching the computer's capabilities, these devices stretch our imaginations to develop new ways of using computers. We'll consider some of the more interesting and exotic technologies later; for now we turn our attention to the output end of the process.

Speech recognition software allows this officer to record spoken notes without using a keyboard.

Output: From Pulses to People

> As a rule, men **worry** more about **what they can't see** than about what they can.
> —Julius Caesar

A computer can do all kinds of things, but none of them is worth anything to us unless we have a way to get the results out of the box. Output devices convert the computer's internal bit patterns into a form that humans can understand. The first computers were limited to flashing lights, teletypewriters, and other primitive communication devices. Most computers today produce output through two main types of devices: monitor screens for immediate visual output and printers for permanent paper output.

Screen Output

The **monitor**, or **video display terminal (VDT)**, serves as a one-way window between the computer user and the machine. Early computer monitors were designed to display characters—text, numbers, and tiny graphic symbols. Today's monitors are as likely to display graphics, photographic images, animation, and video as they are to display text and numbers. Because of the monitor's ever-expanding role as a graphical output device, computer users need to know a bit about the factors that control image size and quality.

Monitor size, like television size, is measured as the length of a diagonal line across the screen; a typical desktop monitor today measures from 15 to 21 inches diagonally, but the actual viewable area is usually smaller. Images on a monitor are composed of tiny dots, called **pixels** (for picture elements). A square inch of an image on a monitor is typically a grid of dots about 72 pixels on each side. Such a monitor has a **resolution** of 72 dots per inch (dpi). The higher the resolution, the closer together the dots and the clearer the image. Another way to describe resolution is to refer to the total number of pixels displayed on the screen. Assuming that two monitors are the same size, the one that places the dots closest together displays more pixels—and creates a sharper, clearer image. When describing resolution in this way, people usually indicate the number of columns and rows of pixels rather than the total number of pixels. For example, a 1,024 × 768 image is composed of 1,024 columns by 768 rows of pixels, for a total of 786,432 pixels.

Resolution isn't the only factor that determines image quality. Computer monitors are limited by **color depth**—the number of different colors they can display at the same time. Color depth is sometimes called **bit depth,** because a wider range of colors per pixel takes up more bits of space in video memory. If each pixel is allotted 8 bits of memory, the resulting image can have up to 256 different colors on screen at a time. (There are 256 unique combinations of 8 bits to use as color codes.) In other words, 8-bit color, common in older PCs, has a color depth of 256. Most graphics professionals use 24-bit color, or *true color,* because it allows more than 16 million color choices

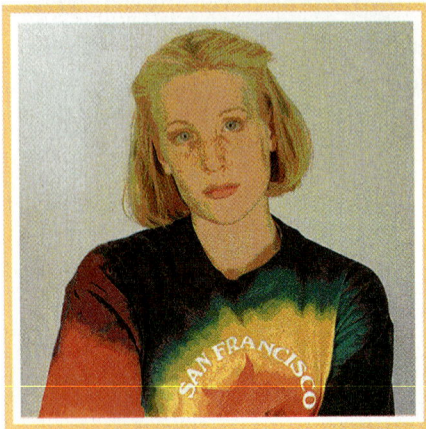 

These four images show the same photograph displayed in four different bit depths: 1, 4, 8, and 16 bits.

per pixel—more than enough for photorealistic images. **Monochrome monitors** can display only monochrome images. **Gray-scale monitors** (which can display black, white, and shades of gray but no other colors) and **color monitors** (which can display a range of colors) have greater color depth. A modern PC or Macintosh can display different combinations of resolution and color depth on the same monitor.

The monitor is connected to the computer by way of the *video adapter*, which is a circuit board installed in a slot inside the main system unit. An image on the monitor exists inside the computer in *video memory*, or **VRAM**, a special portion of RAM dedicated to holding video images. The amount of VRAM determines the maximum resolution and color depth that a computer system can display. The more video memory a computer has, the more detail it can present in a picture.

Most monitors fall into one of two classes: television-style **CRT (cathode-ray tube) monitors** and flat-panel **LCD (liquid crystal display) monitors**. Because of their clarity, speedy response time, and low cost, CRTs still dominate desktops. Lighter, more compact LCDs are used primarily in portable computers. But **overhead projection panels** and **video projectors** also use them to project computer screen images for meetings and classes. As LCDs are dropping in price, they are turning up on more and more desktops; many experts predict they'll eventually replace bulky CRTs on most desks.

Paper Output

Output displayed on a monitor is immediate but temporary. A **printer** can produce a hard copy on paper of any static information that can be displayed on the computer's screen. Printers come in several varieties, but they all fit into two basic groups: **impact printers** and **nonimpact printers**.

Impact printers include line printers and dot-matrix printers. Printers of this type share one common characteristic: They form images by physically striking paper, ribbon, and print hammer together, the way a typewriter does. Mainframes use **line printers** to produce massive printouts; these speedy, noisy beasts hammer out thousands of lines of text per minute. You've undoubtedly seen form letters from banks and stores, bills from utility companies, and report cards from schools

Most desktop computers use CRT monitors because they're inexpensive and they produce high-quality images. But lightweight, flat-screen LCD monitors are becoming more popular on desktops as their prices come down and their image quality improves (right). LCDs are also used in projectors that allow computer screen images to be projected for large viewing audiences (below).

Chapter 3 Hardware Basics: Peripherals

How It Works How It Works How It Works How It Works **How It Works**

3.2 Color Video

The colors in some CRT video images glow because the monitor is a luminous source of light using additive color synthesis—colors are formed by adding different amounts of red, green, and blue light.

Like television sets, computer monitors refresh or update their images many times per second. If a monitor refreshes its image fewer than 70 times per second (70 hertz), the flicker may be enough to cause eye strain, headaches, and nausea. Many monitors slow down their refresh rates if the resolution is increased, so if you're shopping for a monitor, buy one with a refresh rate of more than 70 hertz at the maximum resolution you expect to be using.

Another factor that should figure into your purchasing decision is the monitor's dot pitch—the measurement of how close the holes in the grid are to each other. The smaller the dot pitch, the closer the holes and the sharper the image.

When viewed from a distance of more than a few inches, the three dots visually merge; the color created by this mixing depends on the strength of each of the color electron beams.

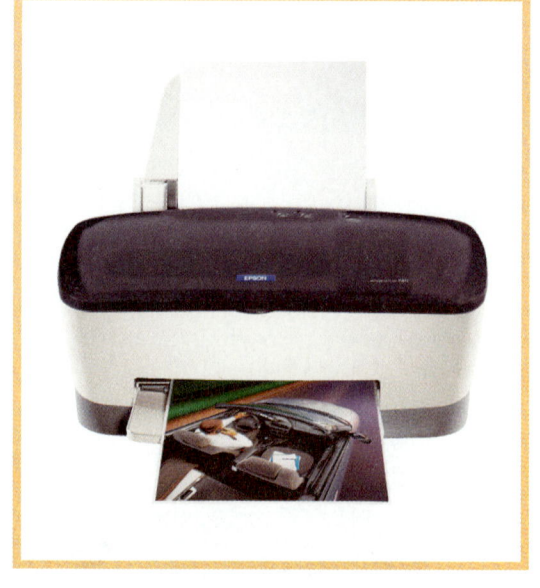

Dot-matrix printer (top left), desktop inkjet printer (top right), portable inkjet printer (bottom left), and laser printer (bottom right). All provide different forms of hard copy output.

that were printed with line printers. Because they're limited to printing characters, line printers are inadequate for applications such as desktop publishing, where graphics are essential.

Dot-matrix printers print text and graphics with equal ease. Instead of printing each character as a solid object, a dot-matrix printer uses pinpoint-sized hammers to transfer ink to the page. The printed page is a matrix of tiny dots, some white and some black (or, for color printers, other colors). It's almost as if the computer were hammering bits directly on the page. The final printout might be a picture, text, or a combination of the two. A typical dot-matrix printer produces printouts with a resolution—relative closeness of dots—of less than 100 dots per inch (dpi). An image displayed on a computer screen looks fine at this resolution, but a 100 dpi printout of a photo or drawing looks rough and ragged. The pixels that make up characters and pictures are obvious to even casual viewers.

Except for those applications, such as billing, where multipart forms need to be printed, **nonimpact printers** have replaced impact printers in most offices. The two main types of nonimpact printers are laser printers and inkjet printers. **Laser printers** can print four to thirty pages per minute of high-quality text and graphical output. Because of their speed, durability, and reliability, they're often shared in office environments. Laser printers use the same technology as photocopy machines: A laser beam creates patterns of electrical charges on a rotating drum; those charged patterns attract black toner and transfer it to paper as the drum rotates. Color laser printers can print multicolor images by mixing different toner shades.

People who work in color tend to use less expensive **inkjet printers**, which spray ink directly onto paper to produce printed text and graphic images. Inkjets generally print fewer pages per minute (one to twelve) than laser printers. But high-quality color inkjet printers cost far less than color laser printers, and many are less expensive than the cheapest black-and-white laser printers. Inkjet printers are also smaller and lighter than laser printers. Portable inkjet printers designed to travel with laptops weigh only a couple of pounds each. Some inkjet printers, called photo printers, are specially optimized to print high-quality photos captured with digital cameras and scanners.

Chapter 3 Hardware Basics: Peripherals

How It Works How It Works How It Works How It Works **How It Works**

3.3 Color Printing

Printed colors can't be as vivid as video colors because printed images don't produce light like a monitor does; they only reflect light. Most color printers use subtractive synthesis *to produce colors: They mix together various amounts of cyan (light blue), magenta (reddish purple), yellow, and black pigments to create a color.*

Most printers, like monitors, are raster devices—*they form images from little dots. The resolution of raster printers is normally measured in dots per inch (dpi). Printers have resolutions of hundreds—or even thousands—of dpi.*

Matching on-screen color with printed color is difficult because monitors use additive color synthesis to obtain the color, whereas printers use subtractive synthesis. Monitors are able to display more colors than printers, though printers can display a few colors that monitors can't. But the range of colors that humans can perceive extends beyond either technology.

You can demonstrate subtractive synthesis by painting overlapping areas of cyan, magenta, and yellow ink. The combination of all three is black; combinations of pairs produce red, green, and blue, which are secondary colors of the subtractive system.

Both laser and inkjet printers produce output with much higher resolution—usually 600 or more dots per inch—than is possible with dot-matrix models. At these resolutions it's hard to tell with the naked eye that characters are, in fact, composed of dots. The best color printers can reproduce photographs with striking accuracy. Because of their ability to print high-resolution text and pictures, nonimpact printers dominate the printer market today.

Multifunction peripherals (**MFP**, also called *all-in-one devices*) take advantage of the fact that different tools can use similar technologies. A multifunction device can combine a scanner, a printer, and a fax modem (described in the Telecommunications and Networking chapter). Such a device can serve as a printer, a scanner, a color photocopy machine, and a fax machine.

For certain scientific and engineering applications, a **plotter** is more appropriate than a printer for producing hard copy. A plotter is an automated drawing tool that can produce large, finely scaled drawings, engineering blueprints, and maps by moving the pen and/or the paper in response to computer commands.

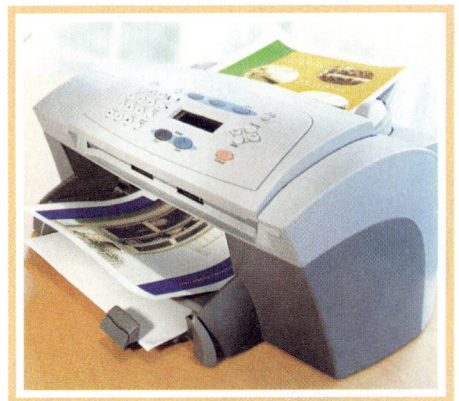

A multifunction peripheral combines a printer with a scanner and a modem so it can serve as a printer, a scanner, a photocopy machine, and a fax machine.

Output You Can Hear

Most modern PCs include sound cards. A **sound card** enables the PC to accept microphone input, play music and other sound through speakers or headphones, and process sound in a variety of ways. (All Macintoshes and some PCs have audio circuitry integrated with the rest of the system so they don't need separate sound cards.) With a sound card, a PC can play digital recordings of all kinds of sounds, from personal recordings made with the PC and a microphone to music downloaded from the Internet.

Most sound cards also include **synthesizers**—specialized circuitry designed to generate sounds electronically. These synthesizers can be used to produce music, noise, or anything in between. A computer also can be connected to a stand-alone music synthesizer, so the computer has complete control of the instrument. Computers can also generate synthesized speech with the right software. Of course, to produce any kind of sound, the computer needs to include or be attached to speakers or headphones.

Moby, like many modern musicians, use computers and electronic synthesizers extensively for composing and performing music.

Controlling Other Machines

In the same way that many input devices convert real-world sights and sounds into digital pulses, many output devices work in the other direction, taking bit patterns and turning them into nondigital movements or measurements. Robot arms, telephone switchboards, transportation devices, automated factory equipment, spacecraft, and a host of other machines and systems accept their orders from computers.

In one example familiar to computer gamers, an enhanced input device delivers output. The force feedback joystick can receive signals from a computer and give tactile feedback—jolts, scrapes, and bumps—that match the visual output of the game or simulation. Many video arcades take the concept further by having the computer shake, rattle, and roll the gamer's chair while displaying onscreen movements that match the action. Output devices that generate synthetic smells are also beginning to appear. If these devices catch on, Web sites might commonly include smells as well as sights and sound. While you're virtually visiting your favorite beach resort you might smell synthetic surf, sand, and sunblock.

Computers control the movements of spacecrafts and virtual reality arcade games using output devices that operate on similar principles.

Of course, computers can send information directly to other computers, bypassing human interaction altogether. The possibilities for computer output are limited only by the technology and the human imagination, both of which are stretching further all the time.

Storage Devices: Input Meets Output

> A **retentive memory** may be a good thing, but **the ability to forget** is the true token of greatness.
> —Elbert Hubbard

Some computer peripherals are capable of performing both input and output functions. These devices, which include tape and disk drives, are the computer's **storage devices**. They're sometimes referred to as *secondary storage* devices, because the computer's memory is its *primary storage*. Unlike RAM, which forgets everything when the computer is turned off, and ROM, which can't learn anything new, storage devices enable the computer to record information semi-permanently so it can be read later by the same computer or by another computer.

Magnetic Tape

Tape drives are common storage devices on most mainframe computers and some PCs. A tape drive can write data onto, and read data off of, a magnetically coated ribbon of tape. The reason for the widespread use of **magnetic tape** as a storage medium is clear: A magnetic tape can store massive amounts of information in a small space at a relatively low cost. The spinning tape reels that symbolized computers in so many old science fiction movies have for the most part been replaced by tape cartridges based on similar technology.

Tape cartridges similar to this one have replaced spinning tape reels as backup storage devices.

Rules of Thumb

Ergonomics and Health

Along with the benefits of computer technology comes the potential for unwelcome side effects. For people who work long hours with computers, the side effects include risks to health and safety due to radiation emissions, repetitive-stress injuries, or other computer-related health problems. Inconclusive evidence suggests that low-level radiation emitted by video display terminals (VDTs) and other equipment might cause health problems, including miscarriages in pregnant women and leukemia. The scientific jury is still out, but the mixed research results so far have led many computer users and manufacturers to err on the side of caution.

More concrete evidence relates keyboarding to occurrences of **repetitive-stress injuries** such as **carpal tunnel syndrome**, a painful affliction of the wrist and hand that results from repeating the same movements over long periods. Prolonged computer use also increases the likelihood of headaches, eyestrain, fatigue, and other symptoms of "techno-stress."

Ergonomics (sometimes called human engineering) is the science of designing work environments that enable people and things to interact efficiently and safely. Ergonomic studies suggest preventative measures you can take to protect your health as you work with computers:

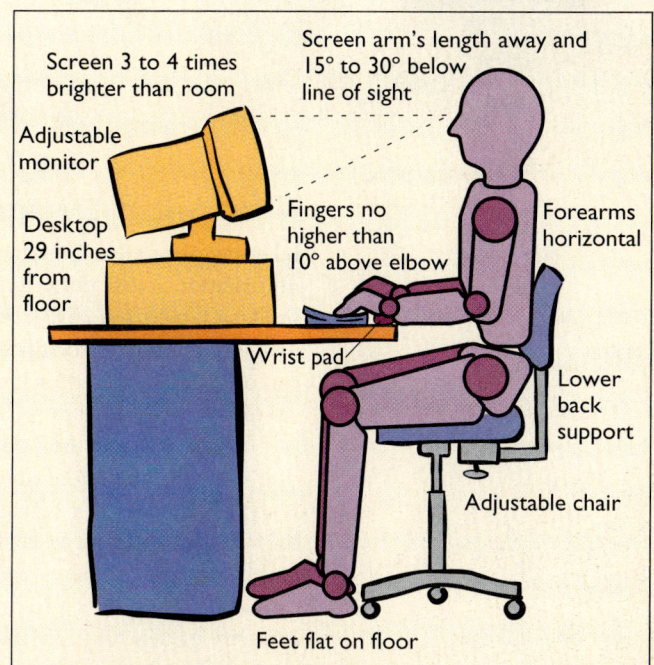

- ▶ **Choose equipment that's ergonomically designed.** When you're buying computer equipment, look beyond functionality. Use magazine reviews, manufacturer's information, and personal research to check on health-related factors, such as monitor radiation and glare, disk-drive noise levels, and keyboard layout. A growing number of computer products, such as split, angled ergonomic keyboards, are specifically designed to reduce the risk of equipment-related injuries.
- ▶ **Create a healthy workspace.** Keep the paper copy of your work at close to the same height as your screen. Position your monitor and lights to minimize glare. Sit at arm's length from your monitor to minimize radiation risks.
- ▶ **Build flexibility into your work environment.** Whenever possible work with an adjustable chair, an adjustable table, an adjustable monitor, and a removable keyboard. Change your work position frequently.
- ▶ **Rest your eyes.** Look up from the screen periodically and focus on a far-away object or scene. Blink frequently. Take a 15-minute break from using a VDT every 2 hours.
- ▶ **Stretch.** While you're taking your rest break, do some simple stretches to loosen tight muscles. Occasional stretching of the muscles in your arms, hands, wrists, back, shoulders, and lower body can make hours of computer work more comfortable and less harmful.
- ▶ **Listen to your body.** If you feel uncomfortable, your body is telling you to change something or take a break. Don't ignore it. Ergonomic keyboards like the split, angled keyboard allow computer users to hold their hands and arms in more natural positions while typing to reduce the risk of repetitive-stress injuries.
- ▶ **Seek help when you need it.** If your wrists start hurting when you work, or you have persistent headaches, or you're feeling some other problem that may be related to excessive computer work, talk to a professional. A medical doctor, chiropractor, physical therapist, or naturopath may be able to help you to head off the problem before it becomes chronic.

Standard-sized internal hard drives and microdrives mounted in removable cartridges are, below the surface, based on similar technology.

Magnetic tape has one clear limitation: Tape is a **sequential access** medium. Whether a tape holds music or computer data, the computer must zip through information in the order in which it was recorded. Retrieving information from the middle of a tape is far too time-consuming for most modern computer applications, because people expect immediate response to their commands. As a result, magnetic tape is used today primarily for backup of data and a few other operations that aren't time-sensitive.

Magnetic Disks

Like magnetic tape, a **magnetic disk** has a magnetically coated surface that can store encoded information; a **disk drive** writes data onto the disk's surface and reads data from the surface. But unlike a tape drive, a **disk drive** can rapidly retrieve information from any part of a magnetic disk without regard for the order in which the information was recorded, in the same way you can quickly select any track on an audio compact disc. Because of their **random access** capability, disks are the most popular media for everyday storage needs.

Most computer users are familiar with the 3.5-inch **diskette** (also called **floppy disk**, or just *disk*)—a small, magnetically sensitive, flexible plastic wafer housed in a plastic case. The diskette is commonly used for transferring small data files between machines because just about every PC includes a disk drive that can read and write on these inexpensive disks. The most notable exception: Macintoshes no longer include diskette drives as standard equipment, because diskettes are too slow and limited for modern multimedia applications. A typical diskette has a capacity of less than 2MB—enough space to hold the words for half of this book, but not enough for even one large detailed photograph.

Virtually all PCs include hard disks as their main storage devices. A **hard disk** is a rigid, magnetically sensitive disk that spins rapidly and continuously inside the computer chassis or in a separate box connected to the computer housing. This type of hard disk is never removed by the user. Information can be transferred to and from a hard disk much faster than from a diskette. A hard disk might hold several gigabytes (thousands of megabytes) of information—more than enough room for every word and picture in this book.

To fill the gap between low-capacity, slow diskettes and nonremovable, fast hard disks, manufacturers have developed high-capacity transportable storage solutions. There are many choices beyond diskettes in **removable cartridge media**. The most popular are listed here:

Iomega's Zip disks are widely used for storing and transporting data that won't fit on old-fashioned diskettes.

- *Zip disks*, developed by Iomega. A Zip disk looks like a thicker version of a standard diskette. The most common Zip disks can hold up to 100 megabytes of data; a newer variety can hold up to 250 MB. Zip drives cannot read or write standard floppy disks, even though they use a similar technology. Zip drives are popular add-ons for PCs and Macintoshes; they're even installed as standard equipment on some models. Their popularity makes Zip disks useful for exchanging large data files between machines.
- *SuperDisks*, developed by Imation. A SuperDisk looks similar to a standard diskette, but it is capable of holding 120 megabytes of data—roughly 80 times as much as a typical diskette. The SuperDisk drive can't read or write data as fast as some other removable storage devices, but it has one big advantage: It can also read and write standard diskettes, so it can replace a standard floppy disk drive in a computer system. Sony offers a similar but less widely used device called a HiFD drive.
- *Jaz disks*, also developed by Iomega. Jaz disks, unlike Zip and SuperDisks, are based on hard disk technology. As a result, they have a much

higher capacity (1 to 2 gigabytes) and faster read/write speeds. Jaz disks are, in effect, removable hard disk cartridges. They're often used for storing and transporting large multimedia files.

▸ *Peerless cartridges*, from Iomega, will likely replace Jaz disks because of their huge 10 to 20 gigabyte capacity and high speed.

▸ *Magneto-optical (MO) disks* use a combination of magnetic disk technology and optical disk technology to store and retrieve information. They're not as fast as hard disks, and they're expensive, but they're extremely reliable and they can hold hundreds of megabytes of data.

Magnetic media aren't the only removable storage options. Today, optical storage technology is widely used for storage and retrieval of information.

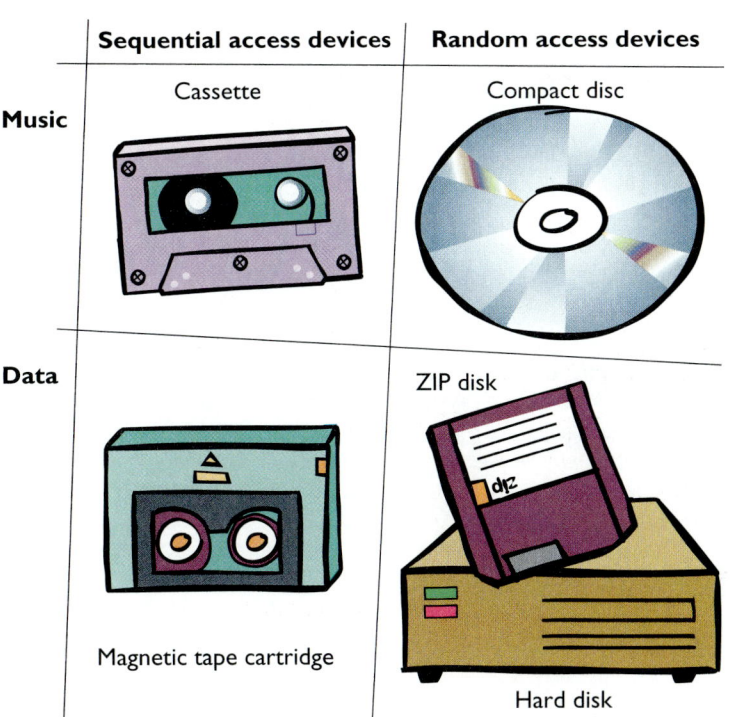

Most stereo systems include sequential access devices—cassette decks—and random access devices—compact disc players. The advantages of random access are the same for stereos as for computers.

Optical Disks

An **optical disk drive** uses laser beams rather than magnets to read and write bits of data on a reflective layer of the disk. A transparent plastic disk surface protects the reflective layer from routine physical damage while letting laser light through. Access speeds are slower for optical disks than for magnetic hard disks. But optical storage is generally highly reliable, especially for long-term storage.

From CD-ROM to DVD-R/CD-RW, there's an alphabet soup of choices in optical disk drives for PCs today. The names can be especially confusing because they aren't consistent. Does *R* stand for Read, Recordable, Rewriteable, or Random? It depends on the context. Many of these drive types will undoubtedly go by the wayside as the cost of the expensive all-purpose drives comes down. But until then, it's helpful to know something about these oddly-named devices.

The most common optical drive in computers is the **CD-ROM drive.** A CD-ROM drive can read data from **CD-ROM** (compact disc—read-only memory) disks—data disks that are physically identical to music compact discs. The similarity of audio and data CDs is no accident; it makes it possible for CD-ROM drives to play music CDs under computer control. A CD-ROM can hold up to about 800 megabytes of data—more raw text than you could type in your lifetime. But because CD-ROM drives are read-only devices, they can't be used as storage devices. Instead, they're mostly used to read commercially pressed CD-ROMs containing everything from business applications to multimedia games and reference libraries.

Many PCs include **CD-RW drives** (sometimes refered to as *CD-R/RW drives*) instead of CD-ROM drives. Like a CD-ROM drive, a CD-RW drive can read data from CD-ROMs and play music from audio CDs. But a CD-RW drive can also **burn**, or record, data onto CD-R and CD-RW disks.

CD-R (compact disc-recordable) disks are *WORM* (write-once, read-many) media. That is, a drive can write onto a blank (or partially filled) CD-R disk, but it can't erase the data once it's burned in. CD-Rs are commonly used to make archival copies of large data files, backup copies of software CDs, and personal music CDs. They're also useful for creating master copies of CD-ROMs and audio CDs for professional duplication.

CD-RW (compact disc-rewritable) disks are more expensive than CD-R media, but they have the advantage of being erasable. A drive can write, erase, and rewrite a CD-RW disk repeatedly. Many people use CD-RW disks instead of removable cartridge media for storing, transporting, and backing up large quantities of data.

CD-RW drives are advertised with three different speeds: a speed for burning CD-Rs, a speed for writing CD-RWs, and a much faster speed for reading CD-ROMs. All three **data transfer rates** are expressed as multiples of 150K per second, the speed of the original CD-ROM drives. A typical drive might have maximum speeds specified as 12X/10X/32X. Actual drives speeds don't always measure up to these values. Even the fastest CD-RW drives are pokey compared to a magentic hard drive.

How It Works

3.4 Disk Storage

Magnetic Disks

Both hard disks and floppy disks are coated with a magnetic oxide similar to the material used to coat cassette tapes and videotapes. The read/write head of a disk drive is similar to the record/play head on a tape recorder; it magnetizes parts of the surface to record information. The difference is that a disk is a digital medium—binary numbers are read and written. The typical hard disk consists of several *platters*, each accessed via a read/write head on a movable *armature*. The magnetic signals on the disk are organized into concentric tracks; the tracks in turn are divided into sectors. This is the traditional scheme used to construct addresses for data on the disk.

Hard disks spin much faster than floppy disks and have a higher storage density (number of bytes per square inch). The *read/write head* of a hard disk glides on a thin cushion of air above the disk and never actually touches the disk.

CD-ROM

A CD-ROM drive contains a small laser that shines on the surface of the disk, "reading" the reflections. Audio CDs and computer CD-ROMs have similar formats; that's why you can play an audio CD with a CD-ROM drive. Information is represented optically—the bottom surface of the CD, under a protective layer of plastic, is coated with a reflective metal film. A laser burns unreflective pits into the film to record data bits. After a pit is burned, it can't be smoothed over and made shiny again; that's why CD-ROMs are read-only.

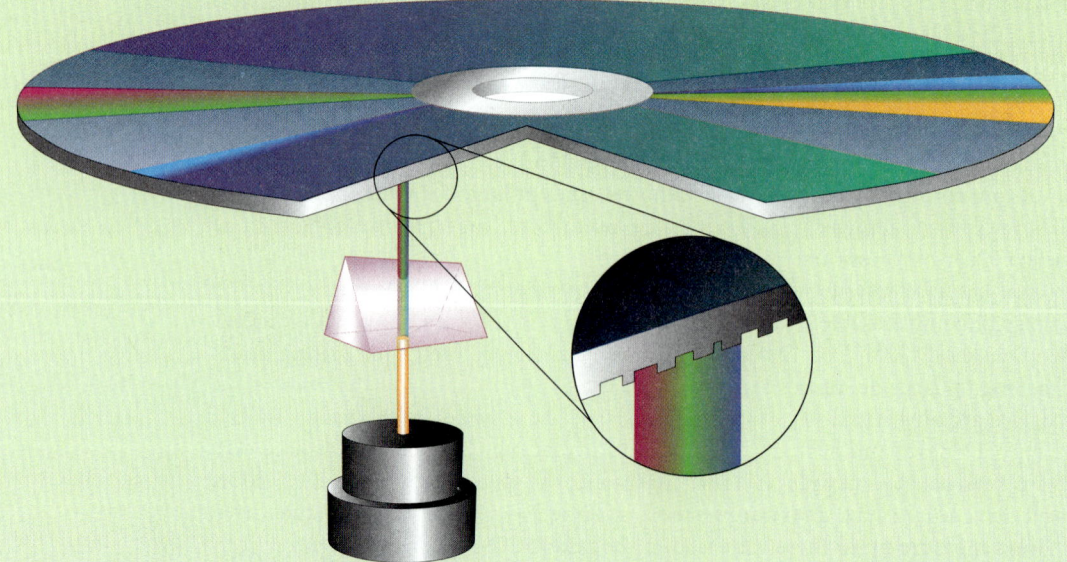

Chapter 3 Hardware Basics: Peripherals   **87**

Works How It Works How It Works How It Works How It Works How It Works

DVD-ROM

A DVD-ROM drive works on the same principle as a CD-ROM drive; the main difference is that the pits are packed much closer together on a DVD, so about seven times as many can fit on the disk surface. (To read these tightly packed bits, the DVD-ROM uses a narrower laser beam.) A DVD can hold even more data—up to 8.5 gigabytes—if it has a second layer of data. On a layered DVD, the top layer is semi-reflective, allowing a second readback laser to penetrate to the layer below. The laser can "see through" the top layer, just as you can see through a picket fence when you look at it from exactly the right angle. For truly massive storage jobs, a DVD can have data on both sides—up to 17 gigabytes. Two-sided DVDs usually have to be turned over for the reader to read both sides; future drives may use additional readback lasers to read the second side without flipping the disk.

CD-RW Drives

CD-RW drives use laser beams to write data on CD-RW disks. But CD-RW media have layers with chemical structures that react to different temperatures created by different types of lasers. To write data, a high-intensity laser beam produces high temperatures that break down the crystalline structure of the original surface. The resulting pits dissipate, rather than reflect, low-level lasers during the process of reading recorded data. To erase data, a laser heats the pits to about 400 degrees, causing them to revert to their original reflective crystalline state.

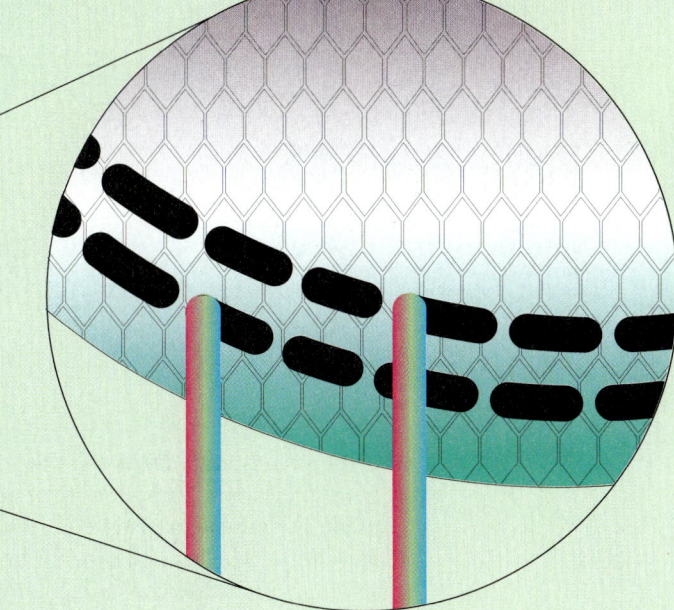

A CD-RW drive can read CD-ROMs, play audio CDs, burn audio CDs, and read and write data onto CD-RW disks.

Several types of DVD drives are also used as replacements for CD-ROM drives in PCs. The **DVD** is the same size as a standard CD-ROM, but can hold between 3.8 and 17 gigabytes of information, depending on how the information is stored. DVD originally stood for *digital video disk*, because the disks were designed to replace VHS tapes in video stores. (Home DVD players *are* extremely popular, but they haven't replaced VHS recorders because they can't be used to record televison programs.) Today many people say DVD stands for *digital versatile disks*, because these high-capacity disks are used to store and distribute all kinds of data.

DVD-ROM drives can play DVD movies, read DVD data disks, read standard CD-ROMs, and play audio CDs. But because they're read-only, they can't record data, music, or movies.

A combination ***DVD/CD-RW drive*** offers the advantages of a DVD-ROM drive and a CD-RW drive in a single unit that can play DVD movies, play audio CDs, record and erase data on CD-RW disks, and burn audio CDs and CD-ROMs. But this type of drive can't record movies or other large files on blank DVDs; it can only record on CD-R and CD-RW media. ***DVD-RAM drives*** can read, erase, and write data (but not DVD video) on multi-gigabyte ***DVD-R*** (but not CD-R or CD-RW) media. The do-it-all ***DVD-R/CD-RW drive*** can read all the standard CD and DVD disk types and record on CD-R, CD-RW, and ***DVD-R*** (recordable) media. With the right software, it can be used to create DVD videos that you can play on DVD movie players. Apple refers to the DVD-R/CD-RW drive as the SuperDrive. Hopefully, the rest of the industry will settle on a name for this versatile drive that goes beyond acronyms.

Common Optical Drives: What They Can Do

Drive type	Read CD-ROM data	Play Audio CDs	Write CD-R data	Record Audio CDs	Write/rewrite CD-RW data	Read DVD-ROM data	Play DVD Movie	Write DVD data	Write/rewrite DVD-RAM data	Record DVD Video
CD-ROM	●	●								
CD-RW	●	●	●	●	●					
DVD-ROM	●	●				●	●			
DVD/CD-RW	●	●	●	●	●	●	●			
DVD-RAM	●	●				●	●	●	●	
DVD-R CD-RW	●	●	●	●	●	●	●	●		●

Solid-State Storage Devices

Until recently, disk drives were the only realistic random-access storage devices for most computer applications. In spite of their popularity, disk drives present problems for today's computer users. The moving parts in disk drives are more likely to fail than other computer components. For airline travelers and others who must depend on battery power for long periods of time, spinning disk drives consume too much energy. Disk drives can be noisy—a problem for musicians and others who use computers for audio applications. And disk drives are bulky when compared with computer memory; they're not practical for palm-sized computers and other applications where space is tight.

Flash memory is a type of erasable memory chip that can serve as a reliable, low-energy, quiet, compact alternative to disk storage. Until recently, flash memory was too expensive for most storage applications. It's still more expensive than disk storage, but flash memory is now practical for many applications. Some flash memory formats are designed for specific applications, such as storing pictures in digital cameras and transferring them to PCs for editing. Sony's *memory stick* is an all-purpose digital storage card about the size of a stick of gum. Most experts believe that flash memory or some other type of **solid state storage** technology—storage with no moving parts—will eventually replace disk and tape storage in computers and other digital devices.

Computer Systems: The Sum of Its Parts

> The computer is by all odds the most **extraordinary** of the **technological clothing** ever devised by man, since it is an **extension** of our **central nervous system**. Beside it **the wheel is a mere hula hoop** . . .
> —Marshall McLuhan, in *War and Peace in the Global Village*

The DiskOnKey fits on a key chain, but can store up to 50 megabytes of data when plugged into a computer's USB port (described in the next section).

Most personal computers fall into one of four basic design classes:

- *Tower systems*—tall, narrow boxes that generally have more expansion slots and bays than other designs.
- Flat "pizza box" systems (sometimes ambiguously referred to as *desktop systems*) designed to sit under the monitor like a platform.
- *All-in-one systems* (like the iMac) combine monitor and system unit into a single housing.
- *Portable computers* include all the essential components, including keyboard and pointing device, in one compact box.

Whatever the design, a PC must allow for attachment of input, output, and storage peripherals. That's where slots, ports, and bays figure in. Now that we've explored the peripherals landscape, we can look again at the ways of hooking those peripherals into the system.

Sony's Memory Stick is a solid-state storage medium that can be used in cameras, audio devices, video equipment, and computers, making it easy for these devices to share information.

Ports and Slots Revisited

The system board, or motherboard, of a computer system generally includes several ports. The most common ports on system boards have been standard on PCs for years. They include the following:

- A **serial port** for attaching a modem or other device that can send and receive messages one bit at a time
- A **parallel port** for attaching a printer or other device that communicates by sending or receiving bits in groups, rather than sequentially
- **Keyboard/mouse ports** for attaching a keyboard and a mouse

Other ports are typically included on expansion boards rather than the system board:

- A **video port** for plugging a color monitor into the video board
- **Microphone, speaker, headphone**, and **MIDI** (musical instrument digital interface) ports for attaching sound equipment to the sound card

All of these ports follow **interface standards** agreed on by the industry so that devices made by one manufacturer can be attached to systems made by other companies. The downside of industry standards is that they can sometimes hold back progress. For example, today's fastest modems outpace the classic serial port, and today's color printers are kept waiting by the pokey parallel port.

This wearable Flash memory card carries 16 megabytes of critical medical information—information that might save a life in an emergency.

This rear view of a tower system unit shows several ports, including some (below) that are included in add-on-boards in slots.

Computer manufacturers and owners use expansion cards to get around the limitations of these standard ports. For example, most modern computers include an *internal modem* in an expansion slot; this modem card adds a standard phone jack as a communication port. For faster connection to a local-area network (LAN), many modern PCs include a *network card* that adds a LAN port. For faster communication with external drives, scanners, and other peripherals, a PC might include a *SCSI* (Small Computer Systems Interface, pronounced "scuzzy") card that adds a SCSI port to the back of the system box. (SCSI ports are standard on older Macintoshes.) The SCSI interface design enables users to daisy-chain (string together) several peripherals and attach them to a single port.

Internal and External Drives

Disk drives generally reside in *bays* inside the system unit. A new PC almost always has a floppy disk drive in one bay, a hard drive in another, and some kind of CD or DVD drive in a third bay. Some PCs have extra bays for additional internal hard drives or removable media. Tall tower models generally have more expansion bays than flat systems designed to sit under monitors. But even if there's no room in the system unit for additional internal drives, external drives can be connected to the system through ports like the SCSI port.

Most portable computers are too small to include three drive bays. But some models have bays that enable you to swap drives. For example, you might remove the CD-ROM drive from a laptop and insert a floppy disk drive so you can save a backup copy of your work. Some models enable you to *hot swap* devices—remove and replace them without powering down. Most portables enable you to attach external peripherals through ports. Some portables can be plugged into docking stations that contain, or are attached to, all the necessary peripherals. When docked, a portable can function like a desktop computer, complete with large-screen monitor, full-sized keyboard, mouse, sound system, and a variety of other peripherals.

This tower system has its side panel removed so you can see the storage bays containing disk drives (top right) and the expansion boards inserted into slots (top left).

Expansion Made Easy: Emerging Interfaces

It's clear that the *open architecture* of the PC—the design that enables you to add expansion cards and peripherals—gives it flexibility and longevity that it wouldn't have otherwise. Many hobbyists have been using the same computer system for years; they just swap in new cards, drives, and even CPUs and motherboards to keep their systems up to current standards. But most computer users today prefer to use their computers, not take them apart. Fortunately, new interface standards are emerging that will enable casual computer users to add the latest and greatest devices to their systems without cracking the box.

A *USB*, or *universal serial bus*, can transmit data at approximately 11 megabits—roughly 100 times faster than the PC serial port—and a newer, faster version is in the works. Up to 126 devices, including keyboards, mice, digital cameras, scanners, and storage devices—can be chained together from a single USB port. USB devices can be hot swapped, so the system instantly recognizes the presence of a new device when it is plugged in. And USB, like SCSI, is *platform independent*, so USB devices work on both PCs and Macintoshes. In fact, this paragraph is being typed on a keyboard that's shared by a PC and a Mac through a USB hub. All new PCs and Macintoshes include at least one USB port. In time, computer manufacturers may phase out other ports made unnecessary by USB's presence. Some, including Compaq, have started producing *legacy-free PCs* that cost less because they use USB ports instead of older serial, parallel, keyboard, mouse, and SCSI ports.

Another interface standard that shows promise is *FireWire*, an extremely high-speed connection standard developed by Apple. Most PC makers refer to FireWire by the less friendly designation, *IEEE 1394*, assigned by the Institute of Electrical and Electronic Engineers when they approved it as a standard. (Sony calls their version iLink.) FireWire can move data between devices at 400 or more megabits per second—far faster than most peripheral devices can handle it. This high speed makes it ideal for data-intensive work like digital video. Most modern digital

Rules of Thumb

Computer Consumer Concepts

The **best computer** for your specific needs is the one that will come on the market **immediately after** you actually purchase some other model.

—Dave Barry, humorist

This book's appendix, CD-ROM, and Internet Web site contain specific information about the nuts and bolts of buying hardware and software to make your own computer system. Of course, any brand-specific advice on choosing computer equipment is likely to be outdated within a few months of publication. Still, some general principles remain constant while the technology races forward. Here are nine consumer criteria worth considering, even if you have no intention of buying your own computer:

▸ **Cost.** Buy what you can afford, but be sure to enable for extra memory, extended warranties, peripherals (printer, extra storage devices, modem, cables, speakers, and so on), and software. If you join a user group or connect to an online shareware site, you'll be able to meet some of your software needs at low (or no) cost. But you'll almost certainly need some commercial software, too. Don't be tempted to copy copyrighted software from your friends or public labs; software piracy is theft, prosecutable under federal laws. (Choosing software isn't easy, but many periodicals and Web sites publish regular reviews to help you sort out the best programs.)

▸ **Capability.** Is it the right tool for the job? Buy a computer that's powerful enough to meet your needs. Make sure the processor is fast enough to handle your demands. If you want to take advantage of state-of-the-art multimedia programs, consider only machines that meet the latest standards. If you want to create state-of-the-art multimedia programs, you'll need a powerful computer that can handle audio and video input as well as output—FireWire (IEEE 1394) if you'll be using a digital video camera. Be sure the machine you buy can do the job you need it to do, now and in the foreseeable future.

▸ **Capacity.** If you plan to do graphic design, publishing, or multimedia authoring, make sure your machine has enough memory and disk storage to support the resource-intensive applications you'll need. Consider adding removable media drives for backup and transport of large files.

▸ **Customizability.** Computers are versatile, but they don't all handle all jobs with equal ease. If you'll be using word processors, spreadsheets, and other mainstream software packages, just about any computer will do. If you have off-the-beaten-path needs (video editing, instrument monitoring, and so on), choose a system with enough slots and ports to enable it to be extended for your work.

▸ **Compatibility.** Will the software you plan to use run on the computer you're considering? Most popular computers have a good selection of compatible software, but if you have specific needs, such as being able to take your software home to run on Mom's computer, study the compatibility issue carefully. Total compatibility isn't always possible or necessary. A typical Windows-compatible computer, for example, probably won't run every "Windows-compatible" program, but it will almost certainly run the mainstream applications that most users need. Many people don't care if all their programs will run on another kind of computer; they just need data compatibility—the ability to move documents back and forth between systems on disk or through a network connection. It's common, for example, for Windows users and Macintosh users to share documents over a network.

▸ **Connectivity.** In today's networked world, it's shortsighted to see your computer as a self-contained information appliance. Make sure you include a high-speed modem and/or network connection in your system so you can take full advantage of the communication capabilities of your computer.

▸ **Convenience.** Just about any computer can do most common jobs, but which is the most convenient for you? Do you value portability over having all the peripherals permanently connected? Is it important to you to have a machine that's easy to install and maintain so you can take care of it yourself? Or do you want to choose the same kind of machine as the people around you so you can get help easily when you need it? Which user interface makes the kind of work you'll be doing easiest?

▸ **Company.** If you try to save money by buying an off-brand computer, you may find yourself the owner of an orphan computer. High-tech companies can vanish overnight. Make sure you'll be able to get service and parts down the road.

▸ **Curve.** Most models of personal computers seem to have a useful life span of just a few years—if they survive the first year or two. If you want to minimize financial risk, avoid buying a computer during the first year of a model's life, when it hasn't been tested on the open market. Also avoid buying a computer that's over the hill; you'll know it because most software developers will have abandoned this model for greener CPUs. In the words of 18th century British poet Alexander Pope, "Be not the first by whom the new are tried, nor yet the last to lay the old aside."

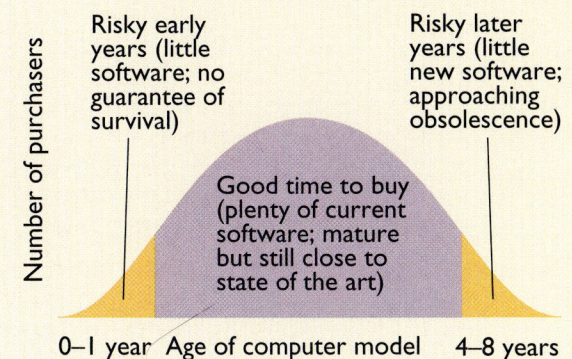

Computer consumer's curve

video cameras have FireWire ports, so they can be connected directly to 1394-equipped PCs. Like USB, FireWire allows multiple devices to be connected to the same port and to be hot swapped. FireWire can also supply power to peripherals so they don't need an external power supply. Because of its speed and versatility, FireWire is expected to be standard equipment on all new PCs soon.

Putting It All Together

A typical computer system might have several different input, output, and storage peripherals. From the computer's point of view, it doesn't matter which of these devices is used at any given time. Each input device is just another source of electrical signals; each output device is just another place to send signals; each storage device is one or the other, depending on what the program calls for. Read from here, write to there—the CPU doesn't care; it dutifully follows instructions. Like a stereo receiver, the computer is oblivious to which input and output devices are attached and operational, as long as they're compatible.

A typical desktop computer system includes a computer and several peripheral devices.

Networks: Systems without Boundaries

Unlike a stereo system, which has clearly defined boundaries, a computer system can be part of a network that blurs the boundaries between computers. When computers are connected in a network, one computer can, in effect, serve as an input device for another computer, which serves as an output device for the first computer. Networks can include hundreds of different computers, each of which might have access to all peripherals on the system. Many public and private networks span the globe by taking advantage of satellites, fiber optic cables, and other communication technologies. Using a modem, a computer can connect to a network through an ordinary phone line. The rise in computer networks is making it more difficult to draw lines between individual computer systems. If you're connected to the Internet, your computer is, in effect, just a tiny part of a global system of interconnected networks.

Software: The Missing Piece

In the span of a few pages we've surveyed a mind-boggling array of computer hardware, but, in truth, we've barely scratched the surface. Nonetheless, all this hardware is worthless without software to drive it. In the next chapter we'll take a look at the software that makes a computer system come to life.

Use It or Lose It

Arthur H. Bell, Ph.D.

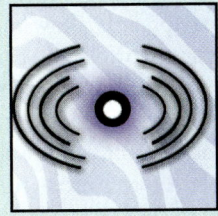

Much has been written about the impact of computer technology on our physical health. Research has raised questions about repetitive-stress injuries, eyestrain, backaches, and other potential hazards of spending too much time in front of a computer. But excessive screen time may also have a negative impact on our social health, too. Arthur H. Bell, Ph.D., is a Professor of Management Communication at the McLaren School of Business, University of San Francisco. In this article, first published in the February, 2000, issue of Adobe *magazine, Bell addresses the problem and suggests ways to keep your communication edge intact.*

I'm worried about a subtle but dangerous occupational hazard. You and I sit in deep communion with our computer monitors for most of our waking hours; our minds may be engaged, but our faces look like out-takes from Night of the Living Dead. (Peek around the office right now. Johnson sits slack-jawed, locked in the tractor beam of his monitor. Williams slumps in her chair, her eyes half-open toward the flitting video images.) What's going on here? A vital component in our repertoire of professional skills is in danger of atrophy—the nonverbal side of our day-to-day communication isn't getting exercise. We're all becoming poster children for the Deadpan Society.

So what? I'm not suggesting that we start smiling and gesturing at our computer monitors. But when we turn way from our CRTs for face-to-face meetings with clients or coworkers, we have increasing trouble jump-starting our nonverbal charms (such as eye contact, facial expressiveness, gestures, and posture). That's bad for business, bad for the team, and bad for individual careers.

Virtually all research on human communication points to the predominant influence of nonverbal cues in interpersonal relations. When nonverbal cues are missing, communication itself breaks down in the workplace. (Results: bad meetings, boring interviews, unproductive contacts with clients, and crossed signals with the boss.)

What you show is as important as what you say in getting your message across. Don't believe it? Put this idea to the test by recalling the last time you returned an article of clothing to a store (or, heaven help you, a software package you've opened). Was it the clerk's words, "Yes, we'll exchange it," or the clerk's expression and tone of voice that communicated the real message and left a lasting impression? We "read" nonverbal signals very accurately. When the dictionary meanings of words conflict with the nonverbal signals that accompany them, we believe the messages sent by the nonverbal signals, not the words.

There's a rueful irony here for specialists in fonts, graphics, and effects. Designers know better than most how important the "look" can be in making an impression and communicating the whole message. Yet they are as prone as anyone to ignore their own nonverbal signals—in effect, their facial graphics—when talking to others in the workplace.

I can't prescribe what your face, eyes, and hands should be doing during nonvirtual communication. But I can share my own short list of reminders when I turn from the monitor to meet with colleagues, students, and clients.

- **Maintain comfortable eye contact.** Shifty, nervous eyes send messages that undercut your words.
- **Use your hands to emphasize ideas.** "Handling" your words in meaningful ways helps others interpret your message.
- **Show obvious interest with your face.** Neutral expressions will be interpreted as signs of disapproval or lack of attention.
- **Lean a bit forward to listen.** The laid-back sprawl communicates a lack of concern and energy.
- **Touch things you're talking about (within limits, of course).** Holding a proposal, picking up the new software release, or touching your finger to numbers on a chart are all high-involvement communication techniques.

The language of nonverbal cues and signals is a must-have for your professional success. And yes, I'm looking right at you and gesturing as I write this.

DISCUSSION QUESTIONS

1. Can you think of examples of recent interactions you've had with other people that support the main points of this article?
2. Do you think computers are, in fact, interfering with our ability to communicate? Explain your answer.

Summary

A computer with just a CPU and internal memory is of limited value; peripherals allow that computer to communicate with the outside world and store information for later use. Some peripherals are strictly input devices. Others are output devices. Some are external storage devices that accept information from and send information to the CPU.

The most common input devices today are the keyboard and the mouse, but a variety of other input devices can be connected to the computer. Trackballs, touch-sensitive pads, touch screens, and joysticks provide alternatives to the mouse as a pointing device. Bar-code readers, optical-mark readers, and magnetic-ink readers are designed to recognize and translate specially printed patterns and characters. Scanners and digital cameras convert photographs, drawings, and other analog images into digital files that the computer can process. Sound digitizers do the same thing to audio information. All input devices are designed to do one thing: convert information signals from an outside source into a pattern of bits that the computer can process.

Output devices perform the opposite function: They accept strings of bits from the computer and transform them into a form that is useful or meaningful outside the computer. Video monitors, including CRTs and LCDs, are almost universally used to display information continually as the computer functions. A variety of printers are used for producing paper output. Sound output from the computer, including music and synthesized speech, is delivered through audio speakers. Output devices also allow computers to control other machines.

Unlike most input and output peripherals, storage devices such as disk drives and tape drives are capable of two-way communication with the computer. Because of their high-speed random access capability, magnetic disks—high-capacity hard disks, inexpensive diskettes, and a variety of removable media—are the most common forms of storage on modern computers. Sequential access tape devices are generally used only to archive information that doesn't need to be accessed often. Optical disks are used mostly as high-capacity, read-only media, but newer types of optical drives can both read and write data. In the future solid-state storage technology will probably replace disks and tapes for most applications.

The hardware for a complete computer system generally includes at least one processor, memory, storage devices, and several I/O peripherals for communicating with the outside world. Network connections make it possible for computers to communicate with one another directly. Networks blur the boundaries between individual computer systems. With the hardware components in place, a computer system is ready to receive and follow instructions encoded in software.

Chapter Review

▼ Key Terms

bar-code reader (p. 72)
CD-R (p. 85)
CD-ROM (p. 85)
CD-ROM drive (p. 85)
CD-RW (p. 85)
CD-RW drive (p. 85)
CRT (cathode-ray tube) monitor (p. 78)
digital camera (p. 75)
digitize (p. 74)
disk drive (p. 84)
diskette (floppy disk) (p. 84)
dot-matrix printer (p. 80)
DVD (p. 88)
DVD-R (p. 88)
DVD-ROM drive (p. 88)
ergonomics (p. 70)
FireWire (IEEE 1394) (p. 89)
flash memory (p. 89)
graphics tablet (p. 72)
handwriting recognition software (p. 73)

hard disk (p. 84)
impact printer (p. 78)
inkjet printer (p. 80)
interface standards (p. 89)
joystick (p. 72)
keyboard (p. 70)
laser printer (p. 80)
LCD (liquid crystal display) monitor (p. 78)
line printer (p. 78)
magnetic disk (p. 84)
magnetic-ink character reader (p. 72)
magnetic tape (p. 82)
monitor (p. 77)
mouse (p. 71)
multifunction peripheral (MFP) (p. 81)
nonimpact printer (p. 80)
optical character recognition (OCR) (p. 73)
optical disk drive (p. 85)
optical-mark reader (p. 72)

pen-based computer (p. 73)
pen scanners (p. 73)
pixel (p. 77)
plotter (p. 81)
pointing stick (TrackPoint) (p. 71)
point-of-sale (POS) terminal (p. 72)
printer (p. 78)
random access (p. 84)
removable cartridge media (p. 84)
repetitive-stress injuries (p. 70)
resolution (p. 77)
scanner (p. 74)
sensor (p. 77)
sequential access (p. 84)
sound card (p. 81)
tape drive (p. 82)
touchpad (trackpad) (p. 71)
touch screen (p. 72)
trackball (p. 71)
USB (universal serial bus) (p. 90)
video display terminal (VDT) (p. 77)

▼ Interactive Quiz Questions

1. The *Computer Confluence* CD-ROM contains self-test quiz questions related to this chapter, including multiple choice, true or false, and matching questions.
2. The *Computer Confluence* Web site, www.prenhall.com/beekman, contains self-test exercises related to this chapter. Follow the instructions for taking a quiz. After you've completed your quiz, you can email the results to your instructor.

   The Web site also contains open-ended discussion questions called Internet Explorations. Discuss one or more of the Internet Exploration questions at the section for this chapter.

▼ Review Questions

1. Provide a working definition for each of the key terms listed in the "Key Terms" section. Check your answers in the glossary.
2. List five input devices and three output devices that might be attached to a PC. Describe a typical use for each.
3. Name and describe three special-purpose input devices people commonly use in public places, such as stores, banks, and libraries.
4. The mouse is impractical for use as a pointing device on a laptop computer. Describe at least three alternatives that are more appropriate.
5. What are the advantages of CRT monitors over LCDs?
6. Name at least two hardware devices that use LCDs because using a CRT would be impractical.
7. What are the advantages of nonimpact printers such as laser printers over impact printers? Are there any disadvantages?
8. Some commonly used peripherals can be described as both input and output devices. Explain.
9. What is the difference between sequential access and random access storage devices? What are the major uses of each?

▼ Discussion Questions

1. If we think of the human brain as a computer, what are the input devices? What are the output devices? What are the storage devices?
2. What kinds of new input and output devices do you think future computers might have? Why?

▼ Projects

1. The keyboard is the main input device for computers today. If you don't know how to touch-type, you're effectively handicapped in a world of computers. Fortunately, many personal computer software programs are designed to teach keyboarding. If you need to learn to type, try to find one of these programs, and use it regularly until you are a fluent typist.
2. Using the inventory of computers you developed in Project 4 in Chapter 1, determine the major components of each (input devices, output devices, storage, and so on).
3. Visit a bank, store, office, or laboratory. List all the computer peripherals you see, categorizing them as input, output, or storage devices.
4. Using computer advertisements in magazines, newspapers, and catalogs, try to break down the cost of a computer to determine, on the average, what percentage of the cost is for the system unit (including CPU, memory, and disk drives), what percentage is for input and output devices, and what percentage is for software. How do the percentages change as the price of the system goes up?

Sources and Resources

Books

Insanely Great: The Life and Times of Macintosh, the Computer That Changed Everything, Reissue Edition, by Steven Levy (New York: Penguin, 2000). Levy is one of the best writers in the field; his style is lively and inviting, even when he's writing about high-tech subjects. In this book he recounts the first ten years of the Macintosh's history.

Infinite Loop: How the World's Most Insanely Great Computer Company Went Insane, by Michael S. Malone (New York: Doubleday, 1999). Malone's book tells the Apple story from the early days of the Apple I through the roller-coaster years of the Macintosh.

The Second Coming of Steve Jobs, by Alan Deutschman (New York: Broadway Books, 2000). This book focuses on Apple's controversial CEO in the years between his reigns at Apple. Jobs is a complex, private person who has achieved fame that rivals rock stars. His story makes good reading.

How Computers Work: 6th Edition, by Ron White (Indianapolis: Que, 2001). This book, described at the end of Chapter 2, provides clear explanations of the inner workings of most commonly used personal computer peripherals.

The Essential Guide to Computer Data Storage: From Floppy to DVD, by Dr. Andrei Khurshudov (Upper Saddle River, NJ: Prentice Hall, 2001). This book provides in-depth explanations of a variety of PC peripherals and interface standards, including magnetic disks, optical disks, and storage for cameras and MP3 music players.

Upgrading PCs: Visual Quickstart Guide, by Bart G. Farkas and Jeff Govier (Berkeley, CA: Peachpit Press, 1999). There are basically two ways to keep up with the rapid-fire changes in PC technology: buy a new computer system every two or three years, or upgrade individual components regularly. This book is designed for people who'd like to be in the upgrade crowd but don't know much about electronic technology. Like other Visual Quickstart books, it clearly and concisely explains procedures with lots of pictures and a minimum of technobabble. If you're comfortable with a screwdriver, you'll probably be comfortable with this book.

Build Your Own Pentium III PC, by Aubrey Pilgrim (New York: McGraw-Hill, 2000). Building your own PC isn't as hard as it sounds—especially if you have a good guide. This book is designed to guide you step-by-step through the process—even if you're not an engineer. In today's competitive PC market, you may not save a lot of money by building your own, but you'll learn a lot—and hopefully have fun along the way.

Troubleshooting, Maintaining, and Repairing PCs, Millennium Edition, by Stephen J. Bigelow (New York: McGraw-Hill, 2000), and **Bigelow's Drive and Memory Troubleshooting Pocket Reference,** by Stephen J. Bigelow (New York: McGraw-Hill, 2000). PCs today are relatively easy to use—as long as nothing goes wrong. When trouble arises, or when it's time to upgrade a component, a PC can be frustrating and bewildering. If you want to—or need to—get inside your PC or its peripherals, Bigelow's hardbound PC reference may help you find your way around. The drive and memory pocket reference has a narrower focus, but a similar style. (In spite of its name, it probably won't fit in your pocket.) Some of the material in these books is highly technical, but that goes with the territory.

Upgrading and Troubleshooting Your Mac, by Gene Steinberg (Berkeley, CA: Osborne/McGraw-Hill, 2000). Macintoshes are generally easier to troubleshoot and repair than other PCs; from the beginning, they've been designed that way. This easy-to-read book is full of answers about making Macs and their peripherals work together.

Mac Answers, Second Edition, by Bob Levitus and Shelly Brisbin (Berkeley, CA: Osborne/McGraw-Hill, 2000). This book offers a wealth of information on Macintoshes and their peripherals in a question-and-answer format. The writing style is clear and friendly.

Real World Scanning and Halftones, by David Blatner and Steve Roth (Berkeley, CA: Peachpit Press, 1998). It's easy to use a scanner, but it isn't always easy to get high-quality scans. This illustrated book covers scanner use from the basics to advanced tips and techniques.

Start with a Digital Camera: A Guide to Using Digital Cameras to Create High-Quality Graphics, by John Odam (Berkeley, CA: Peachpit Press, 1999). This lavishly illustrated book provides an excellent overview of the world of digital photography. Technological issues, aesthetics, and practical shooting tips are all covered.

Desktop Yoga, by Julie T. Lusk (New York: Perigee, 1998). Like any activity, computer work can be hazardous to your health if you don't exercise care and common sense. This book describes stretching and relaxation exercises for desk-bound workers and students. If you spend hours a day in front of a computer screen, these activities can help you to take care of your body and mind.

Disclosure, by Michael Crichton (New York: Ballantine Books, 1977). This book-turned-movie provides an inside look at a fictional Seattle corporation that manufactures computer peripherals. Even though the author has clearly tampered with credibility for the sake of a suspenseful plot, the story provides insights into the roles money and power play in today's high-stakes computer industry.

Periodicals

E-media. This slick trade monthly focuses on storage technologies, including CD-RW and DVD.

Computer Shopper. This massive monthly typically includes a few consumer-oriented articles, but most people read it for the ads—hundreds each month, complete with an index.

World Wide Web Pages

Most computer peripheral manufacturers have World Wide Web pages. The *Computer Confluence* Web site will guide you to many of the most interesting pages.

4 | Software Basics: The Ghost in the Machine

After you read this chapter you should be able to:

▼

Describe three fundamental categories of software and their relationship

Explain the relationship of algorithms to software

Discuss the factors that make a computer application a useful tool

Describe the role of the operating system in a modern computer system

Outline the evolution of user interfaces from early machine-language programming to futuristic virtual-reality interfaces

▲

▼ **In this chapter:**

How programs happen
Why software warranties don't promise much
What the operating system does
How user interfaces change the way we use computers
Concise computer consumer's guide
Self-study questions and projects
Mini-reviews of helpful resources for further study
…and more.

▼ **On the CD-ROM:**

Activities on how Operating Systems work
Video lab on cutting edge software company
Instant access to glossary and key word references
Interactive self-study quizzes
…and more.

▼ **On the Web:**

www.prenhall.com/beekman

Free software sources
Software-related Web sites
Links to Web sites of many important software companies
Self-study exercises
…and more.

Linus Torvalds and the Software Nobody Owns

I had **no idea** what I was doing. I knew I was the **best programmer in the world.** Every 21-year-old programmer knows that. "**How hard can it be**, it's just an **operating system?**"

—Linus Torvalds

When Linus Torvalds bought his first PC in 1991, he never dreamed it would be a critical weapon in a software liberation war. He just wanted to avoid waiting in line to get a terminal to connect to his university's mainframe.

Torvalds, a 21-year-old student at the University of Helsinki in Finland, had avoided buying a PC because he didn't like the standard PC's "crummy architecture with this crummy MS-DOS operating system." The operating system is the basic set of programs that tells the computer what to do; MS-DOS (Microsoft Disk Operating System) was the operating system on most PCs in 1991. But Torvalds had been studying operating systems, and he decided to try to build something on his own.

He based his work on Minix, a scaled-down textbook version of the powerful UNIX operating system. Little by little, he cobbled together pieces of a *kernel*, the part of the system where the real processing and control work is done.

Linus Torvalds

When he mentioned his project on an Internet discussion group, a member offered him space to post it on a university server. Others copied it, tinkered with it, and sent the changes back to Torvalds. The communal work-in-progress became known as **Linux** (usually pronounced "Linn-uks"). Within a couple of years, it was good enough to release as a product.

Instead of copyrighting and selling Linux, Torvalds made it freely available under General Public License (GPL) developed by the Free Software Foundation. According to the GPL, anyone could give away, modify, or even sell Linux, as long as the source code—the program instructions—remain freely available for others to improve. Linux is the best known example of **open source software**; it spearheads the popular open source software movement.

Thousands of programmers around the world have worked on Linux, with Torvalds at the center of the activity. Some do it because they believe there should be alternatives to expensive corporate products; others do it because they can customize the software; still others do it just for fun. As a result of all their efforts, Linux has matured into a powerful, versatile product with millions of satisfied users.

Linux powers Web servers, film and animation workstations, scientific supercomputers, a handful of handheld computers, and even Internet-savvy appliances like refrigerators. Linux is especially popular among people who do heavy-duty computing on a tight budget—particularly in debt-ridden Third World countries.

The success of Linux has inspired Apple, Sun, Hewlett-Packard, and other software companies to release products with open source code. Even the mighty Microsoft is paying attention as this upstart operating system grows in popularity.

Today Torvalds is an Internet folk hero. Web pages pay homage to him, his creation, and the stuffed penguin that has become the Linux mascot. In 1996, he completed his master's degree in computer science and went to work for Transmeta Corp., a chip design company in Silicon Valley. He still spends hours every week online with the Linux legions, improving the operating system that belongs to everybody—and nobody.

Chapters 2 and 3 told only part of the story of how computers do what they do. Here's a synopsis of our story so far:

On one side we have a person—you, me, or somebody else; it hardly matters. We all have problems to solve—problems involving work, communication, transportation, finances, and more. Many of these problems cry out for computer solutions.

On the other side we have a computer—an incredibly sophisticated bundle of hardware capable of performing all kinds of technological wizardry. Unfortunately, the computer *recognizes only zeros and ones*.

A great chasm separates the person who has a collection of vague problems from the stark, rigidly bounded world of the computer. How can humans bridge the gap to communicate with the computer?

That's where software comes in. Software enables people to communicate certain kinds of problems to computers and makes it possible for computers to communicate solutions back to those people.

Modern computer software didn't just materialize out of the atmosphere; it evolved from the plug boards and patch cords and other hardware devices that were used to program early computers like the ENIAC. Mathematician John von Neumann, working with ENIAC's creators, J. Presper Eckert and John Mauchly, wrote a 1945 paper suggesting that program instructions could be stored with the data in memory. Every computer created since has been based on the *stored-program concept* described in that paper. That idea established the software industry and liberated programmers from the tyranny of hardware.

Instead of flipping switches and patching wires, today's programmers write *programs*—sets of computer instructions designed to solve problems—and feed them into the computer's memory through keyboards and other input devices. These programs are the computer's software. Because software is stored in memory, a computer can switch from one task to another and then back to the first without a single hardware modification. For instance, the computer that serves as a word processor for writing this book can, at the click of a mouse, turn into an email terminal, a window into the World Wide Web, a reference library, an accounting spreadsheet, a drawing table, a video-editing workstation, a musical instrument, or a game machine.

What is software, and how can it transform a mass of circuits into an electronic chameleon? This chapter provides some general answers to that question along with details about each of the three major categories of software:

▸ Compilers and other translator programs, which enable programmers to create other software
▸ Software applications, which serve as productivity tools to help computer users solve problems
▸ System software, which coordinates hardware operations and does behind-the-scenes work the computer user seldom sees.

Processing with Programs

> Leonardo **da Vinci** called music **"the shaping of the invisible"** and his phrase is even more apt as a description of **software**.
> —Alan Kay, developer of the concept of the personal computer

Software is invisible and complex. To make the basic concepts clear, we start our exploration of software with a down-to-earth analogy.

Food for Thought

Think of the hardware in a computer system as the kitchen in a short-order restaurant: It's equipped to produce whatever output a customer (user) requests, but it sits idle until an order

The communication gap . . .

(command) is placed. Robert, the computerized chef in our imaginary kitchen, serves as the CPU, waiting for requests from the users/customers. When somebody provides an input command—say, an order for a plate of French toast—Robert responds by following the instructions in the appropriate recipe.

As you may have guessed, the recipe is the software. It provides instructions telling the hardware what to do to produce the output the user desires. If the recipe is correct, clear, and precise, the chef turns the input data—eggs, bread, and other ingredients—into the desired output—French toast. If the instructions are unclear or if the software has **bugs**, or errors, the output may not be what the user wanted.

For example, suppose Robert has this recipe for "Suzanne's French Toast Fantastique."

This seemingly foolproof recipe has several trouble spots. Since step 1 doesn't say otherwise, Robert might include the shells in the "slightly beaten eggs." Step 2 says nothing about separating the six slices of bread before dipping them in the batter; Robert would be within the letter of the instruction if he dipped all six at once. Step 3 has at least two potential bugs. Since it doesn't specify what to fry in butter, Robert might conclude that the mixture, not the bread, should be fried. Even if Robert decides to fry the bread, he may let it overcook waiting for the butter to turn golden brown, or he may wait patiently for the top of the toast to brown while the bottom quietly blackens. Robert, like any good computer, just follows instructions.

> **Suzanne's French Toast Fantastique**
> 1. Combine 2 slightly beaten eggs with 1 teaspoon vanilla extract, ½ teaspoon cinnamon, and ⅔ cup milk.
> 2. Dip 6 slices of bread in mixture.
> 3. Fry in small amount of butter until golden brown.
> 4. Serve bread with maple syrup, sugar, or tart jelly.

Suzanne's French Toast Fantastique: The Recipe

A Fast, Stupid Machine

Our imaginary automated chef may not seem very bright, but he's considerably more intelligent than a typical computer's CPU. Computers are commonly called "smart machines" or "intelligent machines." In truth, a typical computer is incredibly limited, capable of doing only the most basic arithmetic operations (such as 7 + 3 and 15 − 8) and a few simple logical comparisons ("Is this number less than that number?" "Are these two values identical?").

> The **most useful word** in any computer language is **"oops."**
> —David Lubar, in *It's Not a Bug, It's a Feature*

Computers *seem* smart because they can perform these arithmetic operations and comparisons quickly and accurately. A typical desktop computer can do thousands of calculations in the time it takes you to pull your pen out of your pocket. A well-crafted program can tell the computer to perform a sequence of simple operations that, when taken as a whole, print a term paper, organize the student records for your school, or simulate a space flight. Amazingly, everything you've ever seen a computer do is the result of a sequence of extremely simple arithmetic and logical operations done very quickly. The challenge for software developers is to devise instructions that put those simple operations together in ways that are useful and appropriate.

Suzanne's recipe for French toast isn't a computer program; it's not written in a language that a computer can understand. But it could be considered an **algorithm**—a set of step-by-step procedures for accomplishing a task. A computer program generally starts as an algorithm written in English or some other human language. Like Suzanne's recipe, the initial algorithm is likely to contain generalities, ambiguities, and errors.

The programmer's job is to turn the algorithm into a program by adding details, hammering out rough spots, testing procedures, and **debugging**—correcting errors. For example, if we were turning Suzanne's recipe into a program for our electronic-brained short-order cook, we might start by rewriting it like the recipe shown here.

> **Suzanne's French Toast Fantastique**
> 1. Prepare the batter by following these instructions:
>   - 1a. Crack 2 eggs so whites and yolks drop in bowl; discard shells.
>   - 1b. Beat eggs slightly with wire whip, fork, or mixer.
>   - 1c. Mix in 1 teaspoon vanilla extract, ½ teaspoon cinnamon, and ⅔ cup milk.
> 2. Place small amount of butter in frying pan and place on medium heat.
> 3. For each of 6 pieces of bread, follow these steps:
>   - 3a. Dip slice of bread in mixture.
>   - 3b. For each of the two sides of the bread do the following steps:
>   - 3b1. Place the slice of bread in the frying pan with this (uncooked) side down.
>   - 3b2. Wait 1 minute and then peek at underside of bread; if lighter than golden brown, repeat this step.
>   - 3c. Remove bread from fry pan and place on plate.
> 4. Serve bread with maple syrup, sugar, or tart jelly.

Suzanne's French Toast Fantastique: The Algorithm

How It Works

4.1 Executing a Program

Most programs are composed of millions of simple machine language instructions. Here we'll observe the execution of a tiny part of a running program: a series of instructions that performs some arithmetic. The machine instructions are similar to those in actual programs, but the details have been omitted. The computer has already loaded (copied) the program from disk into memory so that the CPU can see it.

The CPU automatically fetches and executes instructions in sequence—from a series of consecutive memory addresses—unless it's told to "jump" somewhere else. The CPU is about to read the next instruction from memory location 100. This instruction and the ones that follow (in locations 101, 102, and 103) tell the CPU to read a couple of numbers from memory (locations 2000 and 2001), add them, and store the result back into memory (location 2002). Translated into English, the instructions look like this:

(100) Get (read) the number at memory address 2000 (not the number 2000, but the number stored in location 2000) and place it in register A.

(101) Get the number at memory address 2001 and place it in register B.

(102) Add the contents of registers A and B, placing the result in register C.

(103) Write (copy) the number in register C to memory address 2002.

For this example, let's suppose that memory location 2000 contains the number 7 and memory location 2001 contains 9.

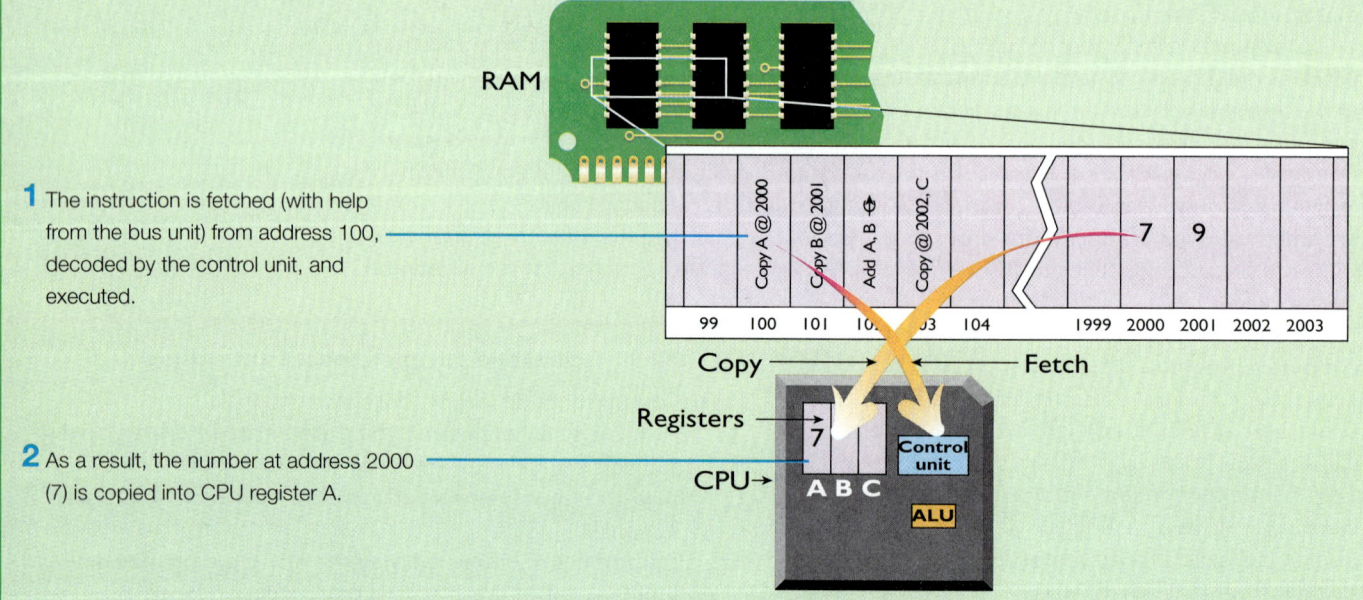

1 The instruction is fetched (with help from the bus unit) from address 100, decoded by the control unit, and executed.

2 As a result, the number at address 2000 (7) is copied into CPU register A.

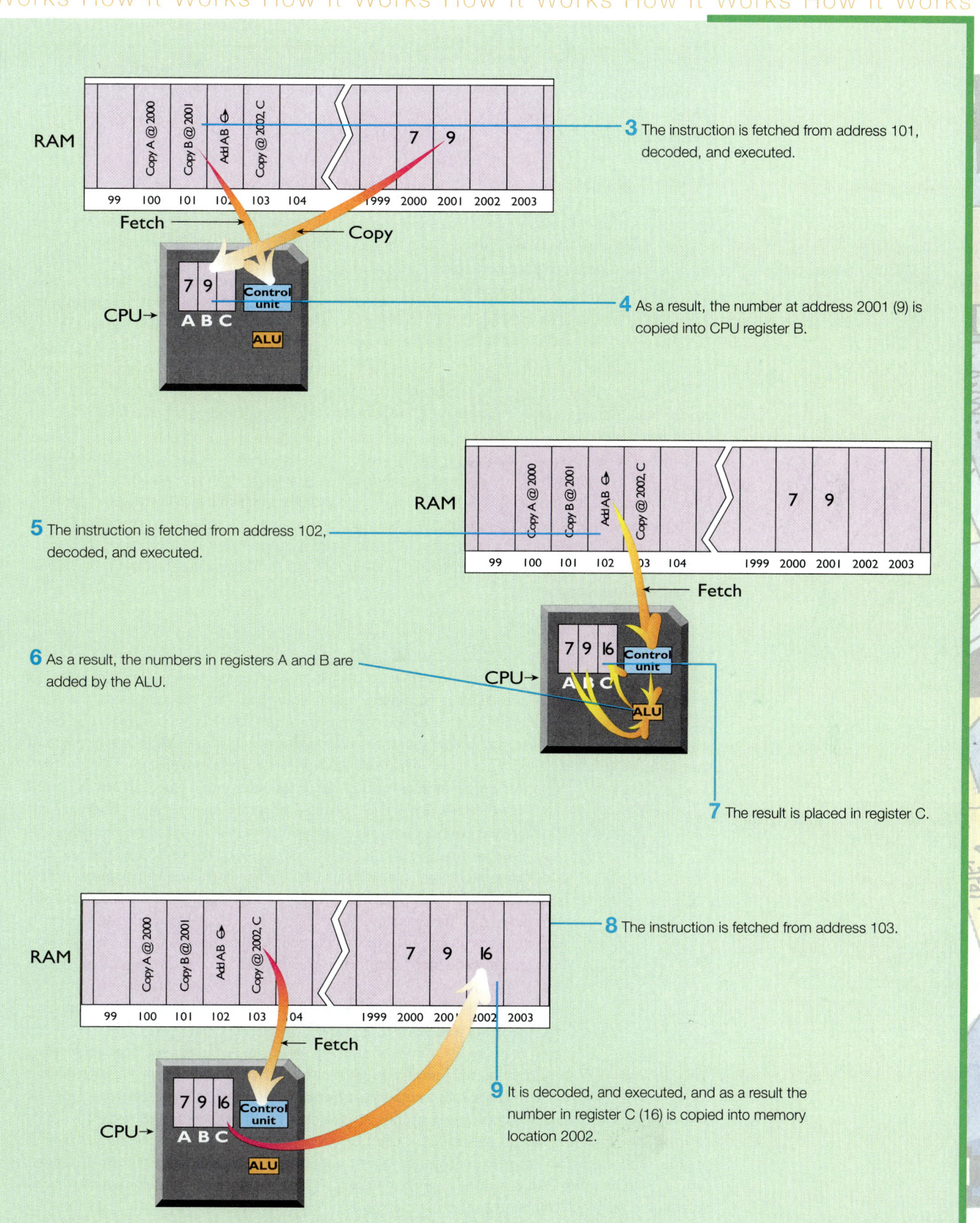

We've eliminated much of the ambiguity from the original recipe. Ambiguity, while tolerable (and sometimes useful) in conversations between humans, is a source of errors for computers. In its current form the recipe contains far more detail than any human chef would want but not nearly enough for a computer. If we were programming a computer (assuming we had one with input hardware capable of recognizing golden brown French toast and output devices capable of flipping the bread), we'd need to go into excruciating detail, translating every step of the process into a series of absolutely unambiguous instructions that could be interpreted and executed by a machine with a vocabulary smaller than that of a 2-year-old child!

The Language of Computers

> The programmer, **like the poet**, works only slightly removed from **pure thought-stuff**. He builds **castles in the air**, creating by exertion of the imagination. Yet the program construct, unlike the poet's words, is real in the sense that **it moves and works**, producing visible outputs **separate from the construct itself**.
> —Frederick P. Brooks, Jr., in *The Mythical Man Month*

Every computer processes instructions in a native **machine language**. Machine language uses numeric codes to represent the most basic computer operations—adding numbers, subtracting numbers, comparing numbers, moving numbers, repeating instructions, and so on. Early programmers were forced to write every program in a machine language, tediously translating each instruction into binary code. This process was an invitation to insanity; imagine trying to find a single mistyped character in a page full of zeros and ones!

Today most programmers use programming languages such as C++, Java, and Visual BASIC that fall somewhere between natural human languages and precise machine languages. These languages, referred to as **high-level languages**, make it possible for scientists, engineers, and businesspeople to solve problems using familiar terminology and notation rather than cryptic machine instructions. For a computer to understand a program written in one of these languages, it must use a translator program to convert the English-like instructions to the zeros and ones of machine language.

To clarify the translation process, let's go back to the kitchen. Imagine a recipe translator that enables our computer chef to look up phrases like "fry until golden brown." Like a reference book for beginning cooks, this translator fills in all of the details of testing and flipping foods in the frying pan, so Robert understands what to do whenever he encounters "fry until golden brown" in any recipe. As long as our computer cook is equipped with the translator, we don't need to include so many details in each recipe. We can communicate at a higher level. The more sophisticated the translator, the easier the job of the programmer. The most common type of translator program is called a **compiler** because it compiles a complete translation of the program in a high-level computer language (such as C++) before the program runs for the first time. The compiled program can run again and again; it doesn't need to be recompiled unless instructions need to be changed.

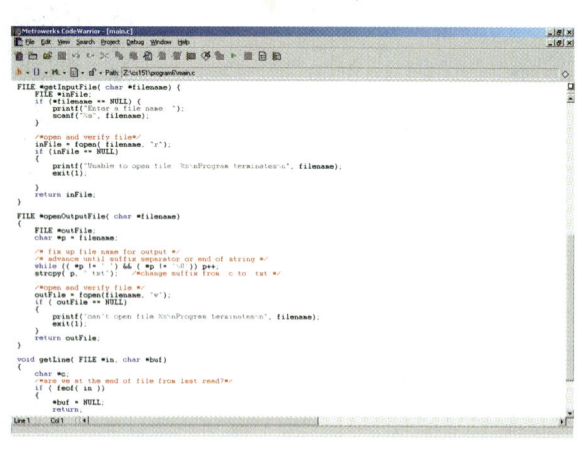

Compilers enable programmers to write in high-level languages such as C.

Programming languages have steadily evolved during the last few decades. Each new generation of languages makes the programming process easier by taking on, and hiding from the programmer, more of the detail work. The computer's unrelenting demands for technical details haven't gone away; they're just handled automatically by translation software. As a result, programming is easier and less error prone. As translators become more sophisticated, programmers can communicate in computer languages that more closely resemble **natural languages**—the languages people speak and write every day.

Even with state-of-the-art computer languages, programming requires a considerable investment of time and brain power. Fortunately, many tasks that required programming two decades ago can now be accomplished with spreadsheets, and graphics programs, and other easy-to-use software applications. Programming languages are still used to solve problems that can't be handled with off-the-shelf software, but most computer users manage to do their work without programming. Programming today is done mainly by professional software developers, who use programming languages to create and refine the applications and other programs the rest of us use.

Software Applications: Tools for Users

Software applications enable users to control computers without thinking like programmers. We now turn our attention to applications.

> The computer is only a **fast idiot**, it has no imagination; it **cannot originate** action. It is, and will remain, **only a tool** to man.
> —American Library Association reaction to the UNIVAC computer exhibit at the 1964 New York World's Fair

Consumer Applications

Computer stores, software stores, and mail-order houses sell thousands of software titles: publishing programs, accounting software, personal-information managers, graphics programs, multimedia tools, educational games, and more. The process of buying computer software is similar to the process of buying music software (CDs or cassettes) to play on a stereo system. But there are some important differences; we'll touch on a few here.

Documentation

A computer software package generally includes printed *documentation* with instructions for installing the software on a computer's hard disk. Some software packages also include tutorial manuals and reference manuals that explain how to use the software. Many software companies have replaced these printed documents with tutorials, reference materials, and *help files* that appear onscreen at the user's request. Most help files are supplemented and updated with *online help* at the company's Web site. Many programs are so easy to use that it's possible to put them to work without reading the documentation. But most programs include advanced features that aren't obvious through trial-and-error experimentation.

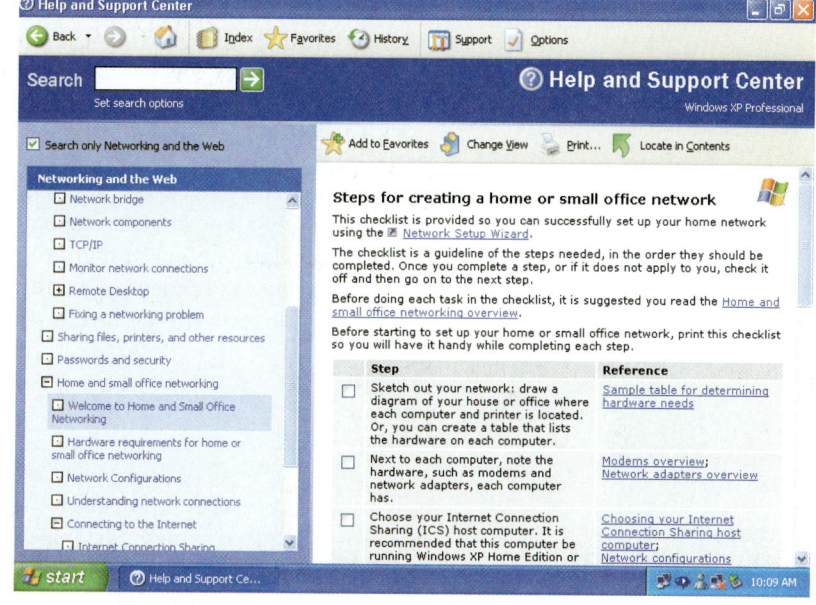

Most modern computer software provides some kind of online help on demand. Microsoft Windows provides context-sensitive help—help windows whose contents depend on what else is currently on the screen. Many software companies, including Microsoft, use Web databases to provide online help.

Upgrading

Most software companies continually work to improve their products by removing bugs and adding new features. As a result, new versions of most popular programs are released every year or two. To distinguish between versions, program names are generally followed by version numbers, such as 6.0 in Photoshop 6.0. Most companies use decimals to indicate minor revisions and whole numbers to indicate major revisions. For example, Adobe Premiere 5.1, a video editing program, includes only a few more features than Premiere 5.0, but Premiere 6.0 is significantly different from version 5.1. Not all software follows this logical convention. For example, the last five versions of Microsoft's consumer operating system have been labeled Microsoft Windows 3.1, Windows 95, Windows 98, Windows Millennium Edition (Windows ME), and Windows XP, Home Edition. When you buy a software program, you generally buy the current version. When a new version is released, you can *upgrade* your program to the new version by paying an upgrade fee to the software manufacturer.

Compatibility

A computer software buyer must be concerned with *compatibility*. When you buy a music CD you don't need to specify the brand of your CD player, because all manufacturers adhere to common industry standards. But no complete, universal software standards exist in the computer world, so a program written for one type of computer system may not work on another. Software packages contain labels with statements such as "Requires Windows 9x, ME, or XP with 128MB of RAM." (An x in a version specification generally means "substitute any number" so "Windows 9x" means "Windows ninety-*something*.") These demands should not be taken lightly; without compatible hardware and software, most software programs are worthless.

Disclaimers

According to the warranties printed on many software packages, the applications might be worthless even if you have compatible hardware and software. Here's the first paragraph from a typical "limited warranty:"

This program is provided "as is" without warranty of any kind. The entire risk as to the result and performance of the program is assumed by you. Should the program prove defective, you—and not the manufacturer or its dealers—assume the entire cost of all necessary servicing, repair, or correction. Further, the manufacturer does not warranty, guarantee, or make any representations regarding the use of, or the result of the use of, the program in terms of correctness, accuracy, reliability, currentness, or otherwise, and you rely on the program and its results solely at your own risk.

Software companies hide behind disclaimers because nobody's figured out how to write error-free software. Remember our problems providing Robert with a foolproof set of instructions for producing French toast? Programmers who write applications such as word-processing programs must try to anticipate and respond to all combinations of commands and actions performed by users under any conditions. Given the difficulty of this task, most programs work amazingly well—but not perfectly.

Licensing

When you buy a typical computer software package, you're not actually buying the software. Instead, you're buying a **software license** to use the program on a single machine. While licensing agreements vary from company to company, most include limitations on your right to copy disks, install software on hard drives, and transfer information to other users. Many companies offer **site licenses**—special licenses for entire companies, schools, or government institutions. A few companies now rent software to corporate and government clients.

Virtually all commercially marketed software is **copyrighted** so it can't be legally duplicated for distribution to others. Some disks (mostly entertainment products) are physically **copy protected** so they can't be copied *at all*. A milder, more common form of copy protection is to require the user to type in his or her name and a product serial number before a newly installed program will work. Because programming is so difficult, software development is expensive. Software developers use copyrights and copy protection to ensure that they sell enough copies of their products to recover their investments and stay in business to write more programs.

Distribution

Software is distributed through direct sales forces to corporations and other institutions. Software is sold to consumers in computer stores, software specialty stores, book and record stores, and other retail outlets. Much software is sold through mail-order catalogs and Web sites. Web distribution makes it possible for some companies to offer software without packaging or disks. For example, you might download (copy) a demo version of a commercial program from a company's Web site or some other source; the demo program is identical to the commercial version, but with some key features disabled. After you try the program and decide you want to buy it, you can contact the company (by phone or through the Web site), pay (by credit card) for the full version of the program, and receive (by email) a code that you can type in to unlock the disabled features of the program.

Not all software is copyrighted and sold through commercial channels. Web sites, user groups, and other sources commonly offer **public domain software** (free for the taking) and **shareware** (free for the trying, with a send-payment-if-you-keep-it honor system) along with demonstration versions of commercial programs. Unlike copyrighted commercial software, public domain software, shareware, and demo software can be legally copied and shared freely.

It may seem strange that anyone would pay several hundred dollars for a product that comes with no war-

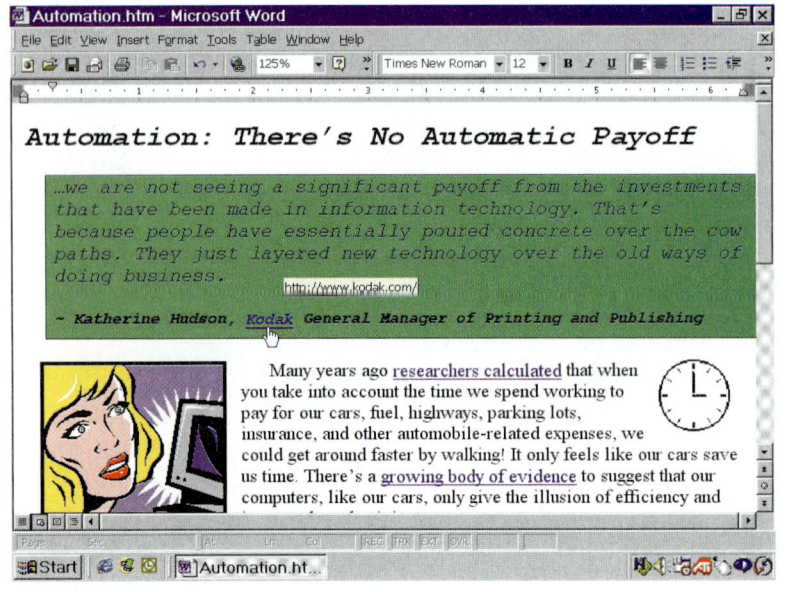

Word processors are based on the visual metaphor of a typewriter, but a modern word processor makes it easy to add graphics, video, and even Web links to an onscreen document.

ranty and dozens of legal restrictions about how you can use it. In fact, the rapidly growing software industry has spawned dozens of programs that have sold millions of copies. Why do so many people buy and use these hit programs? Of course, the answer varies from person to person and from product to product. But in general most successful software products share these two important characteristics:

- *They are built around visual metaphors of real-world tools.* A drawing program turns the screen into a sheet of drawing paper and a collection of drawing tools. Spreadsheets resemble an accountant's ledger sheets. Video editing software puts familiar VCR controls on the screen. But if these programs merely mimicked their real-world counterparts, people would have no compelling reason to use them.
- *They extend human capabilities in some way.* Popular programs enable people to do things that can't be done easily, or at all, with conventional tools. An artist using a graphics program can easily add an eye-catching distortion effect to a drawing and just as easily remove it if it doesn't look right. Spreadsheet programs enable managers to project future revenues based on best guesses and then instantly recalculate the bottom line with a different set of assumptions. And the possibilities opened up by computer video editing are mind-boggling. All kinds of software applications that extend human capabilities are the driving force behind the computer revolution.

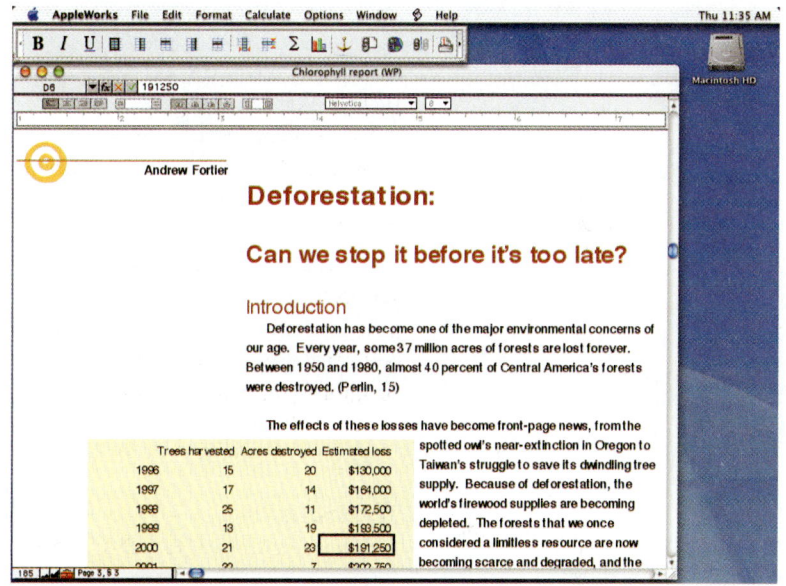

AppleWorks is an integrated application program that combines several popular applications in an easy-to-use package.

Integrated Applications and Suites: Software Bundles

While most software packages specialize in a particular application, such as word processing or photographic editing, low-priced **integrated software** packages include several applications designed to work well together. Popular integrated packages, such as AppleWorks and Microsoft Works, generally include word processing, database, spreadsheet, graphics, telecommunication, and personal information management (PIM) modules.

The parts of an integrated package may not have all the features of their separately packaged counterparts, but integrated packages still offer advantages. They apply a similar look and feel to all of their applications so users don't need to memorize different commands and techniques for doing different tasks. The best integrated programs blur the lines between applications so, for example, you can create a table full of calculations right in the middle of a typed letter without explicitly switching from a word processor to a spreadsheet. *Interapplication communication* enables automatic transfer of data among applications so, for example, changes in a financial spreadsheet are automatically reflected in a graphic table embedded in a word-processed memo.

These advantages aren't unique to integrated packages. Many software companies offer **application suites**—bundles containing several application programs that might also be sold as separate programs. The best-selling suite, Microsoft Office, comes in several different versions designed for different types of users. The core programs of Microsoft Office include Microsoft Word (a word processor), Excel (a spreadsheet program), PowerPoint (a presentation graphics

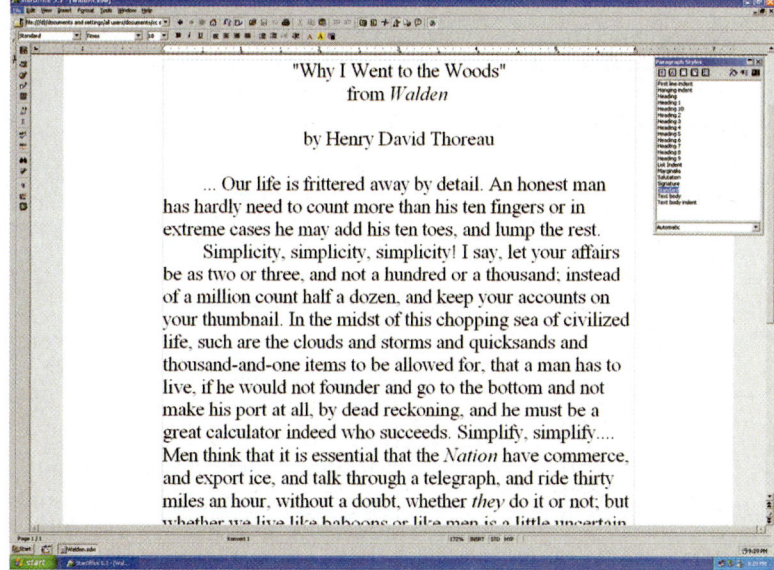

StarOffice is a popular freeware office suite from Sun Microsystems. StarOffice is available for many operating systems.

program), Access (a database program), Outlook (an email/personal-information management program), and Internet Explorer (a Web browser). Microsoft has designed these applications so they have similar command structures and easy interapplication communication. The price of a suite such as Microsoft Office is generally less than the total price of its applications purchased separately, but more than the cost of an integrated package such as Microsoft Works. Suites have more features than integrated programs but also make greater demands on system memory, disk storage, and the CPU. Many older computers simply aren't powerful enough to run a modern application suite. Still, Microsoft Office is the most widely used application package on newer PCs and Macintoshes.

Vertical-Market and Custom Software

Because of their flexibility, word processors, spreadsheets, databases, and graphics programs are used in homes, schools, government offices, and all kinds of businesses. But many computer applications are so job specific that they're of little interest or use to anybody outside a given profession. Medical billing software, library cataloging software, legal reference software, restaurant management software, and other applications designed specifically for a particular business or industry are called **vertical-market** or **custom applications**.

Vertical-market applications tend to cost far more than mass-market applications, because companies that develop the software have very few potential customers through which to recover their development costs. In fact, some custom applications are programmed specifically for single clients. For example, the software used to control the space shuttle was developed with a single customer—NASA—in mind.

Vertical-market software helps this researcher track geographic information.

System Software: The Hardware-Software Connection

> Originally, **operating systems** were envisioned as a way to handle one of the most **complex** input/output operations: **communicating** with a variety of disk drives. But, the operating system quickly **evolved** into an **all-encompassing bridge** between your PC and the software you run on it.
>
> —Ron White, in *How Computers Work*

When you're typing a paper or writing a program, you don't need to concern yourself with the parts of the computer's memory that hold your document, the segments of the word-processing software currently in the computer's memory, or the output instructions sent by the computer to the printer. **System software**, a class of software that includes the *operating system* and *utility programs*, handles these details, and hundreds of others behind the scenes.

What the Operating System Does

Virtually every general-purpose computer today, whether a timesharing supercomputer or laptop PC, depends on an **operating system (OS)** to keep hardware running efficiently and to make the process of communication with that hardware easier. Operating system software runs continuously whenever the computer is on. The operating system provides an additional layer of insulation between you and the bits-and-bytes world of computer hardware. Because the operating system stands between the software application and the hardware, application compatibility is often defined by the operating system as well as the hardware.

The operating system, as the name implies, is a system of programs that performs a variety of technical operations, from basic communication with peripherals to complex networking and security tasks.

Communicating with Peripherals

Some of the most complex tasks performed by a computer involve communicating with screens, printers, disk drives, and other peripheral devices. A computer's operating system includes programs that transparently communicate with peripherals.

Coordinating Concurrent Processing of Jobs

Large, multiuser computers often work on several jobs at the same time—a technique known as *concurrent processing*. State-of-the-art parallel-processing machines use multiple CPUs to process jobs simultaneously. But a typical computer has only one CPU, so it must work on several projects by rapidly switching back and forth between projects. The computer takes advantage of idle time in one process (for example, waiting for input) by working on another program. (Our computerized chef, Robert, might practice concurrent processing by slicing fruit while he waits for the toast to brown.) A timesharing computer practices concurrent processing whenever multiple users are connected to the system. The computer quickly moves from terminal to terminal, checking for input and processing each user's data in turn. If a PC has *multitasking* capabilities, the user can issue a command that initiates a process (for example, to print this chapter) and continue working with other applications while the computer executes the command.

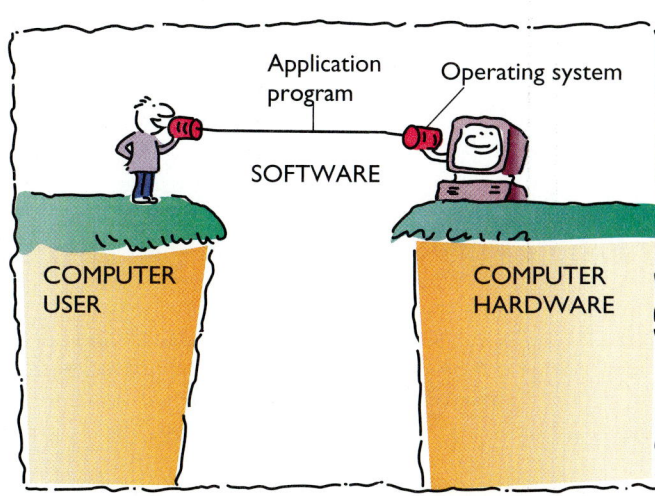

The user's view: When a person uses an application, whether a game or an accounting program, the person doesn't communicate directly with the computer hardware. Instead, the user interacts with the application, which depends on the operating system to manage and control hardware.

Memory Management

When several jobs are being processed concurrently, the operating system must keep track of how the computer's memory is being used and make sure that no job encroaches on another's territory.

Memory management is accomplished in a variety of ways, from simple routines that subdivide the available memory between jobs to elaborate schemes that temporarily swap information between the computer's memory and external storage devices. One common technique for dealing with memory shortages is to set aside part of a hard disk as *virtual memory*. Thanks to the operating system, this chunk of disk space looks just like internal memory to the CPU, even though access time is slower.

Resource Monitoring, Accounting, and Security

Many multiuser computer systems are designed to charge users for the resources they consume. These systems keep track of each user's time, storage demands, and pages printed so accounting programs can calculate and print accurate bills. Each user generally has a unique identification name and password, so the system can track and bill for individual resource usage. Even in environments where billing isn't an issue, the operating system should monitor resources to ensure the privacy and security of each user's data.

Program and Data Management

In addition to serving as a traffic cop, a security guard, and an accountant, the operating system acts as a librarian, locating and accessing files and programs requested by the user and by other programs.

Coordinating Network Communications

Until recently, network communications weren't handled by the typical operating system; they were coordinated by specialized network operating systems. But many modern operating systems are designed to serve as gateways to networks, from the inner office to the Internet. These network communication functions are described in detail in later chapters.

How It Works

4.2 The Operating System

Most of what you see onscreen when you use an application program and most of the common tasks you have the program perform, such as saving and opening files, are being performed by the operating system at the application's request.

When a computer is turned off, there's nothing in RAM, and the CPU isn't doing anything. The operating system (OS) programs must be in memory and running on the CPU before the system can function. When you turn on the computer, the CPU automatically begins executing instructions stored in ROM. These instructions help the system boot, and the operating system is loaded from disk into part of the system's memory.

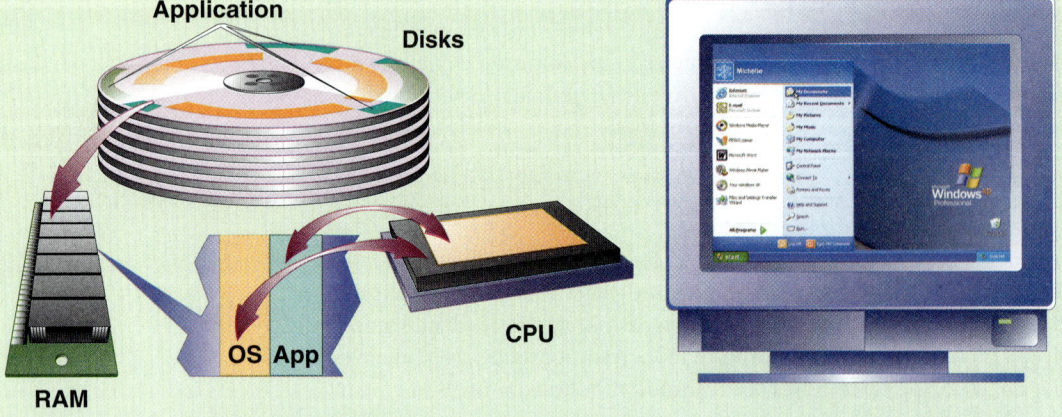

Using the mouse, you "ask" the operating system to load a word processing application program into memory so it can run.

Utility Programs

Even the best operating systems leave some housekeeping tasks to other programs and to the user. **Utility programs** serve as tools for doing system maintenance and repairs that aren't automatically handled by the operating system. Utilities make it easier for users to copy files between storage devices, to repair damaged data files, to translate files so that different programs can read them, to guard against viruses and other potentially harmful programs (as described in the chapter on computer security and risks), to compress files so they take up less disk space, and to perform other important, if unexciting, tasks.

It Works How It Works How It Works How It Works How It Works How It Works

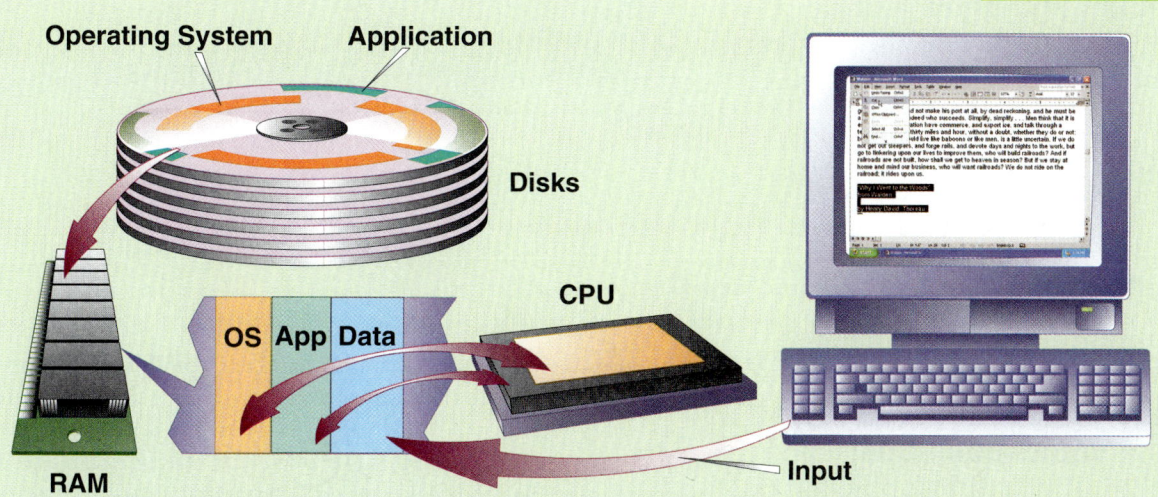

The loaded application occupies a portion of memory, leaving that much less for other programs and data. The OS remains in memory, so it can provide services to the application program, helping it to display onscreen menus, communicate with the printer, and perform other common actions. Because the OS and application are in constant communication, control—the location in memory where the CPU is reading program instructions—jumps all around. If the application calls the OS to help display a menu, the application tells the CPU, "Go follow the menu display instructions at address x in the operating system area; when you're done, return here and pick up where you left off."

To avoid losing your data file when the system is turned off, you save it to the disk—write it into a file on the disk for later use. The OS handles communication between the CPU and the disk drive, ensuring that your file doesn't overwrite other information. (Later, when you reopen the file, the OS locates it on the disk and copies it into memory so the CPU—and therefore any program—can see it and work with it.)

The operating system can directly invoke many utility programs, so they appear to the user to be part of the operating system. For example, *device drivers* are small programs that enable I/O devices—keyboard, mouse, printer, and others—to communicate with the computer. Once a device driver—say, for a new printer—is installed, the printer driver functions as a behind-the-scenes intermediary whenever the user requests that a document be printed on that printer.

Some utility programs are included with the operating system. Others, including many device drivers, are bundled with peripherals. Still others are sold or given away as separate products.

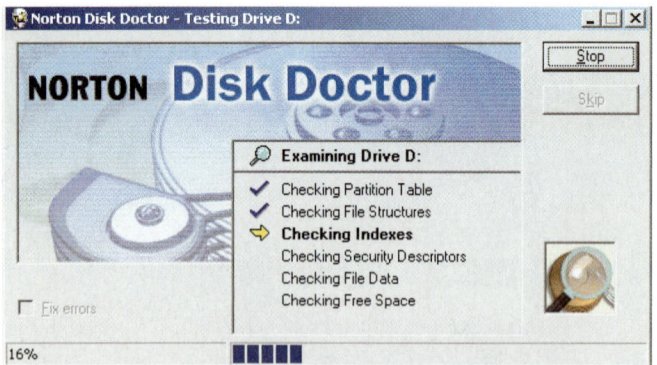

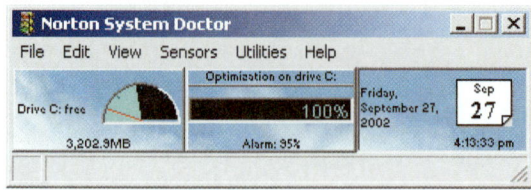

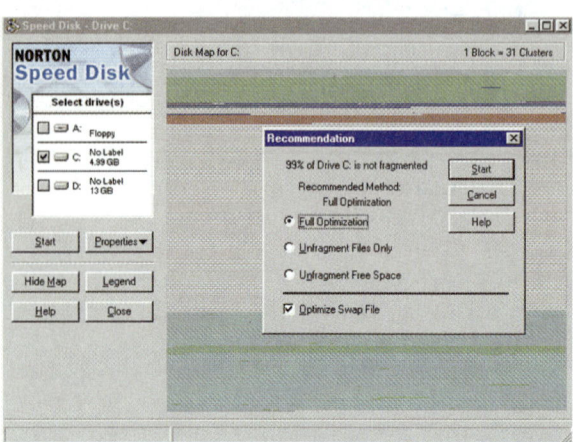

Norton Utilities (from Symantec) is a popular utility package that includes software tools for recovering damaged files, repairing damaged disks, and improving disk performance.

Where the Operating System Lives

Some computers—mostly game machines, handheld computers, and special-purpose computers—store their operating systems permanently in ROM (read-only memory) so they can begin working immediately at start-up time. But since ROM is unchangeable, these machines can't have their operating systems modified or upgraded without hardware transplants. Some computers, including many handheld devices, store their operating system in flash memory so they can be upgraded. But most computers, including all modern PCs, include only part of the operating system in ROM. The remainder of the operating system is loaded into memory in a process called **booting**, which occurs when you turn on the computer. (The term *booting* is used because the computer seems to pull itself up by its own bootstraps.)

Most of the time the operating system works behind the scenes, taking care of business without the knowledge or intervention of the user. But occasionally it's necessary for a user to communicate directly with the operating system. For example, when you boot a PC, the operating system takes over the screen, waiting until you tell it—with the mouse, the keyboard, or some other input device—what to do. If you tell it to open a graphics application, the operating system locates the program, copies it from disk into memory, turns the screen over to the application, and then accepts commands from the application while you draw pictures on the screen.

Interacting with the operating system, like interacting with an application, can be intuitive or challenging. It depends on something called the *user interface*. Because of its profound impact on the computing experience, the user interface is a critically important component of almost every piece of software.

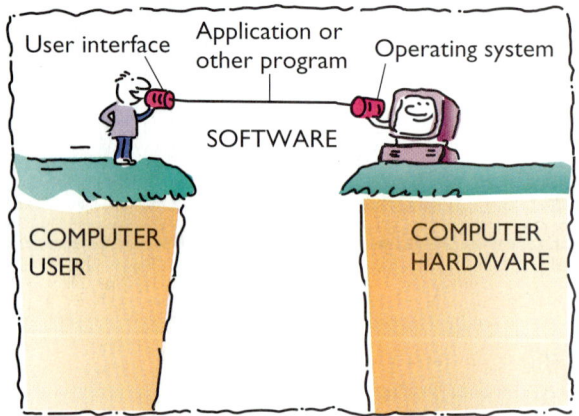

The user's view revisited: The user interface is the part of the computer system that the user sees. A well-designed user interface hides the bothersome details of computing from the user.

The User Interface: The Human–Machine Connection

> The anthropologist Claude Levi-Strauss has called human beings **tool makers** and **symbol makers**. The user interface is potentially the most sophisticated of these constructions, one in which the **distinction between tool and symbol is blurred**.
>
> —Aaron Marcus and Andries van Dam, user interface experts

Early computer users had to spend tedious hours writing and debugging machine-language instructions. Later users programmed in languages that were easier to understand but still technically challenging. Today users spend much of their time working with preprogrammed applications, such as word processors, that simulate and amplify the capabilities of real-world tools. As software evolves, so does the **user interface**—the look and feel of the computing experience from a human point of view.

Character-Based User Interfaces

The earliest PC operating systems, created for the Apple II, the original IBM PC, and other machines, looked nothing like today's Macintosh and Windows operating systems. When IBM introduced its first personal computer in 1981, a typical computer monitor displayed 24 80-column lines of text, numbers, and/or symbols. The computer sent messages to the monitor telling it which character to display in each location on the screen. To comply with this hardware arrangement, the PC's operating system, MS-DOS, was designed with a **character-based interface**—a user interface based on characters rather than graphics.

MS-DOS (Microsoft Disk Operating System, sometimes called just DOS), became the standard operating system on IBM-compatible computers—computers functionally identical to an IBM personal computer and therefore capable of running IBM-compatible software. Unlike the Windows desktop, MS-DOS uses a **command-line interface**: The user types commands, and the computer responds. Some MS-DOS-compatible applications have a command-line interface, but it's more common for applications to have a **menu-driven interface** that enables users to choose commands from onscreen lists called **menus**.

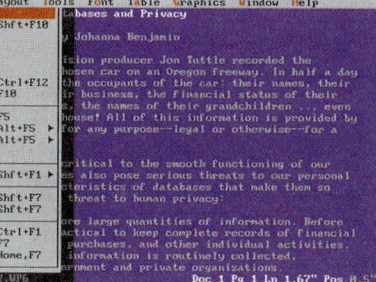

Whether typing commands to the OS or selecting options from menus in applications, MS-DOS users work with a character-based interface.

Graphical User Interface Operating Systems

In the years since the introduction of the IBM-PC, graphic displays have become the norm. A computer with a graphic display is not limited to displaying rows and columns of characters; it can individually control every dot on the screen. When the Apple Macintosh was introduced in 1984, it was the first low-cost computer whose operating system was designed with a graphic display in mind. The **Mac OS** sports a **graphical user interface**—abbreviated **GUI**, pronounced "gooey."

Instead of reading typed commands and file names from a command line, the Macintosh operating system determines what the user wants by monitoring movements of the mouse. With the mouse the user points to **icons** (pictures) that represent applications, **documents** (files, such as term papers and charts created with applications), **folders** (collections of files), and disks. These pictures are arranged on a metaphorical **desktop**—a virtual workspace designed to resemble in some ways the physical desktops we use in day-to-day work. Documents are displayed in **windows**—framed areas that can be opened, closed, and rearranged with the mouse.

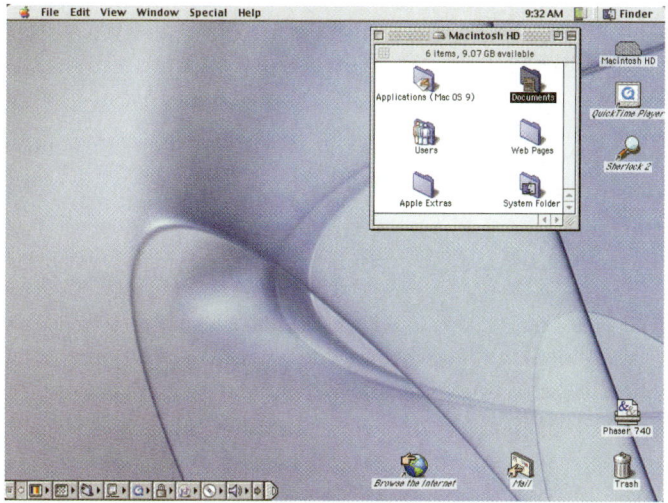
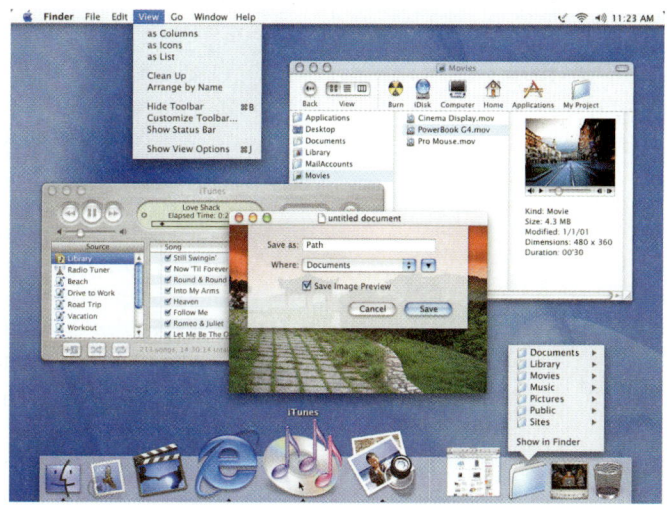

The Mac OS was the first operating system to popularize the graphical user interface. Today's Mac OS X adds several new elements to the traditional windows, icons, and pull-down menus. Shown here are Mac OS 9, the last descendant of the "original" Mac OS, and Mac OS-X, a new operating system released by Apple in 2001.

Windows has replaced MS-DOS as the standard operating system on IBM-compatible PCs. Like the Mac OS, Windows has evolved and added many new features over the years.

The user selects commands from **pull-down menus** at the top of the screen. **Dialog boxes** enable users to specify preferences by simply filling in onscreen blanks and clicking check boxes and buttons. (A User's View box in Chapter 0, ReadMe presents a short session with Mac OS.)

Ironically, the Macintosh has been eclipsed in the GUI operating system market by a product from Microsoft, the company that produces MS-DOS. Originally, **Microsoft Windows** (commonly called *Windows*, or just *Win*) was a type of program, known as a **shell**, that put a graphical face on MS-DOS. The Windows shell stood between the user and the operating system, translating mouse movements and other user input into commands that could be recognized by MS-DOS. With the introduction of Windows 95 in 1995, Microsoft completed the transition of Windows from an operating system shell into an operating system that seldom shows its MS-DOS roots. (A User's View box in Chapter 0, ReadMe presents a short session with Windows.)

Windows and Mac OS have evolved over the years, adding new features to their GUIs to make them easier to use. **Task bars** provide instant one-click access to open applications, making it easy to switch back and forth between different tasks. **Hierarchical menus** organize commands into compact, efficient submenus. **Pop-up menus** can appear anywhere on the screen. Many of these menus are **context-sensitive**—the choices they offer depend on the context.

There are many differences between Windows and Mac OS, but the two have user interfaces that are more alike than different—especially when working with cross-platform applications such as Microsoft Office and Adobe Photoshop. Many users effortlessly switch back and forth between the two operating systems every day.

Why WIMP Won

> The first principle of human interface design,
> whether for a **doorknob** or a **computer**,
> is to keep in mind the **human being** who wants to use it.
> **The technology is subservient to that goal**.
> —Donald Norman, in *The Art of Human-Computer Interface Design*

Graphical user interfaces with windows, icons, menus, and pointing devices (collectively known as *WIMP*) offer several clear advantages from the user's point of view:

▶ *They're intuitive*. Visual metaphors like trash cans and folders are easier for people to understand and learn than typed commands. Users feel safe learning by trial and error, because it's usually easy to predict the results of each action.

▶ *They're consistent*. GUI applications have the same user interface as their operating systems, so users don't need to learn new ways of doing things whenever they switch applications. Many Macintosh and Windows users have mastered dozens of applications without ever consulting a manual.

- *They're forgiving.* Almost every dialog box includes a Cancel button, enabling the user to say, in effect, "Never mind." The **Undo command** can almost always take back the last command, restoring everything the way it was before the current command was issued.
- *They're protective.* When you're about to do something that may have unpleasant consequences (such as replacing the revised version of your term paper with an older version), the software opens a dialog box, reminding you to make sure you're doing what you want before you proceed.
- *They're flexible.* Users who prefer to keep their hands on the keyboard can use keyboard shortcuts instead of mouse movements to invoke most commands. Most actions can be accomplished in several different ways; each user can, in effect, customize the user interface.

Of course, all of this user-friendliness doesn't come free. GUIs and friendly operating systems require more expensive graphics display systems, more memory, more disk space, faster processors, and more complex software. Character-based operating systems have minimal hardware requirements when compared with just about any GUI operating system or shell. But steadily falling hardware prices have made even the least expensive PCs powerful enough to handle GUIs.

Character-based interfaces aren't dead. They're common in VCRs, cell phones, microwave ovens, stereos, and other consumer devices with limited memory and limited options for users. They're also widely used in applications built on older computer systems and in applications that involve transmitting data through networks. In fact, the Internet explosion has fueled growth in popularity of several versions of UNIX, a character-based operating system that is older than any of the operating systems we've looked at so far.

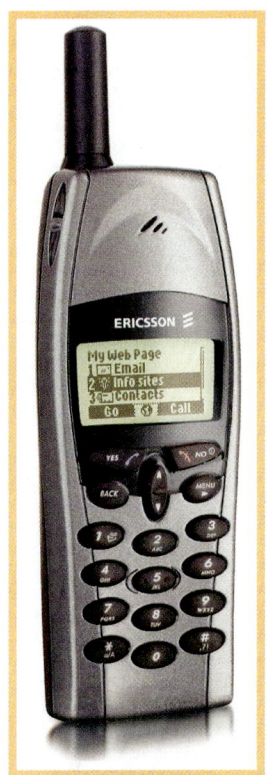

Many consumer devices today, including VCRs, cell phones, and pagers, use character-based user interfaces.

Multiple User Operating Systems: UNIX and Linux

Because of its historical ties to academic and government research sites, the Internet is heavily populated with computers running the **UNIX** operating system. UNIX, developed at Bell Labs in the time before PCs, enables a timesharing computer to communicate with several other computers or terminals at one time. UNIX has long been the operating system of choice for workstations and mainframes in research and academic settings. In recent years it has taken root in many business environments. In spite of competition from Microsoft, UNIX is still the most widely available multiuser operating system today. Some form of UNIX is available for personal computers, workstations, servers, mainframes, and supercomputers.

Unlike the other operating systems listed here, UNIX isn't owned and controlled by a single company. Many commercial brands of UNIX are available, including Sun's Solaris, Hewlett Packard's HP-UX, and IBM's AIX. Linux, described at the beginning of this chapter, is widely distributed for free and supported without cost by a devoted, technically savvy group of users.

At its heart, in all its versions, UNIX is a command-line, character-based operating system. The command-line interface is similar to that of MS-DOS, although the commands aren't the same. For most tasks the UNIX command-line interface feels like a single-user system, even when many users are *logged in*—connected to and using the system. Until recently, some knowledge of UNIX commands was necessary for taking advantage of most Internet services. The character-based UNIX interface is still widely used on Internet servers. The User's View box, *Connecting to a Multiuser UNIX System*, shows how you might use a command-line interface to connect to a multiuser mainframe UNIX system from a terminal. Like the other User's View boxes in this book, it's designed to give you a peek at the process, not a tutorial.

Today's UNIX systems don't just work with typed commands. Several companies, including Sun and IBM, market UNIX variations and shells with graphical interfaces. The User's View box, *Using a Linux GUI*, shows a short Linux session with a GUI shell that looks like a cross between Microsoft Windows and Mac OS.

116 Chapter 4 Software Basics

The User's View

Connecting to a Multiuser UNIX System

SOFTWARE: UNIX operating system.

THE GOAL: *To log into your school's UNIX mainframe from a terminal.*

1 When you press Return, UNIX displays a system message to indicate that it's waiting for you to log in, that is, to provide an ID and password.

2 You type your login name—the one-word name assigned to your computer account (in this example sanchez) and press Enter or Return.

3 The program then prompts you to enter your password so the host computer can verify your identity. When you type your password, it isn't echoed on the screen.

4 After you press Return, UNIX displays a system message to indicate that you've successfully logged in.

5 This UNIX system assumes you're using a VT-100 terminal (or at least a terminal that can emulate, or imitate, a VT-100)—the default type. When you press Return without typing anything else, you're saying that the VT-100 default settings will work with your terminal.

6 On this particular UNIX system you can launch a menu program that enables you to access common commands through menus. But you'll stick with the command-line interface for this example.

```
UNIX(r) System V Release 4.0

login: sanchez
Password:
AFS (R) 3.4 Login
================================================================
=Welcome to node ai.asu.edu - Sparc 20 1000 running Solaris 2.3=
        =This system is only for use authorized by ASU=
================================================================

You have mail.
Terminal type is vt100
Erase is Backspace
type 'menu' without quotes and press the enter key for our menu

ai > ls
AppleVolumes        Mail            dead.letter
Backup              Work            mbox
School              Reports         News
booklist            saved.notes     readme
ai > pine
```

7 This UNIX system responds to commands typed after the ai *prompt*. Different systems have different prompts, but they all mean the same thing: the system is waiting for you to type a command.

8 You type LS to list the files in your current directory. If you misspell or mistype the command, the system responds with an *error message* telling you, in effect, that it doesn't recognize the command. But since you typed it correctly, the system responds by displaying a multicolumn list of files.

Chapter 4 Software Basics 117

The User's View

Using a Linux GUI

SOFTWARE: KDE, Linux, and Corel® WordPerfect® (part of the Corel® WordPerfect® Suite).

THE GOAL: To open and print a term paper, this time with Linux. You'll use KDE, a shell that puts a graphical desktop environment between you and the Linux command-line environment. Then, for the sake of comparison, you'll repeat part of the process with a command-line interface.

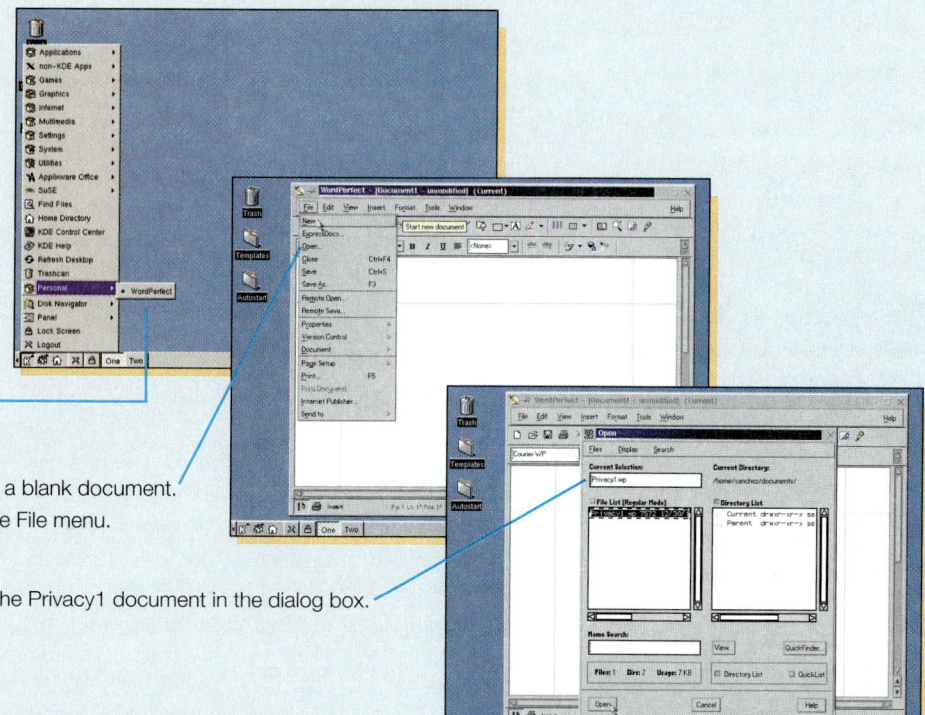

1 KDE has a customizable graphical user interface; here it's configured with familiar features of Windows and the Macintosh OS. You select WordPerfect from the personal pop-up menu that resembles the Windows Start menu.

2 WordPerfect opens with a blank document. You select Open from the File menu.

3 You select the Privacy1 document in the dialog box.

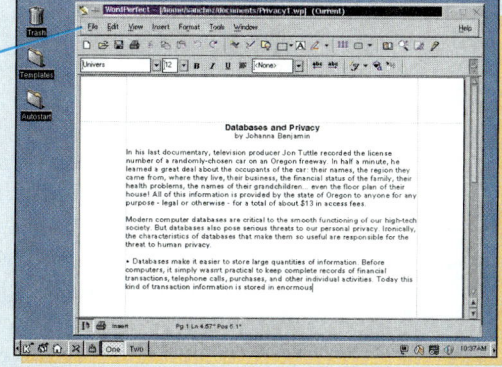

4 When the document opens, you select Print from the File menu, respond to the dialog box, close WordPerfect, and wait for your printout. You'd be done now, except . . .

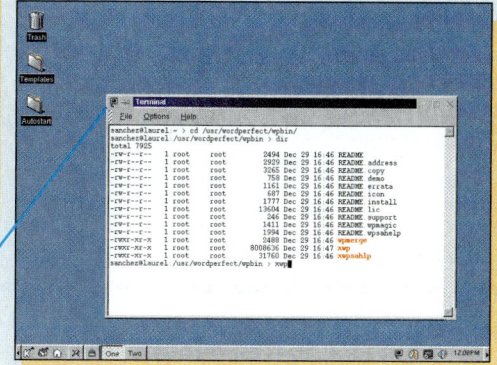

5 You decide to test your Linux literacy by launching the program again, but this time using the operating system's command-line interface. You use a terminal program to connect to a server called Laurel; you type commands to locate the directory and launch WordPerfect.

Hardware and Software Platforms

In most electronic devices the operating system operates invisibly and anonymously. But some operating systems, especially those in PCs, are recognized by name and reputation. The most well-known operating system platforms include:

- *Microsoft Windows XP.* This is Microsoft's flagship product introduced in 2001. For years Microsoft has sold two very different versions of Windows: one for home users and one for businesses. With Microsoft XP, the two product lines have merged into one. There are still different versions of Windows, including one especially designed for servers—computer systems that serve data and programs to networked PCs. But all of these products are based on the same core programs.
- *Microsoft Windows Millennium Edition (Windows ME).* This is Microsoft's last "consumer" operating system before XP. Previous versions of this OS include Windows 98, Windows 95, and Windows 3.1; all are still widely used.
- *Microsoft Windows 2000* and *Windows NT.* These are the predecessors to Windows XP; they were aimed at networked computers that need features not found in the consumer version of Windows.
- *Microsoft Windows CE.* This stripped-down Windows variant is designed mostly for handheld computers—especially the Pocket PC, a Microsoft standard for handheld computers that competes directly with Palm's operating system (see following). Other versions of Win CE have been embedded into car accessories, televisions, and other electronic devices. Several other companies make operating systems for consumer devices and PDAs. But unlike Windows CE, most of these are designed to work on specific devices rather than whole classes of devices.
- *Palm OS.* This OS, originally developed for the Palm Pilot, is now used in handheld devices manufactured by many companies, including Palm, Handspring, Sony, and IBM. Its pen-based user interface is intuitive and convenient to use. The Palm OS has communication capabilities that make it easy to transfer data between a handheld device and another computer. Palm OS is now available in phones and other communication devices.
- *Mac OS X (10).* OS X is the completely new operating system for the Mac introduced in 2001. On the surface OS X sports a stylish, animated user interface that looks strikingly different than previous Mac operating systems. Underneath its friendly exterior OS X is built on UNIX, the powerful OS known for security and stability rather than simplicity. OS X runs only on Macintosh hardware.
- *Mac OS 9.* This is the last in a long line that started with the original Macintosh operating system in 1984. OS 9 and its predecessors run only on Macs.
- *Linux, Sun's Solaris, and other UNIX variations.* Some form of UNIX or LINUX can be found on PCs, Macs, workstations, supercomputers, mainframes, and a variety of other devices. Linux is especially popular because it is free—and freely supported by its partisans. Since Linux doesn't offer as many applications programs as Windows, some people use dual-boot PCs that can switch back and forth between Windows and Linux by simply rebooting.
- *IBM's OS/2.* Originally designed in partnership with Microsoft, OS/2 has been losing market share since IBM took over sole control of the product. OS/2 is now only being updated for existing corporate customers and is no longer in active development. In the operating system wars, even Big Blue has trouble competing with the marketing power of Microsoft.

Operating systems by themselves aren't very helpful to people. They need application software so they can do useful work. But application software can't exist by itself; it needs to be built on some kind of platform. People often use the term **platform** to describe the combination of hardware and operating system software on which application software is built.

The trends are unmistakable. In the early days of the personal computer revolution, there were dozens of different platforms—machines from Apple, Commodore, Tandy, Texas Instruments, Atari, Coleco, and other companies. All of these products have

Compatibility issues: Hardware platforms and software environments. Most personal computers today are built on what's sometimes called the Wintel platform: Some form of the Windows OS running on an Intel (or compatible) CPU. The Macintosh platform—Mac OS software running on PowerPC processors—makes up a much smaller segment of the market. The Linux OS can run on many hardware platforms, including Intel and PowerPC processors, but different versions of Linux aren't necessarily compatible. Other hardware and software platforms represent smaller shares of the market.

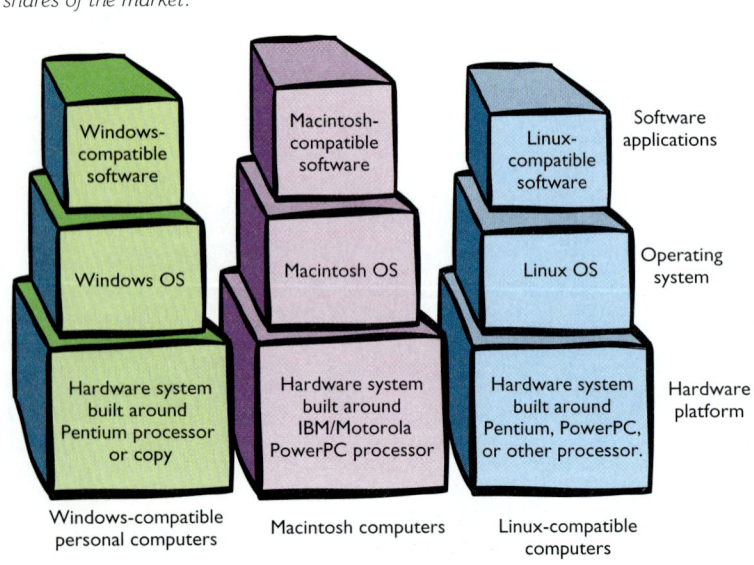

vanished from the marketplace, sometimes taking their parent companies with them. Today's market for new PC hardware and software is dominated by three general platforms: Windows in all its variations, the Mac OS, and various versions of UNIX. UNIX isn't often found in desktop PCs; it's mostly used in servers and high-end workstations. While the Mac commands a hefty share of specialized markets like graphic design, publishing, music, multimedia, and education, it runs far behind Windows in the massive corporate desktop market.

To compete in a Windows-dominated world, Apple works with other companies to offer **emulation** options to make Windows and DOS software run on Macintoshes. One technique involves *software emulation*; a software program creates a *simulated* Windows machine in the Mac, translating all Windows-related instructions into signals the Mac's operating system and CPU can understand. But translation takes time, so software emulation isn't adequate when speed is critical. The other solution, *hardware emulation*, involves adding a circuit board containing an Intel-compatible CPU and additional PC hardware. This board effectively puts a second computer in the Mac's system unit. Emulation technology isn't unique to the Macintosh; there are emulation programs, for example, that enable Windows and Mac programs to run on UNIX-based Sun workstations. Emulation blurs the lines between platforms and enables users to avoid having to choose a single operating system and user interface.

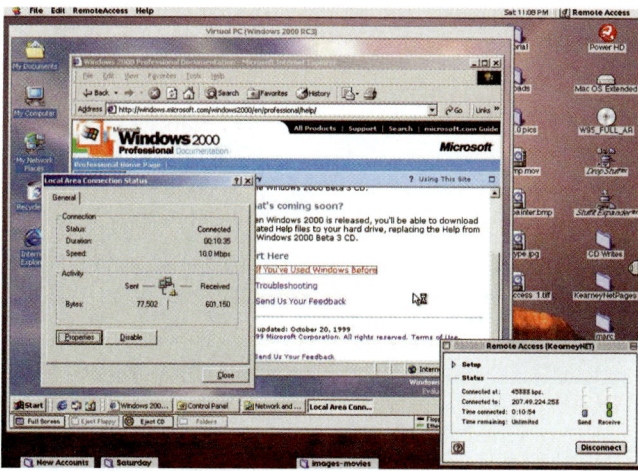

Emulation software enables software written for one computer platform to be used on another. *For example, this Macintosh can run Macintosh and Windows programs simultaneously—and transfer data back and forth between them—using Virtual PC from Connectrix.*

Tomorrow's User Interfaces

As attractive and popular as today's graphical user interfaces are, they're not likely to reign forever. Future user interfaces will be built around technologies that are still in development today. Here are some likely candidates:

> I **hate** computers. **Telepathy** would be better.
> —John Perry Barlow, writer and cofounder of the Electronic Frontier Foundation

- *The end of applications.* As more programs take advantage of interapplication communication, the boundaries between individual applications are likely to blur. Future computer users may not think in terms of word processors, spreadsheets, and such; they'll just use their computers like we use pencils today—as all-purpose tools.
- *Network applications.* With the growing importance of the Internet and other networks, future applications may be more tied to networks than to desktop computer platforms. Computer users are spending less time on their desktops and more time on the Web. Microsoft has responded to that trend with .NET, a strategy that blurs the line between the Web and Microsoft's operating systems and applications. As .NET evolves, more and more software components will be delivered by the network rather than residing on the desktop. Microsoft's .NET strategy is a response to the popularity of **Java**, a platform-neutral computer language developed by Sun Microsystems for use on multiplatform networks. Programs written in Java can run on computers running Windows, Macintosh, UNIX, and other operating systems, provided those computers have **Java virtual machine** software installed. Java **applets**—miniature application pieces designed to work with other applications or applets—are routinely included in World Wide Web pages today to add animation and interactivity. As this technology matures, it may make it possible for computer users to do their work without knowing—or caring—where in the world their software is.
- *Natural-language interfaces.* It's just a matter of time before we'll be able to communicate with computers in English, Spanish, Russian, Japanese, or some other natural language. Today many computers can reliably read subsets of the English language or can be trained to understand spoken English commands and text. Tomorrow's machines should be able to handle much day-to-day work through a natural-language interface, written or spoken. Natural-language processing is discussed in more depth in later chapters.
- *Agents.* Artificial intelligence research will lead to intelligent **agents** that "live" in our computers and act as digital secretaries, anticipating our requests, filling in details in our work, searching networks for critical information, and adjusting the computerized workspace to fit our needs. Today's software agents only begin to suggest future possibilities. The last chapter of this book

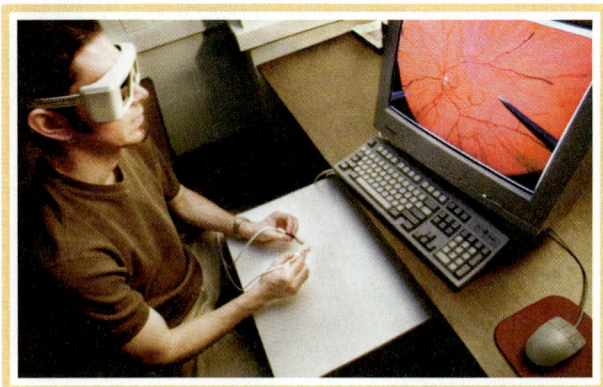 

Virtual reality is used for work and for play; here are two examples. This researcher (left) practices virtual surgery using a type of software that may allow surgeons to practice before performing difficult operations. It may also someday allow surgeons to perform operations on patients thousands of miles away. This virtual thrill ride (right) of Monument Valley, Arizona offers low-risk adventure through simulation software.

describes tomorrow's agents and other futuristic user interface technologies, including the technology of virtual reality.

- *Virtual realities.* Further into the future, many experts predict that user interfaces will become so sophisticated that we'll be hard-pressed to detect the difference between the real world outside the computer and the **virtual reality** created by the computer, except that the virtual reality will enable us to do things that we can't do on the physical plane. Some computer games today provide surprisingly convincing simulations of the experience of driving a car or flying a plane. These games represent the tip of a gigantic iceberg of research into virtual reality software. More sophisticated virtual reality interfaces can be achieved today with specially designed hardware—for input, a glove or body suit equipped with motion sensors, and for output, a helmet with eye-sized screens whose views change as the helmet moves. This equipment, when coupled with appropriate software, enables the user to explore an artificial world of data as if it were three-dimensional physical space. Today's clumsy virtual reality technology is a long way from living up to its name; virtual reality illusions are interesting, but they're poor substitutes for reality. Still, virtual reality has practical applications: Virtual walk-throughs are used by architects and engineers to preview buildings and mechanical assemblies; virtual reality models are used for education and simulations, and virtual worlds are popping up in amusement parks and arcades.

The best known example of the kind of virtual reality researchers are working toward is the Holodeck on TV's *Star Trek*. The Holodeck can create absolutely convincing simulations of anything from a Sherlock Holmes detective story to a 24th-century antimatter generator. No keyboards or screens are in sight; the user interface is a three-dimensional artificial world full of people, places, and things—real or imaginary—that can be seen, touched, talked to, and controlled by one or more "users." Far-fetched? Absolutely. Possible? Maybe. When? Don't sell your keyboard yet....

Rules of Thumb

Green Computing

When compared with heavy industries such as automobiles and energy, the computer industry is relatively easy on the environment. But the manufacture and use of computer hardware and software does have a significant environmental impact, especially now that so many of us are using the technology. Fortunately, you have some control over the environmental impact of your computing activities. Here are a few tips to help minimize your impact:

- **Buy green equipment.** Today's computer equipment uses relatively little energy, but as world energy resources dwindle, less is always better. Many modern computers and peripherals are specifically designed to consume less energy. Look for the Environmental Protection Agency's Energy Star certification on the package.
- **Use a laptop.** Portable computers use far less energy than desktop computers. They're engineered to preserve precious battery power. But if you use a laptop, keep it plugged in when you have easy access to an electrical outlet. Batteries wear out from repeated usage, and their disposal can cause environmental problems of a different sort. (If you're the kind of person who always needs to have the latest and greatest technology, a laptop isn't the greenest choice for you, because laptops are difficult or impossible to upgrade.)
- **Take advantage of energy-saving features.** Most modern systems can be set up to go to sleep (a sort of suspended animation state that uses just enough power to preserve RAM) and turn off the monitor or printer when idle for more than an hour or so. If your equipment has automatic energy-saving features, use them. You'll save energy and money.
- **Turn it off when you're away.** If you're just leaving your computer for an hour or two, you won't save much energy by turning the CPU off. But if you're leaving it for more than a few hours and it's not on duty receiving faxes and email, you'll do the environment a favor by turning it off or putting it to sleep.
- **Save energy, not screens.** Your monitor is probably the biggest power guzzler in your system. A screen saver can be fun to watch, but it doesn't save your screen, and it doesn't save energy, either. As long as your monitor is displaying an image, it's consuming power. Use sleep.
- **Print only once.** Don't print out a rough draft just to proofread; try to get it clean onscreen. (Most people find this one hard to follow 100% of the time; some errors just don't seem to show up until you print.)
- **Recycle your waste products.** When you do have to reprint that 20-page report because of a missing paragraph on page 1, recycle the flawed printout. When your laser printer's toner cartridge runs dry, ship or deliver it to one of the many companies that recycle cartridges. They may even pay you a few dollars for the empty cartridge. When your portable's battery dies, follow the manufacturer's instructions for recycling it. While you're in recycling mode, don't forget all those computer magazines and catalogs.
- **Pass it on.** When you outgrow a piece of hardware or software, don't throw it away. Donate it to a school, civic organization, family member, or friend who can put it to good use.
- **Send bits, not atoms.** It takes far more resources to send a letter by truck, train, or plane than to send an electronic message through the Internet. Whenever possible, use your modem instead of your printer.

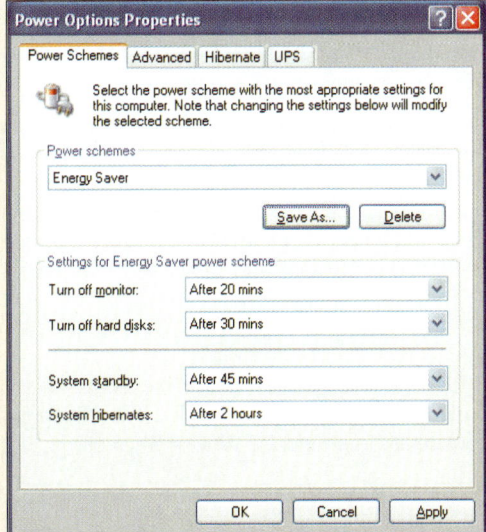

Windows and Macintosh operating systems have energy-saver control panels that can be set to automatically switch the monitor and CPU to low-power sleep modes after specified periods of inactivity.

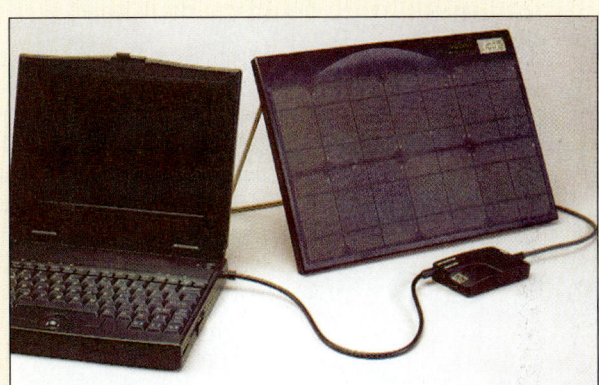

Portable computers consume far less energy than desktop models; this one is powered by the sun using a Neptune Solar Panel.

CrossCurrents

'Read the Manual!' What Manual?

Stephen Manes

Stephen Manes, PC World *Contributing Editor and cohost of PBS series Digital Duo, has been using computers since the days when computer manuals came packaged with new computer software and hardware. In this column from the June 2001 issue of* PC World *magazine, Manes discusses the disappearance of the manual from the box—and what it means to those of us who use this technology.*

Customer service shouldn't begin when you have a problem. It should start when a product is built, so that you don't have to futz around on the Web or wait on hold to get answers. One form of that service is good product design. Another is a great manual.

A what? As hardware and software grow dizzyingly more complicated, the manual—if any—now amounts to a scrap of tissue. The online help that supposedly replaces it inevitably runs out of information just as you close in on what you need to know.

Back in 1982, my first IBM PC—with 64KB of memory, a 4.77-MHz 8088 processor, and DOS—came with loose-leaf manuals that were boxed in linen and full of useful examples. My new 1-GHz Dell Pentium III came with its own box of documentation, but no linen and not much information—even if you count a grand total of ten pages on Microsoft Office 2000 that tout new features but offer virtually no details on how they actually work.

A Vicious Circle

Documentation is getting worse because companies treat it the way they do customer service—as a cost center. Their miserly policies push expenses out to the users. It's a vicious circle: Companies refuse to spend a nickel more than they have to for documentation; faced with useless help, customers learn not to bother with it; and after discovering from surveys and focus groups that nobody uses the manuals, companies make them even worse.

That merry-go-round sends users to sources that actually explain things. Since Microsoft makes money selling books designed to fill the gaping holes in its abysmal manuals, it's no wonder some ugly adjectives characterize documentation circa 2001:

- **Unspecific.** To cut costs, vendors release one-size-fits-all docs to cover 17 similar but not identical models. Before you can use the manual, you need to figure out which facts apply to the product you have—assuming the information is there at all. Want a challenge? Try to get details on the particular CD-RW or DVD drive the computer maker stuck into your machine.

- **Immovable.** Several things are wrong with manuals meant to be read on computer screens. How do you proceed when you need information on what to do when your machine won't boot? Since my computer screen doesn't face my printer or scanner, it's not exactly easy to read online documentation while I'm fiddling with peripherals' front panels. The latest affront to common sense comes from Kyocera, which delivers the detailed manual for its nifty new Palm-based Smartphone on CD-ROM. Maybe you're supposed to bring along a laptop whenever you use the phone.

- **Incomplete.** You need two basic pieces of information to get a home networking gateway to work: the proper settings for your broadband provider, and those for Windows networking. Unless you have experience with networks, you have little chance of getting the settings right from the meager info the ISPs and Microsoft supply. Yet not one of the gateways I've tried offers any real help in these two essential areas. Listen up, manufacturers: Decent documentation might well reduce the number of returns you get from people who simply can't figure out how to set up your product.

- **Unusable.** Professional indexing by a human being has become a quaint concept. At best, you can expect to get full-text searching in an online document, but that's a poor substitute for a real index. More often, though, you get a travesty generated by some half-bright indexing program—or no index at all.

- **Unreal.** How many times have you followed step-by-step directions that were flat-out wrong? If you're lucky, the Readme file or an errata sheet will point out some of the howlers. Better idea: Manufacturers should get the documentation right in the first place, particularly when it's in online form.

The need for documentation grows more acute as consumer products go digital and inherit the complexity of PCs. Much of the problem is poor design: You shouldn't have to read a manual just to dope out some simple function of a VCR or coffeemaker.

But you do. Manuals for those devices stink, too, but at least they don't come on CD-ROM—so far.

DISCUSSION QUESTIONS

1. Why do you think computer manuals have become so scarce?
2. Do you think CD-ROM and Web documentation is an adequate substitute for manuals? Why or why not?

Summary

Software provides the communication link between humans and their computers. Because software is soft—stored in memory rather than hard-wired into the circuitry—it can easily be modified to meet the needs of the computer user. By changing software, you can change a computer from one kind of tool into another.

Most software falls into one of three broad categories: compilers and other translator programs, software applications, and system software. A compiler is a software tool that enables programs written in English-like languages such as BASIC and C to be translated into the zeros and ones of the machine language the computer understands. A compiler frees the programmer from the tedium of machine-language programming, making it easier to write quality programs with fewer bugs. But even with the best translators, programming is a little like communicating with an alien species. It's a demanding process that requires more time and mental energy than most people are willing or able to invest.

Fortunately, software applications make it easy for most computer users today to communicate their needs to the computer without learning programming. Applications simulate and extend the properties of familiar real-world tools like typewriters, paintbrushes, and file cabinets, making it possible for people to do things with computers that would be difficult or impossible otherwise. Integrated software packages combine several applications in a single unified package, making it easy to switch between tools. For situations when a general commercial program won't do the job, programmers for businesses and public institutions develop vertical-market and custom packages.

Whether you're writing programs or simply using them, the computer's operating system is functioning behind the scenes, translating your software's instructions into messages that the hardware can understand. An operating system serves as the computer's business manager, taking care of the hundreds of details that need to be handled to keep the computer functioning. A timesharing operating system has the particularly challenging job of serving multiple users concurrently, monitoring the machine's resources, keeping track of each user's account, and protecting the security of the system and each user's data. Many of those system-related problems that the operating system can't solve directly can be handled by utility programs. Popular operating systems today include several versions of Microsoft Windows, the Mac OS, and several versions of UNIX.

Applications, utilities, programming languages, and operating systems all must, to varying degrees, communicate with the user. A program's user interface is a critical factor in that communication. User interfaces have evolved over the years to the point where sophisticated software packages can be operated by people who know little about the inner workings of the computer. A well-designed user interface shields the user from the bits and bytes, creating an onscreen façade or shell that makes sense to the user. Today the computer industry has moved away from the tried-and-true command-line interfaces toward a friendlier graphical user interface that uses windows, icons, mice, and pull-down menus in an intuitive, consistent environment. Tomorrow's user interfaces are likely to depend more on voice, three-dimensional graphics, and animation to create an artificial reality.

Chapter Review

▼ Key Terms

algorithm (p. 101)
application suite (office suite) (p. 107)
booting (p. 112)
bug (p. 101)
character-based interface (p. 113)
command-line interface (p. 113)
compatibility (p. 105)
compiler (p. 104)
concurrent processing (p. 109)
context-sensitive menus (p. 114)
copyrighted software (p. 106)
custom application (p. 108)
debugging (p. 101)
desktop (p. 113)
dialog box (p. 114)
document (p. 113)
documentation (p. 105)
emulation (p. 119)

folder (p. 113)
graphical user interface (GUI) (p. 113)
hierarchical menus (p. 114)
high-level language (p. 104)
icon (p. 113)
integrated software (p. 107)
Java (p. 119)
Linux (p. 99)
machine language (p. 104)
Mac OS (p. 113)
menu (p. 113)
menu-driven interface (p. 113)
Microsoft Windows (p. 114)
MS-DOS (p. 113)
multitasking (p. 109)
natural language (p. 104)
open source software (p. 99)
operating system (OS) (p. 108)

platform (p. 118)
pop-up menus (p. 114)
public domain software (p. 106)
pull-down menu (p. 114)
shareware (p. 106)
shell (p. 114)
software license (p. 106)
system software (p. 108)
Undo command (p. 115)
UNIX (p. 115)
upgrade (p. 105)
user interface (p. 112)
utility program (p. 110)
vertical-market application (p. 108)
virtual memory (p. 109)
virtual reality (p. 120)
window (p. 113)

124 Chapter 4 Software Basics

▼ Interactive Quiz Questions

1. The *Computer Confluence* CD-ROM contains self-test quiz questions related to this chapter, including multiple choice, true or false, and matching questions.
2. The *Computer Confluence* Web site, www.prenhall.com/beekman, contains self-test exercises related to this chapter. Follow the instructions for taking a quiz. After you've completed your quiz, you can email the results to your instructor.

The Web site also contains open-ended discussion questions called Internet Explorations. Discuss one or more of the Internet Exploration questions at the section for this chapter.

▼ Review Questions

1. Define or describe each of the key terms listed in the Key Terms section. Check your answers in the glossary.
2. What is the relationship between a program and an algorithm?
3. Most computer software falls into one of three categories: compilers and other translator programs, software applications, and system software. Describe and give examples of each.
4. Which must be loaded first into the computer's memory, the operating system or software applications? Why?
5. Write an algorithm for changing a flat tire. Check your algorithm carefully for errors and ambiguities. Then have a classmate or your instructor check it. How did your results compare?
6. Describe several functions of a single-user operating system. Describe several additional functions of a multiuser operating system.
7. What does it mean when software is called IBM-compatible or Macintosh-compatible? What does this have to do with the operating system?
8. Why is the user interface such an important part of software?
9. What is a graphical user interface? How does it differ from a character-based interface? What are the advantages of each?
10. What are the three main platforms for desktop computers today? Briefly describe each of them.

▼ Discussion Questions

1. In what way is writing instructions for a computer more difficult than writing instructions for a person? In what way is it easier?
2. How would using a computer be different if it had no operating system? How would programming be different?
3. Speculate about the user interface of a typical computer in the year 2010. How would this user interface differ from those used in today's computers?
4. If you had the resources to design a computer with a brand new user interface, what would your priorities be? Make a rank-ordered list of the qualities you'd like to have in your user interface.
5. How do you feel about the open software movement? Would you be willing to volunteer your time to write software or help users for free?

▼ Projects

1. Write a report about available computer applications in your field of study or in your chosen profession.
2. Take an inventory of computer applications available in your computer lab. Describe the major uses for each application.

Sources and Resources

Books

Just for Fun: The Story of an Accidental Revolutionary, by Linus Torvalds and David Diamond (New York: Harperbusiness, 2001). *Red Herring* Executive Editor convinced Linus Torvalds to tell his story. The result is this book, a quirky collection of tidbits from the life of the creator of Linux.

Rebel Code: Linux and the Open Source Revolution, by Glyn Moody (New York: Perseus, 2001). This book tells the Linux story in a style that's more conventional, and for many readers, more readable, than the Torvalds/Diamond book.

Windows XP for Dummies, by Andy Rothbone (Indianapolis: Hungry Minds, 2001). The *Dummies* series that started with *DOS*

between lines, indents, tab stops, and *justification* (alignment of text on a line). Still other commands enable you to specify and format multiple columns, tables, footnotes, and *headers* and *footers*—blocks that appear at the top and bottom of every page. You can create *style sheets* containing custom styles for each of the common elements in a document, making it easy to apply (and modify) complex formatting combinations throughout a document. *Automatic formatting (autoformat)* features can take care of some formatting chores—such as indenting numbered lists—while the text is entered.

- *Proofreading the document.* A built-in *spelling checker* can compare the words in your document with the words in a disk-based dictionary, flagging suspect words as potential misspellings and possibly suggesting corrections. Some word processors can fix common misspellings on the fly using *automatic correction (autocorrect).* *Grammar and style checker software* analyzes each word in context, checking for errors of context ("I wood never have guest"), common grammatical errors ("Ben and me went to Boston"), and stylistic foibles ("The book that is most popular"). In addition to pointing out possible errors and suggesting improvements, it can analyze prose complexity using measurements such as sentence length and paragraph length. This kind of analysis is useful for determining whether your writing style is appropriate for your target audience. But spelling checkers, grammar-and-style-checkers, and other electronic advising systems in today's word processors are far from perfect; good writers use a healthy dose of human judgment along with the computer-generated advice.

These fonts represent just a few of the hundreds of typefaces available for personal computers and printers today. The two symbol fonts given, Symbol and Zapf Dingbats, provide special characters not available with other fonts.

Examples of	12-point size	24-point size
Serif fonts	Times Courier	Times Courier
Sans-serif fonts	Helvetica Avant Garde	Helvetica Avant Garde
Script fonts	Zapf Chancery Kuenstler Script	Zapf Chancery Kuenstler Script
Display fonts	Regular Joe Birch Remedy	Regular Joe Birch Remedy
Symbol fonts (Symbol and Zapf Dingbats)	Σψμβολ ✻❂◻❄✣✺■	Σψμβολ ✻❀◻❄✣✺■

- *Saving the document.* Since RAM is not a permanent storage medium, it's important to regularly *save* your document—that is, create a disk file containing your work in progress. If the power fails, or the computer fails, or you accidentally erase part of the text, you can restart the machine (if necessary) and *open* the saved version of your document—copy it back into RAM—to add or edit text.
- *Printing the document.* A simple command causes single or multiple copies of a document to be printed on the selected printer. Also, most word processors today enable you to create documents for publishing on the Web rather than on paper.

Desktop Publishing

Just as word processing changed the writer's craft in the 1970s, the world of publishing was radically transformed in the 1980s, when Apple introduced its first LaserWriter printer and a new company named Aldus introduced a Macintosh program called PageMaker that could take advantage of that printer's high-resolution output capabilities. Publishing—traditionally an expensive, time-consuming, error-prone process—instantly became a viable enterprise for just about anyone with a computer and a little cash.

The User's View

Word Processing

SOFTWARE: *Microsoft Word.*

THE GOAL: To enter, edit, format the text of a classic work to be read in an English class presentation. Most applications today enable you to do common tasks using either menu commands or onscreen buttons. This example illustrates both techniques.

1 You hurriedly enter the text, forgetting to include the title and author at the beginning. You decide to add them to the bottom and move them to the top. You **select text** to be edited using the mouse or the keyboard. Selected text appears highlighted on the screen.

2 Choosing the Cut command from the Edit menu, you tell the computer to cut the selected text from the document and place it in the **Clipboard**—a special portion of memory for temporarily holding information for later use.

3 After using the mouse or arrow keys to reposition the cursor at the beginning of the document, you select the Paste command from the Edit menu. The computer places a copy of the Clipboard's contents at the insertion point; the text below the cursor moves down to make room for the inserted text. This type of **cut-and-paste** editing is possible in most application programs; you can also use it to move text from one document to another. To speed up the process, most applications enable **drag-and-drop** editing so you can simply drag (with the mouse) selected text to another part of the document.

4 To italicize the title *Walden*, you select the characters to be changed . . .

5 . . . choose the Font command from the Format menu . . .

Chapter 5 Computer Applications 131

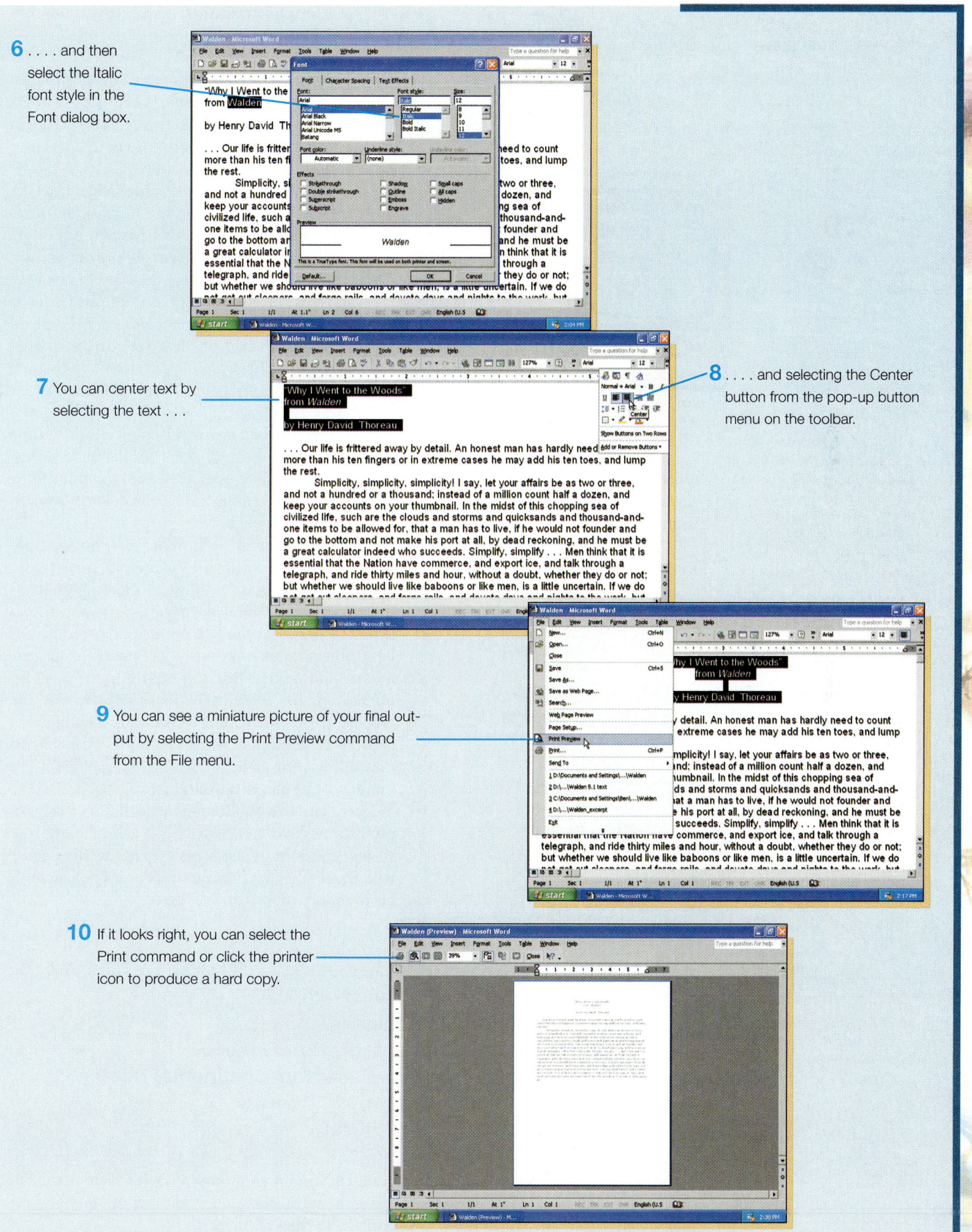

6 . . . . and then select the Italic font style in the Font dialog box.

7 You can center text by selecting the text . . .

8 . . . . and selecting the Center button from the pop-up button menu on the toolbar.

9 You can see a miniature picture of your final output by selecting the Print Preview command from the File menu.

10 If it looks right, you can select the Print command or click the printer icon to produce a hard copy.

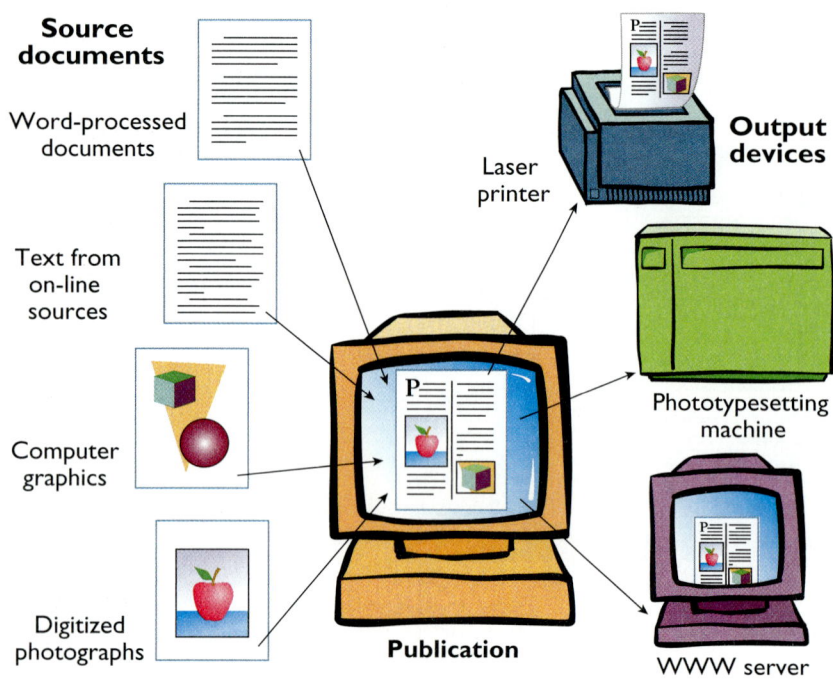

Source documents are merged in a publication document, which can be printed on a laser or inkjet printer, printed on a high-resolution phototypesetter, or even published on the World Wide Web.

The first steps in the publishing process involve producing *source documents*—articles, chapters, drawings, maps, charts, and photographs that are to appear in the publication. Desktop publishers generally use standard word processors and graphics programs to produce most source documents. They use scanners with image editing software to transform photographs and hand-drawn images into computer-readable documents. *Page-layout software*, such as QuarkXpress, PageMaker, or InDesign, is used to combine the various source documents into a coherent, visually appealing publication. Pages are generally laid out one at a time on screen, although most programs have options for automating multiple-page document layout. Documents can be printed on paper, published on the Web, or distributed electronically using "paperless" publishing formats like Adobe's *PDF (portable document format)*.

More than any other application, desktop publishing was responsible for the initial acceptance by large corporations of computers with graphical user interfaces. Desktop publishing saves time and money for corporations large and small and helps to reduce the quantity of publication errors.

But the real winners in the desktop publishing revolution might turn out to be not big businesses but everyday people with something to say. With commercial TV networks, newspapers, magazines, and book publishers increasingly controlled by a few giant corporations, many media experts worry that the free press guaranteed by our First Amendment is seriously threatened by *de facto* media monopolies. Desktop publishing technology offers hope for every individual's right to publish. Writers, artists, and editors whose work is shunned or ignored by large publishers and mainstream media now have affordable publishing alternatives. The number of small presses, alternative periodicals, and independent Web publications is steadily increasing as publishing costs go down. If, as A. J. Liebling suggested, freedom of the press belongs to the person who owns one, that precious freedom is now accessible to more people than ever before.

Spreadsheets and Other Simulation Software

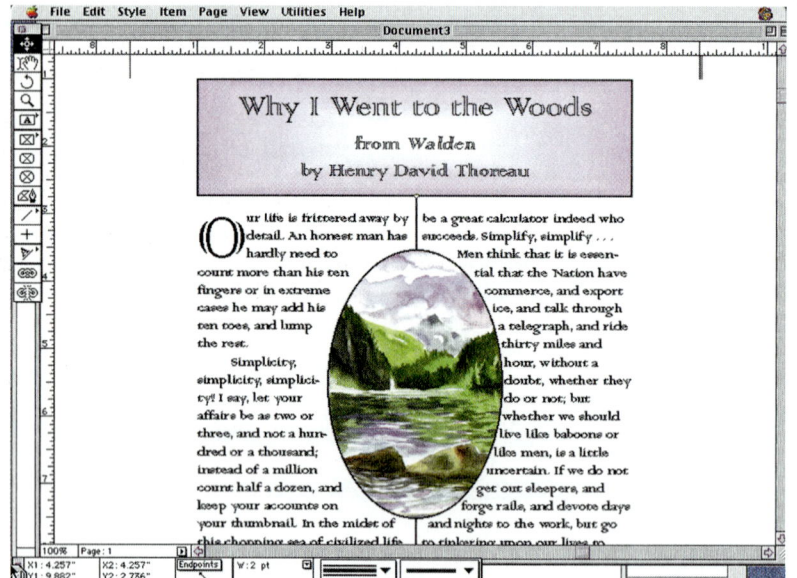

Professional publishing programs, such as QuarkXpress, enable publishers to control precisely the layout of text, graphics, and other elements on pages.

> Compare the **expansion of business** today to the **conquering of the continent** in the nineteenth century. The spreadsheet in that comparison is like the **transcontinental railroad**. It **accelerated the movement,** made it possible, and **changed the course** of the nation.
> —Mitch Kapor, developer of Lotus 1-2-3 spreadsheet software

Numbers are at the heart of applications ranging from accounting to statistical analysis. The most popular number-crunching application is the spreadsheet, but a number of other number manipulation tools are available for solving different types of problems.

Rules of Thumb

Beyond Desktop Tacky!

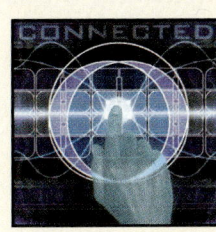

Many first-time users of WYSIWYG word processors and desktop publishing systems become intoxicated with the power at their fingertips. It's easy to get carried away with all those fonts, styles, and sizes and to create a document that makes supermarket tabloids look tasteful. While there's no substitute for a good education in the principles of design, it's easy to avoid tacky-looking documents if you follow a few simple guidelines:

- **Plan before you publish.** Design (or select) a simple, visually pleasing format for your document, and use that format throughout the document.

- **Use appropriate fonts.** Limit your choices to one or two fonts and sizes per page, and be consistent throughout your document. Serif fonts like the one used in the main text of this book generally are good choices for paragraphs of text; the serifs gently guide the reader's eye from letter to letter. Sans-serif fonts, like the one used in the box you are reading, work well for boxed text, tables, headings, and titles. It's generally better to use only one sans-serif font in a document. Make sure all your chosen fonts work properly with your printer.

- **Don't go style-crazy.** Avoid overusing *italics*, **boldface**, ALL CAPS, <u>underlines</u>, and other styles for emphasis. When in doubt, leave it out.

- **Look at your document through your readers' eyes.** Make every picture say something. Don't try to cram too much information on a page. Don't be afraid of white space. Use a format that speaks clearly to your readers. Make sure the main points of your document stand out. Whatever you do, do it for the reader.

- **Learn from the masters.** Study the designs of successful publications. What makes them work? Use design books, articles, and classes to develop your aesthetic skills along with your technical skills. With or without a computer, publishing is an art.

- **Know your limitations.** Desktop publishing technology makes it possible for anyone to produce high-quality documents with a minimal investment of time and money. But your equipment and skills may not be up to the job at hand. For many applications, personal desktop publishing is no match for a professional design artist or typesetter. If you need the best, work with a pro.

- **Remember the message.** Fancy fonts, tasteful graphics, and meticulous design can't turn shoddy ideas into words of wisdom, or lies into the truth. The purpose of publishing is communication; don't try to use technology to disguise the lack of something to communicate.

The Spreadsheet

In the same way a word processor can give a computer user control over words, **spreadsheet software** enables the user to take control of numbers, manipulating them in ways that would be difficult or impossible otherwise. A spreadsheet program can make short work of tasks that involve repetitive calculations: budgeting, investment management, business projections, grade books, scientific simulations, checkbooks, and so on. A spreadsheet can also reveal hidden relationships between numbers, taking much of the guesswork out of financial planning and speculation.

Almost all spreadsheet programs are based on a simple concept: the malleable matrix. A spreadsheet document, called a **worksheet**, typically appears on the screen as a grid of numbered **rows** and alphabetically lettered **columns**. The box representing the intersection of a row and a column is called a **cell**. Every cell in this grid has a unique **address** made up of a row number and column letter. For example, the cell in the upper-left corner of the grid is called cell A1 (column A, row 1). All the cells are empty in a new worksheet; it's up to the user to fill them. Each cell can contain a numeric value, an alphabetic label, or a formula representing a relationship between numbers in other cells.

The User's View

Creating a Simple Worksheet

SOFTWARE: Microsoft Excel.

THE GOAL: To create a computerized version of a worksheet showing projected expenses for one college student's fall term. The design of the worksheet is based on this hand-drawn planning version.

1 The first step is to type descriptive labels for the worksheet title and to label the rows and columns. Typing appears in the **current** or **active cell**—the cell containing the cursor—and in the long window above the worksheet, called the **console** or **formula bar**. You move from cell to cell by clicking with the mouse or by navigating with the keyboard.

2 To make room for row labels, you widen the first column by dragging its border to the right.

3 After typing the labels, you type numeric values to represent dollar values for each category in each month.

4 To change cell formats so numbers are displayed with dollar signs, you select the **range** (rectangular block) of cells by dragging between cells B3 and F11, two opposite corners of the rectangle.

5 Choose the Cells command from the Format menu . . .

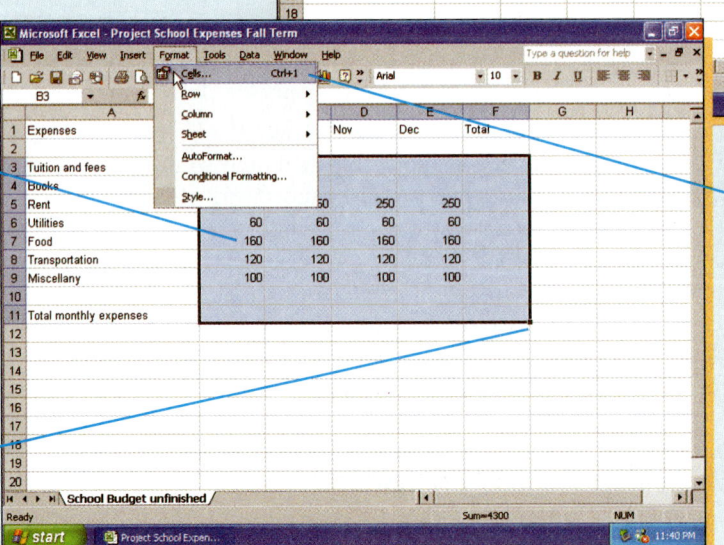

6 ...and then select the Currency format to change the appearance of all values in the range.

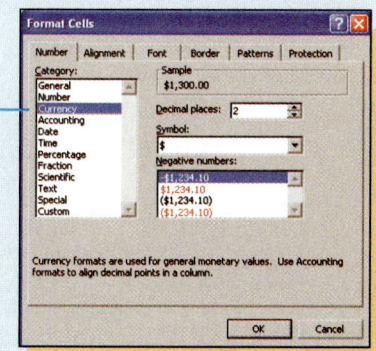

7 You enter a formula to calculate the total expenses for September in cell B11: 5sum(B3:B9). When you press Enter, the formula in the cell is replaced by the calculated value—the sum of the numbers in cells B3 through B9. (The formula is still visible in the formula bar whenever cell B11 is active.)

8 You don't need to repeat this process for the other columns in the worksheet; instead you can replicate this formula in cells C11 through F11. When you select the range of cells from B11 to F11 and apply the Fill Right command, each cell in the block gets a version of this formula automatically adjusted to calculate the total for that cell's column.

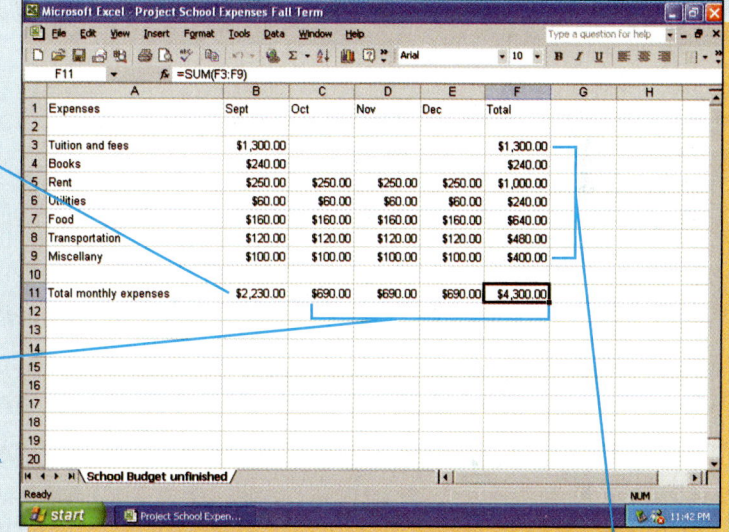

9 A similar process (using the Fill Down command) calculates the totals in column F.

10 After you change the format of some cells to make the worksheet more readable, you decide to change numbers in two of December's cells to enable for holiday gifts and travel.

11 The spreadsheet software automatically recalculates all formulas to reflect the revised input data.

The worksheet may be bigger than what appears on your screen. The program enables you to scroll horizontally and vertically to view the larger matrix. (After Z, columns are labeled with double letters: AA, AB, and so on.)

Values (numbers) are the raw material the spreadsheet software uses to perform calculations. Numbers in worksheet cells can represent wages, test scores, weather data, polling results, or just about anything that can be quantified. To make it easier for people to understand the numbers, most worksheets include labels at the tops of columns and at the edges of rows, such as "Monthly Wages," "Midterm Exam 1," "Average Wind Speed," or "Final Approval Rating." To the computer, these labels are meaningless strings of characters. The label "Total Points" doesn't tell the computer to calculate the total and display it in an adjacent cell; it's just a road sign for human readers. To calculate the total points (or the average wind speed or the final approval rating), the worksheet must contain a formula—a step-by-step procedure for calculating the desired number.

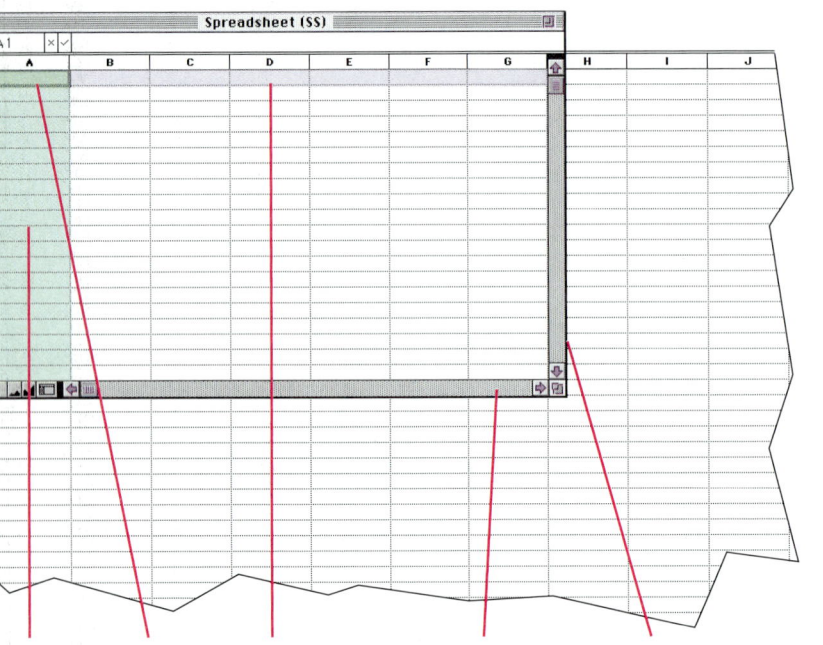

A spreadsheet program is a versatile tool, but it's especially valuable for answering what-if questions: "What if I don't complete the third assignment? How will that affect my chances for getting an A?" "What if I put my savings in a high-yield, tax-sheltered IRA account with a withdrawal penalty? Will I be better off than if I leave it in a low-yield passbook account with no penalty?" "What if I buy a car that gets only 10 miles per gallon instead of a car that gets 40? How much more will I pay altogether for fuel over the next four years?" Because it enables you to change numbers and instantly see the effects of those changes, spreadsheet software streamlines the process of searching for answers to these questions. The User's View box illustrates how you might create a simple worksheet using Microsoft Excel.

Most popular spreadsheet programs include these features:

- *Predefined functions.* A function in a formula instructs the computer to perform some predefined set of calculations. For example, the formula =SQRT(C5) calculates the square root of the number in cell C5. Modern spreadsheet applications have large libraries of predefined functions.
- *Macros.* A spreadsheet's menu of functions, like the menu in a fast-food restaurant, is limited to the most popular selections. For situations where the built-in functions don't fill the bill, most spreadsheets enable the user to capture sequences of steps as reusable macros—custom-designed procedures that you can add to the existing menu of options.
- *Templates.* Even with functions and macros, the process of creating a complex worksheet from scratch can be intimidating. Many users take advantage of worksheet templates that contain labels and formulas but no data values. These reusable templates produce instant answers when you fill in the blanks.
- *Charting capabilities.* Most spreadsheet programs include charting commands that can turn worksheet numbers into charts and graphs automatically. The process of creating a chart is usually as simple as filling in a few blanks in a dialog box. The correct chart can make a set of stale figures come to life, awakening our eyes and brains to trends and relationships that we might not have otherwise seen.

Statistical Software: Beyond Spreadsheets

Spreadsheet software is remarkably versatile, but no program is perfect for every task. Other types of number-manipulation software are available for those situations in which spreadsheets don't quite fit the job. Here are some examples:

- *Accounting and financial management software.* Accounting is a complex concoction of rules, formulas, laws, and traditions, and creating a worksheet to handle the details of the process is difficult and time-consuming. Instead of relying on general-purpose spreadsheets for accounting, most businesses (and many households) use professionally designed **accounting and financial management software.** This specialized software can track income and expenses, chart financial patterns, download bank transaction records, and maintain an audit trail of every transaction. In addition to keeping records, financial management software can automate check writing, bill paying, budgeting, and other routine money matters. Periodic reports and charts can provide detailed answers to questions such as "Where does the money go?" and "How are we doing compared to last year?" Most accounting and financial management programs don't calculate income taxes, but they *can* export records to **tax preparation programs** that do.
- *Mathematics processing software.* Many professionals and students whose mathematical needs go beyond the capabilities of spreadsheets depend on symbolic **mathematics processing software** to grapple with complex equations and calculations. Mathematics processors make it easier for mathematicians to create, manipulate, and solve equations, in much the same way word processors help writers.
- *Statistical analysis software.* **Statistical analysis software** can suggest answers to questions like "Do people who live near nuclear power plants run a higher cancer risk?" by testing the strength of data relationships. Statistical software can also produce graphs showing how two or more variables relate to each other.
- *Scientific visualization software.* **Scientific visualization software** uses shape, location in space, color, brightness, and motion to help us understand relationships that are invisible to us. Scientific visualization takes many forms, all of which involve graphical representation of numerical data. The numbers can be the result of abstract equations, or they can be data gleaned from the real world. Either way, turning the numbers into pictures enables researchers and students to see the unseeable, and sometimes, as a result, to know what was previously unknowable.

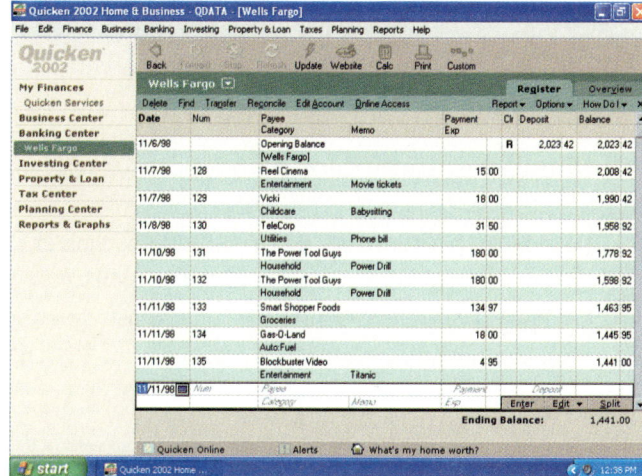

Inexpensive financial management programs for homes and small businesses make the accounting process easier to understand by simulating checks and other familiar documents on the screen. Quicken enables you to track cash, check, and credit card transactions, and use the data in a variety of ways.

Calculated Risks: Computer Modeling and Simulation

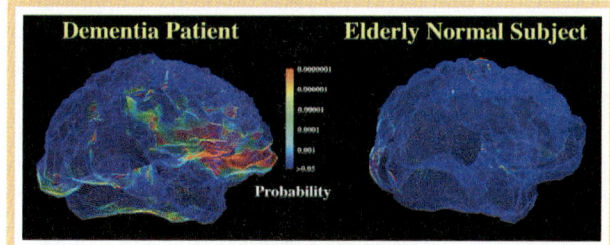
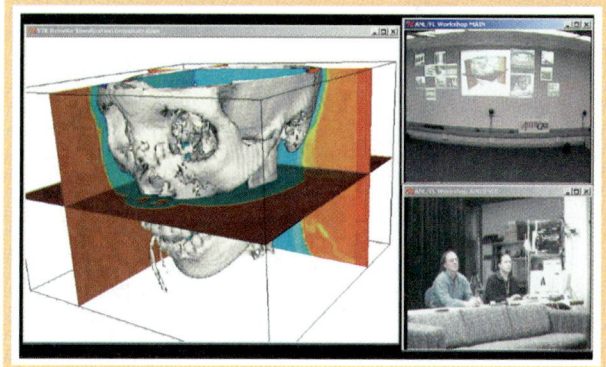

These two visualizations, created at the Laboratory of Neuro Imaging (LONI), map physical differences between a normal human brain and one with a form of dementia (left). Using a tool called Access Grid, researchers work with a shared visualization called the Visible Human (right).

Whether part of a simple worksheet or a complex set of equations, numbers often symbolize real-world phenomena. A well-designed **simulation**, whether constructed with a spreadsheet or another software application, can help people achieve a better understanding of the world outside the computer. A business executive who creates a worksheet to project quarterly profits and losses is simulating changes in the economic world that affect the company. An engineer who uses a mathematics processor to test the stress capacity of a bridge is simulating real-world activity on a real-world bridge.

Computer simulations are widely used for research, forecasting, education, and training. Computer simulations can be safer and less expensive than real-world training and testing. They can also save money. Computer models make visualization possible, and visualization enables researchers and students to see and understand relationships that might otherwise go unnoticed.

The downside of computer simulation can be summed up in three words: Simulation isn't reality. The accuracy of a simulation depends on how closely its mathematical model corresponds to the system being simulated. Mathematical models and simulations are built on assumptions, many of which are difficult or impossible to verify. Some models suffer from faulty assumptions; others contain hidden assumptions that may not even be obvious to their creators; still others go astray simply because of clerical or human errors. **Garbage in, garbage out (GIGO)** is a basic rule of simulation.

A computer simulation, whether generated by a PC spreadsheet or churned out by a supercomputer, can be an invaluable decision-making aid. The risk is that the people who make decisions with computers will turn over too much of their decision-making power to the computer.

Graphics and Multimedia

> **Mastering technology** is only part of what it means to be an artist in the twenty-first century. The other hurdle is **mastering creative expression**, so that art has something substantial to say. **Expression** has been **the one constant** among artists from the Stone Age until now. The only thing that has changed is the **technology**.
> —Steven Holtzman, author of *Digital Mantras*

Computer applications aren't limited to text and numbers. Today millions of people use software tools to work with pictures, sounds, video, and other media types.

Painting and Digital Image Processing

An image on a computer screen is made up of a matrix of **pixels**—tiny dots of white, black, or color arranged in rows. **Painting software** enables you to "paint" pixels on the screen with a pointing device. A typical painting program accepts input from a mouse, joystick, trackball, touch pad, or pen, translating the pointer movements into lines and patterns on the screen. A professional artist might prefer to work with a pen on a pressure-sensitive tablet because it can, with the right software, simulate a traditional paintbrush more accurately than other pointing devices. A painting program typically offers a **palette** of onscreen tools. Some tools mimic real-world painting tools, while others can do things that are difficult, even impossible, on paper or canvas.

Painting programs create **bitmapped graphics** (or, as they're sometimes called, **raster graphics**)—pictures that are, to the computer, simple maps showing how the pixels on the screen should be represented. For the simplest bitmapped graphics, a single bit of computer memory represents each pixel. Since a bit can contain one of two possible values, 0 or 1, each pixel can display one of two possible colors, usually black or white. To display more colors, paint programs allocate more bits of memory per pixel.

Like a picture created with a high-resolution paint program, a digitized photograph or a photograph captured with a digital camera is a bitmapped image. Digital **image processing software** enables the user to manipulate photographs and other high-resolution images with tools similar to those found in paint programs. Digital image processing software makes it easier for photographers to remove unwanted reflections, eliminate red eye, and brush away facial blemishes—to perform the kinds of editing tasks that were routinely done with magnifying glasses and tiny brushes before photographs could be digitized. But digital photographic editing is far more powerful than traditional photo-retouching techniques. With image-processing software, it's possible to distort and combine photographs, creating fabricated images that show no evidence of tampering. Supermarket gossip tabloids routinely use these tools to create sensationalistic cover photos. Many experts question whether photographs should be allowed as evidence in the courtroom now that they can be doctored so convincingly.

2-D and 3-D Drawing

Because high-resolution paint images and photographs are stored as bit maps, they can make heavy storage and memory demands. Another type of graphics program can economically store pictures with virtually *infinite* resolution, limited only by the capabilities of the output device. **Drawing software** stores a picture not as a collection of dots, but as a collection of lines and shapes. When you draw a line with a drawing program, the software doesn't record changes in a pixel map. Instead, it calculates and remembers a mathematical formula for the line. A drawing program stores shapes as shape formulas and text as text. Because pictures are collections of lines, shapes, and other objects, this approach is often called **object-oriented graphics** or **vector graphics**. In effect, the computer is remembering that a blue line segment goes here, a red circle goes here, and a chunk of text goes here instead of remembering that this pixel is blue, this one is red, and this one is white. . . .

With **3-D modeling software,** graphic designers can create three-dimensional objects with tools similar to those found in conventional drawing software. Illustrators who use 3-D software appreciate its flexibility. A designer can create a 3-D model of an object, rotate it, view it from a variety of angles, and take two-dimensional snapshots of the best views for inclusion in final printouts. Similarly, it's possible to walk through a 3-D environment that exists only in the computer's memory, printing snapshots that show the simulated space from many points of view.

For many applications the goal is not a printout but an animated presentation on a computer screen or videotape. Three-dimensional graphics also play an important role in the branch of engineering known as **computer-aided design (CAD)**—the use of computers to design products.

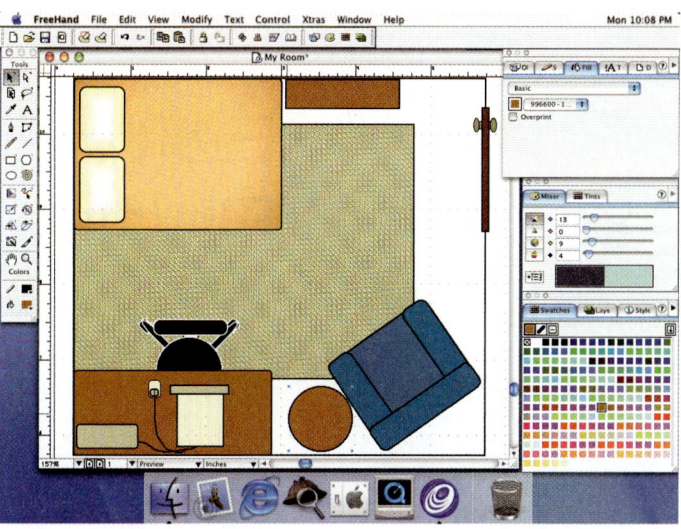

This room floor plan was created with Macromedia Freehand, a powerful professional drawing and illustration program. Each piece of furniture can be moved as an independent object in the drawing.

Presentation Graphics: Bringing Lectures to Life

Presentation graphics software helps to automate the creation of visual aids for lectures, training sessions, sales demonstrations, and other presentations. Presentation graphics programs such as PowerPoint are most commonly used for creating and displaying a series of onscreen slides to serve as visual aids for presentations. Slides might include photographs, drawings, spreadsheet-style charts, or tables. These different graphical elements are usually integrated into a series of **bullet charts** that list the main points of a presentation. Slides can be output as 35mm color slides, overhead transparencies, or handouts. Presentation graphics programs can also display slide shows directly on computer monitors or LCD projectors, including animation and video clips along with still images. Some can convert presentations into Web pages automatically.

Dynamic Media: Animation, Video, and Audio

Most PC applications—painting and drawing programs, word processors, desktop publishers, and so on—were originally designed to produce paper documents. But many types of modern media can't be reduced to pixels on printouts because they contain *dynamic* information—information that changes over time or in response to user input. Today's multimedia computers enable us to create and edit animated sequences, video clips, sound, and music along with text and graphics. Just as words and pictures serve as the raw materials for desktop publishing, dynamic media such as animation, video, audio, and hypertext are important components of interactive multimedia projects.

Macromedia's Director is a popular multimedia program with powerful animation capabilities. The frames in the Cast window show several different views of an object as it moves through the timeline shown in the Score window.

Animation Software

In its simplest form, computer-based **animation** is similar to traditional frame-by-frame animation techniques—each frame is a computer-drawn picture, and the computer displays those frames in rapid succession. But computer animation programs, even low-priced packages aimed at the home market, contain software tools that can do much more than flip pages. They can take much of the tedium out of animation by automating repetitive processes. Instead of drawing every frame by hand, an animator can create key frames and objects and use software to help fill in the gaps—a process known as *tweening*. The most powerful animation programs include tools for working with animated objects in three dimensions, adding depth to the scene on the screen.

The User's View

Editing Photographic Images

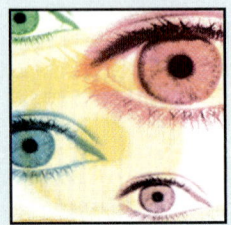

SOFTWARE: Adobe Photoshop with a scanner plug-in.

THE GOAL: To create a cover for a forthcoming CD from an obscure but enthusiastic band.

1 You select your favorite photo of the band from the prints of a recent photo shoot, as well as a photo of a conga drum which you captured with a digital camera. The cover concept combines the band and the drum. The first step is to import the photos—the band photo using a scanner, and the digital camera by transferring the file from your camera to your computer—and save each of them as Photoshop documents.

2 You want to isolate the drum from its background, so you trace around it with the magnetic lasso. You don't have to trace the exact profile of the drum, because the magnetic lasso automatically snaps to the nearest edges.

3 You create a mask, which hides everything except the selected drum.

4 The drum photo can now be placed in front of another background as if it were a set of paper dolls. You drag the drum photo into the window with the band photo, which pastes it into a new layer so it can be moved and modified independently.

Chapter 5 Computer Applications 141

5 You notice that the light in the drum image appears to fall from the opposite direction as the light which falls on the band in the other photo. To create the illusion of uniform lighting for the photos, you flip the drum image along its horizontal axis.

6 You resize the canvas to the dimensions of a standard CD booklet. You also resize the drum layer, squashing, stretching, and distorting it to create the illusion that the viewer is standing just over the drum.

7 One of the band member's faces appears washed out. To correct this problem, you use the digital equivalent of a darkroom tool, the Burn tool, to simulate the process of selectively over-exposing portions of the image.

8 You select the closest section of the drum with the lasso, and tell Photoshop to apply a blur effect to add a sense of depth to the image.

9 You add a title and resize it to match the drum head. Finally, you apply a bulge effect to the text and give it a horizontal slant, so that it matches the perspective of the drum head.

10 You print the final document on a high-resolution printer.

The User's View

Creating Presentation Graphics

SOFTWARE: Microsoft PowerPoint.

THE GOAL: To create visual aids for a talk you're giving for a class. You'll use PowerPoint, a presentation graphics package that's especially designed for this kind of task.

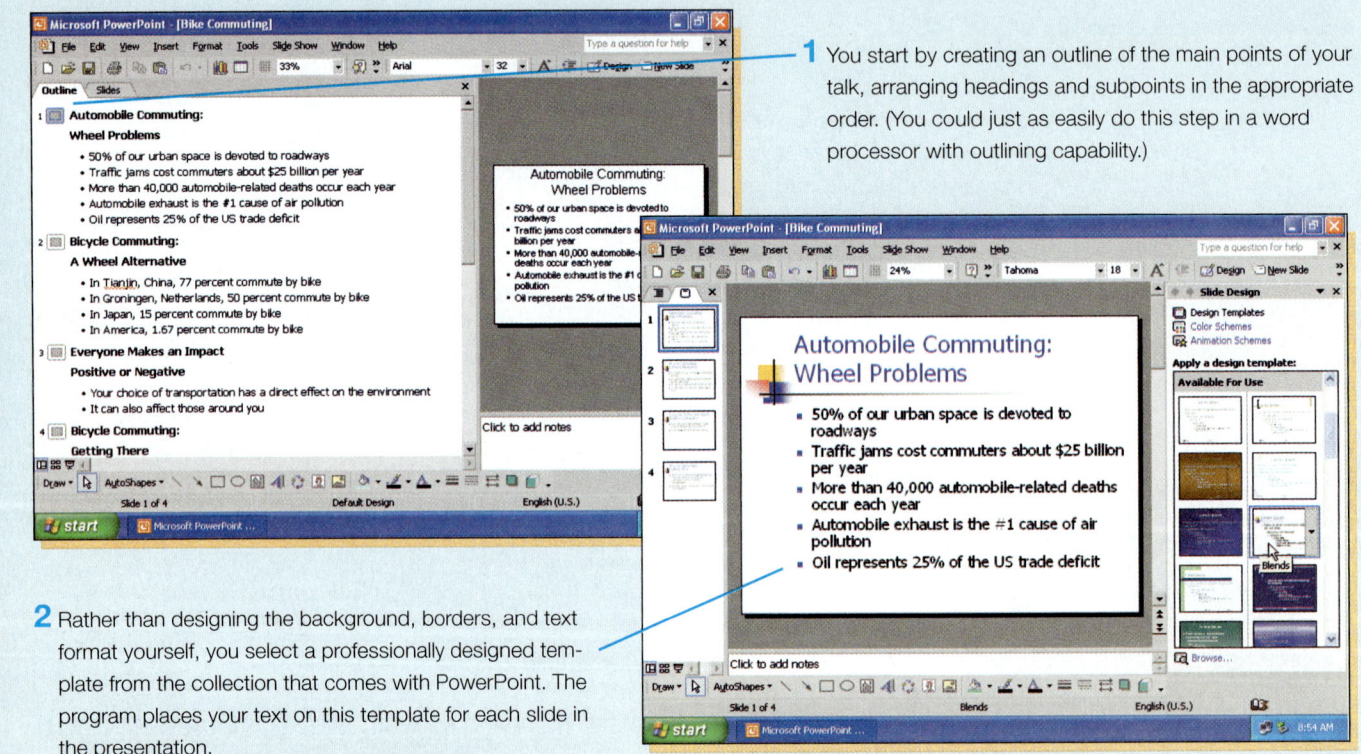

1 You start by creating an outline of the main points of your talk, arranging headings and subpoints in the appropriate order. (You could just as easily do this step in a word processor with outlining capability.)

2 Rather than designing the background, borders, and text format yourself, you select a professionally designed template from the collection that comes with PowerPoint. The program places your text on this template for each slide in the presentation.

Digital Video

Digital video, like text, numbers, and computer graphics, can be treated as data by computers and combined with other forms of data. Conventional television and video images are stored and broadcast as analog (smooth) electronic waves. A *video digitizer* can convert analog video signals from a television broadcast or videotape into digital data. Most video digitizers must be installed as add-on cards or external devices that plug into serial or USB ports. Broadcast-quality digitizers are relatively expensive; low-cost models are available for hobbyists who can settle for less-than-perfect images.

Video professionals and hobbyists who use *digital video cameras* don't need to digitize their video footage before working with it in a computer, because it's already in digital form. Digital video cameras capture and store all video footage as digital data. Most digital video cameras have FireWire (IEEE 1394) ports (see Chapter 3) that can be used to copy raw video footage from tape to a computer and later copy the edited video back from computer to tape. Because digital video can be reduced to a series of numbers, it can be copied, edited, stored, and played back without any loss of quality. Digital video will soon replace analog video for most applications.

Chapter 5 Computer Applications

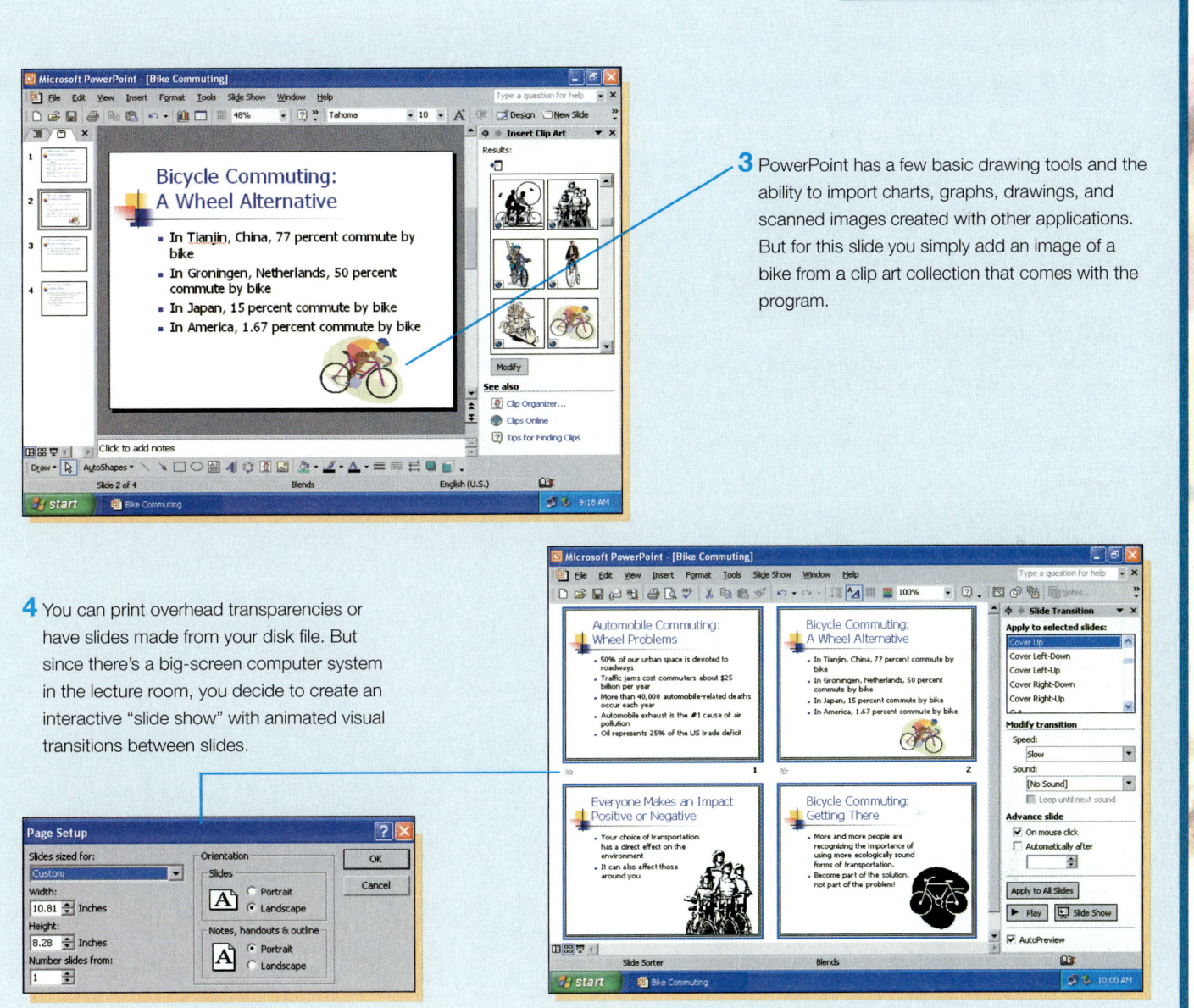

3 PowerPoint has a few basic drawing tools and the ability to import charts, graphs, drawings, and scanned images created with other applications. But for this slide you simply add an image of a bike from a clip art collection that comes with the program.

4 You can print overhead transparencies or have slides made from your disk file. But since there's a big-screen computer system in the lecture room, you decide to create an interactive "slide show" with animated visual transitions between slides.

Video editing software, such as Adobe Premiere and Apple Final Cut Pro, makes it easy to eliminate extraneous footage, combine clips from multiple takes into coherent scenes, splice together scenes, insert visual transitions, superimpose titles, synchronize a soundtrack, and create special effects. Editing software can combine live action with computer animation. After it's edited, the video clip can be "printed" on videotape.

Edited video doesn't need to be exported to tape. Many digital clips end up in multimedia presentations. Onscreen digital movies can add realism and excitement to educational, training, presentation, and entertainment software. Video clips are also common on the Web.

Digital movies can make heavy hardware demands; even a short full-screen video clip can quickly fill a large hard disk or CD-ROM. To save storage space and to allow the processor to keep up with the quickly changing frames, digital movies designed for the Web or CD-ROM are often displayed in small windows with fewer than the standard video rate of 30 frames per second. In addition, **compression** software and hardware are used to squeeze data out of movies so they can be stored in smaller spaces, usually with a slight loss of image quality. General data compression software can reduce the size of almost any kind of data file; specialized image compression software is generally used to compress graphics and video files.

How It Works

5.1 Data Compression

A full-screen 256-color photograph or painting takes about a megabyte of storage—the same as the complete text from a typical paperback book! Graphic images, digital video, and sound files can consume massive amounts of storage space on disk and in memory; they can also be slow to transmit over computer networks. **Data compression** technology allows large files to be temporarily squeezed so they take less storage space and network transmission time. Before they can be used, compressed files must be decompressed. (In the physical world many companies "compress" goods to save storage and transportation costs: When you "just add water" to a can of concentrated orange juice, you're "decompressing" the juice.)

All forms of compression involve removing bits; the trick is to remove bits that can be replaced when the file can be restored. Different compression techniques work best for different types of data.

Suppose you want to store or transmit a large text file. Your text compression software might follow steps similar to those shown here:

1 Each character in the uncompressed ASCII file occupies 8 bits; a seven-character word—invoice, for example—requires 56 bits of storage.

i n v o i c e

(space) p a y a b l e

2 A 2-byte binary number can contain code values ranging from 0 to 65,535—enough codes to stand for every commonly used word in English. This partial code dictionary shows the code values for a few words, including invoice and payable.

Portion of a dictionary		
A	○○○○○○○○	○○○○○○○●
a	○○○○○○○○	○○○○○○●○
aback	○○○○○○○○	○○○○○○●●
abacus	○○○○○○○○	○○○○○●○○
...		
invoice	○○●○○●○●	○○●●●○○○
invoiced	○○●○○●○●	○○●●●○○●
invoke	○○●○○●○●	○○●●●○●○
...		
pay	○●○●○●○●	●○●○○●○○
payable	○●○●○●●○	●○●○○○○●
...		
zygote	●●●●●●●●	●●●●●●●●

3 To compress a file using a code dictionary, the computer looks up every word in the original file, in this example, invoice and payable. It replaces each word with its 2-byte code value. In this example they are % 9 and V ú. The seven-character word now takes up only 16 bits—less than one-third of its original size.

4 In a compressed file, these 2-byte code values would be used to store or transmit the information for invoice and payable, using fewer bits of information either to increase storage capacity or to decrease transmission time.

% 9 V ú

5 To reverse the process of compression, the same dictionary (or an identical one on another computer) is used to decompress the file, creating an exact copy of the original. All the tedious dictionary lookup is performed quickly by a computer program.

Chapter 5 Computer Applications 145

Compression programs usually work on patterns of bits rather than English words. One type of digital video compression stores values for pixels that change from one frame to the next; there's no need to repeatedly store values for pixels that are the same in every frame. For example, the only pixels that change in these two pictures are the ones that represent the unicycle and the shadows.

In general, compression works because most raw data files contain redundancy that can be "squeezed out." **Lossless compression** systems allow a file to be compressed and later decompressed without any loss of data; the decompressed file will be an identical copy of the original file. Popular lossless compression systems include ZIP/PKZIP (DOS/Windows), StuffIt (Macintosh), tar (UNIX), and GIF (general graphics). A **lossy compression** system can usually achieve better compression than a lossless one but may lose some information in the process; the decompressed file isn't always identical to the original. This is tolerable in many types of sound, graphics, and video files but not for most program and data files. JPEG is a popular lossy compression system for graphics files.

MPEG is a popular compression system for digital video. An MPEG file takes just a fraction of the space of an uncompressed video file. Because decompression programs demand time and processing power, playback of compressed video files can sometimes be jerky or slow. Some computers get around the problem with MPEG hardware boards that specialize in compression and decompression, leaving the CPU free for other tasks. **Hardware compression** is likely to be built into most computers as multimedia becomes more commonplace.

The original photographic image (above) is clear with an uncompressed size of 725 KB. The image on the right shows the visible lossy effect of aggressive JPEG compression. But the size of the compressed file is only 19 KB.

146 Chapter 5 Computer Applications

Software can turn a desktop or laptop computer into a video editing and production machine. Video professionals use programs like Apple's Final Cut Pro *(top) and Adobe's* After Effects *(center) to edit video footage and add special effects. Apple's iMovie and iDVD (bottom) are designed to make non-linear video editing and DVD production simple and intuitive for non-professionals.*

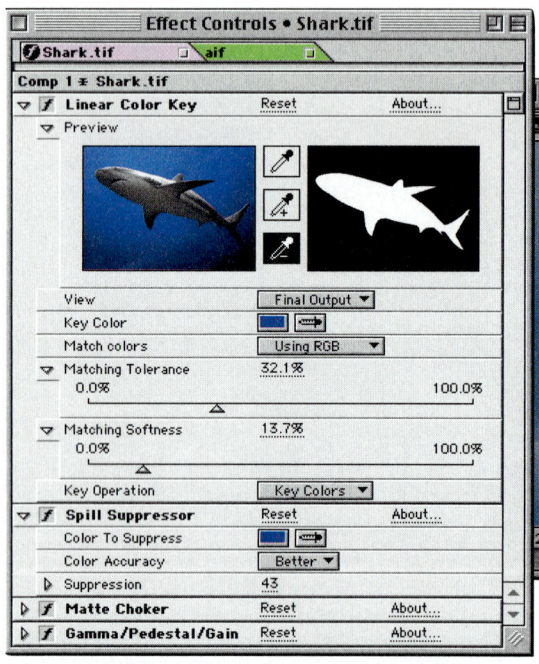

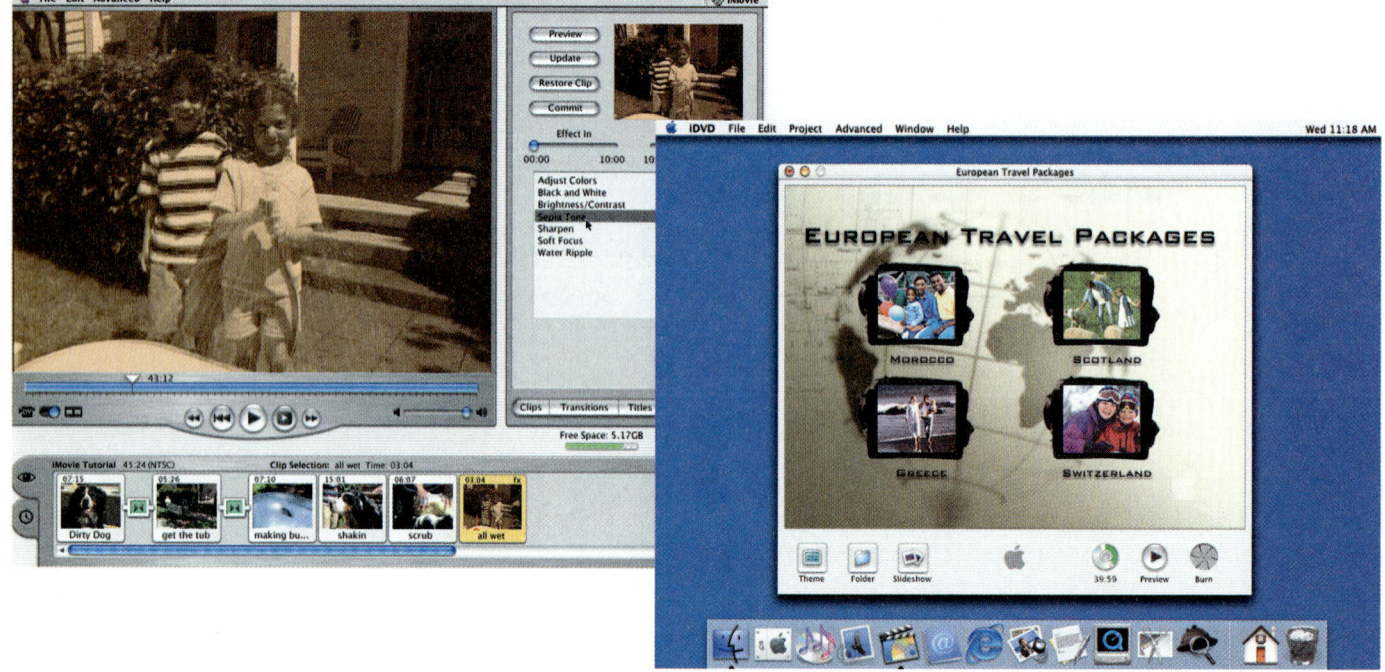

Digital Audio and MIDI

Any sound that can be recorded can be captured with an *audio digitizer* and stored as a *digital audio* data file on a disk. Sound files, like video files, are generally compressed so they don't take up so much disk space. Digitized sound data, like other computer data, can be loaded into the computer's memory and manipulated by software. Sound editing software can change a sound's volume and pitch, add special effects such as echoes, remove extraneous noises, and even rearrange musical passages.

Multimedia computers can also control a variety of electronic musical instruments and sound sources using **MIDI (Musical Instrument Digital Interface)**—a standard interface that allows electronic instruments and computers, regardless of type or brand, to communicate with each other and work together. MIDI is used to send commands to instruments and sound sources—commands that, in effect, say "play this sound at this pitch and this volume for this amount of time. . . ." MIDI commands can be interpreted by a variety of music synthesizers (electronic instruments that synthesize sounds using mathematical formulas) and other electronic musical instruments. But most multimedia PCs can also interpret and execute MIDI commands using sounds built into their sound cards or stored in software form.

Interactive Multimedia

The term **multimedia** generally means using some combination of text, graphics, animation, video, music, voice, and sound effects to communicate. When you watch a typical TV program, you're experiencing a multimedia product. With each second that passes, you are bombarded

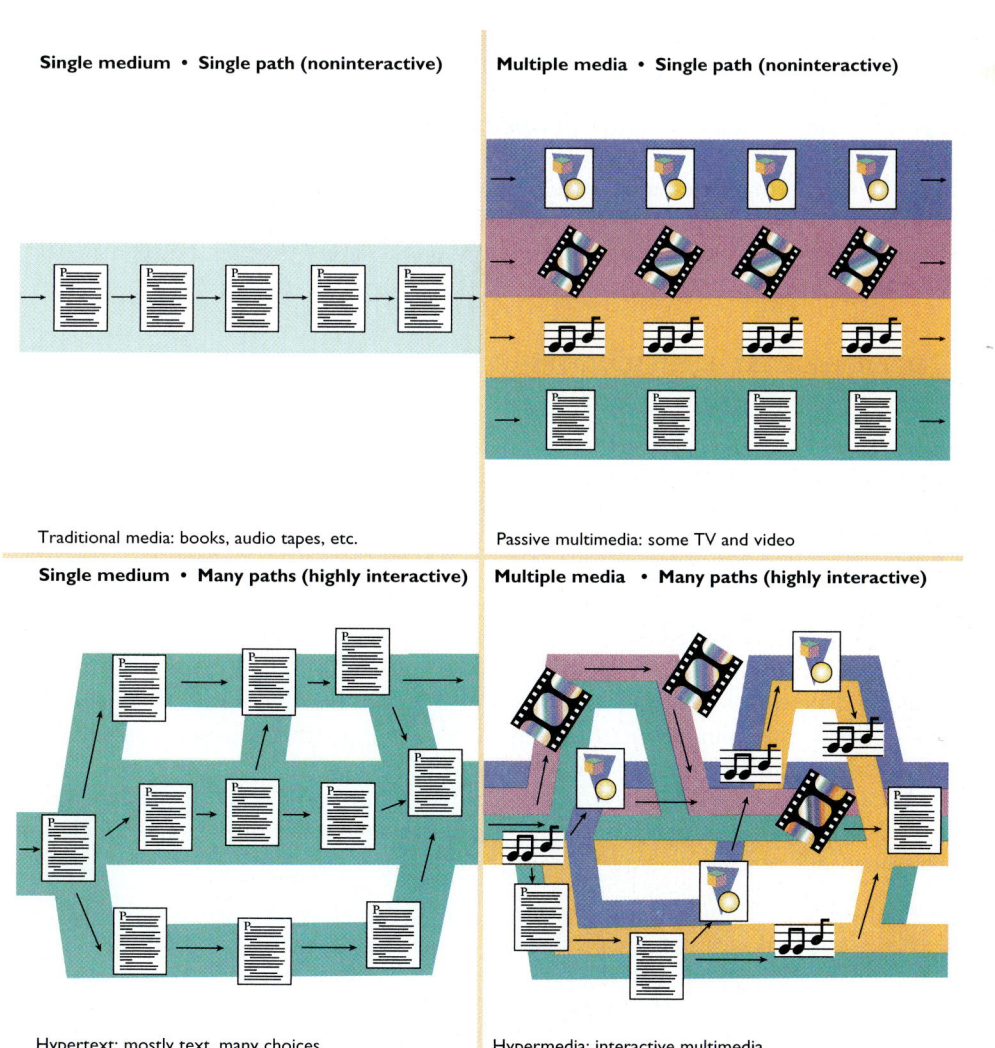

Interactivity and multiplicity: the two dimensions of multimedia.

with millions of bits of information. But television and video are passive media—they pour information into our eyes and ears while we sit and take it all in. We have no control over the information flow. Modern computer technology allows information to move in both directions, turning multimedia into **interactive multimedia**. Unlike TV, radio, and video, interactive multimedia enable the viewer/listener to take an active part in the experience. The best interactive multimedia software puts the user in charge, enabling that person to control the information flow. (Interactive multimedia documents are sometimes referred to as *hypermedia* documents because they combine mixed media with hyperlinking capability.)

Multimedia authoring software is used to create and edit multimedia documents. Like desktop publishing, interactive multimedia authoring involves combining source documents—including graphics, text files, video clips, and sounds—in an aesthetically pleasing format that communicates to the user. Multimedia authoring software, like page layout software, serves as the glue that combines documents created and captured with other applications. But since a multimedia document can change in response to user input, authoring involves specifying not just *what* and *where* but also *when* and *why*.

With the growing interest in the Internet, many people expect the World Wide Web to replace CD-ROMs for most multimedia delivery. Most multimedia authoring tools can create Web-ready multimedia documents. For example, documents created by Authorware and Director can be converted into Web documents using Macromedia's Shockwave technology. Shockwave software compresses multimedia documents so they can appear and respond more quickly on the Web. But even with compression, the Internet isn't fast enough to deliver the high-quality audio and video that's possible with CD-ROM and DVD-ROM. On the other hand, the contents of a disk are static; they can't be continually updated like a Web site—and CD-ROMs don't offer opportunities for communication with other people the way a Web site can. Many multimedia manufacturers today produce *hybrid disks*—media-rich CD-ROMs and DVD-ROMs that automatically draw content and communication from the Web. Hybrid disks hint at the types of multimedia experiences that will be possible without disks through tomorrow's faster Internet.

Whatever form it takes, interactive multimedia technology offers tremendous promise for education, entertainment, and communication in the future. Of course, if we aren't careful, the same technology may further remove us from books, other people, and the natural world around us.

Databases: Electronic File Cabinets

> The next best thing to knowing something is knowing **where to find it**.
> —Samuel Johnson

A **database program** is an information management program that allows people to store, organize, retrieve, communicate, and manage information in ways that wouldn't be possible without computers. Database programs are designed to maintain **databases**—collections of information stored on computer disks. A database can be an electronic version of a phone book, a recipe file, a library's card catalog, an inventory file stored in an office file cabinet, a school's student grade records, a card index containing the names and addresses of business contacts, or a catalog of your CD collection. Just about any collection of information can be turned into a database. People use databases of all sizes and shapes—from massive mainframe database managers that keep airplanes filled with passengers to computerized appointment calendars on palmtop computers and public database kiosks in shopping malls.

Why do people use computers for information-handling tasks that can be done with index cards, three-ring binders, or file folders? Computerized databases offer several advantages over their paper-and-pencil counterparts:

▸ *Databases make it easier to store large quantities of information.* If you have only 20 or 30 compact discs, it makes sense to catalog them in a notebook. If you have 2,000 or 3,000, your notebook may become as unwieldy as your CD collection. With a computerized database, your complete CD catalog can be stored on a single diskette. The larger the mass of information, the bigger the benefit of using a database.

- *Databases make it easier to retrieve information quickly and flexibly.* While it might take a minute or more to look up a phone number in a card file or telephone directory, the same job can be done in seconds with a database. If you look up 200 numbers every week, the advantage of a database is obvious. That advantage is even greater when your search doesn't match your file's organization. For example, suppose you have a phone number on a scrap of paper and you want to find the name and address of the person with that number. That kind of search may take hours if your information is stored in a large address book or file alphabetized by name, but the same search is almost instantaneous with a computerized database.
- *Databases make it easy to organize and reorganize information.* Paper filing systems force you to arrange information in one particular way. Should your book catalog be organized by author, by title, by publication date, or by subject? There's a lot riding on your decision, because if you decide to rearrange everything later, you waste a lot of time. With a database you can instantly switch between these organizational schemes as often as you like; there's no penalty for flexibility.
- *Databases make it easy to print and distribute information in a variety of ways.* Suppose you want to send letters to hundreds of friends inviting them to your post-graduation party. You'll need to include directions to your place for out-of-towners but not for home-towners. A database, when used with a word processor, can print personalized form letters, including extra directions for those who need them, and print preaddressed envelopes or mailing labels in a fraction of the time it would take you to do it by hand and with less likelihood of error. You can even print a report listing invitees sorted by ZIP code so you can suggest possible car pools. (If you want to bill those who attend the party, your database can help with that, too.)

Database Anatomy

For our purposes, a database is a collection of information stored in an organized form in a computer, and a database program is a software tool for organizing storage and retrieval of that information. A variety of programs fit this broad definition, ranging from simple address book programs to massive inventory-tracking systems.

Many terms that describe the components of database systems grew out of the file cabinet terminology of the office. A database is composed of one or more files. A **file** is a collection of related information; it keeps that information together the way a drawer in a file cabinet does. If a database is used to record sales information for a company, separate files might contain the relevant sales data for each year. For an address database, separate files might hold personal and business contacts. It's up to the designer of the database to determine whether information in different categories is stored in separate files on the computer's disk.

The term *file* sometimes causes confusion because of its multiple meanings. A disk can contain application programs, system programs, utility programs, and documents, all of which are, from the computer's point of view, files. But for database users, the term *file* usually means a file that is part of a database—a specific kind of file. In this chapter *file* refers specifically to a data file created by a database program.

A database file is a collection of records. A **record** is the information relating to one person, product, or event. In the library's card catalog database a record is equivalent to one card. In an address book database, a record contains information about one person. A compact disc catalog database would have one record per CD.

Each discrete chunk of information in a record is called a **field**. A record in the library's card catalog database would contain fields for author, title, publisher, address, date, and title code number. Your CD database could break records into fields by title, artist, and so on.

Database Operations

The challenging part of using a database is retrieving information in a timely and appropriate manner. Information is of little value if it's not accessible. One way to find information is to **browse** through the records of the database file just as you would if they were paper forms in a notebook. Most database programs provide keyboard commands, onscreen buttons, and other

The User's View

Selecting, Sorting, and Reporting

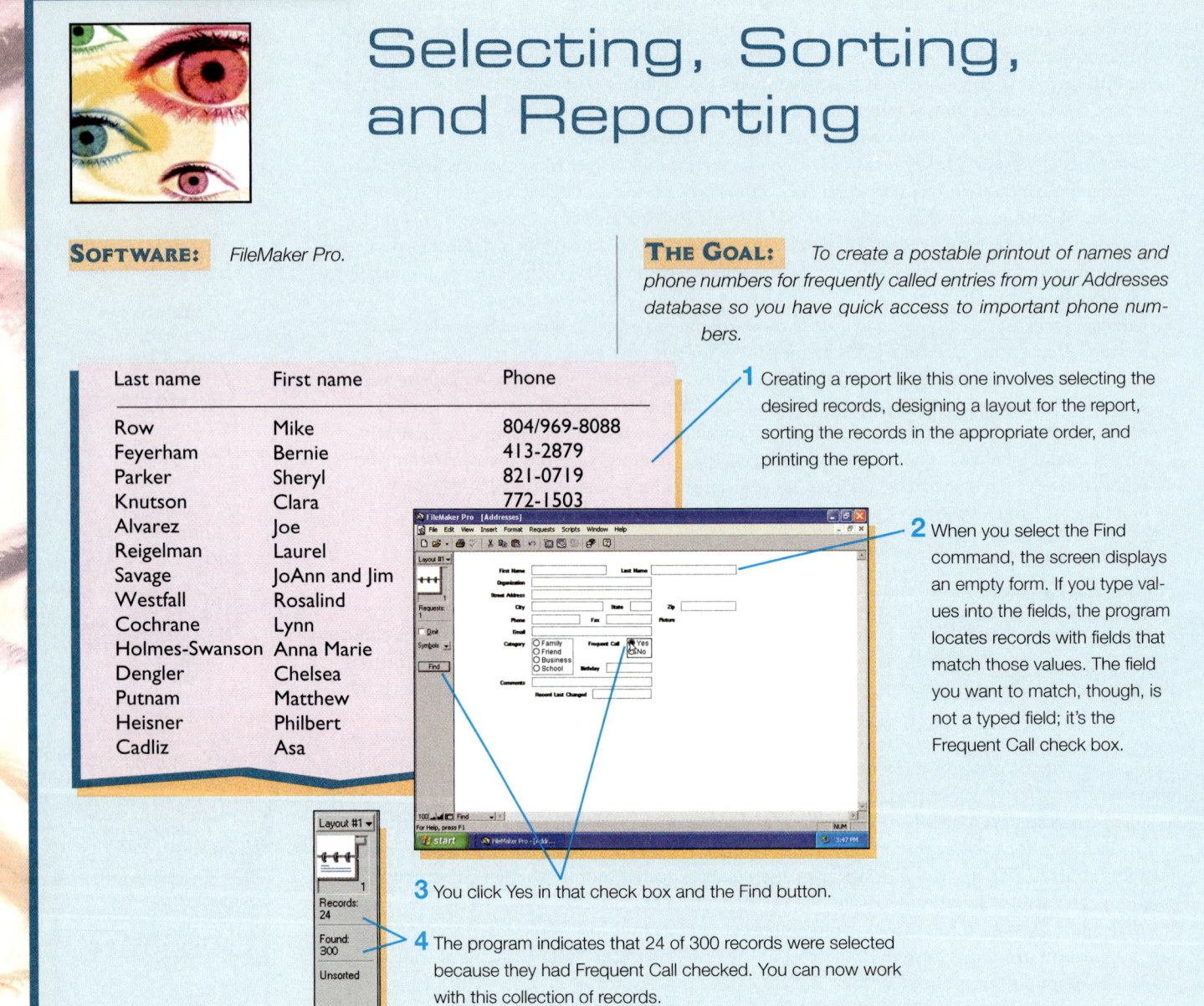

SOFTWARE: FileMaker Pro.

THE GOAL: To create a postable printout of names and phone numbers for frequently called entries from your Addresses database so you have quick access to important phone numbers.

1. Creating a report like this one involves selecting the desired records, designing a layout for the report, sorting the records in the appropriate order, and printing the report.

2. When you select the Find command, the screen displays an empty form. If you type values into the fields, the program locates records with fields that match those values. The field you want to match, though, is not a typed field; it's the Frequent Call check box.

3. You click Yes in that check box and the Find button.

4. The program indicates that 24 of 300 records were selected because they had Frequent Call checked. You can now work with this collection of records.

tools for navigating quickly through records. But this kind of electronic page turning offers no particular advantage over paper, and it's painfully inefficient for large files.

Fortunately, most database programs include a variety of commands and capabilities that make it easy to get the information you need when you need it.

▶ *Database queries.* The alternative to browsing is to ask the database for specific information. In database terminology, an information request is called a **query**. A query may be a simple **search** for a specific record (say, one containing information on Abraham Lincoln) or a request to **select** *all* the records that match a set of criteria (for example, records for all U.S. presidents who served more than one term). Most programs enable the user to specify the rules of the search by filling in a dialog box or a blank onscreen form. Some require the user to type the request using a special *query language* that's more precise than English. Once you've selected a group of records, you can browse through it, produce a printout, or do just about anything else you might do with the complete file.

Chapter 5 Computer Applications

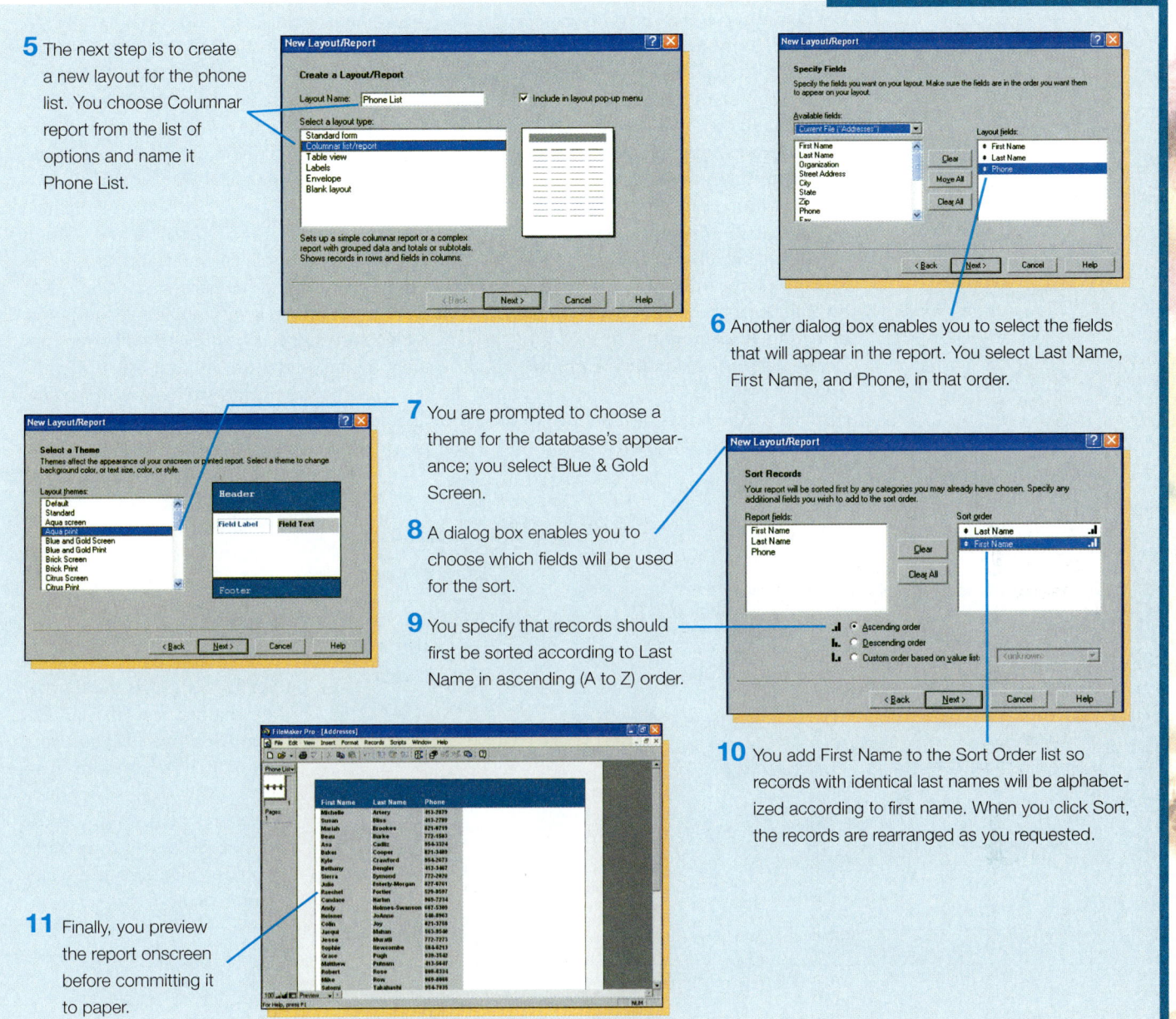

5 The next step is to create a new layout for the phone list. You choose Columnar report from the list of options and name it Phone List.

6 Another dialog box enables you to select the fields that will appear in the report. You select Last Name, First Name, and Phone, in that order.

7 You are prompted to choose a theme for the database's appearance; you select Blue & Gold Screen.

8 A dialog box enables you to choose which fields will be used for the sort.

9 You specify that records should first be sorted according to Last Name in ascending (A to Z) order.

10 You add First Name to the Sort Order list so records with identical last names will be alphabetized according to first name. When you click Sort, the records are rearranged as you requested.

11 Finally, you preview the report onscreen before committing it to paper.

▸ *Sorting data.* Sometimes it's necessary to rearrange records to make the most efficient use of data. For example, a mail-order company's customer file might be arranged alphabetically by name for easy reference, but it must be rearranged in order by ZIP code to qualify for postal discounts on catalog mailings. A **Sort** command enables you to arrange records in alphabetic or numeric order based on values in one or more fields.

▸ *Printing reports, labels, and form letters.* In addition to displaying information on the screen, database programs can produce a variety of printouts. The most common type of database printout is a **report**—an ordered list of selected records and fields in an easy-to-read format. Most business reports arrange data in tables with rows for individual records and columns for selected fields; they often include summary lines containing calculated totals and averages for groups of records. Database programs can also be used to produce mailing labels and customized form letters. Many database programs don't actually print letters; they simply **export data** or transmit the necessary records and fields to word processors with **mail merge** capabilities, which then take on the task of printing the letters.

Special-Purpose Databases

Specialized database software is preprogrammed for specific data storage and retrieval purposes. For example, *geographical information systems (GISs)* enable businesses to combine tables of data such as customer sales lists with demographic information from the U.S. Census Bureau and other sources. The right combination can reveal valuable strategic information. For example, a stock brokerage can pinpoint the best locations for branch offices based on average incomes and other neighborhood data; a cable TV company can locate potential customers who live close to existing lines. Because they can display geographic and demographic data on maps, they enable users to see data relationships that might be invisible in table form.

One broad category of specialized database program goes by a number of names, including **personal information managers (PIMs)** and *electronic organizers*. A personal information manager generally includes an address/phone book, an appointment calendar, and a to-do list function; some PIMs also accept diary entries, personal notes, and other hard-to-categorize tidbits of information. For people on the go, PIMs work especially well with notebook computers or handheld computers. In fact, the market for PIM software has been eclipsed by an even larger market for handheld computers and personal digital assistants with built-in PIM software. For example, software that's built into the Palm OS allows a pocket-sized device to be hot-synched, at the touch of a button, to the PIM software on a desktop PC or Mac. This instant data linking makes it easy to keep up-to-date personal information both in and out of the office. In many organizations, PIMs have been replaced by enterprise information systems such as Microsoft Outlook. These systems enable networked coworkers to share calendars and contacts easily. The Web offers another alternative: Several Web sites provide free PIM software that can be accessed from any Web-accessible computer; many of these enable workgroups to share calendars and other information.

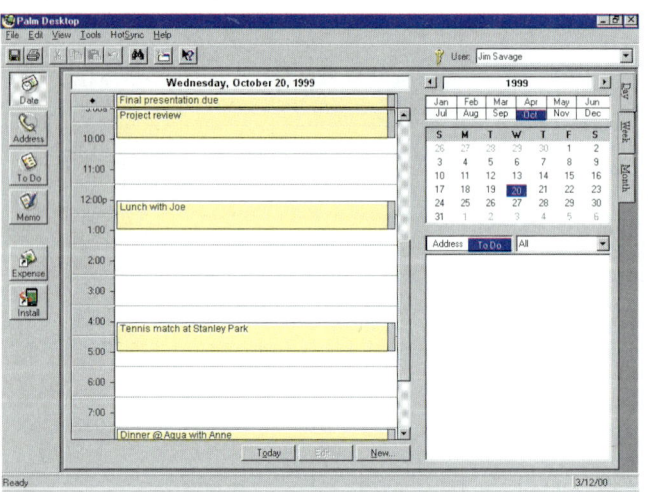
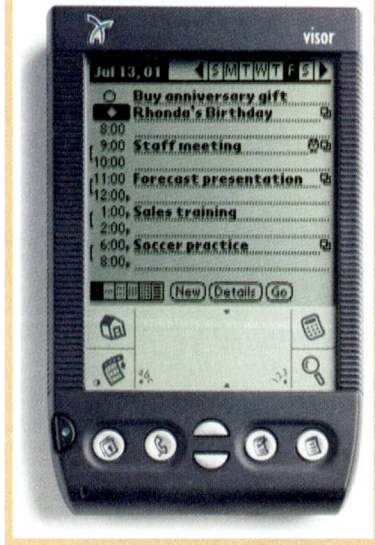

Personal information management software can help you keep track of appointments, phone numbers, and to-do lists. The information is readily accessible as long as your computer is nearby or you can find a way to carry the data with you. Handheld computers like this Handspring Visor can share information with PC programs, so you can carry the essentials with you as you move through your day.

Database Management Systems

Technically speaking, many consumer databases and personal information manager programs aren't really database managers at all; they're file managers. A **file manager** is a program that enables users to work with one file at a time. A true **database management system (DBMS)** is a program or system of programs that can manipulate data in a large collection of files—the database—cross-referencing between files as needed. A DBMS can be used interactively, or it can be controlled directly by other programs. A file manager is sufficient for mailing lists and other common data management applications. But for many large, complex jobs there's no substitute for a true DBMS.

Large databases can contain hundreds of interrelated files. This maze of information could be overwhelming to users if they were forced to deal with it directly. Fortunately, a database management system can shield users from the complex inner workings of the system, providing them with only the information and commands they need to get their jobs done. In fact, a well-designed database puts on different faces for different classes of users.

Clerk's view

Video rental view used by clerks to access renter information, scan bar codes on videos, and print rental invoices

Video store database

Manager's view

- Inventory-tracking view used by managers to check on rental history and inventory for individual movies
- Policy view used by managers to change pricing, membership, and other policies

Technician/programmer's view

Technical view used by programmer to create other user interfaces and custom queries

Clerks, managers, programmers, and customers see different views of a video rental store's database. Customers can browse through listings and reviews of available movies using a touch-screen kiosk. The clerk's view allows only for simple data-entry and check-out procedures. The manager, working with the same database, has control over pricing, policies, and inventory, but can't change the structure or user interface of the database. The programmer can work under the hood to fine-tune and customize the database so it can better meet the needs of other employees and customers.

Databases and Privacy

> If **all records** told the same tale,
> then **the lie** passed into history and **became truth**.
> —George Orwell, in *1984*

We live in an information age, and data is one of the currencies of our time. Businesses and government agencies spend billions of dollars every year to collect and exchange information about you and me. Consumer and marketing information, credit and banking information, tax records, health data, insurance records, political contributions, voter registration, credit card purchases, warranty registrations, magazine and newsletter subscriptions, phone calls, passport registration, airline reservations, automobile registrations, arrests, Internet explorations—they're all recorded in computers, and we have little or no control over what happens to most of those records once they're collected.

The same characteristics that make databases more efficient than other information storage methods—storage capacity, retrieval speed, organizational flexibility, and ease of distribution of information—also make them a threat to our privacy. With networked computers it's easy to compile profiles by combining information from different database files. As long as the files share a single unique field, such as the Social Security number, **record matching** is trivial and quick. And when database information is combined, the whole is often far greater than the sum of its parts.

Sometimes the results are beneficial. Government enforcement agencies use record matching to locate criminals ranging from tax evaders to mass murderers. Because credit bureaus collect data about us, we can use credit cards to borrow money wherever we go. But these benefits come with at least three problems:

Rules of Thumb

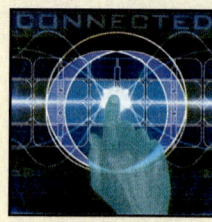

Dealing with Databases

Whether you're creating an address file with a simple file manager or retrieving data from a full-blown relational database management system, you can save yourself a great deal of time and grief if you follow a few commonsense rules:

- **Choose the right tool for the job.** Don't invest time and money in a programmable relational database to computerize your address book, and don't try to run the affairs of your multinational corporation with a $99 file manager.
- **Think about how you'll get the information out before you put it in.** What kinds of files, records, and fields will you need to create to make it easy to find things quickly and print things the way you'll want them? For example, use separate fields for first and last name if you want to sort names alphabetically by last name and print first names first.
- **Start with a plan, and be prepared to change your plan.** It's a good idea to do a trial run with a small amount of data to make sure everything works the way you think it should.
- **Make your data consistent.** Inconsistencies can mess up sorting and make searching difficult. For example, if a database includes residents of Minnesota, Minn., and MN, it's hard to group people by state.
- **Databases are only as good as their data.** When entering data, take advantage of the data-checking capability of your database software. Does the first name field contain nonalphabetic characters? Is the birth date within a reasonable range? Automatic data checking is important, but it's no substitute for human proofreading or for a bit of skepticism when using the database.
- **Query with care.** In the words of Aldous Huxley, "People always get what they ask for; the only trouble is that they never know, until they get it, what it actually is that they have asked for." Here's a real example: A student searching a database of classic rock albums requested all records containing the string "Dylan," and the database program obediently displayed the names of several Bob Dylan albums . . . plus one by Jimi Hendrix called *Electric Ladyland*. Why? Because "dylan" is in Ladyland! Unwanted records can go unnoticed in large database selections, so it's important to define selection rules very carefully.
- **If at first you don't succeed, try another approach.** If your search doesn't turn up the answers you were looking for, it doesn't mean the answers aren't there; they may just be wearing a disguise. For example, if you search a standard library database for "Vietnam War" references, you might not find any. Why? Because the government officially classifies the Vietnam War as a conflict, so references are stored under the subject "Vietnam Conflict." Technology meets bureaucracy!

- *Data errors are common.* A study of 1,500 reports from the three big credit bureaus found errors in 43% of the files.
- *Data can become nearly immortal.* Because files are commonly sold and copied, it's impossible to delete or correct erroneous records with absolute certainty.
- *Data isn't secure.* A *Business Week* reporter demonstrated this in 1989 by using his computer to obtain then Vice President Dan Quayle's credit report. Had he been a skilled criminal, he might have been able to *change* that report.

Protection against invasion of privacy is not explicitly guaranteed by the U.S. Constitution. Legal scholars agree that the **right to privacy**—freedom from interference in the private sphere of a person's affairs—is implied by other constitutional guarantees, although debates rage about what this means. Federal and state laws provide forms of privacy protection, but most of those laws were written years ago. When it comes to privacy violation in America, technology is far ahead of the law.

Democracy depends on the free flow of information, but it also depends on the protection of individual rights. Maintaining a balance is not easy, especially when new information technologies are being developed at such a rapid pace. With information at our fingertips it's tempting to think that more information is the answer. But in the timeless words of populist philosopher Will Rogers, "It's not the things we don't know that get us into trouble, it's the things we do know that ain't so."

Rules of Thumb

Your Private Rights

Sometimes computer-aided privacy violations are nuisances; sometimes they're threats to life, liberty, and the pursuit of happiness. Here are a few tips for protecting your right to privacy.

- **Your Social Security number is yours—don't give it away.** Since your SSN is a unique identifier, it can be used to gather information about you without your permission or knowledge. For example, you could be denied a job or insurance because of something you once put on a medical form. Never write it (or your driver's license number or phone number, for that matter) on a check or credit card receipt. Don't give your SSN to anyone unless they have a legitimate reason to ask for it.
- **Don't give away information about yourself.** Don't answer questions about yourself just because a questionnaire or company representative asks you to. When you fill out any form—coupon, warranty registration card, survey, sweepstakes entry, or whatever—think about whether you want the information stored in somebody else's computer.
- **Say no to direct mail, phone, and email solicitations.** Businesses and political organizations pay for your data so they can target you for mail, phone, and email campaigns. You can remove yourself from many lists using forms from the Direct Mail Marketing Association (www.the-dma.org). If this doesn't stop the flow, you might want to try a more direct approach. Send back unwanted letters along with "Take me off your list" requests in the postage-paid envelopes that come with them. When you receive an unsolicited phone marketing call, tell the caller "I never purchase or donate anything as a result of phone solicitations," and ask to be removed from the list. If they call within 12 months of being specifically told not to, you can sue and recover up to $500 per call according to the Telephone Consumer Protection Act of 1991. Unfortunately, there's no comparable federal law to protect you against junk email yet, so you should be especially careful about giving out your email address if you don't like receiving unsolicited email.
- **Say no to sharing your personal information.** If you open a private Internet account, tell your Internet service provider that your personal data is not for sale. If you don't want your state's Department of Motor Vehicles selling information about you, notify them. A relatively new federal law gives you more control over DMV use of personal data. If you don't want credit agencies sharing personal information, let them know. The Federal Trade Commission's Privacy Web site (www.ftc.gov/privacy) includes clear guidelines and forms for contacting your DMV and credit agencies. The Financial Modernization Act of 1999 allows you to tell your banks and other financial institutions not to share your personal information with other institutions; check with those institutions for details.
- **Say no to pollsters.** Our political system has been radically transformed by polling; most of our "leaders" check the polls before they offer opinions on controversial issues. If you and I don't tell the pollsters what we're thinking, politicians will be more likely to tell us what they're thinking.
- **If you think there's incorrect or damaging information about you in a file, find out.** The Freedom of Information Act of 1966 requires that most records of U.S. government agencies be made available to the public on demand. The Privacy Act of 1974 requires federal agencies to provide you with information in your files relating to you and to amend incorrect records. The Fair Credit Reporting Act of 1970 allows you to see your credit ratings—for free if you have been denied credit—and correct any errors. The three big credit bureaus are Equifax (www.equifax.com), Trans Union (www.tuc.com), and Experian (www.experian.com).
- **To maximize your privacy, minimize your profile.** If you don't want a financial transaction recorded, use cash. If you don't want your phone number to be public information, use an unlisted number. If you don't want your mailing address known, use a post office box.
- **Know your electronic rights.** Privacy protection laws in the United States lag far behind those of other high-tech nations, but they are beginning to appear. For example, the 1986 Electronic Communications Privacy Act provides the same protection that covers mail and telephone communication to some—but not all—electronic communication. The 1988 Computer Matching and Privacy Protection Act regulates the use of government data in determining eligibility for federal benefits.
- **Support organizations that fight for privacy rights.** If you value privacy rights, let your representatives know how you feel, and support the American Civil Liberties Union, Computer Professionals for Social Responsibility, the Electronic Frontier Foundation, Electronic Privacy Information Center, Center for Democracy and Technology, Private Citizen, and other organizations that fight for those rights.

CrossCurrents

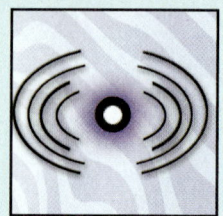

Counterfeit Freedom

Randall E. Stross

After the terrorist attacks of September 11, 2001, security jumped to the forefront of the political landscape. This article, first published in the October 8 Issue of U.S. News and World Report, argues that increased security justified a loss of personal privacy and civil liberties. This controversial point of view was rarely heard before the September 11 massacre.

If we were self-sufficient farmers in a sparsely populated land, or misanthropic hermits, we would not be so vulnerable to the horrors that the few can visit upon the many. But we have become, and will remain, an urban nation, living and working, traveling and spectating, in physical proximity, our exposure to unspeakable violence shared. Until September 11, we had gone about our daily business, cheek by jowl, as strangers to one another, without thinking much about our shared vulnerability. But now we must. And Larry Ellison, the CEO of Oracle, has helped us with a proposal that we adopt a national identification card, with digitized photograph and thumbprint, and tied to a central database, for which Oracle would provide the software for free.

Ellison presented his proposal as a means of improving airline security. We all know that this measure alone is anything but a panacea, that a suicidal terrorist who had entered the country legally and maintained a clean criminal record would not be stopped. Still, would we not feel better when boarding if counterfeit-proof digital ID were required of everyone? We know viscerally that no community has ever deliberately entrusted its well-being to anonymous strangers.

Our current patchwork of ID systems is based on easily forged paper documents and scattered government databases that can't connect with one another. Whether we use Oracle software is unimportant, but the rest of Ellison's proposal incorporates the crucial elements that we must put in place with all possible speed: First, we must insist on biometric authentication, using unique physical characteristics like a fingerprint. This would eliminate identity theft, which increased 16-fold in the mid-1990s, expanding to an estimated 700,000 instances to date. It would also spare law-abiding citizens from wrongful arrest. The Saudi Arabian government complained last month that at least five innocent Saudi citizens had been wrongly identified as suicide bombers.

False choice. Second, we must maintain a single database of identities. The Immigration and Naturalization Service, State Department, Social Security Administration, FBI, IRS, state driver's license bureaus—each could still track different kinds of information. But for a person's physical identity, each should draw upon a single repository. When asked his opinion of the Ellison proposal, Robert Post, a constitutional law professor at the University of California-Berkeley, warned that we should not allow "a terrorist attack to destroy forms of freedom that we have enjoyed." Post did not specify what "freedom" was at risk. We must identify ourselves for any number of activities of daily life, so the only freedom that would be lost with the advent of improved ID technology is the freedom to falsify one's legal identity. I'm sorry, what's the rationale again for that latitude?

If there's prolonged debate about national identity cards, I hope it will not run along the old ruts, the individual's interests versus the state's. This vital matter is really between citizen and fellow citizen, the obligations of community members to one another. In 1620, the residents of Plymouth did not need to carry ID cards; all knew one another. Thus was born the first American ID database, stored not in silicon but in every resident's head.

By the time of the Revolution, the Colonies' largest city, Philadelphia, was a teeming mass of 25,000, and only 5 percent of the population lived in cities. Yet even then, the young country's leaders saw need for government to help citizens do what the individual could no longer do on his own: identify the newcomers swelling the rapidly expanding U.S. community. The first census, in 1790, recorded the names and addresses of heads of families.

Fast-forward to the present. Instead of the 4 million residents of 1790, we are a nation of 285 million, with 30 million foreign visitors a year. Our borders are so porous and the document requirements for employment so flimsy that we also host 6 million to 12 million illegal aliens. One wonders why we haven't furloughed the border guards and swung the gates open, conceding we have effectively lost control of those who come in and, legally speaking, disappear.

Does a national ID card seem Orwellian? Alternatively, we can build biometric authentication into every state-issued driver's license, require similar ID cards of nondrivers and all foreign visitors, and have states share a central database of identities. Uncomfortable with the picture of that database holding your precious identity? Too late. Your identity, plus your phone calls, medical records, bank transactions, credit problems, and minutely detailed listings of purchases all are on file in digital form, as the private sector has embraced databases enthusiastically (making Ellison a very wealthy man). Yet these are outside our oversight. A federal identity database, however, would be ours, accountable to us, governed by rules that we the public direct. We are all inhabitants of a continent-size village. Knowing one another a bit better is a communal necessity.

DISCUSSION QUESTIONS

1. Do you agree that the advantages of a national ID card justify the threat to personal privacy? Explain your answer.
2. What kinds of laws, if any, should be in place to protect your privacy if a national ID card is adopted?

Summary

Applications software can turn a general-purpose computer into a wide variety of specialized tools. Whether you work with words, numbers, pictures, sounds, video, or collections of data, an application program can probably enhance your productivity.

Word processing software enables the writer to edit and format text on the screen before printing. Spelling checkers and grammar and style checkers partially automate the proofreading process, although they leave the more difficult parts of the job to literate humans. Word processors and desktop publishing software and hardware have revolutionized the publishing process by enabling publishers to produce professional-quality text-and-graphics documents at a reasonable cost.

Spreadsheet software can be used for tracking financial transactions, calculating grades, forecasting economic conditions, recording scientific data—just about any task that involves repetitive numerical calculations. The responsiveness and flexibility of spreadsheet software make it particularly well suited for providing answers to what-if questions. Most spreadsheet programs include charting commands to turn worksheet numbers into a variety of graphs and charts.

A variety of other number-crunching applications are available for those situations where a basic spreadsheet program isn't sufficient or convenient to use. Like spreadsheets, most of these applications are simulation tools. Computer simulations offer many advantages for decision makers, but they aren't without risks.

Computer graphics applications include bit-mapped painting programs that enable users to "paint" pixels on the screen and object-oriented drawing programs that store pictures as collections of geometric objects rather than as maps of computer bits. Bit-mapped graphics are used in high-resolution digital image processing software for onscreen photo editing, whereas object-oriented graphics are at the heart of 3-D modeling software. Presentation graphics software automates the process of creating slides, transparencies, handouts, and computer-based presentations.

For animation and digital video work, PCs mimic many of the features of expensive professional workstations at a fraction of the cost. Similarly, today's personal computers can perform a variety of sound and music editing tasks that used to require expensive equipment and numerous musicians. Today's multimedia computer systems make a new kind of software possible—software that uses text, graphics, animation, video, music, voice, and sound effects to communicate. Interactive multimedia software enables the user to control the presentation rather than just watch or listen passively.

Database programs enable users to store, organize, retrieve, communicate, and manage large amounts of information. Database programs enable users to view data in a variety of ways, select particular records, sort records in any order, and print reports, mailing labels, and other custom printouts. While most database programs are general-purpose tools that can be used to create custom databases for any purpose, some are special-purpose tools programmed to do a particular set of tasks. Database management systems (DBMSs) can work with several files at once, cross-referencing information among files when appropriate.

The accumulation of data by government agencies and businesses is a growing threat to our right to privacy. Massive amounts of information about private citizens are collected and exchanged for a variety of purposes. Today's technology makes it easy to combine information from different databases, producing detailed profiles of individual citizens. While there are many legitimate uses for these procedures, there's also a great potential for abuse.

Chapter Review

▼ Key Terms

3-D modeling software (p. 139)
accounting and financial management software (p. 137)
animation software (p. 139)
bitmapped (raster) graphics (p. 138)
bullet charts (p. 139)
clipboard (p. 130)
compression (p. 143)
console (formula bar) (p. 134)
current (active) cell (p. 134)
cut-and-paste (p. 130)

data compression (p. 144)
database (p. 148)
database management system (DBMS) (p. 152)
database program (p. 148)
digital audio (p. 147)
digital video (p. 142)
drag-and-drop (p. 130)
drawing software (p. 138)
editing (p. 128)
field (p. 149)

file (p. 149)
file manager (p. 152)
Find command (p. 128)
font (p. 128)
formatting (p. 128)
formula (p. 136)
grammar and style checker (p. 129)
image processing software (p. 138)
interactive multimedia (p. 148)
MIDI (musical instrument digital interface) (p. 147)

multimedia (p. 147)
multimedia authoring software (p. 148)
object-oriented (vector) graphics (p. 139)
open (p. 129)
outliner (outline view) (p. 128)
page-layout software (p. 132)
painting software (p. 138)
personal information manager (PIM) (p. 152)
pixel(s) (p. 138)
presentation graphics software (p. 139)
query (p. 150)
range (p. 134)
record (p. 149)
record matching (p. 153)
report (p. 151)
right to privacy (p. 154)
save (p. 129)
scrolling (p. 128)
search (p. 150)
search and replace (find and replace) (p. 128)
select (records) (p. 150)
selecting text (p. 130)
simulation (p. 137)
sort (p. 151)
source document (p. 132)
spelling checker (p. 129)
spreadsheet software (p. 133)
word processor (p. 128)
worksheet (p. 133)
WYSIWYG (p. 128)

▼ Interactive Quiz Questions

1. The *Computer Confluence* CD-ROM contains self-test quiz questions related to this chapter, including multiple choice, true or false, and matching questions.
2. The *Computer Confluence* Web site, www.prenhall.com/beekman, contains self-test exercises related to this chapter. Follow the instructions for taking a quiz. After you've completed your quiz, you can email the results to your instructor.
   The Web site also contains open-ended discussion questions called Internet Explorations. Discuss one or more of the Internet Exploration questions at the section for this chapter.

▼ Review Questions

1. Define or describe each of the key words listed in the "Key Words" section. Check your answers in the glossary.
2. What is the difference between a file manager and a database management system? How are they similar?
3. Describe the structure of a simple database. Use the terms *file*, *record*, and *field* in your description.
4. What is a query? Give examples of the kinds of questions that might be answered with a query.
5. What steps are involved in producing a standard multi-column business report from a database?
6. What are the advantages of personal information management software over paper notebook organizers? What are the disadvantages?
7. What does it mean to sort a data file?
8. How can a database be designed to reduce the likelihood of data-entry errors?
9. Describe how record matching is used to obtain information about you. Give examples.
10. Do we have a legal right to privacy? On what grounds?
11. Why are computers important in discussions of invasion of privacy?

▼ Discussion Questions

1. Grade books, checkbooks, and other information collections can be managed with either a database program or a spreadsheet program. How would you decide which type of application is most appropriate for a given job?
2. What have you done this week that directly or indirectly involved a database? How would your week have been different in a world without databases?
3. "The computer is a great humanizing factor because it makes the individual more important. The more information we have on each individual, the more each individual counts." Do you agree with this statement by science fiction writer Isaac Asimov? Why or why not?
4. Suppose you have been incorrectly billed for $100 by a mail-order house. Your protestations are ignored by the company, which is now threatening to report you to a collection agency. What do you do?
5. What advantages and disadvantages does a computerized law enforcement system have for law-abiding citizens?
6. In what ways were George Orwell's "predictions" in the novel *1984* accurate? In what ways were they wrong?

▼ Projects

1. Design a database for your own use. Create several records, sort the data, and print a report.
2. Find out as much as you can about someone (for example, yourself or a public figure) from public records like tax records, court records, voter registration lists, and motor vehicle files. How much of this information were you able to get directly from the Web? How much was available for free?
3. Find out as much as you can about your own credit rating.
4. The next time you order something by mail or phone, try encoding your name with a unique middle initial so you can recognize when the company sells your name and address to other companies. Use several different spellings for different orders if you want to do some comparative research.
5. Determine what information about you is stored in your school computers. What information are you allowed to see? What information are others allowed to see? Exactly who may access your files? Can you find out who sees your files? How long is the information retained after you leave?
6. Keep track of your purchases for a few weeks. If other people had access to this information, what conclusions might they be able to draw about you?

Sources and Resources

Books

To learn the specifics of an application, use a hands-on tutorial for that application. The books listed here can provide you with a broader perspective.

The Non-Designer's Design Book, by Robin Williams (Berkeley, CA: Peachpit Press, 1994). In this popular book, Robin Williams provides a friendly introduction to the basics of design and page layout in her popular, down-to-earth style. The first half of the book illustrates the four basic design principles (proximity, alignment, repetition, and contrast). The second half focuses on using type as a design element. This book is highly recommended for anyone new to graphic design.

Looking Good in Print, Fourth Edition, by Roger C. Parker and Patrick Berry (Scottsdale, AZ: Coriolis, 1998). This book covers the nontechnical side of desktop publishing. Now that you know the mechanics, how can you make your work look good? Parker and Berry clearly describe the basic design tools and techniques and then apply them in sample documents ranging from brochures to books.

Bugs in Writing, by Lynn Dupre (Reading, MA: Addison-Wesley, 1998). This entertaining little book is designed to help computer science and computer information systems students—who presumably already know how to debug their programs—debug their prose. It's a friendly, readable tutorial that can help almost anybody to be a better writer.

Wired Style: Principles of English Usage in the Digital Age, by Constance Hale and Jessie Scanlon (San Francisco: Broadway Books, 2000). Should an email address be italicized when it's included in a paragraph of text? For that matter, is it E-mail, e-mail, or email? Do you back up files or backup files? When you write about IBM, should you use its unabbreviated name? Digital communication changes our language quickly, and the classic grammar and style manuals don't always have the answers. In this sometimes controversial guidebook, the editors of Wired answer these questions, explain their writing and editing philosophies, and provide tips for writing about rapidly evolving technologies and ideas. If you like the informal future-focused style of Wired, you'll appreciate this book.

Scrolling Forward: Making Sense of Documents in the Digital Age, by David M. Levy (Arcade Publishing, 2001). How are computers, the Internet, and digital technology in general changing the notion of documents? The future of books, paper, copyrights, and libraries are discussed in this thought-provoking book.

The Sum of Our Discontent: Why Numbers Make Us Irrational, by David Boyle (Texere, 2001). Computers, television, and other media bombard us with more numbers than most of us can digest. Boyle argues that all those numbers make it harder, not easier, to understand what's going on around us.

Designing Infographics, by Eric K. Meyer (Indianapolis: Hayden Books, 1997). This book provides an excellent overview of the theory and the practice of designing graphs, charts, and other informative illustrations. It covers tools, techniques, forms, and applications of quantitative and informative graphics; there's even a section on statistical ethics.

The Visual Display of Quantitative Information, Envisioning Information, and **Visual Explanations: Images and Quantities, Evidence and Narrative,** by Edward R. Tufte (Cheshire, CT: Graphics Press, 1987, 1990, and 1997, respectively). These three beautiful books make a powerful case for intelligent design of charts, graphics, and other visual aids. Many of the examples in these books show how graphs and charts can be both creative and informative.

Serious Play: How the World's Best Companies Simulate to Innovate, by Michael Schrage (Cambridge, MA: Harvard Business School Press, 1999). "When talented innovators innovate, you don't listen to the specs they quote. You look at the models they've created," says Michael Schrage, MIT Media Lab fellow and *Fortune* magazine columnist. In this book, Schrage looks at the kind of "serious play" being done at innovative companies such as Disney, 3M, Sony, and Hewlett Packard.

Graphic Communications Dictionary, by Daniel J. Lyons (Upper Saddle River, NJ: Prentice Hall, 2000). This is an excellent alphabetic reference for anyone wrestling with the terminology of graphic design.

The Arts and Crafts Computer: Using Your Computer as an Artist's Tool, by Janet Ashford (Berkeley, CA: Peachpit Press, 2001). This lavishly illustrated book covers basic principles of drawing, painting, photography, typography, and design with computers. But unlike other books on computer art, this one goes beyond the computer screen and the printed page as output possibilities. If you want to create original fabric art, greeting cards, labels, decals, bumper stickers, and toys, you'll find a wealth of ideas here.

Looking Good in Presentations: Third Edition, by Molly W. Joss and Roger C. Parker (Scottsdale, AZ: Coriolis Group, 1999). Programs like PowerPoint can help nondesigners create stylish presentations, but they're not foolproof. (How many ugly, boring computer-enhanced presentations have you had to sit through?) This is a great book for anyone creating presentations, from simple slide shows to full-featured multimedia extravaganzas. Starting with "How To Not Be Boring" in Chapter 1, you'll find plenty of tips to make your presentations shine.

The Little Digital Video Book, by Michael Rubin (Berkeley, CA: Peachpit Press, 2001). This compact book should be included with every digital camcorder. It's packed with helpful tips for choosing and organizing equipment, preparing a project, shooting quality footage, editing clips, adding soundtracks, and polishing productions. Highly recommended.

Theoretical Foundations of Multimedia, by Robert S. Tannenbaum (New York: W.H. Freeman, 1998). Multimedia is an ideal profession for a modern Renaissance person. To be truly multimedia literate, a person needs to understand concepts from fields as diverse as computer science, physics, design, law, psychology, and communication. This introductory text/CD-ROM surveys each of these fields from the multimedia perspective, providing valuable conceptual background with practical value.

Understanding Media: The Extensions of Man, by Marshall McLuhan (Cambridge, MA: MIT Press, 1994.) This classic, originally published in 1964, explores the relationship of mass media to the masses. The new introduction in this 30th Anniversary reissue reevaluates McLuhan's visionary work 30 years later.

Multimedia: From Wagner to Virtual Reality, edited by Randall Packer and Ken Jordan (New York: Norton, 2001). This collection of essays by William Burroughs, John Cage, Tim Berners-Lee, and others, offers a broad overview of the historical roots of multimedia.

Database Design for Mere Mortals: A Hands-On Guide to Relational Database Design, by Michael J. Hernandez (Reading, MA: Addison-Wesley, 1997). This book can save time, money, and headaches for anyone who's involved in designing and building a relational database. After defining all of the critical concepts, the author clearly outlines the design process using case studies to illustrate important points.

Object Technology: A Manager's Guide, Second Edition, by David A. Taylor (Reading, MA: Addison-Wesley, 1998). This book clearly explains the basics of object technology in non-technical terms. The author explores object-oriented databases, object-oriented programs, and object-oriented software on networks.

Data Smog: Surviving the Information Glut, by David Shenk (New York: HarperEdge, 1997). It's possible to have too much information at your fingertips. David Shenk's book clearly describes the hazards to individuals and society of all this information.

Surveillance Society: Monitoring Everyday Life (Issues in Society), by David Lyon (Open University Press, 2001). This book intelligently analyzes the deterioration of personal privacy in our information society without getting bogged down in jargon.

Database Nation: The Death of Privacy in the 21st Century, by Simson Garfinkel (Cambridge, MA: O'Reilly, 2000). This is a frightening, sobering account of the erosion of our personal privacy as a result of misuse of technology—databases, on-the-job monitoring, data networks, biometric devices, video surveillance, and more. Garfinkel skillfully mixes chilling true stories and futuristic scenarios with practical advice for reclaiming our individual and collective rights to privacy. Highly recommended.

The Transparent Society: Will Technology Force Us to Choose Between Freedom and Privacy?, by David Brin (Cambridge, MA: Perseus Press, 1998). Brin, a mathematician and award-winning science fiction writer, presents a compelling case that personal privacy is doomed by technology. He argues that our best hope is to provide equal access to all information, rather than let the biggest brothers have the only windows into our lives. Compelling reading.

Periodicals

Artbyte. This stylish magazine explores the world and culture of digital art and design.

DV and **AV Video & Multimedia Producer.** These days video producers have to pay attention to the world of computers and multimedia. These two publications provide current coverage of the converging worlds of video and multimedia.

Keyboard and Electronic Musician. These two magazines are among the best sources for up-to-date information on computers and music synthesis.

The Privacy Journal (www.privacyjournal.net). This widely quoted monthly newsletter covers all issues related to personal privacy.

Organizations

Privacy Foundation (www.privacyfoundation.org). The Privacy Foundation isn't an advocacy group; its mission is to report on technology-based privacy threats and circulate alerts.

Computer Professionals for Social Responsibility (www.cpsr.org). CPSR provides the public and policy-makers with realistic assessments of the power, promise, and problems of information technology. Much of their work deals with privacy-related issues. Their newsletter is a good source of information.

The Electronic Frontier Foundation (www.eff.org). EFF strives to protect civil rights, including the right to privacy, on emerging communication networks.

Electronic Privacy Information Center (www.epic.org). EPIC serves as a watchdog on government efforts to build surveillance capabilities into the emerging information infrastructure.

Web Pages

Check the *Computer Confluence* Web site for links to many of the organizations and publications listed above.

6 Networking and Telecommunication

After you read this chapter you should be able to:

▼

Describe the nature and function of local-area networks and wide-area networks

Discuss the uses and implications of email, teleconferencing, and other forms of online communication

Describe several types of communication services that are available with or without an Internet connection

Describe several types of electronic digital communication that don't necessarily involve personal computers

Describe current and future trends in telecommunications and networking

▲

▼ **In this chapter:**

The roots of the Internet

Why nobody controls the Internet

How the Internet works

Publishing pages on the Web

The next generation Internet and beyond

. . . and more.

▼ **On the CD-ROM:**

A networking activity

Animated demonstrations of important network technology concepts

Video clips of network applications in action

Instant access to glossary and key word references

Interactive self-study quizzes

. . . and more.

▼ **On the Web:**

www.prenhall.com/beekman

Links to network hardware and software resources

In-depth explanations of various network technology concepts

Tips for using email, teleconferences, and other network services effectively

Self-study exercises

. . . and more.

Arthur C. Clarke's Magical Prophecy

1. If an elderly but distinguished scientist says that something is possible he is almost **certainly right**, but if he says that it is impossible he is **very probably wrong.**
2. The only way to find the **limits of the possible** is to go beyond them into the impossible.
3. Any sufficiently advanced technology is **indistinguishable from magic**.

—Clarke's Three Laws

Besides coining Clarke's laws, British writer Arthur C. Clarke has written more than 100 works of science fiction and nonfiction. His most famous work was the monumental 1968 film *2001: A Space Odyssey*, in which he collaborated with movie director Stanley Kubrick. The film's villain, a faceless English-speaking computer with a lust for power, sparked many public debates about the nature and risks of artificial intelligence.

Arthur C. Clarke

HAL, the rebellious computer in the movie *2001: A Space Odyssey*

But Clarke's most visionary work may be a paper published in 1945 in which he predicted the use of *geostationary* **communications satellites**—satellites that match the Earth's rotation so they can hang in a stationary position relative to the spinning planet below, relaying wireless transmissions between locations on the planet below. Clarke's paper pinpointed the exact height of the orbit required to match the movement of the satellite with the planetary rotation. He also suggested that these satellites could replace many telephone cables and radio towers, allowing electronic signals to be beamed across oceans, deserts, and mountain ranges, linking the people of the world with a single communications network.

A decade after Clarke's paper appeared, powerful rockets and sensitive radio receiving equipment made communications satellites realistic. In 1964 the first synchronous TV satellite was launched, marking the beginning of a billion-dollar industry that has changed the way people communicate.

Today Clarke is often referred to as the father of satellite communications. He lives in Sri Lanka, where he continues his work as a writer, but now he uses a personal computer and beams his words around the globe to editors using the satellites he envisioned half a century ago.

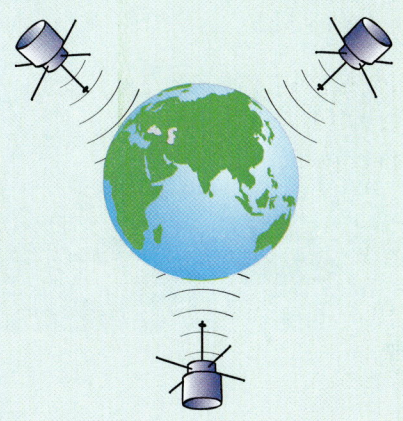

Geostationary communication satellites

The Battle of New Orleans, the bloodiest battle of the War of 1812, was fought two weeks after the war officially ended; it took that long for the cease-fire message to travel from Washington, D.C., to the front line. In 1991, 179 years later, six hard-line Soviet communists staged a coup to turn back the tide of democratic and economic reforms that were sweeping the U.S.S.R. Within hours messages zipped between the Soviet Union and Western nations on telephone and computer networks. Cable television and computer conferences provided up-to-the-minute analyses of events—analyses that were beamed to computer bulletin boards inside the Soviet Union. Networks carried messages among the resistors, allowing them to stay steps ahead of the coup leaders and the Soviet military machine. People toppled the coup and ultimately the Soviet Union—not with guns, but with courage, will, and timely information.

Telecommunication technology—the technology of long-distance communication—has come a long way since the War of 1812, and the world has changed dramatically as a result. After Samuel Morse invented the telegraph in 1844, people could, for the first time, send long-distance messages instantaneously. Alexander Bell's invention of the telephone in 1876 extended this capability to the spoken voice. Today systems of linked computers enable us to send data and software across the room or around the world. The technological transformation has changed the popular definition of the word *telecommunication*, which today means long-distance electronic communication in a variety of forms.

In this chapter we look at the computer as part of a network rather than as a self-contained appliance, and we discuss ways in which such linked computers are used for communication and information gathering. We also consider how networks are changing the way we live and work. In the next chapter we'll delve deeper into the Internet—the global computer network at the heart of the next telecommunication revolution.

Linking Up: Network Basics

> All the **most promising technologies** making their debut now are chiefly due to communication between computers— that is, to **connections** rather than to **computations**. And since **communication is the basis of culture**, fiddling at this level is indeed **momentous**.
>
> —Kevin Kelly, former *Wired* Executive Editor

A student uses a terminal in the library to connect with an online information source.

A computer network is any system of two or more computers that are linked together. Why is networking important? The answers to this question revolve around the three essential components of every computer system:

- *Hardware.* Networks enable people to share computer hardware, reducing costs and making it possible for more people to take advantage of powerful computer equipment.
- *Software.* Networks enable people to share data and software programs, increasing efficiency and productivity.
- *People.* Networks enable people to work together in ways that are otherwise difficult or impossible.

Important information is hidden in these three statements. But before we examine them in more detail, we need to look at the hardware and software that make computer networks possible.

Basic Network Anatomy

> The most desirable interaction with a network is one in which **the network itself is invisible and unnoticeable**. Planners often forget that people do not want to use systems at all—easy or not. What people want is to **delegate** a task and **not to worry about how** it is done.
>
> —Nicholas Negroponte, director of MIT's Media Lab

In Chapter 2, you saw how information travels among the CPU, memory, and other components within a computer as electrical impulses that move along collections of parallel wires called buses. A network extends the range of these information pulses, allowing them to travel to other computers. A computer may have a direct connection to a network—for example, it might be one of many machines linked together in an office—or it might have remote access to a network through a phone line, a television cable system, or a satellite link. Either way, the computer needs some specialized hardware to complete the connection. To connect directly, the computer needs a network interface card; for a remote connection it generally needs a modem or similar device.

The Network Interface

Chapter 2 described personal computer ports—sockets that enable information to pass in and out. Parallel ports, commonly used to connect older printers to a computer, enable bits to pass through in groups of 8, 16, or 32. Serial ports, on the other hand, require bits to pass through one at a time. Most PCs have at least one of each. Macintoshes don't have built-in parallel ports. Older Macs have multipurpose serial ports for connecting to printers, modems, and some networks. The standard serial port on an IBM-compatible computer is designed to attach peripherals such as modems—not to connect directly to networks. Modern Macs and PCs have USB and FireWire (IEEE 1394) ports that are much faster and more flexible than traditional serial and parallel ports.

A network interface card (NIC) adds an additional serial port to the computer—one that's especially designed for a direct network connection. The network interface card controls the flow of data between the computer's RAM and the network cable. At the same time it converts the computer's internal low-power signals into more powerful signals that can be transmitted through the network. The type of card depends on the type of network connection needed. The most common types of networks today require some kind of Ethernet card in each computer. Ethernet is a popular networking architecture developed in 1976 at Xerox. (Most Macintoshes and some PCs include an Ethernet port on the main circuit board and don't need an additional card to connect to an Ethernet network.) Details vary—and there are *many* details—but the same general principles apply to all common network connections.

A network interface card allows a PC to connect to a network.

In the simplest networks two or more computers are linked by cables. But direct connection is impractical for computers that are miles or oceans apart. For computers to communicate over long distances, they need to transmit information through other paths.

Communication á la Modem

The world is outfitted with plenty of electronic communication paths: An intricate network of cables, radio transmitters, and satellites enables people to talk by telephone between just about any two places on the planet. The telephone network is ideal for connecting remote computers, too, except it was designed to carry sound waves, not streams of bits. Before a digital signal—a stream of bits—can be transmitted over a standard phone line, it must be converted to an analog signal—a continuous wave. At the receiving end the analog signal first must be converted back into the bits representing the original digital message. Each of these tasks is performed by a modem (short for modulator/demodulator)—a hardware device that connects a computer's serial port to a telephone line.

A modem converts digital signals from a computer or terminal into analog signals. The analog waves are transmitted through telephone lines to another modem, which converts them back into digital signals.

An internal modem is installed on a circuit board inside the computer's chassis. An external modem sits in a box linked to a serial port. Both types use phone cables to connect to the telephone network through standard modular phone jacks. Modems differ in their transmission speeds, measured in bits per second (bps). Many people use the term *baud rate* instead of bps, but bps is technically more accurate for high-speed modems. Modems today commonly transmit at 28,800 bps to 56.6K (56,600) bps over standard phone lines. In general, communication by

166 Chapter 6 Networking and Telecommunication

An external modem (right) connects to the computer's serial port. An internal modem (left) is installed inside the computer's chassis.

modem is slower than communication between computers that are directly connected on a network. High-speed transmission isn't usually critical for text messages, but it can make a huge difference when the data being transmitted includes graphics, sound, video, and other multimedia elements—the kinds of data commonly found on the Web.

Faster Modem Alternatives

For faster remote connections, many businesses and homes bypass standard modems and use some kind of high-speed alternative. Several competing technologies are available to computer users in many areas: DSL, cable modems, and satellite modems.

- **DSL** uses standard phone lines and is provided by phone companies in many cities.
- **Cable** modems provide fast network connections through cable television networks in many areas.
- **High-speed wireless** connections can connect computers to networks using radio waves rather than wires.
- **Satellite dishes** can deliver fast computer network connections as well as television programs.

These technologies, sometimes called *broadband* technologies, are discussed in more detail later in this chapter and the next chapter.

Networks Near and Far

> **Imagine** how useful an office would be without a door.
> —Doug Engelbart, Internet pioneer, the importance of network connections

A LAN can contain a variety of computers and peripherals that are connected.

Computer networks come in all shapes and sizes, but most can be categorized as either local-area networks or wide-area networks.

A **local-area network (LAN)** is a network in which the computers are physically close to each other, usually in the same building. A typical LAN includes a collection of computers and peripherals; each computer and networked peripheral is an individual *node* on the network. Nodes are connected by cables, which serve as pathways for transporting data between machines. Some LAN cables, known as *twisted pair*, resemble the copper wires in standard telephone cables. Another type of cable, *coaxial cable*, is the same type of cable used to trans-

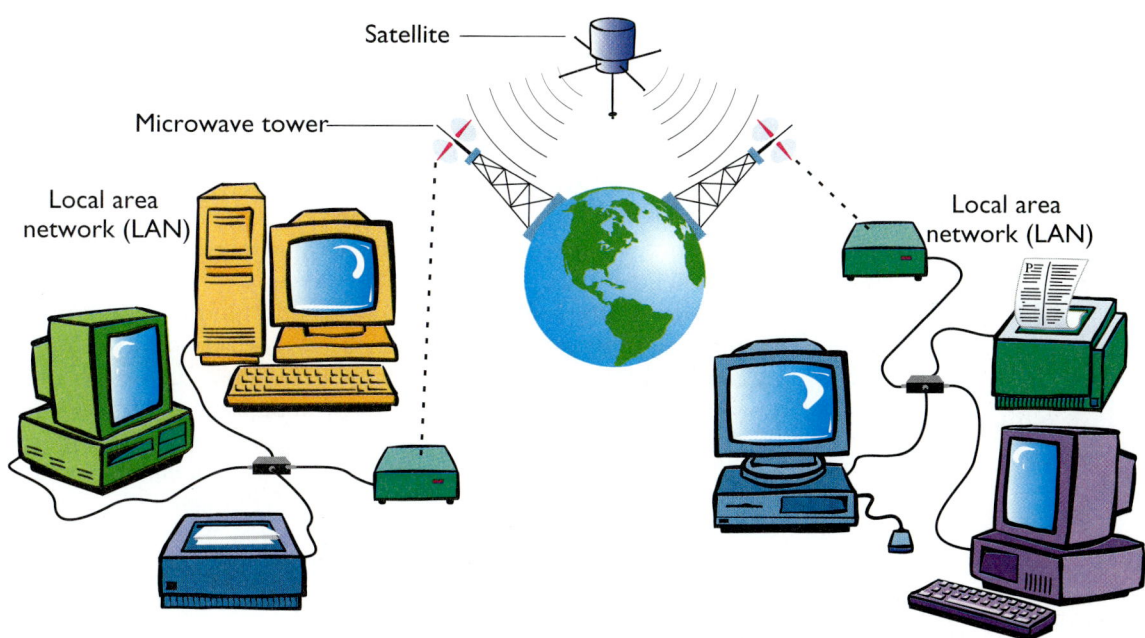

WANs are often made up of LANs linked by phone lines, microwave towers, and communication satellites.

port television signals. Some networks, mostly in homes, use existing household electrical or telephone wiring to transmit data.

In a **wireless network** each node has a tiny radio or infrared transmitter connected to its network port so it can send and receive data through the air rather than through cables. Wireless network connections are especially convenient for workers who are constantly on the move. They're also used for creating small networks in homes and small businesses because they can be installed without digging or drilling.

All computers on a LAN do not have to use the same operating system. For example, a single network might include Macintoshes, Windows PCs, and UNIX workstations. The computers can be connected in many different ways, and many rules and industry-defined standards dictate what will and won't work. Most organizations depend on network administrators to take care of the behind-the-scenes details so others can focus on using the network. For **enterprise network systems**—large, complex networks with hundreds of computers—network administrators depend on network management system software to help them track and maintain healthy networks.

A **metropolitan area network (MAN)** is a service that links two or more LANs within a city. MAN service is typically provided by a telephone or telecommunications company. With a MAN, a company can keep employees linked even if they're blocks away from each other.

A **wide-area network (WAN)**, as the name implies, is a network that extends over a long distance. In a WAN each network site is a node on the network. Data is transmitted long-distance between networks on a collection of common pathways known as a **backbone**. Large WANs are possible because of the web of telephone lines, microwave relay towers, and satellites that span the globe. Most WANs are private operations designed to link geographically dispersed corporate or government offices.

In today's internetworked world, communication frequently happens between LANs and WANs. **Bridges** and **gateways** are hardware devices that can pass messages between networks and, in some cases, translate messages so they can be understood by networks that obey different software protocols. **Routers** are hardware devices or software programs that route messages as they travel between networks via bridges and gateways.

Communication Software

Whether connected by cables, radio waves, or a combination of modems and telephone lines, computers need some kind of **communication software** to interact. To

> Pretty soon you'll have no more idea of **what computer you're using** than you have an idea of **where your electricity comes from**.
> —Danny Hillis, computer designer

communicate with each other, two machines must follow the same **protocol**—a set of rules for the exchange of data between a terminal and a computer or between two computers. One such protocol is transmission speed: If one machine is "talking" at 56,600 bps and the other is "listening" at 28,800 bps, the message doesn't get through. (Most modems can avoid this particular problem by adjusting their speeds to match each other.) Protocols include prearranged codes for messages such as "Are you ready?" "I am about to start sending a data file," and "Did you receive that file?" For two computers to understand each other, the software on both machines must be set to follow the same protocols. Communication software establishes a protocol that is followed by the computer's hardware.

Communication software can take a variety of forms. For users who work exclusively on a local-area network, many communication tasks are taken care of by a **network operating system (NOS)** such as Novell's Netware or Microsoft's Windows XP Server. Just as a personal computer's operating system shields the user from most of the nuts and bolts of the computer's operation, a NOS shields the user from the hardware and software details of routine communication between machines. But unlike a PC operating system, the NOS must respond to requests from many computers and must coordinate communication throughout the network. Today many organizations are replacing their specialized PC-based NOSs with intranet systems—systems built around the open standards and protocols of the Internet, as described in more detail in the next chapter.

The function and location of the network operating system depend in part on the LAN model. Some LANs are set up according to the **client/server model**, a hierarchical model in which one or more computers act as dedicated **servers** and all the remaining computers act as clients. Each server is a high-speed, high-capacity computer containing data and other resources to be shared with client computers. Using NOS server software, the server fulfills requests from clients for data and other resources. In a client/server network the bulk of the NOS resides on the server, but each client has NOS client software for sending requests to servers.

Many small networks are designed using the **peer-to-peer model** (sometimes called *p-to-p* or *P2P*) which enables every computer on the network to be both client and server. In this kind of network every user can make files publicly available to other users on the network. Some desktop operating systems, including many versions of Windows and the Mac OS, include all the software necessary to operate a peer-to-peer network. In practice many networks are hybrids, combining features of the client/server and peer-to-peer models.

Outside of a LAN one of the most common types of communication software is **terminal emulation software**, which enables a personal computer to function as a character-based "dumb" terminal—a simple input/output device for sending messages to and receiving messages from the host computer. A terminal program handles phone dialing, protocol management, and the miscellaneous details necessary for making a PC and a modem work together. With terminal software and a modem, a personal computer can communicate through phone lines with

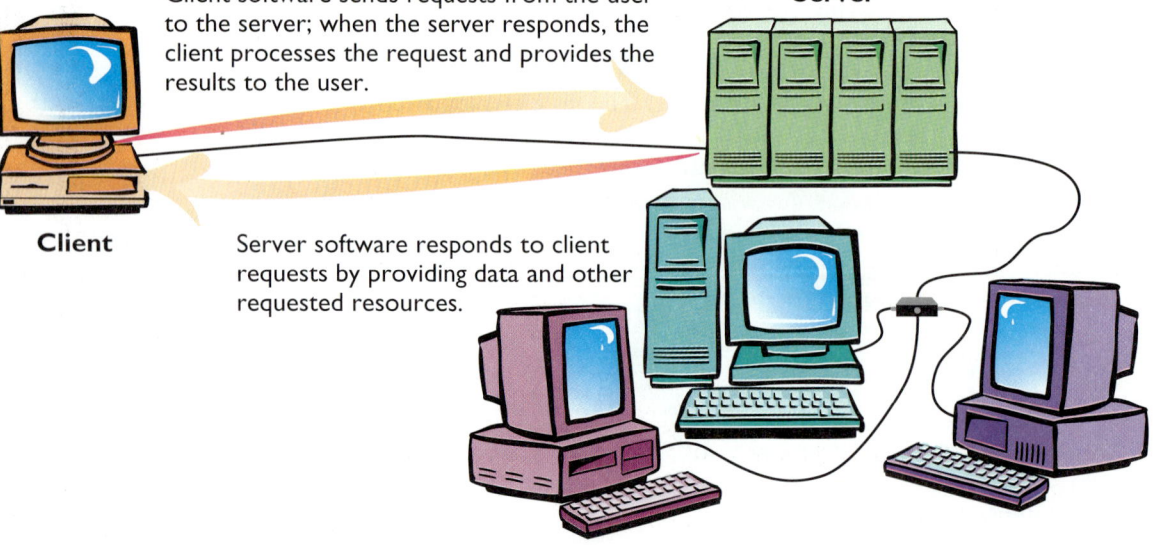

Client/server computing involves two-way communication between client and server programs.

Client software sends requests from the user to the server; when the server responds, the client processes the request and provides the results to the user.

Client

Server

Server software responds to client requests by providing data and other requested resources.

another PC, a network of computers, or, more commonly, a large multiuser computer. The Windows operating system package includes a terminal emulation program.

Basic terminal emulators are fine for bare-bones computer-to-computer connections, but their character-based user interfaces can be confusing to people who are used to point-and-click GUIs. What's more, they can't be used to explore media-rich destinations on and off the World Wide Web. That's why most online explorers today use Web browsers and other specialized graphical client software instead of generic terminal programs.

At the other end of the line the communication software is usually built into the multiuser operating system of the **host system**—the computer that provides services to multiple users. This software enables a timesharing computer to communicate with several other computers or terminals at once. The most widely used host operating system today is UNIX, the 30-year old OS that has many variants, including the non-commercial Linux OS discussed in Chapter 4, "Software Basics: The Ghost in the Machine."

Servers like these can provide software and data for hundreds of networked computers.

The Network Advantage

> A network becomes more valuable as **it reaches more users.**
> —Metcalf's Law, by Bob Metcalf, inventor of Ethernet

With this background in mind let's reconsider the three reasons people use networks:

- *Networks enable people to share computer hardware, reducing costs and making it possible for more people to take advantage of powerful computer equipment.* When computers and peripherals are connected in a LAN, computer users can share expensive peripherals. Before LANs the typical office had a printer connected to each computer. Today it's more common to find a small number of high-quality networked printers shared by a larger group of computers and users. In a client/server network, each printer may be connected to a *print server*—a server that accepts, prioritizes, and processes print jobs. While it may not make much sense for users to try to share a printer on a wide-area network, WAN users often share other hardware resources. Many WANs include powerful mainframes and supercomputers that can be accessed by authorized users at remote sites.

- *Networks enable people to share data and software programs, increasing efficiency and productivity.* In offices without networks people often transmit data and software by sneakernet—that is, by carrying disks between computers. In a LAN one or more computers can be used as **file servers**—storehouses for software and data that are shared by several users. With client software a user can get software and data from any server on the LAN without taking a step. A large file server is typically a dedicated computer that does nothing but serve files. But a peer-to-peer approach, allowing any computer to be both client and server, can be an efficient, inexpensive way to share files on small networks. Of course, sharing computer software on a network can violate software licenses (see Chapter 4) if not done with care. Many, but not all, licenses allow the software to be installed on a file server as long as the number of simultaneous users never exceeds the number of licensed copies. Some companies offer **site licenses** or **network licenses**, which reduce costs for multiple copies or remove restrictions on software copying and use at a network site. (Software copying is discussed in more detail in Chapter 11, "From Internet to Information Infrastructure.") Networks don't eliminate compatibility differences between different computer operating systems, but they can simplify data communication between machines. Users of Windows-compatible computers, for example, can't run Macintosh applications just because they're available on a file server. But they can, in many cases, use data files and documents created on a Macintosh and stored on the server. For example, a poster created with Adobe Illustrator on a Macintosh could be stored on a file server so it can be opened, edited, and printed by users of Illustrator on Windows PCs. File sharing isn't always that easy. If users of different systems use programs with incompatible file formats, they need to use **data translation software** to read and modify each other's files. On WANS the transfer of data and software can save more than shoe leather; it can save time. There's no need to send disks or CDs by overnight

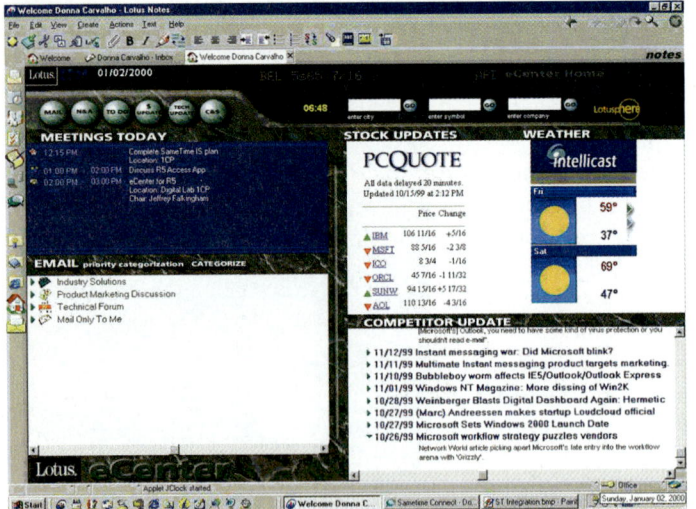

Lotus Notes, the most widely used groupware application, combines distributed databases, email, and document management to facilitate information sharing and workgroup collaboration. Lotus Notes is a client/server application that works on all major operating systems. Notes is compatible with many Internet protocols and services. (Lotus Notes® is a registered trademark of Lotus Development Corporation.)

mail between two sites if both sites are connected to the same network. Typically, data can be sent electronically between sites in a matter of minutes.

▶ *Networks enable people to work together in ways that are difficult or impossible without network technology.* Some software applications can be classified as **groupware**—programs designed to enable several networked users to work on the same documents at the same time. Groupware programs include multi-user appointment calendars, project-management software, database-management systems, and software for group editing of text-and-graphics documents. Many groupware programs today, such as Lotus Notes, are built on Internet protocols, so group members can communicate and share information using Web browsers and other standard Internet software tools.

Workgroups can benefit from networks without groupware packages. Most groupware features—email, message posting, calendars, and the rest—are generally available through Web and PC applications. Still, for large organizations a full-featured groupware package can be easier to manage than a collection of separate programs.

For many LAN and WAN users, network communication is limited to sending and receiving messages. As simple as this might sound, electronic messaging profoundly changes the way people and organizations work. In the next section we take a close look at the advantages and implications of interpersonal communication with computers.

Email, Teleconferences, and Instant Messaging: Interpersonal Computing

> New technology gives us two kinds of **newfound freedom**: The ability to **reach each other** 24/7— and the chance to **avoid one another** as never before.
>
> —Lori Gottlieb, Author of *Stick Figure*

Whether you're connected to a LAN, a WAN, a timesharing mainframe, or the Internet, you probably have access to some kind of **email** system that enables you to send and receive messages to others on the network. Chapter 0, ReadMe, covered the basics of email and illustrated a simple email session.

As explained in that chapter, most email messages are plain ASCII text; formatted documents, pictures, multimedia documents, and other computer files are typically sent as **attachments** that accompany messages. Newer email programs can (optionally) send, receive, edit, and display email messages formatted in HTML, the formatting language used in most Web pages. HTML email messages can include multiple typeface sizes and styles, and the text can be formatted in a variety of ways. The email client software hides the HTML from the sender and the recipient; they just see the formatted message. If the recipient views a formatted message with a mail program that doesn't recognize HTML, the formatting doesn't appear.

A variation of email is the **teleconference**—an online meeting between two or more people. Many teleconferencing systems enable users to communicate in real time, just as they would by telephone. In a typical **real-time teleconference** each participant sits at a computer or terminal, watching the messages appear on the screen as they're typed by other participants and typing comments for others to see immediately. Because of their give-and-take, informal nature, public real-time teleconferences are often called **chat rooms**. Whatever they're called, they tend to be chaotic, and typing responses can seem painfully slow to participants watching the process on the screen. Still, many people enjoy the immediacy of real-time communication.

Instant messaging (IM) adds spontaneity by allowing an online user to create a "buddy list" to determine who on the list is logged on at any given time, and start an instant keyboard conversation with anyone who's available from the list. Instant messaging was popularized by America Online as an entertaining way for members to chat with each other and with others on the Internet. IM services from AOL, Microsoft, and others are extremely popular today. Many businesses now use instant messaging to keep employees connected. IM technology is even built into many mobile phones.

In an **asynchronous teleconference** (sometimes called a *delayed teleconference*), participants type, post, and read messages at their convenience. In effect, participants in a delayed teleconference share an email box for messages related to the group's purposes. The Internet's Usenet **newsgroups**, discussed in the next chapter, are popular examples of asynchronous teleconferences.

Email, instant messaging, and other types of online communication can replace many memos, letters, phone calls, and face-to-face meetings, making organizations more productive and efficient.

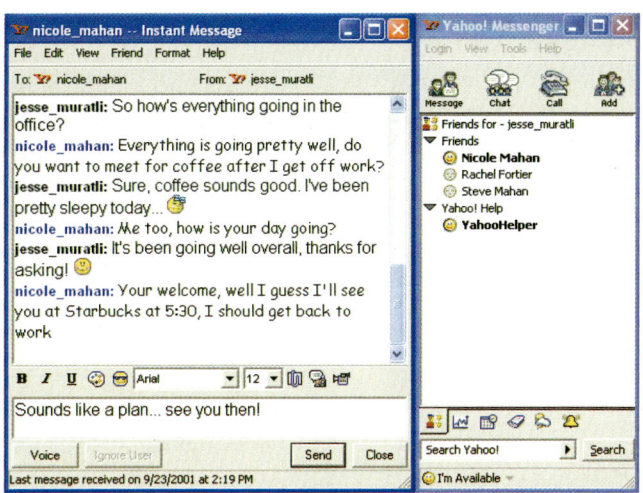

Instant messaging systems allow people to carry on real-time text-based conversations whenever they're online.

The Postal Alternative

The number of email messages now exceeds the number of letters sent through the U.S. Postal Service each year. Most experts expect email to take an even bigger chunk of the post office's business in coming years. Here's why:

- *Email is fast.* A typical email message takes no more than a few minutes from the time it's conceived until it reaches its destination—across the office or across the ocean. Email users often refer to traditional mail as "snail mail."
- *Email doesn't depend on location.* If you send someone an electronic message, that person can log in and read it from a computer at home, at the office, or anywhere in the world.
- *Email facilitates group communication.* In most email systems it's no harder and no more expensive to send a message to several people than to send it to one person. Most systems enable groups to have named distribution lists (sometimes called *aliases*) so a mail message addressed to an alias name (like faculty, office, or sales) is sent automatically to everyone in the group.
- *Email messages are digital data that can be edited and combined with other computer-generated documents.* Because the messages you receive by email are stored in your computer electronically, you can edit text and numbers without having to retype the entire document and without wasting paper. You can easily add text from other documents stored on your computer. When you're finished, you can forward the edited document back to the original sender or to somebody else for further processing.

Bypassing the Telephone

Email and teleconferencing also offer advantages over telephones:

- *Online communication is less intrusive than the telephone.* A ringing phone can interrupt concentration, disrupt a meeting, and bring just about any kind of activity to a standstill. Instead of shouting "Answer me now!" an email message waits patiently in the mailbox until the recipient has the time to handle it.
- *Online communication allows time shifting.* Email users aren't plagued by busy signals, unanswered rings, and message machines. You can receive email messages when you're busy, away, or asleep, and they'll be waiting for you when you have the time to pick them up. Time zones are largely irrelevant to email users.

Minimizing Meetings

Teleconferences and email can drastically reduce the amount of time people spend traveling to and participating in meetings. They offer several advantages for group decision-making:

- *Teleconferences and email enable decisions to evolve over time.* A group can discuss an issue electronically for hours, days, or weeks without the urgency of getting everything settled in a single session. New information can circulate when it's current rather than at the next meeting. Participants have time to think about each statement before responding. When organizations use teleconferences for discussion and information dissemination, meetings tend to be infrequent, short, and to the point.

- *Teleconferences and email make long-distance meetings possible.* Teleconferences can include people from all over the world, and nobody needs to leave home to participate. In fact, a growing number of programmers, writers, and other information workers literally work at home, communicating with colleagues by modem.
- *Teleconferences and email emphasize the message over the messenger.* In companies that rely on email and teleconferences for much of their communication, factors like appearance, race, gender, voice, mannerisms, and title tend to carry less weight than they do in other organizations. Status points go to people with good ideas and the ability to express those ideas clearly in writing.

Online Issues: Reliability, Security, Privacy, and Humanity

> Well there's egg and bacon; egg, sausage and bacon; egg and **spam**; bacon and **spam**; egg, bacon, sausage and **spam**; **spam**, bacon, sausage and **spam**; **spam**, egg, **spam**, **spam**, bacon and **spam**; **spam**, **spam**, **spam**, egg and **spam**; **spam**, **spam**, **spam**, **spam**, **spam**, **spam**, baked beans, **spam**, **spam**, **spam** and **spam**; or lobster thermidor aux crevettes with a mornay sauce garnished with truffle paté, brandy, and a fried egg on top of **spam**.
> —Waitress in *Monty Python's Flying Circus*

Any new technology introduces new problems, and online communication is no exception. Here are some of the most important:

- *Email and teleconferencing are vulnerable to machine failures, network glitches, human errors, and security breaches.* A system failure can cripple an organization that depends on email for critical communications. Internet users have experienced email blackouts caused by power outages, satellite failures, system overloads, and other technological breakdowns. Email attachment viruses like 2000's Love Bug have caused billions of dollars worth of damage worldwide. (See the Chapter "Computer Security and Risks" for more on viruses.)
- *Email can be overwhelming.* Many people receive hundreds of messages a day. Sifting through all those messages can consume hours of time that could have been used in other ways. Email overload has become such a serious problem that some businesses have implemented email-free Fridays to give their employees time to catch up on other work.
- *Email can be unsolicited.* Because it's easy, fast, and free, email is often used to send blanket messages to masses of people without permission. Some of this unsolicited mail is innocent (and not-so-innocent) humor. Some is designed to spread the word for a good cause. (Some "good cause" campaigns are, in fact, fraudulent or misinformed; even so, they continue to circulate.) Most unsolicited email is designed to sell something—weight-loss plans, insurance, vacation homes, cigarettes, pornography, cheap loans, political campaigns, or just about anything that people can pay for with a credit card. Junk email is known as spam because it can be just as annoying and repetitive as the menu in the Monty Python skit quoted above. But spam can also be a security risk, as you'll see in the next two chapters.
- *Email can pose a threat to privacy.* The U.S. Postal Service has a centuries-old tradition of safeguarding the privacy of first-class mail. Electronic communication is not grounded in that tradition. While most email messages are secure and private, there's always a potential for eavesdropping by an organization's system administrators and crafty system snoopers. Many businesses routinely monitor email sent by employees. In 1999 an online bookseller was found guilty of intercepting a competitor's email to gain market advantage. That same year users of Microsoft's popular HotMail service learned that their private email messages and address books could be easily accessed by anyone with a basic knowledge of how Web addresses work. Microsoft corrected the problem, but questions of email security remain.
- *Email can be faked.* Email forgery can be a serious threat on a surprising number of email systems. Some systems have safeguards against sending mail using someone else's ID, but none completely eliminates the threat. In time, it's likely that a digital signature will be encoded into every email message (using cryptography technology described in the Chapter "Computer Security and Risks."). Until then, forgery is a problem.

- *Email works only if everybody plays.* Just as the postal system depends on each of us checking our mailboxes daily, an email system can work only if all subscribers regularly log in and check their mail. Most people develop the habit quickly if they know important information is only available online.
- *Email and teleconferencing filter out many "human" components of communication.* When Bell invented the telephone, the public reaction was cool and critical. Businesspeople were reluctant to communicate through a device that didn't allow them to look each other in the eye and shake hands. While this reaction might seem strange today, it's worth a second look. When people communicate, part of the message is hidden in body language, eye contact, voice inflections, and other nonverbal signals. The telephone strips visual cues out of a message, and this can lead to misunderstandings. Most online communication systems peel away the sounds as well as the sights, leaving only plain words on a screen—words that might be misread if they aren't chosen carefully. What's more, email and teleconferences seldom replace casual "water cooler conversations"—those chance meetings that result in important communications and connections.

Problems notwithstanding, email and electronic messaging have become fixtures in businesses, schools, and government offices everywhere.

Converging Communication Technologies: From Messages to Money

The Internet is at the heart of the telecommunications explosion that's going on today. But many telecommunication services and technologies—online information services, fax machines, voice mail, GPS devices, mobile phones, video teleconferencing systems, ATMs, and more—aren't dependent on the Internet. Each of these applications is built around digital computer technology, and the boundaries that separate them are growing fuzzy as communication technologies converge.

> **Never in history** has distance meant less.
> —Alvin Toffler, in *Future Shock*

Online Information Services

A decade ago, when the Internet was the domain of researchers, thousands of electronic bulletin board systems (BBS) served as modem destinations for online explorers. Most BBSs were small operations operated out of homes. Visitors could post messages and read messages left by others with similar interests, send and receive email, and share software. Today most BBSs have been replaced by Web sites that offer the same services, and more, via the Internet. The same fate has befallen most online databases. Customers who used to connect directly to database services such as Dow Jones News Retrieval Service now retrieve the same information through Web sites on the Internet.

Commercial online services—America Online, CompuServe, and Prodigy—can still be accessed without venturing onto the Internet. Subscribers have access to a variety of services: news, research tools, shopping, banking, games, chat rooms, bulletin boards, email, instant messaging, software libraries. Subscribers can download software—copy it from the host computer to their computers—and upload software—post it on the host system so it's available for others. (Software sharing is part of the community spirit networks, but it's not without problems. Two of these problems, software piracy and viruses, are discussed in the Chapter "Computer Security and Risks.")

The Internet has forced online services to change the way they do business. Customers who used to be content within the confines of a particular service now want to have access to the World Wide Web. Many information services have responded to the Web's popularity by becoming part of it. Before the Web, CompuServe was the largest online information service. In 1997, after several consecutive years of declining enrollment, it converted to a fee-based subscription outpost on the Web. Not long afterward it was purchased by America Online (AOL), now the largest private online service.

AOL's customers use special client software rather than a Web browser to connect and use its services. But the AOL client software includes a Web browser so AOL users can explore the entire Web—not just the offerings inside AOL. AOL also provides space for customers to build

Online services such as AOL offer a variety of services in a privately controlled environment.

My Places
- Customize My Places
- Greetings
- Horoscopes
- Local News
- Maps & Directions
- My Portfolios
- People Directory
- Sports Scores
- Stock Quotes
- What's New on AOL
- White Pages

Have You Tried?
- AOL Anywhere
- People Directory

- AOL Help
- Go to Internet
- Parental Controls

AOL Keyword: Welcome

Rules of Thumb

Online Survival Tips

Whether you log into an information service or the Internet, you're using a relatively new communication medium with new rules. Here are some suggestions for successful online communication:

- **If your online service is metered, do what you can offline.** Do your homework before you log in so you don't have to look things up while the meter is running. Compose, edit, and address messages before you log on. Plan your strategy before you connect.
- **Avoid peak hours.** Online traffic comes in waves. If you avoid the peaks, you'll save time and aggravation.
- **Let your system do as much of the work as possible.** If your email program can sort mail, filter mail, or automatically append a signature file to your mail, take advantage of those features. If you send similar messages over and over, store them, and recycle the relevant text. If you find yourself sending messages to the same group of people repeatedly, create an alias that includes all of those people—a distribution list that can save you the trouble of typing or selecting all those names each time. If you can automate repetitive processes like logging in and downloading mail, do it; the time you invest will be paid back over and over.
- **Store names and addresses in an online address book.** Email addresses aren't always easy to remember and type correctly. If you mistype even a single character, your message will probably either go to the wrong person or *bounce*—come back to you with some kind of undeliverable mail message. An online address book enables you to select addresses without typing them each time you use them.
- **Protect your privacy.** Miss Manners said it well in a 1998 Wired interview: "For email, the old postcard rule applies. Nobody else is supposed to read your postcards, but you'd be a fool if you wrote anything private on one."
- **Cross-check online information sources.** Don't assume that every information nugget you see online is valid, accurate, and timely. If you "hear" something online, treat it with the same degree of skepticism that you would if you heard it in a cafeteria or coffee shop.
- **Be aware and awake.** It's easy to lose track of yourself and your time online. In his book *Virtual Community*, Howard Rheingold advises, "Rule Number One is to pay attention. Rule Number Two might be: Attention is a limited resource, so pay attention to where you pay attention."
- **Avoid information overload.** When it comes to information, more is not necessarily better. Search selectively. Don't waste time and energy trying to process mountains of online information. Information is not knowledge, and knowledge is not wisdom.

and display personal Web pages. By including Internet email and Web services in its package, AOL has become the largest Internet service provider.

Many experts question whether everything-under-one-roof services like AOL can successfully compete with the free-for-all World Wide Web. Others believe there'll always be a place for services that can simplify the online experience. One thing is certain: The Internet will continue to bring changes to these services, and the changes will come rapidly.

Video Teleconferencing

A **video teleconference** enables people to communicate face to face over long distances by combining video and computer technology. In its simplest form video teleconferencing is like two-way television. Each participant sits in a room equipped with video cameras, microphones, and television monitors. Video signals are beamed between sites so that every participant can see and hear every other participant on television monitors. Video teleconferencing is mainly practiced in special conference rooms by groups that meet too often to travel. But some businesses now use video telephones that transmit pictures as well as words through phone lines.

With the addition of a video camera, an interface, and a high-speed network connection, a telephone-capable desktop computer can be used for video teleconferencing. These systems enable callers to see each other on their computer screens while they carry on phone

Video conferencing hardware and software make this long-distance business meeting possible.

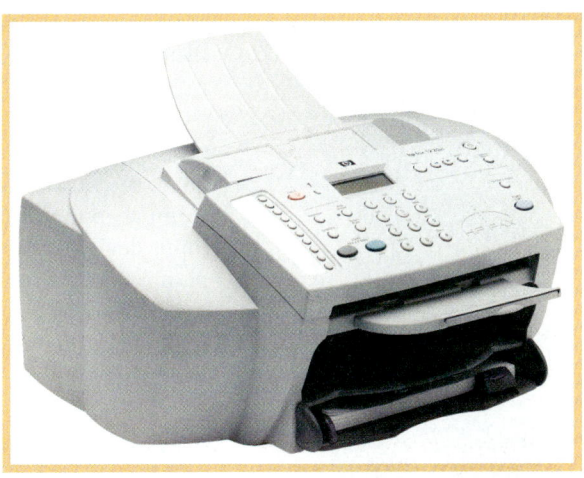

A fax modem (left) enables a personal computer to communicate with a fax machine (right).

conversations over high-speed computer networks, including the Internet. Some enable them to view and edit shared documents while they talk. Today most PC-based video teleconferencing systems suffer from erratic video transmission, but the technology is getting better quickly.

Fax Machines and Fax Modems

A **facsimile (fax) machine** is a fast and convenient tool for transmission of information stored on paper. When you send a fax of a paper document, the sending fax machine scans each page, converting the scanned image into a series of electric pulses and sending those signals over phone lines to another fax machine. The receiving fax machine uses the signals to construct and print black-and-white facsimiles or copies of the original pages. In a sense the two fax machines and the telephone line serve as a long-distance photocopy machine.

A computer can send onscreen documents through a fax modem to a receiving fax machine. The **fax modem** translates the document into signals that can be sent over phone wires and decoded by the receiving fax machine. In effect, the receiving fax machine acts like a remote printer for the document. A computer can also use a fax modem to receive transmissions from fax machines, treating the sending fax machine as a kind of remote scanner. A faxed letter can be displayed on screen or printed to paper, but it can't be immediately edited with a word processor the way an email message can. Like a scanned document, the digital facsimile is nothing more than a collection of black-and-white dots to the computer. Before a faxed document can be edited, it must be processed by optical character recognition (OCR) software.

Voice Mail and Computer Telephony

"Hi. This is Anita Chen. I'm either away from my desk or on another line. Please leave your name, number, and a message. If you prefer to talk to a receptionist, press zero." The **voice mail** system that delivers this recorded message is more than an answering device; it's a voice messaging system with many of the features of an email system.

Your response is recorded in Anita's voice mailbox. When she dials the system number from any telephone and enters her ID number or password on the phone's keypad, she can listen to her messages, respond to them, forward copies to others, and delete unneeded messages. She can do just about anything she could do with an email message except edit messages electronically and attach computer documents.

In spite of its growing popularity, voice mail has detractors. Many people resent taking orders from a machine rather than being able to talk to a human operator. Many callers are frustrated by having to wade through endless voice menus before they can speak to a real person. Office workers often complain about the time-consuming processes of recording and listening to messages.

Voice mail is a familiar example of a growing trend toward **computer telephony integration (CTI)**—the linking of computers and telephones to gain productivity. Many PCs have **telephony** software and hardware that allow them to serve as speakerphones, answering machines, and complete voice mail systems. A typical computer telephony system connects to a standard phone line through a modem capable of handling voice conversations. But it's also possible to

The Kyocera Smartphone is a cell phone and a PDA that uses the Palm OS. Integrated software makes it easy to call contacts from the address book, record notes about phone conversations, and connect to the Internet.

send voice signals through a LAN, a WAN, or the Internet, bypassing the phone companies (and their charges) altogether. So far this kind of network telephony isn't as simple or reliable as commercial phone services, but it may soon pose a threat to phone company profits.

On the mobile front, the line between computers and telephones is especially fuzzy. Many mobile phones can connect to the Internet, do instant messaging, upload and download short email messages, and display miniature Web pages. Handheld PDAs from Palm, Handspring, Compaq, and other companies can do the same things, but with larger screens and friendlier input devices. These handheld computers use software to integrate the functions of a PDA, a phone, and an Internet terminal. Hybrid PDAs and phones involve tradeoffs—do you want to use a boxy PDA as a phone or type email on a tiny phone keypad? But most analysts expect rapid advances in these converging technologies over the next few years—advances such as reliable speech recognition—that will make these devices much more useful for people on the go.

The Global Positioning System

The U.S. Department of Defense **Global Positioning System (GPS)** includes 24 satellites that circle the Earth, carefully spaced so that they can pinpoint any location on the planet. The satellites are positioned so that from any point on the planet, at any time, four satellites will be above the horizon. Each satellite contains a computer, an atomic clock, and a radio. On the ground, a **GPS receiver** can use signals broadcast by three or four visible satellites to determine its position. Handheld GPS receivers can display locations, maps, and directions on small screens; GPS receivers can also be embedded in automobile navigation systems or connected to laptop computers. Members of the U.S. military use GPS receivers to keep track of where they are, but so do scientists, engineers, motorists, hikers, boaters, and others. Many mobile phones include GPS receivers so they can be located quickly when used for emergency calls.

E-Money

When you strip away the emotional trappings, money is just another form of information. Dollars, yen, pounds, and rubles are all just symbols that make it easy for people to exchange goods and services. Money can be just about anything, provided people agree to its value. During the last few centuries, paper replaced metal as the major form of money. Today paper is being replaced by digital patterns stored in computer media. Most major financial transactions take place inside computers, and most money is stored on computer disks and tapes instead of in wallets and safe deposit boxes.

Money, like other digital information, can be transmitted through computer networks. That's why it's possible to withdraw cash from your checking account using an **automated teller machine (ATM)** at a bank, airport, or shopping mall thousands of miles from your home bank. An ATM (not to be confused with the communication protocol with the same initials) is a specialized terminal linked to a bank's main computer through a commercial banking network.

An ATM isn't necessary for **electronic fund transfer** to take place. Many people have paychecks deposited automatically in checking or savings accounts and have bills paid automatically out of those accounts. These automatic transfers don't involve cash or checks; they're done inside computer networks. Many banks allow you to use your home computer or your touch-tone phone to transfer money between accounts, check balances, and pay bills. Electronic fund transfer is one component of **electronic commerce,** or **e-commerce**—commercial activity that takes place through networked computers. E-commerce will be discussed in more detail in later chapters.

A GPS receiver helps this hiker produce an extremely accurate map of the Colorado trail.

Emerging Communication Technologies: Beyond Wires

After more than a century of electric technology, **we have extended our central nervous system** itself in a global embrace, **abolishing both space and time** as far as our planet is concerned.

—Marshall McLuhan, in *Understanding Media*

Until recently, most computer networks depended on wires to transmit electrical signals between computers. But the last decade has seen enormous growth in network technology that carries bits in other ways. In this section, we'll focus on two types of network technology that are dramatically changing the ways people communicate: fiber optic cables and wireless technology. But first, a few words about bandwidth.

Building Bandwidth

Computer networks transmit text, numbers, pictures, sounds, speech, music, video, and money as digital signals. The World Wide Web is fertile ground for mixing of these diverse media. Video on demand, pay-by-the-song music shopping, interactive multiplayer games, real-time auctions, picture phones, customized news feeds, and more are available on the Web—if you don't mind putting up with small, jerky videos, grainy images, and (especially) long waits.

Every day stock traders move billions of dollars in funds electronically through world markets.

The cause of most of these problems on the Internet and other networks is a lack of bandwidth at some point in the path between the sending computer and the receiving computer. The word has a technical definition, but in the world of computer networks bandwidth generally refers to the quantity of information that can be transmitted through a communication medium in a given amount of time. In general, increased bandwidth means faster transmission speeds. Bandwidth is typically measured in kilobits (thousands of bits) or megabits (millions of bits) per second. (Since a byte is 8 bits, a megabit is 1/8 of a megabyte. The text of this chapter is about 1/16 megabyte, or a half megabit of information. A physical medium capable of transmitting 100 megabits per second could theoretically transmit this chapter's text 200 times in one second.) Bandwidth can be affected by many factors, including the physical media that make up the network, the amount of network traffic, the software protocols of the network, and the type of network connection.

Some people find it easier to visualize bandwidth by thinking of a network cable as a highway. One way to increase bandwidth in a cable is to increase the number of parallel wires in that cable—the equivalent of adding more lanes to a freeway. Another way is to increase the speed with which information passes through the cable; this is the same as increasing the speed of the vehicles on the freeway. Of course, it's easier and safer to increase highway speed limits if you have a traffic flow system that minimizes the chance of collisions and accidents; in the same way, more efficient, reliable software can increase network bandwidth. But increasing a highway's throughput doesn't help much if cars pile up at the entry and exit ramps; in the same way, a high-bandwidth network seems like a low-bandwidth network if you're connected through a slow modem.

Fiber Optic Connections

> These are the days of **lasers in the jungle Lasers in the jungle** somewhere. . . .
> —Paul Simon, in "The Boy in the Bubble"

Broadband network connections such as cable modems and DSL are faster than standard modems because they have greater bandwidth. But DSL and cable modems have nowhere near the bandwidth of fiber optic cables that are gradually replacing copper wires in the worldwide telephone network. Fiber optic cables use light waves to carry information at blinding speeds. A single fiber optic cable can transmit half a gigabit (500 *million* bits) per second, replacing 10,000 standard telephone cables!

All-digital fiber optic networks improve the sound quality of phone calls and the speed of long-distance phone response while cutting costs for callers. More importantly, a fiber optic network can rapidly and reliably transmit masses of multimedia data at the same time it's handling voice messages.

Digital fiber optic networks now connect major communication hubs around the world. Many large businesses and government institutions are connected to the global fiber optic network. But most small businesses and homes still depend on copper wires for the "last mile," as it's often referred to in the industry—the link to the closest on-ramp to the fiber optic freeway. Fiber optic communication lines will eventually find their way into most homes, radically changing our lives in the process. These cables will provide two-way links to the outside world for our phones, televisions, radios, computers, and a variety of other devices.

The lines that separate the telephone industry, the computer industry, and the home entertainment industry will blur as voices, video, music, and messages flow back and forth on light waves. Many services we take for granted today—video rentals, cable TV, newspapers, and magazines, for example—will be transformed or replaced by digital high-bandwidth interactive delivery systems of the future. At the same time, entirely new forms of communication are likely to emerge.

Wireless Communication Takes Off

> Wireless technology is a **liberating force**. It will make possible **human-centered computers**. This wasn't possible before because we were **anchored to a PC**, and we had to go to it like going to a temple to **pay our respects**.
>
> —Michael Dertouzos, Director, MIT Laboratory for Computer Science

Different types of networks are built with different physical media; the media play critical roles in determining network performance. The two most important performance variables on the physical layer are bandwidth—the amount of information that can be transmitted in a given amount of time—and maximum operating distance.

A lightning-fast network connection to your desktop is of little use if you're away from your desk most of the time. When bandwidth is less important than mobility and portability, wireless technology can provide practical solutions.

Infrared wireless technology has been around for many years. Many laptops and handheld computers have infrared ports that can send and receive digital information short distances. Infrared technology isn't widely used in networks because of distance and line-of-sight limitations. Still, infrared technology has practical applications—especially for mobile users. For example, Palm users routinely share programs and data by beaming them through infrared links.

One popular wireless LAN technology is known in the industry as **Wi-Fi** or *802.11b*. (Apple refers to its brand of 802.11b as Airport.) This client/server technology allows multiple computers to connect to a LAN through a base station up to 150 feet away. Wi-Fi isn't as fast as a hard-wired Ethernet connection, but it's fast enough for most applications, including multimedia Web downloads. A home Wi-Fi network allows computers to connect from any room without cables. Wi-Fi base stations are showing up in airports, coffee shops, and other public places. On some campuses Wi-Fi networks allow students to effortlessly connect their laptops to the Internet from dorm rooms, classrooms, or tree-lined gardens.

Another type of wireless technology is **Bluetooth**, named for a Danish king who overcame his country's religious differences. Bluetooth technology

NETWORKS ARE BUILT ON PHYSICAL MEDIA

Type	Principal Uses	Maximum Operating Distance (without amplification)	Cost
Twisted pair	Small LANS	300 feet	Low
Coaxial cable	Large LANS	600–2,500 feet	Medium
Fiber optic	Network backbones; WANS	1–25 miles	High
Wireless/infrared	LANS	3–1,000 feet (line of sight)	Medium
Wireless/radio	Connecting things that move	Varies considerably	High

overcomes differences between mobile phones, handheld computers, and PCs, making it possible for all of these devices to communicate with each other regardless of operating system. Bluetooth uses radio technology similar to Wi-Fi, but its transmissions are limited to about 30 feet. In some ways Bluetooth competes with Wi-Fi, but it has the potential to complement a Wi-Fi network. With Bluetooth it's possible to create a **personal area network (PAN)**—a network that links a variety of personal electronic devices so they can communicate with each other. Bluetooth technology is still in the early stages of development. When it becomes widely available and affordable, it will open up all kinds of possibilities:

- A pacemaker senses a heart attack and notifies the victim's mobile phone to dial 911.
- A car radio communicates with parking-lot video cameras to find out where spaces are available.
- A pen scans business cards and sends the information to a PDA inside a briefcase.
- A medical wristband transmits an accident victim's vital information to a doctor's handheld computer.
- A cell phone tells you about specials on clothes (available in your size) as you walk past stores in a mall. (Many fear that this technology will usher in a new era of wireless spam.)

This University of Tennessee student can connect to the Internet using the campus wireless network.

Wi-Fi and Bluetooth aren't part of mainstream culture yet, but wireless communication through mobile phones certainly is. In two decades, mobile phones have gone from simple analog systems to powerful digital devices that can handle Internet data along with voice traffic. In the United States, mobile phones are seldom used to connect to the Internet. Mobile Internet connections are more common in Europe and Asia. In Japan, people routinely use their phones to send and receive email, exchange instant messages, check news headlines, shop, play games, and even do karaoke. The next generation of mobile wireless technology, often called **3G**, promises high-bandwidth connections that will support true multimedia, including real-time video.

The convenience of wireless technology carries a price in security. Wireless networks are far more vulnerable to eavesdropping, data snooping, and hacking than wired networks. Many techniques and tools can help preserve privacy and security, but none of them so far is foolproof. These problems are discussed in more detail in the security chapter.

Many Japanese students use their mobile phones regularly for instant messaging and multiplayer games.

Digital Communication in Perspective

Fiber optic networks and wireless networks are already changing our lives, and the changes will accelerate as these technologies spread. We'll explore these changes in the next chapter as we focus on the Internet—the network of networks at the center of the communication revolution.

Before we do, let's step back and put electronic communication in a larger perspective. As futurist Stewart Brand reminded us in his groundbreaking book, *The Media Lab*:

We can be grateful for the vast dispersed populations of peasant and tribal cultures in the world who have never used a telephone or a TV, who walk where they're going, who live by local subsistence skills honed over millennia. You need to go on foot in Africa, Asia, South America to realize how many of these people there are and how sound they are. If the world city goes smash, they'll pick up the pieces, as they've done before. Whatever happens, they are a reminder that electronic communication may be essential to one kind of living, but it is superfluous to another.

CrossCurrents

Time To Do Everything Except Think

David Brooks

Is there a downside to the digital communication explosion? In this lighthearted article, first published in the April 30, 2001 issue of Newsweek, David Brooks raises some serious questions about being over-connected. Brooks is the author of Bobos in Paradise.

Somewhere up in the canopy of society, way above where normal folks live, there will soon be people who live in a state of perfect wirelessness. They'll have mobile phones that download the Internet, check scores and trade stocks. They'll have Palm handhelds that play music, transfer photos and get Global Positioning System readouts. They'll have laptops on which they watch movies, listen to baseball games and check inventory back at the plant. In other words, every gadget they own will perform all the functions of all the other gadgets they own, and they will be able to do it all anywhere, any time.

Wireless Woman will do a full day's work on the beach in her bikini: her personal digital assistant comes with a thong clip so she can wear it on her way to the pina colada stand. Her phones beep, her pagers flash red lights; when they go off, she looks like a video arcade. Wireless Man will be able to put on his performance underwear, hop in his SUV and power himself up to the top of a Colorado mountain peak. He'll be up there with his MP3 device and his carabiners enjoying the view while conference-calling the sales force, and playing MegaDeath with gamers in Tokyo and Sydney. He'll be smart enough to have enough teeny-tiny lithium batteries on hand to last weeks, and if he swallows them they'd cure depression for life. He's waiting for them to develop a laptop filled with helium that would actually weigh less than nothing, and if it could blow up into an inflatable sex doll he'd never have to come down.

So there he sits in total freedom on that Rocky Mountain peak. The sky is blue. The air is crisp. Then the phone rings. His assistant wants to know if he wants to switch the company's overnight carrier. He turns off his phone so he can enjoy a little spiritual bliss. But first, there's his laptop. Maybe somebody sent him an important email. He wrestles with his conscience. His conscience loses. It's so easy to check, after all . . .

Never being out of touch means never being able to get away. But Wireless Man's problem will be worse than that. His brain will have adapted to the tempo of wireless life. Every 15 seconds there is some new thing to respond to. Soon he has this little rhythm machine in his brain. He does everything fast. He answers emails fast and sloppily. He's bought the fastest machines, and now the idea of waiting for something to download is a personal insult. His brain is operating at peak RPMs.

He sits amid nature's grandeur and says, "It's beautiful. But it's not moving. I wonder if I got any new voice mails." He's addicted to the perpetual flux of the information networks. He craves his next data fix. He's a speed freak, an info junkie. He wants to slow down, but can't.

Today's business people live in an overcommunicated world. There are too many Web sites, too many reports, too many bits of information bidding for their attention. The successful ones are forced to become deft machete wielders in this jungle of communication. They ruthlessly cut away at all the extraneous data that are encroaching upon them. They speed through their tasks so they can cover as much ground as possible, answering dozens of emails at a sitting and scrolling past dozens more. After all, the main scarcity in their life is not money; it's time. They guard every precious second, the way a desert wanderer guards his water.

The problem with all this speed, and the frantic energy that is spent using time efficiently, is that it undermines creativity. After all, creativity is usually something that happens while you're doing something else: when you're in the shower your brain has time to noodle about and create the odd connections that lead to new ideas. But if your brain is always multitasking, or responding to techno-prompts, there is no time or energy for undirected mental play. Furthermore, if you are consumed by the same information loop circulating around everyone else, you don't have anything to stimulate you into thinking differently. You don't have time to read the history book or the science book that may actually prompt you to see your own business in a new light. You don't have access to unexpected knowledge. You're just swept along in the same narrow current as everyone else, which is swift but not deep.

So here's how I'm going to get rich. I'm going to design a placebo machine. It'll be a little gadget with voice recognition and everything. Wireless People will be able to log on and it will tell them they have no messages. After a while, they'll get used to having no messages. They'll be able to experience life instead of information. They'll be able to reflect instead of react. My machine won't even require batteries.

DISCUSSION QUESTIONS

1. Do you think Wireless Woman and Wireless Man are realistic? Explain.
2. Do you agree that speed and efficiency undermine creativity? Explain.

Summary

Networking is one of the most important trends in computing today. Computer networks are growing in popularity because they allow computers to share hardware, allow computers to send software and data back and forth, and enable people to work together in ways that would be difficult or impossible without networks.

LANs are made up of computers that are close enough to be directly connected with cables or wireless radio transmitters/receivers. Most LANs include shared printers and file servers. WANs are made up of computers separated by considerable distance. The computers are connected to each other through the telephone network, which includes cables, microwave transmission towers, and communication satellites. Before it can be transmitted on a phone network, a computer's digital signal is converted to an analog signal using a modem.

Communication software takes care of the details of communication between machines—details like protocols that determine how signals will be sent and received. Network operating systems typically handle the mechanics of LAN communication. Terminal programs enable personal computers to function as character-based terminals when connected to other PCs or to timesharing computers. Other types of specialized client programs have graphical user interfaces and additional functionality. Timesharing operating systems enable multiuser computers to communicate with several terminals at a time.

Email and teleconferencing are the two most common forms of communication between people on computer networks. Email and teleconferencing offer many advantages over traditional mail and telephone communication and can shorten or eliminate many meetings. But because of several important limitations email and teleconferencing cannot completely replace older communication media.

A modem can link a computer to online services that offer shopping, banking, teleconferencing, software downloading, email, games, and other features. But online services are being overshadowed and transformed by the Internet, the global network that provides the same services and many more.

Other kinds of telecommunication, including fax, voice mail, GPS, video teleconferencing, and electronic fund transfer, are built on computer technology. The conversion of the global phone network to fiber optic cables with digital switching makes it possible for phone lines to transmit all kinds of digital data along with phone calls. Increased bandwidth increases communication options on and off the Internet. The lines that separate the telephone, computer, and home entertainment industries will blur as new communication options blossom.

Chapter Review

▼ Key Terms

analog signal (p. 165)
asynchronous teleconference (p. 171)
attachment (p. 170)
bandwidth (p. 177)
bits per second (bps) (p. 165)
bluetooth (p. 178)
bounce (p. 174)
bridges (p. 167)
chat room (p. 170)
client/server model (p. 168)
communication software (p. 167)
digital signal (p. 165)
direct connection (p. 165)
download (p. 173)
electronic commerce (e-commerce) (p. 176)
electronic mail (email) (p. 170)
Ethernet (p. 165)
facsimile (fax) machine (p. 175)
fax modem (p. 175)
fiber optic cable (p. 177)
file server (p. 169)
gateways (p. 167)
Global Positioning System (GPS) (p. 176)
groupware (p. 170)
host system (p. 169)
instant messaging (p. 170)
local-area network (LAN) (p. 166)
modem (p. 165)
network interface card (NIC) (p. 165)
network license (p. 169)
network operating system (NOS) (p. 168)
online service (p. 173)
peer-to-peer model (p. 168)
port (p. 165)
protocol (p. 168)
real-time teleconference (p. 170)
remote access (p. 165)
router (p. 167)
server (p. 168)
site license (p. 169)
spam (p. 172)
telecommunication (p. 164)
teleconference (p. 170)
telephony (p. 175)
terminal emulation software (p. 168)
upload (p. 173)
video teleconference (p. 174)
voice mail (p. 175)
wide-area network (WAN) (p. 167)
Wi-Fi (p. 178)
wireless network (p. 167)

Interactive Quiz Questions

1. The *Computer Confluence* CD-ROM contains self-test quiz questions related to this chapter, including multiple choice, true or false, and matching questions.
2. The *Computer Confluence* Web site, www.prenhall.com/beekman, contains self-test exercises related to this chapter. Follow the instructions for taking a quiz. After you've completed your quiz, you can email the results to your instructor.

   The Web site also contains open-ended discussion questions called Internet Explorations. Discuss one or more of the Internet Exploration questions at the section for this chapter.

Review Questions

1. Define or describe each of the key terms listed in the "Key Terms" section. Check your answers using the glossary.
2. Give three general reasons for the importance of computer networking. (*Hint*: Each reason is related to one of the three essential components of every computer system.)
3. How do the three general reasons listed in Question 2 relate specifically to LANs?
4. How do the three general reasons listed in Question 2 relate specifically to WANs?
5. Under what circumstances is a modem necessary for connecting computers in networks? What does the modem do?
6. Describe at least two different kinds of communication software.
7. How could a file server be used in a student computer lab? What software licensing issues would be raised by using a file server in a student lab?
8. What are the differences between email and instant messaging systems?
9. Describe some things you can do with email that can't be done with regular mail.
10. Describe several potential problems associated with email and teleconferencing.
11. "Money is just another form of information." Explain this statement, and describe how it relates to automated teller machines and electronic fund transfer.
12. Wi-Fi and Bluetooth wireless technologies are designed to serve different purposes than mobile phone technology. Explain this statement.

Discussion Questions

1. Suppose you have an important message to send to a friend in another city, and you can use the telephone, email, real-time teleconference, fax, or overnight mail service. Discuss the advantages and disadvantages of each. See if you can think of a situation for each of the five options in which that particular option is the most appropriate choice.
2. Some people choose to spend several hours every day online. Do you see potential hazards in this kind of heavy modem use? Explain your answer.
3. In the quote at the end of the chapter, Stewart Brand points out that electronic communication is essential for some of the world's people and irrelevant to others. What distinguishes these two groups? What advantages and disadvantages does each have?

Projects

1. Find out about your school's computer networks. Are there many LANs? How are they connected? Who has access to them? What are they used for?
2. Spend a few hours exploring an online service like AOL. Describe the problems you encounter in the process. Which parts of the service are the most useful and interesting?

Sources and Resources

Books

The Communications Miracle: The Telecommunication Pioneers from Morse to the Information Superhighway, by John Bray (New York: Plenum, 1995). This book gives the communication revolution a historical perspective by mixing technical explanations with human stories.

How Networks Work, Millennium Edition, by Frank J. Derfler, Jr., and Les Freed (Indianapolis, IN: Que, 2000). Follows the model popularized with the *How Computers Work* series. It uses a mix of text and graphics to illuminate the nuts and bolts of PC networks.

The Little Network Book, by Lon Poole and John Rizzo (Berkeley, CA: Peachpit Press, 1999). Networking isn't just for professionals anymore. Today's operating systems and network hardware make it (almost) easy to set up a network in a home or small business. This little book clearly explains options, techniques, and technology for setting up and using a network of PCs, Macs, or both.

Networking: A Beginner's Guide, Second Edition, by Bruce Hallberg (Berkeley, CA: Osborne McGraw-Hill, 2001). This book is written for people who know a fair amount about bits and bytes inside a computer but want to learn the ins-and-outs of transmitting those bits and bytes between computers. It's clearly written, but probably too technical for *true* beginners.

The Essential Guide to Networking, by James Edward Keogh (Upper Saddle River, NJ: Prentice Hall, 2000). This book is part of a series of technical *Essential* books for non-technical professionals. This one provides a broad overview of network technology, from LANs and WANs to the Internet and wireless networks.

The Essential Guide to Telecommunications, Third Edition, by Annabel Z. Dodd (Prentice Hall, 2002). This popular book presents a clear, comprehensive guide to the telecommunications industry and technology, including telephone systems, cable systems, wireless systems, and the Internet. If you want to understand how the pieces of our communication networks fit together, this book is a great place to start.

Computer Networks and Internets, Third Edition, by Douglas E. Comer, CD-ROM by Ralph Droms (Upper Saddle River, NJ: Prentice Hall, 2001). This text answers the question, "How do computer networks and internets operate?" Coverage includes LANs, WANs, Internet packets, digital telephony, protocols, client/server interaction, network security, and the underpinnings of the World Wide Web. A CD-ROM and a companion Web site supplement the text.

Telecommunications Systems and Technology, by Michael Khader and William E. Barnes (Upper Saddle River, NJ: Prentice Hall, 2000). This text is a technical overview of telecommunications systems, with in-depth discussions of modems, telephony systems, multimedia communication, TCP/IP, and many other topics.

Wireless Nation: The Frenzied Launch of the Cellular Revolution, by James B. Murray (Perseus Books, 2001). The mobile phone explosion and the PC both burst into our culture in the last decades of the twentieth century, and they came together through the Internet. This book chronicles the rise of mobile communication technology.

Jargon Watch: A Pocket Dictionary for the Jitterati, as overheard by Gareth Branwin (San Francisco: HardWired, 1997). Hard-core computer networkers speak a language all their own—a language rich with opaque acronyms and shorthand descriptors for complex concepts. This tiny book leaves the technical definitions for other references. It focuses instead on "geek speak, exec lingo, and memo slang." If you have any doubt that computers are changing our language, you'll be convinced by reading this collection of colorful, often hilarious phrases. To keep abreast of this ever-changing new language, check the column of the same name in *Wired* magazine.

Telecosm: How Infinite Bandwidth Will Revolutionize Our World, by George Gilder (Free Press, 2000). The thesis of this book is in the title. Gilder is a well-known pundit with a colorful writing style and grand optimism concerning our technological future.

Tyranny of the Moment: Fast and Slow Time in the Information Age, by Thomas Hylland (Pluto Press, 2001). In an age when instantaneous communication has never been easier, time is one of our scarcest commodities. Hylland explores this paradox, and discusses the social and political implications of the evaporation of "slow time."

F2f, by Phillip Finch (New York: Bantam, 1997). As communities form on computer networks, they bring with them many of the problems found in other communities. This suspense thriller captures some of the potential risks of online communities in an exciting, tightly written story.

Film

You've Got Mail. This light comedy, named for AOL's ubiquitous greeting, points out the power of electronic communication to build strong emotional bonds.

Periodicals

Network Magazine focuses on networks with a business perspective.

Computer Telephony and **CTI** are two magazines that cover the rapidly changing territory where computers and telephones meet. Both periodicals are aimed at professionals and include a fair amount of technical material.

Web Pages

Computer networking technology is changing faster than publishers can print books and periodicals about it. The *Computer Confluence* Web site can connect you to up-to-date networking information all over the Internet.

7 | Inside the Internet and the Web

After you read this chapter you should be able to:

▼

Explain how and why the Internet was created

Describe the technology that's at the heart of the Internet

Describe the technology that makes the Web work as a multimedia mass medium

Discuss the tools people use to build Web sites

▲

▼ **In this chapter:**

The roots of the Internet

Why nobody controls the Internet

How the Internet works

Publishing pages on the Web

... and more.

▼ **On the CD-ROM:**

A 3-D model of a global information network

Animated demonstration showing how a Web browser works

Important access to glossary and key word references

Interactive self-study quizzes

... and more.

▼ **On the Web:**

www.prenhall.com/beekman

Articles and books on the Internet's history, structure, and use

Tools for exploring the Internet

Resources for building and publishing multimedia Web pages

Self-study exercises

... and more.

ARPANET Pioneers Build an Unreliable Network...
on Purpose

It's a bit like **climbing a mountain**.
You don't know how far you've come until you **stop and look back**.
—Vint Cerf, ARPANET pioneer and first president of the Internet Society

In the 1960s, the world of computers was a technological Tower of Babel—most computers couldn't communicate with each other. When people needed to move data from one computer to another, they carried or mailed a magnetic tape or a deck of punch cards. While most of the world viewed computers only as giant number crunchers, J. C. R. Licklider, Robert Taylor, and a small group of visionary computer scientists saw the computer's potential as a communication device. They envisioned a network that would enable researchers to share computing resources and ideas.

U.S. military strategists during those Cold War years had a vision, too: They foresaw an enemy attack crippling the U.S. government's ability to communicate. The Department of Defense wanted a network that could function even if some connections were destroyed. They provided a million dollars to Taylor and other scientists and engineers to build a small experimental network. The groundbreaking result, launched in 1969, was called ARPANET, for Advanced Research Projects Agency NETwork. When a half dozen researchers sent the first historic message from UCLA to Doug Engelbart's lab at the Stanford Research Institute, no one even thought to take a picture.

ARPANET was built on two unorthodox assumptions: The network itself was unreliable, so it had to be able to overcome its own unreliability, and all computers on the network would be equal in their ability to communicate with other network computers. In ARPANET there was no central authority because that would make the entire network vulnerable to attack. Messages were contained in software "packets" that could travel independently by any number of different paths, through all kinds of computers, toward their destinations.

The team that built the Internet included, from front to back: Bob Taylor, Vint Cerf, Frank Heart, Larry Roberts, Len Kleinrock, Bob Kahn, Wes Clark, Doug Engelbart, Barry Wessler, Dave Walden, Severo Ornstein, Truett Thach, Roger Scantlebury, Charlie Herzfeld, Ben Barker, Jon Postel, Steve Crocker, Bill Naylor, and Roland Bryan.

ARPANET grew quickly into an international network with hundreds of military and university sites. In addition to carrying research data, ARPANET channeled debates over the Vietnam War and intense discussions about Space War, an early computer game. ARPANET's peer-to-peer networking philosophy and protocols were copied in other networks in the 1980s. Vint Cerf and Bob Kahn, two of the original researchers, developed the protocols that became the standard computer communication language, allowing different computer networks to be linked.

In 1990 ARPANET was disbanded, having fulfilled its research mission and spawned the Internet. In a recent interview, Cerf said about the network he helped create, "It was supposed to be a highly robust technology for supporting military command and control. It did that in the Persian Gulf War. But, along the way, it became a major research support infrastructure and now has become the best example of global information infrastructure that we have."

The ARPANET pioneers have gone on to work on dozens of other significant projects and products. In the words of Bob Kahn, "Those were very exciting days, but there are new frontiers in every direction I can look these days."

The team that designed ARPANET suspected they were building something important. They couldn't have guessed, though, that they were laying the groundwork for a system that would become a universal research tool, a hotbed of business activity, a virtual shopping mall, a popular social hangout, a publisher's clearinghouse of up-to-the-minute information, and one of the most talked about institutions of our time.

The Internet is a technology, a tool, and a culture. Computer scientists originally designed it for computer scientists, and other scientists and engineers are continually adding new features. Consequently, the vocabulary of the Internet often seems like a flurry of technobabble to the rest of us. You don't need to analyze every acronym to make sense of the Internet, but your Net experiences can be far more rewarding if you understand the concepts at the heart of basic netspeak terminology. In this chapter we delve a little deeper into the Internet to make those concepts clearer.

Inside the Internet

> It shouldn't be too much of a surprise that the Internet has evolved into a force **strong enough** to reflect the **greatest hopes and fears** of those who use it. After all, it was designed to **withstand nuclear war**, not just the **puny huffs and puffs** of politicians and religious fanatics.
> —Denise Caruso, digital commerce columnist, *New York Times*

The Internet includes dozens of national, statewide, and regional networks, hundreds of networks within colleges and research labs, and thousands of commercial sites. Most sites are in the United States, but the Internet has connections in almost every country in the world.

The Internet provides hundreds of millions of people with services that include email, network newsgroups, instant messaging, Web publishing, shopping, banking, and research. Many of these services are similar to those provided by America Online and other online services. But the Internet is far bigger than any single network or online service. America Online is, in essence, a members-only club that occupies a tiny corner of the public Internet; members use their AOL accounts to explore the rest of the Web as well as the private AOL areas. More importantly, the Internet is not controlled by any one government, corporation, individual, or legal system. Several international advisory organizations develop standards and protocols for the evolving Internet, but no one has the power to control the Net's operation or evolution. The Internet is, in a sense, a massive anarchy unlike any other organization the world has ever seen.

Counting Connections

Cyber cafes around the world, like this one in China, enable travelers to stay connected to their homes—and the rest of the world. Customers pay by the minute to log into their home servers, keep up with email, and explore the Web.

> No **LAN** is an **island**.
> —Karyl Scott, *InfoWorld* writer

In its early days, the Internet connected only a few dozen computers at U.S. universities and government research centers, and the government paid most of the cost of building and operating it. Today it connects millions of computers in almost every country in the world, and costs are shared by thousands of connected organizations. It's impossible to pin down the exact size of the Internet for several reasons:

- The Internet is growing too fast to track. Millions of new users connect to the Internet every year in the United States alone, and the rest of the world is adding new connections by the minute.
- The Internet is decentralized. There's no Internet Central that keeps track of user activity or network connections. To make matters worse for Internet counters, some parts of the Internet can't be accessed by the general public; they're sealed off to protect private information.
- The Internet doesn't have hard boundaries. There are several ways to connect to the Internet (described later in this chapter); these different types of connections offer different classes of services and different degrees of interactivity. As choices proliferate, it's becoming harder to know exactly what it means to "belong to the Internet."

This last point is worth a closer look. It's easier to understand the different types of Internet access if you know a little bit about the protocols that make the Internet work.

Internet Protocols

The protocols at the heart of the Internet are called **TCP/IP** (Transmission Control Protocol/Internet Protocol). They were developed as an experiment in **internetworking**—connecting different types of networks and computer systems. The TCP/IP specifications were published as **open standards**, not owned by any company. As a result TCP/IP became the "language" of the Internet, allowing cross-network communication for almost every type of computer and network. These protocols are generally invisible to users; they're hidden deep in software that takes care of communication details behind the scenes. They define how information can be transferred between machines and how machines on the network can be identified with unique addresses.

The TCP protocols define a system similar in many ways to the postal system. When a message is sent on the Internet, it is broken into **packets**, in the same way you might pack your belongings in several individually addressed boxes before you ship them to a new location. Each packet has all the information it needs to travel independently from network to network toward its destination. Different packets might take different routes, just as different parcels might be routed through different cities by the postal system. The host systems that use software to decide how to route Internet transmissions are called **routers**, although sometimes less flexible hardware **switches** can do the same routing work faster. Regardless of the route they follow, the

> The most important quality of the Internet is that it lends itself to **radical reinvention**…. In another 10 years, the **only part** of the Internet as we know it now that will have survived will be **bits and pieces** of the underlying Internet protocol. . . .
> —Paul Saffo, director of the Institute for the Future

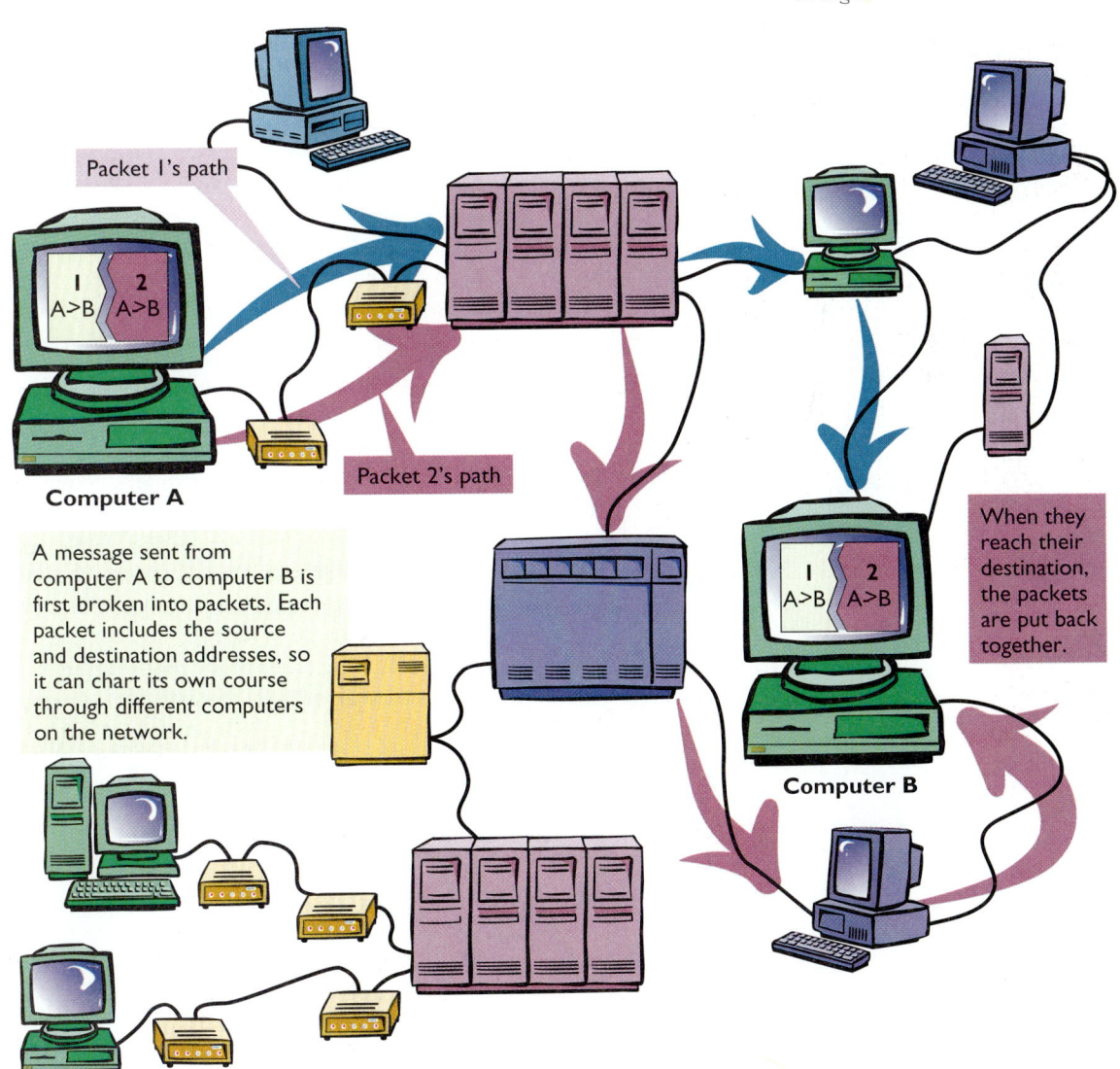

Packet switching gets the message through.

Computer A

A message sent from computer A to computer B is first broken into packets. Each packet includes the source and destination addresses, so it can chart its own course through different computers on the network.

Computer B

When they reach their destination, the packets are put back together.

packets eventually reach their destination, where they are reassembled into the original message. This **packet-switching** model is flexible and robust, allowing messages to get through even when part of the network is down.

The other part of TCP/IP—the IP part—defines the addressing system of the Internet. Every host computer on the Internet has a unique **IP address**: a string of four numbers separated by periods, or, as they say in netspeak, dots. A typical IP address might look like this: 123.23.168.22 ("123 dot 23 dot 168 dot 22"). Every packet includes the IP address of the sending computer and the receiving computer.

Internet Addresses

In practice, people seldom see or use numerical IP addresses, because the Internet's **domain name system (DNS)** translates the IP address into something that's easier for humans to read and remember. The DNS uses a string of names separated by dots to specify the exact Internet location of the host computer.

Internet addresses are classified by **domains**. In the United States the most widely used top-level domains are general categories that describe types of organizations:

- .edu   Educational sites
- .com   Commercial sites
- .gov   Government sites
- .mil   Military sites
- .net   Network administration sites
- .org   Nonprofit organizations

The Internet Ad Hoc Committee recently created seven additional top-level domain names:

- .aero   Air transport organizations
- .biz   Businesses
- .coop   Cooperative businesses such as credit unions
- .info   Information services
- .museum Museums
- .name   Personal registration by name
- .pro   Licensed professionals, including lawyers, doctors, and accountants

Some of these domains, including .com, .net, .org, and .info, are open to anyone without restriction. For example, you could have a Web site or an email address in the .net domain whether or not you're part of a nonprofit organization. Other domains, including .edu and .mil, are restricted so only people in the designated organizations can use them. Outside (and occasionally inside) the United States top-level domains are two-letter country codes, such as .jp for Japan, .th for Thailand, .au for Australia, .uk for United Kingdom, and .us for United States.

The top-level domain name is the last part of the address. The other parts of the address, when read in reverse, provide information that narrows down the exact location on the network. The words in the domain name, like the lines in a post office address, are arranged hierarchically from little to big. They might include the name of the organization, the name of the department or network within the organization, and the name of the host computer.

The domain naming system is used in virtually all email addresses and Web URLs. In a Web address, the URL specifies the IP address of the Web server that houses the page. In an email address, domain name system is used to pinpoint the Internet location of the host computer that contains the user's mail server. The email address includes the user name and the host address, as illustrated at the top of the next page.

Here are some other examples of email addresses using the domain name system:

- president@whitehouse.gov   User *president* whose mail is stored on the host *whitehouse* in the government domain
- crabbyabby@AOL.com   User called *crabbyabby* whose mail is handled by AOL, a commercial service provider
- hazel_filbert@admin.gmcc.ab.ca   User *hazel_filbert* at the *admin* server for Grant MacEwan Community College in Alberta, Canada

Anatomy of an email address.

Internet Access Options

> The **grand design** keeps getting grander.
> A **global computer** is taking shape, and we're all connected to it.
> Stewart Brand, in *The Media Lab*

Computers connect to the Internet through three basic types of connections: direct connections, dial-up connections through modems, and broadband connections through high-speed alternatives to modems.

Direct Connections

In many schools and businesses the computers have a **direct (dedicated) connection** to the Internet through a LAN and have their own IP addresses. A direct connection offers several advantages: You can take full advantage of Internet services without dialing in; your files are stored on your computer, not on a remote host; and response time is much faster, making it possible to transfer large files (like multimedia documents) quickly. Direct connect digital lines come in many varieties, including *T1* connections, which can transmit voice, data, and video at roughly 1.5Mbps, and *T3*, which is even faster. (On some continents a technology called E1 is used instead of T1.)

Dial-up Connections

If your computer isn't directly connected to the Internet, you can temporarily connect to an Internet host through a **dial-up connection**—a connection using a modem and standard telephone lines. The time-honored method—one that works even with ancient equipment and questionable phone lines—is called dial-up terminal emulation. **Terminal emulation software** makes your computer act as a dumb terminal—an input/output device that enables you to send commands to and view information on the host computer. Email messages and other files are stored on the host computer, not your PC. Many Internet services, including most of the Web, are off limits with this kind of connection because of the character-based, command-line interface. Graphics and multimedia files must be specially encoded before they can be transmitted or received.

Software that uses **PPP** (point-to-point protocol) allows a computer connected via modem and phone line to have full Internet access temporarily and a temporary IP address. **Full-access dial-up connections** offer most of the advantages of direct connection, including Web access, but response time is limited by the modem's speed. A typical connection through a modem and **POTS** (plain old telephone service) is much slower (and often less reliable) than a direct Internet connection. While modern modems are theoretically capable of delivering data at 56Kb or faster, they're often much slower when connected to typical noisy phone lines. Modem connections are sometimes called **narrowband connections** because they don't offer much bandwidth when compared to other types of connections.

Broadband Connections

Until a few years ago, a slow dial-up connection was the only alternative to direct Internet for homes and small businesses. Today millions of Internet users connect via DSL, cable modems, and satellites. These modem alternatives are often called **broadband connections** because they have much higher bandwidth than standard modem connections. In some cases, broadband connections offer data transmission speeds comparable to direct connection speeds. Many broadband services offer another big advantage: They're always on. Users of these services don't need to dial in; the Internet is instantly available anytime, like television or radio. The most common broadband alternatives are based on the following different technologies:

- *DSL.* Many phone companies offer **DSL (digital subscriber line),** a technology for bringing high-bandwidth connections to homes and small businesses over ordinary copper telephone lines. (*Jargon alert*: There are several variants of DSL. The term xDSL is sometimes used to refer to all forms of DSL. DSL is faster and cheaper than **ISDN**, a digital service offered by phone companies in the 1990s. Most experts believe ISDN will soon be obsolete.) DSL customers must be geographically close to phone company service hubs. DSL transmission speeds vary considerably. **Downstream traffic**—information from the Internet to the subscriber—sometimes approaches T1 speeds. A graphics-heavy Web page that takes minutes to download through a conventional modem will load in seconds through a DSL connection. **Upstream traffic**—data traveling from the home computer to the Internet—typically travels much slower, but still much faster than standard modem transmission. A DSL signal can share a standard telephone line with voice traffic, so it can remain on without interfering with telephone calls. DSL connections are only available in limited areas, and installation can be complicated and expensive. But DSL's high-speed, always-connected signal brings the advantages of a direct Internet connection to homes and small businesses.
- *Cable modem connections.* Some cable TV companies offer ultra-high-speed Internet connections through **cable modems**. Cable modems allow Internet connections using the same network of coaxial cables that delivers television signals to millions of homes. Like DSL, cable modem service isn't available everywhere. Cable modem speeds can theoretically exceed DSL speeds both downstream and upstream. But because a single cable is shared by an entire neighborhood, transmission speeds can go down when the number of users goes up. What's more, cable modems come from cable TV companies, which often receive them over T1 lines. In the end, cable modem users typically experience data transmission speeds in roughly the same range as high-speed DSL connections.

Some airports have Wi-Fi wireless networks that enable travelers to connect to the Internet while they wait for their flights.

INTERNET CONNECTION SPEEDS

Connection type		Downstream Potential	Downstream Typical	Upstream Typical
Dial-up modems: connection modem (56 K)		56 Kbps	42 to 53 Kbps	33.6 Kbps
T1/E1		1.544 Mbps	1.544 Mbps	1.544 Mbps
T3		44.736 Mbps	44.736 Mbps	44.736 Mbps
ISDN		128 Kbps	64 Kbps to 128 Kbps	64 Kbps to 128 Kbps
DSL/xDSL		6.1 Mbps	512 Kbps to 1.544 Mbps	128 Kbps
Cable modem		27 Mbps	1.5 to 3 Mbps	500 Kbps to 2.5 Mbps
Satellite connection		1.2 Mbps	150 Kbps to 1000 Kbps	50 Kbps to 150 Kbps
Wireless broadband (802.11b)		20 Mbps	5.5 or 11 Mbps	5.5 or 11 Mbps

Speeds vary widely for different types of Internet connections.

- *Satellite connections.* **Satellite Internet connections** are available through many of the same satellite dishes that provide television channels to viewers. Downstream satellite transmission is much faster than conventional modem traffic, although not quite as fast as DSL or cable modem service. For some satellite services, upstream traffic goes through phone lines at standard modem rates. Some newer services use satellites for both upstream and downstream traffic. For many homes and businesses outside of urban centers, satellites provide the only high-speed Internet access options available.
- *Wireless broadband connections.* People packing portable computers can, in some places, temporarily connect to the Internet through **wireless broadband connections**. The wireless broadband technology with the most industry support is referred to by its IEEE certification number, *802.11b*, but also called *Wi-Fi*. This technology, described in the last chapter, allows multiple computers to connect to a base station using short-range radio waves. This technology is used in many homes and offices for sharing Internet connections without cables. Using the same technology, students can connect to the Internet while they move around a wireless-equipped campus, travelers can make Web connections while waiting in some airports, and coffee shops can become Internet cafes for people with wireless receivers in their laptops.

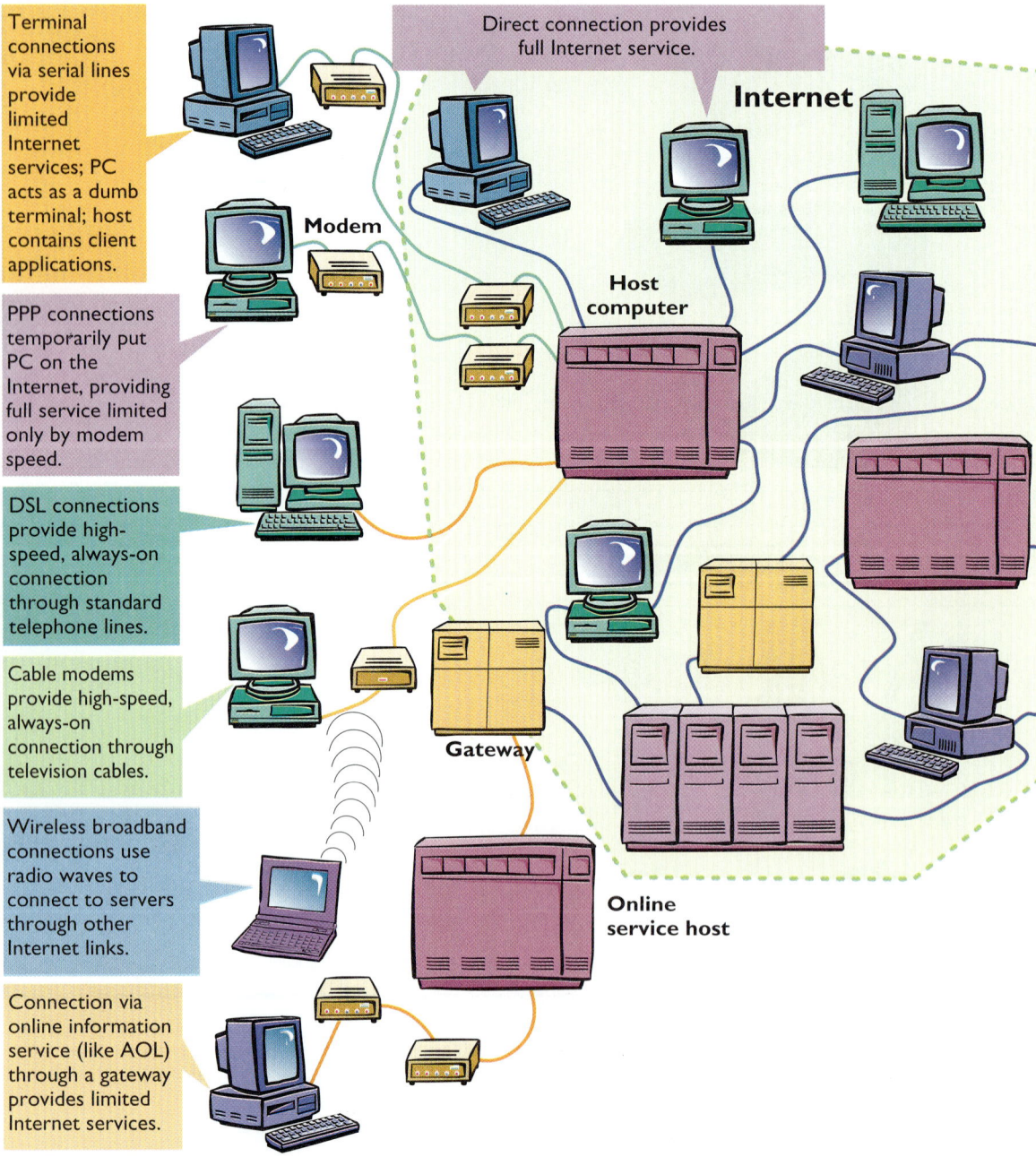

There are many ways to connect a PC to the Internet.

None of these broadband technologies is widely available, but each is rapidly expanding its area of coverage. In the future, many homes and small businesses will have direct connection to the Internet via fiber optic cables. But for now, most Internet users must settle for modem speeds or choose from broadband services available in their areas.

Internet Service Providers

Internet service providers (ISPs) generally offer several connection options at different prices. Local ISPs are local businesses with permanent connections to the Internet. They provide connections to their customers, usually through local telephone lines, along with other services. For example, an ISP might provide an email address, a server for customers to post Web pages, and technical help as part of a service package. National ISPs such as EarthLink offer similar services on a nationwide scale. National ISPs have local telephone numbers in most major cities so travelers can dial into the Net on the road without paying long-distance charges. In some cities inexpensive or free access to the Internet is available through a freenet—a local ISP designed to provide community access to online forums, announcements, and services.

Many private networks and online services (including America Online, CompuServe, and Prodigy) provide Internet access through **gateways**. A gateway is a computer connected to two networks—in this context the Internet and an outside network—that translates communication protocols and transfers information between the two. Some online services, such as MSN, have been rebuilt so they use the same protocols and framework as the Internet; subscribers use standard Web browsers and email programs to access services. Others, such as AOL and CompuServe, use proprietary client software to give subscribers access to their services and to the Internet. These services also enable members to use standard Internet software tools to connect to the Web and check email. Whatever their underlying architecture, online services are essentially ISPs that offer extra services to subscribers.

Inside Internet Applications: The Client/Server Connection

Internet applications, like PC applications, are software tools for users. But working with Internet applications is different from working with word processors or spreadsheets because of the distributed nature of the Internet and the **client/server model** used by most Internet applications. In the client/server model, a client program asks for information, and a server program fields the request and provides the requested information from databases and documents. The client program hides the details of the network and the server from the user.

Different people might access the same server using different client applications with different user interfaces. For example, a user with a direct connection might be using a Web browser with a point-and-click interface to explore a particular server, while another user with a dial-up terminal connection might be typing UNIX commands and seeing only text on screen. A third user might be viewing the same data, a few words at a time, on the tiny screen of a handheld PDA or mobile phone.

Many Internet applications use specialized servers. Some of the most common server types include the following:

- *Email servers*. An **email server** acts like a local post office for a particular Internet host—a business, an organization, or an ISP. For example, a college might have an email server to handle the mail of all students, faculty and staff; their email addresses point to that server. The email server receives incoming mail, stores it, and provides it to the email client programs of the addressees when they request it. Similarly, the email server collects mail from its subscribers and sends those messages toward their Internet destinations. Basically, the email server handles local client requests of two types: "Give me my mail," and "Pick up my mail and send it."
- *File servers*. File servers are common within LANs, but they're also used to share programs, media files, and other computer data across the Internet. The Internet's **file transfer protocol (FTP)** enables users to **download** files from remote servers (sometimes called FTP servers) to their computers—and to **upload** files they want to share from their computers to these archives. When you click a Web link that downloads a file, the Web browser's request is probably handled using FTP. Most files in Net archives are compressed—made smaller using special encoding schemes. File **compression** saves storage space on disk and saves transmission time when files

are transferred through networks. (See Chapter 7, "Graphics, Hypermedia, and Multimedia," for more on compression.) Once files are downloaded to a PC, they have to be decompressed before they can be used. You don't need to know how compression works to take advantage of it; software makes the process automatic and transparent.

- *Application servers.* An **application server** stores applications—PC office applications, databases, or other applications—and makes them available to client programs that request them. An application server might be used within a large company to keep PCs updated with the latest software. Each PC might have a client program that regularly sends requests for updates to the server. The application server might also be housed at an **application service provider (ASP)**—a company that manages and delivers application services on a contract basis. Users of ASPs don't buy applications; they rent them, along with service contracts. Some application servers supply platform-neutral, Web-centered applications rather than OS-specific PC applications. Many industry watchers believe ASPs will eventually provide most of the software we use. For some companies ASPs are part of larger Web-services strategies. Web services are discussed in later chapters.

- *Web servers.* A **Web server** stores Web pages and sends them to client programs—Web browsers—that request them. It may also store and send Web media, including graphics, audio, video, and animation. We'll turn our attention now to the technology behind the Web.

Inside the Web

> The dream behind the Web is of a **common information space** in which we **communicate by sharing** information.
> —Tim Berners-Lee, creator of the World Wide Web

The **World Wide Web (WWW)** is a distributed browsing and searching system originally developed at CERN (European Laboratory for Particle Physics) by Tim Berners-Lee, a visionary scientist who is profiled in the next chapter. He designed a system for giving Internet documents unique addresses, wrote the HTML language for encoding and displaying documents, and built a software browser for viewing those documents from remote locations. Since it was introduced in 1991, the Web has become phenomenally popular as a system for exploring, viewing, and publishing all kinds of information on the Net.

Web Protocols: HTTP and HTML

> The Web was built by millions of people simply **because they wanted it**, without need, greed, fear, hierarchy, authority figures, ethnic identification, advertising, or any form of manipulation. **Nothing like this ever happened** before in history. We can be blasé about it now, but it is **what we will be remembered for**. We have been made aware of a **new dimension** of human potential.
> —Jaron Lanier, virtual reality pioneer

The Web is built around a naming scheme that allows every information resource on the Internet to be referred to using a **uniform resource locator** or, as it's more commonly known, **URL**. Here's a typical URL:

```
http://weatherunderground.com/satellite/vis/1k/US.html/
```

The first part of this URL refers to the protocol that must be used to access information; it might be FTP, news, or something else. It's most commonly *http*, for **hypertext transfer protocol**, the protocol used to transfer Web pages. The second part (the part following the //) is the address of the host containing the resource; it uses the same domain-naming scheme used for email addresses. The third part, following the dot address, describes the path to the particular resource on the host—the hierarchical nesting of directories (folders) that contain the resource.

Most Web pages are created using a language called **HTML (hypertext markup language)**. An HTML *source document* is a text file that includes codes that describe the format, layout, and logical structure of a hypermedia document. HTML is not WYSIWYG (What You See Is What You Get); the HTML codes embedded in the document make it look cryptic and nothing like the final page displayed on the screen. But these codes enable a Web browser to translate an HTML source document into that finished page. Because it's a text file, an HTML document can be easily transmitted from a Web server to a client machine anywhere on the Internet.

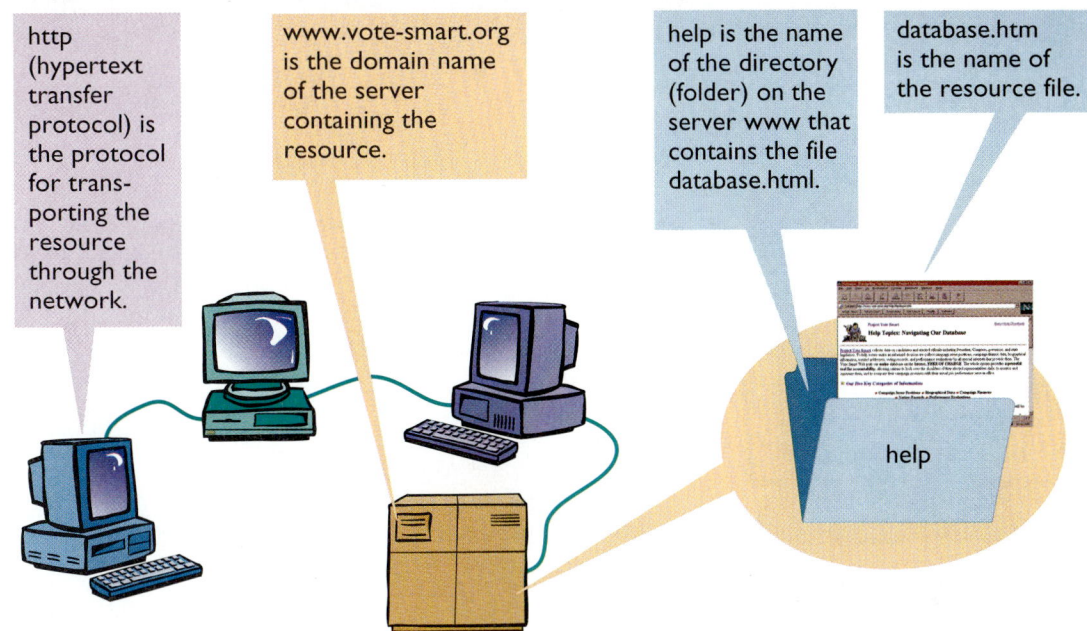

Anatomy of a URL.

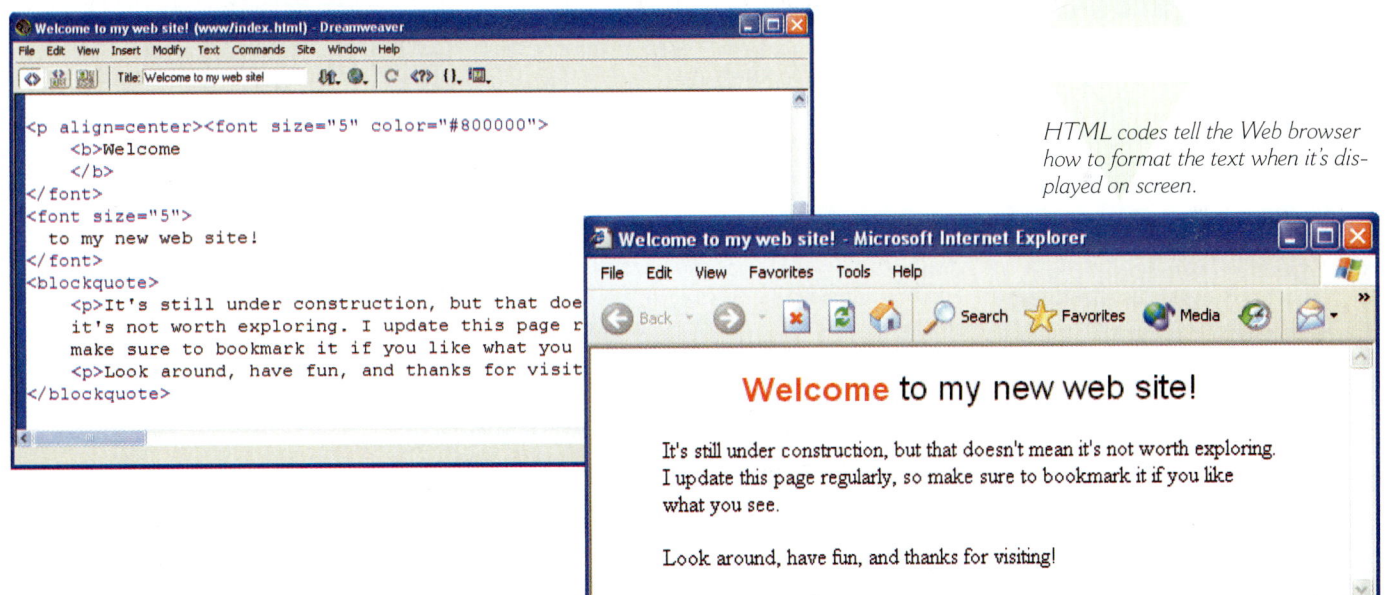

HTML codes tell the Web browser how to format the text when it's displayed on screen.

Publishing on the Web

You can create a Web page with any word processor or text editor; you just type the HTML commands along with the rest of the text. But you don't need to write HTML code to create a Web page. Many programs, including Microsoft Word, PowerPoint, and FileMaker Pro, can automatically convert basic formatting features (including character styles, indentation, and justification) into HTML codes. Some **Web authoring software**, including Macromedia Dreamweaver, Adobe GoLive, and Microsoft FrontPage

> By expanding the number of people who have **the power to transmit knowledge**, the Web might trigger a power shift that **changes everything**.
>
> —Howard Rheingold, author of *Virtual Communities*

How It Works

7.1 The World Wide Web

1. When you type a URL into the address box of your Web browser, the browser sends a message through the Internet to the server with the specified domain name www.requestfiles.com.

2. The server responds by sending the specified file to the client browser. The file is an HTML file containing the text contents of the requested Web page along with HTML codes for formatting and adding other elements to the page. Because HTML files are all text, they're small and easy to transmit through the Internet.

3. The browser reads the HTML file and interprets the HTML commands, called *tags*, embedded in angle brackets <like this>. It uses the formatting tags to determine the look and layout of the text on the page. For example, <H1> indicates a level-one heading to be displayed in large text; <1> indicates italics, and so on.

Server

4. The HTML file doesn't contain pictures; it's a text file. But it does contain a tag specifying where a picture file is stored and where in the page it is to be displayed. The server responds to this tag by sending the requested graphics files.

Server

5. The HTML file also contains a tag indicating a hyperlink to another document with a URL on another server. When the user clicks that link, a message is sent to the new server; and the process of building a Web page in the browser window starts anew.

work like page layout programs that desktop publishers use. You can lay out text and graphics exactly the way you want them to look, and the authoring program creates an HTML document that looks like your original layout when viewed through a Web browser. The best of these Web authoring programs enable you to manage entire Web sites using tools that can automate repetitive edits, apply formatting styles across pages, and check for bad links. Some have tools for connecting large sites to databases containing critical, rapidly changing content.

Once an HTML document is completed, it needs to be uploaded onto a Web server before it's visible on the Web. Many ISPs provide Web server space as part of their subscription service; other companies rent Web server space to individuals and organizations. By default, most Web pages have URLs that include the ISP or Web server domain names—names like http://hometown.aol.com/shjoobedebop/index.htm. Many businesses, organizations, and individuals pay an annual fee to a *domain name registry* company for names that match and are easier to remember and use. Many customized domain names resemble company or product names—for example, www.prenhall.com or www.computerconfluence.com.

From Hypertext to Multimedia

Way back in the early 1990s (!) the first Web pages were straight hypertext. Within a couple of years graphics were common, and a few cutting-edge Web sites enabled browsers to download scratchy video and audio clips to their hard disks. Today color graphics and animation are everywhere, and a typical Web site can contain any or all of these:

> We are still a **multimedia organism**. If we want to push the envelope of complexity further, we have to use **all of our devices** for accessing information—not all of which are **rational**.
> —Psychologist Mihaly Csikszentmihalyi

- *Tables*—spreadsheet-like grids whose rows and columns contain neatly laid out text and graphical elements. Tables with invisible cell borders are often used as simple alignment tools.
- *Frames*—subdivisions of a Web browser's viewing area that enable visitors to scroll and view different parts of a page—or even multiple pages—simultaneously.
- *Forms*—pages that visitors who want to order goods and services, respond to questionnaires, enter contests, express opinions, or add comments to ongoing discussions can fill in.
- *Animation*—based on a variety of technologies, from simple repetitive GIF animations to complex interactive animations created with authoring tools such as Flash.
- *Search engines*—tools for locating what you're looking for on a site. Most of these site-specific search engines are based on the same technology as Web-wide search engines. Many site builders license search engines from search engine companies.
- *Downloadable audio* clips—compressed sound files that you must download onto your computer's hard disk before the browser or some other application can play them. Some types of audio compression cause significant sound quality degradation. The MP3 compression format is popular because compressed music files sound almost the same as uncompressed originals. MP3 files can be played using a variety of software programs and portable MP3 players. The next two chapters discuss applications and implications of MP3 technology.
- *Downloadable video* clips—compressed video files that you can download and view on a computer. Many are small, short, and jerky, but quality is rapidly improving as new video compression technologies mature.
- *Streaming audio* files—sounds that play without being completely downloaded to the local hard disk. Some streaming files play automatically while you view a page providing background music and sound effects. Others, such as sound samples at music stores, play on request. Unlike downloaded media files, you can view or hear streaming media files within seconds, because they play while you're downloading them. For the same reason, streaming media files don't need to be limited to short clips. Concert-length streaming programs are common. High-quality streaming music requires a fast connection and can be interrupted by Internet traffic jams.
- *Streaming video* files—video clips that play while you're downloading them. Streaming video is even more dependent on high-bandwidth connection than streaming audio.
- *Real-time streaming audio* broadcasts, or Webcasts—streaming transmission of radio broadcasts, concerts, news feeds, speeches, and other sound events as they happen.
- *Real-time streaming video* Webcasts—similar to streaming audio Webcasts, but with video.
- *3-D environments*—drawn or photographed virtual spaces you can explore with mouse clicks.

The User's View

Building a Web Site

SOFTWARE: Macromedia Dreamweaver and Microsoft Internet Explorer.

THE GOAL: To create a Web site to represent a small service business.

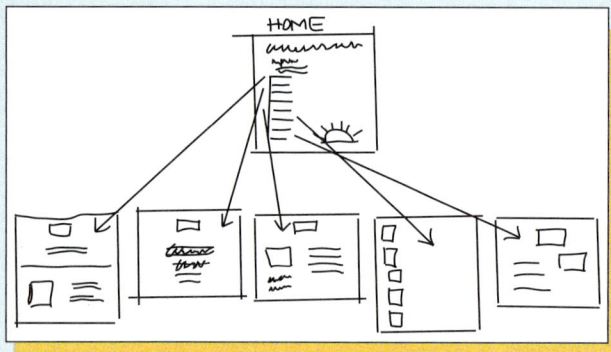

1. The first step in publishing, whether on paper or on the Web, is to plan the layout for the publication. Since a Web site is a hypertext document, a flowchart can make it easier to plan the links between pages.

2. A sketch can help you crystallize your ideas for the layout of each page.

3. Once the plan is complete, you collect, digitize, and edit the source documents—the images, articles, and other elements that will make up the finished publication.

4. Because your Web site will contain only standard HTML code, you could create the site using any text editor, inserting appropriate HTML codes into the text. But you use Dreamweaver, a Web authoring tool that enables you to design the page with a WYSIWYG editor that automatically creates HTML code.

5. After you define a directory (folder) as the temporary home for your site, you create a new page. Using the Page Properties command, you define the basic characteristics of the page: name, location, default fonts, text link colors, and background color. You select colors that match the dominant colors in your most important graphical images.

6. Your sketch calls for a column of links on the left side of the page, so you create a table, which enables you to align pictures and text neatly in rows and columns.

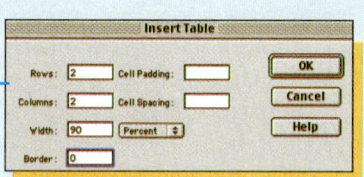

7. You select the table and change its background color to green from the Properties palette.

8. You type the titles for your navigation banner. You format the text using commands similar to those of a word processor. Dreamweaver converts your commands to HTML codes.

9. You select a title in your navigation banner, and specify the file name for the new page that will be linked to that text.

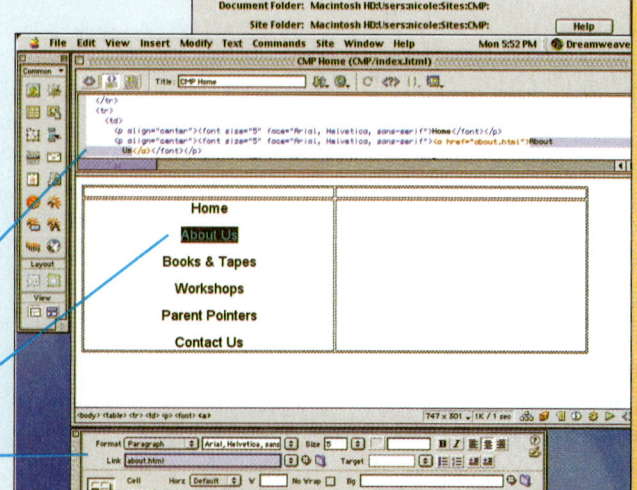

Chapter 7 Inside the Internet and the Web   199

View The User's View The User's View The User's View

10 You create links for the rest of the titles in the column, and place an image you created earlier above the links.

11 You realign the borders of the table and make them invisible. The dotted line borders are visible in the Dreamweaver editor, but they won't show up when the page is displayed in a Web browser.

12 You select the two empty cells, change their background color to white, and merge them, leaving you with one large cell to contain the content specific to each page of your site.

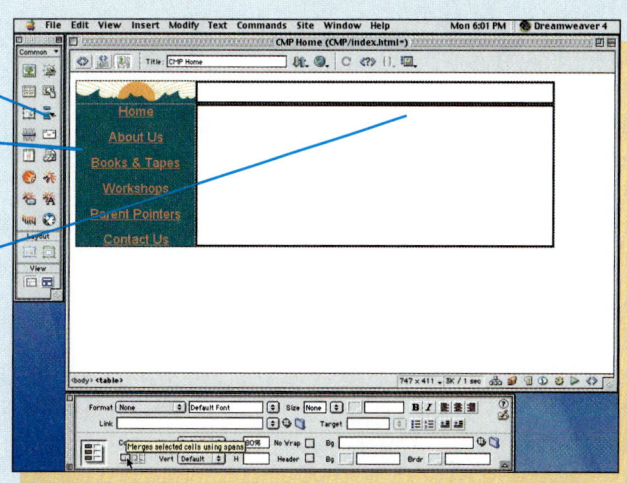

13 You want all the pages in the site to share the elements you have created so far, so you save a copy of the page, which you'll use as the starting point for all the pages in your site.

14 You place another image in the empty cell of the home page, then type a welcome message beneath it.

15 To begin work on the next page, you make another copy of your template file, and rename it with the name that you entered into the Link bar earlier. You add images, text, and other elements to the page, just as you did on the home page.

16 After you complete the pages, you preview them in a browser, which uses the HTML codes to construct a page that's similar to the design you created. You make sure to test the links before loading the entire site onto the Web server so they can be viewed by the world.

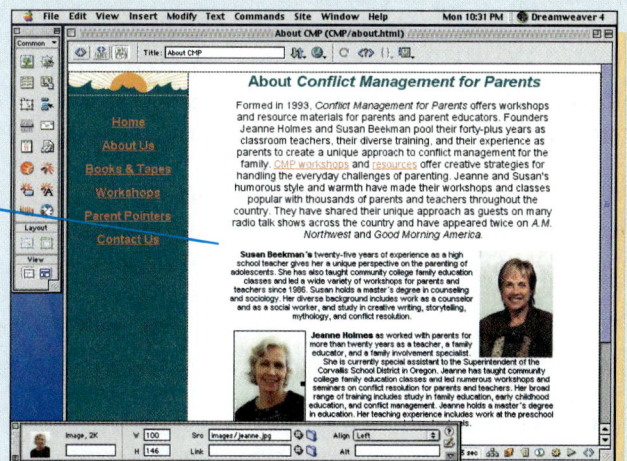

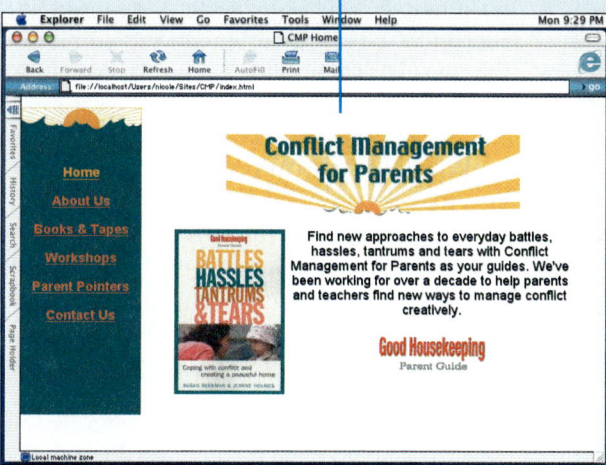

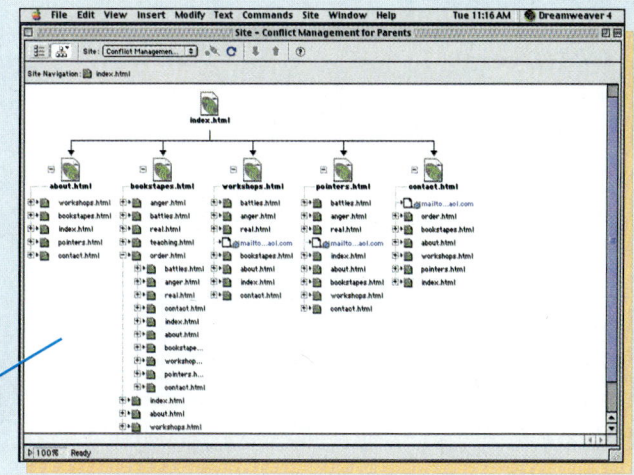

17 After thoroughly testing the site with different browsers, you compare this site map, created by Dreamweaver, with the original design. You're ready to load the site onto your Web server so the world can view it.

Streaming media are available from a variety of Web sites. rollingstone.com (left) offers music videos on request. live365.com (right) provides live audio feeds from hundreds of radio stations around the word.

▸ **Personalization**—customization of content made possible because sites can remember information about guests from visit to visit. Some sites use login names and passwords to remember visitors. Others track and remember using **cookies**—small files deposited on the visitor's hard disk. Cookies can make online shopping and other activities more efficient and rewarding, but they can also pose a threat to personal privacy.

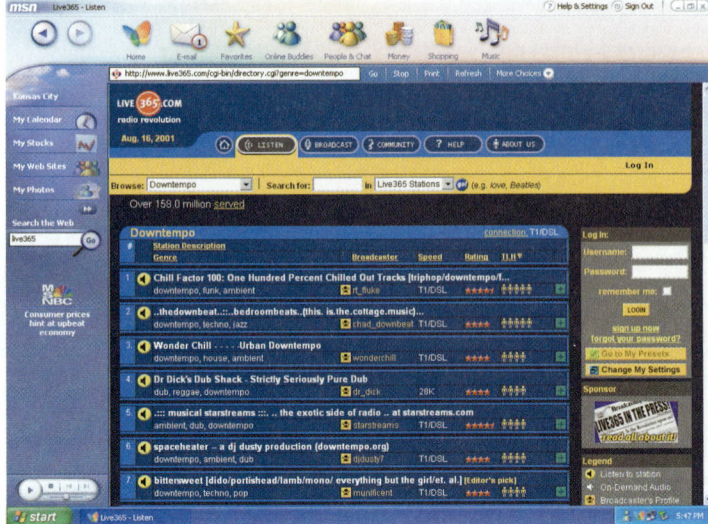

Today new Web ideas appear at an astounding rate—so fast that browser makers have trouble keeping up. Fortunately, the most popular browsers can be enhanced with **plug-ins**—software extensions that add new features. When a company introduces a Web innovation—say, a new type of animation—it typically makes a free browser plug-in available to users. Once you download the plug-in and install it in your browser, you can take advantage of any Web pages that include the innovation. Popular plug-ins become standard features in future browser versions, so you don't need to download and install them. Even if a browser can't play or display a particular type of graphics, animation, audio, or video by itself, it might be able to offload the task to a **helper application**—a separate program designed to present that particular media type.

The most popular free cross-platform plug-ins and helper applications include the following:

This 3D pool game is one of many interactive multimedia Web applications provided at shockwave.com

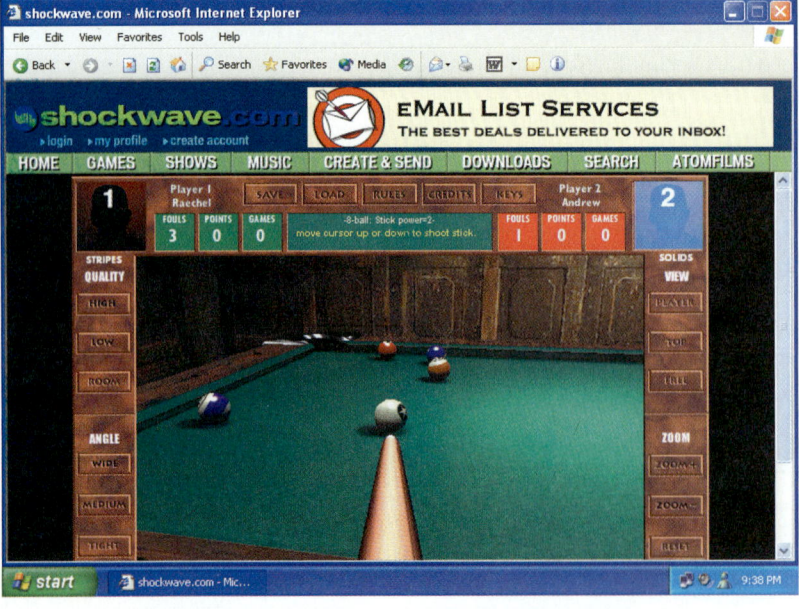

▸ RealPlayer (Real) is one of the most popular programs for playing streaming audio and video, including live Webcasts. RealPlayer movies and sound files are encoded in proprietary formats so they can't be played with other media players.
▸ Windows Media Player (Microsoft) is a direct competitor to RealPlayer, delivering streaming media in proprietary formats that aren't compatible with other players.
▸ QuickTime (Apple) also delivers cross-platform streaming media in proprietary formats. But QuickTime excels at providing high-quality multimedia for CD-ROMs, broadband downloads, and other delivery systems where bandwidth is less of an issue.
▸ Shockwave/Flash (Macromedia) plug-ins enable Web browsers to present compressed interactive multimedia documents and animations created with Flash, Director, and other authoring tools.
▸ Acrobat (Adobe) displays documents in **Portable Document Format (PDF)** so they look the same

Rules of Thumb

Weaving Winning Web Sites

It's easy to create a Web site—just about anybody with an Internet connection can do it. It's not so easy to create an effective Web site—one that communicates clearly, attracts visitors, and achieves its goals. Here are a few pointers for making your Web publications work.

- **Start with a plan.** The Web is littered with Web sites that seem pointless. Many of those sites were probably constructed without clear plan or purpose. Start with clear goals and design your entire site with those goals in mind.
- **Write for the Web.** Most people won't read long, scrolling documents on computer screens. Limit each page to a couple of screens worth of text. Provide clearly marked links to pages with more details for people who need them. And don't forget to check your spelling and grammar.
- **Keep it simple.** Web pages that are cluttered with blinking text, busy backgrounds, repetitive animations, and garish graphics tend to lose their visitors quickly. Stick with clean lines and clear design if you want people to stick around.
- **Keep it consistent.** Every page in your site should look like it's related to the other pages in your site. Fonts, graphical elements, colors, buttons, and menus should be consistent from page to page.
- **Make it obvious.** Your visitors should be able to tell within a few seconds how your site works. Unless you're building a puzzle palace, make sure the buttons and structure of your site are intuitive.
- **Keep it small.** Large photographs, complex animations, video clips, and sounds can make your Web site big and slow to load. People with standard modem connections won't want to wait two minutes for your graphically heavy Web page to load. If you need lots of pictures, use an image-editing program to optimize them for the Web.
- **Keep it honest.** Anybody can publish a Web site, without the benefit of an editor. Check your facts before you share your pages with the world.
- **Offer contact information.** Web communication shouldn't be one-way. Provide an email address or a form to enable your visitors to contact you.
- **Think like a publisher and a multimedia designer.** The rules of publishing and design, discussed in earlier chapters, apply to Web publishing, too.
- **Test before you publish.** Show your work to others—preferably people in your target audience—and watch their reactions carefully. If they get lost, confused, bored, or upset, you probably have more work to do before launching the final site.
- **Think before you publish.** It's easy to publish Web pages for the world—at least that part of the world that uses the Web. Don't put anything on your Web pages that you don't want the world to see; you may, for example, be asking for trouble if you publish your home address, your work schedule, and a photo of the expensive computer system in your study.
- **Keep it current.** It's easy to build a Web site, and it's even easier to forget to keep it up to date. If your Web site is worth visiting, it's worth revising. If the contents of your site are constantly in need of revision, consider using a database to house the data so you can automatically update the site when the data changes.

on the screen as on paper, even if the documents are viewed on computers that don't have the same fonts installed.

HTML was originally designed to share scientific research documents—not to deliver media-rich documents in which design is as important as content. By popular demand, the HTML standard has been revised several times to incorporate new features. Newer versions of HTML, sometimes called *dynamic HTML*, allow HTML code to modify itself automatically under certain circumstances. Dynamic HTML supports cascading style sheets that can define formatting and layout features that aren't recognized in older versions of HTML.

Dynamic HTML also recognizes *scripts*—short programs—that can add interactivity, animation, and other dynamic features to Web pages. One common use of scripts is to add *rollovers* to onscreen buttons, so they visibly change when the pointer rolls over them. Scripts are typically written in *JavaScript*, a scripting language developed by Netscape. Microsoft's *VBScript* is also used for writing scripts, but VBScript code doesn't work on non-Microsoft browsers. Web pages that take advantage of the latest dynamic HTML features can be more interesting and interactive, but only if they are viewed with newer full-featured browsers. Unscrupulous Web programmers can use scripts to embed viruses and other unwanted elements into your computer. We'll explore these risks in the Security chapter.

Dynamic Web Sites: Beyond HTML

> If you thought a Web site consisted of **HTML** pages organized as a directory, **go back to the 20th century**. A successful Web site today consists primarily of **XML** code and a **database**.
> —Dana Blankenhorn, coauthor of *Web Commerce: Building a Digital Business*

HTML is flexible, but it's designed for page layout, not programming. By itself, it can't support online shopping, financial transaction processing, library catalogs, daily newspapers, search engines, and other applications with masses of rapidly changing data. This kind of dynamic Web site requires two things that HTML can't easily deliver: a database to store the constantly changing content of the site, and custom programming to make the appropriate data available to visitors through the Web site. A *database-driven Web site* can display dynamic, changeable content without having constantly redesigned pages. For example, an online store's Web site doesn't have a separate HTML page for each catalog item. Instead, it has pages that are coded to display product information drawn from a database that can be continually updated. The Web site is a *front end* for the database; it serves as the visitor's window into the database.

The REI.com Web site uses a massive database to store catalog items, inventory information, customer data, and transaction information. The dynamic Web site displays data based on visitor input.

Programmers use a variety of programming languages for creating dynamic Web sites. The Perl language is particularly popular for programming Web servers. *Java*, an object-oriented programming language developed by Sun Microsystems, is probably the best-known language for Web programming. (Java and JavaScript have little in common except their names. JavaScript is a simple scripting language for enhancing HTML Web pages; Java is a full-featured cross-platform programming language.) Small Java programs are called *applets* because they're like tiny applications. Java applets can be automatically downloaded onto your client computer through almost any modern Web browser. A Java applet is platform independent; it runs on a Windows PC, a Mac, a UNIX workstation, or anything else as long as the client machine has Java Virtual Machine (JVM) software installed. This JVM software is built into most modern browsers and is available for free download.

Microsoft offers several alternatives to Java. The oldest is *ActiveX*, a collection of programming technologies and tools for creating *controls* or *components*—programs that are similar in many ways to Java applets. ActiveX components require a compatible browser, such as Internet Explorer, to run properly. Another Microsoft technology, *C#*, is a programming language similar to Java in many ways, but it lacks Java's cross-platform capabilities.

Many experts expect *XML (extensible markup language)*, which includes all of HTML's features plus many additional, powerful programming extensions to replace HTML. XML enables Web developers to control and display data the way they now control text and graphics. Forms, database queries, and other data-intensive operations that can't be completely constructed with standard HTML are much easier with XML. In effect, XML combines a programming language with a page layout language. XML is at the heart of Microsoft's .NET and other competing strategies for developing Web services. Web services will be discussed in later chapters.

XML isn't the only markup language that's emerging to go beyond the capabilities of HTML. *XHTML*, a sort of cross between HTML and XML, is backward compatible with HTML, making it easier to upgrade older sites. A subset of XHTML called XHTML basic is especially designed to work with phones, PDAs, and other small-screen wireless devices. XHTML and XHTML basic are designed to work together, so that sites designed with XHTML automatically work on handheld devices. XHTML isn't yet widely used, but it has strong support from the wireless industry and from the World Wide Web Consortium (W3C), an organization that sets standards for the Web. W3C is also developing a standard for *SMIL (synchronized multimedia integration language)*, an HTML-like language designed to make it possible to link time-based streaming media so, for example, sounds, video, and animation can be tightly integrated with each other.

Putting Protocols to Work

In this chapter we've examined the technology that makes the Internet tick. Of course, we've only scratched the surface—the technology of the Internet is far too complex to cover in detail in an overview like this one. Still, it's satisfying to know that everything you do with the Internet is based on technological foundations described in this chapter. In the next chapter we'll survey the ways people are putting this technology to work to enhance communication, connection, and commerce. We'll also look at some of the ethical, legal, and social issues raised by the Internet as it grows and changes.

Machine Net
Cathy Benko

Networks aren't just for people anymore. Advances in networking technology, including wireless technology, are making it practical to connect machines so they can communicate directly with each other. In this article, first published in the February 7, 2000 issue of The Industry Standard, Cathy Benko of Deloitte Consulting discusses the machine-to-machine network revolution.

> "In the bowling alley of tomorrow, there will even be machines that wear rental shoes and throw the ball for you. Your sole function will be to drink beer."
>
> Dave Barry

A lot of people have predicted that a time will come when machines become more important than humans. What few predicted was that machines would seize power on the Net.

In fact, more and more machines are using sophisticated artificial intelligence programs to talk to one another online—without human interference. Until now, the Net has been the most human-centric technology ever. Starting with the browser, every new Internet development has made it easier to send email, surf the Web, shop online and conduct business. Few technologies have worked so hard to be human-friendly.

Now it's the machines' turn to catch up. Within the next few years, Internet connections between machines will outnumber the connections made by man.

Just as the Net has reshaped business, so it will reshape relationships between machines. Air conditioners will send messages to the electric company. Truck fleets will stay linked to headquarters. Wired VCR clocks will set themselves.

Sending simple messages from one machine to another is just the beginning. At the experiment stage is a gizmo that reads email for U.S. congressmen and summarizes the correspondence by issue—a clever device that elected officials probably wouldn't want to boast about.

Such newly empowered machines suggest the Net is headed in a direction we haven't previously considered. The growing adoption of handheld devices has made it possible to think in terms of communicating through the Net anywhere, anytime. What may be more revolutionary is the notion of machines and databases communicating without our help.

Want to make a virtual visit to the future? Visit www.echelon.com/demo, where you can use your mouse to pull down the blinds and turn on a lamp in a mock living room at the headquarters of network control designer **Echelon (ELON)** in Palo Alto, Calif. It's a first step toward a future where you can log on at work to see if you left the iron on in your bedroom—and turn it off if you did. And it's not far from there to putting refrigerators, cars and phones online.

Industrial and commercial applications involving power may be the first to market. GE Lighting, for instance, is exploring "intelligent office" control systems, connecting lighting; heating, ventilation and air conditioning; fire and security; and electrical systems. Expect IT managers to find themselves in charge of utilities, too.

The current incarnation of the Net is all about bringing information to us. But as machines demand more online time, and then become the most voracious users of bandwidth, the Net will reconfigure itself to cater to their needs.

This opens an immense and still embryonic market. Surging demand will surface for products that let machines do things better and faster than we can. With increasingly advanced artificial intelligence software, vending machines will let delivery vans know when they need to be replenished; copy machines will notify overnight delivery computers when an order is ready for pickup; manufacturers' shop floors will use digital cameras and the Internet to coordinate production schedules. In homes, simple devices will set electricity use based on time of day and temperature. For consumers, these new machines will make user-friendly PCs seem hostile by comparison.

Who—or what—uses the Net won't be the only change. It has long been the conventional wisdom that the Internet was primarily about people—and until now, that has largely been true. The Internet's playing field, however, is about to become a lot more crowded and complex.

For many apps, the PC remains a slow, complex tool. A machine-to-machine dialogue promises to change that. A customer-friendly era is coming online—and some of those customers will be machines.

DISCUSSION QUESTIONS

1. Do you think these predictions are realistic? Explain your answer.
2. How do you think these changes will effect your life? Will there be both negative and positive effects?

Summary

The Internet is a network of networks that connects all kinds of computers around the globe. It grew out of a military research network designed to provide reliable communication even if part of the network failed. The Internet uses standard protocols to allow internetwork communication to occur. No single organization owns or controls the Internet.

You can connect to the Internet in any of several ways; these ways provide different degrees of access to Internet services. A direct connection provides the most complete and fastest service, but users can also access most Internet information through modem connections. Broadband connections approach direct connection speeds, but they aren't universally available. Several online services have gateways to the Internet; these gateways enable users to access Internet information resources and send and receive Internet mail.

Most Internet applications are based on the client/server model. The user interface for these applications varies depending on the type of connection and the type of client software used by the user. A user might type UNIX commands to a host computer or use point-and-click tools on a personal computer.

Millions of people use Web browsers to explore interconnected Web pages published by private companies, public institutions, and individuals. The earliest Web pages were simple hypertext pages; today the Web contains thousands of complex, media-rich structures that offer visitors a wealth of choices. The World Wide Web uses a set of protocols to make a variety of Internet services and multimedia documents available to users through a simple point-and-click interface. Web pages are generally constructed using a language called HTML. Many Web authoring tools automate the coding of HTML pages, making it easy for nonprogrammers to write and publish their own pages. Other languages and techniques are being developed to extend the power of the Web in ways that go beyond the capabilities of HTML. Today, most large interactive Web sites are database-driven, so content can be updated automatically.

Chapter Review

▼ Key Terms

application server (p. 194)
application service provider (ASP) (p. 194)
broadband connection (p. 190)
cable modem (p. 190)
client/server model (p. 193)
compression (p. 193)
cookies (p. 200)
database-driven web site (p. 202)
dial-up connection (p. 190)
direct (dedicated) connection (p. 189)
download (p. 193)
DSL (digital subscriber line) (p. 190)
email server (p. 193)

extensible markup language (XML) (p. 202)
file transfer protocol (FTP) (p. 193)
gateway (p. 193)
helper application (p. 200)
HTML (hypertext markup language) (p. 194)
Internet service provider (ISP) (p. 193)
internetworking (p. 187)
Java (p. 202)
JavaScript (p. 201)
narrowband connection (p. 190)
open standards (p. 187)
packet switching (p. 188)

plug-in (p. 200)
satellite connections (p. 192)
streaming audio (p. 197)
streaming video (p. 197)
TCP/IP (p. 187)
upload (p. 193)
uniform resource locator (URL) (p. 194)
WWW (p. 194)
web-authoring software (p. 195)
Web server (p. 194)
wireless broadband connection (p. 192)

▼ Interactive Quiz Questions

1. The *Computer Confluence* CD-ROM contains self-test quiz questions related to this chapter, including multiple choice, true or false, and matching questions.
2. The *Computer Confluence* Web site, www.prenhall.com/beekman, contains self-test exercises related to this chapter. Follow the instructions for taking a quiz. After you've completed your quiz, you can email the results to your instructor.

   The Web site also contains open-ended discussion questions called Internet Explorations. Discuss one or more of the Internet Exploration questions at the section for this chapter.

▼ Review Questions

1. Define or describe each of the key terms listed in the "Key Terms" section. Check your answers using the glossary.
2. Why is it hard to determine how big the Internet is today? Give several reasons.
3. Why are TCP/IP protocols so important to the functioning of the Internet? What do they do?
4. How does the type of Internet connection influence the things you can do on the Internet?
5. Explain the relationship between the client/server model and the fact that different users might experience different interfaces while accessing the same data.
6. What do email addresses and URLs have in common?
7. Why is file compression important on the Internet?
8. Briefly describe several software tools that can be used to develop Web pages.

▼ Discussion Questions

1. How did the Internet's Cold War origin influence its basic decentralized, packet-switching design? How does that design affect the way we use the Net today? What are the political implications of that design today?
2. Why is the World Wide Web important as a publishing medium? In what ways is the Web different from any publishing medium that's ever existed before?

▼ Projects

1. Search the Web for articles related to the history and evolution of the Internet. Create a summary report on paper or on the Web.
2. Create a Web site on a subject of interest to you and link it to other Web sites. (When you're trying to decide what information to include in your home page, remember that it will be accessible to millions of people all over the world.)

Sources and Resources

Books

There are thousands of books on the Internet. Many of them promise to simplify and demystify the Net, but they don't all deliver. The Internet is complex and ever-changing. The following list contains a few particularly good titles, but you should also look for more current books released since this book went to press.

When Wizards Stay Up Late, by Katie Hafner and Matthew Lyon (New York: Simon and Schuster, 1998). If you want to learn more about the birth of the Internet, this book is a great place to start. The authors describe the people, challenges, and technical issues in clear, entertaining prose.

The Whole Internet: The Next Generation, by Kiersten Conner-Sax and Ed Krol (Sebastapol, CA: O'Reilly, 1999). In 1992 Ed Krol turned his online Internet guide into one of the first true guidebooks to the Net. It provided explorers with the technical knowledge necessary to get around on the pre-Web Internet. This completely rewritten edition is less technical, but just as practical. It's packed with useful information and advice on everything from shopping at auctions to stopping spam.

How the Internet Works, Millennium Edition, by Preston Gralla (Indianapolis: Que, 1999). If you like the style of *How Computers Work*, you'll appreciate *How the Internet Works*. You won't learn how to use the Net, but you'll get a colorful tour of what goes on behind the scenes when you connect. There's a surprising amount of technical information in this graphically rich, approachable book.

TCP/IP Clearly Explained, Third Edition, by Pete Loshin (Boston: AP Professional, 1999). If you want to dig deeper into the protocol that makes the Internet tick, this book, by a former *Byte* magazine editor, should help.

HTML 4 for the World Wide Web Visual QuickStart Guide, Fourth Edition, by Elizabeth Castro (Berkeley, CA: Peachpit Press, 2000). There are dozens of books on HTML, but few offer the clear, concise, comprehensive coverage of this bestseller. Castro does a marvelous job of presenting just enough information on each topic, and presenting it in an understandable way. If you want to build your own Web pages, this is a great place to start. Even if you know the basics of HTML, you'll appreciate the coverage of "advanced" topics like DHTML and CGI. Once you've read it, you'll almost certainly want to keep it as a reference.

Perl and CGI for the World Wide Web Visual QuickStart Guide, by Elizabeth Castro (Berkeley, CA: Peachpit Press, 1999). When you fill out a form on a Web page, it's likely that your input is processed by a script that's written in PERL following the CGI protocol. Castro's book takes up where her popular HTML book leaves off, introducing the basics of PERL and CGI for first-time scripters.

JavaScript for the World Wide Web Visual QuickStart Guide, Third Edition, by Tom Negrino and Dori Smith (Berkeley, CA: Peachpit Press, 1999). JavaScript is the most popular cross-platform scripting language for Web pages. A little bit of JavaScript can turn a static Web page into a dynamic interactive page. This book provides a quick introduction to the language, including applications involving forms, frames, files, graphics, and cookies. If you're ready to move beyond basic HTML, this book can help.

HTML: The Complete Reference, Second Edition, by Thomas A. Powell (Berkeley, CA: Osborne/McGraw Hill, 1999). This massive book includes a well-designed, in-depth tutorial and a comprehensive reference section. It covers beginning HTML and many more advanced topics.

Philip and Alex's Guide to Web Publishing, by Philip Greenspun (San Francisco: Morgan Kaufmann Publishers, Inc., 1999). This is a quirky, wordy, opinionated, and informative exposition on creating Web sites that work. Greenspun covers a great deal of territory here, including building a site, tracking users, publicizing a site, interfacing with relational databases, and handling finances. The author's color photos allow this book to hold its own on the coffee table. (Alex, the author's dog, appears on the cover; beyond that, it's not clear what he contributed to the book.)

Web Style Guide: Basic Design Principles for Creating Web Sites, by Patrick J. Lynch and Sarah Horton (New Haven: Yale University Press, 1999). Yale University was one of the first institutions to publish a Web style guide on the Web. This book, like that site, offers a clear, thoughtful discussion of techniques for designing effective Web sites.

The Non-Designer's Web Book, by Robin Williams and John Tollett (Berkeley, CA: Peachpit Press, 1997). Web publishing, like desktop publishing, can be hazardous if you don't have a background in design. Robin Williams and John Tollett provide a crash course in design for first-time Web authors. They assume you're using an authoring tool that hides the nuts and bolts of HTML; if you're not, you'll need to learn HTML elsewhere.

Great Web Architecture, by Clay Andres (Sebastapol, CA: IDG Books, 1999). There's more to Web design than making pretty pages. This book explores and explains the underlying structure of successful Web sites.

Community Building on the Web, by Amy Kim (Berkeley, CA: Peachpit Press, 2000). Some of the most successful Web sites today offer more than information—they offer a sense of community. In this book the designer of some of the best Web community sites shares strategy, philosophy, and technology secrets for building a successful Web community. If you want your Web site to be a satisfying group experience for visitors, read this book.

World Wide Web: Beyond the Basics, edited by Dr. Marc Abrams (Upper Saddle River, NJ: Prentice Hall, 1998). If you already know how to build Web pages and use search engines, and want to learn more about the technical side of the Web, this book can help. It covers history, technology, security, and other topics with academic depth that goes beyond typical Web books.

Periodicals

Inter@ctive Week. This weekly publication provides comprehensive coverage of all things interactive and online, with a special focus on the Web.

Internet World. This news magazine is aimed at Webmasters and others who make a business of the Internet.

Internet Week. This weekly also covers the Internet from a professional business perspective.

Web Techniques. This technical monthly goes into detail on constructing Web sites that work.

Web Pages

The World Wide Web is especially good at providing information about itself. Whether you want to learn HTML, see the latest Web traffic reports, or explore the technological underpinnings of the Net, you'll find Web links at the *Computer Confluence* Web site (**www.prenhall.com/beekman**) that can help.

8 From Internet to Information Infrastructure

After you read this chapter you should be able to:

▼

Describe several software tools for navigating and using the Internet

Discuss several important social and political issues raised by the Internet

Explain how the Internet and other telecommunication technologies are evolving into an all-encompassing information infrastructure

Discuss the future of the Internet in particular and cyberspace in general

▲

▼ **In this chapter:**

Internet communication beyond email

How Napster changed the Net

The dark side of the Internet

Publishing pages on the Web

Next generation Internet and beyond

. . . and more.

▼ **On the CD-ROM:**

Video clips featuring Web pioneers

Animated demonstration of peer-to-peer computing

Access to glossary and key word references

Interactive self-study quizzes

. . . and more.

▼ **On the Web:**

<u>www.prenhall.com/beekman</u>

Tools for exploring the Internet

Resources for communicating through the Internet

Discussions of important Internet issues

Self-study exercises

. . . and more.

Tim Berners-Lee Weaves the Web for Everybody

The whole idea you can have some idea and make it happen means that dreamers all over the world should take heart and not stop.

—Tim Berners-Lee, creator of the World Wide Web

The Internet has long been a powerful communication medium and a storehouse of valuable information. But until recently, few people mastered the cryptic codes and challenging languages that were required to unlock the Internet's treasures. The Net was effectively off limits to most of the world's people. Tim Berners-Lee changed all that when he single-handedly invented the World Wide Web and gave it to all of us.

Tim Berners-Lee was born in London in 1955. His parents met while programming the Ferranti Mark I, the first commercial computer. They encouraged their son to think unconventionally. He developed a love for electronics, and even built a computer out of spare parts and a TV set when he was a physics student at Oxford.

Berners-Lee took a software engineering job at CERN, the European Particle Physics Laboratory in Geneva, Switzerland. While he was there, he developed a program to help him track all of his random notes. He tried to make the program, called Enquire, deal with information in a "brain like way." Enquire was a primitive hypertext system that allowed related documents on his computer to be linked with numbers rather than mouse clicks. (In 1980 PCs didn't have mice.)

Tim Berners-Lee

Berners-Lee wanted to expand the concept of Enquire so he could link documents on other computers to his own. His idea was to create an open-ended distributed hypertext system with no boundaries, so scientists everywhere could link their work together.

The World Wide Web was born at CERN in Geneva, Switzerland

Over the next few years he single handedly built a complete system to realize his dream. He designed the URL scheme for giving every Internet document a unique address. He developed HTML, the language for encoding and displaying hypertext documents on the Web. He created HTTP, the set of rules that allow hypertext documents to be linked across the Internet. And he built the first software browser for viewing those documents from remote locations.

When he submitted the first paper describing the Web to a conference in 1991, the conference organizers rejected it because the Web seemed too simple to them. They thought that Berners-Lee's ideas would be a step backward when compared to hypertext systems that had been developed by Ted Nelson, Doug Engelbart, and others over the previous 25 years. It's easy to see now that the simplicity of the Web was a strength, not a weakness.

Rather than trying to own his suite of inventions, Berners-Lee made them freely available to the public. Suddenly, vast tracts of the Internet were open to just about anyone who could point and click a mouse. The Web's popularity spread like a virus, and the Internet was forever changed.

When he created the Web, Tim Berners-Lee turned the Internet into a mass medium. Few people in history have had so great an impact on the way we communicate. In the words of writer Joshua Quittner, Tim Berners-Lee's accomplishments are "almost Gutenbergian."

Tim Berners-Lee now works in an unassuming office at MIT, where he heads the World Wide Web Consortium (W3C). The W3C is a standards-setting organization dedicated to helping the Web evolve in positive directions rather than disintegrating into incompatible factions. The work of Tim Berners-Lee and the W3C will help ensure that the World Wide Web continues to belong to everyone.

In the last chapter, we looked at the hardware, software, and protocols at the core of the Internet and the Web. People have built an amazing variety of powerful, useful, and novel applications on top of these core technologies. In this chapter we'll examine some of those applications and the ways people use them. Later in this chapter we'll survey some of the issues raised by this rapidly evolving technology. We'll end the chapter with a look into the future—a future in which the Internet is much more intimately involved in our lives.

Internet Applications: Communication and Connection

> **No other medium** gives every participant the capability to communicate **instantly** with thousands and thousands of people.
> —Tracy LaQuey, in *The Internet Companion*

We'll begin our survey of Internet applications by examining Web search engines and portals in a little more detail. Then we'll review several types of interpersonal communication tools on the Net. Next we'll take a look at peer-to-peer computing, grid computing, and push technology, and the ways people are using those technologies. Finally, we'll look at e-commerce applications, including Web services, and their impact on business.

Search Engines

With its vast storehouses of information, the Web is like a huge library. Unfortunately, the Web is a poorly organized library; you might find information on a particular topic almost anywhere. (What can you expect from a library where nobody's in charge?) That's why search engines are among the Web's most popular tools.

You're probably familiar with at least one Web search engine, but you may not know much about how it works. All search engines are designed to make it easier to find information on the Web, but they don't all function the same way. A typical search engine uses *web crawlers* or *spiders*—software robots that systematically explore the Web, retrieve information about pages, and index the retrieved information in a database. Different search engines use different search and indexing strategies. For example, one search engine might record detailed information about keywords in documents, while another might pay more attention to links to and from other documents. For some search engines, researchers organize and evaluate Web sites in databases; other search engines are almost completely automated.

Most search engines enable you to type queries using keywords, just as you might locate information in other types of databases. You can construct complex queries using *Boolean logic* (for example, American AND Indian BUT NOT Cleveland), quotations, and other tools for refining queries. Some search engines enable you to narrow your search repeatedly by choosing subcategories from a hierarchical *directory* or *subject tree*, as described in Chapter 0. Whatever search technique you use, you're eventually presented with a rank-ordered list of Web pages. A page might go undetected by one search engine and appear at the top of a list on another. That's why many researchers use *meta-search engines* such as MetaCrawler, OneSeek, and Apple's Sherlock—software tools that conduct parallel searches using several different search engines and directories. Of course, getting more hits isn't necessarily better. The best search engines provide you with relatively few high-quality results rather than overwhelming you with marginally relevant links.

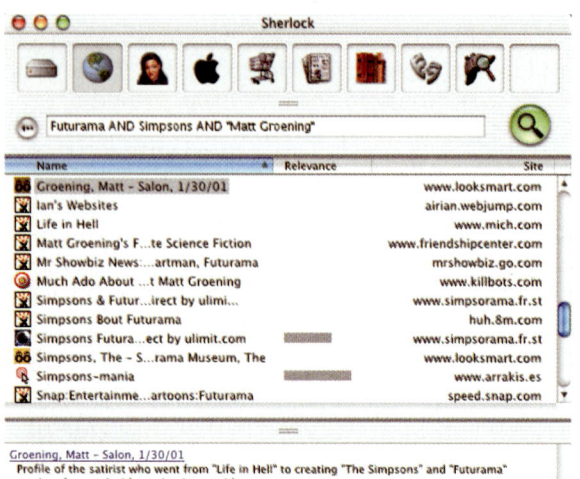

Sherlock 2, a meta-search engine built into the Mac OS, coordinates searches using multiple search engines.

Some popular search engines are designed to search for specific types of information. Specialized search engines can help you locate email addresses and phone numbers; others can help you find the lowest prices on the Web. These specialized search engines generally use technology that's very similar to general search engine technology.

Most search engines have access to less than one percent of the pages on the Web. The rest are out of reach of the public or stored in databases that can't be searched by conventional search engines. Some newer search engines, including *invisibleweb.com*, can provide access to information in those databases. Web search technology continues to evolve with the Web.

Portals

Many Web sites that started out as search engines have evolved into **portals**—Web entry stations that offer quick and easy access to a variety of services. Popular general-interest portals include Yahoo!, Excite, Lycos, AltaVista, Netscape Netcenter, and MSN. **Consumer portals** includes search engines, email services, chat rooms, references, news and sports headlines, shopping malls, other services, and advertisements—many of the same things found in online services such as AOL. You can personalize many of the portals so they automatically display local weather and sports scores, personalized TV and movie listings, news headlines related to particular subjects, horoscopes, and ads to meet your interests. Most browsers enable users to choose a home page that opens by default when the browser is launched; portals are designed with this feature in mind.

In addition to these general interest portals, the Web has a growing population of specialized portals. **Corporate portals** on intranets serve the employees of particular corporations. **Vertical portals**, or **vortals**, like vertical market software (Chapter 4) target members of a particular industry or economic sector. For example, **webmd.com** is a portal for medically minded consumers and health-care professionals. A growing number of specialized portals are competing to be your browser's home page.

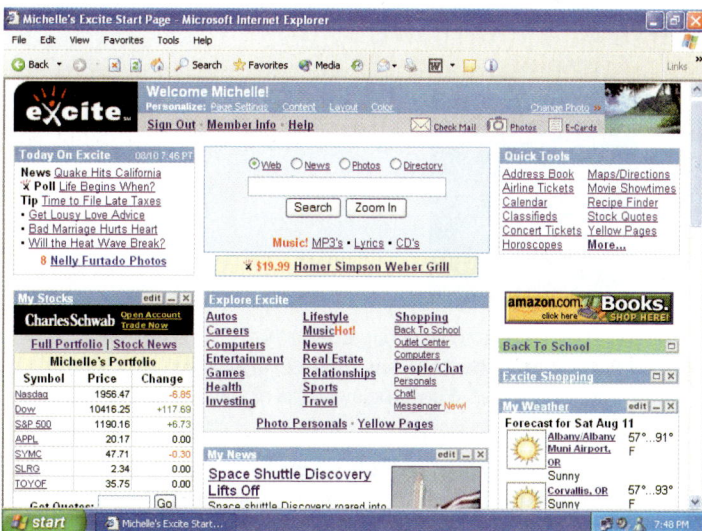

Like other portals, Excite can be personalized to highlight weather, news, sports, and financial headlines the user specifies.

Email on the Internet

The most popular Internet application is one of the oldest—email. There's no single way to send and receive Internet mail. What you see on the screen depends on the type of Internet connection you have and the mail program you use. If you have a dial-up connection to a UNIX-based host, you might send and receive mail using the UNIX mail program Pine, an easy-to-use program developed at the University of Washington. Because it's character-based, Pine works with almost any kind of Internet connection. Users with full Internet connections have many more mail software options, including graphical programs such as Microsoft Outlook Express and Qualcomm Eudora Pro. These programs enable PCs to download and handle mail locally rather than depending on a host as a post office. Many email services, including several free ones, are designed to be accessed through Web browsers rather than separate email client programs.

Email programs have a variety of user interfaces. Pine (top) is a character-based UNIX program that can be used on a terminal or PC. Eudora (bottom left) is a cross-platform commercial email program that is powerful and easy to use. Hotmail is a free email service that is accessible through Web browsers.

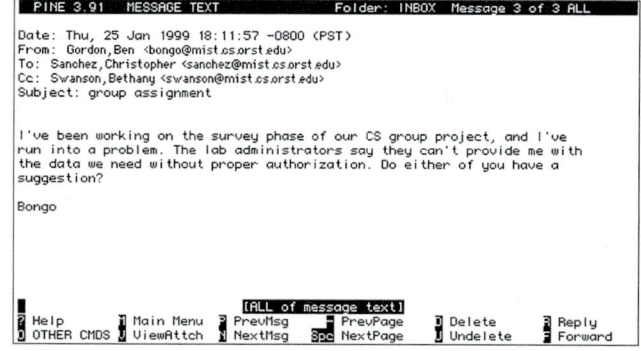

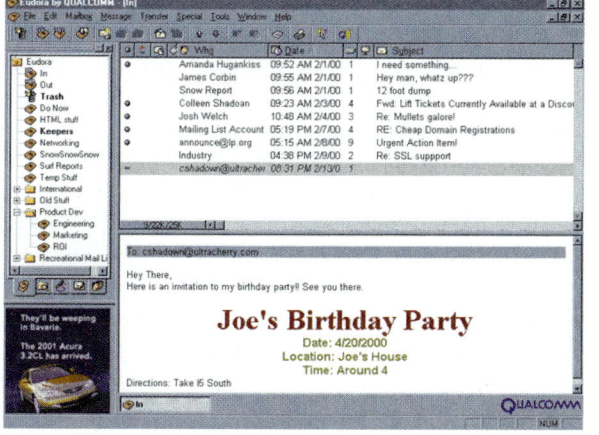

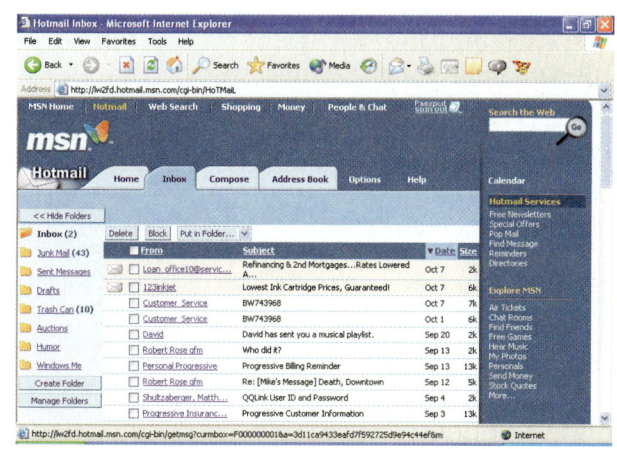

Rules of Thumb

Working the Web

The Web is so easy to navigate that it's tempting to just dive in. But like a large library, the Web has more to offer if you learn a few tricks and techniques. Your goals should dictate your Web strategy.

- **Get to know your search engines.** Try several, choose your favorites, and learn the more advanced search features so you can minimize the time it takes to find what you're looking for. Searchenginewatch (www.searchengingwatch.com) is a good source of information about search engines.
- **Be specific when you search.** A search engine is more likely to give you the answer you're looking for if you search for "Epson USB scanner" than if you just type "scanner".
- **Know your plusses and minuses.** In most search engines you can use a plus sign to signify that you want pages that contain all words. For example, "+Alaska +oil +wildlife" searches pages that contain all three words. On the other hand, a minus sign usually means "not". For example, "cancer –astrology" locates pages that contain "cancer" but not "astrology". When you use these symbols, you're using basic Boolean algebra—the logical basis of database queries.
- **Be selective.** As Robert P. Lipshutz wrote in *Mobile Computing*, "A few tidbits of accurate, timely and useful information are worth much more than a ream of random data, and bad information is worse than no information at all." When you're assessing a Web page's credibility, consider the author, the writing, the references, and the page sponsor's objectivity and reliability. Be aware that many of the most popular search engines charge companies to be listed prominently in their directories, and that some give top billing to their own services and partners.
- **Triangulate.** A traditional navigation technique for sailors, triangulation involves using two points, other than yourself, to establish location. Xerox Chief Scientist John Seely Brown suggests that the same concept should be applied to the turbulent waters of the Web. Don't assume something is true because one Web source tells you so, unless you're sure the source is rock solid.
- **Organize your favorites.** When you find a page worth revisiting, record it on your list of favorites or bookmarks. Browsers enable you to organize your lists by category—a strategy that's far more effective than just throwing them all in a digital shoebox.
- **Protect your privacy.** Many Web servers keep track of all kinds of data about you: what site you visited before you came, where you clicked, and more. When you fill out forms to enter contests, order goods, or leave messages, you're providing more data for your hosts. Don't divulge any private information about yourself. And make sure you don't leave tracks that you're ashamed of as you hip-hop around the Web.
- **Be conscious of cookies and bugs.** Many Web servers send **cookies** to your browser when you visit them or perform other actions. Cookies are tidbits of information about your session that can be read later; they enable Web sites to remember what they know about you between sessions. Cookies make personalized portals and customized shopping experiences possible. Unfortunately, Cookies can also provide all kinds of possibilities for snoopers who want to know how you spend your time online. By default, most browsers don't tell you when they leave a cookie. It's easy to change browser settings so your browser will refuse all cookies, accept cookies only from selected sites, or ask you, on a cookie-by-cookie basis, whether to accept or refuse cookies. Unfortunately, you can't easily turn off **Web bugs**—one-pixel graphic images that are programmed to send information about your Web use back to their creators.
- **Online shopping isn't always better.** In increasing numbers shoppers are abandoning brick-and-mortar stores for click-and-mortar Web stores. Online shops and auctions can save you money, especially if you comparison shop. But when a product doesn't work as advertised, or when you have after-sale questions, a Web merchant might not be as helpful as a local shopkeeper. Some don't even accept phone queries. If your purchase will require person-to-person communication before or after the sale, you're probably better off patronizing a local merchant.
- **Shop with bots.** Bots are software robots, or agents, that can explore the Web and report back their findings. Several bots (such as mySimon at www.mySimon.com) are designed to help you find low prices by searching the databases of hundreds of merchants.
- **Shop with care.** The Web, like the nondigital world, has its share of less-than-honest merchants. Use services such as bizrate (www.bizrate.com) to evaluate questionable merchants before you lay your digital money down. If you're dealing with a private party or an unknown merchant, consider using a transaction service such as Paypal (www.paypal.com) to serve as a safe temporary depository for funds until the purchased product reaches you.
- **Remember why you're there.** The Web's extensive hyperlinks make it all too easy to wander off course when you're searching for important information. If you're using the Web to save time, stay focused or you may find that the Web costs more time than it saves.

Standard Internet mail messages are plain ASCII text. Plain text messages can be viewed with any mail client program, including those in email-capable PDAs and phones. Many email programs can also send and receive documents formatted with HTML—the language commonly used to create Web pages. HTML messages can include text formatting, pictures, and links to Web pages. But not all email programs can handle HTML email, and not all email users *want* HTML email. HTML encoding can slow down an email program. An HTML email message can also carry a **Web bug**—an invisible piece of code that silently notifies the sender about when the message was opened and may report other information about their machine or email software at the same time. Web bugs, which operate through specially encoded one-pixel graphics files, are increasingly common in commercial Web pages as well as HTML email messages.

Most email programs can send and receive formatted word processor documents, pictures, and other multimedia files as **attachments** to messages. Attachments need to be temporarily converted to ASCII text using some kind of encoding scheme before they can be sent through Internet mail. Most modern email programs take care of the encoding and decoding automatically. Of course, attachments aren't practical with many PDAs, cell phones, and other text-only email devices. And attachments can contain viruses and other unwelcome surprises, as described in the next chapter.

The Handspring Treo is a wireless device designed to send and receive email without a PC. The Treo also serves as a PDA, a wireless phone, and a wireless Web browser.

Mailing Lists

Email is a valuable tool for communicating one-to-one with individuals around the globe, but it's also useful for communicating one-to-many. **Mailing lists** enable you to participate in email discussion groups on special-interest topics. Lists can be small and local, or large and global. They can be administered by a human being or automatically administered by programs with names like Listserv and Majordomo. Each group has a mailing address that looks like any Internet address.

You might belong to one student group that's set up by your instructor to carry on discussions outside of class, another group that includes people all over the world who use Macromedia Flash to animate Web pages, a third that's dedicated to saving endangered species in your state, and a fourth for customers of an online bookstore. When you send a message to a mailing list address, every subscriber receives a copy. And, of course, you receive a copy of every mail message sent by everyone else to those lists.

Subscribing to a busy list might mean receiving hundreds of messages each day. To avoid being overwhelmed by incoming mail, many list members sign up to receive them in daily digest form; instead of receiving many individual messages each day, they receive one message that includes all postings. But digest messages can still contain lots of repetitive, silly, and annoying messages. Some lists are **moderated** to ensure that the quality of the discussion remains high. In a moderated group, a designated moderator acts as an editor, filtering out irrelevant and inappropriate messages and posting the rest.

Network News

You can participate in special-interest discussions without overloading your mailbox by taking advantage of **newsgroups**. A newsgroup is a public discussion on a particular subject consisting of notes written to a central Internet site and redistributed through a worldwide newsgroup network called Usenet. You can check into and out of a newsgroup discussion whenever you want; all messages are posted on virtual bulletin boards for anyone to read anytime. There are groups for every interest and taste . . . and a few for the tasteless. Newsgroups are organized hierarchically, with dot names like rec.music.makers.percussion and soc.culture.french. You can explore network newsgroups through several Web sites, including Google, or with a newsreader client program.

Many newsgroups contain the same kind of free-flowing discussions you'll find in Internet mailing lists, but there are two important differences:

▶ Listserv mail messages are delivered automatically to your mailbox, but you have to seek out information in newsgroups.

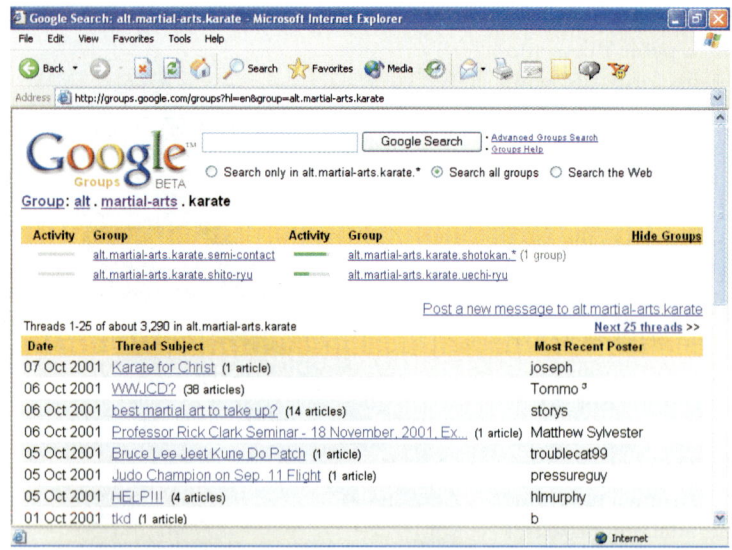

Google.com's newsreader enables you to view newsgroups by category (top) and view messages posted within those categories (bottom).

- Mailing list messages are sent to a specific group of people, whereas newsgroup messages are available for anyone to see . . . for years to come.

Newsgroup discussions can get bogged down by repetitive questions from newcomers, childish rants, off-topic trivia, and other counterproductive messages. **Moderated newsgroups** contain only messages that have been filtered by designated moderators. The moderator discards inappropriate messages, making it easier for others to find the information they're looking for. Yahoo, MSN, AOL, and other portals and information services have discussion groups that are similar to Usenet newsgroups; the main difference is that they aren't distributed as widely.

Real-Time Communication

> For **time** is the **longest distance** between two points.
>
> —Tennessee Williams

Mailing lists and newsgroups are delayed or **asynchronous communication** because the sender and the recipients don't have to be logged in at the same time. The Internet offers programs for **real-time communication**, too. **Instant messaging** has been possible since the days of text-only Internet access. Internet relay chat (IRC) and Talk enable UNIX users to exchange instant messages with their online friends and coworkers. But newer, easier to use messaging systems from AOL/Netscape, Microsoft, Yahoo, ICQ, and others have turned instant messaging into one of the most popular Internet activities. Instant messaging programs enable users to create buddy lists, check for "buddies" who are logged in, and exchanged typed messages and files with those who are. Most of these programs are available for free.

Some chat rooms and multiplayer games on the Web use graphics to simulate real-world environments. Participants can represent themselves with **avatars**—graphical "bodies" that might look like simple cartoon sketches, elaborate 3-D figures, or exotic abstract icons.

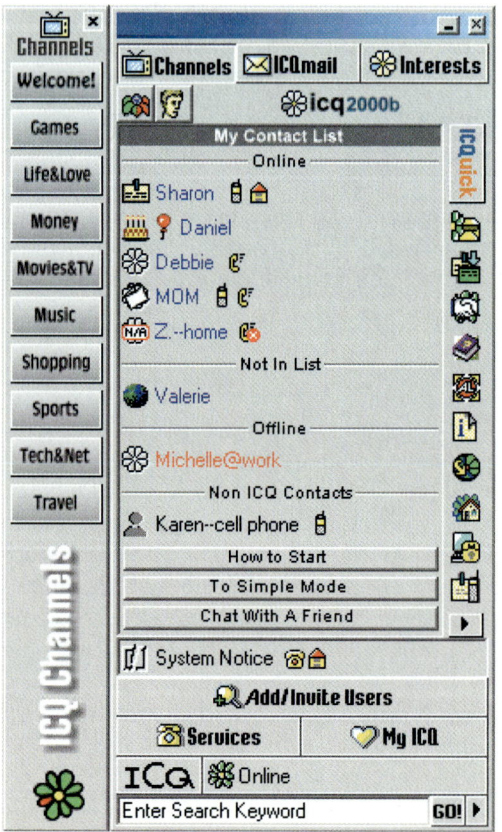

ICQ, one of the most popular instant messaging services on the Internet, enables users to communicate in real time with friends and colleagues.

For more conventional communication, many programs enable you to use a computer's microphone and speaker to turn the Internet into a toll-free long-distance telephone service. Most **Internet telephony (IP telephony)** programs work only when both parties are running the same program at the same time, and they're not nearly as trouble-free as traditional long-distance service. Still, many experts predict that this kind of technology will soon pose a serious competitive threat to the current telephone infrastructure.

Several programs make it possible to carry on two-way **video teleconferences**—provided you have a video camera and a high-speed Internet connection for each computer. With high-powered hardware, it's even possible to have multiperson videoconferences through the Web. The video images may be small, grainy, and jerky, but they're bound to get better as the technology matures.

Rules of Thumb

Netiquette

The Internet is a new type of community that uses new forms of communication. Like any society the Net has rules and guidelines of acceptable behavior. If you follow these rules of **netiquette**, you'll be doing your part to make life on the Net easier for everybody—especially yourself.

- **Say what you mean, and say it with care.** Once you send something electronically, there's no way to call it back. Compose each message carefully, and make sure it means what you intend it to mean. If you're replying to a message, double-check the heading to make sure your reply is going only to those people you intend to send it to. Even if you took only a few seconds to write your message, it may be broadcast far and wide and be preserved forever in online archives.

- **Keep it short.** Include a descriptive subject line, and limit the body to a screen or two. If you're replying to a long message, include a copy of the relevant part of the message—but not the whole message. Remember that many people receive hundreds of email messages each day and they're more likely to read and respond to short ones.

- **Proofread your messages.** A famous *New Yorker* cartoon by Peter Steiner shows one dog telling another, "On the Internet no one knows you're a dog." You may not be judged by the color of your hair or the clothes you wear when you're posting messages, but that doesn't mean appearances aren't important. Other people will judge your intelligence and education by the spelling, grammar, punctuation, and clarity of your messages. If you want your messages to be taken seriously, present your best face.

- **Don't assume you're anonymous.** Your messages can say a lot about you, Those messages might be seen by more than your intended audience, and they won't necessarily go away when you want them to. Researcher Jonathan G.S. Koppell suggests a more contemporary caption for the *New Yorker* cartoon mentioned above: "On the Internet, everyone knows you're an aging, overweight, malamute-retriever mix living in the southwest, and with a preference for rawhide."

- **Learn the "nonverbal" language of the Net.** A simple phrase like "Nice job!" can have very different meanings depending on the tone of voice and body language behind it. Since body language and tone of voice can't easily be stuffed into a modem, online communities have developed text-based substitutes, sometimes called **emoticons**. Here are a few:

:-)	These three characters represent a smiling face. (To see why, look at them with this page rotated 90° to the right.) "Smilie" suggests the previous remark should not be taken seriously. (The dash is optional.)
;-)	This winking smilie usually means the previous remark was flirtatious or sarcastic.
:-(	This frowning character suggests something is bothering the author—probably the previous statement in the message.
:-I	This character represents indifference.
:-.	This usually follows an extremely biting sarcastic remark.
:-P	This one is sticking its tongue out as if to say, "I'm grossed out!"
\<g\>	People who don't like smilies use this to say "grin."
ROTFL	This is short for "rolling on the floor laughing"; it's one of hundreds of keystroke-saving acronyms.
BTW	This one means "by the way."
IMHO	This one says "in my humble opinion."
Flame on	This statement, inspired by a comic book hero, warns readers that the following statements are inflammatory.
Flame off	This means the tirade is over.
\<rant\>	The angle brackets make this emoticon look like HTML, the page description language of the Web; this one means "beginning of rant."
\</rant\>	Using the HTML convention, this means "end of rant."

- **Keep your cool.** Many otherwise timid people turn into raging bulls when they're online. The facelessness of Internet communication makes it all too easy to shoot from the hip, overstate arguments, and get caught up in a digital lynch-mob mentality. There's nothing wrong with expressing your emotions, but broadside attacks and half-truths can do serious damage to your online relationships. Online or off, freedom of speech is a right that carries responsibility.

- **Don't be a source of spam.** It's so easy to send multiple copies of email messages that it's tempting broadcast too widely. Target your messages carefully; if you're trying to sell tickets to a local concert or advertise your garage sale, don't tell the whole world. If you *do* send a mass mailing, hide the recipient list to protect the privacy of your recipients. One way is to send the message to yourself and put everyone else in the bcc (blind carbon copy) field. And if you send repeated mass mailings, make sure you *always* include a message telling people how they can get off your list.

- **Send no-frills mail.** Even if your email program makes it easy to use fancy formatting, embed HTML, and include attachments, it's usually better to err on the side of simplicity. Graphics and fancy formatting make message files bigger and slower to download. Many people turn off the HTML capabilities of their email programs to protect themselves from Web bugs (HTML code that sends messages back to the sender). And many email veterans fear attachments because of the risk of email viruses. If you don't need the extra baggage, why not leave it out?

- **Lurk before you leap.** People who silently monitor mailing lists and newsgroups without posting messages are called **lurkers**. There's no shame in lurking, especially if you're new to a group—it can help you to figure out what's appropriate. After you've learned the culture and conventions of a group, you'll be better able to contribute constructively and wisely.

- **Check your FAQs.** Many newsgroups and mailing lists have **FAQs** (pronounced "facks")—posted lists of **frequently asked questions**. These lists keep groups from being cluttered with the same old questions and answers, but only if members take advantage of them.

- **Give something back.** The Internet includes an online community of volunteers who answer beginner questions, archive files, moderate newsgroups, maintain public servers, and provide other helpful services. If you appreciate their work, tell them in words and show them in actions—do your part to help others in the Internet community.

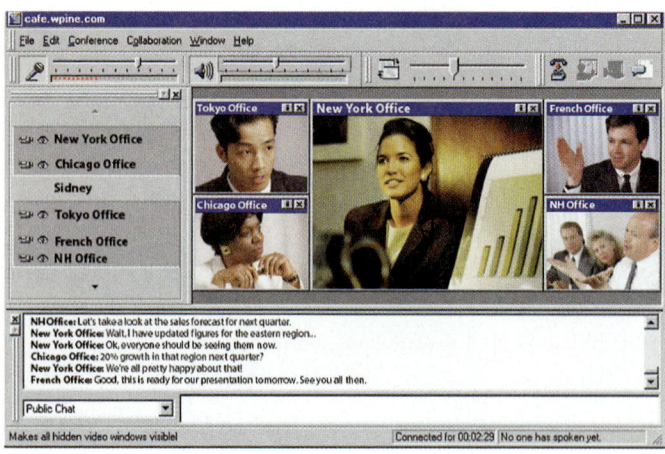

CU-SeeMe enables real-time audio/visual communication over the Internet.

Push Technology

> We think we "surf" the Web now,
> but what we really do is hopscotch across fragile stepping-stones of texts, or worse,
> spelunk in a vast unmapped cave of documents.
> Only when **waves of media** begin to cascade behind our screens—
> huge swells of unbrowsable stuff—will we truly surf.
> —Kevin Kelly and Gary Wolf, former Wired editors

The Web was built with **pull technology**—browsers on client computers pull information from server machines. With pull technology the browser needs to initiate a request before any information is delivered. But for some applications, it makes more sense to have information delivered automatically to the client computer. That's the way **push technology** works. (Microsoft used the term *Webcasting* for their brand of push technology. But today Webcasting more commonly refers to streaming audio and video feeds from radio stations, TV stations, and others on the Web.) With push technology you subscribe to a service or specify the kinds of information you want to receive and the server delivers that information periodically and unobtrusively. Maybe you want up-to-the-minute weather maps displayed in a small window in the corner of your screen. You might prefer to see news headlines (on subjects of your choice) scroll across the top of your screen. You may want to automatically receive new product descriptions from selected companies. Or you might like to have the software on your hard disk automatically upgraded when upgrades are posted on the Web. All of this is possible with push technology.

Technically speaking, today's push technology is really pull technology in disguise. Your computer quietly and automatically pulls information from selected Web servers based on your earlier requests or subscriptions. As convenient as they are, push programs have the same basic problem as Web search engines: They give you what they think you want, but they may not be very smart. Their ability to deliver what you really need—without bombarding you with unwanted data—will get better as artificial intelligence technology improves. In the meantime, push technology is used mostly for in-house delivery of information on intranets. Email continues to be the single form of push technology that has been embraced by almost all Internet users.

Peer-to-Peer and Grid Computing

> The genie does not go back in the bottle—**period**.
> —Tom Peters, business guru and best-selling author

Of all the companies that came out of nowhere during the dot-com boom of the late '90s, Napster generated the most conversation—and controversy. When 19-year-old college student Shawn Fanning put a friendly user interface and a fresh spin on decades-old file-sharing technology, he created a virtual swap meet for students and others who wanted to share MP3 music files. Almost overnight Napster became one of the hottest Internet destinations, with millions of users downloading and sharing MP3s daily using Napster's software. In May of 2000, a tech company hired by the rock band Metallica revealed that 322,000 Napster users were illegally distributing their music. The Recording Industry Association of America sued the company because its software enabled users to download copyrighted recordings without paying the record companies or artists.

The Napster servers didn't contain those illegal recordings—it just displayed links to recordings scattered all over the Net. People who used Napster practiced **peer-to-peer (P2P) computing**—or, more specifically, **peer-to-peer file sharing**—by making music files on their hard drives available to others rather than posting them on central servers. In April of 2001, a U.S. District Judge ruled that Napster was violating federal copyright law and forced the company to change its software so that users no longer had free access to copyrighted recordings. Napster changed its software and its business model, but the peer-to-peer music exchange lived on through other programs and Web sites. The popular Gnutella file-sharing system avoids Napster's legal problems by allowing users to share music, movies, and other files without going through a central directory. According to some experts, Gnutella's rapid growth suggests that it may become a Web standard.

Technologies like Gnutella make it difficult—or impossible—for laws to contain the peer-to-peer file-sharing phenomenon. Recording artists are divided on the issue; some encourage fans to share their music, while others fear that sharing will make it difficult for many musicians to support themselves. (Copyright and intellectual property issues are discussed in more detail in the next chapter.)

Music sharing is just one application of peer-to-peer computing. The technology is being applied to a growing number of diverse applications. Books, movies, and computer software are shared using Napster-like technology—and with the same legal and ethical concerns. Businesses use P2P for group collaboration, for Web searches, and for sharing updates to virus-control software, among other things.

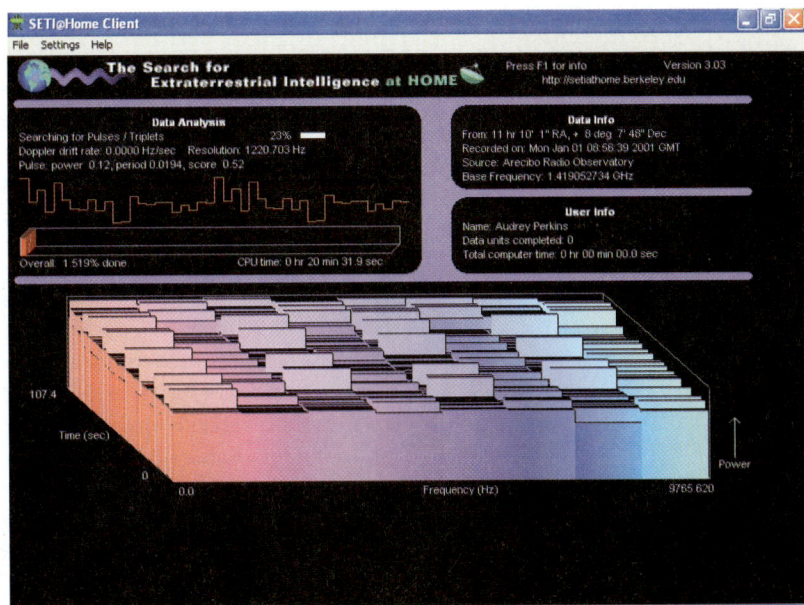

The SETI@Home program starts after a PC sits idle for a few minutes; this animated screensaver shows the program in action.

A related technology—**grid computing**—is, like P2P, a form of *distributed computing*. But grid computing isn't about sharing files; it's about sharing processing power. The best-known example is SETI@Home (setiathome.ssl.berkeley.edu/), a program that puts PCs all over the Internet together into a sort of virtual supercomputer that analyzes space telescope data in the search for extraterrestrial life. The SETI@Home program, when installed on a PC, uses the computer's idle time to do calculations and send the results back to SETI headquarters. Millions of PCs around the world can do the work of a million-dollar supercomputer in much less time. A similar program called FightAIDS@home (fightaidsathome.com) enables PCs to contribute spare processing cycles to the fight against AIDS.

Grid computing may soon extend far beyond these processor-sharing programs to a new Internet model that resembles a utility grid. IBM and other companies are supporting initiatives to build a grid computing environment where anyone can plug in from anywhere and rent processing power and software from anywhere on the Net. Grid computing applications are currently being used by the U.S. Department of Defense, the U.S. Department of Energy, NASA, the U.K National Grid, and a variety of academic and scientific communities.

Intranets, Extranets, and Electronic Commerce

> Our customers are moving at **Internet speed**. They need us to respond at Internet speed.
> —Laurie Tucker, Federal Express vice president

For many businesses, Internet protocols and software are almost as important as the Net itself. Members of these organizations communicate through **intranets**—self-contained intraorganizational networks that are designed using the same technology as the Internet. A typical intranet offers email, newsgroups, file transfer, Web publishing, and other Internet-like services, but not all of these services are available to people outside the organization. For example, an intranet Web document might be accessible only to company employees—not to the entire Internet community. If an intranet has a gateway connection to the Internet, the gateway probably has some kind of *firewall* to prevent unauthorized communication and to secure sensitive internal data.

Some private TCP/IP networks are designed for outside use by customers, clients, and business partners of the organization. These networks, often called **extranets**, are typically for **electronic commerce (e-commerce)**—business transactions through electronic networks. Most use **electronic data interchange (EDI)**—a decade-old set of specifications for ordering, billing, and paying for parts and services over private networks.

Some extranets are **virtual private networks** that use encryption software (described in the next chapter) to create secure "tunnels" through the public Internet. Others use their own lines or lease lines that aren't subject to the traffic and security problems of the public Internet. Extranets are especially useful for **business-to-business (B2B)** e-commerce—transactions that involve businesses providing goods or services to other businesses.

Business-to-consumer (B2C) e-commerce generally involves transactions that take place on the Internet, rather than an extranet, because consumers don't have access to private extranets. The Internet has spawned a wide variety of B2C businesses, including

- *Online catalog sales.* Online catalogs save paper, but they offer other advantages for consumers, including search engines, immediate availability reports, custom orders, and instant updates. But some types of merchandise don't lend themselves to online sales, and online customers can be frustrated by confusing user interfaces and minimal customer support.
- *Auctions.* The Internet makes long-distance auctions practical, allowing people to bid on all kinds of items. Some retail outlets use auctions to move clearance merchandise; some sites sell everything through auctions.
- *Reverse auctions.* Some sites allow customers to request goods or services and have merchants bid on prices. Everything from airline tickets to legal services is offered through reverse auctions.
- *Comparison shopping.* Specialized search engines search the Web for the lowest prices.
- *Financial services.* Checks, credit cards, stocks are all available online.

B-to-C sites can offer a high degree of personalization—for example, suggesting products similar to the ones already ordered by a customer, or remembering a customer's personal preferences and sizes between visits. But personalization raises privacy and security concerns in many customers. (Security issues are discussed in detail in the next chapter.)

E-commerce is changing the way many companies do business. But e-commerce isn't cheap or easy. Profits have proven to be elusive for many online companies. Like the brick-and-mortar world, the Internet presents challenges along with opportunities for enterprising business people.

Web Services

> The **network** is the **computer**.
> —advertising slogan used by Sun Microsystems, Inc., in the 1990s

Software costs can be daunting for companies that have to build e-commerce sites from the ground up. Several of the computer industry's biggest companies, including IBM, Hewlett Packard, Microsoft, Oracle, and Sun, are developing software tools to make e-commerce solutions easier to build and maintain. These systems have different names and features, but they all fall into a software category called **Web services**. Web services involve new kinds of Web-based applications that can be assembled quickly using existing *software components*. Component technology can, for example, make it easy to plug a shopping-cart component into an existing Web site, or to design applications that can be accessed through a variety of Web-enabled devices. XML plays an important role in most Web services systems currently under development.

Unfortunately, the industry hasn't agreed on the details of this emerging technology. Sun, Hewlett Packard, and IBM are using Java to build their cross-platform service tools. Microsoft's .NET is being built using C#, a proprietary language that (so far) runs only on Windows platforms. The Free Software Foundation is working on a UNIX version of Microsoft's .NET technology, hoping to keep .NET from being a proprietary system. Meanwhile, the W3C is attempting to create standards that the entire industry can embrace.

Complete Web Services systems are still many years away. But they offer great hope for companies struggling with the challenges of creating successful e-commerce sites.

The Evolving Internet

> In the short term, the **impact** of new technologies like the Internet will be **less than the hype** would suggest. But in the long term, it will be vastly **larger than we can imagine** today.
> —Paul Saffo, director of the Institute for the Future

The Internet started as a small community of scientists, engineers, and other researchers who staunchly defended the noncommercial, cooperative charter of the network. Today the Net has swollen into a community of millions, including everybody from children to corporate executives. The rate of growth is so great that it raises questions about the Internet's ability to keep up; the amount of information transmitted may eventually be more than the Net can handle.

The U.S. government no longer assumes primary responsibility for Internet expansion. Many funding and administrative duties have been passed on to private companies, allowing businesses to commercialize the Net. In 1995, for the first time, the number of commercial host sites on the Net exceeded the number of noncommercial sites. In the 3-year period that followed, the Net experienced a hundredfold increase in monthly traffic.

Internet2 and the Next Generation Internet

As the Internet evolves into the network of the masses, congestion becomes more problematic for the scientists and researchers who made up the original Internet community. The U.S. government, working in conjunction with several large corporations, launched *Internet2* in 1998 to provide faster network communications for universities and research institutions. A related effort from DARPA, the *Next Generation Internet (NGI)*, will consist of a nationwide web of optical fiber integrated with intelligent management software to maintain high-speed connections.

Internet2 will eventually be capable of transmitting data at 9.6 billion bits per second—enough to send all 30 volumes of the Encyclopedia Britannica in 1 second. Internet2 isn't available for commercial or recreational use; it is reserved for research and academic work. Participating universities are building virtual laboratories, digital libraries, telemedicine research facilities, and distance learning applications that take advantage of its tremendous bandwidth. The rest of us will undoubtedly inherit the technologies developed for Internet2.

Internet Issues: Ethical and Political Dilemmas

> **The Internet** still hasn't figured out how to **conduct itself in public**.... Everybody is trying to **develop the rules** by which they can conduct themselves in order to keep a **civil operation** going and not **self-destruct**.
> —George Lucas, filmmaker

The commercialization of the Internet has opened a floodgate of new services to users. People are logging into the Internet to view weather patterns, book flights, buy stocks, sell cars, track deliveries, listen to radio broadcasts from around the world, conduct videoconferences, coordinate disaster recovery programs, and do countless other private and public transactions. The Internet saves time, money, and lives, but it brings problems, too.

Computer Addiction

For a few hard-core networkers the world on the other side of the modem is more real and more interesting than the everyday physical world. One Alaskan reader wrote to advice columnist Ann Landers: "Computer chat lines can become every bit as addictive as cocaine. I have been hooked on both, and it was easier to get off coke." While this may seem strange, it's not unique. Many people feel the same way about television, spectator sports, or romance novels. Internet addiction, like any addiction, can be a serious problem—for individuals and for society. The problem is growing as more people go online, and no quick fixes are in sight.

Freedom's Abuses

Commercialization has brought capitalism's dark side to the Internet. Electronic junk mail scams, get-rich-quick hoaxes, online credit-card thefts, email forgery, child pornography hustling, illegal gambling, Web site sabotage, online stalking, and other sleazy activities abound. The Internet has clearly lost its innocence.

Some of these problems have at least partial technological solutions. Concerned parents and teachers can now install *filtering software* that, for the most part, keeps children out of Web sites that contain inappropriate content. Commercial Web sites routinely use encryption so customers can purchase goods and services without fear of having credit-card numbers stolen by electronic eavesdroppers. Several software companies and banks are developing systems for circulating *digital cash* on the Internet to make online transactions easier and safer. To protect against email forgery, many software companies are working together to hammer out standards for *digital signatures* using encryption techniques described in the next chapter.

Many problems associated with the rapid growth and commercialization of the Internet are social problems that raise important political questions. Online hucksterism and pornography have prompted government controls on Internet content, including the 1996 Communications Decency Act. Opponents to this law and other proposed controls argue that it's important to preserve the free flow of information; they stress the need to protect our rights to free speech and privacy on the Net. In 1996 the U.S. Supreme Court declared the Communications Decency Act unconstitutional, arguing that "the interest in encouraging freedom of expression in a democratic society outweighs any theoretical but unproven benefit of censorship." Nevertheless, the legal battle is certain to continue.

In December of 2000, Congress passed the Children's Internet Protection act. The act requires public libraries and schools that receive certain types of federal funding install content filters on computers with Internet access. Like the Communications Decency Act, the Children's Internet Protection Act faces legal challenges based on the First Amendment to the Constitution.

Questions about human rights online probably won't be resolved by legislators and judges, though. The Internet's global reach makes it nearly impossible for a single government to regulate it. Even if the governments of the world agree to try to restrict information flow, the Net seems to have developed a mind of its own. The same decentralized, packet-switching technology that was designed to protect government messages from enemy attack today protects civilian messages from government or corporate control. In the words of Internet pioneer John Gilmore, "The Net interprets censorship as damage and routes around it."

Universal Access Issues

During the 1990s the U.S. government pushed for the development of a National Information Infrastructure (NII)—an affordable, secure, high-speed network to provide "universal service" for all Americans. Probably the biggest roadblock to realizing the dream of NII is the **digital divide** that separates computer haves from have-nots.

As part of the nonprofit Tech Corps program, these computer professionals volunteer their time and skills to help students and teachers put technology to good use.

Today a little more than half of the U.S. population has easy access to the Internet—a subset of America that excludes most poor people and minorities. Government programs to wire schools, libraries, and other public facilities have increased access for disadvantaged populations. But many Internet services that used to be free for all are now available to only paying customers. Families can't buy computers or Internet service if they're having trouble paying the rent. The problem of equal access isn't likely to go away without combined efforts of governments, businesses, and individuals.

Even if America achieves a universal access NII, access issues still confront the rest of the world. The Internet is a global infrastructure, but huge populations all over the world are locked out. Many experts fear that we'll leave those populations behind as we move further into the information age. This kind of information stratification could be harmful to all of us unless we find ways to unlock the Internet for everybody who wants it.

Internet Everywhere:
The Invisible Information Infrastructure

> In the future, **everything with a digital heartbeat** will be connected to the Internet.
> —Scott McNealy, CEO of Sun Microsystems

Where is it all heading? Vint Cerf, one of the Internet's founders, thinks it's headed for space. He's putting much of his time and energy into a project called InterPlaNet, which he hopes will extend the Internet to the other planets in our solar system. According to the plan, electronic "post offices" will orbit other planets, routing messages between space explorers, both human and robot.

Back on Earth, technology forecaster Paul Saffo suggests a blurring of the boundaries between the Web and interpersonal communication applications. When we visit a Web site that's being explored by hundreds of other people, we'll actually be able to experience their presence and interact with them in ways that go beyond today's simple chat rooms. In Saffo's words, "We're going to shift away from a model of people accessing information to a model of people accessing other people in an information-rich environment. The information will become the wallpaper surrounding conversational space."

We may be sharing Web space with more people in the future, but we'll also be sharing it with all kinds of gadgets. Today we think of the Web as a network of computers, but the Web isn't just for PCs, mainframes, and servers anymore. A variety of Internet appliances, network computers, set-top boxes, PDAs, mobile phones, and other devices are being connected to the Internet in offices and homes. Everything from coffee makers to traffic lights may be routinely connected to the Web soon. Consider the possibilities:

You tell your alarm clock to wake you in time to catch the 8:00 A.M. flight to Washington. At 5:00 A.M. the clock checks the airline's Web site and determines that the flight has been delayed an hour. It also checks online traffic reports and finds that traffic is light. The clock resets your wakeup time accordingly, giving you an extra hour of sleep. As usual, it turns on the heat and the coffee maker 10 minutes before it wakes you. On the way to the airport, your car routes you around a congested construction spot. When you arrive at the airport, it tells you where to find a vacant parking spot close to the terminal.

Whether you consider this future fantasy appealing or appalling, the technology is on the horizon. One thing is clear: The Web is changing so fast it's impossible for anybody to predict exactly what it will look like even a few months from today.

Cyberspace: The Electronic Frontier

> Cyberspace. **A consensual hallucination** experienced daily by billions of legitimate operators, **in every nation**, by children being taught mathematical concepts. . . . A graphic representation of data abstracted from the banks of **every computer in the human system**. **Unthinkable complexity**. Lines of light ranged in the nonspace of the mind, clusters and constellations of data. Like city lights, receding. . . .
>
> —William Gibson, in *Neuromancer*

Science fiction writers suggest that tomorrow's networks will take us beyond the Internet into an artificial reality that has come to be known as **cyberspace**, a term coined by William Gibson in his visionary novel *Neuromancer*.

In *Neuromancer*, as in earlier works by Vernor Vinge and others, travelers experience the universal computer network as if it were a physical place, a shared virtual reality, complete with sights, sounds, and other sensations. Gibson's cyberspace is an abstract, cold landscape in a dark and dangerous future world. Vinge's novella *True Names* takes place in a network hideaway where adventurous computer wizards never reveal their true names or identities to each other. Instead, they take on mythical identities with supernatural abilities.

Today's computer networks are still light-years from the futuristic visions of Vinge and Gibson. But the Net today *is* a primitive cyberspace—a world where messages, mathematics, and money can cross continents in seconds. People from all over the planet meet, develop friendships, and share their innermost thoughts and feelings in cyberspace.

John Perry Barlow, co-founder of the Electronic Frontier Foundation has called the online world an "electronic frontier," suggesting parallels to America's Old West. Until recently the electronic frontier was populated mostly by free-spirited souls willing to forgo creature comforts. These digital pioneers built the roads and towns that are used today by less adventurous settlers and business interests.

In spite of its rapid commercialization, the electronic frontier is far from tame. Network nomads pick digital locks and ignore electronic fences. Some explore nooks and crannies out of a spirit of

Cindy Price and Josh Marquis met on an AOL message board devoted to the O. J. Simpson murder trial in 1995. They married in 1996.

adventure. Others steal and tamper with private information for profit or revenge. Charlatans and hustlers operate outside the law. Law enforcement agencies and lawmakers occasionally overreact.

There's a strong sentiment on the Net toward keeping controls to a minimum. Netizens commonly argue that the Web will always be free of control because of the way it's constructed. It's true that governments have so far had trouble regulating many Internet activities. But there's no guarantee that the free-spirited Internet will always remain that way.

In *The Code and Other Laws of Cyberspace*, Lawrence Lessig claims that, because of commerce and other forces, an architecture of control is being built into the Net—control by government and by businesses intent on maximizing Net profits. Lessig argues that the code—the way the Net is programmed—will determine how much freedom we have in the future Internet. "We can build, or architect, or code cyberspace to protect values we believe are fundamental, or we can build, or architect, or code cyberspace to allow those values to disappear. There is no middle ground. There is no choice that does not include some kind of *building*."

There are parallels in the nondigital world. Many city planning experts argue that industrialized nations have systematically (if not consciously) rebuilt their cities so that, in many places, it's just about impossible to live without a car. These car-centered cities have generated revenue for businesses and governments, and they've brought a new sense of freedom to many citizens. But for the poor, the disabled, the young, the old, and others who can't drive, these cities are anything but free. At the same time, other cities have thriving masses of car-free people. Design choices (and nonchoices) made decades ago determine the livability of our cities today.

In the same way, the design decisions being made today by software architects, corporate managers, government officials, and concerned citizens will determine the nature of our Internet experiences in the future. Will portals guide us to corporate-approved information sources? Will netizens feel free to express controversial opinions and criticize powerful institutions without fear of lawsuits and prosecution? Will paths through cyberspace be accessible to everyone? As Mark Stefik says in *Internet Dreams: Archetypes, Myths, and Metaphors*, "Different versions of [cyberspace] support different kinds of dreams. We choose, wisely or not."

The Day I got Napsterized

Steven Levy

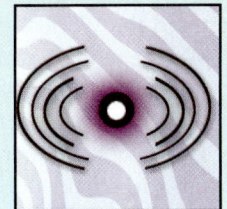

Steven Levy has eloquently written for years about free speech and privacy on the Internet. In this article, first published in the May 28, 2001 issue of Newsweek, *Levy brings the discussion to a personal level.*

As a spectator, I found it easy to be sanguine about the raging Internet intellectual-property debates. I'd tempered my ecstasy during the heady exultations of the "information wants to be free"-bies, and kept my emotional powder dry as apocalyptic content owners warned that wanton file-sharing would mean the death of creativity. Basically, my take was that the Net had simply opened up a powerful mode of distribution, most fully realized in the Napsterlike peer-to-peer (P2P) model, where everybody could help spread the word (and the music). Artists and merchants alike would eventually figure out how to reap bucks from that bounty, and until then I'd sit back and enjoy the fun as Metallica and Courtney Love duked it out.

That was before I got P2P'd. And like facing a hangman's noose, being pirated on the Net has a way of focusing one's attention.

I first got wind of my own Napsterish problem a few months back when I stumbled on a message posted in an Internet discussion group that mentioned my 1984 book *Hackers*. Some helpful soul informed the group that one could get the whole tome free, simply by going to a certain Web site. Huh?

Indeed, the entire text of *Hackers* was posted for all the world to download. And the Web address revealed a most unexpected host for the giveaway: Stanford University. How did my copyrighted work find its way there? A few minutes of clicking revealed that this particular server had some connection to the chair of the university's program in history and philosophy of science, Tim Lenoir. So I called him to ask if he'd any idea who'd done this.

"I scanned your book," he said. Then came the apologies. The professor professed to be a big fan of my work, and (erroneously) assuming that it was out of print, spent a few hours to suck the words from each page of my book, submit it to a program that converted it to text and posted it for the benefit of his students only. The fact that anyone in the world could get to it, he said, was a mistake: he had not intended Stanford University to become an unofficial global distributor of *Hackers*, charging nothing and, of course, paying no royalties. Lenoir promised to remove the book from the site, and we had a pretty good conversation about what might be fair use of electronic texts in an educational setting. By the time I hung up the phone, I felt somewhat less violated. Still, I wondered whether his "mistake" had cost me book sales.

My benign outlook dissolved about a week later when I received an email from an English reader informing me that "in some kind of ironic but illegal turn, your book *Crypto* has been ... posted onto the newsgroup alt.binaries.e-book." This was the work I had published just weeks before, still selling briskly at $25.95 a pop! I knew all too well where the aforementioned irony came from. One topic I'd discussed in *Crypto* was the use of cyberanonymity, a means of cloaking the origin of an electronic missive. The purloiner of my own book called himself Stormysky, and carefully hid his tracks. Using those techniques, a number of Internet repositories had emerged as thriving underground book dumps where free-riders could download the texts of hundreds of recent tomes. Author Harlan Ellison calls the alt-scanners "rodents without ethic or understanding." A talk with my publisher's lawyer was even more dispiriting. "We're seeing this problem all the time," he moaned; he'd had little success in stemming the tide of purloined works by the likes of Tom Clancy. (So what were my chances?)

Though the technologies of anonymity wouldn't let me trace this particular rodent, it was possible to send him email. Stormysky replied promptly, assuring me that he'd posted my book not to hurt me but to express his notion that the Internet was about sharing—and also as a protest against the intention of publishers to lock up intellectual property on the Net. If publishers have their way, Stormysky warned, they would limit the uses of books so that traditional consumer rights—lending a book to a friend, or even getting access to the book after a specified period—might be lost.

I actually agree with those sentiments, but also think I'm entitled to some payment for my work—and wonder what will happen when electronic reading devices become more convivial, and downloaders of these files won't pay a penalty in eyestrain. Unfortunately, my new friend's protest contradicted his belief that "authors should receive monetary compensation for their creations." Grappling with this concept, he graciously agreed not to post any more of my work to newsgroups.

Forgive me, Stormy, if I'm feeling less than grateful. But I do appreciate the wake-up call. For authors like me—as musicians have already learned—the intellectual-property wars cannot be a spectator sport. I need to speak up more forcefully on the issues, and petition vociferously for creative business models—even if they require drastically altering the ones that have evolved over decades. Publishers mainly want control, and the consumers mainly want convenience and value, if not freebies. But it's the artists who are on the firing line, eager to win audiences but concerned about maintaining our credit ratings. We have to muscle our way into the center of the quest for a solution that somehow exploits the distribution power of the Net while assuring that our audiences pay us something for the experience. Otherwise, we'll just be P'd on.

DISCUSSION QUESTIONS

1. What do you think of Stormysky's argument that the Internet should be about sharing?
2. Under what circumstances would it be okay, in your opinion, to scan a book and post it? To download it?.

Summary

A variety of applications are built on the protocols of the Internet and the World Wide Web. For example, people who use the Web depend on search engines to find the information they need. Search engines use a combination of automated searching and indexed databases to catalog Web resources.

The most popular Internet communication service, email, uses a standard email addressing scheme so users on different networks can communicate. Mailing lists and newsgroups enable group discussions, debates, and information sharing on particular subjects. Other communication tools enable real-time instant messaging, voice communication, and even video teleconferencing.

Peer-to-peer computing was popularized by Napster, but its applications go beyond music sharing. Many businesses are exploring ways to apply P2P technology. Grid computing goes beyond P2P computing by enabling people to share processor power with others. Some organizations are working to build a grid-computing model that would make the Internet work like a shared utility.

E-commerce is built on Internet technology. Businesses use the Internet and the Web for business-to-business and business-to-customer communication. Many businesses have private networks, called intranets, based on Internet technology. Extranets are also private networks based on the same technology; extranets enable businesses to connect with their partners and customers without going through public Internet channels.

As the Internet grows and changes, issues of privacy, security, censorship, criminal activity, universal access, and appropriate Net behavior are surfacing. Even more questions will arise when all kinds of electronic devices are attached to the Web, communicating with each other from our homes, our offices, and our vehicles. We have many questions to answer as the Internet evolves from an electronic frontier into a futuristic cyberspace.

Chapter Review

▼ Key Terms

asynchronous communication (p. 214)
attachment (email) (p. 213)
business-to-business (B2B) (p. 218)
business-to-consumer (B2C) (p. 218)
cookies (p. 212)
cyberspace (p. 221)
digital cash (p. 219)
digital divide (p. 220)
electronic commerce (e-commerce) (p. 217)
extranet (p. 217)

FAQ (frequently asked question) (p. 215)
filtering software (p. 219)
grid computing (p. 217)
instant messaging (p. 214)
Internet telephony (p. 214)
Internet2 (p. 219)
intranet (p. 217)
mailing list (p. 213)
netiquette (p. 215)
newsgroup (p. 213)

peer-to-peer (P2P) computing (p. 216)
portal (p. 211)
pull technology (p. 216)
push technology (p. 216)
real-time communication (p. 214)
video conferences (p. 214)
virtual private networks (p. 218)
Web services (p. 218)

▼ Interactive Quiz Questions

1. The *Computer Confluence* CD-ROM contains self-test quiz questions related to this chapter, including multiple choice, true or false, and matching questions.
2. The *Computer Confluence* Web site, www.prenhall.com/beekman, contains self-test exercises related to this chapter. Follow the instructions for taking a quiz. After you've completed your quiz, you can email the results to your instructor.

   The Web site also contains open-ended discussion questions called Internet Explorations. Discuss one or more of the Internet Exploration questions at the section for this chapter.

▼ Review Questions

1. Define or describe each of the key terms listed in the "Key Terms" section. Check your answers using the glossary.
2. Why is netiquette important? Give some examples of netiquette.
3. How might you use remote login while visiting another school? What about file transfer? How might the Web make remote login unnecessary?
4. Why is file compression important on the Internet?
5. Why is the World Wide Web important as a publishing medium? In what ways is the Web different from any publishing medium that has ever existed before?
6. Briefly describe several software tools that can be used to develop Web pages.
7. How does push technology differ from standard Web page delivery techniques? How is it used?
8. What new services are available as a result of the commercialization of the Internet? What new problems are arising as a result of that commercialization?

▼ Discussion Questions

1. As scientists, engineers, and government officials develop plans for the future of the Internet, they wrestle with questions about who should have access and what kinds of services to plan for. Do you have any ideas about the kinds of things they might want to consider?
2. Do you know anyone who has experienced Internet addiction? If so, can you describe the experience?
3. How do you think online user interfaces will evolve as bandwidth and processing power increase? Describe what cyberspace will feel like in the year 2010, in the year 2050, and beyond.

▼ Projects

1. Research peer-to-peer and grid-computing applications to determine how they're used. Write a report summarizing your findings.
2. Read several books and articles about cyberspace, and write a paper comparing them. Better yet, write a hypertext document, and publish it on the Web.

Sources and Resources

Books

These books, along with the ones listed in the last chapter, represent a sampler of good Internet resources.

Weaving the Web, by Tim Berners-Lee. (San Francisco: Harper San Francisco, 1999). This is the story of the creation of the Web straight from the word processor of the man who did it. Few people in history have had more impact on the way we communicate than this unassuming man.

How the Web Was Born, by James Gillies and Robert Cailliau. (London: Oxford University Press: 2000). This book provides another account of the events leading up to and following the creation of the Web. The authors provide a context that helps explain how Englishman Tim Berners-Lee made critical decisions in shaping the Web.

The World Wide Web: A Mass Communication Perspective, by Barbara K. Kaye and Norman J. Medoff (Mountain View, CA: Mayfield Publishing Company, 1999). This book examines the relationship of the Web to radio, TV, newspapers and other mass media and discusses issues raised by the emergence of Web communication.

From Anarchy to Power: The Net Comes of Age, by Wendy M. Grossman (New York University Press, 2001). The Internet has gone through a radical transition in just a few years. This book chronicles the changes and comments on the profound social and political impact of those changes.

Search Engines for the World Wide Web Visual QuickStart Guide, Third Edition, by Alfred and Emily Glossbrenner (Berkeley, CA: Peachpit Press, 2001). There's plenty of information on the Web; the trick is finding what you need when you need it. This little book tells you what you need to choose and use search engines efficiently and effectively. It covers the big six general-purpose Web search engines along with a healthy sampling of specialty sites for locating anything from automobiles to Zip codes. Highly recommended.

The Invisible Web: Uncovering Information Sources Search Engines Can't See, by Gary Prince and Chris Sherman (CyberAge Books, 2001). If the information you need is stowed in a Web database, a standard search engine can't find it. This book will tell you what you need to know to track down the Web's hidden treasures.

Harley Hahn's Internet and Web Yellow Pages, 2002 Edition, by Harley Hahn (Berkeley, CA: Osborne/McGraw Hill, 2001). Many books attempt to catalog the contents of the Web, but most of them can't compete with the currency and convenience of online Web search tools. Harley Hahn's popular directory combines solid research and a careful selection process with useful tips, clever insights, and amusing asides. The result is a book that's both fun and informative. The built-in CD-ROM contains the text in clickable hypertext format.

Stopping Spam: Stamping Out Unwanted Email and News Postings, by Alan Schwartz and Simson Garfinkel (Cambridge: O'Reilly, 1998). Spam can be a serious problem for casual computer users and systems administrators alike. This book outlines the problem and provides guidance for anyone who wants a spam-free Internet diet.

Sending Your Government a Message: Email Communication Between Citizens and Government, by C. Richard Neu, Robert H. Anderson, and Tora K. Bikson (Santa Monica, CA: Rand, 1999) and **Universal Access to E-Mail,** by Robert H. Anderson, Tora K. Bikson, Sally Ann Law, and Bridger M. Mitchell (Santa Monica, CA: Rand, 1999). These two books, from the influential Rand research organization, address the critical issue of email access. *Sending Your Government a Message* focuses on citizen access to U.S. government's agencies; *Universal Access* deals with email access in general. Both books discuss current public policy and make recommendations for future policy. *Sending Your Government a Message* includes a list of government email addresses. Both texts are available online, along with other Rand publications, at www.rand.org/publications/electronic.

Peer-to-Peer: Harnessing the Power of Disruptive Technologies, edited by Andy Oram (O'Reilly and Associates, 2001). This collection of essays discusses the philosophy, applications, and implications of peer-to-peer technology, from music sharing to CPU sharing and beyond.

The Code and Other Laws of Cyberspace, by Lawrence Lessig (New York: Basic Books, 1999. This important book presents a strong argument that we might lose our liberty on the Internet unless we consciously work to preserve it. The way we build the Net today will determine what's possible in cyberspace tomorrow. Lessig, a lawyer, is an excellent writer with something important to say.

Crypto Anarchy, Cyberstates, and Pirate Utopias, edited by Peter Ludlow (MIT Press, 2001). This lively, thought-provoking collection of essays presents a cyberspace made up of virtual communities that are outside of the circles of corporate and political power.

True Names: and the Opening of the Cyberspace Frontier, by Vernor Vinge and James Frenkel (New York: Tor Books, 2000). In 1981 (three years before the original publication of *Neuromancer*) Vernor Vinge's critically acclaimed novella, *True Names,* described a virtual world inside a computer network. Vinge didn't use the term "cyberspace," but his visionary story effectively invented the concept. This book includes the wonderful original *True Names* novella and a collection of articles by cyberspace pioneers about the past, present, and future of cyberspace.

Neuromancer, by William Gibson (New York: Ace Books, 1995). Gibson's 1984 cyberpunk classic spawned several sequels, dozens of imitations, and a new vocabulary for describing a high-tech future. Gibson's future is gloomy and foreboding, and his futuristic slang isn't always easy to follow. Still, there's plenty to think about here.

Snow Crash, by Neal Stephenson (New York: Bantam, 1992). This science fiction novel lightens the dark, violent cyberpunk future vision a little with Douglas Adams–style humor. Characters regularly jack into the Metaverse, a shared virtual reality network that is in many ways more real than the physical world where they live. The descriptions of this alternate reality heavily influenced the design of many VR-like Web sites today.

Periodicals

Yahoo! Internet Life. This monthly magazine attempts to keep readers abreast of the technology and culture of the Internet. Of course, many Internet travelers aren't satisfied reading paper news that's two or three months old when they can get up-to-the-minute information online.

Net Economy. This monthly covers the impact of the Internet on business and the economy.

Web Pages

To learn more about the Web, turn to the Web. Emerging technologies and applications abound; you'll find links at the *Computer Confluence* Web site (www.prenhall.com/beekman).

9 | Computer Security and Risks

After you read this chapter you should be able to:

▼

Describe several types of computer crime and discuss possible crime-prevention techniques

Describe the major security issues facing computer users, computer system administrators, and law enforcement officials

Describe how computer security relates to personal privacy issues

Describe how security and computer reliability are related

▲

▼ **In this chapter:**

Who are the real computer criminals?

Who owns information?

How to protect your computer from viruses and other attacks

Ethics and the law—where are the gaps?

Can we really have security?

… and more.

▼ **On the CD-ROM:**

An interactive look at cryptography

An animated illustration of viruses in action

Instant access to glossary and key word references

Interactive self-study quizzes

… and more.

▼ **On the Web:**

www.prenhall.com/beekman

Articles and books on computer crime, hackers, and law enforcement

Tips for protecting yourself from electronic mischief and malice

Discussions of intellectual property and other legal issues related to information technology

Self-study exercises

… and more.

Kempelen's Amazing Chess-Playing Machine

Check.
—The only word ever spoken by
Kempelen's chess-playing machine

In 1760 Wolfgang Kempelen, a 49-year-old Hungarian inventor, engineer, and advisor to the court of Austrian Empress Maria Theresa, built a mechanical chess player. This amazing contraption defeated internationally renowned players and earned its inventor almost legendary fame.

Kempelen's chess-playing machine

A Turkish-looking automaton sat behind a big box that supported a chessboard and chess pieces. The operator of the machine could open the box to "prove" there was nothing inside but a network of cogwheels, gears, and revolving cylinders. After every 12 moves, Kempelen wound the machine up with a huge key. Of course, the chess-playing machine was actually a clever hoax. The real chess player was a dwarf-sized person, who controlled the mechanism from inside and was concealed by mirrors when the box was opened. The tiny player couldn't see the board, but he could tell what pieces were moved by watching magnets below the chessboard.

Kempelen had no intention of keeping the deception going for long; he thought of it as a joke and dismantled it after its first tour. But he became a slave to his own fraud, as the public and the scientific community showered him with praise for creating the first "machine-man." In 1780 the Emperor Joseph II ordered another court demonstration of the mechanical chess player, and Kempelen had to rebuild it. The chess player toured the courts of Europe, and the public became more curious and fascinated than ever.

After Kempelen died in 1804, the machine was purchased by the impresario Maelzel, who showed it far and wide. In 1809 it challenged Napoleon Bonaparte to play. When Napoleon repeatedly made illegal moves, the machine-man brushed the pieces from the table. Napoleon was delighted to have unnerved the machine. When he played the next game fairly, Napoleon was badly beaten.

The chess-playing machine came to America in 1826, where it attracted large, paying crowds. In 1834 two different articles—one by Edgar Allen Poe—revealed the secrets of the automated chess player. Poe's investigative article was insightful but not completely accurate; one of his 17 arguments was that a true automatic player would invariably win.

After Maelzel's death in 1837, the machine passed from hand to hand until it was destroyed by fire in Philadelphia in 1854. During the 70 years that the automation was publicly exhibited, its "brain" was supplied by 15 different chess players, who won 294 of 300 games.

With his elaborate and elegant deception, Kempelen might be considered the forerunner of the modern computer criminal. Kempelen was trapped in his fraud because the public wanted to believe that the automated chess player was real. Desire overtook judgment in thousands of people, who were captivated by the idea of an intelligent machine.

More than two centuries later, we're still fascinated by intelligent machines. In 1997 people all over the world watched (many via the Web) as IBM's Deep Blue computer trounced Garry Kasparov, the reigning international chess champion. But modern computers don't just play games; they manage our money, our medicine, and our missiles. We're expected to trust information technology with our wealth, our health, and even our lives. The many benefits of our partnership with machines are clear. But blind faith in modern technology can be foolish and, in many cases, dangerous. In this chapter we examine some of the dark corners of our computerized society: legal dilemmas, ethical issues, and reliability risks. All of these issues are tied to a larger question: How can we make computers more secure so that we can feel more secure in our daily dealings with them?

Online Outlaws: Computer Crime

> Computers are **power**, and **direct contact** with power can bring out the **best** or **worst** in a person.
> —Former computer criminal turned corporate computer programmer

Like other professions, law enforcement is being transformed by information technology. The FBI's National Crime Information Center provides police with almost instant information on crimes and criminals nationwide. Investigators use PC databases to store and cross-reference clues in complex cases. Using pattern recognition technology, automated fingerprint identification systems locate matches in minutes rather than months. Computers routinely scan the New York and London stock exchanges for connections that might indicate insider trading or fraud. Texas police use an intranet to cross-reference databases of photographs, fingerprints, and other crime-fighting information. *Computer forensics* experts use special software to scan criminal suspects' hard disks for digital "fingerprints"—traces of deleted files containing evidence of illegal activities. All of these tools help law enforcement officials ferret out criminals and stop criminal activities.

Like guns, people use computers to break laws as well as uphold them. Computers are powerful tools in the hands of criminals, and computer crime is a rapidly growing problem.

A police officer uses his mobile computer to check records in a central crime database.

The Computer Crime Dossier

> Some will rob you with a **six gun**, and some with a **fountain pen**.
> —Woody Guthrie, in "Pretty Boy Floyd"

Today the computer has replaced both the gun and the pen as the weapon of choice for many criminals. **Computer crime** is often defined as any crime accomplished through knowledge or use of computer technology.

Nobody knows the true extent of computer crime. Many computer crimes go undetected. Those that are detected often go unreported because businesses fear that they can lose more from negative publicity than from the actual crimes.

According to a 2001 survey of more than 500 companies and government agencies by the FBI and the Computer Security Institute, 85 percent detected computer security breaches in the preceding 12 months. These breaches included system penetration by outsiders, theft of information, changing data, financial fraud, vandalism, stealing of passwords, and preventing legitimate users from gaining access to systems. According to the survey, financial losses due to security breaches topped $377 million. By conservative estimates, businesses and government institutions lose billions of dollars every year to computer criminals.

The majority of computer crimes are committed by company insiders who aren't reported to authorities, even when they are caught in the act. To avoid embarrassment, many companies cover up computer crimes committed by their own employees and managers. These crimes are typically committed by clerks, cashiers, programmers, computer operators, and managers who have no extraordinary technical ingenuity. The typical computer criminal is a trusted employee with no criminal record who is tempted by an opportunity such as the discovery of a loophole in system security. Greed, financial worries, and personal problems motivate this person to give in to temptation.

Of course, not all computer criminals fit this profile. Some are former employees seeking revenge on their former bosses. Some are high-tech pranksters looking for a challenge. A few are corporate or international spies seeking classified information. Organized crime syndicates are turning to computer technology to practice their trades. Sometimes entire companies are found guilty of computer fraud. For example, Equity Funding, Inc., used computers to generate thousands of false insurance policies that later were sold for over $27 million.

The 2001 survey suggests that the explosive growth of Internet commerce is changing the demographics of computer crime: 70 percent reported that Internet connections were frequent points of attack; only 31 percent said that internal systems were frequent points of attack.

Comparing this survey with previous annual surveys shows unmistakable trends: Internet security breaches are on the rise, internal security breaches are on the rise, and computer crime in general is on the rise. All of these increases are happening in spite of increased security and law-enforcement efforts.

Theft by Computer

Theft is the most common form of computer crime. Computers are used to steal money, goods, information, and computer resources. Here are a few examples:

> Every system has **vulnerabilities**.
> Every system can be **compromised**.
> —Peter G. Neumann, in *Computer Related Risks*

- A part-time college student used his touch-tone phone and personal computer to fool Pacific Telephone's computer into ordering phone equipment to be delivered to him. He started a business, hired several employees, and pilfered about a million dollars' worth of equipment before he was turned in by a disgruntled employee. (After serving two months in jail, he became a computer security consultant.)
- A former automated teller machine repairman illegally obtained $86,000 out of ATMs by spying on customers while they typed in passwords and then creating bogus cards to use with the passwords.
- In 1988 several million dollars of assets at a major U.S. bank were illegally transferred to a private Swiss bank account. The transfer was noticed because a computer glitch on that particular day forced employees to check transactions manually; the automated procedure normally used wouldn't have noticed the suspicious transaction.
- In 1999 the *London Times* revealed that several London banks had paid millions of pounds in ransoms to hackers who threatened to cripple their computer systems if they didn't pay. The banks paid rather than admitting publicly that their systems weren't secure against attack.
- In 1999 two brothers in China were sentenced to death for using computers to redirect about $30,000 to bank accounts they controlled.
- In 1999 an employee of PairGain posted an anonymous announcement on a Yahoo stock board; the message claimed that PairGain was about to be purchased by another company for nearly twice its current market value. Investors drove the stock price up about 40 percent before they learned they had been bilked out of thousands of dollars by a bogus message. An FBI task force retraced the perpetrator's electronic footprints and arrested him for stock manipulation a week later. This kind of pump-and-dump stock manipulation has been committed dozens of times since the PairGain crime.
- In 2000 intruders broke into Creditcards.com, stole 55,000 credit card numbers, and held them for ransom. When their extortion attempt failed, they posted the numbers on the Web. The company has since created a more secure Web site.
- In 2001 two young Russian men were arrested for breaking into several U.S. company networks, stealing sensitive information, and demanding ransom for it. The FBI captured the pair by using a fake computer security company as bait. When they demanded payment from the bogus company, FBI agents agreed. The two men were arrested when they landed in the United States to collect their bounty.
- In May of 2001 Operation Cyber Loss, the FBI's crackdown on Internet fraud, netted 88 people in 10 days. According to the FBI, 56,000 people were defrauded of more than $117 million during the scams.

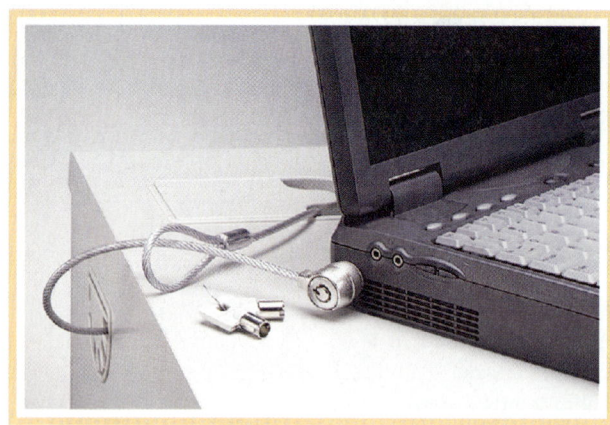

A portable computer is easy prey for a thief unless it's locked to something solid and stationary.

Some types of computer crime are so common that they've been given names. A common student scam uses a process called **spoofing** to steal passwords. The typical spoofer launches a program that mimics the mainframe computer's login screen on an unattended terminal in a public lab. When an unsuspecting student types an ID and password, the program responds with an error message and remembers the secret codes.

Sometimes thieves use computers and other tools to steal whole *identities*. By collecting personal information—credit-card numbers, driver's license numbers, Social Security numbers, and a few other tidbits of data—a thief can effectively pose as someone else, even committing crimes in that person's name. **Identity theft** doesn't require a computer; many identity thieves get sensitive information by dumpster diving—rummaging through company and personal trash. But computers generally play a role in the process. Identity theft often involves **social engineering**—slang for the use of deception to get individuals to reveal sensitive information.

The steady increase in electronic commerce has been accompanied by an increase in online fraud. Online auctions seem to be particularly fertile grounds for criminals. "The ePrivacy and Security Report" from market-research company eMarketer.com estimated that 87 percent of online fraud cases in 2000 were related to online auctions, with the average cost per victim being around $600.

One common type of computer theft today is the actual theft of computers. Laptop and handheld computers make particularly easy prey for crooks—especially in airports and other high-traffic, high-stress locations.

All of these crimes are expensive—for businesses, law enforcement agencies, and taxpayers and consumers who ultimately must pay the bills. But as crimes go, the types of theft described so far are relatively uncommon. The same can't be said of the most widely practiced type of computer-related theft: software piracy.

Software Piracy and Intellectual Property Laws

> Information wants to be free. Information also wants to be expensive. **Information wants to be free** because it has become so cheap to distribute, copy, and recombine—**too cheap to meter**. **It wants to be expensive** because it can be **immeasurably valuable** to the recipient. **That tension will not go away**.
>
> —Stewart Brand, in *The Media Lab*

Software piracy—the illegal duplication of copyrighted software—is rampant. Millions of computer users have made copies of programs they don't legally own. Now that many software companies have given in to user demands and removed physical copy protection from their products, copying software is as easy as duplicating a cassette tape or photocopying a book. Unfortunately, many people aren't aware that copying software, recorded music, and books can violate federal laws protecting intellectual property.

The Piracy Problem

The software industry, with a world market of more than $50 billion a year, loses billions of dollars every year to software pirates. The Business Software Alliance (BSA) estimates that more than one-third of all software in use is illegally copied, costing the software industry tens of thousands of jobs. Piracy can be particularly hard on small software companies. Developing software is just as difficult for them as it is for big companies like Microsoft and Oracle, but they often lack the financial and legal resources to cover their losses to piracy.

Software industry organizations, including the BSA and SPA Anti-Piracy (a division of the Software & Information Industry Association), work with law enforcement agencies to crack down on piracy. At the same time they sponsor educational programs to make computer users aware that piracy is theft, because laws can't work without citizen understanding and support.

Software piracy is a worldwide problem, with piracy rates highest in developing nations. In China approximately 95 percent of all new software installations are pirated; in Vietnam the piracy rate is 97 percent. A few Third World nations refuse to abide by international copyright laws. They argue that the laws protect rich countries at the expense of underdeveloped nations. In 1998, the Argentine Supreme Court ruled that the country's copyright laws don't apply to computer software.

Intellectual Property and the Law

Legally, the definition of **intellectual property** includes the results of intellectual activities in the arts, science, and industry. **Copyright** laws have traditionally protected forms of literary expression; **patent** law has protected mechanical inventions, and **contract** law has covered trade secrets. Software doesn't fit neatly into any of these categories under the law. Copyright laws protect most commercial software programs, but a few companies have successfully used patent laws to protect software products.

The purpose of intellectual property laws is to ensure that mental labor is justly rewarded and to encourage innovation. Programmers, inventors, scientists, writers, editors, filmmakers, and musicians depend on ideas and the expression of those ideas for their incomes. Ideas are information, and information is easy to copy. Intellectual property laws are designed to protect these professionals and encourage them to continue their creative efforts so society can benefit from their future work.

Most of the time, these laws help to achieve their goals. A novelist can devote two or three years of her life to writing a masterpiece, confident that she won't find bootleg copies for sale on street corners when she finishes it. A movie studio can invest millions of dollars in a film, knowing that the investment will be returned, a little at a time, through ticket sales and video rentals. An inventor can work long hours to create a better mousetrap and know that MegaMousetrap City won't steal her idea.

But sometimes intellectual property laws are applied in such a way that they may stifle the innovation and creativity they're designed to protect. In 1999 Amazon.com was awarded a controversial patent for "one-click shopping." Similarly, SightSound patented all paid downloads of "desired digital video or digital audio signals," RealNetworks patented streaming audio and video, and British Telecom claims to hold a 1976 patent that covers every Web hyperlink! Most experts agree that these ideas are too simple and broad to be owned by one company. And in many cases, the patent owner isn't the inventor of the concept—Douglas Engelbart demonstrated hyperlinking as early as 1967 at Stanford Research Institute. Such broad patents generally end up in court, where legal experts and technology experts debate the merits and scope of the ideas and the laws designed to protect them. Meanwhile, legislators attempt to update the laws.

Most existing copyright and patent laws, which evolved during the age of print and mechanical inventions, are outdated, contradictory, and inadequate for today's information technology. Many laws, including the Computer Fraud and Abuse Act of 1984, clearly treat software piracy as a crime. The NET (No Electronic Theft) Act of 1997 closed a narrow loophole in the law that allowed people to give away software on the Internet.

The Digital Millennium Copyright Act (DMCA) of 1998 represents the most comprehensive reform of U.S. copyright law in a generation. The DCMA includes several controversial provisions that need to be clarified by the courts. According to the law, it is illegal to write a program that circumvents copy protection schemes, whether or not that program is used to copy DVDs, electronic books, or other protected material illegally. The DMCA also makes it a crime to share information about how to crack copy protection. Critics argue that the law suppresses freedom of speech, academic freedom, and the principle of *fair use*—the time-honored right to make copies of copyrighted material for personal and academic use and for other noncompetitive purposes.

In matters of software, the legal system is sailing in uncharted waters. Whether dealing with issues of piracy or monopoly, lawmakers and judges must struggle with difficult questions about innovation, property, freedom, and progress. The questions are likely to be with us for quite a while.

In this 1999 scene, Moscow police attempted to make a dent in the illegal software market by destroying mountains of pirated software.

Software Sabotage: Viruses and Other Invaders

> **The American government** can stop me from going to the U.S., but they **can't stop my virus**.
> —Virus creator

Another type of computer crime is sabotage of hardware or software. The word **sabotage** comes from the early days of the Industrial Revolution, when rebellious workers shut down new machines by kicking wooden shoes, called sabots, into the gears. Modern computer saboteurs commonly use software rather than footwear to do destructive deeds. The names given to the saboteurs' destructive programs—viruses, worms, and Trojan horses—sound more like biology than technology, and many of the programs even mimic the behavior of living organisms.

Trojan Horses

A **Trojan horse** is a program that performs a useful task while at the same time carrying out some secret destructive act. As in the ancient story of the wooden horse that carried Greek soldiers through the gates of Troy, Trojan horse software hides an enemy in an attractive package. Trojan horse programs are often posted on shareware Web sites with names that make them sound like games or utilities. When an unsuspecting bargain hunter downloads and runs such a program, it might erase files, change data, or cause some other kind of damage. Some network saboteurs use Trojan horses to pass secret data to other unauthorized users.

One type of Trojan horse, a **logic bomb**, is programmed to attack in response to a particular logical event or sequence of events. For example, a programmer might plant a logic bomb that is designed to destroy data files if the programmer is ever listed as terminated in the company's personnel file. A logic bomb might be triggered when a certain user logs in, a special code is entered in a database field, or a particular sequence of actions is performed by the user. If the logic bomb is triggered by a time-related event, it is called a *time bomb*. A widely publicized virus included a logic bomb that was programmed to destroy PC data files on Michelangelo's birthday.

Trojan horses can cause serious problems in computer systems of all sizes. To make matters worse, many Trojan horses carry software viruses.

Viruses

A biological virus is unable to reproduce by itself, but it can invade the cells of another organism and use the reproductive machinery of each host cell to make copies of itself; the new copies leave the host and seek out new hosts to repeat the process. A software **virus** works in the same way: It spreads from program to program, or from disk to disk, and uses each infected program or disk to make more copies of itself. Virus software is usually hidden in the operating system of a computer or in an application program. Some viruses do nothing but reproduce; others display messages on the computer's screen; still others destroy data or erase disks.

A virus is usually operating-system specific. Windows viruses invade only Windows disks, Macintosh viruses invade only Macintosh disks, and so on. There are exceptions: **Macro viruses** attach themselves to documents that contain *macros*—embedded programs to automate tasks. Macro viruses can be spread across computer platforms if the documents are created and spread using cross-platform applications—most commonly the applications in Microsoft Office. Macro viruses can be spread through innocent-looking email attachments. Viruses spread through email are sometimes called *email viruses*.

One of the most widely publicized email viruses was 1999's Melissa virus. Melissa's method of operation is typical of email viruses: An unsuspecting computer user receives an "Important message" from a friend: "Here is that document you asked for . . . don't show it to anyone else ;-)." The attached Microsoft Word document contains a list of passwords for Internet pornography sites. It contains something else: a macro virus written in Microsoft Office's built-in Visual Basic scripting language. Once the document is opened, the macro virus goes to work, sending a copy of the email message and infected document to the first 50 names on the user's Outlook address book. Within minutes, 50 more potential Melissa victims receive messages apparently from someone they know—the user of the newly infected computer. Melissa spread like wildfire among Windows systems, infecting 100,000 systems in just a few days. Melissa wasn't designed to do damage to systems, but the flurry of messages brought down some email servers. A nationwide search located the probable author of the Melissa virus, a 30-year-old New Jersey resident with a fondness for a topless dancer named Melissa.

Shortly after Melissa faded from the headlines, a similar, but more destructive, virus named Chernobyl infected more than 600,000 computers worldwide. South Korea alone suffered 300,000 attacks; about 15 percent of their PCs were damaged by the virus, at a cost of $250 million. In May of 2000, a Melissa-like virus called Love Bug spread from a PC in the Philippines around the world through innocent-looking "I Love You" email message attachments. In a matter of hours, the Love Bug caused billions of dollars in lost productivity and damage to computer systems.

Origination
A programmer writes a tiny program—the virus—that has destructive power and can reproduce itself.

Transmission
Most often, the virus is attached to a normal program; unknown to the user, the virus spreads to other software.

Reproduction
The virus is passed by disk or network to other users who use other computers. The virus remains dormant as it is passed on.

Infection
Depending on how it is programmed, a virus may display an unexpected message, gobble up memory, destroy data files or cause serious system errors.

How a virus works.

Worms

Like viruses, **worms** (named for tapeworms) use computer hosts to reproduce themselves. But unlike viruses, worm programs travel *independently* over computer networks, seeking out uninfected workstations in which to reproduce. A worm can reproduce until the computer freezes from lack of free memory or disk space. A typical worm segment resides in memory rather than on disk, so the worm can be eliminated by shutting down all of the workstations on the network.

The first headline-making worm was created as an experiment by a Cornell graduate student in 1988. The worm was accidentally released onto the Internet, clogging 6,000 computers all over the United States, almost bringing them to a complete standstill and forcing operators to shut them all down so every worm segment could be purged from memory. The total cost, in terms of work time lost at research institutions, was staggering. The student was suspended from school and was the first person convicted of violating the Computer Fraud and Abuse Act.

In the summer of 2001, a worm called Code Red made worldwide headlines. Code Red didn't attack PCs; its target was Internet servers running Microsoft server software. The U.S. government and Microsoft issued warnings about the worm and made free software patches available to protect servers. Even so, many servers were crippled by the repeated attacks from the worm, including servers owned and operated by Microsoft.

Virus Wars

The popular press usually doesn't distinguish among Trojan horses, viruses, and worms; they're all called computer viruses. Whatever they're called, these rogue programs make life more complicated and expensive for people who depend on computers. Researchers have identified more than 18,000 virus strains, with 200 new ones appearing each month. At any given time, about 250 virus strains exist in the wild—in circulation.

Modern viruses can spread faster and do more damage than viruses of a few years ago for several reasons. The Internet, which speeds communication all over the planet, also speeds virus

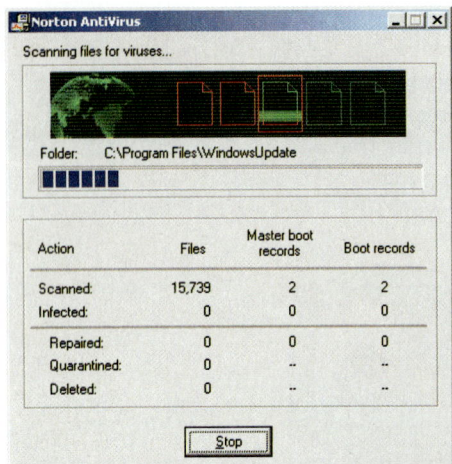

Antivirus software scans files for viruses; updates with new virus "signatures" are downloadable from the software company's Web site.

transmission. Web pages, macros, and other technologies give virus writers new places to hide their creations. And increased standardization on Microsoft applications and operating systems has made it easier for viruses to spread. Just as natural mixed forests are more resistant to disease than are single-species tree farms, mixed computing environments are less susceptible to crippling attacks than is an organization in which everyone uses the same hardware and software.

When computers are used in life-or-death situations, as they are in many medical and military applications, invading programs can even threaten human lives. The U.S. government and several states now have laws against introducing these programs into computer systems.

Antivirus programs (also called *vaccine* or *disinfectant programs*) are designed to search for viruses, notify users when they're found, and remove them from infected disks or files. Most antiviral programs continually monitor system activity, watching for and reporting suspicious virus-like actions. But no antivirus program can detect every virus, and these programs need to be frequently revised to combat new viruses as they appear. Most antivirus programs can automatically download new virus-fighting code from the Web as new virus strains appear. But it can take several days for companies to develop and distribute patches for new viruses—and destructive viruses can do a lot of damage in that time.

The virus wars continue to escalate as virus writers develop new ways to spread their works. After a rash of 1999 email viruses, most users learned not to open unidentified email attachments. But before the year was over, a worm called BubbleBoy (named for an episode of TV's *Seinfeld*) demonstrated that a system could be infected by email even if the mail wasn't opened. Some viruses have even been developed to infect HTML code in Web pages or HTML email messages. HTML viruses can't (so far) infect your computer if you're viewing an infected Web page on another computer; the infected HTML code must be downloaded onto your machine. Still, HTML viruses are reminders that the virus wars are far from over.

Hacking and Electronic Trespassing

The Hacker Ethic

Access to computers—and anything which might teach you something about the way the world works—should be **unlimited** and **total**.
Always yield to the **Hands-on Imperative**.
1. All information should be **free**.
2. **Mistrust Authority—Promote Decentralization**.
3. Hackers should be judged by their **hacking**, not bogus criteria such as degrees, age, race, or position.
4. You can create **art and beauty** on a computer.
5. Computers can **change your life** for the better.
—Steven Levy, in *Hackers: Heroes of the Computer Revolution*

I don't drink, smoke, or take drugs. I don't steal, assault people, or vandalize property. **The only way** in which I am really **different** from most people is in my fascination with the ways and means of learning about **computers that don't belong to me**.
—Bill "The Cracker" Landreth, in *Out of the Inner Circle*

In the late 1970s, timesharing computers at Stanford and MIT attracted informal communities of computer fanatics who called themselves *hackers*. In those days a hacker was a person who enjoyed learning the details of computer systems and writing clever programs, referred to as hacks. Hackers were, for the most part, curious, enthusiastic, intelligent, idealistic, eccentric, and harmless. Many of those early hackers were, in fact, architects of the microcomputer revolution.

Over the years the idealism of the early hacker communities was at least partly overshadowed by cynicism, as big-money interests took over the young personal computer industry. At the same time the term *hacking* took on a new, more ominous connotation in the media. While many people still use the term to describe software wizardry, it more commonly refers to unauthorized access to computer systems. Old-time hackers insist that this electronic trespassing is really *cracking*, or criminal hacking, but the general public and popular media don't recognize the distinction between hackers and crackers. Today's stereotypical hacker, like his early counterparts, is a young, bright, technically savvy, white, middle-class male who, in addition to programming his own computer, may break into others.

Of course, not all young computer wizards break into systems, and not all electronic trespassers fit the media stereotype. Still, hackers aren't just a media myth; they're real, and there are lots of them. Electronic trespassers enter corporate and government computers using stolen passwords and security holes in operating system software. Sometimes they use modems to dial up the target computers directly; in other cases they "travel" to their destinations through the Internet and other networks.

Many hackers are merely motivated by curiosity and intellectual challenge; once they've cracked a system, they look around and move on without leaving any electronic footprints. Some hackers claim to be acting in the public good by pointing out security problems in commercial software products. Some malicious hackers use Trojan horses, logic bombs, and other tricks of the trade to wreak havoc on corporate and government systems. A growing number of computer trespassers are part of electronic crime rings intent on stealing credit-card numbers and other sensitive, valuable information. This kind of theft is difficult to detect and track because the original information is left unchanged when the copy is stolen.

Cliff Stoll discovered an international computer espionage ring because of a 75-cent accounting error.

According to the FBI, an Internet hack happens every 30 seconds. Hackers have defaced the Web sites of the White House, the U.S. Senate, the Department of the Interior, presidential candidates, countless online businesses, and even a hacker's conference. Sometimes Web sites are simply defaced with obscene or threatening messages; sometimes they're replaced with satirical substitutes; sometimes they're vandalized so they don't work properly. *Webjackers* hijack legitimate Web pages and redirect users to other sites—anywhere from pornographic sites to fraudulent businesses.

Denial of service (DoS) attacks bombard servers and Web sites with so much bogus traffic that they're effectively shut down, denying service to legitimate customers and clients. In a *distributed denial of service (DDoS) attack* the flood of messages comes from many compromised systems distributed across the Net. In a single week in February, 2000, Yahoo, E*TRADE, eBay, and Amazon Web sites were crippled by denial of service attacks, costing their owners millions of dollars in business. Two months later a 15-year-old Canadian boy nicknamed "Mafia Boy" was arrested after he bragged online about causing the breakdowns. His expensive pranks didn't require any special expertise; he reportedly downloaded all of the software he used from the Internet.

The most famous case of electronic trespassing was documented in Cliff Stoll's best-selling book, *The Cuckoo's Egg*. While working as a system administrator for a university computer lab in 1986, Stoll noticed a 75-cent accounting error. Rather than letting it go, Stoll investigated the error. He uncovered a system intruder who was searching government, corporate, and university computers across the Internet for sensitive military information. It took a year and some help from the FBI, but Stoll eventually located the hacker—a German computer science student and part of a ring of hackers working for the KGB. Ironically, Stoll captured the thief by using standard hacker tricks, including a Trojan horse program that contained information on a fake SDI Net (Strategic Defense Initiative Network).

This kind of online espionage is becoming commonplace as the Internet becomes a mainstream communication medium. A more recent front-page-story-turned-book involved the 1995 capture of Kevin Mitnick, the hacker who had stolen millions of dollars' worth of software and credit-card information on the Net. By repeatedly manufacturing new identities and cleverly concealing his location, Mitnick successfully evaded the FBI for years. But when he broke into the computer of computational physicist Tsutomu Shimomura, he inadvertently started an electronic cat-and-mouse game that ended with his capture and conviction. Shimomura was able to defeat Mitnick because of his expertise in computer security—the protection of computer systems and, indirectly, the people who depend on them.

Computer Security: Reducing Risks

In the **old world**, if I wanted to attack something physical, there was **one way to get there**. You could put guards and guns around it, **you could protect it**. But a database—or a control system—usually has multiple pathways, **unpredictable routes to it**, and seems intrinsically **impossible to protect**. That's why most efforts at computer security have been **defeated**.
— Andrew Marshall, military analyst

With computer crime on the rise, computer security has become an important concern for system administrators and computer users alike. **Computer security** refers to protecting computer systems and the information they contain against unwanted access, damage, modification, or destruction. According to a 1991 report of the Congressional Research Service, computers have two inherent characteristics that leave them open to attack or operating error:

1. A computer does exactly what it is programmed to do, including reveal sensitive information. Any system that can be programmed can be reprogrammed by anyone with sufficient knowledge.
2. Any computer can do only what it is programmed to do. "[I]t cannot protect itself from either malfunctions or deliberate attacks unless such events have been specifically anticipated, thought through, and countered with appropriate programming."

Computer owners and administrators use a variety of security techniques to protect their systems ranging from everyday low-tech locks to high-tech software scrambling.

Physical Access Restrictions

One way to reduce the risk of security breaches is to make sure that only authorized personnel have access to computer equipment. Organizations use a number of tools and techniques to identify authorized personnel. Computers can perform some security checks; human security guards perform others. Depending on the security system, you might be granted access to a computer based on

- *Something you have*—a key, an ID card with a photo, or a *smart card* containing digitally encoded identification in a built-in memory chip
- *Something you know*—a password, an ID number, a lock combination, or a piece of personal history, such as your mother's maiden name
- *Something you do*—your signature or your typing speed and error patterns
- *Something about you*—a voice print, fingerprint, retinal scan, facial feature scan, or other measurement of individual body characteristics; these measurements are collectively called **biometrics**.

Because most of these security controls can be compromised—keys can be stolen, signatures can be forged, and so on—many systems use a combination of controls. For example, an employee might be required to show a badge, unlock a door with a key, and type a password to use a secured computer.

In the days when corporate computers were isolated in basements, physical restrictions were sufficient for keeping out intruders. But in the modern office, computers and data are almost everywhere, and networks connect computers to the outside world. In a distributed, networked environment, security is much more problematic. It's not enough to restrict physical access to mainframes when personal computers and network connections aren't restricted. Additional security techniques—most notably passwords—are needed to restrict access to remote computers.

Passwords

Passwords are the most common tool used to restrict access to computer systems. Passwords are effective, however, only if they're chosen carefully. Most computer users choose passwords that are easy to guess: names of partners, children, or pets; words related to jobs or hobbies; and consecutive characters on keyboards. One survey found that the

Biometric devices provide high levels of computer and network security because they monitor human body characteristics that can't be stolen. The U-Match Bio-Link Mouse (top) checks the thumbprint of the user against a database of prints approved for access. IriScan's PC Iris (bottom) can compare the patterns in the iris of the user against a database of employees or other legitimate network users.

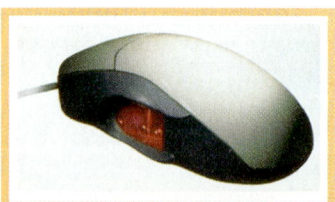

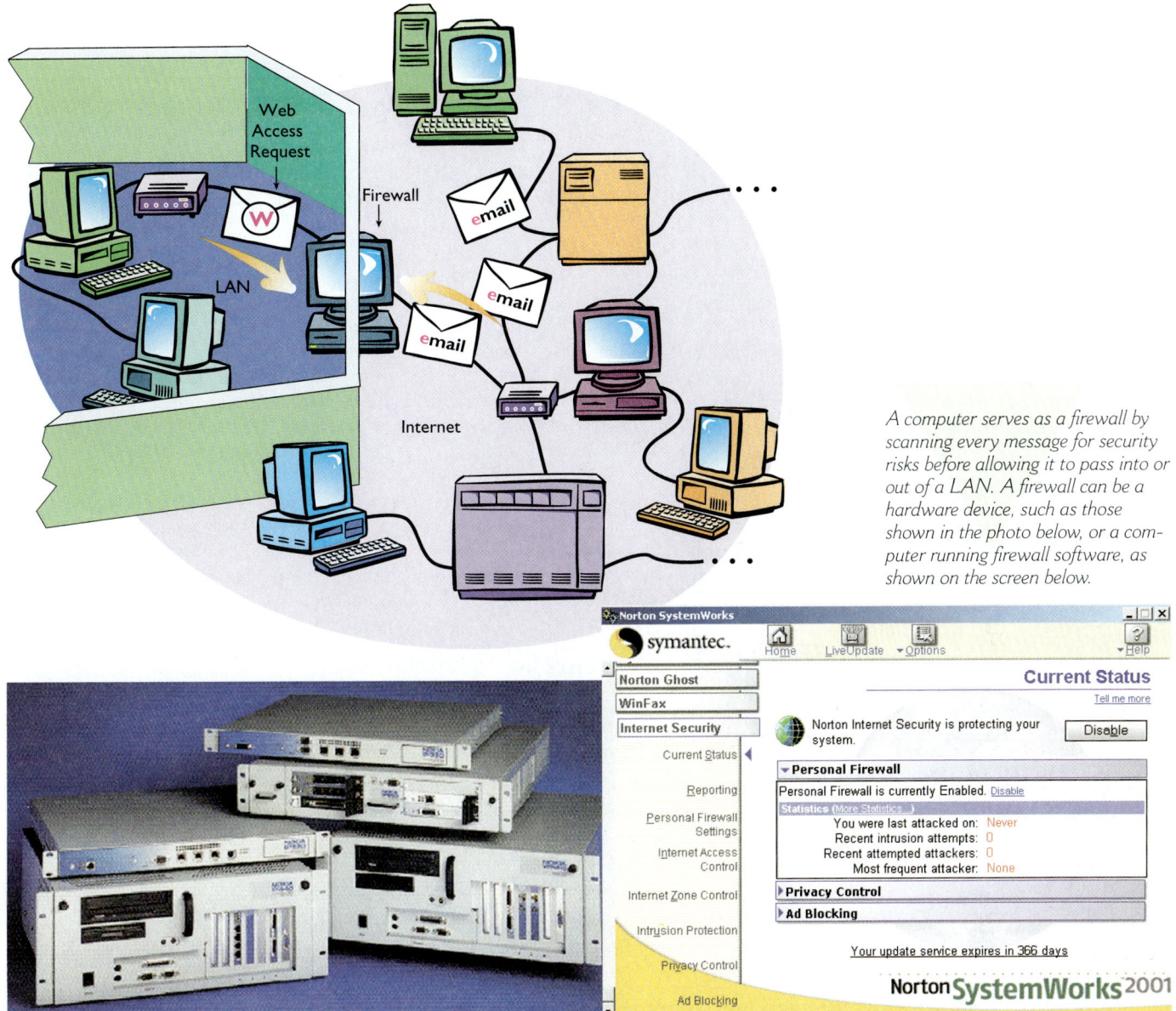

A computer serves as a firewall by scanning every message for security risks before allowing it to pass into or out of a LAN. A firewall can be a hardware device, such as those shown in the photo below, or a computer running firewall software, as shown on the screen below.

two favorite passwords in Britain were "Fred" and "God"; in America they were "love" and "sex." Hackers know and exploit these clichés; cautious users avoid them. Many security systems refuse to enable users to choose any real words or names as passwords so hackers can't use dictionary software to guess them systematically. Even the best passwords should be changed frequently.

Access-control software doesn't need to treat all users identically. Many systems use passwords to restrict users so they can open only files related to their work. In many cases, users are given read-only access to files that they can see but not change.

To prevent unauthorized use of stolen passwords by outsiders, many companies use callback systems. When a user logs in and types a password, the system hangs up, looks up the user's phone number, and calls back before providing access.

Firewalls, Encryption, and Audits

Many data thieves do their work without breaking into computer systems; instead, they intercept messages as they travel between computers on networks. Passwords are of little use for hiding email messages when they're traveling through phone lines or Internet gateways. Still, Internet communication is far too important to sacrifice in the name of security. Many organizations use **firewalls** to keep their internal networks secure while enabling communication with the rest of

How It Works

9.1 Cryptography

If you want be sure that an email message can be read only by the intended recipient, you must either use a secure communication channel or secure the message.

Mail within many organizations is sent over secure communication channels—channels that can't be accessed by outsiders. But you can't secure the channels used by the Internet and other worldwide mail networks; there's no way to shield messages sent through public telephone lines and airwaves. In the words of Mark Rotenberg, director of the Electronic Privacy Information Center, "Email is more like a postcard than a sealed letter."

If you can't secure the communication channel, the alternative is to secure the message. You secure a message by using a crypto-system to encrypt it—scramble it so it can be decrypted (unscrambled) only by the intended recipient.

Almost all cryptosystems depend on a key—a password-like number or phrase that can be used to encrypt or decrypt a message. Eavesdroppers who don't know the key have to try to decrypt it by brute force—by trying all possible keys until the right one is guessed.

Some cryptosystems afford only modest security: A message can be broken after only a day or week of brute force cryptanalysis on a supercomputer. More effective systems would take a supercomputer billions of years to break the message.

The traditional kind of cryptosystem used on computer networks is called a symmetric secret key system. With this approach the sender and recipient use

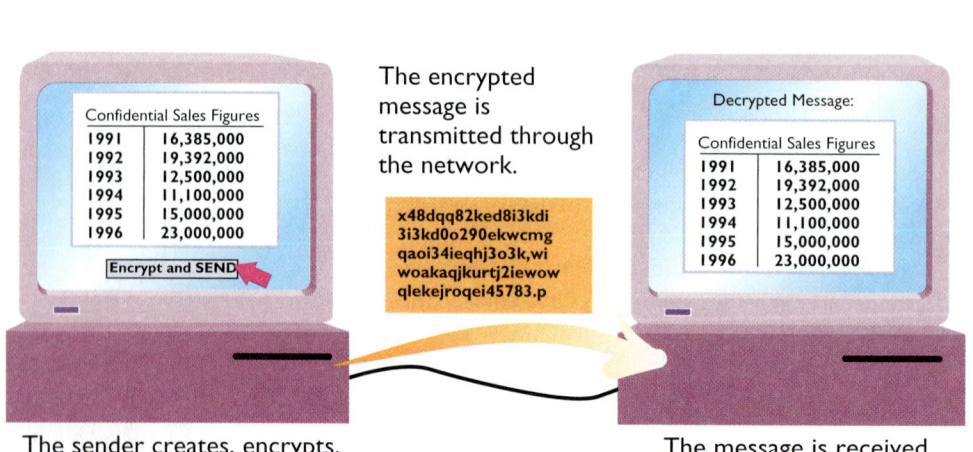

The encryption process.

the Internet. The technical details of firewalls vary considerably, but they're all designed to serve the same function: to guard against unauthorized access to an internal network. In effect, a firewall is a gateway with a lock—the locked gate opens only for information packets that pass one or more security inspections. Firewalls aren't just for large corporations anymore. Without firewall hardware or software installed, a home computer with an always-on DSL or cable modem connection can be easy prey for Internet snoopers.

the same key, and they have to keep the shared key secret from everyone else.

The biggest problem with symmetric secret key systems is key management. If you want to communicate with several people and ensure that each person can't read messages intended for the others, then you'll need a different secret key for each person. When you want to communicate with someone new, you have the problem of letting them know what the key is. If you send it over the ordinary communication channel, it can be intercepted.

In the 1970s, cryptographers developed public key cryptography to get around the key management problems. The most popular kind of public key cryptosystem, RSA, is being incorporated into most new network-enabled software. Phillip Zimmerman's popular shareware utility called PGP (for Pretty Good Privacy) uses RSA technology.

Each person using a public key cryptosystem has two keys: a private key known only to the user and a public key that is freely available to anyone who wants it. Thus a public key system is asymmetric: A different key is used to encrypt than to decrypt. Public keys can be published in phone directories, Web pages, and advertisements; some users include them in their email signatures.

If you want to send a secure message over the Internet to your friend Sue in St. Louis, you use her public key to encrypt the message. Sue's public key can't decrypt the message; only her private key can do that. The private key is specifically designed to decrypt messages that were encrypted with the corresponding public key.

Since public/private key pairs can be generated by individual users, the key distribution problem is solved. The only keys being sent over an insecure network are publicly available keys.

You can use the same technology in reverse (encrypt with the private key, decrypt with the public key) for message authentication: When you decrypt a message, you can be sure that it was sent from a particular person on the network. In the future, legal and commercial documents will routinely have digital signatures that will be as valid as handwritten ones.

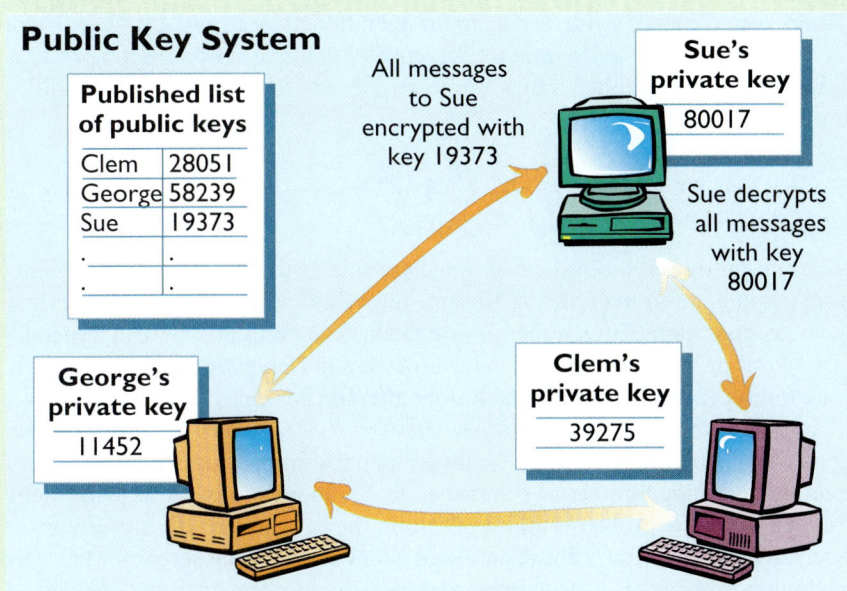

Of course, the firewall's digital drawbridge has to let some messages pass through; otherwise there could be no communication with the rest of the Internet. How can those messages be secured in transit? To protect transmitted information, many organizations and individuals use **encryption** software to scramble their transmissions. When a user encrypts a message by applying a secret numerical code, called an *encryption key*, the message can be transmitted or stored as an indecipherable garble of characters. The message can be read only after it's been reconstructed with a matching key.

For the most sensitive information, passwords, firewalls, and encryption aren't enough. A diligent spy can "listen to" the electromagnetic signals that emanate from the computer hardware and, in some cases, read sensitive information. To prevent spies from using these spurious broadcasts, the Pentagon has spent hundreds of millions of dollars on a program called Tempest to develop specially shielded machines.

Audit-control software is used to monitor and record computer transactions as they happen so auditors can trace and identify suspicious computer activity after the fact. Effective audit-control software forces every user, legitimate or otherwise, to leave a trail of electronic footprints. Of course, this kind of software is of little value unless someone in the organization monitors and interprets the output.

An uninterruptible power supply (UPS) protects against both power surges and momentary power failures.

Backups and Other Precautions

Even the tightest security system can't guarantee absolute protection of data. A power surge or a power failure can wipe out even the most carefully guarded data in an instant. An **uninterruptible power supply (UPS)** can protect computers from data loss during power failures; inexpensive ones can protect even home computers from short power dropouts. **Surge protectors** don't help during power failures, but they can shield electronic equipment from dangerous power spikes.

Of course, disasters come in many forms. Sabotage, human errors, machine failures, fire, flood, lightning, and earthquakes can damage or destroy computer data along with hardware. Any complete security system should include a plan for recovering from disasters. For mainframes and PCs alike, the best and most widely used data recovery insurance is a system of making regular **backups**. For many systems data and software are backed up automatically onto disks or tapes, usually at the end of each workday. Most data processing shops keep several *generations* of backups so they can, if necessary, go back several days, weeks, or years to reconstruct data files. For maximum security, many computer users keep copies of sensitive data in several different locations. A storage device called a **RAID (redundant array of independent disk)** enables multiple hard disks to operate as a unit. RAID systems can, among other things, automatically *mirror* data on multiple disks, effectively creating instant backups.

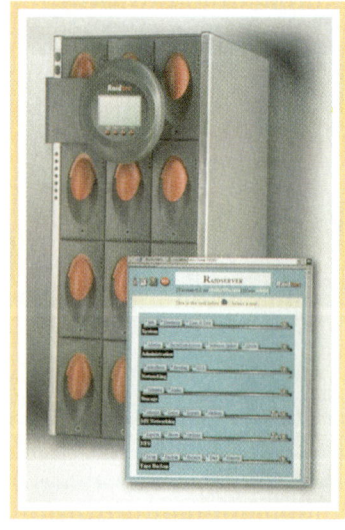

A RAID such as this NAS RAID server stores redundant copies of data so that the data can be saved even if a disk crashes.

Human Security Controls: Law, Management, and Ethics

Security experts are constantly developing new technologies and techniques for protecting computer systems from computer criminals. But at the same time, criminals continue to refine their craft. In the ongoing competition between the law and the lawless, computer security generally lags behind. In the words of Tom Forester and Perry Morrison in *Computer Ethics*, "Computer security experts are forever trying to shut the stable door after the horse has bolted."

Ultimately, computer security is a human problem that can't be solved by technology alone. Security is a management issue, and a manager's actions and policies are critical to the success of a security program. An alarming number of companies are lax about computer security. Many managers don't understand the problems and don't think they are at risk. It's important for managers to understand the practical, ethical, and legal issues surrounding security. Managers must make their employees aware of security issues and security risks. If managers don't defend against security threats, information can't be secure.

Security, Privacy, Freedom, and Ethics: The Delicate Balance

> In this age of advanced technology, **thick walls** and **locked doors** cannot guard our **privacy** or safeguard our **personal freedom**.
> —Lyndon B. Johnson, 36th president of the United States, February 23, 1974

It's hard to overstate the importance of computer security in our networked world. Destructive viruses, illegal interlopers, crooked coworkers, software pirates, and cyber-vandals can erode trust, threaten jobs, and make life difficult for everyone. But sometimes computer security measures can create problems of their own. Complex access procedures, virus-protection programs, intellectual property laws, and other security measures can, if carried too far, interfere with people getting their work done. In the extreme, security can threaten individual human rights.

When Security Threatens Privacy

As we've seen in other chapters, computers threaten our personal privacy on several fronts. Corporate and government databases accumulate and share massive amounts of information about us against our will and without our knowledge. Internet-monitoring programs and software snoopers track our Web explorations and read our electronic mail. Corporate managers use monitoring software to measure worker productivity and observe their onscreen activities. Government security agencies secretly monitor telephone calls and data transmissions.

When security measures are used to prevent computer crime, they usually help protect privacy rights at the same time. When a hacker invades a computer system, legitimate users of the system might have their private communications monitored by the intruder. When an outsider breaks into the database of a bank, the privacy of every bank customer is at risk. The same applies to government computers, credit bureau computers, and any other computer containing data on private citizens. The security of these systems is important for protecting people's privacy.

But in some cases security and law enforcement can pose threats to personal privacy. Here are some examples:

- In 1990 Alana Shoar, email coordinator for Epson America, Inc., found stacks of printouts of employee email messages in her boss's office—messages that employees believed were private. Shortly after confronting her boss, she was fired for "gross misconduct and insubordination." She filed a class-action suit, claiming that Epson routinely monitored all email messages. Company officials denied the charges but took a firm stand on their right to any information stored on, sent to, or taken from their business computers. The courts ruled in Epson's favor. Since then, many other U.S. court decisions have reinforced a company's right to read employee email stored on company computers.
- In 1995 the U.S. government passed legislation requiring new digital phone systems to include additional switches that allow for electronic surveillance. This legislation protects the FBI's ability to wiretap at the expense of individual privacy. Detractors have pointed out that this digital "back door" could be abused by government agencies and could also be used by savvy criminals to perform illegal wiretaps. Government officials argue that wiretapping is a critical tool in the fight against organized crime.
- The digital manhunt that led to the arrest of the programmer charged with authoring the Melissa virus was made as a direct result of information provided by America Online Inc. A controversial Microsoft document identification technology—the Global Unique Identifier, or GUID—may also have played a role. While virtually everyone was happy when the virus's perpetrator was apprehended, many legal experts feared that the same techniques will be used for less lofty purposes.
- In 2000 the U.S. government found Microsoft guilty of gross abuses of its monopolistic position in the software industry. The government's case included hundreds of private email messages between Microsoft employees—messages that contradicted Microsoft's public testimony.
- A 2001 U.S. law required that future mobile phones include GPS technology for transmitting the phone's location to a 911 operator in the case of an emergency call. Privacy activists fear that government agents and criminals will use this E911 technology to track the movements of phone owners.
- In response to the terrorist attacks of September 11, 2001, the U.S. Congress quickly drafted and passed the USA Patriot Act, a sweeping act that redefined terrorism and the government's authority to combat it. The act defined "cyberterrorism" to include computer crimes that cause at least $5,000 in damage or destroy medical equipment. It increased the FBI's latitude to use wiretap technology to monitor suspects' Web browsing and email without a judge's order. Critics argued that this law could easily be used to restrict the freedom and threaten the privacy of law-abiding citizens.

One of the best examples of a new technology that can simultaneously improve security and threaten privacy is the *active badge* (sometimes called the *smart badge*). Researchers at the University of Cambridge and nearby Olivetti Research Center are developing and wearing microprocessor-controlled badges that broadcast infrared identification codes every 15 seconds. Each badge's code is picked up by a nearby network receiver and transmitted back to a badge-location database that is constantly being updated. Active badges are used for identifying, finding, and remembering:

- *Identifying.* When an authorized employee approaches a door, the door recognizes the person's badge code and opens. Whenever anyone logs into a computer system, the badge code identifies the person as an authorized or unauthorized user.

- *Finding.* An employee can check a computer screen to locate another employee and find out with whom that person is talking. With active badges there's no need for a paging system, and "while you were away" notes are less common.
- *Remembering.* At the end of the day, an active-badge wearer can get a minute-by-minute printout listing exactly where he's been and whom he's been with.

Is the active badge a primitive version of the communicator on TV's *Star Trek* or a surveillance tool for Big Brother? The technology has the potential to be either or both; it all depends on how people use it. Active badges, like other security devices and techniques, raise important legal and ethical questions about privacy—questions that we, as a society, must resolve sooner or later.

Justice on the Electronic Frontier

> Through our scientific genius, we have **made this world a neighborhood**; now through our moral and spiritual development, we must **make of it a brotherhood**.
> —The Rev. Martin Luther King, Jr.

An active badge transmits signals that enable a network to identify, locate, and track the badge wearer. This active badge from Versus Technology also includes a button that can be programmed to send a message to a pager, open a door, or perform another task.

Federal and state governments have responded to the growing computer crime problem by creating new laws against electronic trespassing and by escalating enforcement efforts. Hackers have become targets for nationwide anti-crime operations. Dozens of hackers have been arrested for unauthorized entry into computer systems and for the release of destructive viruses and worms. Many have been convicted under federal or state laws. Others have had their computers confiscated with no formal charges filed.

Some of the victims of these sting operations claim that they broke no laws. In one case a student was arrested because he published an electronic magazine that carried a description of an emergency 911 system allegedly stolen by hackers. Charges were eventually dropped when it was revealed that the "stolen" document was, in fact, available to the public.

Cases like this raise questions about how civil rights apply in the "electronic frontier." How does the Bill of Rights apply to computer communications? Does freedom of the press apply to online magazines in the same way it applies to paper periodicals? Can an electronic bulletin board operator or Internet service provider be held responsible for information others post on a server? Can online pornography be served from a house located in a neighborhood with anti-porn laws?

Laws like the Telecommunications Act of 1996 attempt to deal with these questions by outlining exactly what kinds of communications are legal online. Unfortunately, these laws generally raise as many questions as they answer. Shortly after passage a major section of the Telecommunications Act, called the Communications Decency Act, was declared unconstitutional by the Supreme Court. The debates continue inside and outside of the courts.

The Digital Millennium Copyright Act of 1998 (discussed earlier in this chapter) hasn't (so far) been found unconstitutional, but it has resulted in several lawsuits that raise serious human rights questions. In the summer of 2001, a Russian programmer and graduate student named Dmitry Sklyarov was arrested by the FBI after he spoke at a computer security conference in Las Vegas. His alleged crime was writing—not using—a program that cracks Adobe's copy protection scheme for e-books. After a Web-wide demonstration against the arrest and Adobe, the company publicly came out in favor of freeing Sklyarov.

The same law was used to silence Professor Edward Felton in 2001. The Princeton University computer scientist was threatened with a lawsuit from the Recording Industry Association of America if he presented a paper analyzing the system that encodes digital music; he withdrew the paper. Several months later Felton published the paper and the RIAA recanted its threat—but not its right to threaten similar suits in the future.

The DMCA was even used to file a suit against *2600* magazine because of a single Web site link. A Norwegian 15-year-old had written code allowing DVD movies to be played on Linux

Rules of Thumb

Safe Computing

Even if you're not building a software system for the DOJ or the FBI, computer security is important. Viruses, disk crashes, system bombs, and miscellaneous disasters can destroy your work, your peace of mind, and possibly your system. Fortunately, you can protect your computer, your software, and your data from most hazards.

- **Share with care.** A computer virus is a contagious disease that spreads when it comes in contact with a compatible file or disk. Viruses spread rapidly in environments where disks and files are passed around freely, as they are in many student computer labs. To protect your data, keep your disks to yourself, and don't borrow disks from others. When you do share a 3.5-inch disk, physically write-protect it (by moving the plastic slider to uncover the square hole) so a virus can't attach to it.

Write-protect opening

- **Beware of email bearing gifts.** Many viruses hide in attachments to email messages that say something like "Here's the document you asked for. Please don't show anyone else." Don't open unsolicited email attachments; just throw them away.
- **Handle shareware and freeware with care.** Other viruses enter systems in Trojan horse shareware and freeware programs. Treat public domain programs and shareware with care; test them with a disinfectant program before you install them on your hard disk. Contrary to popular belief, you can't get a virus by reading an email message. But a virus can be embedded in an email attachment, so scan attached files before opening them.
- **Don't pirate software.** Even commercial programs can be infected with viruses. Shrink-wrapped, virgin software is much less likely to be infected than pirated copies. Besides, software piracy is theft, and the legal penalties can be severe.
- **Disinfect regularly.** Virus protection programs are available for all kinds of systems, often for free. Use up-to-date virus protection software regularly if you work in a high-risk environment like a public computer lab.
- **Treat your removable disks as if they contained something important.** Keep them away from liquids, dust, pets, and (especially) magnets. Don't put your disks close to phones, speakers, and other electronic devices that contain hidden magnets. (Magnets won't harm CD-ROMs or DVD-ROMs, but scratches can make them unusable.)
- **Take your passwords seriously.** Choose a password that's not easily guessable, not in any dictionary, and not easy for others to remember. Don't post it by your computer, and don't type it when you're being watched. Change your password occasionally—immediately if you have reason to suspect it has been discovered.
- **If it's sensitive, lock it up.** If your computer is accessible to others, protect your private files with passwords and/or encryption. Many operating systems and utilities include options for adding password protection and encrypting files. If others need to see the files, lock them so they can be read but not changed or deleted. If secrecy is critical, don't store the data on your hard disk at all. Store it on removable disks and lock it away in a safe place.
- **If it's important, back it up.** Regularly make backup copies of every important file on different disks than the original. Keep copies of critical disks in different locations so that you have backups in case disaster strikes.
- **If you're sending sensitive information through the Internet, consider encryption.** Use a utility or a program like freeware PGP (Pretty Good Privacy) to turn your message into code that's almost impossible to crack.
- **Don't open your system to interlopers.** If you've got an always-on Internet connection—T1, DSL, or cable modem—consider using firewall hardware or software to detect and lock out snoopers. Set your file sharing controls so access is limited to authorized visitors.
- **Prepare for the worst.** Even if you take every precaution, things can still go wrong. Make sure you aren't completely dependent on the computer for really important things.

computers—code that broke the DVD copy protection scheme. *2600*'s Web site included a link to another site containing the program. (*The New York Times* Web site contained a link to the same site, but was not sued by the recording industry.)

When Congress passed the Telecommunications Act of 1996 and the Digital Millennium Copyright Act of 1998, they were attempting to make U.S. law more responsive to the issues of the digital age. But each of these laws introduced new problems by threatening rights of citizens—problems that have to be solved by courts and by future lawmakers. These laws illustrate the difficulty lawmakers face when protecting rights in a world of rapid technological change.

Rules of Thumb

Computer Ethics

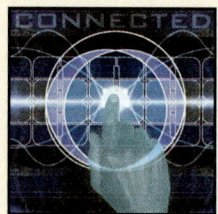

Ethics is moral philosophy—philosophical thinking about right and wrong. Many people base their ethical beliefs on religious rules such as the Ten Commandments or the Buddhist Eightfold Path. Others use professional codes such as the doctor's Hippocratic Oath, which includes the often quoted "First do no harm." Still others use personal philosophies with principles such as "It's okay if a jury of observers would approve." But in today's changing world, deciding how to apply the rules isn't always easy. Sometimes the rules don't seem to apply directly, and sometimes they contradict each other. (How should you "Honor thy father" if you learn that he's using the home computer to embezzle money from his employer? Is it okay to allow a friend who's broke to borrow your Microsoft Office CD for a required class project?) These kinds of *moral dilemmas* are central questions in discussions of ethics. Information technology poses moral dilemmas related to everything from copying software to reporting a coworker's sexually explicit screen saver or racist email.

Computer ethics can't be reduced to a handful of rules—the gray areas are always going to require thought and judgment. But principles and guidelines can help to focus thinking and refine judgments when dealing with technology-related moral dilemmas. The ACM **Code of Ethics**, reprinted in the Appendix of this book, is the most widely known code of conduct specifically for computer professionals. The ACM Code is worth understanding and applying even if you don't plan to be a "computer professional." Who shouldn't "Contribute to Society and Human Well-Being" or "Honor Confidentiality"? But these principles take on new meaning in an age of email and databases.

Here are some other guidelines that might help you to decide how to "do the right thing" when faced with ethical dilemmas at school, at work, or at home:

- **Know the rules and the law.** Many laws, and many organizational rules, are reflections of moral principles. For example, almost everyone agrees that *plagiarism*—presenting somebody else's work as your own—is wrong. It's also a serious violation of rules in most schools. And if the work is copied without permission, plagiarism can become copyright infringement, a serious legal offense . . . whether or not the work explicitly says that it is copyrighted.
- **Don't assume that it's okay if it's legal.** Our legal system doesn't define what's right and wrong. How can it, when we don't all agree on morality? The law is especially lax in areas related to information technology, because the technology changes too fast for lawmakers to keep up. It's ultimately up to each individual to act with conscience.
- **Think scenarios.** If you're debating between different actions, think about what might happen as a result of your actions. If you suspect your employer is falsifying spreadsheets to get around environmental regulations, what's likely to happen if you snoop around on his computer and blow the whistle on him? What's likely to happen if you don't? What are your other alternatives?
- **When in doubt, talk it out.** Discuss your concerns with people you trust—ideally, people with wisdom and experience dealing with similar situations. For example, if you're unsure about the line between getting computer help from a friend and cheating on homework, ask an instructor.
- **Make yourself proud.** How would you feel if you saw your actions on the front page of *The New York Times*, your company newsletter, or your family's hometown newspaper? If you'd be embarrassed or ashamed, you probably should choose another course of action.
- **Remember the golden rule: Do unto others as you would have them do unto you.** This universal principle is central to every major spiritual tradition, and it is amazingly versatile. One example: Before you download that bootleg MP3 file of that up-and-coming singer, think about how you'd feel about bootleggers if you were the singer.
- **Take the long view.** It's all too easy to be blinded by the rapid-fire rewards of the Internet and computer technology. Consider this guiding principle from a Native American tradition: In every deliberation, consider the impact of your decision on the next seven generations.

Security and Reliability

> If the automobile had followed the same development cycle as the computer, a **Rolls Royce would today cost $100**, get a million miles per gallon, and **explode once a year**, killing everyone inside.
>
> —Robert X. Cringely, *InfoWorld* columnist

So far our discussion of security has focused mainly on protecting computer systems from trespassing, sabotage, and other crimes. But security involves more than criminal activity. Some of the most important security issues have to do with creating systems that can withstand software errors and hardware glitches.

Bugs and Breakdowns

Computer systems, like all machines, are vulnerable to fires, floods, and other natural disasters, as well as breakdowns caused by failure of hardware components. But in modern computers, hardware problems are relatively rare when compared with software failures. By any measure bugs do more damage than viruses and computer burglars put together. Here are a few horror stories:

- On November 20, 1985, the Bank of New York's computer system started corrupting government securities transactions. By the end of the day, the bank was $32 billion overdrawn with the Federal Reserve. Before the system error was corrected, it cost the bank $5 million in interest.
- In September, 1999, the Mars Climate Orbiter burned up as it approached Mars because controllers had mixed up British and metric units. Three months later, the Mars Polar Lander went silent 12 minutes before touchdown. Investigators suspect software errors are at least partly responsible for this spectacular mission failure.
- Programs on NASA observation satellites in the 1970s and 1980s rejected ozone readings because the programmers had assumed when they wrote the programs that such low numbers could not be correct. It wasn't until British scientists reported ozone-level declines that NASA scientists reprocessed the data and confirmed the British findings that the earth's ozone layer was in danger.
- The Therac 25 radiation machine for tracking cancers was thoroughly tested and successfully used on thousands of patients before a software bug caused massive radiation overdoses, resulting in the partial paralysis of one patient and the death of another.
- On January 15, 1990, AT&T's 30-year-old signaling system software failed, bringing the long-distance carrier's network to its knees. Twenty million calls failed to go through during the next 18 hours before technicians found the problem: a single incorrect instruction hiding among a million lines of code.
- On February 25, 1991, 28 American soldiers were killed and 98 others wounded when an Iraqi Scud missile hit a barracks near Dhahran, Saudi Arabia. A tiny bug in a Patriot missile's software threw off its timing just enough to prevent it from intercepting the Scud. Programmers had already fixed the bug, and a new version of the software was being shipped to Dhahran when the attack occurred.

Every year brings new stories of breakdowns and bugs with catastrophic consequences. But it wasn't until 1999 that a computer bug—the Y2K (year 2000) bug, or millennium bug—became an international sensation. For decades programmers commonly built two-digit date fields into programs to save storage space, thinking "Why allow space for the first two digits when they never change?" But when 1999 ended, those digits did change, making many of those ancient programs unstable or unusable. Programmers knowledgeable in COBOL, FORTRAN, and other ancient computer languages repaired many of the programs. But others couldn't be repaired and had to be completely rewritten.

Businesses and governments spent more than 100 billion dollars trying to head off Y2K disasters. Many individuals bought generators and guns, stockpiled food and water, and prepared for a collapse of the computer-controlled utility grids that keep our economy running. When the fateful day arrived, the Y2K bug caused many problems, ranging from credit card refusals to malfunctioning spy satellites. But for most people, January 1, 2000, was business as usual. It's debatable whether disasters were averted by billions of dollars worth of preventive maintenance, or whether the Y2K scare stories were overblown. The truth is undoubtedly somewhere between these two extremes. In any event, Y2K raised public consciousness about their dependence on fickle, fragile technology.

Given the state of the art of programming today, three facts are clear:

1. It's impossible to eliminate all bugs. Today's programs are constructed of thousands of tiny pieces, any one of which can cause a failure if it's incorrectly coded.

These South Koreans, like people all around the world, stocked up on food and cooking gas cans to prepare for possible emergency shortages as a result of Y2K computer failures.

2. Even programs that appear to work can contain dangerous bugs. Some bugs are easy to detect and correct because they're obvious. The most dangerous bugs are difficult to detect and may go unnoticed by users for months or years.
3. The bigger the system, the bigger the problem. Large programs are far more complex and difficult to debug than small programs, and the trend today is clearly toward large programs. For example, Microsoft Windows 95 has 11 million lines of code, and was considered huge at the time; Windows 2000 has close to 29 million!

As we entrust complex computerized systems to do everything from financial transaction processing to air traffic control, the potential cost of computer failure goes up. In the last decade, researchers have identified hundreds of cases in which disruptions to computer system operations posed some risk to the public, and the number of incidents has doubled every two years.

Computers at War

> Massive networking makes the U.S. the **world's most vulnerable target**.
> —John McConnell, former NSA director

Nowhere are the issues surrounding security and reliability more critical than in military applications. To carry out its mission effectively, the military must be sure its systems are secure against enemy surveillance and attack. At the same time, many modern military applications push the limits of information technology farther than they've ever been before.

Smart Weapons

The United States has invested billions of dollars in the development of **smart weapons**—missiles that use computerized guidance systems to locate their targets. A command-guidance system enables a human operator to control the missile's path while watching a missile's-eye view of the target on a television screen. A missile with a homing guidance system can track a moving target without human help, using infrared heat-seeking devices or visual pattern recognition technology. Weapons that use "smart" guidance systems can be extremely accurate in pinpointing enemy targets under most circumstances. In theory smart weapons can greatly reduce the amount of civilian destruction in war if everything is working properly.

One problem with high-tech weapons is that they reduce the amount of time people have to make life-and-death decisions. As decision-making time goes down, the chance of errors goes up. In one tragic example, an American guided missile cruiser on a peacetime mission in the Persian Gulf used a computerized Aegis fleet defense system to shoot down an Iranian Airbus containing 290 civilians. The decision to fire was made by well-intentioned humans, but those humans had little time—and used ambiguous data—to make the decision.

Autonomous Systems

Even more controversial is the possibility of people being left out of the decision-making loop altogether. Yet the trend in military research is clearly toward weapons that demand almost instantaneous responses—the kind that only computers can make. An **autonomous system** is a complex system that can assume almost complete responsibility for a task without human input, verification, or decision making.

The most famous and controversial autonomous system is the Strategic Defense Initiative (SDI)—former President Ronald Reagan's proposed "Star Wars" system for shielding the United States from nuclear attack. The SDI system, as planned, would have used a network of laser-equipped satellites and ground-based stations to detect and destroy attacking missiles shortly after launch, before they had time to reach their targets. SDI weapons would have to be able to react almost instantaneously, without human intervention. If they sensed an attack, these system computers would have no time to wait for the president to declare war, and no time for human experts to analyze the perceived attack.

SDI generated intense public debates about false alarms, hardware feasibility, constitutional issues, and the ethics of autonomous

In today's weapon systems, such as those based on the North America Aerospace Defense Command (NORAD) Cheyenne Mountain Complex in Colorado Springs, Colorado, computers are critical components in the command and control process.

weapons. But for many who understand the limitations of computers, the biggest issue is software reliability. SDI's software system would require tens of millions of lines of code. The system couldn't be completely tested in advance because there's no way to simulate accurately the unpredictable conditions of a global war. Yet to work effectively, the system would have to be absolutely reliable. In a tightly coupled worldwide network, a single bug could multiply and expand like a speed-of-light cancer. A small error could result in a major disaster. Many software engineers have pointed out that absolute reliability simply isn't possible now or in the foreseeable future.

In spite of years of political haggling, system failures, and cost overruns, an SDI-like system is still in the works, and systems reliability issues remain. Supporters of automated missile-defense systems argue that the technical difficulties can be overcome in time, and the U.S. government continues to invest billions in research toward that end. Whether or not a "smart shield" is ever completed, it has focused public attention on critical issues related to security and reliability.

Warfare in the Digital Domain

Even as the U.S. government spends billions of dollars on smart missiles and missile defense systems, many military experts suggest that future wars may not be fought in the air, on land, or at sea. The front lines of the future may, instead, be in cyberspace. By attacking through vast interconnected computer networks, an enemy could conceivably cripple telecommunications systems, power grids, banking and financial systems, hospitals and medical systems, water and gas supplies, oil pipelines, and emergency government services without firing a shot.

Several recent examples highlight our vulnerability:

- In 1994 Swedish hackers broke into telecommunications systems in central Florida and blocked several 911 systems by automatically dialing their numbers repeatedly. Anyone who called 911 with a legitimate emergency was greeted with a busy signal until the attack ended.
- In 1996 a juvenile hacker disabled a key phone computer servicing a Massachusetts airport, paralyzing the airport control tower for six hours.
- In 1998 Israeli police working with the FBI, the U.S. Air Force, and NASA arrested three Israeli teens who successfully hacked into Department of Defense computers in both countries.
- During the 2000 U.S. election, dozens of politically motivated Web attacks occurred for various causes, parties, and countries. The attacks included Web site vandalism, denial of service attacks, and system snooping.

None of these crimes resulted in serious damage or injury. But terrorists, spies, or criminals might use the same techniques to trigger major disasters.

Recognizing the growing threat of system sabotage, Attorney General Janet Reno created the *National Infrastructure Protection Center* in early 1998. The NIPC's state-of-the-art command center is housed at FBI headquarters. The center includes representatives of various intelligence agencies (the departments of defense, transportation, energy, and treasury), and representatives of several major corporations.

Corporate participation is critical because private companies own many of the infrastructure systems that are most vulnerable to attack. Unfortunately, many businesses are slow to recognize the potential threat to their systems. They embrace the efficiency that networks bring, but they don't adequately prepare for attack through those networks.

In the wake of the terrorist attacks of September, 2001, George W. Bush formed The President's Critical Infrastructure Board consisting of cabinet members and top presidential aids. The cyberterrorism panel was designed to protect utilities and critical public services that depend on information networks.

Network attacks are all but inevitable, and such attacks can have disastrous consequences for all of us. In a world where computers control everything from money to missiles, computer security and reliability are too important to ignore.

Is Security Possible?

Computer thieves. Hackers. Software pirates. Computer snoopers. Viruses. Worms. Trojan horses. Wiretaps. Hardware failures. Software bugs. When we live and work with computers, we're exposed to all kinds of risks that didn't exist in the precomputer era. These risks make computer security especially important and challenging.

Because computers do so many amazing things so well, it's easy to overlook the problems they bring with them and to believe that they're invincible. But like Kempelen's chess-playing machine, today's computers hide the potential for errors and deception under an impressive user interface. This doesn't mean we should avoid using computers, only that we should remain skeptical, cautious, and realistic as we use them. Security procedures can reduce but not eliminate risks. In today's fast-moving world absolute security simply isn't possible.

Now, Weapons of Mass Disruption?

George F. Will

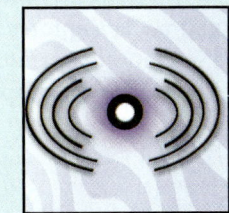

The terrorist attacks of September 11, 2001, used passenger airliners as crude, but powerful, weapons of mass destruction. In this article, first published in the October 29, 2001, issue of Newsweek, George Will tells us to expect a wave of terrorism that uses hardware, software, and computer expertise as weapons.

Americans have received their marching orders. They have been told to stiffen their sinews, summon up their blood—and go to the mall. And a movie. This summons to normality is akin to the rallying cry on the eve of Agincourt. However, energetic everydayness, even lightheartedness, is suddenly a serious duty. Just as there is at all times a moral obligation to be intelligent, there is today an obligation to be cheerful.

It would be irrational for Americans to begin acting as though terrorists are capable of making daily life hazardous for Americans generally. Acting that way would cripple the country's social and economic vigor, its defining assets. And an even more important reason for not allowing current problems to knock America off its normally jaunty stride is that the nation's equilibrium may soon be tested by even bigger problems.

When in 1820 the argument about the admission of Missouri to the Union as a slave state aggravated sectional animosities, Jefferson called the crisis a "fire bell in the night," awakening the nation to the possibility of worse to come. Last week's fire bell was anthrax, a small sample of what can be called the terrorism of substances, biological and chemical. There have been hearings, reports and books on these subjects, but complacent democracies are educated primarily by events, not exhortations—the British did not bring Churchill to power until Hitler approached the English Channel ports.

What might be the next alarm bell to ring? Of course, a truck bomb would intensify national nervousness by making things that are ubiquitous—trucks—seem ominous. And high explosives directed against, say, Hoover Dam would not only complicate life in the Southwest, it would underscore the unsettling message that even big things can be pulverized. However, it is time to think about attacks using things not solid and directed against things not as solid as skyscrapers or dams.

Consider cyberterrorism, assaults that can be undertaken from anywhere on the planet against anything dependent on or directed by flows of information. Call this soft terrorism. Although it can put lives in jeopardy, it can do its silent, stealthy work without tearing flesh or pulverizing structures. It can be a weapon of mass disruption rather than mass destruction, as was explained by the President's Commission on Critical Infrastructure Protection in its 1997 report on potential cyberattacks against the "system of systems" that is modern America.

"Life is good in America," the report says, "because things work. When we flip the switch, the lights come on. When we turn the tap, clean water flows." Now suppose a sudden and drastic shrinkage of life's "taken for granted" quotient. The report notes that terrorist attacks have usually been against single targets—individuals, crowds, buildings. But today's networked world of complexity and interconnectedness has vast new vulnerabilities with a radius larger than that of any imaginable bomb blast.

Terrorists using computers might be able to disrupt information and communications systems and, by doing so, attack banking and financial systems, energy (electricity, oil, gas) and the systems for the physical distribution of America's economic output.

Hijacked aircraft and powdered anthrax—such terrorist tools are crude and scarce compared with computers, which are everywhere and inexpensive. Wielded with sufficient cunning, they can spread the demoralizing helplessness that is terrorism's most important intended byproduct. Computers as weapons, even more than intercontinental ballistic missiles, render irrelevant the physical geography—the two broad oceans and two peaceful neighbors—that once was the basis of America's sense of safety.

A threat is a capability joined with a hostile intent. In early summer 1997 the U.S. military conducted a threat-assessment exercise, code-named Eligible Receiver, to test the vulnerabilities of "borderless cyber geography." The results confirmed that in a software-driven world, an enemy need not invade the territory, or the air over the territory, of a country in order to control or damage that country's resources.

The attack tools are on sale everywhere: computers, modems, software, telephones. The attacks can shut down services or deliver harmful instructions to systems. And a cyberattack may not be promptly discovered. The report says, "Computer intrusions do not announce their presence the way a bomb does."

Already "subnational" groups—terrorists, organized crime—are taking advantage of legal and widely available "strong encryption" software that makes their communications invulnerable to surveillance. How invulnerable? John Keegan, the British military analyst, quotes William Crowell, former deputy director of the largest U.S. intelligence agency, the National Security Agency: "If all the personal computers in the world were put to work on a single [strongly encrypted] message, it would still take an estimated 12 million times the age of the universe to break a single message."

Now suppose a state or group or state-supported group used similar cybermarvels to attack, say, U.S. banking and financial systems, or the production and distribution of electric power. Americans know how impotent, and infuriated, they feel when a thunderstorm knocks out electrical power for even a few hours. The freezer defrosts, the Palm handheld cannot be recharged, "SportsCenter" is missed. War is hell. And speaking of war:

. . . If we are supposed to stiffen our sinews and summon up our blood for a battle, it would be well to remember that the Battle of Agincourt, for which Shakespeare's Henry V exhorted the stiffening and summoning, was won in 1415 by the skill of English archers wielding longbows, the high technology of the day.

DISCUSSION QUESTIONS

1. The author seems to be arguing that computer technology will be the major weapon in the next wave of terrorism. Do you agree? Explain your answer.
2. What do you think we should do to prepare to defend ourselves against cyberterrorism?

Summary

Computers play an ever-increasing role in fighting crime. At the same time, law enforcement organizations are facing an increase in computer crime—crimes accomplished through special knowledge of computer technology. Most computer crimes go undetected, and those that are detected often go unreported. But by any estimate computer crime costs billions of dollars every year.

Some computer criminals use computers, modems, and other equipment to steal goods, money, information, software, and services. Others use Trojan horses, viruses, worms, logic bombs, and other software tricks to sabotage systems. According to the media, computer crimes are committed by young, bright computer wizards called hackers. Research suggests, however, that hackers are responsible for only a small fraction of computer crimes. The typical computer criminal is a trusted employee with personal or financial problems and knowledge of the computer system. The most common computer crime, software piracy, is committed by millions of people, often unknowingly. Piracy is a violation of intellectual property laws, which, in many cases, lag far behind the technology.

Because of rising computer crime and other risks, organizations have developed a number of computer security techniques to protect their systems and data. Some security devices, such as keys and badges, are designed to restrict physical access to computers. But these tools are becoming less effective in an age of personal computers and networks. Passwords, encryption, shielding, and audit-control software are all used to protect sensitive data in various organizations. When all else fails, backups of important data are used to reconstruct systems after damage occurs. The most effective security solutions depend on people at least as much as on technology.

Normally, security measures serve to protect our privacy and other individual rights. But occasionally, security procedures threaten those rights. The trade-offs between computer security and freedom raise important legal and ethical questions.

Computer systems aren't just threatened by people; they're also threatened by software bugs and hardware glitches. An important part of security is protecting systems—and the people affected by those systems—from the consequences of those bugs and glitches. Since our society uses computers for many applications that put lives at stake, reliability issues are especially important. In modern military applications, security and reliability are critical. As the speed, power, and complexity of weapons systems increase, many fear that humans are being squeezed out of the decision-making loop. The debate over high-tech weaponry is bringing many important security issues to the public's attention for the first time.

Chapter Review

▼ Key Terms

access-control software (p. 239)
active badge (p. 243)
antivirus program (p. 236)
audit-control software (p. 241)
autonomous system (p. 248)
backup (p. 242)
biometrics (p. 238)
code of ethics (p. 246)
computer crime (p. 230)
computer security (p. 238)
contract (p. 233)

copyright (p. 233)
denial of service (DoS) attacks (p. 237)
encryption (p. 241)
ethics (p. 246)
firewall (p. 239)
hacker (p. 236)
identity theft (p. 232)
intellectual property (p. 233)
logic bomb (p. 234)
password (p. 238)

patent (p. 233)
sabotage (p. 234)
social engineering (p. 232)
smart weapon (p. 248)
software piracy (p. 232)
uninterruptible power supply (UPS) (p. 242)
virus (p. 234)
worm (p. 235)

▼ Interactive Quiz Questions

1. The *Computer Confluence* CD-ROM contains self-test quiz questions related to this chapter, including multiple choice, true or false, and matching questions.
2. The *Computer Confluence* Web site, www.prenhall.com/beekman, contains self-test exercises related to this chapter. Follow the instructions for taking a quiz. After you've completed your quiz, you can email the results to your instructor.

   The Web site also contains open-ended discussion questions called Internet Explorations. Discuss one or more of the Internet Exploration questions at the section for this chapter.

▼ Review Questions

1. Define or describe each of the key terms listed in the "Key Terms" section. Check your answers using the glossary.
2. Why is it hard to estimate the extent of computer crime?
3. Describe the typical computer criminal. How does he or she differ from the media stereotype?
4. What is the most common computer crime? Who commits it? What is being done to stop it?
5. What are intellectual property laws, and how do they apply to software?
6. Describe several different types of programs that can be used for software sabotage.
7. What are the two inherent characteristics of computers that make security so difficult?
8. Describe several different computer security techniques, and explain the purpose of each.
9. Every afternoon at closing time, the First Taxpayer's Bank copies all the day's accumulated transaction information from disk to tape. Why?
10. In what ways can computer security protect the privacy of individuals? In what ways can computer security threaten the privacy of individuals?
11. What are smart weapons? How do they differ from conventional weapons? What are the advantages and risks of smart weapons?

▼ Discussion Questions

1. Are computers morally neutral? Explain your answer.
2. Suppose Whizzo Software Company produces a program that looks, from the user's point of view, exactly like the immensely popular BozoWorks from Bozo, Inc. Whizzo insists that it didn't copy any of the code in Bozo-Works; it just tried to design a program that would appeal to BozoWorks users. Bozo cries foul and sues Whizzo for violation of intellectual property laws. Do you think the laws should favor Bozo's arguments or Whizzo's? Why?
3. What do you suppose motivates people to create computer viruses and other destructive software? What do you think motivates hackers to break into computer systems? Are the two types of behavior related?
4. Some people think all mail messages on the Internet should be encrypted. They argue that, if everything is encrypted, the encrypted message won't stand out, so everybody's right to privacy will be better protected. Others suggest that this would just improve the cover of criminals with something to hide from the government. What do you think, and why?
5. Would you like to work in a business where all employees were required to wear active badges? Explain your answer.
6. How do the issues raised in the debate over SDI apply to other large software systems? How do you feel about the different issues raised in the debate?

Projects

1. Talk to employees at your campus computer labs and computer centers about security issues and techniques. What are the major security threats according to these employees? What security techniques are used to protect the equipment and data in each facility? Are these techniques adequate? Report on your findings.

2. Perform the same kind of interviews at local businesses. Do businesses view security differently than your campus personnel?

Sources and Resources

Books

A Gift of Fire: Social, Legal, and Ethical Issues in Computing, by Sara Baase (Upper Saddle River, NJ: Prentice-Hall, 1997). This book offers a thorough, easy-to-read overview of the human questions facing us as a result of the computer revolution: privacy, security, reliability, accountability, and the rest. A revised edition should be available by the time you read this.

Cyberethics: Morality and Law in Cyberspace, by Richard Spinello (Jones and Bartlett, 2000). This book surveys most of the big issues of computer ethics: intellectual property, privacy, security, free speech, and others. Case studies help make theoretical concepts concrete.

Readings in CyberEthics, edited by Richard A. Spinello and Herman T. Tavani (Jones and Bartlett, 2001). This collection of papers and articles includes sections on freedom of expression, property, privacy, and other critical subjects related to information technology.

Computer Network Security and CyberEthics, by Joseph Migga Kizza (McFarland & Co., 2001). This book clearly analyzes the causes, cost, and consequences of computer crime and cracking.

Web Security: A Step-by-Step Reference Guide, by Lincoln D. Stein (Reading, MA: Addison-Wesley, 1997). The explosive growth of the Web has created a variety of new security problems and risks. This book explains in clear language many of the technical problems related to Web security. It also offers practical advice for Web administrators and users who want to protect themselves from attacks and privacy violations.

Secrets and Lies: Digital Security in a Networked World, by Bruce Schneier (New York: Wiley, 2000). Mathematician and computer security expert Schneier tells you in clear, lively prose how to think like a computer thief so you can protect yourself and your organization from that thief.

The Hundredth Window: Protecting Your Privacy and Security in the Age of the Internet, by Charles Jennings and Lori Fena (Free Press, 2000). The Internet is only as secure as its weakest link. This practical book can help you to understand where the weakest links are and how to protect your privacy online.

Virtual Private Networks for Dummies, by Mark Merkow (Foster City, CA: IDG Books, 1999). In spite of its title, this book provides a great deal of technical information on setting up secure Internet connections and communications. Coverage includes cryptography, privacy, reliability, and e-commerce.

Internet Cryptography, by Richard E. Smith (Reading, MA: Addison-Wesley, 1997). Cryptography is the most effective tool for protecting privacy and preserving security on the Internet. This book explains the ins and outs of cryptography, with plenty of practical details for people who need to protect their data as it moves around on the Net.

Cyberwars: Espionage on the Internet, by Jean Guisnel (New York: Plenum, 1997). If you need proof that the Internet has graduated from its role as a research assistant, read Cyberwars. Guisnel, a respected French journalist, exposes the emerging online battle zones where spies, saboteurs, government agents, drug traffickers, and others wage virtual wars. Even though we can't see them happening, we're all victims of the fallout from these dangerous battles.

Digital Copyright Protection, by Peter Wayner (Boston: AP Professional, 1997). This somewhat technical book provides information and advice on several ways of protecting digital information on the Web and elsewhere.

Hackers: Heroes of the Computer Revolution, by Steven Levy (New York: Delta, 1994). This book helped bring the word "hackers" into the public's vocabulary. Levy's entertaining account of the golden age of hacking gives a historical perspective to today's anti-hacker mania.

The Cuckoo's Egg, by Cliff Stoll (New York: Pocket Books, 1989, 1995). This best-selling book documents the stalking of an interloper on the Internet. International espionage mixes with computer technology in this entertaining, engaging, and eye-opening book.

Takedown: The Pursuit and Capture of Kevin Mitnick, America's Most Wanted Computer Outlaw—by the Man Who Did It, by Tsutomu Shimomura with John Markoff (New York: Hyperion Books, 1996) and *The Fugitive Game*, by Jonathon Littman (New York: Little, Brown and Co., 1997). These two books chronicle the events leading up to and including the capture of Kevin Mitnick, America's number one criminal hacker. Takedown presents the story from the point of view of the security expert who captured Mitnick. The Fugitive Game is written from a more objective journalistic point of view.

Cyberpunk—Outlaws and Hackers on the Computer Frontier, Updated Edition, by Katie Hafner and John Markoff (New York: Simon & Schuster, 1995). This book profiles three hackers whose exploits caught the public's attention: Kevin Mitnick, a California cracker who vandalized corporate systems; Pengo, who penetrated U.S. systems for East German espionage purposes; and Robert Morris, Jr., whose Internet worm brought down 6,000 computers in a matter of hours.

The Hacker Crackdown: Law and Disorder on the Electronic Frontier, by Bruce Sterling (New York: Bantam Books, 1992). Famed cyberpunk author Sterling turns to nonfiction to tell both sides of the story of the war between hackers and federal law enforcement agencies. The complete text is available online along with rest-of-the-story updates.

Computer-Related Risks, by Peter Neumann (Reading, MA: Addison-Wesley, 1995). Neumann runs the popular and eye-opening comp.risks forum on the Internet. This book draws on that forum and Neumann's expertise, providing an exhaustive technical survey of the risks we face as a result of our dependence on computer technology. The hundreds of documented examples range from humorous to horrifying, and they're tied together with Neumann's intelligent assessment of the broader problems and possible solutions.

Ender's Game, by Orson Scott Card (New York: Tor Books, 1999). This award-winning, entertaining science fiction opus has become a favorite of the cryptography crowd because of its emphasis on encryption to protect privacy.

The Blue Nowhere, by Jeffery Deaver (New York: Simon & Schuster, 2001). This suspenseful thriller involves a sadistic hacker who invades his victim's computers, meddles with their lives, and lures them to their deaths. Though fictional, the novel presents a terrifyingly accurate analysis of the lack of privacy and security on the internet.

The Postman, by David Brin (New York: Bantam, 1990). This entertaining science fiction novel weaves a tale of the future that raises many of the same issues raised by Kempelen's chess-playing machine. The disappointing 1997 movie bears little resemblance to the novel.

Periodicals

Many popular magazines, from *Newsweek* to *Wired*, provide regular coverage of issues related to privacy and security of digital systems. Most of the periodicals listed here are newsletters of professional organizations that focus on these issues.

Information Security (www.infosecuritymag.com). This magazine focuses on security problems and solutions. Some of the articles are technical, but most are accessible to anyone with an interest in security issues.

The CPSR Newsletter, published by Computer Professionals for Social Responsibility (P.O. Box 717, Palo Alto, CA 94302, 415/322-3778, fax 415/322-3798, email: cpsr@csli.stanford.edu). An alliance of computer scientists and others interested in the impact of computer technology on society, CPSR works to influence public policies to ensure that computers are used wisely in the public interest. Their newsletter has intelligent articles and discussions of risk, reliability, privacy, security, human rights, work, war, education, the environment, democracy, and other subjects that bring together computers and people.

EFFector, published by the Electronic Frontier Foundation (155 Second St., Cambridge, MA 02141, 617/864-0665, fax 617/864-0866, email: effnews-request@eff.org). This electronic newsletter is distributed by EFF, an organization "established to help civilize the electronic frontier." EFF was founded by Mitch Kapor (see Chapter 6) and John Perry Barlow to protect civil rights and encourage responsible citizenship on the electronic frontier of computer networks.

Ethix: The Bulletin of the Institute for Business, Technology, and Ethics (www.ethix.org, email: contact@ethix.org). The IBTE is a relatively new nonprofit corporation working to transform business through appropriate technology and ethical values.

Web Pages

As you might suspect, the Net is the best source of up-to-the-minute information on computer security and related issues. Public and commercial organizations maintain Web pages devoted to these issues, and dozens of newsgroups contain lively ongoing discussions on controversial topics. Check the *Computer Confluence* Web site for the latest links.

10 Information Age Issues: Inventing the Future

After you read this chapter you should be able to:

▼

Explain how the emerging information economy differs from earlier social and economic systems

Describe several ways computers and robots have changed the nature and quality of jobs, both positively and negatively

List several trends in information technology that are likely to continue for a few more years

Outline several research areas that may produce breakthroughs in computer technology in the next few decades

Describe some of the social and psychological risks of the information age

Speculate about the long-term future of the information age

▲

▼ **In this chapter:**

How to predict the future
How technology transforms cultures, economies, and jobs
Technology over the horizon
Important, difficult questions
The gift of fire
. . . and more.

▼ **On the CD-ROM:**

Video clips showing the impact of computers and robots in the workplace
Virtual reality on video
Emerging technology
Interactive self-study quizzes
. . . and more.

▼ **On the Web:**
www.prenhall.com/beekman

A robot playground
Information economy analysis and trends
Resources for telecommuters and other "boundaryless" workers
Statistics and analysis of the impact of technology on employment
Resources for protecting our planet while using computers
Links to the labs
Discussions of biotechnology, microtechnology, and nanotechnology
Self-study exercises
. . . and more.

256

Alan Kay Invents the Future

> The best way to predict the future
> is to **invent it**.
> —Alan Kay

Alan Kay has been inventing the future for most of his life. Kay was a child prodigy who composed original music, built a harpsichord, and appeared on NBC as a "Quiz Kid." Kay's genius wasn't reflected in his grades; he had trouble conforming to the rigid structure of the schools he attended. After high school he worked as a jazz guitarist and an Air Force programmer before attending college.

His Ph.D. project was one of the first microcomputers, and one of several that Kay would eventually develop. In 1968 Kay was in the audience when Douglas Engelbart stunned the computer science world with a futuristic demonstration of interactive computing. Inspired by Engelbart's demonstration, Kay led a team of researchers at Xerox PARC (Palo Alto Research Center in California) in building the computer of the future—a computer that put the user in charge.

Working on a back-room computer called the Alto, Kay developed a bit-mapped screen display with icons and overlapping windows—the kind of display that became standard two decades later. Kay also championed the idea of a friendly user interface. To test user friendliness, Kay frequently brought children into the lab, "because they have no strong motivation for patience." With feedback from children, Kay developed the first painting program and Smalltalk, the groundbreaking object-oriented programming language.

Alan Kay

In essence, Kay's team developed the first personal computer—a single-user desktop machine designed for interactive use. But Kay, who coined the term "personal computer," didn't see the Alto as one. In his mind a true personal computer could go everywhere with its owner, serving as a calculator, a calendar, a word processor, a graphics machine, a communication device, and a reference tool. Kay's vision of what he called the Dynabook is only now, three decades later, appearing on the horizon.

Xerox failed to turn the Alto into a commercial success. But when he visited PARC, Apple's Steve Jobs (see Chapter 3) was inspired by what he saw. Under Jobs a team of engineers and programmers built on the Xerox ideas, added many of their own, and developed the Macintosh—the first inexpensive computer to incorporate many of Kay's far-reaching ideas. Kay became a research fellow at Apple, where he called the Macintosh "the first personal computer good enough to criticize." Today virtually all PCs have user interfaces based on Kay's groundbreaking work.

Alan Kay's Dynabook was the early prototype for the modern personal computer.

Today Kay works as a research fellow for Disney, where he applies his vision to emerging technologies in communication, entertainment, and education. Kay continues his crusade for users, especially small users. He says, as with pencil and paper, "it's not a medium if children can't use it." In a recent collaborative research project, Kay and MIT researchers worked with school children to design artificial life forms in artificial environments inside the computer. Like many of Kay's research projects, the Vivarium project had little relationship to today's computer market. This kind of blue-sky research doesn't always lead to products or profits. But for Alan Kay it's the way to invent the future.

The future is being invented every day by people like Alan Kay—people who can see today the technology that will be central to tomorrow's society. We're racing into a future shaped by information technology. In this chapter we examine the impact of information technology on today's workplace. Then, using current research as a springboard, we'll imagine how information technology might evolve and how that technology might affect our future.

Into the Information Age

> It is the business of the future to be **dangerous**... The **major advances in civilization** are processes that all but **wreck** the **societies** in which they occur.
> —Alfred North Whitehead

Every so often civilization dramatically changes course. Events and ideas come together to transform radically the way people live, work, and think. Traditions go by the wayside, common sense is turned upside down, and lives are thrown into turmoil until a new order takes hold. Humankind experiences a *paradigm shift*—a change in thinking that results in a new way of seeing the world. Major paradigm shifts take generations because individuals have trouble changing their assumptions about the way the world works.

Before the 20th century, humanity experienced two major paradigm shifts directly related to the world of work: the agricultural revolution and the industrial revolution. During the *agricultural revolution*, which took place over several centuries about 10,000 years ago, people learned to domesticate animals, grow their own grains, and use plows and other agricultural tools. The result was a society in which most people lived and worked on farms, exchanging goods and services in nearby towns. During the *industrial revolution*, which happened about a century ago, people gradually moved from the farm to the factory.

Twentieth-century information technology produced what's been called a second industrial revolution as people turned from factory work to information-related work. In today's *information economy* clerical workers outnumber factory workers, and most people earn their living working with words, numbers, and ideas. Instead of planting corn or making shoes, most of us shuffle bits in one form or another. As we roar through the information age, we're riding a wave of social change that rivals any that came before.

Technology was central to each of these transformations. The agricultural economy grew from the plow, the industrial revolution was sparked by

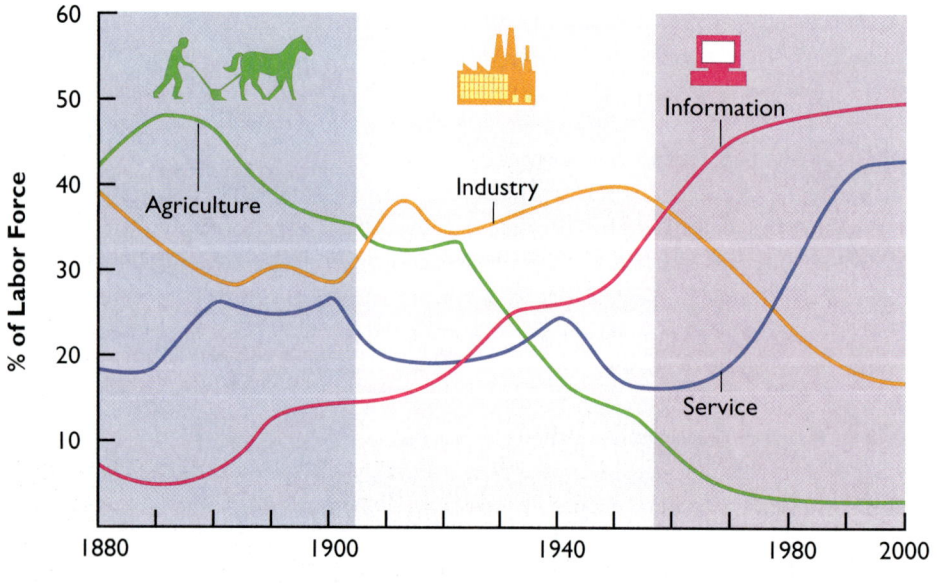

In a single century, the workforce moved from the farm, to the factory, and then to the office.

machines, and the information age is so dependent on computers that it's often called the computer age.

Countless words have been written about the effects of computer technology on our work, our schools, our home life, and our society. Many writers focus on emerging technologies and the new possibilities they offer: possibilities for improved communication, personal expression, information access, and productivity. Others focus on computer technology as a source of suffering, oppression, and alienation. Both utopian and anti-utopian visions are based on speculation about the future. Researchers who study the current impact of computer technology report that the truth, so far, lies between these two extremes.

Where Computers Work

> Businessmen **go down** with their businesses because they like the **old way** so well they cannot **bring themselves to change.**
> —Henry Ford

It's becoming harder all the time to find jobs that haven't been changed in some way by computers. To get a perspective on how computers affect the way we work, we consider the three computerized workplaces that have attracted the most attention: the automated factory, the automated office, and the electronic cottage.

The Automated Factory

Today's **automated factories** bear little resemblance to the factories that spearheaded the industrial revolution. Computers help track inventory, time the delivery of parts, control the quality of the production, monitor wear and tear on machines, and schedule maintenance. Engineers use **CAD** (computer-aided design) and **CAM** (computer-aided manufacturing) technologies to design new products and the machines that build those products. In most automated factories robots work alongside humans, but in some state-of-the-art factories the only function of human workers is to monitor and repair robots.

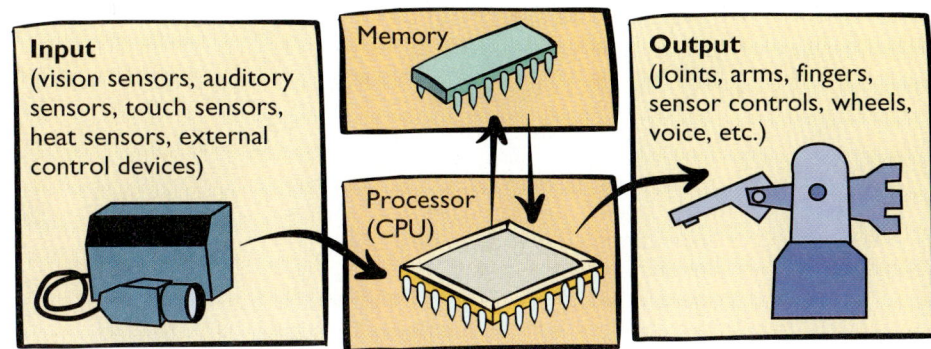

A robot is, in effect, a computer with exotic peripherals.

As exotic as they might seem, robots are similar to other kinds of computer technology people use every day. While a typical computer performs mental tasks, a **robot** is a computer-controlled machine designed to perform specific manual tasks. The most important hardware differences between robots and other computers are the input and output peripherals. Instead of sending output to a screen or a printer, a robot sends commands to joints, arms, and other moving parts. Most modern robots include some kind of input sensors that allow them to correct or modify their actions based on feedback from the outside world.

Today's robots are constrained by the limitations of artificial intelligence software. The most sophisticated robot today can't tie a pair of shoelaces, understand the vocabulary of a three-year-old child, or consistently tell the difference between a cat and a dog. From a management point of view robots offer several advantages: They can save money, improve quality, increase productivity, and tackle jobs that wouldn't be safe or practical for humans. Today hundreds of thousands of industrial robots do welding, part fitting, painting, and other repetitive tasks in factories all over the world.

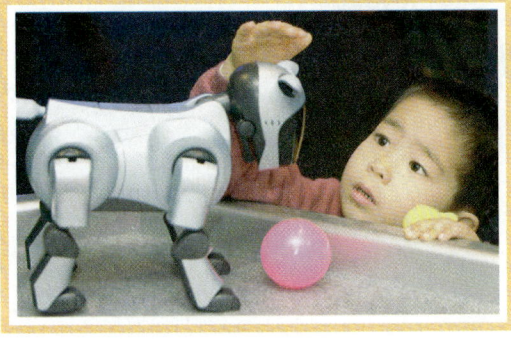

Mobile robots are practical for a variety of jobs, including defusing a bomb (upper left). The walking robot (center left) and the Japanese piano-playing robot (lower right) aren't as practical, but they vividly demonstrate that today's technology can produce machines with great flexibility and dexterity. Sony's Aibo (lower left) is a commercially available programmable electronic pet that develops its own personality depending on how its owner plays with it.

How It Works

10.1 Information Flow in a Management Information System

A retail chain processes a tremendous amount of data daily. Depending on how it is handled, this information can be either overwhelming or enlightening. To make the best use of the information, many chains use management information systems to aid in decision-making. This example follows the many paths of information through the Frostbyte Outdoor Outfitters Corporation.

When a new shipment arrives, a clerk records it using a terminal; inventory and accounting files are updated automatically.

Top-level managers use reports that summarize long-term trends to analyze overall business strategies.

The MIS uses a variety of inputs to produce reports for managers at all levels.

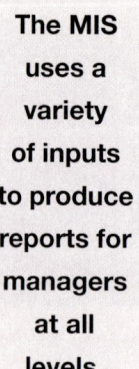
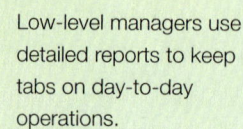

Midlevel managers use summary and exception reports to spot trends and unusual circumstances.

When a clerk punches a sale into the terminal, a database records changes in financial and inventory files.

Low-level managers use detailed reports to keep tabs on day-to-day operations.

Chapter 10 Information Age Issues

How It Works

On-demand reports integrate information and show relationships. Example: impact of cold weather on ski sales.

Sales Volume vs. Average Temperature as of 6/30/02

	Jan.	Feb.	Mar.	Apr.	May	June
Sales Volume	1798	1700	1609	1532	1302	1216
Sales	$24,398	$24,673	$22,468	$21,003	$18,068	$16,328
Average Temperature	24	32	41	48	58	71

Year-End Sales by Item: Top 20 as of 12/31/02

ITEM	SOLD UNITS	RETURNED UNITS	TOTAL UNITS	TOTAL SALES
Beaver Kayaks	58	3	55	$12,375
Possum Packs	1240	212	1028	$20,046
Possum Parkas	1003	323	680	$17,000
Rhinoceros Hiking Boots	1162	429	733	$47,645
Snoreswell Sleeping Bags	923	62	861	$39,175

Summary reports show departmental totals or trends. Example: most popular footwear.

Items Temporarily Out of Stock as of 12/31/02

ITEM	OUT SINCE	DATE AVAILABLE
Fancy Flashlights	12/31/99	1/4/00
Foxy Flannels	12/31/99	1/2/00
Snappy Tents	12/02/99	1/2/00

Exception reports reflect unusual relationships. Example: out-of-stock gear.

Daily Sales Register by Type: 7/31/02

ITEM	UNITS	SALES
Parkas	62	$1209
Flashlights	154	$1540
Tents	2	$500
Hiking Boots	78	$65

Detail reports give complete, detailed information on routine operations. Example: daily orders.

The Automated Office

Modern offices, like modern factories, have been transformed by computers. Many **automated offices** have evolved along with their computers. In the age of networks the challenge for a company's *chief information officer (CIO)* and *chief technology officer (CTO)*—the chief decision-makers concerning enterprise computer systems and technology—is to integrate all kinds of computers, from mainframes to PCs, into a single, seamless system. This approach, often called *distributed computing* (or *enterprise computing*), allows PCs, workstations, minicomputers, and mainframes to coexist peacefully and complement each other. Many organizations have added *thin clients*—*network computers*, *Internet appliances*, and similar devices—to the mix. These low-cost, low-maintenance machines allow workers to access critical network information without the overhead of a PC or workstation.

Groupware is software that allows groups of users to share calendars, send messages, access data, and work on documents simultaneously. Many groupware applications focus on the concept of *workflow*—the path of information as it flows through a workgroup. With groupware and telecommunication, workgroups don't need to be in the same room, or even the same time zone. Most groupware applications take advantage of HTML, XML, and other Internet technologies, making it easier for organizations to create workgroup-oriented intranets.

Modern managers use **management information systems (MIS)** to help them with planning, organizing, staffing, directing, and controlling their organizations. The term *management information system* (which is often shortened to simply *information system*) is commonly defined as a computerized system that includes procedures for collecting data, a database for storing data, and software tools for analyzing data and producing a variety of reports for different levels of management.

Several other types of software systems are available to help managers make decisions. **Decision support systems** provide mathematical models of business systems to aid managers in decision-making. **Project management software** helps coordinate, schedule, and track complex work projects. Expert systems, which use artificial intelligence techniques to simulate experts, can provide expert advice in limited areas.

The Electronic Cottage

Before the industrial revolution most people worked in or near their homes. Today's telecommunications technology opens up new possibilities for modern workers to return home for their livelihood. For hundreds of thousands of writers, programmers, accountants, data-entry clerks, and other information workers, **telecommuting** by modem replaces hours of commuting by car in rush hour traffic.

Novelist Richie Swanson, winner of the Peace Writing award, works at home in his boat house.

Futurist Alvin Toffler popularized the term **electronic cottage** to describe a home where technology allows a person to work at home. Toffler and others predict that the number of telecommuters will skyrocket in the coming decades. Telecommuting makes sense—it's easier to move information than people. Telecommuting can save energy, reduce pollution, reduce congestion, save time, allow for more flexible schedules, and increase worker productivity.

Of course, telecommuting isn't for everybody. Jobs that require constant interaction with coworkers, customers, or clients aren't conducive to telecommuting. Working at home requires self-discipline. Most telecommuters report that the ideal work situation involves commuting to the office 1 or 2 days each week and working at home on the others.

And even workers who don't telecommute are finding all kinds of innovative ways to put computers to work—and play—in their homes.

> My father had worked for the same firm for 12 years. **They fired him**. They replaced him with a **tiny gadget** this big that does everything that my father does only it **does it much better**. The **depressing thing** is my mother ran out and bought one.
> —Woody Allen

Computers and Jobs

When we think about automated factories, computer-supported cooperative work, management information systems, and electronic cottages, it's easy to imagine utopian visions of computers in the workplace of tomorrow. But the real world isn't always picture perfect, and many workers today are experiencing computers in less positive ways. Workers complain of job elimination, stress, depersonalization, fatigue, boredom, overwork, and a variety of health problems attributed to computers.

Computer Monitoring

One particularly controversial aspect of office automation is **computer monitoring**—using computer technology to track, record, and evaluate worker performance, often without the knowledge of the worker. Monitoring systems can provide a manager with instant, onscreen reports showing the number of keystrokes for each clerk, the length of each phone call placed by an employee, details of Web wanderings, and the total amount of idle time for each computer. Some network software even allows a manager to view a copy of any worker's screen secretly at any time.

Privacy issues aside, computer monitoring can have a powerful negative impact on morale. Because employees can't tell when they're being monitored, many workers experience a great deal of stress and anxiety. The boss can be seen as an invisible eavesdropper rather than as a team leader. Monitored workers tend to assume that "if it's not being counted, it doesn't count." The result of this assumption is that quantity may become more important than quality. Millions of workers are monitored by computer, including factory workers, telephone operators, truck drivers, and, in some cases, managers. According to one study, more than one-fourth of American clerical workers are monitored by computer.

Employment and Unemployment

Three decades ago when Woody Allen joked about a gadget replacing his father, automation was generating a great deal of public controversy. Job automation may not be a hot topic in comedy clubs today, but it's still an important issue for millions of workers whose jobs are threatened by machines.

Today's automobile factories are highly automated.

Automation has threatened workers since the earliest days of the industrial revolution. In the early 19th century an English labor group called the **Luddites** smashed new textile machinery; they feared that the machines would take jobs away from skilled craftsmen. The Luddites and similar groups in other parts of Europe failed to stop the wheels of automation. Modern workers have been no more successful than their 19th-century counterparts in keeping computers and robots out of the workplace. Every year brings new technological breakthroughs that allow robots and computers to do jobs formerly reserved for humans.

Of course, computer technology creates new jobs, too. But many displaced workers don't have the education or skills to program computers, design robots, install networks, or even read printouts. Those workers are often forced to take low-tech, low-paying service jobs as cashiers or custodians, if they can find jobs at all. Technology may be helping to create an unbalanced society with two classes: a growing mass of poor uneducated people and a shrinking class of affluent educated people.

Cautiously Optimistic Forecasts

Nobody knows for sure how computer technology will affect employment in the coming decades. A number of studies suggest that, at least for the next few years, technology will stimulate economic growth. This growth will produce new jobs, but it will also bring long, painful periods of adjustment for many workers. Demand for factory workers, clerical workers, and other semiskilled and unskilled laborers will drop dramatically as their jobs are automated or moved to Third World countries where wages are low. At the same time the demand for professionals—especially engineers and teachers—will rise sharply.

According to detailed computer models constructed at the Institute for Economic Analysis at New York University, there will be plenty of jobs in the early 21st century. The question is whether we'll have enough skilled workers to fill those jobs. In other words, economic growth will depend on whether we have a suitably trained workforce. The single most important key to a positive economic future, according to this study, is education.

Will We Need a New Economy?

In the long run, education may not be enough. It seems likely that, at some time in the future, machines will be able to do most of the jobs people do today. We may face a future of *jobless growth*—a time when productivity increases not because of the work people do but because of the work of machines. If productivity isn't tied to employment, we'll have to ask some hard questions about our political, economic, and social system:

- Do governments have an obligation to provide permanent public assistance to the chronically unemployed?
- Should large companies be required to give several months' notice to workers whose jobs are being eliminated? Should they be required to retrain workers for other jobs?
- Should large companies be required to file "employment impact statements" before replacing people with machines in the same way they're required to file environmental impact statements before implementing policies that might harm the environment?
- If robots and computers are producing most of society's goods and services, should all of the profits from those goods go to a few people who own the machines?
- If a worker is replaced by a robot, should the worker receive a share of the robot's "earnings" through stocks or profit sharing?
- The average work week 150 years ago was 70 hours; for the last 50 years it has been steady at about 40. Should governments and businesses encourage job-sharing and other systems that allow for less-than-40-hour jobs?
- What will people do with their time if machines do most of the work? What new leisure activities should be made available?
- How will people define their identities if work becomes less central to their lives?

These questions force us to confront deep-seated cultural beliefs and economic traditions, and they don't come with easy answers. They suggest that we may be heading into a difficult period when many old rules don't apply anymore. But if we're successful at navigating the troubled waters of transition, we may find that automation fulfills the dream expressed by Aristotle more than 2,000 years ago:

If every instrument could accomplish its own work, obeying or anticipating the will of others . . . if the shuttle could weave, and the pick touch the lyre, without a hand to guide them, chief workmen would not need servants, nor masters slaves.

Tomorrow Never Knows

> **Everything** that can be invented has been invented.
> —Charles H. Duell, director of the U.S. Patent Office, 1899

> **Who the hell** wants to hear actors talk?
> —Harry M. Warner, Warner Bros. Pictures, 1927

> There is **no likelihood** man can ever tap the power of the atom.
> —Robert Millikan, winner of the Nobel Prize in Physics, 1923

There is no denying the importance of the future. In the words of scientist Charles F. Kettering, "We should be concerned about the future because we will have to spend the rest of our lives there." However, important or not, the future isn't easy to see. History is full of stories of people who couldn't imagine the impact of new technology. Who could have predicted in 1950 the profound effects, both positive and negative, television would have on our world?

From Research to Reality: 21st-Century Information Technology

> You can count **how many seeds** are in the apple, but not **how many apples** are in the seed.
> —Ken Kesey, author of *One Flew over the Cuckoo's Nest*

According to Alan Kay, there are four ways to predict the future. The best way is to invent the future, but it's not the only way.

Another way to predict the future is to take advantage of the fact that it generally takes 10 years to go from a new idea in the research laboratory to a commercial product. In today's highly competitive high-tech industry, many companies are able to shave some years off the research-to-product interval. In any case, today's research can give us an idea of the kinds of products we will be using in a few years. Of course, many researchers work behind carefully guarded doors, and research often takes surprising turns.

A third way is to look at products from the past and see what made them succeed. According to Kay, "There are certain things about human beings that if you remove, they wouldn't be human any more. For instance, we have to communicate with others or we're not humans. So every time someone has come up with a communications amplifier, it has succeeded the previous technology." The pen, the printing press, the telephone, the television, the personal computer, and the Internet are all successful communication amplifiers. What's next?

Finally, Kay says, we can predict the future by recognizing the four phases of any technology or media business: hardware, software, service, and way of life. These phases apply to radio, television, video, audio, and all kinds of computers.

- *Hardware.* Inventors and engineers start the process by developing new hardware. But whether it's a television set, a personal computer, or a global communication network, the hardware is of little use without software.
- *Software.* The next step is software development. Television programs, audio recordings, video games, databases, and Web pages are examples of software that give value to hardware products.
- *Service.* Once the hardware and software exist, the focus turns to service. Innovative hardware and clever software aren't likely to take hold unless they serve human needs in some way. The personal computer industry is now in the service phase, and the companies that focus on serving their customers are generally the most successful.
- *Way of life.* The final phase happens when the technology becomes so entrenched that people don't think about it any more; they only notice if it isn't there. We seldom think of pencils as technological tools. They're part of our way of life, so much so that we'd have trouble getting along without them. Similarly, the electric motor, which was once a major technological breakthrough, is now all but invisible; we use dozens of motors every day without thinking about them. Computers are clearly headed in that direction.

The 1930 movie Just Imagine *presented a bold, if not quite accurate, vision of the future; here Maureen O'Sullivan sits in her personal flying machine.*

Kay's four ways of predicting the future don't provide a foolproof crystal ball, but they can serve as a framework for thinking about tomorrow's technology. In the next section we turn our attention to research labs, where tomorrow's technology is being invented today. We examine trends and innovations that will shape future computer hardware and software. Then we look at how this technology will serve users as it eventually disappears into our way of life.

Tomorrow's Hardware: Trends and Innovations

> The only thing that has consistently grown faster than hardware in the last 40 years is **human expectation**.
> —Bjarne Stroustrup, AT&T Bell Labs, designer of the C++ programming language

The rapid evolution of computer hardware over the last few decades is nothing short of extraordinary. The relay-based Mark I computer (discussed in Chapter 1) could do only a few calculations each second. Today's personal computers are more than a million times faster! Computer speed today typically is measured in **MIPS (millions of instructions per second)**, where an instruction is the most primitive operation performed by the processor—moving a number to a memory location, comparing two numbers, and the like. The fastest machines can process more than a *billion* instructions per second! Most experts expect the computer *price-to-performance ratio* (the level of performance per unit cost) to double every year or two for several more years.

Technological advances emerging from laboratories will accelerate current trends and push computer technology in entirely new directions. Here are just a few examples:

- *Alternative chip technologies.* Many research labs are experimenting with alternatives to today's silicon chips. For example, IBM researchers have developed plastic chips that are more durable and energy efficient than silicon chips. Chip makers Intel, Motorola, and AMD are working with the U.S. government in a Virtual National Laboratory (VNL) to develop new laser etching technology called extreme ultraviolet lithography (EUVL) that could reduce chip size and increase performance radically. Other researchers are working on more radical research technologies. Superconductors that transmit electricity without heat could increase computer speed a hundredfold. Unfortunately, superconductor technology generally requires a super-cooled environment, which isn't practical for most applications. A more realistic alternative is the **optical computer**, which transmits information in light waves rather than electrical pulses. Optical computers outside research labs are currently limited to a few narrow applications such as robot vision. But when the technology is refined, general-purpose optical computers may process information hundreds of times faster than silicon computers.

- *Alternative storage technologies.* Smaller disks that hold more—the trend will continue, producing hard disks that can store astronomical quantities of data. But solid state storage breakthroughs will threaten the dominance of disks in a few years. For example, Cambridge University researchers funded by Hitachi have developed a "single-electron" memory chip the size of a thumbnail that can store all the sounds and images of a full-length feature film. This experimental chip consumes very little power and retains memory for up to 10 years when the power is switched off.

- *Alternative architectures.* Some of the most revolutionary work in computer design involves not what's inside the processors, but how they're put together. One example is IBM's Blue Gene, a supercomputer being developed to help scientists crack the secrets of proteins in the human body. Blue Gene will have 1 million small, simple processors, each capable of handling 8 threads of instructions simultaneously. The processors won't have power-hungry embedded caches, but they will have built-in memory to improve speed. The network of processors will be self-healing—it will detect failed components, seal them off, and direct work elsewhere. If it works as planned, Blue Gene will be the first "petaflop" computer, capable of handling 1 quadrillion (1,000,000,000,000,000) instructions per second—2 million times more than today's PC!

- *Alternative output displays.* The CRT's days are numbered. Flat-panel screens are commonplace today. Soon we'll be using ultra-high-resolution displays that are thin enough to hang on walls like pictures and efficient enough to run on batteries for days. Goggle displays—the visual equivalent to headphones—will be common for portable PC users who want to shut the rest of the world out. Those who need to see what's going on around them *and* inside their computer can wear eyeglasses with built-in transparent heads-up displays. Researchers at MIT's Media Lab, Xerox PARC, and elsewhere are working on pages made of **electronic (digital) paper** that can be read like printed pages, erased, and reused. Electronic paper is likely to find applications

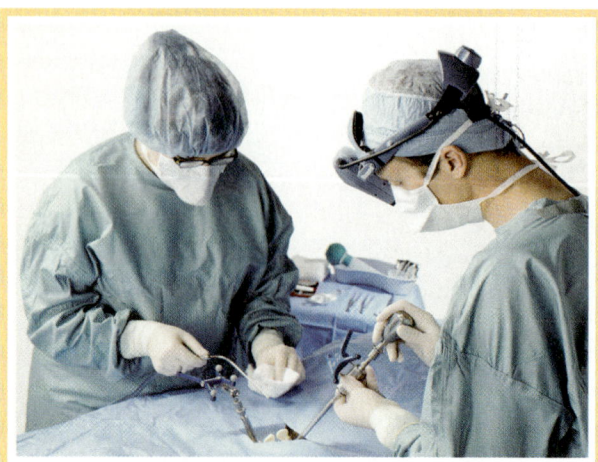

This surgeon's retinal scanner display makes video images and the patient's vital signs continually visible throughout the surgical procedure.

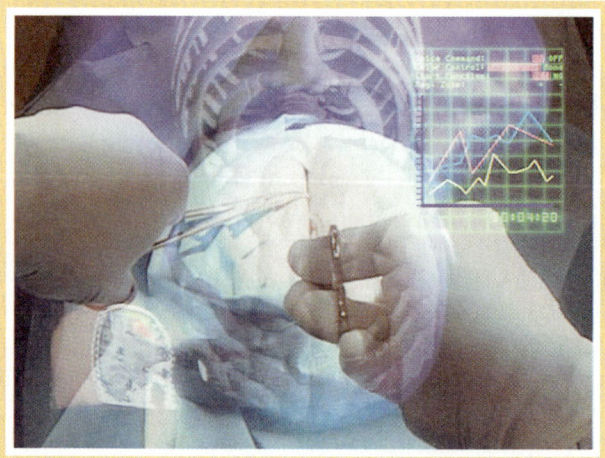

in newspapers that automatically update, magazines that display animated images, textbooks that can be revised rather than replaced, and wall-sized folding digital displays.

- *Alternative input devices: sensors*. Technology forecaster Paul Saffo predicts that the next major breakthroughs will occur as researchers develop—and companies market—inexpensive **sensors** that allow digital devices to monitor the analog world. Temperature sensors, optical sensors, motion sensors, and other types of sensors already make it possible for computers to track a variety of real-world activities and conditions. But as these technologies mature, more sophisticated devices will serve as eyes, ears, and other types of sense organs for computer networks.

This page of electronic paper is being reloaded with a fresh image.

Tomorrow's Software: Evolving Applications and Interfaces

> Our goal was **bug-free**. The new goal is **resiliency**.
> It is much more important to recover from exceptions than to avoid them.
> —Bob Frankston, co-inventor of the spreadsheet program, in *Beyond Calculation*

In computer research, software continues to be the hardest part. Computer scientists are currently working on several programming technologies that make it easier to create more reliable software faster.

These include:

- *Visual programming environments* that allow programmers to do much of the tedious work of program development by filling in dialog boxes and working with icons and menus,
- *Object-oriented programming languages* that allow programs to be constructed from software objects that include data and instructions, and
- *Component software technologies* that allow programmers to use and reuse interchangeable components in different programs.

However, computer scientists aren't even close to developing tools that will allow programmers to produce error-free software quickly.

Still, software technology is advancing rapidly, especially when viewed through the eyes of the user. Twenty years ago the typical computer could be operated only by a highly trained professional, and using a computer was pretty much synonymous with programming a computer; today computers are so easy to use that they're sold at shopping malls and operated by preschoolers.

The graphical user interface pioneered by Xerox and popularized by Apple and Microsoft has become an industry standard, making it possible for users to move back and forth between computer types almost as easily as drivers can adjust to different brands of cars. (Imagine what would happen if Ford or GM moved the brake pedal to the opposite side of the accelerator in next year's models.) But experts expect user interfaces to continue to evolve for a while before they settle down into the kind of long-lasting standard we're used to in automobiles. Today's **WIMP** (windows, icons, menus, and pointing devices) interface is easier to learn and use than earlier character-based interfaces, but it's not the end of the user interface evolution. Researcher Raj Reddy uses another acronym to describe emerging user interface technologies: **SILK**, for speech, image, language, and knowledge capabilities. SILK incorporates many important software technologies:

- *Speech and language.* While we still don't have a language-translating telephone or a foolproof dictation-taking "talkwriter," speech technology is rapidly maturing into a practical alternative to keyboard and mouse input. **Voice recognition** systems are used for security systems, automated voicemail systems, hands-free Web navigation, and other applications. New applications are being developed and marketed every day. With or without speech, **natural-language processing** of English-like commands will be part of future user interfaces. Researchers expect that we'll soon be using programs that read documents as we create them, edit them according to our instructions, and file them based on their content.

- *Image.* In the last decade computer graphics have become an integral part of the computing experience. Tomorrow's graphics won't just be still, flat images; they'll include three-dimensional models, animation, and video clips. Today's two-dimensional desktop interfaces will give way to three-dimensional workspace metaphors complete with 3-D animated objects—virtual workspaces unlike anything we use today. **Virtual reality (VR)** user interfaces will create the illusion that the user is immersed in a world inside the computer—an environment that contains both scenes and the controls to change those scenes.

In Argonne's CAVE (left), a scientist can interactively study the relationships between the nucleic acids of the molecule. In a similar CAVE (right) at the Center for Supercomputer Applications at the University of Illinois, graduate student Paul Rajlich plays CAVE Quake II, a 3-D video game he created using VR technology.

- *Knowledge.* Many experts predict that knowledge will be the most important enhancement to the user interface of the future. Advances in the technology of knowledge—that elusive quality discussed in Chapter 13—will allow engineers to design *self-maintaining systems*—systems that can diagnose and correct common problems without human intervention. Advances in knowledge will make user interfaces more friendly and forgiving. Intelligent applications will be able to decipher many ambiguous commands and correct common errors as they happen. But more importantly, knowledge will allow software agents to really be of service to users.

Tomorrow's Service: Truly Intelligent Agents

> I don't want to sit and move stuff around on my screen all day and look at figures and have it recognize my **gestures** and listen to my **voice**.
> I want to tell it what to do and then go away; I don't want to babysit this computer.
> I want it to act **for me, not with me**.
> —Esther Dyson, computer industry analyst and publisher

At Xerox PARC Alan Kay and his colleagues developed the first user interface based on icons—images that represent tools to be manipulated by users. Their pioneering work helped turn the computer into a productivity tool for millions of people. Today Alan Kay claims future user interfaces will be based on agents rather than tools.

Agents are software programs designed to be managed rather than manipulated. An intelligent software agent can ask questions as well as respond to commands, pay attention to its user's work patterns, serve as a guide and a coach, take on its owner's goals, and use reasoning to fabricate goals of its own.

Many PC applications include *wizards* and other agent-like software entities to guide users through complex tasks and answer questions when problems arise. The Internet is home to a rapidly growing population of *bots*—software robots that crawl around the Web collecting information, helping consumers make decisions, answering email, and even playing games. But today's wizards, bots, and agents aren't smart enough to manage the many details that a human assistant might juggle. In time, agents may teach us new applications, act as personal messengers, manage our appointments and keep track of our communications, defend our systems from viruses and intruders, and protect our privacy.

Agents are often portrayed with human characteristics; *2001*'s Hal and the computers on TV's *Star Trek* are famous examples. Of course, agents don't need to look or sound human—they just need to possess considerable knowledge and intelligence.

Future agents may possess a degree of sensitivity, too. Researchers at MIT and IBM are developing *affective computers* that can detect the emotional states of their users and respond accordingly. Affective computers use sensors to determine a person's emotional state. Sensors range from simple audiovisual devices to mouse-embedded sensors that work like lie detectors, monitoring pulse or skin resistance. Early research has shown limited success at identifying emotions, but the machines still have much to learn. They can't for example, tell the difference between love and hate, because, from a physiological point of view, they look pretty much the same!

Tomorrow's Way of Life: Transparent Technology

> In the first computing revolution, the ratio of people to computers was **N-to-1**.
> In the second revolution, personal computers insisted the ratio be **1-to-1— one person, one computer**. In the third revolution, we are exploring the impact of having **computers everywhere**, many per person, **1-to-N**.
> —Bob Metcalfe, inventor of Ethernet and founder of 3Com

Since Alan Kay coined the term *personal computer* at Xerox PARC, hundreds of millions of personal computers have been sold. Ironically, many researchers at PARC today think that it's time to move beyond the personal computer because it commands too much of our attention. The goal of these researchers is to make computers disappear so people can use them without thinking about them.

Embedded Intelligence

Computers are already making their way into inconspicuous corners of our lives. Dozens of household appliances and tools have built-in computers. Even our cars are processing megabytes of information as we drive them down the road. Along with the trend toward accessing centrally stored information through networks, we're experiencing another trend: embedding intelligence in the machines that surround us.

There's no end to the possibilities for embedded intelligence. Several companies have introduced dashboard PCs that can function as car stereos, play CD-ROMs, recognize limited spoken commands, alert drivers to incoming email messages, read those messages aloud, store and retrieve contacts and appointments, dial telephone numbers, and recite turn-by-turn directions using GPS-based navigation systems. Some automobile-based PCs include GPS-based security systems that track the vehicle in the event of theft or other emergency.

In Japan computer technology has even found its way into the bathroom. A number of Japanese fixture manufacturers sell smart toilets—computer-controlled, paperless toilets. The newest models automatically collect and store information on blood pressure, pulse, temperature, urine, and weight. The information can be displayed on a LCD display, accumulated for months, and even transmitted by modem to a medical service. Users of these smart toilets get a mini-checkup whenever they visit the bathroom. Body-monitoring features give the toilet an entirely new function—a function that will undoubtedly save lives.

Ubiquitous Computers

When computers show up in our toilets, we're clearly entering an era of *ubiquitous computers*—computers everywhere. For several years researchers at Xerox PARC, Cambridge University, Olivetti, and elsewhere have been experimenting with technology that will make computers even more ubiquitous.

The best known computer in their futuristic office is the *active badge*—a clip-on computerized ID badge that continually reports its location to record-keeping databases and to others in the organization. But ubiquitous computing won't be limited to offices. PARC's Mark Weiser describes an experimental office equipped with intelligent devices: "Doors open only to the right badge wearer, rooms greet people by name, telephone calls can be automatically forwarded to wherever the recipient may be, receptionists actually know where people are, computer terminals retrieve the preferences of whoever is sitting at them, and appointment diaries write themselves."

From Internet to Omninet

Connectivity is a critical part of ubiquitous computing. When computers are embedded in everything, they need to be able to talk to each other—and to us. By connecting embedded

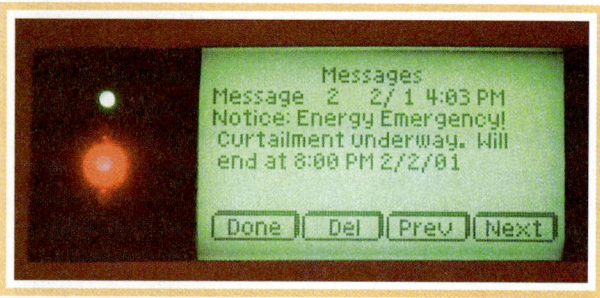

This thermostat, which can control such household items as air conditioning, heating, lights, and appliances, can be monitored and controlled via the Internet.

computers to the Net, we give them voices and ears. All of these smart, connected devices will certainly change the Internet. As more machines become connected, the Net will evolve from today's loose digital fishnet into a tightly woven, seamless fabric that surrounds us. In the words of Leonard Kleinrock, the UCLA computer scientist who set up the first ARPANET node three decades ago, "Tech will be everywhere, always there, always on, just the way electricity is there for you." Human communication will be a tiny fraction of the traffic on the Net—the great majority will be machines communicating with other machines on behalf of humans. MIT AI lab director Rodney Brooks says, "It won't be that you go onto the Internet—the network will come to you." Brooks is part of MIT's Oxygen, a research project that attempts to make computing as plentiful and ubiquitous as the air we breathe.

Ubiquitous computers offer convenience and efficiency beyond anything that's come before. They also raise issues of privacy, intimacy, and independence. These issues will grow in importance as we move further into the information age. But they may seem insignificant when compared with the questions we'll face when the streams of information technology and biotechnology converge in the future.

The Day after Tomorrow: Information Technology Meets Biology

> Our future is technological; but it will not be a world of **gray steel**. Rather our technological future is headed toward a **neo-biological civilization**.
> —Kevin Kelly, in *Out of Control*

The information age won't last forever. Analysts Stan Davis and Bill Davidson predict in their book *2020 Vision* that a bio-economy will replace the information economy sometime around the year 2020. Whether or not they're right, biotechnology and microtechnology will become more intertwined with computer technology in the coming decades.

Borrowing from Biology

Ubiquitous computing will require new ways of thinking about, and developing, hardware and software. At the University of California, researchers on a project called Endeavor attempt to chart our course into the digital ocean of the future. According to Professor Randy Katz, the lead investigator of Endeavor, "The supercomplex system of the future has to be able to organize itself so it can be more robust in its behavior, deal with failure, and then pick up the pieces and move on." In other words, the network of the future will be more like a biological system. Neural nets, described in Chapter 13, allow individual computers to learn from experience because their design is inspired by biological nervous systems. Many researchers are experimenting with **genetic algorithms**—algorithms that evolve through many generations, creating survival-of-the-fittest programs. Paul Saffo, director of the Institute for the Future, suggests a biological imperative, too: "The network of today is engineered, and the network of 2050 is grown."

These tiny mirrors can rotate up and down to switch data in an optical network. More than 500 mirrors are fabricated on less than a square inch of silicon.

Microtechnology

The incredible miniaturization achieved in the computer industry is allowing researchers to use **microtechnology** to develop micromachines—machines on the scale of a millionth of a meter. Microscopic moving parts are etched in silicon using a process similar to that of manufacturing computer chips. Major universities, corporations (including IBM and AT&T), government labs (including Sandia Labs), and small start-up companies are doing research in what are sometimes called microelectromechanical systems (MEMS). For example, engineers at the University of California at Berkeley have built a motor twice as wide as a human hair that runs on static electricity. Japanese researchers have constructed a microcar not much bigger than a grain of rice.

So far most applications of microtechnology have been microsensors: tiny devices that can detect pressure, temperature, and other environmental qualities. Microsensors are used in cars, planes, and spacecraft, but they show promise in medicine, too. Researchers at Johns Hopkins University have developed a smart pill that combines a thermometer with a transmitter so it can broadcast temperatures as it travels through a human digestive tract. This pill is a first step toward other pills that might play more active roles inside our bodies. Scientists speculate that tiny machines may someday be able to roam through the body, locating and destroying cancer cells and invading organisms!

Nanotechnology

If microtechnology is carried to its extreme, it becomes **nanotechnology**—the manufacture of machines on a scale of a few billionths of a meter. Nanomachines would have to be constructed atom by atom using processes drawn from particle physics, biophysics, and molecular biology. Researchers at UCLA, Yale, Rice, and other facilities are working on molecular-scale electronics (moletronics) that could eventually produce a breed of computers that performs *billions* of times faster than today's fastest machines. Hewlett Packard's Stanley Williams and others are working on technology that may soon allow wires and switches to chemically assemble themselves at the molecular level, eliminating the need to etch circuits onto chips.

In 2001 IBM researchers built the first computer circuit contained within a single molecule. The circuit was created using carbon nanotubes—tiny cylindrical molecules with semiconductor properties similar to those found in silicon chips. That same year scientists at Bell Labs—the birthplace of the first transistor in 1947—created a transistor from a single molecule. These technological breakthroughs could carry the computing industry past the silicon dead end that's threatening to overturn Moore's Law within a few years. They may be stepping stones on the road to **quantum computers**—computers based on the properties of atoms and their nuclei and the laws of quantum mechanics.

Quantum computers are still decades away. But computers based on microtechnology and nanotechnology may be just a few years in the future. Many researchers think that molecular circuits could be produced at a fraction of the cost of today's complex microprocessors, because they're built through a purely chemical, or "self-assembly," process, similar to growing a crystal. "If we can truly make this kind of technology manufacturable . . . we'll have computing that's cheap enough to throw away," says Yale scientist Mark Reed.

Using another approach, biophysicists are studying natural molecular machines like the protein rotor that spins a bacterium's flagellum tail, hoping to use their findings to create molecular motors. Scientists at MIT are attempting to get E. coli bacteria to respond like circuits. At the same time, geneticists are gradually unlocking the secrets of DNA—biology's self-replicating molecular memory devices. These and other research threads may lead scientists to the breakthrough that will enable them to create atomic assembler devices that can construct nanomachines. Submicron computers, germ-sized robots, self-assembling machines, intelligent clothes, alchemy . . . the possibilities are staggering and the potential risks terrifying.

Artificial Life

For many researchers the ultimate goal is to create **artificial life**—synthetic organisms that act like natural living systems. Some artificial life researchers create simple software organisms that exist only in computer memory; many of these organisms are similar to computer viruses. Other researchers build colonies of tiny insect robots that communicate with each other and respond to changes in their environment. Artificial life researchers grapple with an array of problems, including the question of definition: Where exactly is the line between a clever machine and a living organism?

Advances in artificial intelligence, robotics, genetics, biotechnology, and microtechnology may someday make the line disappear altogether. Computers and robots will undoubtedly continue to take on more functions that have been traditionally reserved for humans. They may even grow and reproduce using carbon-based genetic technology borrowed from human biology. If they become smart enough to build intelligent machines themselves, almost anything is possible.

This speculation raises questions about the relationship between humans and the machines they create. It's important that we think about those questions while the technology is evolving because our answers may help us to determine the course of that evolution.

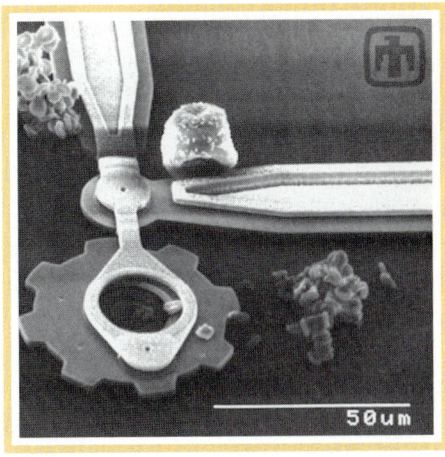

This micromachine isn't much larger than red blood cells (lower right and top left) or a grain of pollen (top right).

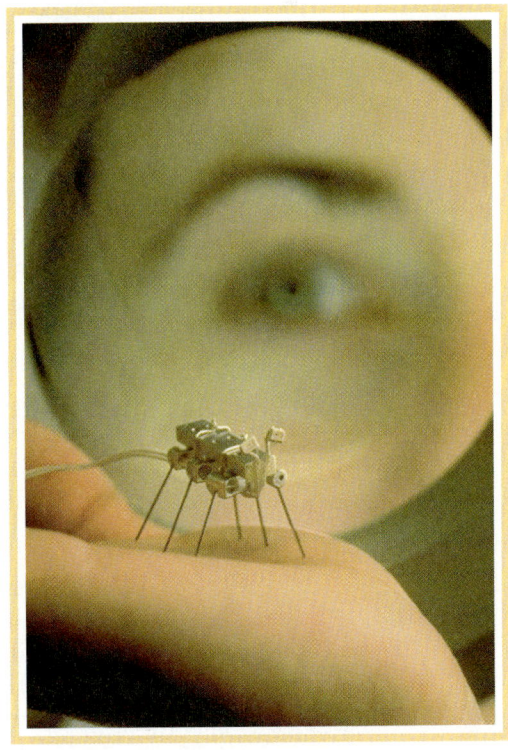

Tiny insect robots like these may be the forerunners of silicon-and-steel artificial life forms.

Human Questions for a Computer Age

> The **important thing** to forecast is not the automobile but the **parking problem**; not the television but the **soap opera**.
> —Isaac Asimov

> It's the **end of the world** as we know it and **I feel fine**.
> —R.E.M.

In earlier chapters we examined many social and ethical issues related to computer technology, including privacy, security, reliability, and intellectual property. These aren't the only critical issues before us. Before closing we'll briefly raise some other important, and as yet unanswered, questions of the information age.

Will Computers Be Democratic?

> The higher the technology, the **higher the freedom**. Technology enforces certain solutions: satellite dishes, computers, videos, international telephone lines force pluralism and freedom onto a society.
> —Lech Walesa

> When machines and computers, profit motives, and property rights are considered **more important than people**, the giant triplets of **racism**, **materialism**, and **militarism** are incapable of being conquered.
> —Martin Luther King, Jr.

In 1990, a spontaneous protest exploded across computer networks in reaction to the threat to privacy posed by Marketplace, a new CD-ROM product containing consumer information on millions of Americans. The firestorm of protest forced Lotus Development Corporation to cancel distribution of the product. In Santa Monica, California, homeless people used public access terminals in the library to lobby successfully for more access to public showers. In France, student organizations used computer networks to rapidly mobilize opposition to tuition increases. In 1999, environmentalists, labor organizations, human rights groups, and a handful of anarchists used the Internet to mobilize massive protests at the World Trade Organization's Seattle meeting. The protests brought many issues surrounding the secretive WTO into the global spotlight for the first time.

Computers are often used to promote the democratic ideals and causes of common people. Many analysts argue that modern computer technology is, by its very nature, a force for equality and democracy. On the other hand, many powerful people and organizations use information technology to increase their wealth and influence.

Will personal computers and the Internet empower ordinary citizens to make better lives for themselves? Or will computer technology produce a society of technocrats and technopeasants? Will computerized polls help elected officials better serve the needs of their constituents? Or will they just give the powerful another tool for staying in power? Will networks revitalize participatory democracy through electronic town meetings? Or will they give tyrants the tools to monitor and control citizens?

Will the Global Village Be a Community?

> Progress in commercial information technologies will improve productivity, bring the world closer together, and **enhance the quality of life**.
> —Stan Davis and Bill Davidson, in *2020 Vision*

> The **real question** before us lies here: do these instruments further **life and its values** or not?
> —Lewis Mumford, 1934

A typical computer today contains components from dozens of countries. The modern corporation uses computer networks for instant communication among offices scattered around the world. Information doesn't stop at international borders as it flows through networks that span the globe. Information technology enables organizations to overcome the age-old barriers of space and time, but questions remain.

In the post–Cold War era, will information technology be used to further peace, harmony, and understanding? Or will the intense competition of the global marketplace simply create new kinds of wars—information wars? Will electronic interconnections provide new opportunities for economically depressed countries? Or will they simply make it easier for information-rich countries to exploit developing nations from a distance? Will information technology be used to promote and preserve diverse communities, cultures, and ecosystems? Or will it undercut traditions, cultures, and roots?

Will We Become Information Slaves?

The information age has redefined our environment; it's almost as if the human species has been transplanted into a different world. Even though the change has happened almost overnight, most of us can't imagine going back to a world without computers. Still, the rapid changes raise questions.

> Our inventions are wont to be **pretty toys** which distract our attention from serious things. They are but improved means to an **unimproved end**.
> —Henry David Thoreau

> **Computers are useless**. They can only give you answers.
> —Pablo Picasso

Can human bodies and minds adapt to the higher stimulation, faster pace, and constant change of the information age? Will our information-heavy environment cause us to lose touch with the more fundamental human needs? Will we become so dependent on our "pretty toys" that we can't get by without them? Will we lose our sense of purpose and identity as our machines become more intelligent? Or will we learn to balance the demands of the technology with our biological and spiritual needs?

Standing on the Shoulders of Giants

When we use computers, we're standing on the shoulders of Charles Babbage, Ada King, Alan Turing, Grace Hopper, Doug Engelbart, Alan Kay, and hundreds of others who invented the future for us. Because of their foresight and effort we can see farther than those who came before us.

> If I have seen farther than other men, it is because **I stood on the shoulders of giants**.
> —Isaac Newton

In Greek mythology Prometheus (whose name means "forethought") stole fire from Zeus and gave it to humanity, along with all arts and civilization. Zeus was furious when he discovered what Prometheus had done. He feared that fire would make mortals think they were as great as the gods and that they would abuse its power. Like fire, the computer is a powerful and malleable tool. It can be used to empower or imprison, to explore or exploit, to create or destroy. We can choose. We've been given the tools. It's up to all of us to invent the future.

Prometheus brings fire from the heavens to humanity.

CrossCurrents

Borg in the Mirror

By Peter Cochrane

Throughout this book we've examined the convergence—the confluence—of information and communication technologies. In October, 1999, Forbes ASAP *published a special issue on* The Great Convergence. *It this article from that issue, Peter Cochrane speculates about the next convergence—the coming together of human and machine. Cochrane suggests that we will need help from implanted devices to survive a future filled with information. Cochrane is the head of research at British Telecommunications and holds the Collier Chair for the Public Understanding of Science & Technology at the University of Bristol. He is the author of* Tips for Time Travelers.

It's easy to imagine a future where information merges onto one global network. In one way or another, the Internet will absorb radio, television, personal computers, telephones, cameras, and so on.

But this is a baby step.

The next real technological advance is a radical symbiosis between humans and machines. The future will be about the creation of networked machinery and digital intelligence to help us deal with a world that's changing faster than our "wet ware" (brains) has evolved to accommodate. And that future demands a subsumption of technology itself into our carbon forms.

Just think of the millions of people with pacemakers, cochlear implants, pain relief modules, and other forms of electronics already embedded in their bodies. Their numbers remind us that we don't just use information technology to communicate, entertain, sell, and trade but to sustain life itself.

Right now, at the frontier of this research are paraplegics with chips implanted in their heads that interpret their brain signals, allowing them to control their computers by thinking—and, in the process, pioneering a new communications channel. Experiments with silicon retinal implants have also been encouraging. Early work on the use of silicon tracks to bypass spinal and other massive nervous system damage is also producing positive results. Waiting in the wings is the artificial pancreas. So is the internal pharmacy: Imagine confidently traveling the world knowing you carry a drugstore inside your own body that is ready to dispense, electronically, the right antibiotic on demand.

On the far horizon is the possibility of using silicon brain implants to enhance our memory and computational skills, and even to enable us to directly interface with machines. Impossible? On the contrary, the idea is about as wild as the crystal set radio of 1914 evolving to become the mobile phone of 1984. I remember suggesting in 1996 that chip implants would eradicate the need for keys, passports, drivers' licenses, identity cards, money, bank accounts, and central medical records. Two years later Professor Kevin Warwick at the University of Reading (in the U.K.) had a chip implanted in his arm to open doors automatically, allowing him access to secure buildings and to be tracked by his secretary. I now hear that diplomats are having similar electronic implants to counteract abduction. Obvious extensions would of course include the tagging of prisoners and criminals.

But medical and security purposes aside, the real reason we will invite computers into our brains is that we increasingly face problems far too complex for the human mind and intellect to solve—even to contemplate.

We need a third intelligence to help us cope with a world of growing complexity that has far outstripped our biological evolution. The future is not about hunting and throwing spears. Nor is it about communicating with a modest number of people about a limited tract of knowledge. We need to assimilate more information and make decisions faster. A century ago a doctor could have read every published discourse on every aspect of medicine. The same was true for chemists, physicists, and engineers. Today a doctor could spend every waking hour reading the research papers on urology alone and still not be fully up to date. What chance for managers and politicians? Not a lot! We know less and less about more and more. Yet business, government, academia, and many other disciplines demand that we know ever more.

To cope and thrive in the future we will need to comprehend more but also see patterns between areas of knowledge—from understanding the ramifications of complex drug interactions to the dynamics of global pollution processes to thinking in 10 dimensions. The key to survival is not to understand certain things in minute detail but to comprehend everything well enough to make wise decisions. We need help.

Just contemplate the cost of some recent decisions that were made on the basis of a very poor understanding of the issues involved: mad cow disease, nuclear power, the contraceptive pill and thrombosis, genetically modified foods. In each case, what's been missing (and critical) has been our ability to understand what was happening and what was about to happen. The consequences of such ignorance are often tragic. If our brains are insufficient and not up to the task, then we have to create a third intelligence to help. And this has to be more than a pocket calculator or a PC—it will require a leap in cognition about us and our world.

Before we can create this third intelligence, our machines must be given a range of sensory inputs from our world and the neural ability to create their own perceptions. Right now, a laptop has far more computational power than an ant but nothing of the intelligence. To overcome this obstacle, we will have to allow computer chips to become part of us, and allow ourselves to become part of machines. All of this prompts people to ask: Will machines be able to read our minds? Will we ever tap into the vast resources of a giant machine's "mind"? Will we be able to communicate with machines just by thinking? The answer to all is a guarded yes. In each of these areas we already have evidence that some of this is possible.

But the question that interests me is: Will machines understand and think as we do? Personally, I hope not. We need to increase the diversity, as well as the depth, of thinking and not constrain it by imposing the limited domain of biology.

DISCUSSION QUESTIONS

1. What are your answers to the questions posed in the last two paragraphs of this article?
2. Do you think we will "invite computers into our brain?" How do you feel about the prospect?

Summary

Our civilization is in the midst of a transition from an industrial economy to a post-industrial information economy. The transition, or paradigm shift, is having a profound influence on the way we live and work, and it is likely to challenge many of our beliefs, assumptions, and traditions. Computers and information technology are central to the change.

The modern, automated factory uses computers at every level of operation. Computer-aided design, computer-aided manufacturing, robots, automated assembly lines, and automated warehouses all combine to produce factories that need very few laborers. Far more people work in offices than in factories, and computers are critically important in the modern office. Many offices today use networked personal computers and workstations for decentralized enterprise computing. Managers use management information systems and other information tools to help them plan, organize, staff, direct, and control their organizations. A growing number of workers use computers and modems to work at home part- or full-time. Telecommuting has many benefits for information workers, their bosses, and society as a whole. Still, telecommuting from home is not for everybody.

The impact of computers varies from job to job. Computer monitoring is a particularly controversial procedure that raises issues of privacy and, in many cases, lowers worker morale. But the biggest problem of automation may be the elimination of jobs. So far most displaced workers have been able to find other jobs in our expanding economy. But automation will almost certainly produce unemployment and pain for millions of people unless society is able to provide them with the education they'll need to take the new jobs created by technology. Automation may ultimately force us to make fundamental changes in our economic system.

Predicting the future isn't easy, but it's important. One of the best ways to predict the future of technology for the next decade or two is to examine the work being done in research labs today. Information and communication technology industries generally go through four phases: hardware, software, service, and way of life.

Tomorrow's computers will continue current trends toward smaller, more powerful, faster, cheaper machines. We can expect significant advances in processors, architecture, peripherals, networks, wireless networks, and sensors.

Software reliability will remain elusive, but user interfaces will continue the trend toward ease of use. Today's graphical user interfaces will gradually give way as speech, natural language, 3-D images, animation, video, artificial intelligence, and even virtual reality become more pervasive.

Perhaps the most important new user interface technology is the intelligent agent. Agents will be managed rather than manipulated by users. They'll carry out users' wishes and anticipate their needs. Perhaps most important, agents will serve as filters between users and the masses of information on networks. Networks will offer a multitude of services, including real-time customizable shopping services, customizable phone services, and computerized television services.

We're heading into an era of ubiquitous computers—computers that are hardly noticeable because they're everywhere. Embedded computers will improve our everyday tools and, in some cases, give them entirely new functions.

Further into the future, information technology may become intertwined with microtechnology and biotechnology. The results may blur the line between living organisms and intelligent machines. We must be aware of the potential risks and benefits of future technology as we chart our course into the future.

Chapter Review

▼ Key Terms

agent (p. 268)
artificial life (p. 271)
automated factory (p. 259)
automated office (p. 262)
bot (p. 268)
computer monitoring (p. 263)
distributed computing (p. 262)
electronic cottage (p. 262)

groupware (p. 262)
information economy (p. 258)
management information system (MIS) (p. 262)
microtechnology (p. 270)
MIPS (millions of instructions per second) (p. 265)
nanotechnology (p. 271)

natural-language processing (p. 267)
optical computer (p. 266)
paradigm shift (p. 258)
robot (p. 259)
sensor (p. 267)
telecommuting (p. 262)
virtual reality (VR) (p. 268)
voice recognition (p. 267)

▼ Interactive Quiz Questions

1. The *Computer Confluence* CD-ROM contains self-test quiz questions related to this chapter, including multiple choice, true or false, and matching questions.
2. The *Computer Confluence* Web site, www.prenhall.com/beekman, contains self-test exercises related to this chapter. Follow the instructions for taking a quiz. After you've completed your quiz, you can email the results to your instructor.

   The Web site also contains open-ended discussion questions called Internet Explorations. Discuss one or more of the Internet Exploration questions at the section for this chapter.

▼ Review Questions

1. Define or describe each of the key terms above. Check your answers using the glossary.
2. How is the information revolution similar to the industrial revolution? How is it different?
3. What are the major components of the modern automated factory?
4. What distinguishes a robot from a desktop computer?
5. What are the advantages and disadvantages of telecommuting from the point of view of the worker? Management? Society?
6. Why is education critical to our future as we automate more jobs?
7. What are the four phases of any technology or media business? Describe how each of these applies to two or more forms of modern electronic technology.
8. Describe several new technologies that may produce significant performance improvements in future computers.
9. What did Raj Reddy mean when he said software will evolve from WIMP to SILK?
10. Why is the windows-and-icons GUI likely to be replaced by an agent-based user interface? What will this mean for computer users?
11. Explain the concept of ubiquitous computers. Give examples of how it might apply in the office of the future and in the home of the future.
12. How might biology, microtechnology, and computer technology become intertwined in the future?

▼ Discussion Questions

1. What evidence do we have that our society is going through a paradigm shift?
2. Many cities are enacting legislation to encourage telecommuting. If you were drafting such legislation, what would you include?
3. What do you think are the answers to the questions raised at the end of the section on automation and unemployment? How do you think most people would feel about these questions?
4. Some of the most interesting technological ideas are emerging from interdisciplinary labs at MIT, Carnegie Mellon University, Xerox, and elsewhere—labs where scientists, engineers, artists, and philosophers work together on projects that break down the traditional intellectual barriers. Why do you think this is so?
5. Will virtual reality replace TV, as Arthur C. Clarke suggests? If it does, is that a good thing?
6. What kinds of questions might be raised if humans develop biologically based computers? How might these computers change our society?
7. Discuss the questions raised in the section called "Human Questions for a Computer Age." Which of those questions are the most important? Which are hardest to answer?

▼ Projects

1. Interview several people whose jobs have been changed by computers, and report on your findings.
2. Think about how computers have affected the jobs you've held. Report on your experiences.
3. Imagine a future in which computers and information technology are forces of evil. Then imagine a future in which computers and information technology are used to further the common good. Write a paper describing both. Whether you use short-story style or essay style, include enough detail so that it's clear how the technology impacts human lives.
4. Write a letter to a long-lost classmate dated 50 years from today. In that letter describe your life during the past 50 years, including the ways computer technology affected it.

Sources and Resources

Books

Dealers of Lightning: Xerox Parc and the Dawn of the Computer Age, by Michael Hiltzik (Harper Business, 2000). This book chronicles the story of a band of brilliant computer visionaries and their groundbreaking work at Xerox—work that defined much of what we take for granted when we use computers today.

The Structure of Scientific Revolutions, Third Edition, by Thomas Kuhn (Chicago: University of Chicago Press, 1996). This landmark book introduced the term "paradigm shift." Kuhn shows how scientific progress is built on paradigm shifts—radical new world views that challenge and threaten the status quo. The social dynamics described here apply to business, technology, and countless other human endeavors.

The Friction Free Economy, by Ted Lewis (New York: Harper Business, 1997). Lewis explains the complexity of the new information-based economy in an enthusiastic, entertaining, understandable way. Whether you're a curious student, a potential investor, or a budding entrepreneur, this book will help you to better understand the new economy and its new rules.

Computerization and Controversy: Value Conflicts and Social Choices, Second Edition, edited by Charles Dunlop and Rob Kling (Boston: Academic Press, 1996). This collection includes carefully researched academic studies as well as insightful articles from the popular press. The coverage of computers in the workplace is particularly good.

Making the Information Society: Experiences, Consequences, and Possibilities, by James W. Cortada (Prentice Hall, 2002). Why is the information revolution so strongly identified with America? This book examines the cultural and social context of the information revolution in America, past, present, and future.

Utopian Entrepreneur, by Brenda Laurel (MIT Press, 2001). Brenda Laurel, a pioneer in user interface design and PC software development, wrote this book as a guide for those seeking socially positive work in the information age. Human values meet electronic commerce in this refreshing book.

The Hacker Ethic and the Spirit of the Information Age, by Pekka Himanen (New York: Random House, 2001). This book argues that Linus Tovalds, Steve Wozniak, and other pioneers of the information revolution are defining a new work ethic based on curiosity, passion, and sharing rather than duty and guilt. Whether or not you agree with the arguments, you'll probably find the presentation worthwhile.

Electronic Commerce: A Managerial Perspective, by Efraim Turban, Jae Lee, David King, and H. Michael Chung (Upper Saddle River, NJ: Prentice Hall, 2000). This text covers the rapidly changing field of electronic commerce, including intranets, extranets, marketing, business-to-business transactions, electronic payment, and more. Case studies and examples supplement the theoretical material.

White Collar Sweatshop: The Deterioration of Work and Its Rewards in Corporate America, by Jill Andresky Fraser (New York: Norton, 2000). This book stretches the sweatshop metaphor beyond data entry warehouses, arguing that modern management techniques are oppressive to all but the top executives in many high-tech companies.

Dot Calm: The Search for Sanity in a Wired World, by Debra A. Dinnocenzo and Richard B. Swegan (Berrett-Koehler, 2001). This is a guide for coping with the pace and pressure of a high-tech work environment. It provides practical tips and techniques that apply to a variety of work situations.

The End of Work, by Jeremy Rifkin (New York: Putnam, 1994). This book discusses the changing nature of work and the disappearance of jobs as we know them. Information technology isn't the only cause, but it plays a critical role in these changes.

Beyond Calculation: The Next Fifty Years of Computing, by Peter J. Denning and Robert M. Metcalfe (New York: Copernicus, 1997). 1997 marked the 50th anniversary of the transistor and of the Association for Computing Machinery, the premier organization for computer professionals. To mark the occasion, many of the pioneers who helped create the technology wrote articles predicting what the next 50 years might bring. This fascinating book is a collection of 20 speculative articles. Some deal exclusively with technology; others focus on social implications.

The Media Lab: Inventing the Future at MIT, by Stewart Brand (New York: Viking, 1988). This is the book that brought the MIT Media Lab into the public eye. In spite of its age, the book does an admirable job of describing a future radically transformed by the interweaving of the computer, communication, and entertainment industries. It also provides an insightful look at technology researchers in action.

Being Digital, by Nicholas Negroponte (New York: Viking, 1996). The director of the MIT Media Lab wrote thought-provoking columns for *Wired* for many years. This collection of columns provides an optimistic, intelligent vision of a digital future.

When Things Start to Think, by Neil Gershenfeld (New York: Henry Holt and Company, 1999). Another researcher at MIT's Media Lab provides a peek at recent research projects and a glimpse of a future in which computers disappear into everyday objects. As you might expect, Gershenfeld doesn't dwell on the dark side of this emerging technology, but his future visions make for clear, interesting reading.

The Unfinished Revolution: Human-Centered Computers and What They Can Do for Us, by Michael L. Dertouzos (Harper Business, 2001). Dertouzos was the longtime head of the MIT Computer Science Department and a respected writer. This book, completed shortly before his death in 2001, argues that computers of the future will need to be better able to adapt to humans—not the other way around.

The Age of Intelligent Machines, by Raymond Kurzweil (Cambridge, MA: MIT Press, 1992). If you want to learn more about AI, this award-winning book is a great resource in spite of its age. With clear prose, beautiful illustrations, and intelligent articles by the masters of the field, Kurzweil explores the historical, philosophical, academic, aesthetic, practical, fanciful, and speculative sides of AI. Kurzweil knows the field from first-hand experience; he has successfully developed and marketed several "applied AI" products, from reading machines for people with visual impairments and electronic musical instruments to expert systems. A companion video is also available.

The Age of Spiritual Machines, by Raymond Kurzweil (New York: Penguin USA, 2000). While *The Age of Intelligent Machines* surveys the past and present of AI, *The Age of Spiritual Machines* boldly looks into a possible future. Will humans really be able download themselves into machine bodies and brains? If this kind of question interests you, you'll enjoy this book.

Taming the Beast: Choice and Control in the Electronic Jungle, by Jason Ohler (Bloomington, IN: Technos Press, 1999). This book examines our relationship with technology with wit, intelligence, common sense, and sound advice. Ohler follows in the tradition of Marshall McLuhan, examining the unseen impact of our media creations on our lives.

The Art of the Long View, by Peter Schwartz (New York: Doubleday, 1996). Scenario planning is a particularly useful tool for highlighting the powerful forces that shape the future and choosing strategies that play out well in a variety of possible futures. Schwartz is a master of scenario planning, and this book describes his methodology and provides examples.

Out of Control: The New Biology of Machines, Social Systems, and the Economic World, by Kevin Kelly (Reading, MA: Addison-Wesley, 1996). Artificial life, artificial intelligence, genetic engineering, virtual reality, and nanotechnology blur the line between the "born" and the "made." Kevin Kelly's powerful, wonderfully readable book explores this line and provides fertile ground for speculation on all kinds of technological, social, and ethical questions.

Minds, Machines, and the Multiverse: The Quest for the Quantum Computer, by Julian Brown (Simon & Schuster, 2000). Quantum computers may someday make today's binary machines seem as obsolete as slide rules. This book explores the mind-boggling possibilities for this future technology.

The Age of Access: The New Culture of Hypercapitalism Where All of Life is a Paid-for Experience, by Jeremy Rifkin (New York: Penguin Books, 2000). In his latest book, Rifkin argues that we're shifting from an economy based on ownership of physical possessions to one based on paying for experiences. He warns of an approaching era in which giant companies charge us for almost every human experience.

Amusing Ourselves to Death: Public Discourse in the Age of Show Business, by Neil Postman (New York: Viking Press, 1986), **Technopoly: The Surrender of Culture to Technology** (New York: Vintage Books, 1993), and **The End of Education: Redefining the Value of School,** by Neil Postman (New York, Knopf, 1995). In these books, noted social critic Neil Postman takes on schools and technology, two powerful forces that are shaping our lives. In *Amusing Ourselves to Death*, Postman argues that television has injured, and is injuring, our ability to think, by reducing every public discourse to just another form of entertainment. In *Technopoly* he argues that our tools, especially computers, no longer play supporting roles; instead, they radically shape our culture, our families, and our world views. In *The End of Education*, he presents a picture of modern education in which economic utility has become the defining principle. Postman presents compelling problems and suggests possible solutions in these important books.

High Tech, High Teach: Technology and Our Search for Meaning, John Naisbitt with Nana Naisbitt and Douglas Philips (New York: Broadway Books, 1999). In this book the author of *Megatrends* examines a future in which technology saturates every aspect of American society. What impact will this "Technologically Intoxicated Zone" have on our lives and consciousness? How will our relationship with technology evolve? These are the kinds of questions *High Tech, High Teach* tackles.

Periodicals

Smart Business for the New Economy. In the '90s *PC Computing* focused on PC technology and business applications. But in the new decade, the PC is no longer the focal point of the "new" economy. In early 2000, *PC Computing* changed its name and broadened its focus to all kinds of information technology that have an impact on business and economy.

Information Week. This weekly news magazine focuses on business and the technology that drives it.

Upside. This monthly is aimed at managers, entrepreneurs, and others who want to track the business side rather than the technological side of the computer industry.

Forbes ASAP. This publication provides a thinking person's perspective on the high-tech workplace. Each year's "Big Issue" includes dozens of essays by famous and not-so-famous writers on a particular theme. (Some of those essays are reprinted in Crosscurrents in this text.)

Fast Company. This is another thought-provoking magazine that deals with the human issues of business in the digital age.

Small Business Computing. This magazine provides computer coverage for those businesses that aren't part of the Fortune 500.

mBusiness. This monthly covers the emerging mobile workforce and the technology that keeps them connected from the road.

Home Office Computing. This one is geared more toward people who use their computers to work at home.

Syllabus. This magazine focuses on higher education and technology. Themes of issues range from multimedia tools to distance education on the Web.

T.H.E. Journal (Technological Horizons in Education). This magazine covers both K–12 and higher education with a mixture of product announcements and articles.

Technos: Quarterly for Education and Technology. This publication by the *Journal of the Agency for Instructional Technology* bills itself as "a forum for the discussion of ideas about the use of technology in education, with a focus on reform." Most of the articles are clearly pro-technology, but many deal with controversial issues. Example: a roundtable discussion called "Violence, Games, and Art."

Technology & Learning. This magazine, aimed at K–12 educators, focuses on uses of technology to enhance education.

Family PC. This magazine is aimed mostly at parents who want to help their kids put computers to good use.

Communications of the ACM. This technical journal is a good source for learning about research in computer science and related fields.

Scientific American. This venerable monthly is the most popular science magazine. It's well known for articles that present scientific and engineering research in a manner that is accessible to nonscientists.

Technology Review: MIT's Magazine of Innovation (www.techreview.com). This magazine isn't just another collection of academic research briefs. It's a colorful, engaging periodical that illuminates current technological research and future trends.

Shift (www.shift.com). This relatively new Canadian magazine covers just about the same beat as *Wired*, listed in Chapter 1. But in recent years *Wired* has become more conservative, with articles about venture capital and stock options taking up more pages. So far, *Shift* seems to have a younger, sassier, more irreverent approach to covering the digital culture.

World Wide Web

The World Wide Web is evolving rapidly in amazing ways, but there are still no direct links to the future. The Web links on the *Computer Confluence* page allow you to explore Xerox PARC, the MIT Media Lab, and other organizations dedicated to inventing the future. Other links transport you into speculative discussions about tomorrow's technology and its implications.

The Concise Computer Consumer's Guide

Buying a computer can be an intimidating process, but it doesn't need to be. With the right information, you should have no trouble finding the right system.

Chapter 3, "Hardware Basics: Peripherals," introduces several general principles that apply to just about any personal computer purchase (see Rules of Thumb box, "Computer Consumer Concepts"). But when you're actually ready to buy a system, you'll need more specific information to help you narrow down the myriad of options and choose the system that best meets your needs. The next few pages provide information on each component in a typical computer system; you can use this information to create a profile of an ideal computer system. The CD-ROM includes an interactive Consumer's Guide that can walk you through the process of creating this profile.

Because of the volatile nature of the computer marketplace, the consumer's guides in this book and CD-ROM can't tell you everything you need to know. You'll need more current information to help you turn your ideal system profile into a detailed brand-specific shopping list. The *Computer Confluence* Web site points you toward up-to-the-minute, consumer-oriented information. Use this Web data along with anything you can glean from magazines, knowledgeable friends, and other sources.

If money were no object, you could purchase a fully loaded, top-of-the-line system with every imaginable peripheral. If, like most of us, you're working with a limited budget, you'll need to be more discriminating. You'll need to figure out exactly which features and components you need, which ones you might want to add later, and which ones you won't need at all. If you have a clear idea of how you're going to use your system, you can assess the trade-offs involved in choosing features and options. For example, if you're a graphics artist, youprobably want to put more of your budget into a high-quality monitor if it means scrimping on audio speakers.

When shopping for a computer, you need to address several questions:

Is portability important? Portable computers are more expensive than desktop computers of equivalent capabilities. They also aren't as expandable as desktop boxes, so they aren't approprate when specialized boards need to be installed. If you want to add peripherals to a

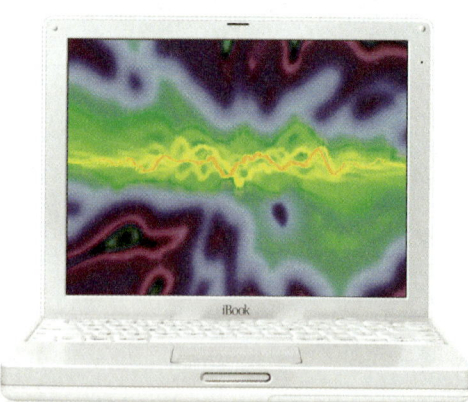

portable, they generally have to be external peripherals connected by USB or other cables. You have to decide whether the convenience of portability outweighs the additional expense and limited expandability.

Should you buy a Windows PC or a Macintosh? This is a highly personal decision; you'll probably meet partisans for both camps who argue with the passion of a religious zealot. The truth is that, while there are still critical differences between the two operating systems, both are capable of serving the needs of most users. If you don't already have a strong preference, check with others in your chosen field to see what they use and why. In general, Windows machines predominate in business, whereas Macs have loyal followings in publishing, graphics, and multimedia. Consider the kinds of software you want to use and find out what's available on each system. Spend some time getting to know both types of systems to see which you prefer.

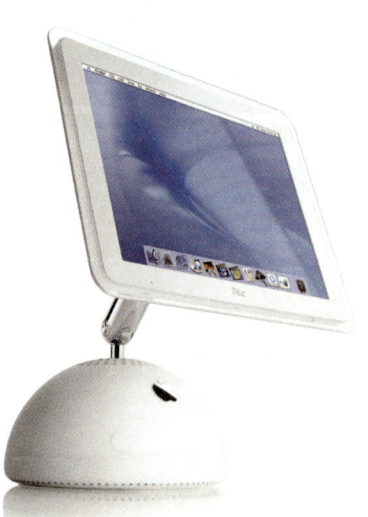

What is your budget? If you have less than $800 to spend, you probably have to get a used computer or an extremely limited system. If you mostly need a word-processing and Web-surfing machine, an older system may be all you need. But most older systems can't run the latest software and have limited expansion options. If you have $800 to $1500 in your computer budget, you can buy a new system with standard capabilities that can handle today's most popular applications. If you can spend more than $1500, you can choose a high-performance system that can run many of the more demanding applications. In general, more expensive computer packages contain higher-quality peripherals as well.

Where do you buy a computer? Many people shop locally at computer specialty stores, superstores, and home electronic stores because of the local service, ease of repairs, and warranty replacements. Others choose mail-order companies for their competitive prices. Mail-order shopping can save money, but it can also mean additional hassles and risks if you don't do your homework or if you choose the wrong company. Leading computer magazines often rate mail-order companies for their service, prices, and reliability. Internet newsgroups can also help you find good deals and businesses with good reputations.

How do you plan to use your computer? Here's a list of computer applications. Which of these applications is most important to you? The applications you choose determine, to a large degree, what your ideal system looks like.

Desktop Productivity Applications
Word processing
Spreadsheet
Database
Publishing
Desktop publishing
Web publishing

Games
Simulations
Multiplayer gaming
Virtual reality

Communications
Online service access
Email
Internet/Web access
Voice mail/Fax

Technical Applications
CAD
Mathematical
Statistics
Programming languages

Financial Applications
Personal finance/Online banking
Accounting

Multimedia/Graphics
Graphic art
Animation
Video
Music
Presentation graphics
Multimedia authoring

CPU

Buy the fastest CPU you can afford. RAM also affects the overall performance of your computer, but it's generally easier to add RAM later than to upgrade a CPU. System speeds are meaured in megahertz, but megahertz don't tell the whole story. The architecture of the chip and the system board can have a profound effect on system speed. A late-model CPU such as a Pentium 4 or a Power PC G4 can easily outperform a CPU with an older design, even if the older CPU has a comparable clock speed. Computer magazines often run benchmark tests to compare CPU performance of common tasks. If you don't have access to their results, do some comparative testing yourself.

Disk Storage

Most new computers come with a single floppy disk drive, a 10- to 30-gigabyte hard drive, and a CD-ROM or DVD-ROM drive; unless your computing needs are minimal, you probably won't be satisfied with a system that doesn't include these basic components. If you're planning on doing graphic design, digital audio, multimedia authoring, or other storage-intensive jobs, you'll probably also want some kind of removable high-capacity disk drive for transporting and backing up large files, a CD-RW drive for creating CD-ROMs, and/or a DVD-R/CD-RW drive for reading and writing on high-capacity DVD disks.

RAM

Certain applications, especially those that manipulate digital images or audio, demand a great deal of RAM. In general, you should plan on getting a computer with at least 64 or 128 megabytes of RAM—more if you plan to use memory-intensive applications.

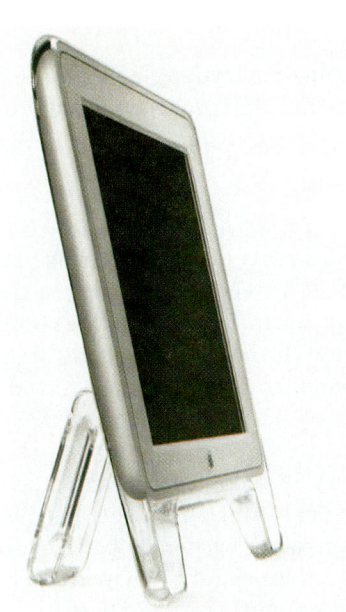

Video Monitor

The quality of the images you can display on your computer is a function not only of the monitor but also of the video adapter inside your system unit. If you plan to make extensive use of intricate color images, you will want a large-screen monitor (17" or greater) capable of supporting a resolution of at least 1024 3 768 pixels, a color depth of 16 million colors, and a noninterlaced refresh rate of at least 75 hertz. If you can afford it, you might consider a space-saving, energy-saving flat-screen monitor. Of course, the video card needs to support your chosen monitor's features and should contain at least 4MB of video RAM.

Input Devices

All computer systems have a keyboard and a pointing device, most commonly a mouse. Many keyboards are now ergonomically designed to reduce the risk of repetitive motion strain. Some users prefer a trackball to the mouse. If you plan to do much graphic design work, consider adding a pressure-sensitive graphics tablet to your system; it's far easier and more accurate to draw with a stylus than a mouse. For serious game playing, a joystick easily beats the mouse. Newer digital joysticks provide superior performance over their analog counterparts and offer more accurate control. If you plan to work with photographic images, you'll need a scanner, a digital camera, or both. A high quality scanner is less expensive and more versatile than a comparable digital camera, assuming you already have a non-digital camera.

Modem/Communications

Since much Web content is graphics intensive, you shouldn't consider anything less than a 56.6 Kbps modem for Web surfing. In many areas, cable modems and DSL connections can provide high-speed Internet access.

Ports and Slots

Until recently, virtually all PCs had standard serial and parallel ports for adding peripherals and several slots for adding internal devices and boards. Most newer PCs, following in the mouseprints of the Apple iMac, include high-speed, hot-swappable USB and FireWire (IEEE 1394) ports designed to work with the latest peripherals. (FireWire is ideal for, among other things, serious digital video editing, because it allows the computer to communicate directly with a digital video camera.)

Some new PCs include older slots and ports alongside the USB and FireWire ports; others are "legacy-free" models with only newer, faster ports. If you're buying all new peripherals, legacy-free machine makes sense; USB and FireWire peripherals are generally better than older models, and there's no reason to pay for ports you'll never use. But if you have a collection of aging peripherals, you'll probably want a machine that supports those peripherals.

Printer

Today's low-cost inkjet printers can produce excellent high-resolution printouts; many are capable of printing photo-quality color images. If your focus is digital photography, you may want to buy a printer that's optimized for photographs. If you'll be working exclusively with text and numbers, you might prefer a laser printer. Laser printers produce excellent printouts of text and black-and-white line art at a lower cost per page.

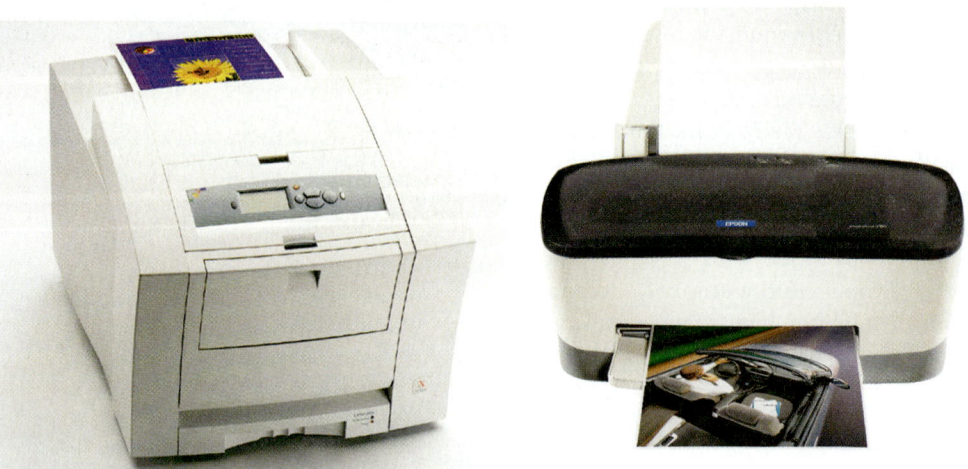

Sound Card/Speakers

All modern PCs and Macintoshes have built-in 16-bit sound cards capable of playing CD-quality audio and MIDI files. Advanced sound cards also supply wave table synthesis and the ability to create and play back studio-quality digital sound samples. These sound cards often contain extensive ROM with megabytes of prerecorded sound samples and expandable RAM banks. No sound system would be complete without a set of amplified, magnetically shielded speakers. The best systems include a separate bass subwoofer for more realistic nondirectional sound.

Software

Most systems come with systems software installed on the hard disk; some come with a number of preinstalled applications programs. Unless your system includes all the software you need, you have to spend part of your computer budget on software. If your software budget is modest, you may be able to meet most or all of your needs with an inexpensive integrated application such as Microsoft Works or AppleWorks. These all-purpose programs cost much less than more powerful office suites, and they demand much less disk space. Of course, integrated applications and software suites can't handle everybody's software needs. Multimedia work, engineering, and other specialized applications require specialized software. Don't overlook shareware and public domain software if your budget is tight.

Add-Ons

There are numerous hardware add-ons that appeal to different special interests. Depending on your needs, you may want to add a flatbed scanner for scanning text and graphics, a digital camera for digitizing real-world images, a MIDI keyboard for playing your own music, or a digital video camera for recording and manipulating full-motion digital video.

One popular type of peripheral is actually another computer—a handheld computer. Devices like the Palm, the Handspring Visor, and the Pocket PC enable you to carry critical information with you when you're away from your desk. You can use one of these handheld PCs to schedule appointments, track tasks, record short notes, do calculations, look up phone numbers, and read files while you're away from your PC. When you return it to its cradle, it can hot-synch with the desktop machine, making sure the most current information is on both computers. The stylus input of these devices is less than ideal for taking notes. But a folding keyboard can make a handheld computer into a supremely portable note-taking machine.

ACM Appendix

ACM Code of Ethics and Professional Conduct (Adopted by ACM Council October 16, 1992)

Commitment to ethical professional conduct is expected of every member (voting members, associate members, and student members) of the Association for Computing Machinery (ACM).

This Code, consisting of 24 imperatives formulated as statements of personal responsibility, identifies the elements of such a commitment. It contains many, but not all, issues professionals are likely to face. Section 1 outlines fundamental ethical considerations, while Section 2 addresses additional, more specific considerations of professional conduct. Statements in Section 3 pertain more specifically to individuals who have a leadership role, whether in the workplace or in a volunteer capacity such as with organizations like ACM. Principles involving compliance with this Code are given in Section 4.

The Code shall be supplemented by a set of Guidelines, which provide explanation to assist members in dealing with the various issues contained in the Code. It is expected that the Guidelines will be changed more frequently than the Code.

The Code and its supplemented Guidelines are intended to serve as a basis for ethical decision making in the conduct of professional work. Secondarily, they may serve as a basis for judging the merit of a formal complaint pertaining to violation of professional ethical standards.

It should be noted that although computing is not mentioned in the imperatives of Section 1, the Code is concerned with how these fundamental imperatives apply to one's conduct as a computing professional. These imperatives are expressed in a general form to emphasize that ethical principles which apply to computer ethics are derived from more general ethical principles.

It is understood that some words and phrases in a code of ethics are subject to varying interpretations, and that any ethical principle may conflict with other ethical principles in specific situations. Questions related to ethical conflicts can best be answered by thoughtful consideration of fundamental principles, rather than reliance on detailed regulations.

1. General moral imperatives
2. More specific professional responsibilities
3. Organizational leadership imperatives
4. Compliance with the code

1. General Moral Imperatives

As an ACM member I will...

1.1 Contribute to Society and Human Well-Being

This principle concerning the quality of life of all people affirms an obligation to protect fundamental human rights and to respect the diversity of all cultures. An essential aim of computing professionals is to minimize negative consequences of computing systems, including threats to health and safety. When designing or implementing systems, computing professionals must attempt to ensure that the products of their efforts will be used in socially responsible ways, will meet social needs, and will avoid harmful effects to health and welfare.

1.1

Chapter 1: pp. 37–42 Living with Computers; pp. 40–42 Living with Computers: Implications: Social and Ethical Issues; p. 43 CrossCurrents: "Tech's Double Edge Sword"

Chapter 3: p. 69 Steve Wozniak, Steve Jobs, and the Garage that Grew Apples; p. 83 Rules of Thumb: Ergonomics and Health

Chapter 4: pp. 99 Linus Torvalds and the Software Nobody Owns; p. 121 Rules of Thumb: Green Computing

Chapter 6: pp. 170–173 Email, Teleconferences, and Instant Messaging: Interpersonal Computing: On-Line Issues: Reliability, Security, Privacy, and Humanity

Chapter 7: p. 204 CrossCurrents: "Machine Net"

Chapter 8: p. 223 CrossCurrents: "The Day I Got Napsterized"

Chapter 9: pp. 246–250 Security and Reliability; p. 246 Rules of Thumb: Computer Ethics

Chapter 10: p. 257 Alan Kay Invents the Future; pp. 272–274 Human Questions for a Computer Age; p. 274 CrossCurrents: "Borg in the Mirror"

1.2

Chapter 1: pp. 40–42 Living with Computers: Implications: Social and Ethical Issues

Chapter 4: pp. 105–107 Software Applications: Tools for Users: Consumer Applications; p. 121 Rules of Thumb: Green Computing

Chapter 5: pp. 137–138 Calculated Risks: Computer Modeling and Simulation

Chapter 8: pp. 218–220 The Evolving Internet: Internet Issues: Ethical and Political Dilemmas

Chapter 9: pp. 230–237 On-Line Outlaws: Computer Crime; pp. 230–236 On-Line Outlaws: Software Sabotage: Viruses and Other Invaders; p. 245 Rules of Thumb: Safe Computing; pp. 246–249 Security and Reliability: Computers at War; p. 251 CrossCurrents: "Now Weapons of Mass Disruption"

Chapter 10: pp. 272–273 Human Questions for a Computer Age

1.3

Chapter 4: pp. 105–107 Software Applications: Tools for Users: Consumer Applications

Chapter 9: p. 229 Kempelen's Amazing Chess Playing Machine; pp. 230–237 On-Line Outlaws: Computer Crime

Chapter 10: pp. 272–273 Human Questions for a Computer Age

In addition to a safe social environment, human well-being includes a safe natural environment. Therefore, computing professionals who design and develop systems must be alert to, and make others aware of, any potential damage to the local or global environment.

1.2 Avoid Harm to Others

"Harm" means injury or negative consequences, such as undesirable loss of information, loss of property, property damage, or unwanted environmental impacts. This principle prohibits use of computing technology in ways that result in harm to any of the following: users, the general public, employees, and employers. Harmful actions include intentional destruction or modification of files and programs leading to serious loss of resources or unnecessary expenditure of human resources such as the time and effort required to purge systems of "computer viruses."

Well-intended actions, including those that accomplish assigned duties, may lead to harm unexpectedly. In such an event the responsible person or persons are obligated to undo or mitigate the negative consequences as much as possible. One way to avoid unintentional harm is to carefully consider potential impacts on all those affected by decisions made during design and implementation.

To minimize the possibility of indirectly harming others, computing professionals must minimize malfunctions by following generally accepted standards for system design and testing. Furthermore, it is often necessary to assess the social consequences of systems to project the likelihood of any serious harm to others. If system features are misrepresented to users, coworkers, or supervisors, the individual computing professional is responsible for any resulting injury.

In the work environment the computing professional has the additional obligation to report any signs of system dangers that might result in serious personal or social damage. If one's superiors do not act to curtail or mitigate such dangers, it may be necessary to "blow the whistle" to help correct the problem or reduce the risk. However, capricious or misguided reporting of violations can, itself, be harmful. Before reporting violations, all relevant aspects of the incident must be thoroughly assessed. In particular, the assessment of risk and responsibility must be credible. It is suggested that advice be sought from other computing professionals. See principle 2.5 regarding thorough evaluations.

1.3 Be Honest and Trustworthy

Honesty is an essential component of trust. Without trust an organization cannot function effectively. The honest computing professional will not make deliberately false or deceptive claims about a system or system design, but will instead provide full disclosure of all pertinent system limitations and problems.

A computer professional has a duty to be honest about his or her own qualifications, and about any circumstances that might lead to conflicts of interest.

Membership in volunteer organizations such as ACM may at times place individuals in situations where their statements or actions could be interpreted as carrying the "weight" of a larger group of professionals. An ACM member will exercise care to not misrepresent ACM or positions and policies of ACM or any ACM units.

1.4 Be Fair and Take Action Not to Discriminate

The values of equality, tolerance, respect for others, and the principles of equal justice govern this imperative. Discrimination on the basis of race, sex, religion, age, disability, national origin, or other such factors is an explicit violation of ACM policy and will not be tolerated.

Inequities between different groups of people may result from the use or misuse of information and technology. In a fair society, all individuals would have equal opportunity to participate in, or benefit from, the use of computer resources regardless of race, sex, religion, age, disability, national origin or other such similar factors. However, these ideals do not justify unauthorized use of computer resources nor do they provide an adequate basis for violation of any other ethical imperatives of this code.

1.5 Honor Property Rights Including Copyrights and Patents

Violation of copyrights, patents, trade secrets and the terms of license agreements is prohibited by law in most circumstances. Even when software is not so protected, such violations are contrary to professional behavior. Copies of software should be made only with proper authorization. Unauthorized duplication of materials must not be condoned.

1.6 Give Proper Credit for Intellectual Property
Computing professionals are obligated to protect the integrity of intellectual property. Specifically, one must not take credit for other's ideas or work, even in cases where the work has not been explicitly protected by copyright, patent, etc.

1.7 Respect the Privacy of Others
Computing and communication technology enables the collection and exchange of personal information on a scale unprecedented in the history of civilization. Thus there is increased potential for violating the privacy of individuals and groups. It is the responsibility of professionals to maintain the privacy and integrity of data describing individuals. This includes taking precautions to ensure the accuracy of data, as well as protecting it from unauthorized access or accidental disclosure to inappropriate individuals. Furthermore, procedures must be established to allow individuals to review their records and correct inaccuracies.

This imperative implies that only the necessary amount of personal information be collected in a system, that retention and disposal periods for that information be clearly defined and enforced, and that personal information gathered for a specific purpose not be used for other purposes without consent of the individual(s). These principles apply to electronic communications, including electronic mail, and prohibit procedures that capture or monitor electronic user data, including messages, without the permission of users or bona fide authorization related to system operation and maintenance. User data observed during the normal duties of system operation and maintenance must be treated with strictest confidentiality, except in cases where it is evidence for the violation of law, organizational regulations, or this Code. In these cases, the nature or contents of that information must be disclosed only to proper authorities.

1.8 Honor Confidentiality
The principle of honesty extends to issues of confidentiality of information whenever one has made an explicit promise to honor confidentiality or, implicitly, when private information not directly related to the performance of one's duties becomes available. The ethical concern is to respect all obligations of confidentiality to employers, clients, and users unless discharged from such obligations by requirements of the law or other principles of this Code.

2. More Specific Professional Responsibilities
As an ACM computing professional I will . . .

2.1 Strive to Achieve the Highest Quality, Effectiveness and Dignity in Both the Process and Products of Professional Work
Excellence is perhaps the most important obligation of a professional. The computing professional must strive to achieve quality and to be cognizant of the serious negative consequences that may result from poor quality in a system.

2.2 Acquire and Maintain Professional Competence
Excellence depends on individuals who take responsibility for acquiring and maintaining professional competence. A professional must participate in setting standards for appropriate levels of competence, and strive to achieve those standards. Upgrading technical knowledge and competence can be achieved in several ways: doing independent study; attending seminars, conferences, or courses; and being involved in professional organizations.

2.3 Know and Respect Existing Laws Pertaining to Professional Work
ACM members must obey existing local, state, province, national, and international laws unless there is a compelling ethical basis not to do so. Policies and procedures of the organizations in which one participates must also be obeyed. But compliance must be balanced with the recognition that sometimes existing laws and rules may be immoral or inappropriate and, therefore, must be challenged. Violation of a law or regulation may be ethical when that law or rule has inadequate moral basis or when it conflicts with another law judged to be more important. If one decides to violate a law or rule because it is viewed as unethical, or for any other reason, one must fully accept responsibility for one's actions and for the consequences.

1.4
Chapter 1: pp. 40–42 Living with Computers: Implications: Social and Ethical Issues

Chapter 10: pp. 262–264 Computers and Jobs; pp. 272–273 Human Questions for a Computer Age

1.5
Chapter 3: p. 91 Rules of Thumb: Computer Consumer Concepts

Chapter 4: pp. 105–107 Software Applications: Tools for Users: Consumer Applications

Chapter 6: pp. 164–170 Linking Up: Network Basics: The Network Advantage

Chapter 9: pp. 230–233 On-Line Outlaws: Computer Crime: Software Piracy and Intellectual Property Laws; pp. 242–245 Security, Privacy, Freedom, and Ethics: The Delicate Balance: Justice on the Electronic Frontier

1.6
Chapter 9: pp. 230–233 On-Line Outlaws: Computer Crime: Software Piracy and Intellectual Property Laws; pp. 242–245 Security, Privacy, and Freedom: The Delicate Balance: Justice on the Electronic Frontier

1.7
Chapter 1: pp. 40–42 Living with Computers: Implications: Social and Ethical Issues

Chapter 4: pp. 108–109 System Software: The Hardware-Software Connection: What the Operating System Does

Chapter 5: p. 155 Rules of Thumb: Your Private Rights; p. 156 CrossCurrents: "Counterfeit Freedom"

Chapter 6: pp. 170–173 Email, Teleconferences, and Instant Messaging: Interpersonal Computing: On-Line Issues: Reliability, Security, Privacy, and Humanity

Chapter 8: p. 212 Rules of Thumb: Working the Web

Chapter 9: pp. 238–239 Computer Security: Reducing Risks: Physical Access Restrictions, Passwords; pp. 242–245 Security, Privacy, Freedom and Ethics: The Delicate Balance; p. 245 Rules of Thumb: Safe Computing

Chapter 10: pp. 262–264 Computers and Jobs

1.8

Chapter 5: p. 155 Rules of Thumb: Your Private Rights; p. 156 CrossCurrents: "Counterfeit Freedom"

Chapter 6: pp. 170–173 Email, Teleconferences, and Instant Messaging: Interpersonal Computing: On-Line Issues: Reliability, Security, Privacy, and Humanity

Chapter 9: p. 245 Rules of Thumb: Safe Computing

Chapter 10: pp. 262–264 Computers and Jobs

2.1

Chapter 4: p. 122 CrossCurrents "'Read the Manual!' What Manual?"

Chapter 5: p. 133 Rules of Thumb: Beyond Desktop Tacky!; pp. 137–138 Calculated Risks: Computer Modeling and Simulation; p. 154 Rules of Thumb: Dealing with Databases

2.2

Chapter 10: pp. 258–264 Where Computers Work

2.3

Chapter 9: pp. 230–237 On-Line Outlaws: Computer Crime; pp. 242–245 Security, Privacy, Freedom and Ethics: The Delicate Balance: Justice on the Electronic Frontier

Chapter 10: pp. 272–273 Human Questions for a Computer Age

2.5

Chapter 5: pp. 137–138 Calculated Risks: Computer Modeling and Simulation

2.6

Chapter 4: pp. 105–107 Software Applications: Tools for Users: Consumer Applications

2.7

Chapter 1: pp. 37–42 Living with Computers

Chapter 2: p. 64 CrossCurrents: "Bit Literacy"

Chapter 9: pp. 242–245 Security, Privacy, Freedom and Ethics: The Delicate Balance: Justice on the Electronic Frontier; pp. 246–250 Security and Reliability

2.8

Chapter 6: pp. 170–173 Email, Teleconferences, and Instant Messaging: Interpersonal Computing: On-Line Issues: Reliability, Security, Privacy, and Humanity

Chapter 9: pp. 236–237 On-Line Outlaws: Computer Crime: Hacking and Electronic Trespassing; p. 245 Rules of Thumb: Safe Computing

2.4 Accept and Provide Appropriate Professional Review

Quality professional work, especially in the computing profession, depends on professional reviewing and critiquing. Whenever appropriate, individual members should seek and utilize peer review as well as provide critical review of the work of others.

2.5 Give Comprehensive and Thorough Evaluations of Computer Systems and Their Impacts, Including Analysis of Possible Risks

Computer professionals must strive to be perceptive, thorough, and objective when evaluating, recommending, and presenting system descriptions and alternatives. Computer professionals are in a position of special trust, and therefore have a special responsibility to provide objective, credible evaluations to employers, clients, users, and the public. When providing evaluations the professional must also identify any relevant conflicts of interest, as stated in imperative 1.3.

As noted in the discussion of principle 1.2 on avoiding harm, any signs of danger from systems must be reported to those who have opportunity and/or responsibility to resolve them. See the guidelines for imperative 1.2 for more details concerning harm, including the reporting of professional violations.

2.6 Honor Contracts, Agreements, and Assigned Responsibilities

Honoring one's commitments is a matter of integrity and honesty. For the computer professional this includes ensuring that system elements perform as intended. Also, when one contracts for work with another party, one has an obligation to keep that party properly informed about progress toward completing that work.

A computing professional has a responsibility to request a change in any assignment that he or she feels cannot be completed as defined. Only after serious consideration and with full disclosure of risks and concerns to the employer or client, should one accept the assignment. The major underlying principle here is the obligation to accept personal accountability for professional work. On some occasions other ethical principles may take greater priority.

A judgment that a specific assignment should not be performed may not be accepted. Having clearly identified one's concerns and reasons for that judgment, but failing to procure a change in that assignment, one may yet be obligated, by contract or by law, to proceed as directed. The computing professional's ethical judgment should be the final guide in deciding whether or not to proceed. Regardless of the decision, one must accept the responsibility for the consequences.

However, performing assignments "against one's own judgment" does not relieve the professional of responsibility for any negative consequences.

2.7 Improve Public Understanding of Computing and Its Consequences

Computing professionals have a responsibility to share technical knowledge with the public by encouraging understanding of computing, including the impacts of computer systems and their limitations. This imperative implies an obligation to counter any false views related to computing.

2.8 Access Computing and Communication Resources Only When Authorized To Do So

Theft or destruction of tangible and electronic property is prohibited by imperative 1.2—"Avoid harm to others." Trespassing and unauthorized use of a computer or communication system is addressed by this imperative. Trespassing includes accessing communication networks and computer systems, or accounts and/or files associated with those systems, without explicit authorization to do so. Individuals and organizations have the right to restrict access to their systems so long as they do not violate the discrimination principle (see 1.4). No one should enter or use another's computer system, software, or data files without permission. One must always have appropriate approval before using system resources, including communication ports, file space, other system peripherals, and computer time.

3. Organizational Leadership Imperatives

Background Note: This section draws extensively from the draft IFIP Code of Ethics, especially its sections on organizational ethics and international concerns. The ethical obligations of organizations tend to be neglected in most codes of professional conduct, perhaps because these codes are written from the perspective of the individual member. This dilemma is addressed by stating these imperatives from the perspective of the organizational leader. In this context "leader" is viewed as any organizational member who has leadership or educational responsibilities. These imperatives generally may apply to organizations as well as their leaders. In this context "organizations" are corporations, government agencies, and other "employers" as well as volunteer professional organizations.

As an ACM member and an organizational leader, I will . . .

3.1 Articulate Social Responsibilities of Members of an Organizational Unit and Encourage Full Acceptance of those Responsibilities

Because organizations of all kinds have impacts on the public, they must accept responsibilities to society. Organizational procedures and attitudes oriented toward quality and the welfare of society will reduce harm to members of the public, thereby serving public interest and fulfilling social responsibility. Therefore, organizational leaders must encourage full participation in meeting social responsibilities as well as quality performance.

3.2 Manage Personnel and Resources to Design and Build Information Systems that Enhance the Quality of Working Life

Organizational leaders are responsible for ensuring that computer systems enhance, not degrade, the quality of working life. When implementing a computer system, organizations must consider the personal and professional development, physical safety, and human dignity of all workers. Appropriate human-computer ergonomic standards should be considered in system design and in the workplace.

3.3 Acknowledge and Support Proper and Authorized Uses of an Organization's Computing and Communication Resources

Because computer systems can become tools to harm as well as to benefit an organization, the leadership has the responsibility to clearly define appropriate and inappropriate uses of organizational computing resources. While the number and scope of such rules should be minimal, they should be fully enforced when established.

3.4 Ensure that Users and those Who Will Be Affected by a System Have Their Needs Clearly Articulated During the Assessment and Design of Requirements; Later the System Must Be Validated to Meet Requirements

Current system users, potential users and other persons whose lives may be affected by a system must have their needs assessed and incorporated in the statement of requirements. System validation should ensure compliance with those requirements.

3.5 Articulate and Support Policies that Protect the Dignity of Users and Others Affected by a Computing System

Designing or implementing systems that deliberately or inadvertently demean individuals or groups is ethically unacceptable. Computer professionals who are in decision making positions should verify that systems are designed and implemented to protect personal privacy and enhance personal dignity.

3.6 Create Opportunities for Members of the Organization to Learn the Principles and Limitations of Computer Systems

This complements the imperative on public understanding (2.7). Educational opportunities are essential to facilitate optimal participation of all organizational members. Opportunities must be available to all members to help them improve their knowledge and skills in computing, including courses that familiarize them with the consequences and limitations of particular types of systems. In particular, professionals must be made aware of the dangers of building systems around oversimplified models, the improbability of anticipating and designing for every possible operating condition, and other issues related to the complexity of this profession.

3.1

Chapter 2: p. 49 Thomas J. Watson, Sr., and the Emperor's New Machines

Chapter 5: p. 127 Bill Gates Rides the Digital Wave

Chapter 10: pp. 262–264 Computers and Jobs

3.2

Chapter 2: p. 49 Thomas J. Watson, Sr., and the Emperor's New Machines

Chapter 3: p. 83 Rules of Thumb: Ergonomics and Health

Chapter 10: pp. 258–264 Where Computers Work; pp. 262–264 Computers and Jobs

3.3

Chapter 9: pp. 236–237 On-Line Outlaws: Computer Crime: Hacking and Electronic Trespassing; pp 238–242 Computer Security: Reducing Risks

Chapter 10: pp. 262–264 Computers and Jobs

3.4

Chapter 10: pp. 262–264 Computers and Jobs

3.5

Chapter 10: pp. 262–264 Computers and Jobs

4. Compliance with the Code
As an ACM member I will...

4.1 Uphold and Promote the Principles of this Code
The future of the computing profession depends on both technical and ethical excellence. Not only is it important for ACM computing professionals to adhere to the principles expressed in this Code, each member should encourage and support adherence by other members.

4.2 Treat Violations of this Code as Inconsistent with Membership in the ACM
Adherence of professionals to a code of ethics is largely a voluntary matter. However, if a member does not follow this code by engaging in gross misconduct, membership in ACM may be terminated.

This Code and the supplemental Guidelines were developed by the Task Force for the Revision of the ACM Code of Ethics and Professional Conduct: Ronald E. Anderson, Chair, Gerald Engel, Donald Gotterbarn, Grace C. Hertlein, Alex Hoffman, Bruce Jawer, Deborah G. Johnson, Doris K. Lidtke, Joyce Currie Little, Dianne Martin, Donn B. Parker, Judith A. Perrolle, and Richard S. Rosenberg. The Task Force was organized by ACM/SIGCAS and funding was provided by the ACM SIG Discretionary Fund. This Code and the supplemental Guidelines were adopted by the ACM Council on October 16, 1992.

©1998 Association for Computing Machinery, Inc.

Glossary

1394 See IEEE 1394.
802.11b See WI-FI.

access-control software Software that only allows user access according to the user's needs. Some users can only open files that are related to their work. Some users are allowed read-only access to files they can see but not change. *Chapter 9*

access time The amount of time, measured in nanoseconds, it takes for a CPU to retrieve a unit of data from memory. Also the amount of time, measured in milliseconds, it takes for a CPU to retrieve a unit of data from a disk drive. *Chapter 2*

accounting and financial management software Software especially designed for financial and accounting tasks. The software sets up accounts, keeps track of money flow between accounts, records transactions, adjusts balances in accounts, provides an audit trail, automates routine tasks such as check writing, and produces reports. *Chapter 5*

active badge (smart badge) A microprocessor-controlled ID badge that broadcasts infrared identification codes to a network receiver that updates a badge-location database. *Chapter 9, Chapter 10*

active cell The cell containing the cursor in a spreadsheet. *Chapter 5*

ActiveX A collection of programming technologies and tools that can be used to create programs that are similar in many ways to Java applets. *Chapter 7*

address In a spreadsheet, the location of a cell, determined by row number and column number. *Chapter 5*

affective computers Computers that use sensors to detect the emotional states of their users and respond accordingly. *Chapter 10*

agent A software program that can ask questions, respond to commands, pay attention to its user's work patterns, serve as a guide and a coach, take on its owner's goals, and use reasoning to fabricate goals of its own. *Chapter 10*

agricultural revolution: The time period where people learned to domesticate animals, grow their own grains, and use plows and other agricultural tools. *Chapter 10*

algorithm A set of step-by-step instructions that, when completed, solves a problem. *Chapter 4, Chapter 9*

All-in-one device See multifunction peripheral

alpha testing Initial testing of a system. Also called "pre-beta testing." *Chapter 9*

analog signal A continuous wave. *Chapter 6*

analysis The phase of the systems development life cycle in which details are fleshed out before design begins. *Chapter 9*

Analytical engine The first computer, conceived by Charles Babbage. Programmed with punch cards, it included functions of input, output, processing, and storage. *Chapter 1*

animation The process of simulating motion with a series of still pictures. *Chapter 5*

antivirus program A program designed to search for viruses, notify users when they're found, and remove them from infected files. *Chapter 9*

applet A small compiled program designed to run inside another application—typically a Web browser. *Chapter 4, Chapter 9*

application program (application) Software tool that allows a computer to be used for specific purposes. *Chapter 0, Chapter 1*

application server A specialized server that stores applications and makes them available to client programs that request them. *Chapter 10*

application service provider (ASP) A company that manages and delivers application services on a contract basis. *Chapter 7*

application suite (office suite) A collection of several related application programs that are also sold as separate programs. *Chapter 4*

architecture Design that determines how individual components of the CPU are put together on the chip. More generally used to describe the way individual components are put together to create a complete computer system. *Chapter 2*

arithmetic logic unit (ALU) The part of the CPU that performs data calculations and comparisons. *Chapter 2*

armature The part of a disk drive that moves the read/write head across the disk surface. *Chapter 3*

artificial life Synthetic organisms that act like natural living systems. *Chapter 10*

ASCII (American Standard Code for Information Interchange) A code that represents characters as 8-bit codes. Allows the binary computer to work with letters, digits, and special characters. *Chapter 2*

assembler Translates assembly-language instructions into machine-language instructions. *Chapter 9*

asynchronous communication Delayed communication, such as that used for newsgroups and mailing lists, where the sender and the recipients don't have to be logged in at the same time. *Chapter 6, Chapter 8*

asynchronous teleconference An online meeting between two or more people in which participants type, post, and read messages at their convenience. *Chapter 6*

attachment (email) A way to send formatted word processor documents, pictures, and other multimedia files via email. *Chapter 6, Chapter 8*

audio digitizer Hardware device or software program that captures a sound and stores it as a data file on a disk. *Chapter 5*

audit-control software Monitors and records computer transactions as they happen so auditors can trace and identify suspicious computer activity after the fact. *Chapter 9*

295

Glossary

automated factory A factory that uses extensive computer systems, robots, and networks to streamline and automate many jobs. *Chapter 10*

automated office An office that uses extensive computer systems and networks to streamline information flow and automate many processes. *Chapter 10*

automated teller machine (ATM) A device that enables users to remotely access and deposit money from their bank accounts through the use of a network. *Chapter 6*

automatic correction (autocorrect) Catches and corrects common typing errors. *Chapter 5*

automatic footnoting Word-processing feature that automatically places footnotes where they belong on the page. *Chapter 5*

automatic formatting (autoformat) Automatically applies formatting to the text. *Chapter 5*

automatic hyphenation Word-processing feature that automatically divides long words that fall at the ends of lines. *Chapter 5*

automatic speech recognition See speech recognition.

automation The practice of replacing jobs performed by humans with jobs performed by computers and robots. *Chapter 10*

avatar A graphical body that is used to represent a person in a virtual meeting place; can range from a simple cartoon sketch to an elaborate 3-D figure or an exotic abstract icon. *Chapter 8*

B2B See business-to-business (B2B).

B2C See business-to-consumer (B2C).

backbone A collection of common pathways used to transmit large quantities of data between networks in a wide-area network (WAN). *Chapter 6*

backup The process of saving data—especially for data recovery. Many systems automatically back up data and software onto disks or tapes. *Chapter 9*

backward compatible Able to run software written for older CPUs. Also, when referring to a software program, able to read and write files compatible with older versions of the program. *Chapter 2*

bandwidth The quantity of information that can be transmitted through a communication medium in a given amount of time. *Chapter 6*

bar-code reader A reading tool that uses light to read universal product codes, inventory codes, and other codes created out of patterns of variable-width bars. *Chapter 3*

basic input/output system (BIOS) Firmware programs in ROM *Chapter 2*

batch spelling checker Checks all the words in your document in a batch when you issue the appropriate command. *Chapter 5.*

baud rate An older measurement of modem speed; today bits per second (bps) is a more accurate term. *Chapter 6*

bay An open area in the system box for disk drives and other peripheral devices. *Chapter 2*

binary A choice of two values, such as yes and no or zero and one. *Chapter 2*

binary number system A system that denotes all numbers with combinations of two digits. *Chapter 2*

biometrics Measurements of individual body characteristics, such as a voice print or fingerprint; sometimes used in computer security. *Chapter 9*

bit Binary digit. The smallest unit of information. A bit can have two values—0 or 1. *Chapter 2*

bit-mapped (raster) graphics Graphics in which images are stored and manipulated as organized collections of pixels rather than as shapes and lines. Contrast with object-oriented graphics. *Chapter 5*

bits per second (bps) The standard unit of measure for modem speed. *Chapter 6.*

bits per second (bps) A measurement to describe the transmission speed of a modem. *Chapter 6*

Bluetooth A type of wireless technology that enables mobile phones, handheld computers, and PCs to communicate with each other regardless of operating system. *Chapter 6*

Boolean logic A complex query structure supported by most search engines; one example is "American AND Indian BUT NOT Cleveland." *Chapter 8*

booting Loading the non-ROM part of the operating system into memory. *Chapter 4*

bot A software robot that crawls around the Web collecting information, helping consumers make decisions, answering email, and even playing games. *Chapter 10*

bounce The automatic return of an undeliverable email message to its sender. *Chapter 6*

bridge A hardware device connected that can pass messages between networks. *Chapter 6*

bps See bits per second.

broadband connection An Internet connection such as DSL or cable modem that offers higher bandwidth, and therefore faster transmission speed, than standard modem connections. *Chapter 7*

browse The process of finding information in a database or other data source, such as the World Wide Web. *Chapter 5*

bug An error in programming. *Chapter 4*

bullet charts Graphical elements, such as drawings and tables, integrated into a series of charts that list the main points of a presentation. *Chapter 5*

bulletin board system (BBS) An online version of the bulletin board. *Chapter 6*

burn To record data onto CD-R and CD-RW disks. *Chapter 3*

bus Group of wires on a circuit board. Information travels between components through a bus. *Chapter 2*

business-to-business (B2B) E-commerce transactions that involve businesses providing goods or services to other businesses. *Chapter 8*

business-to-consumer (B2C) E-commerce transactions that involve businesses providing goods or services to consumers. *Chapter 8*

button (command button) A hot spot on a screen that responds to mouse clicks. A button can be programmed to perform one of many tasks, such as opening a dialog box or launching an application. *Chapter 0, Chapter 5*

byte Grouping of 8 bits. *Chapter 2*

cable modem A type of broadband Internet connection that uses the same network of coaxial cables that delivers TV signals. *Chapter 7,*

C# A programming language similar to Java in many ways, but without Java's cross-platform capabilities. *Chapter 7*

CAD See computer-aided design.

CAI See computer-aided instruction.

CAM See computer-aided manufacturing.

card See expansion slot.

carpal tunnel syndrome An affliction of the wrist and hand that results from repeating the same movements over long periods. *Chapter 3*

cathode ray tube (CRT) monitor A television-style monitor that is used as the output device for many desktop computers. *Chapter 3*

CD-R (compact disk–recordable) An optical disk you can write information on, but you cannot remove the information. *Chapter 3*

CD-ROM (compact disc—read-only memory) A type of optical disk that contains data that cannot be changed; CD-ROMs are commonly used to distribute commercial software programs. *Chapter 0, Chapter 3.*

CD-ROM drive A common optical drive in computers that can read data fromCD-ROM disks, *Chapter 3*

CD-RW (compact disk–rewritable) An optical disk that allows writing, erasing, and rewriting. *Chapter 3*

CD-RW Drive A disk drive that can read and write on rewritable optical disks. *Chapter 3*

cell The intersection of a row and a column on the grid of a spreadsheet. *Chapter 5*

central processing unit (CPU) Part of the computer that processes information, performs arithmetic calculations, and makes basic decisions based on information values. *Chapter 0, Chapter 2*

character-based interface A user interface based on text characters rather than graphics. *Chapter 4*

charting capabilities Commands that can turn worksheet numbers into charts and graphs automatically. *Chapter 5*

chat room Public real-time teleconference. *Chapter 6*

chief information officer (CIO) Along with chief technology officers (CTOs), the chief decision makers concerning enterprise computer systems and technology in a business enterprise. *Chapter 10*

chief technology officer (CTO) Along with chief information officers (CIOs), the chief decision makers concerning enterprise computer systems and technology in a business enterprise. *Chapter 10*

CIM See computer-integrated manufacturing.

circuit board Houses the CPU, along with other chips and electronic components in a computer. *Chapter 2*

click The action of pressing a button on a mouse. *Chapter 0, Chapter 1, Chapter 3*

client/server model For a local-area network, a hierarchical model in which one or more computers act as dedicated servers and all the remaining computers act as clients. The server fills requests from clients for data and other resources. *Chapter 6*

client/server model For Internet applications, a client program asks for information, and a server program fields the request and provides the requested information from databases and documents. The client might reside on a personal computer or the host computer, and the server might reside on the same host computer or another host computer elsewhere on the network. *Chapter 8*

clipboard A special portion of memory for temporarily holding information for later use. *Chapter 5*

clock The timing device producing electrical pulses for synchronizing the computer's operations. *Chapter 2*

CMOS (complementary metal oxide semiconductor) A special low-energy kind of RAM that can store small amounts of data for long periods of time on batter power. CMOS RAM is used to store the date, time and calendar in a PC. CMOS RAM is called parameter RAM in Macintoshes. *Chapter 2.*

coaxial cable A type of cable used to connect nodes in computer networks. The same type of cable is also to transport television signals into homes. *Chapter 6*

code of ethics Code of conduct specifically for computer professionals and developed by the ACM (Association for Computing Machinery). *Chapter 9*

color depth (bit depth) The number of bits devoted to each pixel. *Chapter3*

columns Along with rows, comprise the grid of a spreadsheet. *Chapter 5*

command-line interface User interface that requires the user to type text commands on a command-line to communicate with the operating system. *Chapter 4*

communication software Software that enables computers to interact with each other over a phone line or other network. *Chapter 6*

communications satellite A satellite used to relay information between points on Earth. A typical communications satellite is geostationery; it matches the earth's rotation so it can hang in a stationary position relative to the spinning planet below. *Chapter 6*

compatibility The ability of a software program to run on a specific computer system. Also, the ability of a hardware device to function with a particular type of computer. *Chapter 2, Chapter 4*

compiler A translator program that translates an entire program from a high-level computer language before the program is run for the first time. *Chapter 4*

complex instruction set computer processors (CISC) Instruction sets included in modern computers. Slower and less efficient than processors designed to execute fewer instructions. *Chapter 2*

compression Making files smaller using special encoding schemes. File compression saves storage space on disk and saves transmission time when files are transferred through networks. *Chapter 5, Chapter 7*

computed field In a database, a field containing formulas similar to spreadsheet formulas; they display values calculated from values in other numeric fields. *Chapter 8*

computer-aided design (CAD) The use of computers to design products. *Chapter 5, Chapter 10*

computer-aided manufacturing (CAM) When the design of a product is completed, the numbers are fed to a program that controls the manufacturing of parts. For electronic parts the design translates directly into a template for etching circuits onto chips. Also called CIM, or computer integrated manufacturing. *Chapter 10*

computer crime Any crime accomplished through knowledge or use of computer technology. *Chapter 9*

computer monitoring Using computer technology to track, record, and evaluate worker performance, often without the knowledge of the worker. *Chapter 10*

computer security Protecting computer systems and the information they contain against unwanted access, damage, modification, or destruction. *Chapter 9*

computer telephony integration (CTI) The linking of computers and telephones to gain productivity; voicemail is one example.

concurrent processing A large computer working on several jobs at the same time. The computer uses multiple CPUs to process jobs simultaneously. *Chapter 4*

console (formula bar, edit line) In spreadsheet software, the long window above the worksheet where typing appears. *Chapter 5*

consumer portal A portal that includes search engines, email services, chat rooms, references, news and sports headlines, shopping malls, other services, and advertisements—many of the same things found in online services such as AOL. *Chapter 8*

context-sensitive menus Menus offering choices that depend on the context. *Chapter 4.*

contract (law) A type of law that covers trade secrets. *Chapter 9*

cookies small files deposited on a user's hard disk by Web sites, enabling sites to remember what they know about their visitors between sessions. *Chapter 10, Chapter 8*

copy-protected software Software that prevents a disk from being copied. *Chapter 4*

copyright (law) A type of law that traditionally protects forms of literary expression. *Chapter 9*

copyrighted software Software that is legally protected against duplication. *Chapter 4*

corporate portal A specialized portal on an intranet that serves the employees of a particular corporation. *Chapter 8*

CPU See central processing unit.

cracking Unauthorized access and/or vandalism of computer systems; short for criminal hacking. *Chapter 9*

cradle Device used in docking handheld computers that enables them to share information with desktop and laptop PC's. *Chapter 1*

CRT See cathode ray tube monitor.

current cell (active cell) The cell containing the cursor in a spreadsheet. *Chapter 5*

cursor A line or rectangle, sometimes flashing, that indicates your location on the screen or in a document. *Chapter 3, Chapter 5*

custom application An application programmed for a specific purpose, typically for a specific client. *Chapter 4*

cut-and-paste Copying or deleting text from one point and pasting it into another point in the document. *Chapter 5*

cyberspace A term used to describe the Internet and other on-line networks, especially the artificial realities and virtual communities that form on them. First coined by William Gibson in his novel, *Neuromancer*. *Chapter 8*

data Information in a form that can be read, used, and manipulated by a computer. *Chapter 1, Chapter 2*

data compression Reduces the size of a data file so it can be stored in a smaller space. *Chapter 5*

data compression See compression.

data transfer rate The speed at which data is transferred, using a CD-RW drive. *Chapter 3*

data translation software Software tthat enables users of different systems with incompatible file formats to read and modify each other's files *Chapter 6*

database A collection of information stored in an organized form in a computer. *Chapter 5*

database-driven Web site A Web site that uses database technology to present information dynamically based on current conditions and client requests. *Chapter 7*

database management system (DBMS) A program or system of programs that can manipulate data in a large collection of files (the database), cross-referencing between files as needed. *Chapter 5*

database program A software tool for organizing the storage and retrieval of the information in a database. *Chapter 5*

DBMS See database management system.

debugging Finding and correcting errors—bugs—in computer software. *Chapter 4*

decision support system (DSS) A computer system that supports managers in decision-making tasks. *Chapter 10*

decode unit Takes the instruction read by the prefetcher an translates it into a form suitable for the the CPU's internal processing. *Chapter 2*

dedicated (special-purpose) computer Computer that performs specific tasks, such as controlling temperature and humidity in an office building. *Chapter 1*

delayed teleconference See asynchronous teleconference.

deleting text Removing text from the document. *Chapter 5*

demo software A program, usually available for free trial download, that is identical to a commercial program except that it has some key features disabled. *Chapter 4*

denial of service (DoS) attacks A type of computer vandalism that bombards servers and Web sites with so much bogus traffic that they're effectively shut down, denying service to legitimate customers and clients. *Chapter 9*

desktop A visual representation of a desktop in a graphical user interface where the user performs tasks. *Chapter 0, Chapter 4*

desktop publishing (DTP) Software used mainly to produce print publications. Also, the process of using desktop publishing software to produce publications. *Chapter 5*

desktop system A computer system designed to sit on a desktop. *Chapter 3*

device drivers Small programs that allow input/output devices to communicate with the computer. *Chapter 4.*

dialog box In a graphical user interface, a box that enables the user to communicate with the computer. *Chapter 4*

dial-up connection A temporary connection to an Internet host that uses a modem and standard telephone lines. *Chapter 7*

digital Information made up of discrete units that can be counted. *Chapter 2*

digital audio Format that allows sound files to be stored. *Chapter 5*

digital camera A camera that captures images and stores them as bit patterns on disks or other digital storage media instead of using film. *Chapter 3*

digital cash A system for purchasing goods and services on the Internet without using credit cards. *Chapter 8*

digital divide A term that describes the divide between the people who do and do not have access to the Internet. *Chapter 8*

digital image processing software Enables the user to manipulate photographs and other high-resolution images. *Chapter 5*

digital signal A stream of bits. *Chapter 6*

digital signature A developing identity verification standard that uses encryption techniques to protect against email forgery. *Chapter 8*

digital video Video reduced to a series of numbers and can be edited, stored, and played back without loss of quality. *Chapter 5*

digital video camera A video camera that captures footage in digital form so that clips can be transferred to and from a computer for editing with no loss of quality. *Chapter 5*

digitize Converting information into a digital form that can be stored in the computer's memory. *Chapter 3*

DIMM (Dual in-line memory module) *Chapter 2*

direct (dedicated) connection A dedicated, direct connection to the Internet through a LAN, with the computer having its own IP address. *Chapter 6, Chapter 7*

directory A logical container used to group files and other directories. Also called a folder. *Chapter 4*

disinfectant program See antivirus program

disk drive Device used to retrieve information from a disk and, in some cases, to transfer data to it. *Chapter 3*

diskette (floppy disk) A small, magnetically sensitive, flexible plastic wafer housed in a plastic case, used as a storage device. *Chapter 0, Chapter 3*

distributed computing Integrating all kinds of computers, from mainframes to PCs, into a single, seamless system. *Chapter 8, Chapter 10*

distributed denial of service (DDoS) attack A denial of service attack in which the flood of messages comes from many compromised systems distributed across the Net. *Chapter 9*

DNS See domain name system.

docking station A device for expanding a laptop computer so that it has the power and flexibility of a desktop. *Chapter 1*

documentation Instructions for installing the software on a computer's hard disk. *Chapter 4.*

documents Files, such as term papers and charts created with applications. *Chapter 0, Chapter 4*

domain A class of Internet addresses indicated by a suffix such as .com, .gov, or .net. *Chapter 7*

domain name registry A company that provides its customers with domain names that are easier to remember and use.

domain name system (DNS) A system that translates a computer's numerical IP address into an easier-to-remember string of names separated by dots. *Chapter 7*

dot-matrix printer An old-fashioned impact printer that uses pinpoint-size hammers to transfer ink to the page. The printed page is a matrix of tiny dots. *Chapter 3*

Double-click To click a mouse button twice in rapid succession. *Chapter 0*

download To copy software from an online source to a local computer. *Chapter 6, Chapter 7*

downloadable video Compressed video files that can be downloaded and viewed on a computer. *Chapter 7*

downstream traffic Information transmitted from the Internet to the subscriber. *Chapter 7*

drag To move the mouse while holding the mouse button down. Used for moving objects, selecting text, drawing, and other tasks. *Chapter 0, Chapter 3*

drag-and-drop Editing feature that enables the user to move selected text or an object by dragging it (with the mouse) from one part of the screen to another. *Chapter 5*

drawing software Stores a picture as a collection of lines and shapes. Also stores shapes as shape formulas and text as text. *Chapter 5*

drum scanner A scanner used in publishing applications where image quality is critical. *Chapter 3*

DSL (digital subscriber line) A type of broadband connection to the Internet offered by phone companies. *Chapter 6, Chapter 7*

DSS (decision support system) A computer system that supports managers in decision-making tasks. *Chapter 10*

DTP (desktop publishing) See desktop publishing. *Chapter 5*

dual-boot PC A PC that can switch back and forth between two operating systems by rebooting. *Chapter 4*

DVD (digital video disk or digital versatile disk) Popular type of high-capacity optical disk used in both consumer video playback machines and computers. *Chapter 3*

DVD-R Recordable DVD disk. *Chapter 3*

DVD-CD-RW drive A disk drive that combines the capabilities of a DVD-ROM drive and a CD-RW drive in a single unit. *Chapter 3*

DVD-RAM A type of optical disk with multigigabyte capacity that can be read, written, and erased. *Chapter 3*

DVD-ROM A type of optical disk with read-only capability that is the size of a CD-ROM but that holds much more information. *Chapter 3*

DVD-Rom drive An optical disk drive that can read high-capacity DVD disks. *Chapter 3*

dynamic HTML A relatively new version of HTML that supports formatting and layout features that aren't supported in standard HTML. *Chapter 7*

e-commerce See electronic commerce (e-commerce).

EDI See Electronic Data Interchange.

editing Inserting, deleting, copying, and moving text and other data within a document, and from one document to another. *Chapter 5*

electronic book (ebook) A handheld device that displays digital representations of the contents of books. *Chapter 5*

electronic commerce (e-commerce) Business transactions through electronic networks. *Chapter 6, Chapter 8*

electronic cottage A home in which modern technology enables a person to work at home. *Chapter 10*

electronic data interchange (EDI) A set of specifications for conducting basic business transactions over private networks. *Chapter 8*

electronic funds transfer Automatic money transfers made inside computer networks, not through the use of cash or checks. *Chapter 6*

electronic mail (email) Allows Internet users to send mail messages, data files, and software programs to other Internet users and to users of most commercial networks and online services. *Chapter 0, Chapter 1, Chapter 6*

electronic organizer See personal information manager.

electronic paper (e-paper) A flexible experimental output device that can be read like printed paper, erased, and reused. *Chapter 5, Chapter 10*

email See electronic mail.

email server A specialized server that acts like a local post office for a particular Internet host. *Chapter 8*

email virus A virus spread via email. *Chapter 9*

embedded computer Computer that is embedded into a consumer product, such as a wristwatch or game machine, to enhance those products. Also used to control hardware devices. *Chapter 1*

emulation A process that enables programs to run on a noncompatible operating system. *Chapter 4*

encryption Protects transmitted information by scrambling the transmissions. When a user encrypts a message by applying a secret numerical code (encryption key), the message can be transmitted or stored as an indecipherable garble of characters. The message can be read only after it's been reconstructed with a matching key. *Chapter 9*

enterprise network systems Large, complex networks with hundreds of computers that are tracked and maintained with network management system software. *Chapter 6*

e-paper See electronic paper.

equation solver A feature of some spreadsheet programs that determines data values. *Chapter 6*

Ethernet A popular networking architecture developed in 1976 at Xerox. *Chapter 6*

ethics A moral philosophy of right and wrong. Computer ethics involve principles and guidelines to help users focus on the many technology-related dilemmas of our time. *Chapter 9*

ergonomics The science of designing work environments that enable people and things to interact efficiently and safely. *Chapter 3*

error message Message from the operating system or application that tells the user an error has occurred. *Chapter 4*

ethics A moral philosophy of right and wrong. Computer ethics involve principles and guidelines to help users foucs on the many technology-related dilemmas of our time. *Chapter 9*

expansion cards A special-purpose circuit board that can be inserted in one of a computer's expansion slots. *Chapter 2*

expansion slots An area inside the computer's housing that holds special-purpose circuit boards. *Chapter 2*

export data Transmitting records and fields from a database program to another program. *Chapter 5*

exporting The process of transmitting records and fields from a program, such as a database program, into a form that can be read and processed by another program. *Chapter 5*

extranet A private TCP/IP network designed for outside use by customers, clients, and business partners of an organization. These networks are typically for electronic commerce. *Chapter 7, Chapter 8*

facsimile (fax) A technology that allows images of paper documents to be transmitted through telephone lines to a destination where they can be printed or displayed on a computer screen. *Chapter 6*

300 Glossary

fair use The time-honored right to make copies of copyrighted material for personal and academic use and for other noncompetitive purposes. *Chapter 9*

FAQ (frequently asked questions) A list of frequently asked questions is posted for many newsgroups and mailing lists. The FAQs keep the groups from being cluttered with the same old questions and answers, if their members take advantage of them. *Chapter 8*

fax modem Hardware peripheral that enables a computer to send onscreen documents to a receiving fax machine by translating the document into signals that can be sent over phone wires and decoded by the receiving fax machine. *Chapter 6*

feedback loop In a computer simulation, the user and the computer responding to data from each other. *Chapter 6*

fiber optic cable High-capacity cable that uses light waves to carry information at blinding speeds. *Chapter 6*

field Each discrete chunk of information in a database record. *Chapter 5*

file An organized collection of related information stored in a computer-readable form. *Chapter 2, Chapter 5*

file manager A program that enables users to manipulate files on their computers. *Chapter 5*

file server In a LAN, a computer used as a storehouse for software and data that are shared by several users. *Chapter 6*

file transfer protocol (FTP) A communications protocol that enables users to download files from remote servers to their computers and to upload files they want to share from their computers to these archives. *Chapter 7*

filtering software Software that, for the most part, keeps offensive and otherwise inappropriate Web content from being viewed by children, on-duty workers, and others. *Chapter 8*

find and replace See search and replace.

Find command A command used to locate a particular word, string of characters, or formatting in a document. *Chapter 5*

firewall Software or hardware that guards against unauthorized access to an internal network; keeps internal networks secure while allowing communication with the rest of the Internet. *Chapter 9*

FireWire See IEEE 1394.

firmware A program, usually for special-purpose computers, stored on a ROM chip so it cannot be altered. *Chapter 1*

flash memory A type of erasable memory chip used in cell phones, pagers, portable computers, and handheld computers, among other things. *Chapter 2, Chapter 3*

flatbed scanner Scanner that looks and works like a photocopy machine, except that it creates computer files instead of paper copies. *Chapter 3*

floppy disk (diskette) A small, magnetically sensitive, flexible plastic wafer housed in a plastic case, used as a storage device. *Chapter 3*

folder A container for files and other folders. Also called a directory. *Chapter 4*

font A size and style of typeface. *Chapter 5*

footer Block of information that appears at the bottom of every page in a document, displaying repetitive information such as an automatically calculated page number. *Chapter 5*

form On the Web, a page (or part of a page) that enables visitors to enter information into fields; *Chapter 7*

formatting The function of software, such as word processing software, that enables users to change the appearance of a document by specifying the font, point size, and style of any character in the document, as well as the overall layout of text and graphical elements in the document *Chapter 5*

formula Step-by-step procedure for calculating a number on a spreadsheet. *Chapter 5*

formula bar In spreadsheet software, the long window above the worksheet where typing appears. *Chapter 5*

frame In animation, one still picture in a video or animated sequence. *Chapter 10*

frame In Web design, subdivisions of a Web browser's viewing area that enable visitors to scroll and view different parts of a page—or even multiple pages—simultaneously. *Chapter 7*

FTP See file transfer protocol.

full-access dial-up connection Enables a computer connected via modem and phone line to temporarily have full Internet access and a temporary IP address. *Chapter 7*

function A predefined set of calculations, such as SUM and AVERAGE, in spreadsheet software. *Chapter 5*

gateway A computer connected to two networks that translates communication protocols and transfers information between the two. *Chapter 7*

geostationary Matching the Earth's rotation in a stationary position relative to the spinning planet below. *Chapter 6*

genetic algorithm An algorithm that automatically evolves through many generations. *Chapter 6, Chapter 10*

GB See gigabyte.

geographical information system (GIS) A specialized database that combines tables of data with demographic information and displays geographic and demographic data on maps. *Chapter 5*

generation One cycle of backups; many data-processing shops keep several generations of backups so they can, if necessary, go back several days, weeks, or years to reconstruct data files. *Chapter 9*

generations of computers Designations for major changes in hardware. First-generation computers were built around vacuum tubes. Second-generation computers used transistors. Integrated circuits characterized third-generation computers. The invention of the microprocessor marked the beginning of fourth-generation computers. *Chapter 1*

gigabyte (GB) Approximately 1000MB. *Chapter 2*

GIGO Garbage in, garbage out. Valid output requires valid input. *Chapter 5*

GIS See geographical information system.

Global Positioning System (GPS) A defense department system with 24 satellites that can pinpoint any location on the Earth. *Chapter 6*

GPS See Global Positioning System.

GPS receiver A device that can use Global Positioning System signals to determine its location and communicate that information to a person or a computer. *Chapter 6*

grammar and style checker Component of word-processing software that analyzes each word in context, checking for content errors, common grammatical errors, and stylistic problems. *Chapter 5*

graphical user interface (GUI) A user interface based on graphical displays. With a mouse, the user points to icons that represent files, folders, and disks. Documents are displayed in windows. The user selects commands from menus. *Chapter 4*

graphics tablet A pressure-sensitive touch tablet used as a pointing device. The user presses on the tablet with a stylus. *Chapter 3*

gray-scale monitor Monitor that displays black, white, and shades of gray but no other colors. *Chapter 3*

grid computing A form of distributed computing in which not files but processing power is shared between networked computers. *Chapter 8*

groupware Software designed to be used by work groups rather than individuals. *Chapter 5, Chapter 6, Chapter 10*

GUI See graphical user interface.

H

hacker Someone who uses computer skills to gain unauthorized access to computer systems. Also sometimes used to refer to particularly talented, dedicated programmer. *Chapter 9*

hacking Electronic trespassing and vandalism. *Chapter 9*

hand-held computer A portable computer small enough to be tucked into a jacket pocket. *Chapter 1*

handwriting recognition software Software that translates the user's handwritten forms into ASCII characters. *Chapter 3*

hard copy A paper copy, produced by a printer, of any information that can be displayed on the screen. *Chapter 3*

hard disk A rigid, magnetically sensitive disk that spins rapidly and continuously inside the computer chassis or in a separate box attached to the computer housing. Used as a storage device. *Chapter 0, Chapter 3*

hardware Physical parts of the computer system. *Chapter 0, Chapter 1*

hardware compression Compression using hardware rather than software. *Chapter 5*

header Block that appears at the top of every page in a document, displaying repetitive information such as a chapter title. *Chapter 5*

help file A documentation file that appears onscreen at the user's request. *Chapter 4*

helper application A program designed to help users view particular types of graphics, animation, audio, or video that can't be played by the browser. *Chapter 7*

hierarchical menus Menus that organize commands into compact, efficient submenus. *Chapter 4*

high-level language A programming language that falls somewhere between natural human languages and precise machine languages, developed to streamline and simplify the programming process. *Chapter 4*

high-performance computer See supercomputer.

home page The main entry page to a Web site. *Chapter 7*

host system A computer that provides services to multiple users. *Chapter 6*

hot swap To remove and replace peripheral devices without powering down the computer and peripherals. Some modern interface standards such as USB and FireWire, allow hot-swapping. *Chapter 3*

hot sync Synchronizing of data, typically between a handheld compter and a desktop PC. *Chapter 5*

HTML See Hypertext Markup Language.

HTTP (hypertext transfer protocol) The internet protocol used to transfer Web pages. *Chapter 7*

hybrid disks Media-rich CD-ROMs and DVD-ROMS that automatically draw content and communication from the Web. *Chapter 5*

hyperlink A word, phrase, or picture that acts as a button, enabling the user to explore the Web or a multimedia document with mouse clicks. *Chapter 0, Chapter 7*

hypermedia The combination of text, numbers, graphics, animation, sound effects, music, and other media in hyperlinked documents. *Chapter 5, Chapter 7*

hypertext An interactive cross-referenced system that allows textual information to be linked in nonsequential ways. A hypertext document contains links that lead quickly to other parts of the document or to related documents. *Chapter 7*

Hypertext Markup Language (HTML) An HTML document is a text file that includes codes that describe the format, layout, and logical structure of a hypermedia document. Most Web pages are created with HTML. *Chapter 7*

I

IEEE 1394 An industry standard for relatively new, extremely fast serial communications protocol, especially well suited for multimedia applications such as digital video. Apple computer, which developed the standard, refers to IEEE 1394 as FireWire. *Chapter 4*

icon In a graphical user interface, a picture that represents a file, folder, or disk. *Chapter 4*

identity theft Use of stolen information to assume the identity of another individual. *Chapter 9*

image processing software Software that enables the user to manipulate photographs and other high-resolution images. *Chapter 5*

impact printer Printer that forms images by physically striking paper, ribbon, and print hammer together. *Chapter 3*

industrial revolution The transition of society from an agricultural economy to an industrial economy. *Chapter 6, Chapter 10*

information Anything that can be communicated. *Chapter 2*

information appliance Network computer or other Internet-capable device used in offices and homes. *Chapter 1*

information economy An economy based on information-related work. *Chapter 10*

information systems manager A manager whose responsibilities revolve around an organizations computer systems and networks. *Chapter 10*

Infrared technology A type of wireless networking that uses ports that can send and receive digital information short distances. Not widely used in networks because of distance and line-of-sight limitations, but practical for mobile users.

inkjet printer A nonimpact printer that sprays ink directly onto paper to produce printed text and graphic images. *Chapter 3*

input Information taken in by the computer. *Chapter 1*

input device Device for accepting input, such as a keyboard. *Chapter 1, Chapter 2*

inserting text Adding text at any point in a document. *Chapter 5*

insertion bar Indicates your location in a document. *Chapter 5*

instant messaging A technology that enables users to create buddy lists, check for "buddies" who are logged in, and exchange typed messages and files with those who are. *Chapter 6, Chapter 8*

instruction Computer code telling the CPU to perform a specific action. *Chapter 2*

instruction set A vocabulary of instructions that can be executed by a specific processor. Generally newer processors can process instructions used by earlier models in the same CPU family. *Chapter 2*

integrated circuit A chip containing hundreds, thousands, or even millions of transistors. *Chapter 1*

integrated software Software packages that include several applications designed to work well together. *Chapter 4*

intellectual property The results of intellectual activities in the arts, science, and industry. *Chapter 9*

interactive multimedia Multimedia that enables the user to take an active part in the experience. *Chapter 5*

interactive spelling checker A spelling checker that checks each word as it's typed, sometimes marking each mistyped word by underlining it. *Chapter 5*

interface standards Standards agreed upon by the computer industry to ensure that devices made by one manufacturer can be attached to systems made by other companies. *Chapter 3*

internal modem A modem that is built into the system unit. *Chapter 3.*

Internet (Net) A global interconnected network of thousands of networks linking academic, research, government, and commercial institutions, and other organizations and individuals. *Chapter 0, Chapter 1, Chapter 7*

Internet appliances Non-PC devices such as set-top boxes that are connected to the Internet. *Chapter 8*

Internet service provider (ISP) A business that provides its customers with connections to the Internet along with other services. *Chapter 7*

Internet telephony (IP telephony) A combination of software and hardware technology that enables the Internet to, in effect, serve as a telephone network. Internet telephony systems can use standard telephones, computers, or both to send and receive voice messages. *Chapter 7*

Internet2 An alternative Internet-style network that provides faster network communications for universities and research institutions. *Chapter 8*

internetworking Connecting different types of networks and computer systems. *Chapter 10*

intranet A self-contained intraorganizational network that is designed using the same technology as the Internet. *Chapter 1, Chapter 8*

IP address A unique string of four numbers separated by periods that serves as a unique address for a computer on the Internet. The IP address of the host computer and sending computer is included with every packet of information that traverses the Internet. *Chapter 7*

ISDN A digital broadband service offered by phone companies. Because it is slower and more expensive than DSL and other broadband options, ISDN is not widely used today. *Chapter 6*

ISP See Internet service provider.

J

Java A platform-neutral, object-oriented programming language developed by Sun Microsystems for use on multiplatform networks. *Chapter 4, Chapter 7*

JavaScript A Web scripting language similar to, but otherwise unrelated to, Java. *Chapter 7*

Java virtual machine Software that gives a computer the capability to run Java programs. *Chapter 4*

jobless growth A period of time when productivity increases not because of the work people do but because of the work of machines. *Chapter 10*

joystick A gearshift-like device used as a controller for arcade-style computer games. *Chapter 3*

justification The alignment of text on a line: left justification (smooth left margin and ragged right margin), right justification, full justification (both margins are smooth), and center justification. *Chapter 5*

K

K See kilobyte

keyboard Input device, similar to a typewriter keyboard, for entering data and commands into the computer. *Chapter 0, Chapter 1, Chapter 3*

keyboard/mouse ports Ports for attaching keyboard and mouse to most older PCs. *Chapter 3*

kilobyte (K) About 1000 bytes of information. *Chapter 2*

L

label In a spreadsheet, a text entry that provides information on what a column or row represents. *Chapter 5*

LAN See local area network.

laptop computer A flat-screen, battery-powered portable computer that you can rest on your lap. *Chapter 1*

laser printer A nonimpact printer that uses a laser beam to create patterns of electrical charges on a rotating drum. The charged patterns attract black toner and transfer it to paper as the drum rotates. *Chapter 3*

LCD See liquid crystal display monitor.

Legacy-free PCs PCs using USB ports *Chapter 3*.

line printer An impact printer used by mainframes to produce massive printouts. They print characters only, not graphics. *Chapter 3*

links See hyperlinks.

Linux An operating system based on UNIX, maintained by volunteers, and distributed for free. Linux is used mostly in servers and embedded computers, but is growing in popularity as a PC operating system. *Chapter 4*

liquid crystal display (LCD) monitor A flat-panel display monitor typically used for portable computers. *Chapter 3*

local-area network (LAN) A network in which the computers are close to each other, usually in the same building. Typically includes a collection of computers and peripherals; each computer and shared peripheral is an individual node on the network. *Chapter 1, Chapter 6*

logic bomb A program designed to attack in response to a particular logical event or sequence of events. A type of software sabotage. *Chapter 9*

login name A one-word name that you type to identify yourself when connecting—logging in—to a secure a computer system or network. Sometimes called user name. *Chapter 0, Chapter 6, Chapter 7*

lossless compression Systems allowing files to be compressed and later decompressed without a loss of data. *Chapter 5*

lossy compression system A type of compression in which some quality is lost in the process of compression and decompression. *Chapter 5*

Luddites A group of 19th Century workers who smashed new textile machinery to protect their jobs; today the term is often used to describe someone who opposes new technology in general. *Chapter 10*

lurker A person who silently monitors mailing lists and newsgroups without posting messages. *Chapter 8*

M

machine language The language that computers use to process instructions. Machine language uses numeric codes to represent basic computer operations. *Chapter 4*

Mac OS The operating system for the Apple Macintosh computer. *Chapter 4*

macro Custom-designed embedded procedure program that automates tasks in application programs. *Chapter 5*

macro virus A virus that attaches itself to and is transmitted through macros embedded in documents; usually spread via email. *Chapter 9*

magnetic disk Storage medium with random-access capability, accessed by the computer's disk drive. *Chapter 3*

magnetic-ink character reader Reads numbers printed with magnetic ink on checks. *Chapter 3*

magnetic tape A storage medium used with a tape drive to store large amounts of information in a small space at relatively low cost. *Chapter 3*

magneto-optical (MO) disks A type of removable media that uses a combination of magnetic disk technology and optical disk technology. *Chapter 3*

mailing list An email discussion group on special-interest topics. All subscribers receive messages sent to the group's mailing address. *Chapter 8*

Glossary

mail merge A feature of a word processors or other program that enables it to merge names and addresses from a database mailing list into personalized form letters and mailings. *Chapter 5*

mainframe computer Expensive, room-size computer, used mostly for large computing jobs. *Chapter 1*

management information systems (MIS) Systems that provide timely, reliable, and useful information to managers in business, industry, and government. MIS specialists apply the theoretical concepts of computer science to real-world, practical business problems. *Chapter 10*

mathematics processing software Software designed to deal with complex equations and calculations. A mathematics processor enables the user to create, manipulate, and solve equations easily. *Chapter 5*

MB See megabyte.

megabit (Mb) Approximately 1,000bits—one eighth the size of a megabyte. *Chapter 2*

megabyte (MB) Approximately 1000K, or 1 million bytes. *Chapter 2*

megahertz (MHz) A unit of measurement for a computer's clock speed; millions of clock cycles per second. *Chapter 2*

memory Stores programs and the data they need to be instantly accessible to the CPU. *Chapter 0, Chapter 2*

memory-mapped I/O Information for input and output stored in special areas of memory. *Chapter 2*

menu An onscreen list of command choices. *Chapter 0, Chapter 4*

menu bar Part of the user interface. A bar that contains menus of choices. *Chapter 0*

menu-driven interface User interface that enables users to choose commands from onscreen lists called menus. *Chapter 4*

meta-search engine A software tool that conducts parallel searches using several different search engines and directories. *Chapter 7*

metropolitan area network (MAN) A service that links two or more LANs within a city. *Chapter 6*

MHz See megahertz.

microcomputer Small computer made possible by the microprocessor. Now known as a personal computer. *Chapter 1*

microcomputer revolution Period that began in the mid-1970s when several companies introduced small microcomputers that were as powerful as their larger predecessors. *Chapter 1*

micro-electro-mechanical systems (MEMS) Microscopic electricity-powered machines using a process similar to that of manufacturing computer chips. *Chapter 10*

microprocessor Critical components of a complete computer, housed on a silicon chip. *Chapter 1, Chapter 2*

Microsoft Windows The most popular and powerful PC operating system; uses a graphical user interface. *Chapter 4*

microtechnology Technology that allows the development of micromachines, machines on the scale of a millionth of a meter. *Chapter 10*

middleware Connectivity software linking the client and server machines, providing easy access to information. *Chapter 8*

MIDI (Musical Instrument Digital Interface) A standard interface that allows electronic instruments and computers to communicate with each other and work together. *Chapter 5*

millisecond A thousandth of a second. *Chapter 2*

MIPS (millions of instructions per second) A measurement of computer speed, where an instruction is the most primitive operation performed by the processor—moving a number to a memory location, comparing two numbers, and the like. *Chapter 10*

mirror To automatically duplicate copies of data to multiple disks, effectively creating instant backups. *Chapter 9*

MIS See management information systems.

MO See magneto-optical disks.

modeling The use of computers to create abstract models of objects, organisms, organizations, and processes. *Chapter 5*

modem Modulator/demodulator. A hardware device that connects a computer to a telephone line. *Chapter 6*

moderated (news group or mailing list) Monitored by a moderator who filters out inappropriate or off-topic messages so subscribers don't need to receive or read them. *Chapter 8*

monitor An output device that displays text and graphics onscreen. *Chapter 3*

monochrome monitor Monitor that displays two colors, usually black and white. *Chapter 3*

monospaced font A font in which all characters are equal width, like a typewriter's characters. *Chapter 5*

moral dilemma A predicament for which rules and ethics don't seem to apply, or to contradict one another. *Chapter 9*

Moore's Law The prediction made in 1965 by Gordon Moore that the power of a silicon chip of the same price would double about every 18 months for at least two decades. *Chapter 1*

mouse A handheld input device that, when moved around on a desktop or table, moves a pointer around the computer screen. *Chapter 0, Chapter 3*

motherboard The circuit board that contains a computer's CPU. Also called a system board. *Chapter 2*

moving text Transporting a block of text from one part of a document to another, or from one document to another. *Chapter 5*

MP3 A method of compression that can squeeze a music file to a fraction of its original CD file size with only slight loss of quality. *Chapter 7*

MS-DOS (Microsoft Disk Operating System) An operating system with character-based user interface; it was widely used in the 1980s and early 1990s but has been superceded by Windows. *Chapter 4*

Multifunction peripheral (MFP) A device utilizing the fact that different tools can ukse similar technologies. For example, a multifunction device might combine a scanner, a printer, and a fax modem, to serve as a printer, a scanner, a color photcopy machine, and a fax machine. Also called an all-in-one-device. *Chapter 3*

multimedia Using some combination of text, graphics, animation, video, music, voice, and sound effects to communicate. *Chapter 5*

multimedia authoring software Enables the creation and editing of multimedia documents. *Chapter 5*

multiprocessing See parallel processing.

multitasking Concurrent processing for personal computers. The user can issue a command that initiates a process and continue working with other applications while the computer follows through on the command. *Chapter 4*

N

Nanosecond A billionth of a second; a common unit of measurement for read and write access time to RAM. *Chapter 2*

nanotechnology The manufacture of machines on a scale of a few billionths of a meter. *Chapter 10*

narrowband connection A dial-up Internet connection; named because it doesn't offer much bandwidth when compared to other types of connections. *Chapter 7*

National Infrastructure Protection Center A state-of-the-art command center created to fight the growing threat of system sabotage. The center includes representatives of various intelligence agencies (the departments of defense, transportation, energy, and treasury), and representatives of several major corporations. *Chapter 9*

natural-language Language that people speak and write every day. *Chapter 4*

natural-language processing Applications that involve English-like commands. *Chapter 10*

navigating Moving to different parts of a document. *Chapter 5*

Net (Internet) A global interconnected network of thousands of networks linking academic, research, government, and commercial institutions, and other organizations and individuals. *Chapter 1, Chapter 7*

netiquette Rules of etiquette that apply to Internet communication. *Chapter 8*

network A computer system that links two or more computers. *Chapter 6*

network card A network interface card that adds a LAN port to a PC. *Chapter 3*

network computer (NC) A computer designed to function as part of a network rather than as a PC. *Chapter 1, Chapter 10*

network interface card (NIC) Card that adds an additional serial port to a computer. The port is especially designed for a direct network connection. *Chapter 6*

network license License for multiple copies or removing restrictions on software copying and use at a network site. *Chapter 6*

network operating system (NOS) Server operating system software for a local-area network. *Chapter 6*

network revolution The emergence of networks (clusters of computers linked together for communication and to share resources) and the beginning of the era of interpersonal computing. *Chapter 1*

newsgroup Ongoing public discussions on a particular subject consisting of notes written to a central Internet site and redistributed through a worldwide newsgroup network called. Usenet. You can check into and out of them whenever you want; all messages are posted on virtual bulletin boards for anyone to read anytime. *Chapter 8*

newsreader A client program that enables you to read newsgroups. Both text-based and graphical newsreaders are available. *Chapter 8*

Next Generation Internet (NGI) A future nationwide web of optical fiber integrated with intelligent management software to maintain high-speed connections. *Chapter 8*

NGI See Next Generation Internet (NGI).

NIC See network interface card.

node Each computer and shared peripheral on a local-area network. *Chapter 6*

nonimpact printer A printer that produces characters without physically striking the page. *Chapter 3*

nonvolatile memory Memory for permanent storage of information. *Chapter 2*

NOS See network operating system.

notebook computer Another term for laptop computer. *Chapter 1*

object-oriented (vector) graphics The storage of pictures as collections of lines, shapes, and other objects. *Chapter 5*

OCR See optical character recognition.

office suite (application suite) Software bundle containing several application programs that are also sold as separate programs. *Chapter 4*

online Connected to the computer system and ready to communicate. *Chapter 6*

online banking use of the Internet to conduct basic banking transactions *Chapter 5*

online database A commercial, public, or private database that can be accessed through telecommunication lines. *Chapter 6*

online help Documentation and help available through a software company's Web site. *Chapter 4*.

online service A service that enables hundreds of users at a time to send and receive information. America Online is an example. *Chapter 6*

OOP (object-oriented programming) See object-oriented programming (OOP).

open To load a file into an application program's workspace so it can be viewed and edited by the user. *Chapter 4, Chapter 5*

open architecture A design that allows expansion cards and peripherals to be added to a basic computer system. *Chapter 3*

open source software Software that can be distributed and modified freely by users; Linux is the best-known example. *Chapter 4*

open standards Standards not owned by any company. *Chapter 7*

opening a document Copying a document file from disk into memory using an application program. *Chapter 5*

operating system (OS) A system of programs that perform a variety of technical operations, providing an additional layer of insulation between the user and the bits-and-bytes world of computer hardware. *Chapter 0, Chapter 4*

optical character recognition (OCR) Locating and identifying printed characters embedded in an image, allowing the text to be stored as an editable document. OCR can be performed by wand readers, pen scanners, and OCR software. *Chapter 3*

optical computer A computer that transmits information in light waves rather than electrical pulses. *Chapter 10*

optical disk A high-capacity, highly reliable storage medium. *Chapter 3*

optical disk drive A disk drive that uses laser beams to read and write bits of information on the surface of an optical disk. *Chapter 3*

optical-mark reader A reading device that uses reflected light to determine the location of pencil marks on standardized test answer sheets and similar forms. *Chapter 3*

OS See operating system.

outliner Software that facilitates the arrangement of information into hierarchies or levels of ideas. Some word processors include outline views that serve the same function as separate outliners. *Chapter 5*

outlining Arranging information into hierarchies or levels of ideas. *Chapter 5*

output Information given out by the computer. *Chapter 1*

output device Device for sending information from the computer, such as a monitor or printer. *Chapter 2*

overhead projection panel Equipment using lCD's to project computer screen images. *Chapter 3*

P2P See peer to peer model

packet A collection of information that travels as a unit through the Internet. Internet messages are broken into packets that travel independently to their destinations. *Chapter 7*

packet switching The standard technique used to send information over the Internet. A message is broken into packets that travel independently from network to network toward their common destination, where they are reunited. *Chapter 7*

page-description language A language used by many drawing programs that describes text fonts, illustrations, and other elements of the printed page.

page-layout software In desktop publishing, used to combine various source documents into a coherent, visually appealing publication. *Chapter 5*

painting software Enables you to paint pixels on the screen with a pointing device. *Chapter 5*

palette   A collection of colors available in drawing software. *Chapter 5*

palmtop computer   A handheld computer, sometimes called a personal digital assistant or PDA. *Chapter 1*

Palm OS   The operating system for palm and palm-compatible handheld computers. *Chapter 4*

paperless office   An office of the future in which magnetic and optical archives will replace reference books and file cabinets,

paradigm shift   A change in thinking that results in a new way of seeing the world. *Chapter 10*

parallel port   A standard port on most PCs for attaching a printer or other device that communicates by sending or receiving bits in groups, rather than sequentially. *Chapter 3. Chapter 6*

parallel processing   Using multiple processors to divide jobs into pieces and work simultaneously on the pieces. *Chapter 2*

parameter Ram   CMOS RAM, a special low-energy kind of RAM used to store the date, time and calendar in Macintoshes. *Chapter 2*

password   A string of letters and numbers known only by you. A password is only effective as a security measure if it's chosen carefully. *Chapter 0, Chapter 6, Chapter 9*

patent (law)   A type of law that protects mechanical inventions. *Chapter 9*

PC   See personal computer.

PC card   A credit-card-size card that can be inserted into a slot to expand memory or add a peripheral to a computer; commonly used in portable computers. Sometimes called by its original name, PCMCIA. *Chapter 2*

PDA   See personal digital assistant.

PDF (Portable Document Format)   Allows documents of all types to displayed on any computer screen, including the original formatting. *Chapter 5, Chapter 7*

peer-to-peer (P2P) computing   See peer-to-peer model.

peer-to-peer file sharing   Enabling networked users to make files on their hard drives available to others rather than posting them on central servers. *Chapter 8*

peer-to-peer model   A LAN model that allows every computer on the network to be both client and server. *Chapter 6*

peer-to-peer network   A system of two or more computers that allows each to function as a client or a server. *Chapter 6*

pen-based computer   A keyboardless machine that accepts input from a stylus applied directly to a flat-panel screen. *Chapter 3*

pen scanner   Wireless pen-shaped scanners that can perform optical character recognition. *Chapter 3*

peripheral   Input, output, and secondary storage devices. *Chapter 2*

Perl (Practical Extraction and Reporting Language)   A Web scripting language that is particularly well-suited for writing scripts to process text—for example, complex Web forms.

personal communicator   See personal digital assistant. *Chapter 6*

personal computer (PC)   A small, powerful, relatively low-cost microcomputer. *Chapter 0, Chapter 1*

personal digital assistant (PDA)   A pocket-sized computer used to organize appointments, tasks, notes, contacts, and other personal information. Sometimes called handheld computer or palmtop computer. Many PDAs include additional software and hardware for wireless communication. *Chapter 1, Chapter 6*

personal information manager (PIM)   A specialized database program that automates an address/phone book, an appointment calendar, a to-do list, and miscellaneous notes. Also called an electronic organizer. *Chapter 5*

PIM   See personal information manager.

pixel   A picture element (dot) on a computer screen or printout. Groups of pixels compose the images on the monitor and the output of a printout. *Chapter 3, Chapter 5*

plagiarism   The act of presenting someone else's work as one's own. *Chapter 9*

platform   The combination of hardware and operating system software upon which application software is built. *Chapter 4*

platform independent   The ability of a peripheral device to work on multiple platforms. For example, a USB disk drive could be used wit both Macintosh and Windows computers. *Chapter 3*

platter   A flat disc that is the part of the hard disk that holds information. *Chapter 3*

plotter   An automated drawing tool that produces finely scaled drawings by moving pen and/or paper in response to computer commands. *Chapter 3*

plug-in   A software extension that adds new features. *Chapter 7*

point-of-sale (POS) terminal   A terminal with a wand reader, barcode scanner, or other device that captures information at the checkout counter of a store. *Chapter 3*

point size   Measurement of characters, with one point equal to 1/72 inch. *Chapter 5*

pointing stick   A tiny joystick-like device embedded in the keyboard of a laptop computer. *Chapter 3*

pop-up menu   A menu that can appear anywhere on the screen. *Chapter 3, Chapter 4*

port   Socket that allows information to pass in and out. *Chapter 2, Chapter 6*

portable computer   A small, battery-powered computer such as a laptop computer. *Chapter 1*

Portable Document Format (PDF)   Allows documents of all types to be stored, viewed, or modified on any Windows or Macintosh computer, making it possible for many organizations to reduce paper flow. *Chapter 5*

portal   A Web site designed as a Web entry station, offering quick and easy access to a variety of services. *Chapter 8*.

POS   See point-of-sale terminal.

PostScript   A standard page-description language. *Chapter 5, Chapter 10*

Plain Old Telephone Service (POTS) Used with a modem for narrowband dial-up Internet connections. *Chapter 7*

PPP (point-to-point protocol)   A protocol that enables a computer to connect to the Internet via modem and temporarily have full Internet access and IP address. *Chapter 7*

prefetch unit   Part of the CPU that fetches the next several instructions from memory. *Chapter 2*

presentation graphics software   Automates the creation of visual aids for lectures, training sessions, and other presentations. Can include everything from spreadsheet charting programs to animation editing software, but most commonly used for creating and displaying a series of onscreen slides to serve as visual aids for presentations. *Chapter 5*

price-to-performance ratio   The level of performance per unit cost. *Chapter 10*

print server   A server that accepts, prioritizes prioritizes, and processes print jobs. *Chapter 6*

printer   Output device that produces a paper copy of any information that can be displayed on the screen. *Chapter 0, Chapter 3*

processor   Part of the computer that processes information, performs arithmetic calculations, and makes basic decisions based on information values. *Chapter 2*

program   Instructions that tell the hardware what to do to transform input into output. *Chapter 1, Chapter 4*

project management software   Coordinates, schedules, and tracks complex work projects. *Chapter 10*

prompt   Part of the user interface, characters (such as C:\) that prompt the user to enter information. *Chapter 4*

306 Glossary

proportionally spaced font   Fonts that allow more room for wide characters such as W than for narrow characters such as I. *Chapter 5*

protocol   A set of rules for the exchange of data between a terminal and a computer or between two computers. *Chapter 6*

public domain software   Free software that is not copyrighted, offered through World Wide Web sites, electronic bulletin boards, user groups, and other sources. *Chapter 4*

pull-down menu   In a graphical user interface, a menu located at the top of the screen or window and accessed with a mouse or with keyboard shortcuts. Also called drop-down menu. *Chapter 4*

pull technology   Technology in which browsers on client computers pull information from server machines. The browser needs to initiate a request before any information is delivered. *Chapter 8*

push technology   Technology in which information is delivered automatically to a client computer. The user subscribes to a service and the server delivers that information periodically and unobtrusively. Contrast with pull technology. *Chapter 8*

quantum computer   A computer based on the properties of atoms and their nuclei and the laws of quantum mechanics. *Chapter 10*

query   An information request. *Chapter 5*

query language   A special language for performing queries, more precise than the English language. *Chapter 5*

RAID (redundant array of independent disk)   A storage device that allows multiple hard disks to operate as a unit. *Chapter 9*

RAM   See random access memory.

random access   Storage method that allows information retrieval without regard to the order in which it was recorded. *Chapter 3*

random access memory (RAM)   Memory that stores program instructions and data temporarily. *Chapter 2*

range   A rectangular block of cells. *Chapter 5*

raster (bit-mapped) graphics   Painting programs create raster graphics that are, to the computer, simple maps showing how the pixels on the screen should be represented. *Chapter 5*

read-only memory (ROM)   Memory that includes permanent information only. The computer can only read information from it; it can never write any new information on it. *Chapter 2*

read/write head   The mechanism that reads information from, and writes information to, the spinning platter in a hard disk or disk drive. *Chapter 3*

real-time communication   Internet communication that enables you to communicate with other users who are logged on at the same time. *Chapter 8*

real-time streaming audio   Streaming transmission of radio broadcasts, concerts, news feeds, speeches, and other sound events as they happen. *Chapter 7*

real-time streaming video   Similar to streaming audio Webcasts, but with video. *Chapter 7*

real-time teleconference   An online meeting between two or more people in which participants sit at a computer or terminal, watching messages appear on the screen as they're typed by other participants, and typing comments for others to see immediately. *Chapter 6*

record   In a database, the information relating to one person, product, or event. *Chapter 5*

record matching   Compiling profiles by combining information from different database files by looking for a shared unique field. *Chapter 5*

reduced instruction set computer (RISC)   Processor designed to omit instructions that are seldom used, for the purpose of increasing speed. *Chapter 2*

register   Subdivision of the ALU in the CPU, usually 32 or 64 bits in size. *Chapter 2*

remote access   Network access via phone line, TV cable system, or wireless link. *Chapter 6*

remote login   Enables users on one system to access other host systems across the network. *Chapter 7*

removable cartridge media   High-capacity transportable storage device. Storage media designed to be removed and transported easily, including Zip, Jaz, and Orb disks. *Chapter 3*

repetitive-stress injuries   Injuries, such as carpal tunnel syndrome, caused by repeating the same movements over long periods of time. *Chapter 3*

report   A database printout that is an ordered list of selected records and fields in an easy-to-read form. *Chapter 5*

resolution   Density of pixels, measured by the number of dots per inch. *Chapter 3*

right to privacy   Freedom from interference into the private sphere of a person's affairs. *Chapter 5*

RISC   See reduced instruction set computer.

robot   A computer controlled machine designed to perform specific manual tasks. *Chapter 10*

rollover   A common use of Web scripting, used to make onscreen buttons visibly change when the pointer rolls over them. *Chapter 7*

ROM   See read-only memory.

ROM cartridge   A removable permanent storage device used by some home video game machines. *Chapter 2*

router   A program or device that decides how to route Internet transmissions. *Chapter 6, Chapter 6*

rows   Along with columns, comprise the grid of a spreadsheet. *Chapter 5*

sabotage   A malicious attack on work, tools, or business. *Chapter 9*

satellite connection   H-speed Internet service via communication satellite. *Chapter 7*

saving a document   Making a disk file of your work for later retrieval. *Chapter 5*

scanner   An input device that makes a digital representation of any printed image. See flatbed scanner, slide scanner, drum scanner, and sheet-fed scanner. *Chapter 3.*

scientific visualization software   Uses shape, location in space, color, brightness, and motion to help us understand relationships that are invisible to us, providing graphical representation of numerical data. *Chapter 5*

scrolling   The movement of lines on and off the screen as you move through a document. *Chapter 5*

script   A short program that can add interactivity, animation, and other dynamic features to a Web page or multimedia document. *Chapter 7*

SCSI (Small Computer Systems Interface)   An interface design enabling several peripherals to by strung together and attached to a single port. *Chapter 3*

search   Looking for a specific record. *Chapter 5*

search and replace   Finding selected words or phrases throughout a document and replacing them with a different word or phrase. *Chapter 5*

search engine   A program for locating information on the Web. *Chapter 0, Chapter 1*

search tool   See search engine.

select (records) Looking for all records that match a set of criteria. *Chapter 5*

selecting text Highlighting text, usually by dragging the cursor across it. *Chapter 5*

self-maintaining system A system that can diagnose and correct common problems without human intervention. *Chapter 10*

sensing device Monitors temperature, humidity, pressure, and other physical quantities to provide data used in robotics, environmental climate control, and other applications. *Chapter 3*

sensor A device that enables digital machines to monitor a physical quantity of the analog world—temperature, humidity, pressure, or some other quantities—to provide data used in robotics, environmental climate control, and other applications *Chapter 3, Chapter 10*

sequential access Storage method that requires the user to retrieve information by zipping through it in the order in which it was recorded. *Chapter 3*

serial port A standard port on most PCs for attaching a modem or other device that can send and receive messages one bit at a time. *Chapter 3, Chapter 6*

server A computer especially designed to provide software and other resources to other computers over a network. *Chapter 1*

server In a local-area network under the client/server model, a high-speed, high-capacity computer containing data and other resources to be shared with client computers. *Chapter 6*

set-top box A special-purpose computer designed to provide Internet access and other services using a standard television set and (usually) a cable TV connection. *Chapter 1*

shareware Software that is free for the trying, with a send-pay-ment-if-you-keep-it honor system. *Chapter 4*

sheet-fed scanner Small scanner that accepts pages one at a time through a sheet feeder. *Chapter 3.*

shell A program that puts a graphical face on top of a command line interface such as that of MS-DOS. *Chapter 4*

silicon chip Hundreds of transistors packed into an integrated circuit on a piece of silicon. *Chapter 1*

SILK Acronym for emerging user interface technologies: speech, image, language, and knowledge capabilities. *Chapter 10*

simulation A computer model of a real-life situation. *Chapter 5*

SIMMs Single in-line memory module. *Chapter 2*

site license License for multiple copies or removing restrictions on software copying and use at a network site. *Chapter 4, Chapter 6*

slide scanner A scanner for slides and negatives only. *Chapter 3*

slot Area in the computer's housing for inserting special-purpose circuit boards. *Chapter 2*

smart badge See active badge (smart badge).

smart weapon A missile that uses computerized guidance systems to locate its target. *Chapter 9*

smart whiteboard An input device that enters notes from a whiteboard to a PC. *Chapter 3*

SMIL (synchronized multimedia integration language) An HTML-like markup language designed to make it possible to link time-based streaming media so, for example, sounds, video, and animation can be tightly integrated with each other.

social engineering Slang for the use of deception to get individuals to reveal sensitive information. *Chapter 9*

software Instructions that tell the hardware what to do to transform input into output. *Chapter 0, Chapter 1*

software components Pieces of existing software that can be used to assemble Web services quickly. Component technology can, for example, make it easy to plug a shopping-cart component into an existing Web site. *Chapter 8*

software license An agreement allowing the use of a software program on a single machine. *Chapter 4*

software piracy The illegal duplication of copyrighted software. *Chapter 9*

solid-state storage Storage, such as flash memory, with no moving parts. Solid-state storage is likely to replace disk storage in the future. *Chapter 3*

sort Arrange records in alphabetic or numeric order based on values in one or more fields. *Chapter 5*

sound card A circuit board that allows the PC to accept microphone input, play music and other sound through speakers or headphone, and process sound in a variety of ways. *Chapter 3*

source document In desktop publishing, the articles, chapters, drawings, maps, charts, and photographs that are to appear in the publication. Usually produced with standard word processors and graphics programs. *Chapter 5*

source document In Web publishing, the original document containing the HTML code that produces a finished Web page. *Chapter 5, Chapter 7*

spam Internet junk mail. *Chapter 6, Chapter 7*

special-purpose (dedicated) computer A computer that performs a specific task, such as controlling temperature and humidity in an office building. *Chapter 1*

speech recognition The identification of spoken words and sentences by a computer, making it possible for voice input to be converted into text files. *Chapter 5*

spelling checker A built-in component of a word processor or a separate program that compares words in a document with words in a disk-based dictionary and flags words not found in the dictionary. May operate in batch mode, checking all the words at once, or interactive mode, checking one word at a time. *Chapter 5*

spider See Web crawler.

spoofing A process used to steal passwords online. A spoofer launches a program that mimics a mainframe computer's login screen on an unattended terminal in a public lab. When an unsuspecting person types an ID and password, the program responds with an error message and remembers the secret codes. *Chapter 9*

speaker independence The ability of automatic speech-recognition software to recognize speech without being trained to a speaker. *Chapter 5*

spreadsheet software Enables the user to control numbers, manipulating them in various ways. The software can manage budgeting, investment management, business projections, grade books, scientific simulations, checkbooks, financial planning and speculation, and other tasks involving numbers. *Chapter 5*

SQL A query language available for many different database management systems. More than a query language, SQL also accesses databases from a wide variety of vendors. *Chapter 5*

statistical analysis software Specialized software that tests the strength of data relationships, produces graphs showing how two or more variables relate to each other, uncovers trends, and performs other statistical analyses. *Chapter 5*

storage device Long-term repositories for data. Disks and tape drives are examples. *Chapter 2, Chapter 3*

style sheet Custom styles for each of the common elements in a document. *Chapter 5*

stylus A device used for pointing or writing with handheld computers and PDAs. *Chapter 3*

subnotebook computer A portable computer, smaller than a notebook or laptop, about the size of a hardbound book. *Chapter 1*

supercomputer A super-fast, super-powerful, and super-expensive computer used for applications that demand maximum power. *Chapter 1*

superscalar architecture The architecture of many processors that allows them execute multiple instructions simultaneously. *Chapter 2*

surge protector A device that protects electronic equipment from sudden power surges. *Chapter 9*

switch Hardware that decides how to route Internet transmissions. Switches are similar to software routers, but faster and less flexible. *Chapter 7*

synthesizer A device that can produce—synthesize—music and other sounds electronically. A synthesizer might be a stand-alone musical instrument or part of the circuitry on a computer's sound card. *Chapter 3*

system board The circuit board containing the computer's CPU. Often called motherboard. *Chapter 2.*

system software Software that handles the details of computing. Includes the operating system and utility programs. *Chapter 4*

system unit The box that contains a computer's main circuitry and storage devices. *Chapter 1*

T1 A direct connect digital line that can transmit voice, data, and video at roughly 1.5Mbps. *Chapter 7*

T3 A direct connect digital line that transmits voice, data, and video even faster than a T1 connection. *Chapter 7*

table A grid of rows and columns; on many Web pages tables with hidden grids are used to align graphical images. *Chapter 7*

tape drive Storage device that uses magnetic tape to store information. *Chapter 3*

task bar A button bar that provides one-click access to open applications and tools, making it easy to switch back and forth between different tasks. *Chapter 4*

tax preparation software Provides a prefabricated worksheet where the user enters numbers into tax forms. Calculations are performed automatically, and the completed forms can be sent electronically to the IRS. *Chapter 5*

TB See terabyte.

TCP/IP (Transmission Control Protocol/Internet Protocol) Protocols developed as an experiment in internetworking, now the language of the Internet, allowing cross-network communication for almost every type of computer and network. *Chapter 7*

telecommunication Long-distance electronic communication in a variety of forms. *Chapter 6*

telecommuting Home information workers, especially those who commute by modem. *Chapter 10*

teleconference An online meeting between two or more people. *Chapter 6*

telemedicine The practice of doctors using the Web to work with patients who are outside the hospital walls in remote locations.

telephony Technology that enables computers to serve as speakerphones, answering machines, and complete voice mail systems. *Chapter 6*

Telnet The protocol that makes remote login through a command line interface possible. *Chapter 7*

template In desktop publishing, professionally designed empty documents that can be adapted to specific user needs. *Chapter 5*

template In spreadsheet software, a worksheet that contains labels and formulas but no data values. The template produces instant answers when you fill in the blanks. *Chapter 5*

terabyte (TB) Approximately 1 million megabytes. *Chapter 2*

terminal Combination keyboard and screen that transfers information to and from a mainframe computer. *Chapter 1, Chapter 6*

terminal emulation Software that allows a PC to act as a dumb terminal—an input/output device that enables the user to send commands to and view information on the host computer. *Chapter 6, Chapter 7*

text editing Refining text and correcting errors. *Chapter 5*

text formatting Controlling the format and style of a document. *Chapter 5*

3-D modeling software Software that enables the user to create 3-D objects. The objects can be rotated, stretched, and combined with other model objects to create complex 3-D scenes. *Chapter 5, Chapter 6*

thin client A network computer, Internet appliance, or other device designed to connect to the Internet but not perform all the other tasks performed by a PC. *Chapter 10*

time bomb A logic bomb that is triggered by a time-related event. *Chapter 9*

timesharing Technique by which mainframe computers communicate with several users simultaneously. *Chapter 1*

touchpad (trackpad) A small flat-panel pointing device that is sensitive to light pressure. The user moves the pointer by dragging a finger across the pad. *Chapter 3*

touch screen Pointing device that responds when the user points to or touches different screen regions. *Chapter 3*

trackball Pointing device that remains stationary while the user moves a protruding ball to control the pointer on the screen. *Chapter 3*

track point A small handle that sits in the center of the keyboard, responding to finger pressure by moving the mouse in the direction it is pushed. *Chapter 3*

transistor Performs the same function as the vacuum tube by transferring electricity across a tiny resistor. *Chapter 1*

Trojan horse A program that performs a useful task while at the same time carrying out some secret destructive act. A form of software sabotage. *Chapter 9*

tweening The automatic creation of in-between frames in an animation. *Chapter 5*

twisted pair A type of LAN cable that resembles the copper wires in standard telephone cables. *Chapter 6*

typeface A style of characters used for printing. *Chapter 5*

ubiquitous computers Computers everywhere. *Chapter 10*

Unicode A 65,000-character set for making letters, digits, and special characters fit into the computer's binary circuitry. *Chapter 2*

uninterruptible power supply (UPS) A hardware device that protects computers from data loss during power failures. *Chapter 9*

Universal product codes (UPC's) Codes created from patterns of variable-width bars that send scanned information to a mainframe computer. *Chapter 3.*

Universal serial bus (USB) A cross-platform interface that can transmit data faster than the traditional PC serial port. *Chapter 3; Chapter 6*

UNIX An operating system that allows a timesharing computer to communicate with several other computers or terminals at once. UNIX is the most widely available multi-user operating system in use. It is also widely used on Internet hosts. *Chapter 4, Chapter 7*

upgrade A new and improved version of a software program. *Chapter 4*

upload To post software or documents to an online source so they're available for others. *Chapter 6, Chapter 7*

upstream traffic Information transmitted from the subscriber to the Internet. *Chapter 7*

URL (uniform resource locator) The address of a Web site. *Chapter 0, Chapter 1, Chapter 7*

USB see Universal serial Bus

user interface The look and feel of the computing experience from a human point of view. *Chapter 4*

user name See login name.

utility program Tools for doing system maintenance and some repairs that are not automatically handled by the operating system. *Chapter 4*

vaccine program See antivirus program.

values The numbers that are the raw material used by spreadsheet software to perform calculations. *Chapter 5*

VBScript A Web scripting language. *Chapter 7*

VDT See video display terminal.

vector (object-oriented) graphics The storage of pictures as collections of lines, shapes, and other objects. *Chapter 5*

vertical-market application A computer application designed specifically for a particular business or industry. *Chapter 4*

vertical portal (vortal) A specialized portal that, like vertical market software, is targeted at members of a particular industry or economic sector. *Chapter 8*

video adapter A circuit board installed inside the main system unit connecting the monitor to the computer. *Chapter 3*

video digitizer Converts analog video signals into digital data. *Chapter 5*

video display terminal (VDT) Output device that displays text and graphics and receives messages from the computer. *Chapter 3*

video editing software Software for editing digital video, including titles, sound, and special effect. *Chapter 5*

video memory (VRAM) A special portion of RAM dedicated to holding video images. *Chapter 3*

video port A port for plugging a color monitor into a computer's video board. *Chapter 3*

video projector A projector that can project computer screen images for meetings and classes. *Chapter 3*

video teleconference Face-to-face communication over long distances using video and computer technology. *Chapter 3, Chapter 6*

virtual memory Use of part of a computer hard disk as a substitute for RAM. *Chapter 4*

virtual private network A network that uses encryption software to create secure "tunnels" through the public Internet. *Chapter 8*

virtual reality Technology that creates the illusion that the user is immersed in a world that exists only inside the computer, an environment that contains both scenes and the controls to change those scenes. *Chapter 4, Chapter 10*

virus Software that spreads from program to program, or from disk to disk and uses each infected program or disk to make more copies of itself. A form of software sabotage. *Chapter 9*

visual programming Allows programmers to create large portions of their programs by drawing pictures and pointing to onscreen objects, eliminating much of the coding of traditional programming. *Chapter 9*

voice input Use of a microphone to speak commands and text data to a computer, which uses speech recognition software to interpret the input. *Chapter 3*

voice mail A telephone-based messaging system with many of the features of an email system. *Chapter 6*

voice recognition systems used for applications such as automated voicemail systems, security systems, and hands-free Web navigation. *Chapter 10*

volatile memory Memory, such as RAM, that loses its contents when it loses electrical power. *Chapter 2*

VRAM See video memory.

WAN See wide area network.

wand reader A reading device that uses light to read alphabetic and numeric characters written in a specially designed typeface found on sales tags and credit card slips. *Chapter 3*

Web authoring software Software that facilitates creating of Web pages, typically by making the process similar to desktop publishing. *Chapter 7*

Web browser An application program that enables you to explore the Web by clicking hyperlinks in Web pages stored on Web sites. *Chapter 0, Chapter 1, Chapter 7*

Web bug An invisible piece of code embedded in HTML-formatted email that is programmed to send information about its receiver's Web use back to its creator. *Chapter 8, Chapter 9*

Web casting Delivering of streaming audio or video via the Web. Sometimes refers to push technology. *Chapter 8*

Web crawler A software robot that systematically explores the Web, retrieves information about pages, and indexes the retrieved information in a database. *Chapter 8*

Web page A single document on the World Wide Web (WWW), made up of text and images and interlinked with other documents. *Chapter 0, Chapter 1, Chapter 10*

Web server A server that stores Web pages and sends them to client programs—Web browsers—that request them. *Chapter 7*

Web services New kinds of Web-based applications that can be assembled quickly using existing software components, *Chapter 8*

Web site A collection of related Web pages stored on the same server. *Chapter 0, Chapter 1, Chapter 7*

what-if question A feature of spreadsheet software that allows speculation by providing instant answers to hypothetical questions. *Chapter 5*

WI-FI A popular wireless LAN technology that allows multiple computers to connect to a LAN through a base station up to 150 feet away. Often referred to as 802.11b. *Chapter 6, Chapter 7*

wide-area network (WAN) A network that extends over a long distance. Each network site is a node on the network. *Chapter 1, Chapter 6*

WIMP Windows, icons, menus, and pointing devices. *Chapter 10*

Windows See Microsoft Windows.

window In a graphical user interface, a framed area that can be opened, closed, and rearranged with the mouse. Documents are displayed in windows. *Chapter 4*

wireless broadband connection See WI-FI.

wireless keyboard A keyboard that uses infrared signals rather than wires to communicate with a computer. *Chapter 3*

wireless network A network in which a node has a tiny radio or infrared transmitter connected to its network port so it can send and receive data through the air rather than through cables. *Chapter 6*

wizard A software help agent that walks the user through a complex process. *Chapter 5, Chapter 10*

word processing Software that allows users to create typset documents by entering, editing, formatting, and printing text. *Chapter 5*

word size The number of bits a CPU can process at one time, typically 8, 16, 32, or 64. *Chapter 2*

worksheet A spreadsheet document that appears on the screen as a grid of numbered rows and columns. *Chapter 5*

workstation A high-end desktop computer with massive computing power but is less expensive than a minicomputer. Workstations are the most powerful of the desktop computers. *Chapter 1*

World Wide Web (WWW, Web)   Part of the Internet, a collection of multimedia documents created by organizations and users worldwide. Documents are linked in a hypertext Web that allows users to explore them with simple mouse clicks. *Chapter 0, Chapter 1, Chapter 7*

worm   A program that uses computer hosts to reproduce itself. Worm programs travel independently over computer networks, seeking out uninfected workstations to occupy. A form of software sabotage. *Chapter 9*

writeback   The final phase of execution, in which the bus unit writes the results of the instruction back into memory or some other device. *Chapter 2*

WYSIWYG (What you see is what you get)   With a word processor, the arrangement of the words on the screen represents a close approximation to the arrangement of words on the printed page. *Chapter 5*

XHTML   Markup language that combines features of HTML and XML; its advantage is its backward compatibility with HTML. *Chapter 7*

XML (extensible markup language)   A language that enables Web developers to control and display data the way they control text and graphics. Forms, database queries, and other data-intensive operations that can't be completely constructed with standard HTML are much easier with XML. *Chapter 7*

Y2K bug (millennium bug)   The international sensation about the two-digit date problem when the year changed from 1999 to 2000. *Chapter 9*

Credits

Chapter 0

- p. 3   top right: © Ed Kashi
  center: Courtessy of Vaughn Rogers
  bottom: Keith Brofsky/Getty Images Inc./PhotoDisc
- p. 5   Courtesy of International Business Machines
- p. 9   top right: Dennis O'Clair
  center left: Jose Pelaez
  center right: Nucor Corporation
  bottom left: SuperStock, Inc.
  bottom right: Corbis Digital Stock
- pp. 10–11   all screens courtesy of Microsoft Corporation
- p. 12   screens courtesy of Microsoft Corporation and Apple Computers, Inc.
- p. 13   Getty Images, Inc.
- p. 14   AP/WorldWide Photos
  right: The Image Works
- p. 15   © 2001 America Online, Inc. Used with permission.
- p. 18   top screens: Courtesy of Google.com
  bottom screens: Courtesy of Yahoo.com

Chapter 1

- p. 25   top right: Library of Congress
  center: Culver Pictures, Inc.
  bottom right: Culver Pictures, Inc.
- p. 26   top: Getty Images Inc.
  center: Robert Polidori Photography
  bottom: © 2001 Eric Millette, all rights reserved
- p. 28   right: Photograph courtesy of the Hagley Museum and Library, Wilmington, Delaware
  left: AP/Wide World Photo
- p. 29   top: Courtesy of AT&T Archives
  bottom: AT&T Archives
- p. 30   top center: AP/Wide World Photo
  center right: Carlos Osorio/AP/Wide World Photo
  center left: Lonnie Duka/Getty Images Inc.
  bottom: © CORBIS Stock Market
- p. 31   top left: © Steve Chenn/CORBIS
  top right: Christopher Bissell/Getty Images Inc.
  center: Ric Feld/AP/Wide World Photo
- p. 32   top left: Photo Researchers, Inc.
  bottom left: Apple Computer, Inc.
  bottom right: Courtesy of International Business Machines
- p. 33   top left: Apple Computer, Inc.
  top right: Courtesy of International Business Machines
  left: © 2001 Handspring Inc.
  center: Scott Pollard
  right: AP/Wide World Photo
- p. 34   left: Peter Menzel Photography
  center: H. Montgomery Strategic Design, Inc.
  right: Naokazu Oinuma/AP/Wide World Photo
- p. 35   top left: TimePix
  top center: TimePix
  top right: TimePix
  bottom: NCA Meida Technology Resources, University of Illinois at Urbana-Champaign
- p. 36   top: Dado Galdieri/AP/Wide World Photo
  center: Wyse Technology
  bottom: Trylon Communications
- p. 41   Hank Morgan/Rainbow
- p. 42   Wayne R. Billenduke/Getty Images Inc.

Chapter 2

- p. 49   Library of Congress
- p. 50   Image Works
- p. 52   Photo Courtesy of the Computer Museum
- p. 57   top right: Intel Corporation
  center: Getty Images Inc.
  bottom left: Intel Corporation
  bottom right: Intel Corporation
- p. 61   top right: James A. Folts Photography
  bottom right: Sierra Wireless, Inc.

Chapter 3

- p. 69   Apple Computer, Inc.
- p. 70   bottom center: Courtesy of International Business Machines
  bottom left: © CORBIS
- p. 71   top left: Think Outside, Inc.
  top center: Matias Corporation
  top right: Brodeur Worldwide for Research In Motion
  center: Eleksen Ltd.
  bottom left: Reprinted with permission from Microsoft Corporation
  bottom right: Greg Wieting
- p. 72   top left: Apple Computer, Inc.
  top center: Courtesy of International Business Machines
  top right: Logitech Inc.
  bottom left: Courtesy of Kensington Technology Group
  bottom center: Wacom Technology Corporation
  bottom right: MicroTouch Systems Inc.
- p. 73   top left: James A. Folts Photography
  top right: AP/Wide World Photos
  bottom: C Technologies US inc.
- p. 74   top left: Handspring, Inc.
  top right: AP/Wide World Photos
  center: Virtual Ink Corporation
  bottom left: Walt and Company Communications
  bottom right: MMW Group
- p. 75   top left: Olympus America Inc.
  top center: Nikon Inc.
  top left: Handspring, Inc.
  center left: Courtesy of Sony Electronics, Inc.
  center right: iRez Technologies, LLC
- p. 77   Lernout & Hauspie Speech Products, Inc.
- p. 78   top left and right, center left and right: James A. Folts Photography
  bottom left: Infocus
  bottom right: Apple Computer, Inc.
- p. 80   top left: Epson America, Inc.
  top right: Epson America, Inc.
  left center: Pentax Corporation
  bottom: Techtronix, Inc.
- p. 81   Hewlett-Packard Company
- p. 82   top left: © CORBIS Sygma
  center left: NASA Headquarters
  center right: © CORBIS
  bottom left: Ecrix Corporation
- p. 84   top left: Courtesy of Western Digital Corporation
  top right: Courtesy of International Business Machines
  bottom left: Iomega Corporation
- p. 88   Courtesy of Western Digital Corporation
- p. 89   top right: DiskOn Key (M-Systems)
  center right: Lexar Media, USA
  bottom right: SanDisk

311

Credits

- p. 90   top left: James A. Folts Photography
  bottom left: James A. Folts Photography
- p. 92   Dell Computer Corporation

Chapter 4
- p. 99   Rueters/Mike Blake/Getty Images
- p. 105   Courtesy of the Microsoft Corporation
- p. 106   Courtesy of the Microsoft Corporation
- p. 107   top right: Courtesy of Apple Computers, Inc.
  bottom right: Courtesy of Sun Systems Inc.
- p. 108   Index Stock Imagery Inc.
- p. 112   All screen shots courtesy of Symantec Corporation
- p. 113   top right screen shots courtesy of Microsoft Corporation
  bottom right screen shots courtesy of Apple Computers, Inc.
- p. 114   Courtesy of Microsoft Corporation
- p. 115   Ericsson
- p. 119   Courtesy of Microsoft Corporation
- p. 120   top left: AP/Wide World Photos
  top right: Chris Rogers/Rainbow/PictureQuest
- p. 121   Portable Energy System by Sunwize Technologies

Chapter 5
- pp. 127–128   courtesy of the Microsoft Corporation
- pp. 130–131   all screens courtesy of Microsoft Corporation
- pp. 134–135   all screens courtesy of Microsoft Corporation
- p. 137   top right: Courtesy of Intuit, Inc.
  bottom left: courtesy of the Argonne National Laboratory
  bottom right: University of California, Los Angeles
- p. 139   screens courtesy of MacroMedia, Inc.
- pp. 142–143   courtesy of the Microsoft Corporation
- pp. 144–145   courtesy of Adobe Systems, Inc.
- p. 146   top: courtesy of Apple Computers, Inc.
  center: courtesy of Adobe Systems, Inc.
  bottom: courtesy of the Microsoft Corporation
- pp. 150–151   courtesy of Apple Computers, Inc
- p. 152   left: Handspring, Inc.
  right: courtesy of Palm, Inc.
- p. 153   top left: James A. Folts Photography
  top right: James A. Folts Photography
  center: James A. Folts Photography

Chapter 6
- p. 163   top right: Jeff Greenwald
  center: Photofest
- p. 164   AP/Wide World Photos
- p. 165   3COM/U.S. Robotics
- p. 166   top left: ZOOM Telephonics, Inc.
  top right: U.S. Robotics Corporation
- p. 169   courtesy International Business Machines
- p. 170   courtesy of Lotus Development Corporation
- p. 174   © CORBIS Stock Market
- p. 175   top left: ZOOM Telephonics Inc.
  top right: Hewlett-Packard Company
- p. 176   top: Kyocera Wireless Corporation
  bottom: AP/Wide World Photos
- p. 177   Jean Miele/CORBIS Stock Market
- p. 178   top: Champlain Cable Corporation
  second from top: courtesy of Inmac
  middle: Optical Cable Corp
  second from bottom: Extended Systems
  bottom: Proxim, Inc.
- p. 179   top right: AP/Wide World Photos
  center: Getty Images Inc.

Chapter 7
- p. 185   © Clark Quinn
- p. 186   AP/Wide World Photos
- p. 190   © CORBIS
- p. 191   top: U.S. Robotics Corporation
  second from top: Belken Components
  third from top: Cisco Systems
  fourth from top: Eicon Networks Inc.
  fifth from top: Cisco Systems
  sixth from top: ZOOM Telephonics, Inc.
  second from bottom: © CORBIS
  bottom: Proxim, Inc.
- pp. 198–199   courtesy of MacroMedia and Microsoft Corporation
- p. 200   top left: Courtesy of Rollingstone.com
  top right; Courtesy of Live365, Inc
  bottom: Courtesy of Shockwave.com
- p. 202   Courtesy of REI

Chapter 8
- p. 209   top right: © Sam Ogden
  center: © CORBIS
- p. 210   Courtesy of Apple Computer, Inc.
- p. 211   top right: Courtesy of Excite
- p. 213   Handspring, Inc.
- p. 214   Courtesy Google.com
- p. 216   Courtesy of CUseeme.com, Networks.com
- p. 220   Tech Corps.
- p. 221   TimePix

Chapter 9
- p. 230   © CORBIS
- p. 232   Kensington Microware
- p. 233   Ivan Sekretarev/AP/Wide World Photos
- p. 236   Courtesy of Symantec Corporation
- p. 237   Maggie Hallahan/Network Images
- p. 238   center left: Cramer Sweeney/IrisScan, Inc.
  bottom left: Iridian Technologies, Inc.
- p. 239   center left: Courtesy of Network Associates
  center right: CheckPoint Technologies Software, Inc.
- p. 242   top left: American Power Conversion Corporation
  center: Raidtec Corporation
- p. 244   top left: ©2001 Versus Technology, Inc.
  center: ©2001 Versus Technology, Inc.
- p. 247   © AFP/CORBIS
- p. 248   © Mark Leffingwell/AFP/CORBIS

Chapter 10
- p. 257   top right : John Barr/Getty Images, Inc.
  left: Xerox Palo Alto Research Center
- p. 259   top left: Spencer Grant/Index Stock Imagery, Inc.
  center left: peter Menzel, Photography
  bottom left: AP/World Wide Photos
  top right: Peter Menzel, Photography
- p. 260   top left: Scott Barrow/SuperStock, Inc.
  bottom left: PhotoEdit
  top right: Network Productions/Rainbow
  center right: Tim Brown/Getty Images Inc.
  bottom right: Terry Vine/Getty Images Inc.
- p. 262   AP/World Wide Photos
- p. 263   George Haling/Science Source/Photo Researchers
- p. 265   © The Kobal Collection
- p. 266   top left: Microvision, Inc.
  top right: Microvision, Inc.
- p. 267   center: E Ink Corporation
- p. 268   top left: Argonne National Laboratory
  top right: Bill Sherman/Paul J. Rajlich
- p. 270   top: AP/World Wide Photos
  bottom: Lucent Technologies/Bell labs
- p. 271   top: Courtesy Sandia National Laboratories
  bottom: Peter Menzel Photography
- p. 373   ©Bettman/CORBIS

Index

A

abacus, 27
access time, 61
access, Internet, universal access issues, 220
access, restricting
    audit-control software, 241
    encryption, 240–241
    firewalls, 239
    passwords, 238–239
    physical devices/biometrics, 238
access-control software, 239
accounting software, 137
ACM Code of Ethics, 246
active badges, 243–244, 269
Active X, 202
addiction to computer/Internet use, 42
additive color synthesis, 79
address book, 150–151
addresses
    ISPs (Internet Service Providers), 16
    spreadsheet cells, 133, 136
affective computers, 269
agents
    software, 268–269
    artificial intelligence, 119
agricultural revolution, 258
Aiken, Howard, 49
AIX operating sustem (IBM), 115
algorithms, 101
    genetic algorithms, 270
aliases, 14
aligning text, 129
all-in-one computer systems, 89
Allen, Paul, 127
America Online (AOL), 173
    client software, 173–174
    sending email on, 15
American Standard Code for Informatio Interchange. *See* ASCII code
analog signals, 165
Analytical Engine, 25–27
animation software, 139
animations on Web pages, 197
animators, computers for, 31
anonymizers, use of, by terrorists, 43
antivirus software, 236
Apple Computer, Inc., 69. *See also* specific products
Apple I, 69
Apple II, 69–70
Apple Mouse, 71

applets, 119, 202
Appleworks, 107
application servers, 194
application service providers (ASPs), 194
applications, 8, 37
    algorithms for, 101
    artificial intelligence, 40
    consumer applications, 105
    consumer software
        advantages of using, 106–107
        compatibility issues, 105
        distributing, 106
        documentation, 105
        integrated applications/suites, 107–108
        licenses, 106
        upgrades, 105
        vertical market/custom software, 108
        warranties, disclaimers, 106
    customized problem-solving, 40
    databases, 37
    desktop publishing, 37
    graphics, 40
    multimedia, 40
    opening, 8
    productivity software, 100
    programming, binary notation for, 54
    running, how it works, 102–103
    spreadsheets, 37
    system software, 100, 108
        memory management software, 109
        network communications coordination, 109
        operating systems, 108–109, 112
        parallel processing/multitasking coordination, 109
        peripherals communications, 109
        program/data management, 109
        resource monitoring, 109
    telecommunications/networking, 40
    translator programs, compilers, 100, 104
    utility programs, 110
    word processing, 37
    See also operating systems, 122
architecture, 57
    computer, developments in, 266
    open, 90
arithmetic, binary, 52–54
armature, in disk drives, 86
ARPANET (Advanced Research Projects Agent NETwork), 34, 185–186
artificial intelligence, 40
    agents for, 119
    implications for human control, 42

    machine-to-machine networks, 204
artificial life, 271
artificial reality, 221
ASCII character set, 54–55
ASCII text, 213
ASPs (application service providers), 194
asynchronous teleconferencing, 171
Atanasoff, John, 28
Atanasoff-Berry Computer (ABC, 1939), 28
ATMs (automated teller machines), 176
attachments, 14
    email, 170, 213
auctions, online, 218
auctions, reverse, 218
audio, digital, 147
audio digitizers, 75–77, 147
audio input, slots/ports for, 89
audio/video clips, on Web pages, 197
audit-control software, 241
authoring software, multimedia, 148
autocorrect features, 129
autoformatting, 129
automated offices/factories, 259, 262–263
    computer monitoring, 263
    effects on jobs/job security, 263–264
automated teller machines (ATMs), 176
automatic formatting features, 129
automation of work, andcomputer use, 41
autonomous weapon systems, 248–249
avatars, 214

B

Babbage, Charles, 25–27
Back button (Web pages), 17
backbones (WANs), 167
backups, 242
    storage media for, 84
backward compatibility, 57
bandwidth, 177–178
banking, electronic, 176
bar-code readers, 72–73
Barlow, John Perry, 221
baud rates (bps), 165
bays, 61, 90
BBS (electronic bulletin board systems), 173
Berners-Lee, Tim, 194, 209
binary
    digits. *See* bits
    information, 51–52
    number systems, 52–54

313

binary arithmetic, 52–54
  program/software instructions using, 54
  text in, 54
bio-digital technology, 42
bio-economy, 270
bio-terrorism, 43
biometric devices, 238
bit depth, 77
bitmapped graphics, 138
bits
  bytes, 52, 56
  defined, 51
  in ASCII code, 54
bizrate, 212
Bluetooth wireless technology, 178–179
bookmarks (Web pages), 17
Boolean logic, 210, 212
booting process, 112
bots, 212
  Web, 268
bouncing email, 174
bps (bits per second), 165
Brand, Stewart, 179
bridges, 167
broadband connections, 190, 192–193
broadband technologies, 166
browsers/browsing
  Web, 16
  databases, 149
bugs, 101
  Web, 212–213
bundled software, 107
burning data, 85
buses, 61
business-to-business (B2B) e-commerce, 218
business-to-consumer (B2C) e-commerce, 218
bytes, 52
  8-bit, 53
  defined, 56
  gigabyte, 56
  kilobytes, 56
  megabytes, 56
  multiple, 53
  terabyte, 56

C

C programming language, 104
C# programming language, 202, 218
C++ programming language, 104
cable modems, 166, 190–191
cabling, for LANs, networks, 166, 178
CAD (computer-aided design), 139, 259
CAM (computer-aided manufacturing), 259
cameras
  digital, 75
  digital video, 142
  video digitizer, 75
cards, 61
carpal tunnel syndrome, 83
cars, computers in, 34
cascading style sheets (dynamic HTML), 201
catalogs, online, 218

cathode ray tube (CRT) monitors, 78
CD-R (compact disk recordable) disk drives, 85
CD-ROM (compact disk-read-only memory) disk drives, 5, 85–86
CD-ROM cover, creating using Photoshop, 140–141
CD-RW (compact disk-rewritable) disk drives, 5, 85, 87–88
cell ranges (worksheets), 134
cells (worksheets), 133
  active cells, 134–135
central processing units (CPUs), 4, 50, 56–57, 65
  compatibility issues, 57
  how they work, 58–59
  memory
    access time, 61
    CMOS (complementary metal oxide semiconductor), 61
    Flash memory, 61
    how it works, 62–63
    RAM (random access memory), 60–61, 65
    ROM (read-only memory), 61, 65
  speed issues, 57
    architecture, 57
    clocks, 57
    parallel processing/multiprocessing, 60
    word size, 60
Cerf, Vint, 185, 220
change, technological, rate of, 37
character sets, 55
character-based user interfaces, 113, 115
  MS-DOS, 113
  UNIX operating system, 115–116
characters, non-Roman, Unicode for, 54
charts, charting tools spreadsheets, 136
chat rooms, 170
chess-playing machines, 229–230
chief information officers (CIOs), 262
chief technology officers (CTOs), 262
Chinese languages, Unicode for, 54
chip technologies, developments in, 266
CIOs (chief information officers), 262
circuit boards, 56
Clarke, Arthur C., 163
clicking (mouse), 7
client software (AOL), 173–174
client/server model, 168
  with Internet connections, 193
Clipboard, 130
clock speed, 57
clocks, 57
CMOS (complementary metal oxide semiconductor), 61
coaxial cable, 166, 178
code of ethics, 246
coding, 104. *See also* programming languages
color depth, 77–78
color printing, 81
color video, 79
Colossus (1943), 28
columns (spreadsheets), 133
command-line interfaces, 113
commands, 101

communications, interpersonal, role in terrorism, 43
communications ports, 90
communications satellites, 163
communications technologies, 50. *See also* digital communications
  data transfer speeds, 56
  email, 35, 170–171, 211, 213
  disadvantages/risks of using, 172–173
  fax modems, 175
  financial transaction software, 176
  GPS (Global Positioning System) receivers, 176
  hardware for
    information/Internet appliances, 36
    network computers, 36
    set-top boxes, 36
  Internet, 34–35
    growth/spread of, 35–36
    mailing lists, 213
    netiquette, 215
    newsgroups, 171, 213–214
    World Wide Web (WWW), 35
  instant messaging, 170–171, 214, 216
  inter-application, 107
  intranets, 36
  networks
    LANs (local-area networks), 34
    software for coordinating, 109
    WANs (wide-area networks), 34
  software, 167–168
  teleconferencing, 170–172
  telephony software, 175
  terminal emulators, 168–169
  transmission speeds, 90
  video teleconferencing, 174–175
  voice mail, 175
communications, wireless, 178–179
compact disk recordable (CD-R) disk drives, 85
compact disk-read-only memory (CD-ROM) disks, 85
compact disk-rewritable (CD-RW) disk drives, 85, 88
comparison shopping, search engines for, 218
compatibility issues, platforms, 118
compatiblity, software, 105
compiled programs, 104
compilers, 100, 104
component software technologies, 267
components of computers, 50
  central processing units (CPUs), 58–59
  compatibility issues, 57
  CPUs, 65
  input devices, 50
  memory, 60–63, 65
  memory/storage devices, 50
  output devices, 50
  peripherals, 61, 63
  processor/central processing unit (CPU), 50, 56–57
  speed issues, 57, 60
compressing files and transmission rates, 193
compression, data, 144–145
compression software, 143
CompuServe, 173
computer addiction, 219

Index   315

computer-aided design (CAD), 139
    and manufacturing (CAD/CAM), 259
computer architecture, 57
computer consumers, rules of thumb for, 91
computer crashes, 41
computer crime, 230–231.
    electronic trespassing
        denial of service (DoS) attacks, 237
        hacking/cracking, 236–237
        Webjackers, 237
    laws against, 244–245
    software piracy, 232–233
    software sabotage, 234
        Trojan horses, 234
        viruses, 234–236
        worms, 235
    theft, 231–232
        identity theft, 232
        of computers, 232
    tips for preventing, 245
computer literacy, 37
Computer Matching and Privacy Protection Act (1988), 155
computer monitoring, 263
computer programs. *See* applications
computer security. *See* security issues/tools
computer systems
    integrating components, 92
    networks, 92
computer technology, ethical issues/risks, 40
    automation/dehumanization, 41
    bio-digital technology, 42
    computer/Internet addictions, 42
    crashes/system failures, 41
    high-tech crime, 40
    human control over smart computers, 42
    information abuse, 41
    intellectual property rights, 41
    privacy, 40–41
    role in terrorist attacks, 43
    technological dependency, 41
computer telephony integration (CTI), 175
computer terminals, 30–31
computers. *See also* applications; components
    basic activities/functions, 25, 27
        processing information, 50
        producing output, 50
        receiving input, 50
        storing data/information, 50
    educational uses, 21
    hardware, 27
    history
        abacus, 27
        Aiken's Mark I, 28
        Alan Kay, 257–258
        Apple Computer, Inc., 69
        ARPANET, 185
        Atanasoff-Berry Computer, 28
        Babbage's Analytical Engine, 25–27
        Colossus, 28
        early goals, 27
        ENIAC (mid 1940's), 28
        founding of Apple Computer Inc., 69
        IBM PC., 69
        Internet development, 209
        Linus Torvalds and Linux, 99
        Mark I, 49
        microprocess-based generations, 29
        of Microsoft, 127
        silicon chip-based generation, 29
        transistor-based generation, 29
        UNIVAC I, 28
        vacuum tube-based generation, 28–29
        Watson family and IBM, 49
        Zuse's programmable digital computer, 27
    limited capacity of, 101
    modern dependence on, 26, 30
    software, 27
    types of
        handheld computers, 32–33
        laptop computers, 32
        mainframes, 30–31
        minicomputers, 31
        network computers, 36
        notebook computers, 32–33
        personal computers (PC), 32
        personal data assistants (PDAs), 33
        Pocket PCs, 33
        portable computers, 32
        servers, 31
        special-purpose/embedded, 33
        supercomputers, 31
        workstations, 31
    uses for, 40
        as gateways to Internet/intranets, 36
    versatility, 27
computing, interpersonal, 34
concurrent processing, 109
connectivity, connections, 164
    bandwith issues, 177
        fiber optic cables, 177–178
    communication software, 167–169
    communications ports, 90
    connection types, 165
    direct connections, 13
    Internet
        broadband, 190, 192–193
        connection speeds, 191
        dial-up, 190
        direct (dedicated), 189
        TCP/IP protocol for, 187–188
    networks, 92
    hardware requirements, 165–166
    LANs, cabling for, 166, 178
    wireless communications, 178–179
console bar (worksheets), 134
consumer applications, 105
    advantages of using, 106–107
    compatibility issues, 105
    distributing, 106
    documentation, 105
    integrated applications/suites, 107–108
    software licenses, 106
    upgrades, 105
    vertical-market/custom software, 108
    warranties, disclaimers, 106
consumer portals, 211
context-sensitive help, 105
cookies, 200, 212
copy protection, 106
copyright laws
    intellectual property rights, 233
    software piracy, 232–233
copyrighting, 106

corporate portals, 211
costs, portable computers, 33
Countess of Lovelace. *See* King, August Ada
counting systems, ancient cultures, 27
CPUs. *See* central processing units
cracking, 236–237
cradles, for handheld computers, 32
crashes, system, 41
crime. *See* computer crime, 230
crime, high-tech, 40
crime-fighting, use of computers in, 230
Cronkite, Walter, 28
CRT (cathode ray tube) monitors, 78
cryptography, 43
cryptosystems, 240
CTI (computer telephony integration), 175
CTOs (chief technology officers), 262
CU-SeeMe videoconferencing, 216
cultural integrity, effects of computers on, 272
current cells (worksheets), 134
cursor (arrow) keys, 6
cursors, 11
custom software, 108
customer service, 122
cut-and-paste technique, 130
Cyber cafés, 186
cyberspace, 221
cyberterrorism, 243, 249, 251

data, 27
    defined, 54
    defining, 51
    in spreadsheets, 136
    storing, 50
data access, and information abuse, 41
data analysis. *See also* databases
    large-scale, workstations for, 31
    personal computers (PC), 32
data compression, 144–145
data management software, 109
data presentation
    charts, 136
    scientific visualization software, 137
data processing, 50
data transfer rates, 85
data transfer speeds, 56
data translation software, 169
database-driven Web sites, 202
database management systems (DBMS), 152–153
database programs, 148
databases, 37, 148
    address book example, 150–151
    database management systems (DBMS), 152–153
    geographical information systems (GIS), 152
    managing, tips for, 154
    personal information managers (PIMS), 152
    privacy issues, 153–154
        basic do's and don'ts, 155
        national identity cards, 156
    reports, 151

316 Index

searching, querying, 149–150
sorting data in, 151
structure of, 149
uses for, 148–149
Web sites as front ends for, 202
when/how to use, 154
DBMS (database management system), 152–153
debugging, 101
decision support systems, 262
dedicated computers, 33
dedicated connections, 189
Deep Blue (IBM), 230
dehumanization, and computer use, 41
delayed teleconferencing, 171
Delete key, 6
Dell Computer, Inc., computer assembly process, 50
demo software, 106
denial of service (DoS) attacks, 237
dependency, technological, 41
depth, color/bit, 77–78
design issues, desktop publishing, 133
designing Web sites, 201
desktop computer systems, 89
desktop computers, 30
desktop PCs, standard components, 5
desktop publishing, 37
desktop publishing programs, 132
    design issues, 133
    source documents, 132
desktops
    components, 113
    Macintosh, 12
    Linux systems, 117
    Windows, task bar, 10
device controllers, 82
device drivers, 111
dial-up connections, 190
dialog boxes, 114
digital audio, 147
digital cameras, 75
digital cash, 219
digital communications
    advantages of using, 169–172
    hardware requirements, 165
    modems, 165–166
    social/societal implications, 180
digital divide, 220
digital facsimiles, 175
digital fiber optic networks, 177–178
digital information, 51
Digital Millennium Copyright Act of 1998 (DMCA), 233, 244
digital money, 176
digital movies, 143
digital paper, 266
digital signals, 165
digital signatures, 219
digital versatile disks (DVD) disk drives, 88
digital video, 142–143
    compression systems for, 145
digital video cameras, 142
digitizers, audio, 147
digitizers, video, 142
digitizing, 76
    graphics/images, 74–75

physical data, 77
sound, 75, 77
DIMMs (dual in-line memory modules), 62
direct (dedicated) connections, 13, 165, 189
Direct Mail Marketing Association, 155
Director (Macromedia), 139
directories, hierarchical, 210
directory trees (search engines), 18
disclaimers, software, 106
disinfectant programs, 236
disk drives, 84
    internal versus external, 90
diskette drive, 5
diskettes, 5, 84
display systems, computer-driven, 30
distributed computing, 262
    grid computing, 217
    P2P (peer-to-peer) file sharing, 216–217, 223
distributed denial of service (DDos) attacks, 237
distributing software, 106
DNS (Domain Name System), 188
docking stations, 32–33
documentation
    declining quality of, 122
    for software, 105
documents, 8, 113
    desktop publishing source documents, 132
    word processing
        adding text, 128
        creating example document, 130
        formatting, 128
        navigating, 128
        printing, 129
        proofreading tools, 129
domain name registries, 197
Domain Name System (DNS), 188
domains, 188
DoS (denial of service) attacks, 237
dot-matrix printers, 80
double-clicking (mouse), 7
downloading files, 193
downloading software, 173
downstream traffic, 190
drag-and-drop technique, 130
dragging (mouse), 7
drawing software, 138–139
Dreamweaver (Macromedia), 195
    creating Web site using, 198–199
drivers, device, 111
drum scanners, 75
DSL (digital subscriber line)/xDSL connections, 166, 190
    connection speeds, 191
dual in-line memory modules (DIMMs), 62
DVD (digital versatile disks) disk drives, 88
DVD-CD-RW disk drives, 88
DVD-R/CD-RW disk drive, 88
DVD-RAM disk drives, 88
DVD-ROM disk drives, 87–88
Dvorak keyboards, 70
Dynabook, 257
dynamic HTML, 201
dynamic media, 139
    animations, 139
    digital audio, 147

digital video, 142–143
interactive multimedia, 147–148
dynamic Web sites, 202–203

E

e-commerce (electronic commerce), 176, 217
    B2B (business to business), 218
    B2C (business to consumer), 218
    Web services, 218
e-mail. *See* email, 14
East Asian language keyboards, 55
Echelon technology, 204
Eckert, J. Presper, 28, 100
EDI (electronic data interchange) technology, 217
editing documents
    cut-and-paste technique, 130
    drag-and-drop technique, 130
    text in word processing documents, 130
    word processor documents, 128
editing software, video editing, 143
8-bit color depth, 78
802.11b (wireless broadband) connections, 192
electronic bulletin board systems (BBS), 173
electronic commerce (e-commerce), 217
Electronic Communications Privacy Act (1986), 155
electronic cottage, 262
electronic data interchange (EDI) technology, 217
electronic data transfer, 169
electronic devices, computers in, 33
Electronic Frontier Foundation, 221
electronic funds transfer, 176
electronic mail. *See* email
electronic organizers, 152
electronic paper, 266–267
electronic trespassing
    denial of service (DoS) attacks, 237
    hacking/cracking, 236–237
    Webjacking, 237
email (electronic mail, e-mail), 14, 16
    addresses, 188
    applications for, 211
    composing and sending, 15
    encryption, how it works, 240–241
    etiquette for using, 215
    and the growth in Internet use, 35
    forgery, 172
    mailing lists, 213
    messages
        ASCII text files, 213
        attachments, 213
        bugs in, 213
    origins of, 35
    servers, 193
    systems, 170
        comparison with "snail" mail, 171
        comparison with telephone communications, 171
        disadvantages/risks of using, 172–173
        privacy issues, 174
        teleconferencing using, 171–172
        tips for using effectvely, 174

Index **317**

unwanted, filtering software for, 219
viruses, 234, 236
on wireless devices, 213
embedded computers, 33, 269–270
artificial life, 271
microtechnology, 270–271
nanotechnology, 271
emoney, 176
emoticons, 215
emulation options, 119
encryption, 240–241
energy-saving computer use, 121
Engelbart, Doug, 185
engineers, workstations for, 32
ENIAC (Electronic Numerical Integrator and Computer), 28
Enquire, 209
Enter key, 6
enterprise computing, 262
enterprise network systems, 167
environmental sensors, digitizing data from, 77
erasable memory, 89
ergonomic keyboards, 70, 83
ergonomics, 83
error messages, in UNIX systems, 116
errors, 101
Ethernet cards, 165
Ethernet connections, T1 and T3 connection speeds, 191
ethic, hacker, 236
ethical issues, 40, 246
bio-digital technology, 42
computer addiction, 219
computer monitoring, 263
distributed computing/file-sharing, 216
electronic communications, dehumanization and, 173
globalization of computer use, 43
high-tech crime, 40
human control over smart computers, 42
identity theft, 219
Internet controls, 221
privacy, 40–41
security versus privacy, 242–244
ubiquitous computing, 272–274
unwanted mail, 219
wireless communications, 180
Eudora Pro (Qualcomm), 211
Excel (Microsoft), creating example worksheet using, 134–135
expansion boards, 90
ports/slots on, 89
expansion cards, 61
expansion slots, 61
exporting, database data, 151
external drives, 5
external ports, 61
extranets, 217
eye strain, avoiding, 83

F

facsimilie (fax) machines, 175
factories, automated, 259, 263
effects on jobs/job security, 263–264
fair use, 233
Fanning, Shawn, 216

FAQs (frequently asked questions), 215
favorites (Web pages), 17
fax machines, 175
fax modems, 175
Felton, Edward, 244
fiber optic cables, 177–178
fields (database), 149
FightAIDS@home, 217
file compression, 193
file managers, 152–153
file servers, 169, 193
file sharing, 216–217, 223
file transfer protocol (FTP), 193
FileMaker Pro, creating address book using, 150–151
files, 56
database, 149
sharing, file servers for, 193
filtering software, 219
Final Cut Pro (Apple), 143
financial data analysis, computers for, 31
financial management software, 137
financial services, online, 218
financial transaction software, 176
find and replace feature (wor dprocessors), 128
Find command, 128
firewalls, 239
FireWire (IEEE 1394) ports, 142, 165
FireWire technology, 90
firmware, 33
flaming, 215
Flash memory, 61, 89, 112
flatbed scanners, 74
floppy disk drive, 5
floppy disks, 84
folders, 113
folding membrane keyboard, 71
fonts, 128
footers/headers, 129
forgery, email, 172
formatting
autoformatting, 129
documents, design issues, 133
text, 128
forms, on Web pages, 197
formula bar (worksheets), 134
formulas, in spreadsheets, 136
macros, 136
predefined functions, 136
Forward button (Web pages), 17
4-bit color depth, 78
frames, on Web pages, 197
fraud and email, 172
Free Software Foundation, 99, 218
Freehand (Macromedia), 139
freeware (public domain software), 106
frequently asked questions (FAQs), 215
FrontPage (Microsoft), 195
FTP (file transfer protocol), 193
full-access dial-up connections, 190
function keys (f-keys), 6
functions (spreadsheets), 136
future developments
artificial life, 271
hardware
alternative architectures, 266
alternative chip technologies, 266
alternative input technologies, 267

alternative output technologies, 266–267
alternative storage technologies, 266
speed enhancements, 265
microtechnology, 270–271
nanotechnology, 271
preparing for, 265
software
agent software, 268–269
knowledge technology, 268
programming enhancements, 267
user interface enhancements, 267
ubiquitous computers, 269–270

G

game machines, computers in, 33
garbage in, garbage out rule (GIGO), 138
Gates, Bill, 127
gateways, 167, 193
GB (gigabyte), 56
General Public License (GPL), 99
genetic algorithms, 270
geographical information systems (GIS), 152
geostationary communications satellites, 163
Gibson, William, 43, 221
GIF file compression, 145
gigabyte (GB, gig), 56
GIS (geographical information systems), 152
Glick, Jeremy, 43
Global Positioning System (GPS) receivers, 176
globalization
of computer use, ethical issues, 43
effects of computers on, 272
Gnutella file-sharing system, 216
golf cart computer, 26
GoLive (Adobe), 195
Google.com, newsreader, 214
GPL (General Public License), 99
GPS (Global Positioning System) receivers, 176
Graffiti system rules, 74
grammar checking tools, 129
graphic designers, computers for, 31
graphical user interfaces (GUIs), 113
advantages of using, 114–115
components, 113
features, 114
Mac OS, 113
UNIX/Linux operating systems, 115
KDE desktop, 117
Windows, 114
graphics
adding to Web pages, 197, 200
animations, 139
bitmapped, 138
CAD (computer aided design), 139
digital video, 142–143
digitizing, 74–75
displaying
color depth, 77–78
monitors, 77
drawing software, 138–139

Index

image processing software, 138
    photograph example, 140–141
painting software, 138
presentations, 139
3-D modeling, 139
graphics applications, 40
graphics tablets, 72
gray-scale monitors, 78
Greek language, Unicode for, 54
green (energy-saving) computing, 121
grid computing, 217
groupware applications, 262
groupware programs, 170
guidance systems, military, 248
GUIs. *See* graphical user interfaces

H

hacking, hackers, 236–237
    legal penalties faced by, 244
half keyboards, 71
handheld computers, 32–33
    docking cradles, 32
    input devices, 71
Handspring Visor PDA, 74
    keyboard for, 71
handwriting recognition software, 74
hard disk drives, 84
hard disks, 5
hardware, 4, 27
    basic components, 50
        central processing units (CPUs), 50, 56–59, 65
        compatibility issues, 57
        input devices, 50
        memory, 50, 60–63, 65
        output devices, 50
        peripherals, 61, 63
        speed issues, 57, 60
    central processing unit (CPU), 4
    connectivity, 165
    future developments
        alternative architectures, 266
        alternative chip technologies, 266
        alternative input technologies, 267
        alternative output technologies, 266–267
        alternative storage technologies, 266
        speed enhancements, 265
    Internet connections
        information/Internet appliances, 36
        network computers, 36
        set-top boxes, 36
    MFDs (multifunction peripherals), 81
    modems, 34, 165–166
    monitors, 77–78
    motherboards, ports/slots, 89–90
    plotters, 81
    printers, 78, 80
    selecting, rules of thumb for, 91
    sound cards/synthesizers, 81
    storage devices, 82, 84–85, 88–89
    video adapters, 78
hardware compression, 145
hardware emulation, 119
hardware phase of development, 265
Harvard University, 28
headers/footers, 129

Hebrew language, Unicode for, 54
help files, 105
help systems
    declining quality of, 122
    program documentation, 105
helper applications, 200
Hewlett-Packard Corporation, 69
hierarchical directories, 210
hierarchical menus, 114
high-level languages, 104
high-performance computers, 31
high-tech crime, 40
hits, 18
home pages, portals as, 211
host names, 16
host systems, 169
hot swap devices, 90
household appliances, computer-controlled, 270
HP-UX operating system (Hewlett Packard), 115
HTML (hypertext markup language), 194–195
    development of, 209
    documents
        creating, 195
        uploading/publishing, 197
    dynamic HTML, 201
    tags, 196
http (hypertext transfer protocol), 194
    development of, 209
human error, security risks from, 247
Huxley, Aldous, 154
hybrid disks, 148
hyperlinks, 17
hypermedia, 148
hypertext, 16
    development of, 209
hypertext links, 35
hypertext markup language (HTML). *See* HTML
hypertext transfer protocol (http), 194
    development of, 209

I

I-beam icon, 7
IBM Corportation
    development of Mark I automatic calculator (1944), 28
    introduction of PC, 69
    response to Atanasoff's 1939 computer concept, 28
    Watson family leadership at, 49
IBM hardware, 32
IBM OS/2, 118
icons, 113
identity theft, 219, 232
IEEE 1394 (FireWire) ports, 142, 165
IEEE 1394 data transmission standard, 90
iMac computers, 89
image processing software, 138
    photograph example, 140–141
images, digitizing, 74–75
Imation SuperDisks, 84
inboxes, 14
industrial revolution, 258

information
    binary, 51–52
    computer processing of, 50
    defining, 51
    digital, 51
    digitizing, 74–75, 77
information abuse issues, 41
information age, 258
information flow, example of, 260–261
information overloading, email and, 172
information services, 173–174
information slavery, 273–274
information systems, 262
information/Internet appliances, 36
infrared wireless technology, 178
inkjet printers, 80
innovation, preparing for, 265
input
    memory-mapped, 63
    receiving, 50
input commands, 101
input devices, 5, 50
    audio input, 81
    digitizers
        audio, 75, 77
        cameras, 75
        digital cameras, 75
        scanners, 74–75
        sensors, 77
        video digitizers, 75
    keyboards, 70
    pointing devices
        graphics tablets, 72
        joysticks, 72
        mice, 71
        pointing sticks, 71
        touch screens, 72
        touchpads, 71
        trackballs, 71
    reading tools, 72
        bar-code readers, 72
        magnetic-ink character readers, 72
        optical character recognition (OCR) tools, 73–74
        handwriting recognition software, 74
        optical-mark readers, 72
input function, 25, 27
input technologies, developments in, 267
insertion points, 11
instant messaging, 170–171, 214, 216
institutional computing, 30
instruction sets (CPUs), 57–59
integrated applications, 107–108
integrated circuits, 29
Intel Corporation, 29
intellectual property laws, 233
intellectual property rights, 41
interapplication communication, 107
interface standards, 89
interfaces, network
    hardware for, 165
    modems, 165–166
interfaces, user. *See* user interfaces
internal drives, 5
International Business Machines Corporation. *See* IBM Corporation
Internet. *See also* World Wide Web (WWW)
    and computer addiction, 219
    commercialization of, 219

computer crime, 231
connection hardware
    information/Internet appliances, 36
    network computers, 36
    set-top boxes, 36
connection types
    broadband, 190, 192–193
    dial-up connections, 190
    direct (dedicated) connections, 189
    connection speeds, 191
decentralization/fluidity of, 186
ethical and security issues, 219–222
growth/spread of, 35–36, 222
history, 185–186, 209
origins of, 34–35
services, 186
size of, 186
underlying networks, 186
unwanted email/solicitations, filtering, 219
World Wide Web (WWW), 35
Internet 2, 219
Internet appliances, 221, 262
Internet applications
    application servers, 194
    client/server model, 193
    email, 211, 213
    email servers, 193
    file servers, 193
    grid computing, 217
    instant messaging, 214, 216
    mailing lists, 213
    P2P (peer-to-peer) file sharing, 216–217, 223
    search engines, 210, 212
    Usenet newsgroups, 213–214
    Web servers, 194
Internet Dreams (Stefik), 222
Internet Explorer (Microsoft), 127
    creating Web site using, 198–199
Internet security. See computer crime; security issues/tools
Internet service providers (ISPs), 14, 193
Internet telephony (IP telephony), 214
internetworking protocols, TCP/IP, 187–188
interpersonal computing, 34–36
InterPlaNet, 220
intranets, 36, 217
Iomega Zip/Jaz disk drives, 84
Iowa State University, 28
IP (Internet) telephony, 214
IP addresses, 188
ISDN connections, 190–191
ISP addresses, 16
ISPs (Internet service providers), 14, 193
italicizing text, 130
Itanium (Intel), 60

J

Jacquard, Joseph-Marie Charles, 25
Japaneses language, Unicode for, 54
Java programming language, 104, 119, 202
Java Virtual Machine (JVM), 119
    software, 202
JavaScript, 201–202
Jaz disk drives (Iomega), 84

jobless growth, 263
jobs, effects of automation on, 263–264
Jobs, Steven, 69
Joy, Bill, 43
joysticks, 72
JPEG file compression, 145
justifying text, 129
JVM (Java Virtual Machine) software, 202

K

K (kilobyte), 56
Kahn, Bob, 185
Kay, Alan, 257–258
KB (kilobyte), 56
KDE desktop (Linux), 117
Kempelen, Wolfgang, 229
kernel, 99
keyboards, 5, 70
    East Asian languages, 55
    ergonomic, 83
    for handheld computers, 71
    how to use, 6
    ports for, 89
kilobits (Kbs), 177
kilobyte (KB), 56
King, Augusta Ada (Countess of Lovelace), 25
knowledge technology, enhancements of, 268

L

labels (spreadsheets), 136
Laden, Osama bin, 43
languages, query, 150
LANs (local area networks), 34, 166–167
    client/server model, 168
    NOS (network operating systems), 168
    peer-to-peer model, 168
laptop computers (laptops), 32
    connecting to peripherals/networks, 32
    docking station, 32–33
laser printers, 80
Latin 1 character set, 55
layout software, 132
LCD (liquid crystal display) monitors, 78
legacy-free PCs, 90
legal issues, 244–245
    distributed computing/file-sharing, 216
    Internet controls, 221
Lessig, Lawrence, 222
licenses, software, 106
Licklider, J. C. R., 185
life, artificial, 271
line printers, 78
links, 17
links, hypertext, 35
Linux, graphical user interface for, 115
    KDE desktop, 117
Linux operating system, 99, 118, 169
Lipshutz, Robert P., 212
liquid crystal display (LCD) monitors, 78
Listserv, 213
local area networks (LANs), 34, 166–167
    client/server model, 168
    NOS (network operating systems), 168
    peer-to-peer model, 168
logging in, 14, 115
logic bombs, 234
login names, 14
loom, programmable, 25
lossless compression systems, 145
lossy compression systems, 145
Luddites, 263
lurking, 215

M

Mac OS, 8, 113
    OS 9, 118
    OS X (10), 118
    using Word with, 12
machine language, 104
machine-to-machine networks, 204
Macintosh computers, 32, 69
    hardware
        Apple iMac, 32
        Apple Powerbook G4, 33
    Kay's contributions to, 257
macro viruses, 234
macros functions (spreadsheets), 136
magnetic disk drives, 84, 86
magnetic tape, 82, 84
magnetic-ink character readers, 72
magneto-optical (MO) disks, 85
mail boxes, 14
mail merge, 151
mail programs, 170
mailing lists, 213
mainframe computers, 30
    supercomputers, 31
    terminals, 30–31
    timesharing, 31
Majordomo, 213
malleable matrices (spreadsheet programs), 133
management information systems (MIS), 262
    information flow process, 260–261
managing
    databases, 154
    memory, software for, 109
    programs/data, software for, 109
    resource usage, software for, 109
MANs (metropolitan area networks), 167
manuals, computer, declining quality of, 122
marine biology, use of computers in, 30
Mark I automatic calculator (Aiken, 1944), 28
Mark I computer, 49
Markkula, A.C., 69
math processing programs, 137
matrices, malleable (spreadsheet programs), 133
Mauchley, John, 28, 100
MB (megabyte), 56
media, dynamic, 139
    animations, 139
    digital audio, 147
    digital video, 142–143
    interactive multimedia, 147–148
meetings. See teleconferencing

megabits (Mbs), 56
megabyte (MB, meg), 56
megahertz (MHz), 57
memory, 50
    access time, 61
    CMOS (complementary metal oxide semiconductor), 61
    Flash memory, 61, 89, 112
    how it works, 62–63
    RAM (random access memory), 60–61, 65
    ROM (read-only memory), 61, 65
    software for managing, 109
    storage, hard disks, 5
    system, 5
    virtual memory, 109
    VRAM (video memory), 78
Memory Stick (Sony), 89
memory-mapped I/O, 63
menu-driven interfaces, 113
menus
    hierarchical, 114
    pop-up, 114
    pull-down, 114
meta-search engines, 210
MetaCrawler, 210
metropolitan area networks (MANs), 167
MFPs (multifunction peripherals), 81
MHz (megahertz), 57
micro-drives, 84
microchips, 29
microcomputers, 29
microprocessor chips, 56
microprocessors, 4, 29
    commercial uses for, 29
    microcomputer revolution, 29
    startup/development costs, 29
Microsoft, history of, 127
Microsoft Disk Operating System (MS-DOS), creation of, 127
Microsoft Mouse, 71
Microsoft Office suite, 107
Microsoft Windows operating system, 8. *See also* Windows
microtechnology, 270–271
MIDI (Musical Instrument Digital Interface), 147
military applications
    autonomous systems, 248–249
    cyberwarfare, 249, 251
    smart weapons, 248
millennium bug, 247
milliseconds, 61
minicomputers, 31
Minix, 99
MIPS (millions of instructions per second), 265
MIPS family, 60
mirroring data, 242
MIS (management information systems), 262
    information flow process, 260–261
MITS Altair computer, 52
MO (magneto-optical) disks, 85
mobile communications, 176
Mobile Computing (Lipshutz), 212
modeling software, 137–138
    3-D modeling, 139

modems, 13, 34, 92, 165–166
    cable modems, 190
    connection speeds, 190
    internal, 90
moderated mailing lists, 213
moderated newsgroups, 214
monitoring, computer, 263
monitors, 5, 77
    bit depth, 77
    color depth, 77
    color video, 79
    monochrome/gray scale, 78
    pixels, 77
    resolution, 77
    screen types, 78
    touch-screens, 72
    true color, 77
    video adapters, 78
monochrome monitors, 78
Moore's Law, 29
Moore, Gordon (Intel), 29
morale, workplace, effect of computer monitoring on, 263
motherboards, 56–57
    memory modules on, 62
    ports/slots on, 89–90
mouse devices, 5, 71
    how to use, 7
    ports for, 89
movies, digital, 143
MP3 files
    downloading, 197
    filesharing, Napster technology for, 216, 223
MPEG file compression, 145
MS-DOS (Microsoft Disk Operating System), 113
    creation of, 127
multi-processing, 60
multifunction peripherals (MFPs), 81
multimedia, 147–148
    applications, 40
    authoring software, 148
    on Web pages, 197
    plug-ins for, 200
multitasking, 109
Musical Instrument Digital Interface (MIDI), 147
mySimon, 212

N

nanobots, 21
nanotechnoogy, 42, 271
Napster, 216
    peer-to-peer (P2P) file sharing, 216, 223
narrowband connections, 190
NAS RAID server, 242
National Crime Information Center (FBI), 230
national identity cards, privacy issues, 156
National Information Infrastructure (NII), 220
National Infrastructure Protection Center (NIPC), 249
national security, military applications, 248–249, 251

natural language, 104
natural-language interfaces, 119
natural-language processing, 267
navigating
    Web pages, 17
    word processor documents, 128
    worksheets, 136
NCs (network computers), 36
.NET technology (Microsoft), 218
net PCs, 36
Net, the. *See* Internet
netiquette, 215
Netware (Novell), 168
network cards, 90
network computers, 36
network interface cards (NICs), 165
network interfaces, hardware for, 165–166
network licenses, 169
network operating system (NOS), 168
networking, networks. *See also* Internet
    applications for, 40
    bridges and gateways, 167
    cabling, 178
    client/server model, 168
    communication software, 167–168
        terminal emulators, 168–169
    communications coordination software, 109
    connectivity, 164–165
        hardware, 165
        modems, 165–166
    direct connections, 13
    e-commerce, 218
    email, 35
    extranets, 217
    information processing using, 34
    intranets, 36, 217
    LANs (local-area networks), 34, 166–168
        network operating systems, 168
    machine-to-machine, 204
    metropolitan area networks (MANs), 167
    peer-to-peer model, 168
    reasons for using, 169
    servers, 31
    terminal emulation software, 168–169
    user interfaces for, 119
    virtual private networks, 218
    WANs (local area networks), 34
    wide area networks (WANs), 167
    work groups, 170
    workstations, 31
Neumann, John von, 100
Neuromancer (Gibson), 221
newsgroups, 171, 213–214
Next Generation Internet (NGI), 219
NGI (Next Generation Internet), 219
NICs (network interface cards, 165
nodes (LANs), 166
non-Internet communications programs
    fax machines, 175
    fax modems, 175
    financial transaction software, 176
    GPS (Global Positioning System) receivers, 176
    online information services, 173–174
    telephony software, 175
    video teleconferencing, 174–175
    voice mail, 175

non-Roman characters, Unicode for, 54
nonvolatile memory, 61
North America Aerospace Defense Command (NORAD), 248
Norton Utilities (Symantec), 112
NOS (network operating system), 168
notebook computers, 32–33
    docking stations, 32–33
    subnote books, 32
number systems, 27

O

object-oriented graphics, 139
object-oriented programming languages, 267
OCR (optical character recognition) tools, 73–74
offices, automated, 262
    computer monitoring, 263
    effects on jobs/job security, 263–264
Olson, Barbara, 43
Omninet, 269
on-line help, 105
1-bit color depth, 78
OneSeek, 210
online auctions, 218
online catalogs, 218
online information services, 173
    Internet access using, 173–174
    tips for using effectively, 174
online services, 193
open architecture, 90
open source software, 99
open standards, 187
opening applicaitons, 8
operating systems (OS), 8, 108–109, 112
    how they work, 110–111
    IBM OS/2, 118
    Linux, KDE desktop for, 117
    Mac OS 9, 118
    Mac OS X, 118
    MS-DOS, 127
    Palm OS, 118
    UNIX, 115–116
    UNIX/Linux systems, 118
    Windows 2000/NT, 118
    Windows CE, 118
    Windows ME, 118
    Windows XP, 118
optical character recognition (OCR) tools, 73–74
optical computers, 266
optical disk drives, 85–88
optical media, data transfer rates, 85
optical-mark readers, 72
OS. *See* operating systems
Outline views (outliners), 128
Outlook Express (Microsoft), 211
output
    databases, 151
    memory-mapped, 63
    producing, 50
output devices, 5, 50
    audio output, 81
    device controllers, 82
    monitors, 77–78
    multi-function peripherals (MFPs), 81
    plotters, 81
    printers, 78, 80
output function, 25, 27
output technologies, developments in, 266–267
ovens, computers in, 33
overhead projection panels, 78

P

P2P (peer-to-peer) file sharing, 216–217, 223
packet-switching model, 188
packets (TCP/IP), 187
page-layout software, 132
painting software, 138
palettes (painting software), 138
Palm OS, 118
    software, 74
Palm Pilot, operating system, 118
palmtop computers, 33
PANs (personal area networks), 179
paradigm shifts, 258
parallel ports, 89, 165
parallel processing, 60
    coordination software, 109
passwords, 12, 238–239
    stealing, 231–232
patent laws, 233
Paypal, 212
PC (IBM), 69
PC cards, 62
PC clones, 69
PC Iris (IriScan), 238
PCs (personal computers), 4, 32
    standard components, 5
PDAs (personal digital assistants), 73–74
PDF (Portable Document Format, Adobe), 132, 200
peer-to-peer (P2P) file sharing, 216–217, 223
peer-to-peer model, 168
peerless cartridges (Iomega), 85
pen scanners, 73
    PDAs (personal digital assistants), 73–74
Pentium 4 chip (Intel), 57
Pentium CPUs, 60
peripherals, 5, 51, 63
    bays, 61
    buses, 61
    communicating with, software for, 109, 111
    connecting laptops/notebooks to, 32
    device controllers, 82
    expansion tools, 90, 92
    hot swap devices, 90
    input devices
        digitizers, 74–75, 77
        keyboards, 70
        pointing devices, 71–72
        reading tools, 72–74
    integrating, 92
    keyboards, 5–6
    monitors, 5, 77–79
    mouse devices, 5, 7
    output devices
        MFPs (multifunction peripherals), 81
        monitors, 77–78
        plotters, 81
        printers, 78, 80
    ports/slots for, 89–90
    printers, 5, 78, 80
    selecting, rules of thumb for, 91
    sound cards/synthesizers, 81
    storage devices, 82, 84–85, 88–89
personal area networks (PANs), 179
personal communications, use of computers for, 30
personal computer era, 30
personal computers (PCs), 4, 29, 32
    standard components, 5
    development of, 257
personal computing
    Apple computers, 69
    early Apple computers, 69
    IBM PCs, 69
personal data assistants (PDAs), 33
personal digital assistants (PDAs), 73–74
personal information managers (PIMS), 152
personal information, protecting, 155
PGP (Pretty Good Privacy), 241
photo printers, 80
photographs, editing using Photoshop, 140–141
Photoshop (Adobe), editing photographs using, 140–141
physical data, digitizing, 77
PIMS (personal information managers), 152
Pine email program (UNIX), 211
piracy, software issues, 232–233, 245
    computer crime versus civil rights, 244–245
    legal versus ethical values, 246
Pixar, Inc., 69
pixels, 138
    dot-matrix printer output, 80
    screen resolution, 77
platform independence, programming languages, 119
platform-independent peripherals, 90
platforms, 118. *See also* operating systems
platters, 86
plotters, 81
plug-ins, for Web browsers, 200
Pocket PCs, 33
Poe, Edgar Allen, 229
point size (fonts), 128
point-of-sale (POS) terminals, 72
pointing devices
    graphics tablets, 72
    joysticks, 72
    mice, 71
    pointing sticks, 71
    touch screens, 72
    touchpads, 71
    trackballs, 71
pointing sticks, 72
police work, computers in, 30
pollsters, responsding to, 155
pop-up menus, 114
portable computers, 32, 89
    drive bays, 90
    input devices, 71–72
    laptop computers, 32
    notebook computers, 32

Index

portable printers for, 80
theft of, 232
Windows CE for, 118
Portable Document Format (PDF, Adobe), 132, 200
portable inkjet printers, 80
portals (Internet), 18
portals (Web), 211
ports, 61, 89–90, 165
FireWire (IEEE 1394), 142
interface standards, 89
POS (point-of-sale) terminals, 72–73
POTS (plainold telephone service), 190
power users, 4
PowerPC family, 60
PowerPoint (Microsoft), 139
creating a presentation using, 142–143
PPP (point-to-point protocol), 190
predefined functions (spreadsheets), 136
Premiere (Adobe), 143
presentation graphics software, 139
presentations
charts, spreadsheet tools for, 136
creating using PowerPoint, 142–143
price-to-performance ratio, 265
primary storage, 50, 82. See also memory
Print Preview command (Word), 131
printers, 5
impact printers, 78, 80
nonimpact printers, 80–81
printing
color printing, 81
documents, 129, 131
privacy issues, 40–41, 272
computer monitoring, 263
databases, 153–154
basic do's and don'ts, 155
email, 172
national identity cards, 156
security versus privacy, 242–244
Web-related, cookies, 200
privacy rights, 154
problem-solving applications, 40
processing function, 25
processor-sharing. See grid computing, 217
processors, 50, 56–57
central processing units (CPUs), 58–59
compatibility issues, 57
memory
access time, 61
CMOS (complementary metal oxide semiconductor), 61
Flash memory, 61
how it works, 62–63
RAM (random access memory), 60–61, 65
ROM (read-only memory), 61, 65
speed issues, 57
architecture, 57
clock speed, 57
CPUs, 65
parallel processing/multiprocessing, 60
word size, 60
Prodigy, 173
productivity applications, 100, 105. See also consumer applications
program management software, 109
programmable loom, 25

programmers, 100
programming
algorithms, 101
binary notation for, 54
environments, visual, 267
errors, security risks from, 247
languages, 104
compilers, 100, 104
machine language, 104
natural languages for, 104
programs, 37, 100
instructions, 54
project management software, 262
projectors, 78
prompts, UNIX command lines, 116
proofreading, word processor tools for, 129
property rights, intellectual, 41
protocols
communications, 168
Internet, PPP (point-to-point protocol), 190
internetworking, TCP/IP, 187–188
public domain software (freeware), 106
public key cryptosystems, 241
pull technology, 216
pull-down menus, 114
push technology, 216

quantum computers, 271
QuarkXpress, 132
queries, on search engines, 210
query languages, 150
querying databases/queries, 150
Quick Time (Apple), 200
QWERTY keyboards, 70–71

radio wireless technology, 178
RAID (redundant array of independent disk) device, 242
railroad control room, 26
RAM (random access memory), 60–61, 65
random access, disk drives, 84
random access memory (RAM), 60–61, 65
raster devices, 81
raster graphics, 138
read-only memory (ROM), 61, 65
read/write heads, in disk drives, 86
reading tools, 72
bar-code readers, 72
magnetic-ink character readers, 72
optical character recognition (OCR) tools, 73–74
optical-mark readers, 72
real-time communications, 214, 216
real-time streaming audio/video, 197
real-time teleconferencing, 170
RealPlayer, 200
receiving input, 50
recording CD-R/RW disks, 85
records (database), 149
remote access, 13, 165
removable cartridge media, 84–85
removable media, 5

repetitive stress injury, 70
reports (database), 151
resolution
drawing software, 138
painting software, 138
printer output, 80–81
screen, 77
resources, system, software for managing, 109
restricting access
audit-control software, 241
encryption, 240–241
firewalls, 239
passwords, 238–239
physical devices/biometrics, 238
Revere, Paul, 51
right to privacy, 154
right-clicking (mouse), 7
risks, from computer technology, 40
automation/dehumanization, 41
bio-digital technology, 42
computer/Internet addictions, 42
crashes/system failures, 41
high-tech crime, 40
information abuse, 41
intellectual property right issues, 41
privacy issues, 40–41
role in terrorist attacks, 43
smart computers and human control, 42
technological dependency, 41
Roberts, Steve, 3
robots, 259
artificial life, 271
computer controls for, 82
Rogers, Vaughn, 3
rollovers, 201
ROM (read-only memory), 61, 65
routers, 167, 187
rows (spreadsheets), 133
RSA cryptosystem, 241
running applications, 102–103

sabotage, software, 234
Trojan horses, 234
viruses, 234–236
worms, 235
safe computing, tips for, 245
Saffo, Paul, 220
satellite Internet connections, 192
connection speeds, 191
satellite modems, 166
satellites, communications, 163
saving documents, 129
scanners, 73–76
scanning photographs, 140
scientific data analysis, computers for, 31
scientific visualization software, 137
screen resolution, 77
screen types, monitors, 78
scripts (dynamic HTML), 201
scrolling, 128
SCSI (Small Computer Systems Interface) ports, 90
SDI (Strategic Defense Initiative, 248–249
search and replace feature (word processors), 128

search engines, 17–18, 210
   on Web pages, 197
   specialized
      comparison shopping, 218
      financial services, 218
   using effectively, 212
searching, databases, 150

secondary storage, 82
security issues/tools. *See also* computer crime
   antivirus programs, 236
   audit-control software, 241
   backups, 242
   databases, 153–154
      privacy, 155
   email systems, privacy/unauthorized access, 172
   encryption, 240–241
   firewalls, 239
   human/programming errors, 247
   identity theft, 219
   legal issues, 244–245
   limitations of, 250
   passwords, 238–239
   physical access restrictions, 238
   power-protection devices, 242
   safe computing tips, 245
   security policies, 242
   security risks, 238
      cyberterrorism, 249, 251
   security versus privacy, 242–244
   software for managing, 109
   viruses, 172
   wireless communications, 179
security, national, military applications, 248–249, 251
self-maintaining systems, 268
sensors, 267
   microsensors, 270–271
   environmental, 77
sequential access devices, 84–85
serial ports, 89, 165
servers, 31, 168
   email servers, 193
service phase of development, 265
SETI grid computing project, 217
shareware, 106
sharing information. *See* networking
sheet-fed scanners, 75
shell programs, 114
Sherlock/Sherlock 2 (Apple), 210
Shockwave/Flash technology (Macromedia), 148, 200
shopping bots, 212
silicon chips, 29
   advantages of using, 29
   microprocessor chips, 56
Silicon Valley, 29
SILK (speech, image, language and knowledge) interface, 267
SIMMs (single in-line memory modules), 62
simulation software, 137–138
single in-line memory modules (SIMMs), 62
site licenses, 106, 169
16-bit color depth, 78
64-bit processors, 60

sizes, of files, 56
Sklyarov, Dmitri, 244
slide scanners, 74
slide shows, creating using PowerPoint, 142–143
slides (presentations), 139
slots, 61, 89–90
   interface standards, 89
smart cards, 238
smart weapons, 248
smart whiteboards, 74
smell generators, 82
SMIL (synchronized multimedia integration language), 203
sneakernet, 169
social engineering, 232
social issues
   computers and democracy, 272
   democracy, effects of computers on, 272
   globalization, 272
   information slavery, 273–274
   workforce changes, 258, 262–264
social security number, protecting, 155
software, 8, 27, 100. *See also* applications
   accounting/financial management programs, 137
   animation programs, 139
   commercial applications, 107–108
   consumer applications, 105–107
   database management systems (DBMS), 152–153
   database programs, 148
   desktop publishing, 129
   digital audio, 147
   digital video, 142–143
   drawing software, 138–139
   future developments, 267–269
   groupware, 262
   image processing, 138, 140–141
   interactive multimedia, 147–148
   as intellectual property, 233
   mathematics processing programs, 137
   modeling, simulations, 137–138
   open source, 99
   page-layout software, 132
   painting, 138
   presentation graphic, 139
   productivity applications, 100
   project management software, 262
   scientific visualization, 137
   spreadsheets, 133
   statistical programs, 136–137
   system applications, 100–109
   3-D modeling software, 139
   translator programs, compilers, 100, 104
   utility programs, 110
   what it does, 101
   word processors, 128
software emulation, 119
software errors. *See* programming errors, 247
software phase of development, 265
software piracy, 232–233
software sabotage, 234
   Trojan horses, 234
   viruses, 234–236
   worms, 235
Solaris operating system (Sun), 115
solid state storage devices, 88–89

Solove, David, 30
sorting, database data, 151
sound
   digital audio, 147
   digitizing, 75, 77
sound cards, 81
source documents
   desktop publishing, 132
   HTML, 194
space program, impetus for computer development, 29
spam, 172, 215
SPARC CPU family, 60
speakers, 81
special-purpose computers, 33
speech recognition software, 75, 77
speed
   of computers, enhancements in, 265
   data transmission, 177–178
   electronic data transfer, 169
   memory access, 61
   of CPUs, 57
      clocks, 57
      parallel/multiprocessing, 60
      word size, 60
spelling checkers, 129
Sperry Corporation, 28
spiders, 210
spoofing, 232
spreadsheets, 37, 133
   charting tools, 136
   formulas, 136
      macros, 136
      predefined functions, 136
   templates, 136
   worksheets, 133–136
"Star Wars" defense system, 248–249
StarOffice suite, 107
Start menu, 10
statistical software, 37, 136–137
Stefik, Mark, 222
steganography, use of, by terrorists, 43
stereo systems, sequential access devices in, 85
stereos, computers in, 33
Stoll, Cliff, 237
storage
   devices, 50, 82
      for backup data, 242
      CD-ROMs, 85
      DVDs, 88
      how they work, 86
      magnetic disk drives, 84
      magnetic tape, 82, 84
      optical disk drives, 85, 88
      how they work, 86
      RAID (redundant array of independent disk) device, 242
      solid state, 88–89
   memory
      access time, 61
      CMOS (complementary metal oxide semiconductor), 61
      Flash memory, 61
      RAM (random access memory), 60–61, 65
      ROM (read-only memory), 61, 65
storage function, 25
storage technologies, developments in, 266

storing, data/information, 50
Strategic Defense Initiative (SDI), 248–249
streaming audio/video files, 197
stretching, importance of, 83
StuffIt file compression, 145
style checking tools, 129
style sheets, 129
styluses, for touch-screen monitors, 72
subject trees, 210
    search engines, 18
subnotebooks, 32
subtractive synthesis, 81
suites, software, 107–108
supercomputers, 31
SuperDisks (Imation), 84
SuperDrive (Apple), 88
surge protectors, 242
switches, 187
symbols, coding, Unicode for, 54
synchronized multimedia integration language (SMIL), 203
synthesizers, 81
system boards, 56
system failures, 41
system memory, 5
system software, 8, 100, 108
    memory management software, 109
    network communications coordination, 109
    operating systems, 108–109, 112
    parallel processing/multitasking coordination, 109
    peripheral communications software, 109
    program/data management, 109
    resource monitoring, 109
    utility programs, 110
system units, 4
    basic designs, 89
    bays, 90
    expanding, 90, 92
    ports/slots, 89–90

T

T1 and T3 connections, 189
tables, on Web pages, 197
Tablet PC, 74
tags (HTML), 196
tar file compression, 145
task bars, 114
    Windows desktop, 10
tax preparation software, 137
Taylor, Robert, 185
TB (terabyte), 56
TCP/IP (Transmission Contol Protocol/Internet Protocol), 187–188
Tech Corps program, 220
technological change, 37. See also computer technology
technological dependency, 41
technological development, phases of, 265
telecommunication applications, 40
telecommunications, 164. See also communications programs
    connection types, 165
    digital communications, 183
Telecommunications Act of 1996, 244–245

telecommuting, 262
teleconferencing, 170–171
    advantages of using, 171–172
    disadvantages/risks of using, 172–173
    video, 174–175
telephones
    comparison with email communications, 171
telephony software, 175
television control room, 26
televisions, network computer comparison, 36
templates, for spreadsheets, 136
terabyte (TB), 56
terminal emulation software, 168–169, 190
terminals, 30–31
    point-of-sale (POS), 72
terrorism, 43
text
    ASCII code for, 54
    binary codes for, 54
    selecting in word processing documents, 130
    Unicode for, 54
    word processor
        editing, 128
        entering, 128
        formatting text, 128
text links, 16
The Code and Other Laws of Cyberspace (Lessig), 222
The Cuckoo's Egg (Stoll), 237
theft, 231–232
thin clients, 36, 262
32-bit processors, 60
3-D environments, on Web pages, 197
three-dimensional (3-D) modeling software, 139
time bombs, 234
timesharing, 31, 34
Toffler, Alvin, 262
top-level domains, 188
Torvalds, Linus, 99
touch-screen monitors, 72
touchpads, 71–72
tower systems, 89
toys, computers in, 33–34
trackballs, 71–72
trackpads, 71
TrackPoint (IBM), 71
transistors, invention of (1948), 28
translator programs, 100
    compilers, 104
    how they work, 104
Transmission Control Protocol/Internet Protocol (TCP/IP), 187–188
transmission speeds
    and bandwidth, 177
    fiber optic cables, 177–178
    modems, 165
    wireless communications, 178–179
trespassing, electronic
    denial of service (DoS) attacks, 237
    hacking/cracking, 236–237
    Webjacking, 237
Trojan horses, 234
true color, 77
True Names (Vinge), 221
Turing, Alan, 28

tweening, 139
24-bit color depth, 77
twisted pair cabling, 166, 178
typefaces. See fonts, 128

U

ubiquitous computing, 269–270
    artificial life, 271
    biological paradigms, 270
    ethical/social issues, 272–274
    microtechnology, 270–271
    nanotechnology, 271
Undo command, 115
Unicode character sets, 54–55
uniform resource locators (URLs), 194
uninterruptible power supplies (UPS), 242
UNIVAC I (1951), 28
universal access, 220
universal product codes (UPCs), readers for, 72
universal serial bus (USB) ports, 90
UNIX operating system, 99, 115–116, 118, 169
UNIX system, Pine email program, 211
unsolicited email, 172
UPC (universal product code) readers, 72
upgrades, software, 105
upgrading, portable computers, 33
uploading files, 193
uploading software, 173
upstream traffic, 190
URLs (uniform resource locators), 16, 188, 194
    development of, 209
USA Patriot Act, 243
USB (Universal Serial Bus) ports, 90, 165
Usenet newsgroups, 213–214
user interfaces, 112
    character-based, 113, 115
        MS-DOS, 113
    enhancements of, 267
    graphical (GUI), 113
        advantages of using, 114–115
        features, 114
        Mac OS, 113
        Windows, 114
    Linux operating system, 115
        KDE desktop, 117
    trends in, 119–120
    UNIX operating system, 115–116
user names, 14
users, 100
    logging in, 115
utility programs, 108, 110

V

vaccine programs, 236
values (spreadsheets), 136
VBScripts (Micrtosoft), 201
VDTs (video display terminals), 77
vector graphics, 139
vertical portals (vortals), 211
vertical-market software, 108
video adapters, 78
video cassette recorders, computers in, 33

video digitizers, 75, 142
video, digital, 142–143
    compression systems for, 145
video display terminals (VDTs), 77
video editing software, 143
video memory (VRAM), 78
video ports, 89
video projectors, 78
video teleconferencing, 174–175, 214
videoconferencing, 75, 214
Vinge, Vernor, 221
virtual memory, 109
virtual private networks, 218
virtual reality (VR), 42
    games, device controllers for, 82
    interfaces, 120
    user interfaces, 268
viruses, 172, 234–236
    protecting against, 236
    tips for avoiding, 245
visual aids, creating using PowerPoint, 142–143
Visual BASIC programming language, 104
visual programming environments, 267
visualization software
    modeling, 137–138
    scientific visualization, 137
voice input, digitizing, 75
voice mail systems, 175
voice recognition systems, 267
volatile memory, 61
VRAM (video memory), 78

W3C (World Wide Web Consortium), 209
Walsh, Patricia, 3
WANs (wide area networks), 34, 167
warranties, software, 106
Watson, Thomas J., Jr., 49
Watson, Thomas J., Sr., 37, 49
"way of life" phase of development, 265
weapon systems
    autonomous systems, 248–249
    smart weapons, 248
Web, the. See World Wide Web (WWW); see also Internet
Web authoring software, 195
Web authoring tools, 198
Web bots, 268
Web browsers, 16, 35
    Internet Explorer, 127
    launching of portals by, 211
    multimedia plug-ins for, 200
Web bugs, 212–213
Web commerce, 36
web crawlers, 210
Web pages, 16, 194–195

creating, 195
    multimedia on, 197, 200
    navigating, 17
    storing, Web servers for, 194
    uploading/publishing, 197
Web portals, 211
Web-ready multimedia documents, 148
Web search engines, 210
Web servers, 194
Web services, 218
Web sites, 16
    computer hardware manufacturers, 67
    creating, 198–199
    database-driven, 202
    Direct Mail Marketing Association, 155
    dynamic, 202–203
    effective, design tips, 201
    management tools for, 197
    on-line help, 105
    software manufacturers/developers, 125
    uploading files to, 197
Webcasts, 197, 216
Webjacking, 237
what-if questions, answering using spreadsheets, 136
whiteboards, smart, 74
Wi-Fi wireless technology (802.11b), 178, 192
wide-area networks (WANs), 34
WIMP (winodws, icons, menus and pointing device) interface, 267
windows (desktops), 113–114
Windows Media Player (Microsoft), 200
Windows, Microsoft (Windows), 114
    Windows 2000/NT, 118
    Windows CE, 118
    Windows Millennium Edition (Windows ME), 118
    Windows XP, 118
Windows operating system (Microsoft), 8
Windows terminals, 36
Windows XP Server (Microsoft), 168
wireless broadband connections, 192
wireless communications, 166, 178–179
    ethical implications of, 180
wireless devices, email on, 213
wireless keyboards, 70
wireless networks, 167
wizards, 268
Word (Microsoft)
    creating document using, 130
    opening and using with Mac OS, 12
    opening and using with Windows systems, 10–11
word processing, 37
    creating example document, 130
    editing text, 128
    entering text, 128
    formatting text, 128

Outline views, 128
    printing documents, 129
    proofreading tools, 129
    saving documents, 129
    software for, 128
word processors, 106
word size, 60
work environments, ergonomic considerations, 83
work groups, 170
workers' rights issues, and computer use, 41
workflow management software, 262
workforce, changes in, 258
worksheets (spreadsheets), 133, 136
    cell ranges, 134
    creating in Excel, 134–135
workstations, 31
World War II, development of computer during, 27
World Wide Web, commercialization of, 219
    ethical and security issues, 219–222
World Wide Web (WWW), 16, 35
    creation of, 194
    how it works, 196
    hypertext links, 35
    portals, 211
    pull technology, 216
    push technology, 216
    search engines, 17–18, 210
    URLs (uniform resource locators), 194
    Web browsers, 35
    Web pages, 194–195
        creating, 195
        multimedia, 197, 200
        publishing, 197
World Wide Web Consortium (W3C), 209
WORM (write-once, read-many) media, 85
worms, 235
Wozniak, Steve, 69
wristwatches, computers in, 33
Wurman, Richard Saul, 51
WWW. See World Wide Web
WYSIWYG (What You See Is What You Get), 128

XHTML markup language, 202
XML (extensible markup language), 202
    with Web services, 218
Y2K bug, 247
Yahoo Instant Messanger, 171
Zip disk drives, 5, 84
ZIP/PKZIP file compression, 145
Zuse, Konrad, 27